D0163931

M is... **M**aximizing Your Grade!

LOOK INSIDE THIS BOOK FOR:

■ Active Review Cards

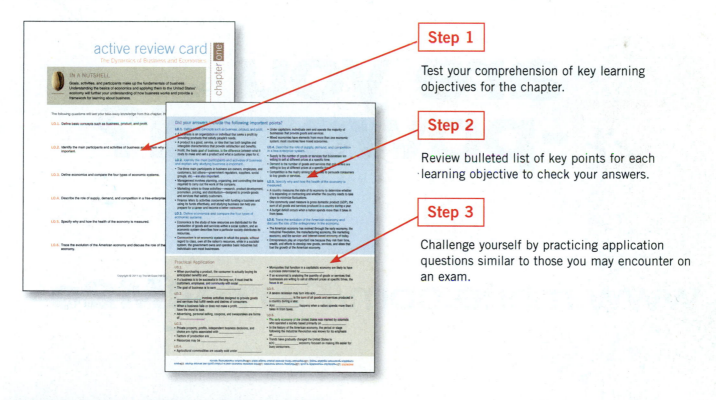

Step 1

Test your comprehension of key learning objectives for the chapter.

Step 2

Review bulleted list of key points for each learning objective to check your answers.

Step 3

Challenge yourself by practicing application questions similar to those you may encounter on an exam.

■ Your Access to Online Resources

• Graded Interactives—scored and tracked interactive exercises

• Study Tools—practice quizzes, interactive flashcards, and narrated presentations

• iPod Content—quizzes, narrated presentations, and more formatted for iPod

• Applications—end of chapter application and study assignments

www.mhhe.com/FerrellM2e

start here.

business

second edition

O.C. Ferrell
University of New Mexico

Geoffrey A. Hirt
DePaul University

Linda Ferrell
University of New Mexico

McGraw-Hill Irwin

M: BUSINESS

Published by McGraw-Hill/Irwin, a business unit of The McGraw-Hill Companies, Inc., 1221 Avenue of the Americas, New York, NY, 10020. Copyright © 2011, 2009 by The McGraw-Hill Companies, Inc. All rights reserved. No part of this publication may be reproduced or distributed in any form or by any means, or stored in a database or retrieval system, without the prior written consent of The McGraw-Hill Companies, Inc., including, but not limited to, in any network or other electronic storage or transmission, or broadcast for distance learning.

Some ancillaries, including electronic and print components, may not be available to customers outside the United States.

This book is printed on acid-free paper.

3 4 5 6 7 8 9 0 QDB/QDB 1 0 9 8 7 6 5 4 3 2 1

ISBN 978-0-07-351174-0
MHID 0-07-351174-9

Vice president and editor-in-chief: *Brent Gordon*
Publisher: *Paul Ducham*
Executive editor: *Doug Hughes*
Director of development: *Ann Torbert*
Senior development editor: *Christine Scheid*
Vice president and director of marketing: *Robin J. Zwettler*
Senior marketing manager: *Sarah Schuessler*
Vice president of editing, design and production: *Sesha Bolisetty*
Senior project manager: *Susanne Riedell*
Lead production supervisor: *Michael R. McCormick*
Interior designer: *Cara Hawthorne, cara david DESIGN*
Senior photo research coordinator: *Lori Kramer*
Photo researcher: *Keri Johnson*
Senior media project manager: *Jen Lohn*
Cover design: *Cara Hawthorne, cara david DESIGN*
Typeface: *10/12 Minon Pro Regular*
Compositor: *Laserwords Private Limited*
Printer: *Quad/Graphics*

Library of Congress Control Number: 2009940705

brief contents

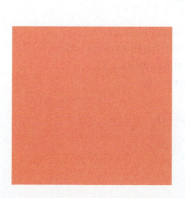

contents

part 3

Managing for Quality and Competitiveness

part 4

Creating the Human Resource Advantage

part 5

Marketing: Developing Relationships

part 6 ● ●

Financing the Enterprise

business

THE DYNAMICS OF BUSINESS (and) ECONOMICS

CHAPTER 1

Introduction We begin our study of business by examining the fundamentals of business and economics in this chapter. First, we introduce the nature of business, including its goals, activities, and participants. Next, we describe the basics of economics and apply them to the United States' economy. Finally, we establish a framework for studying business in this text.

 LO1

Define basic concepts such as business, product, and profit.

THE NATURE OF BUSINESS

A **business** tries to earn a profit by providing products that satisfy people's needs. The outcome of its efforts are **products** that have both tangible and intangible characteristics that provide satisfaction and benefits. When you purchase a product, what you are buying is the benefits and satisfaction you think the product will provide. A Subway sandwich, for example, may be purchased to satisfy hunger; a Porsche Cayenne sport utility vehicle, to satisfy the need for transportation and the desire to present a certain image.

●● learning OBJECTIVES

LO1   Define basic concepts such as business, product, and profit.

LO2   Identify the main participants and activities of business, and explain why studying business is important.

LO3   Define economics and compare the four types of economic systems.

LO4   Describe the role of supply, demand, and competition in a free-enterprise system.

LO5   Specify why and how the health of the economy is measured.

LO6   Trace the evolution of the American economy, and discuss the role of the entrepreneur in the economy.

Most people associate the word *product* with tangible goods—an automobile, computer, loaf of bread, coat, or some other tangible item. However, a product can also be a service, which results when people or machines provide or process something of value to customers. Dry cleaning, photo processing, a checkup by a doctor, a performance by a movie star or basketball player—these are examples of services. A product can also be an idea. Consultants and attorneys, for example, generate ideas for solving problems.

The Goal of Business

The primary goal of all businesses is to earn a **profit,** the difference between what it costs to make and sell a product and what a customer pays for it. If a company spends $2.00 to manufacture, finance, promote, and distribute a product that it sells for $2.75, the business earns a profit of 75 cents on each product sold. Businesses have the right to keep and use their profits as they choose—within legal limits—because profit is the reward for the risks they take in providing products. Not all organizations are businesses. **Nonprofit organizations,** such as Greenpeace, Special Olympics, and other charities and social causes, do not have the fundamental purpose of earning profits, although they may provide goods or services.

To earn a profit, a person or organization needs management skills to plan, organize, and control the activities of the business and to find and develop employees so that it can make products consumers will buy. A business also needs marketing expertise to learn what products consumers need and want and to develop, manufacture, price, promote, and distribute those products. Additionally, a business needs financial resources and skills to fund, maintain, and expand its operations. Other challenges for businesspeople include abiding by laws and government regulations; acting in an ethical and socially responsible manner; and adapting to economic, technological, and social changes. Both for-profit and nonprofit organizations engage in management, marketing, and finance activities to help reach their goals.

To achieve and maintain profitability, businesses have found that they must produce quality products, operate efficiently, and be socially responsible and ethical in dealing with customers, employees, investors, government regulators, the community, and society. Because these groups have a stake in the success and outcomes of a business, they are sometimes called **stakeholders.** Many businesses, for example, are concerned about how the production and distribution of their products affect the environment. Hewlett-Packard Company recycled nearly 250 million pounds of hardware and print cartridges globally in 2007, an increase of almost 50 percent over the previous year and the equivalent of more than double the weight of the *Titanic*. Concerns about landfills becoming high-tech graveyards plague many electronics firms. Television manufacturers worry as consumers trade their bulky TVs for high-definition, flat-screen versions.[1] Other businesses are concerned about the quality of life in the communities in which they operate. Cummins Inc., an Indiana-based manufacturing firm with operations around the world has helped to develop a technical school

TerraCycle, founded by two former Princeton students, is a U.S. firm dedicated to preserving the environment. The company's flagship product, TerraCycle Plant Food, is an all-natural, all-organic liquid plant food made from waste (worm excrement) and packaged in reused soda bottles.

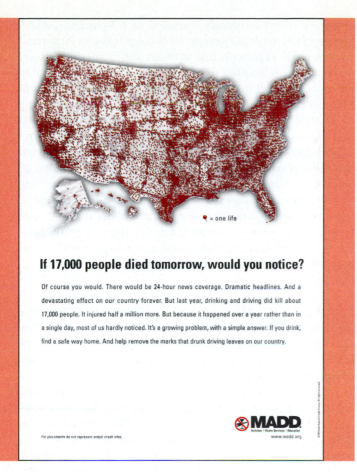

If 17,000 people died tomorrow, would you notice?

Of course you would. There would be 24-hour news coverage. Dramatic headlines. And a devastating effect on our country forever. But last year, drinking and driving did kill about 17,000 people. It injured half a million more. But because it happened over a year rather than in a single day, most of us hardly noticed. It's a growing problem, with a simple answer. If you drink, find a safe way home. And help remove the marks that drunk driving leaves on our country.

● = one life

Pin placements do not represent actual crash sites.

MADD
Activism | Victim Services | Education
www.madd.org

The goal of nonprofit organizations, including MADD (Mothers Against Drunk Driving), isn't to accumulate profits. MADD's mission is to sell the idea of not drinking and driving, and it uses its resources to promote that message.

in Soweto, South Africa, to aid with education and skill development in a previously disadvantaged community.[2] Others are concerned with promoting business careers among African American, Hispanic, and Native American students. The Diversity Pipeline Alliance is a network of national organizations that work toward preparing students and professionals of color for leadership and management in the 21st century workforce. The Pipeline assists individuals in getting into the appropriate college, pursuing a career in business, or earning an advanced degree in business.[3] Still other companies such as The Home Depot have a long history of supporting natural disaster victims from Hurricanes Andrew to Katrina. Other companies, such as U-Haul, are finding

ways to provide services to assist storm victims. In Arkansas, U-Haul offered 30 days of free storage to victims of tornados and floods.[4]

 LO2

Identify the main participants and activities of business, and explain why studying business is important.

The People and Activities of Business

Figure 1.1 shows the people and activities involved in business. At the center of the figure are owners, employees, and customers; the outer circle includes the primary business activities—management, marketing, and finance. Owners have to put up resources—money or credit—to start a business. Employees are responsible for the work that goes on within a business. Owners can manage the business themselves or hire employees to accomplish this task. The president of Procter & Gamble, Alow Latley, does not own the company but is an employee who is responsible for managing all the other employees in a way that earns a profit for investors, who are the real owners. Finally, and most importantly, a business's major role is to satisfy the customers who buy its goods or services. Note also that people and forces beyond an organization's control—such as legal and regulatory forces, the economy, competition, technology, and ethical and social concerns—all have an impact on the daily operations

| FIGURE | 1.1 | Overview of the Business World |

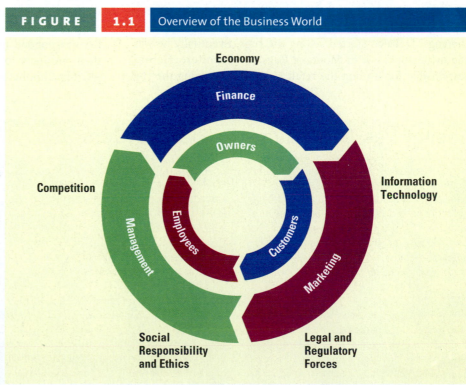

of businesses. You will learn more about these participants in business activities throughout this book. Next, we will examine the major activities of business.

management
Notice that in Figure 1.1 management and employees are in the same segment of the circle. This is because management involves coordinating employees' actions to achieve the firm's goals, organizing people to work efficiently, and motivating them to achieve the business's goals. NASCAR has been a family-run business since its inception. Brian France, current chairman and CEO, is following in the footsteps of his father and grandfather in providing leadership for the sport. NASCAR is now the second most popular spectator sport in the country outperforming fan numbers and viewership for the IRL (Indianapolis Racing League).[5] Management is also concerned with acquiring, developing, and using resources (including people) effectively and efficiently. Under CEO Eric Schmidt's leadership, Google will continue to advance broadband adoption in all forms, knowing that broadband users visit Google sites more often. In a partnership with Dell, Google is preloaded on tool bars and as desktop search software to generate more traffic and, consequently, ad revenue for Google.[6]

Production and manufacturing is another element of management. In essence, managers plan, organize, staff, and control the tasks required to carry out the work of the company or nonprofit organization. We take a closer look at management activities in Parts 3 and 4 of this text.

To illustrate the importance of management, consider a rug and furniture retailer in Bozeman, Montana. Mark DeFalco, who started his career in Colorado in the jewelry business cutting and polishing turquoise, found himself trading jewelry for rugs on Navajo reservations. As he realized the value of the rugs, DeFalco started selling the rugs. Eventually he was the owner/operator of Montana Rugs and Furniture. He was responsible for finding the retail location, managing the rug inventory which ultimately consisted of 60 percent Turkish tribal and Orientals, 20 percent Navajo replicas and 20 percent Western-style rugs, with fine antiques and home furnishings make up the remaining inventory. In buying and managing the inventory, DeFalco had to be aware of the market for rugs with the average sales price of $7,500 with some rugs selling for $30,000. With an annual growth rate of 30 percent since its opening in 2003, DeFalco had to hire a larger staff and move into a larger location in 2005. In 2008, DeFalco decided to sell the business using the guidelines for valuing a rug retailer: 20 percent of revenue plus the value of the inventory. The selling price for Montana Rugs is $1.64 million. DeFalco's decision to sell was based on a desire to retire and a belief that someone "younger and smarter" could maximize the potential of the business. Consequently, making decisions to ensure the business achieves its short- and long-term goals is a vital part of management.[7]

marketing
Marketing and consumers are in the same segment of Figure 1.1 because the focus of all marketing activities is satisfying customers. Marketing includes all the activities designed to provide goods and services that satisfy consumers' needs and wants. Marketers gather information and conduct research to determine what customers want. Using information gathered from marketing research, marketers plan and develop products and make decisions about how much to charge for their products and when and where to make them available. In response to growing concerns over childhood obesity, Kellogg's has agreed to phase out advertising to children under the age of 12, unless those cereals are healthy (low calorie, low sugar and salt). In addition, Kellogg's will stop using cartoon and licensed characters such as Shrek to promote its products to children.[8] Other food producers have responded to consumer health concerns by modifying their products to make them healthier. Pepsico, for example, has eliminated all transfats from its line of snack chips

Tesla Fires Up Dreams of Electric Cars

Although we may be familiar with electric cars primarily via science fiction, they have in fact been in production for over a century. They have been kept out of the mainstream in part because of resistance from oil companies and traditional car companies, but also because of inadequate battery technology. Companies now are using the same type of lithium-ion batteries powering computers and cell phones, and this type works much better than do traditional batteries.

Tesla, manufacturer of an elite electric sports car and a new electric sedan, uses lithium-ion technology. Founded in 2003 by Martin Eberhard and Marc Tarpenning and supported by multimillionaire Elon Musk, Tesla is fairly new in the electric car arena and has made amazing progress. In a recent blog, Elon Musk stated that the company is backlogged with orders and is already profitable. The Tesla Roadster retails for $101,500, and the Model S sedan, slated for release in 2012, will retail for a much more affordable $49,000.

Although the cars are expensive, Tesla produces practical, competitive, eco-friendly cars. Unlike most hybrids, which accelerate slowly and do not perform well against gas-powered cars, the Roadster surges to 60 mph in 4.7 seconds and runs for about 220 miles on one battery charge. The Model S will have a 300-mile range, and the Roadster and Model S are just the beginning.[9] ❖

Q: Discussion Questions

1. How does the development of the Tesla Roadster contribute to developing green initiatives in the auto industry?

2. Why do you think that major auto companies such as General Motors, Ford, and Chrysler have been so slow in developing electric cars?

3. If Tesla is successful with its electric sports car, will it be a role model and influence the future of the electric car in our society?

through a full conversion to nonhydrogenated oils. Such a move reduces consumers' risk of coronary disease.[10] Marketers use promotion—advertising, personal selling, sales promotion (coupons, games, sweepstakes, movie tie-ins), and publicity—to communicate the benefits and advantages of their products to consumers and increase sales. Nonprofit organizations also use promotion. For example, the National Fluid Milk Processor Promotion Board's "milk mustache" advertising campaign has featured Mischa Barton, Jeff Gordon, Tony Hawk, Peyton and Eli Manning, and Gisele Bunschen, as well as animated "celebrities" such as Garfield.[11] We will examine marketing activities in Part 5 of this text.

finance Owners and finance are in the same part of Figure 1.1 because although management and marketing have to deal with financial considerations, it is the primary responsibility of the owners to provide financial resources for the operation of the business. Moreover, the owners have the most to lose if the business fails to make a profit. Finance refers to all activities concerned with obtaining money and using it effectively. People who work as accountants, stockbrokers, investment advisors, or bankers are all part of the financial world. Owners sometimes have to borrow money to get started or attract additional owners who become partners or stockholders. A mentoring group called 8 Wings helps women entrepreneurs obtain funding by assisting them in perfecting their business plan, preparing their presentation to potential funding sources, and introducing them to potential investors and other business contacts. The 8 Wings partners typically take stock or options in the companies they help.[12] Owners of small businesses in particular often rely on bank loans for funding. Part 6 of this text discusses financial management.

Why Study Business?

Studying business can help you develop skills and acquire knowledge to prepare for your future career, regardless of whether you plan to work for a multinational *Fortune* 500 firm, start your own business, work for a government agency, or manage or volunteer at a nonprofit organization. The field of business offers a variety of interesting and challenging career opportunities throughout the world, such as human resources management, information technology, finance, production and operations, wholesaling and retailing, and many more.

Studying business can also help you better understand the many business activities that are necessary to provide satisfying goods and services—and that these activities carry a price tag. For example, if you buy a new compact disk, about half of the price goes toward activities related to distribution and the retailer's expenses and profit margins. The production (pressing) of the CD represents about $1, or a small percentage of its price. Most businesses charge a reasonable price for their products to ensure that they cover their production costs, pay their employees, provide their owners with a return on their

Did the "Got Milk?" campaign featuring famous celebrities and their milk mustaches get you to drink more milk?

investment, and perhaps give something back to their local communities. Bill Daniels founded Cablevision, building his first cable TV system in Casper, Wyoming in 1953, and is now considered "the father of cable television." Upon Daniels's passing in 2000, he had established a foundation that currently has funding of $1.4 billion and supports a diversity of causes from education to business ethics. During his career Daniels created the Young American Bank where children could create bank accounts and learn about financial responsibility and this remains the world's only charter bank for young people. He created the Daniels College of Business through a donation of $20 million to the University of Denver. During his life, he affected many individuals and organizations and his business success has allowed his legacy to be one of giving and affecting communities throughout the United States.[13] Thus, learning about business can help you become a well-informed consumer and contributing member of society.

Business activities help generate the profits that are essential not only to individual businesses and local economies but also to the health of the global economy. Without profits, businesses find it difficult, if not impossible, to buy more raw materials, hire more employees, attract more capital, and create additional products that in turn make more profits and fuel the world

When you buy a Coldplay CD, about half of the price goes toward activities related to distribution, retail expenses, and profit margins.

economy. Understanding how our free-enterprise economic system allocates resources and provides incentives for industry and the workplace is important to everyone.

 LO3

Define economics and compare the four types of economic systems.

THE ECONOMIC FOUNDATIONS OF BUSINESS

To continue our introduction to business, it is useful to explore the economic environment in which business is conducted. In this section, we examine economic systems, the free-enterprise system, the concepts of supply and demand, and the role of competition. These concepts play important roles in determining how businesses operate in a particular society.

Economics is the study of how resources are distributed for the production of goods and services within a social system. You are already familiar with the types of resources available. Land, forests, minerals, water, and other things that

are not made by people are **natural resources. Human resources,** or labor, refers to the physical and mental abilities that people use to produce goods and services. **Financial resources,** or capital, are the funds used to acquire the natural and human resources needed to provide products. Because natural, human, and financial resources are used to produce goods and services, they are sometimes called *factors of production.*

Economic Systems

An **economic system** describes how a particular society distributes its resources to produce goods and services. A central issue of economics is how to fulfill an unlimited demand for goods and services in a world with a limited supply of resources. Different economic systems attempt to resolve this central issue in numerous ways, as we shall see.

Although economic systems handle the distribution of resources in different ways, all economic systems must address three important issues:

1. What goods and services, and how much of each, will satisfy consumers' needs?

2. How will goods and services be produced, who will produce them, and with what resources will they be produced?

3. How are the goods and services to be distributed to consumers?

Communism, socialism, and capitalism, the basic economic systems found in the world today (Table 1.1), have fundamental differences in the way they address these issues.

communism Karl Marx (1818–1883) first described **communism** as a society in which the people, without regard to class, own all the nation's resources. In his ideal political-economic system, everyone contributes according to ability and receives benefits according to need. In a communist economy, the people (through the government) own and operate all businesses and factors of production. Central government planning determines what goods and services satisfy citizens' needs, how the goods and services are produced, and how they are distributed. However, no true communist economy exists today that satisfies Marx's ideal.

On paper, communism appears to be efficient and equitable, producing less of a gap between rich and poor. In practice, however, communist economies have been marked by low standards of living, critical shortages of consumer goods, high prices, and little freedom. Russia, Poland, Hungary, and other Eastern European nations have turned away from communism and toward economic systems governed by supply and demand rather than by central planning. However, their experiments with alternative economic systems have been fraught with difficulty and hardship. China, North Korea, and Cuba continue to apply communist principles to their economies, but these countries are also enduring economic and political change. Consequently, communism is declining and its future as an economic system is uncertain.

socialism Closely related to communism is **socialism,** an economic system in which the government owns and operates basic industries—postal service, telephone, utilities, transportation, health care, banking, and some manufacturing—but individuals own most businesses. Central planning determines what basic goods and services are produced, how they are produced, and how they are distributed. Individuals and small businesses provide other goods and services based on consumer demand and the availability of resources. As with communism, citizens are dependent on the government for many goods and services.

Most socialist nations, such as Sweden, India, and Israel, are democratic and recognize basic individual freedoms. Citizens can vote for political offices, but central government planners usually make decisions about what is best for the nation. People are free to go into the occupation of their choice, but they often work in government-operated organizations. Socialists believe their system permits a higher standard of living than other economic systems, but the difference often applies to the nation as a whole rather than to its individual citizens. Socialist economies profess egalitarianism—equal distribution of income and social services. They believe their economies are more stable than those of other nations. Although this may be true, taxes and unemployment are generally higher in socialist countries. Perhaps as a result, many socialist countries are also experiencing economic turmoil.

capitalism **Capitalism,** or **free enterprise,** is an economic system in which individuals own and operate the majority of businesses that provide goods and services. Competition, supply, and demand determine which goods and services are produced, how they are produced, and how they are distributed. The United States, Canada, Japan, and Australia are examples of economic systems based on capitalism.

There are two forms of capitalism: pure capitalism and modified capitalism. In pure capitalism, also called a **free-market system,** all economic decisions are made without government intervention. This economic system was first described by Adam Smith in *The Wealth of Nations* (1776). Smith, often called the father of capitalism, believed that the "invisible hand of competition" best regulates the economy. He argued that competition should determine what goods and services people need.

● **COMMUNISM** first described by Karl Marx as a society in which the people, without regard to class, own all the nation's resources

● **SOCIALISM** an economic system in which the government owns and operates basic industries but individuals own most businesses

● **CAPITALISM, OR FREE ENTERPRISE** an economic system in which individuals own and operate the majority of businesses that provide goods and services

● **FREE-MARKET SYSTEM** pure capitalism, in which all economic decisions are made without government intervention

TABLE 1.1 Comparison of Communism, Socialism, and Capitalism

	Communism	Socialism	Capitalism
Business ownership	Most businesses are owned and operated by the government.	The government owns and operates major industries; individuals own small businesses.	Individuals own and operate all businesses.
Competition	None. The government owns and operates everything.	Restricted in major industries; encouraged in small business.	Encouraged by market forces and government regulations.
Profits	Excess income goes to the government.	Profits earned by small businesses may be reinvested in the business; profits from government-owned industries go to the government.	Individuals are free to keep profits and use them as they wish.
Product availability and price	Consumers have a limited choice of goods and services; prices are usually high.	Consumers have some choice of goods and services; prices are determined by supply and demand.	Consumers have a wide choice of goods and services; prices are determined by supply and demand.
Employment options	Little choice in choosing a career; most people work for government-owned industries or farms.	Some choice of careers; many people work in government jobs.	Unlimited choice of careers.

Source: "Gross Domestic Product or Expenditure, 1930–2007," *InfoPlease* (n.d.), www.infoplease.com/ipa/A0104575.html (accessed March 9, 2009).

Smith's system is also called *laissez-faire* ("to leave alone") *capitalism* because the government does not interfere in business.

Modified capitalism differs from pure capitalism in that the government intervenes and regulates business to some extent. One of the ways in which the United States and Canadian governments regulate business is through laws. Laws such as the Federal Trade Commission Act, which created the Federal Trade Commission to enforce antitrust laws, illustrate the importance of the government's role in the economy.

mixed economies No country practices a pure form of communism, socialism, or capitalism, although most tend to favor one system over the others. Most nations operate as **mixed economies,** which have elements from more than one economic system. In socialist Sweden, most businesses are owned and operated by private individuals. In capitalist United States, the federal government owns and operates the postal

A number of basic individual and business rights must exist for free enterprise to work. These rights are the goals of many countries that have recently embraced free enterprise.

1. Individuals must have the right to own property and to pass this property on to their heirs. This right motivates people to work hard and save to buy property.

2. Individuals and businesses must have the right to earn profits and to use the profits as they wish, within the constraints of their society's laws and values.

3. Individuals and businesses must have the right to make decisions that determine the way the business operates. Although there is government regulation, the philosophy in countries like the United States and Australia is to permit maximum freedom within a set of rules of fairness.

4. Individuals must have the right to choose what career to pursue, where to live, what goods and services to purchase, and

> **"Demand is the number of goods and services that consumers are willing to buy at different prices at a specific time."**

service and the Tennessee Valley Authority, an electric utility. In Great Britain and Mexico, the governments are attempting to sell many state-run businesses to private individuals and companies. In once-communist Russia, Hungary, Poland, and other Eastern European nations, capitalist ideas have been implemented, including private ownership of businesses.

The Free-Enterprise System

Many economies—including those of the United States, Canada, and Japan—are based on free enterprise, and many communist and socialist countries, such as China and Russia, are applying more principles of free enterprise to their own economic systems. Free enterprise provides an opportunity for a business to succeed or fail on the basis of market demand. In a free-enterprise system, companies that can efficiently manufacture and sell products that consumers desire will probably succeed. Inefficient businesses and those that sell products that do not offer needed benefits will likely fail as consumers take their business to firms that have more competitive products.

more. Businesses must have the right to choose where to locate, what goods and services to produce, what resources to use in the production process, and so on.

Without these rights, businesses cannot function effectively because they are not motivated to succeed. Thus, these rights make possible the open exchange of goods and services.

 L04

Describe the role of supply, demand, and competition in a free-enterprise system.

The Forces of Supply and Demand

In the United States and in other free-enterprise systems, the distribution of resources and products is determined by supply and demand. **Demand** is the number of goods and services that consumers are willing to buy at different prices at a specific time. From your own experience, you probably recognize

Gasoline prices rose and fell sharply in recent years, changing consumers' driving habits. Supply and demand may have played a role, but some people believe the run-up was caused in part, by speculators bidding prices up.

that consumers are usually willing to buy more of an item as its price falls because they want to save money. Consider handmade rugs, for example. Consumers may be willing to buy six rugs at $350 each, four at $500 each, but only two at $650 each. The relationship between the price and the number of rugs consumers are willing to buy can be shown graphically, with a *demand curve* (see Figure 1.2).

Supply is the number of products that businesses are willing to sell at different prices at a specific time. In general, because the potential for profits is higher, businesses are willing to supply more of a good or service at higher prices. For example, a company that sells rugs may be willing to sell six at $650 each, four at $500 each, but just two at $350 each. The relationship

between the price of rugs and the quantity the company is willing to supply can be shown graphically with a *supply curve* (see Figure 1.2).

In Figure 1.2, the supply and demand curves intersect at the point where supply and demand are equal. The price at which the number of products that businesses are willing to supply equals the amount of products that consumers are willing to buy at a specific point in time is the **equilibrium price.** In our rug example, the company is willing to supply four rugs at $500 each, and consumers are willing to buy four rugs at $500 each. Therefore, $500 is the equilibrium price for a rug at that point in time, and most rug companies will price their rugs at $500. As you might imagine, a business that charges more than $500 (or whatever the current equilibrium price is) for its rugs will not sell many and might not earn a profit. On the other hand, a business that charges less than $500 accepts a lower profit per rug than could be made at the equilibrium price.

If the cost of making rugs goes up, businesses will not offer as many at the old price. Changing the price alters the supply curve, and a new equilibrium price results. This is an ongoing process, with supply and demand constantly changing in response to changes in economic conditions, availability of resources, and degree of competition. For example, gasoline prices rose sharply in 2008 in response to a shrinking supply of gasoline and crude oil and rising demand. In contrast to the oil boom, in 2008, there were nearly 1 million homes in foreclosure and over 3 million homeowners were behind in their mortgage payments. The inventory of homes for sale grew rapidly and prices fell because of the large supply of house on the market.[14] Prices for goods and services vary according to these changes in supply and demand. This concept is the force that drives the distribution of resources (goods and services, labor, and money) in a free-enterprise economy.

Critics of supply and demand say the system does not distribute resources equally. The forces of supply and demand prevent sellers who have to sell at higher prices (because their costs are high) and buyers who cannot afford to buy goods at the equilibrium price from participating in the market. According to critics, the wealthy can afford to buy more than they need, but the poor are unable to buy enough of what they need to survive.

The Nature of Competition

Competition, the rivalry among businesses for consumers' dollars, is another vital element in free enterprise. According to Adam Smith, competition fosters efficiency and low prices by forcing producers to offer the best products at the most

| FIGURE | 1.2 | Equilibrium Price of Handmade Rugs |

Prices of Rugs (dollars)

$800
650
500
350
200
0

Equilibrium Price

Supply Curve

Demand Curve

1   2   3   4   5   6   7

Handmade Rugs

reasonable price; those who fail to do so are not able to stay in business. Thus, competition should improve the quality of the goods and services available or reduce prices. For example, thanks to smart design and excellent timing, Apple dominates the market for downloadable music with its iTunes online service and iPod MP3 player. However, many companies have set their sights on capturing some of the firm's market share with new products of their own. Wal-Mart and Napster have launched online music services, while many rival computer firms have introduced MP3 players with new features and/or lower prices.

Within a free-enterprise system, there are four types of competitive environments: pure competition, monopolistic competition, oligopoly, and monopoly.

Pure competition exists when there are many small businesses selling one standardized product, such as agricultural commodities like wheat, corn, and cotton. No one business sells enough of the product to influence the product's price. And because there is no difference in the products, prices are determined solely by the forces of supply and demand.

Monopolistic competition exists when there are fewer businesses than in a pure-competition environment and the differences among the goods they sell is small. Aspirin, soft drinks, and vacuum cleaners are examples of such goods. These products differ slightly in packaging, warranty, name, and other characteristics, but all satisfy the same consumer need. Businesses have some power over the price they charge in monopolistic competition because they can make consumers aware of product differences through advertising. Consumers value some features more than others and are often willing to pay higher prices for a product with the features they want. For example, Advil, a nonprescription pain reliever, contains ibuprofen instead of aspirin. Consumers who cannot take aspirin or who believe ibuprofen is a more effective pain reliever may not mind paying a little extra for the ibuprofen in Advil.

An **oligopoly** exists when there are very few businesses selling a product. In an oligopoly, individual businesses have control over their products' price because each business supplies a large portion of the products sold in the marketplace. Nonetheless, the prices charged by different firms stay fairly close because a price cut or increase by one company will trigger a similar response from another company. In the airline industry,

 Competition, the rivalry among businesses for consumers' dollars, is another vital element in free enterprise.

for example, when one airline cuts fares to boost sales, other airlines quickly follow with rate decreases to remain competitive. Oligopolies exist when it is expensive for new firms to enter the marketplace. Not just anyone can acquire enough financial capital to build an automobile production facility or purchase enough airplanes and related resources to build an airline.

When there is one business providing a product in a given market, a **monopoly** exists. Utility companies that supply electricity, natural gas, and water are monopolies. The government permits such monopolies because the cost of creating the good or supplying the service is so great that new producers cannot compete for sales. Government-granted monopolies are subject to government-regulated prices. Some monopolies exist because of technological developments that are protected by patent laws. Patent laws grant the developer of new technology a period of time (usually 17 years) during which no other producer can use the same technology without the agreement of the original developer. The United States granted the first patent in 1790, and the patent office received 440,000 patent applications in 2006.[15] This monopoly allows the developer to recover research, development, and production expenses and to earn a reasonable profit. Examples of this type of monopoly are the dry-copier process developed by Xerox and the self-developing photographic technology created by Polaroid. Both companies operated for years without competition and could charge premium prices because no alternative products existed to compete with their products. Through continuous development, Polaroid maintains market dominance. Xerox's patents have expired, however, and many imitators have forced market prices to decline.

● ● **LO5**

Specify why and how the health of the economy is measured.

Economic Cycles and Productivity

expansion and contraction Economies are not stagnant; they expand and contract. **Economic expansion** occurs when an economy is growing and people are spending

● INFLATION a condition characterized by a continuing rise in prices

● ECONOMIC CONTRACTION a slowdown of the economy characterized by a decline in spending and during which businesses cut back on production and lay off workers

● RECESSION a decline in production, employment, and income

● UNEMPLOYMENT the condition in which a percentage of the population wants to work but is unable to find jobs

more money. Their purchases stimulate the production of goods and services, which in turn stimulates employment. The standard of living rises because more people are employed and have money to spend. Rapid expansions of the economy, however, may result in **inflation,** a continuing rise in prices. Inflation can be harmful if individuals' incomes do not increase at the same pace as rising prices, reducing their buying power. Zimbabwe has the highest inflation rate at over 165,000 percent.[16]

Economic contraction occurs when spending declines. Businesses cut back on production and lay off workers, and the economy as a whole slows down. Contractions of the economy lead to **recession**— a decline in production, employment, and income. Recessions are often characterized by rising levels of **unemployment,** which is measured as the percentage of the population that wants to work but is unable to find jobs. Figure 1.3 shows the overall unemployment rate in the civilian labor force over the past 89 years. Rising unemployment levels tend to stifle demand for goods and services, which can have the effect of forcing prices downward, a condition known as *deflation*. The United States has experienced numerous recessions, the most recent ones occurring in 1990–1991, 2001, and 2008–2009. Japan has also experienced numerous recessions in the last decade.

The meltdown of the worldwide financial system and the crash of the U.S. stock market in 2008 caused a severe recession, leading to U.S. unemployment rates not seen for decades.

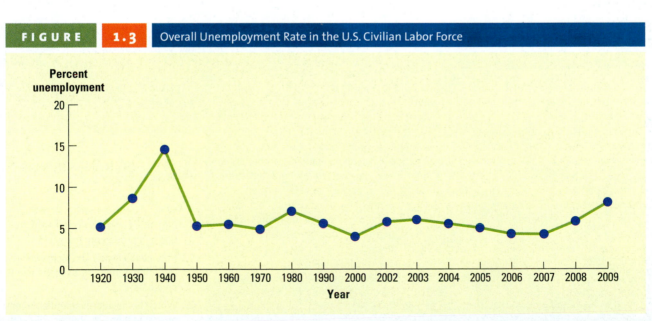

| FIGURE | 1.3 | Overall Unemployment Rate in the U.S. Civilian Labor Force |

Source: "Unemployment Rate," Bureau of Labor Statistics Data, http://data.bls.gov/PDQ/servlet/SurveyOutputServlet?data_tool=latest_numbers&series_id=LNS14000000 (accessed March 9, 2009).

A severe recession may turn into a **depression,** in which unemployment is very high, consumer spending is low, and business output is sharply reduced, such as occurred in the United States in the early 1930s.

Economies expand and contract in response to changes in consumer, business, and government spending. War also can affect an economy, sometimes stimulating it (as in the United States during World Wars I and II) and sometimes stifling it (as during the Vietnam and Persian Gulf wars). Although fluctuations in the economy are inevitable and to a certain extent predictable, their effects—inflation and unemployment—disrupt lives, and thus governments try to minimize them.

measuring the economy Countries measure the state of their economies to determine whether they are expanding or contracting and whether corrective action is necessary to minimize the fluctuations. One commonly used measure is **gross domestic product (GDP)**—the sum of all goods and services produced in a country during a year. GDP measures only those goods and services made within a country and therefore does not include profits from companies' overseas operations; it does include profits earned by foreign companies within the country being measured. However, it does not take into account the concept of GDP in relation to population (GDP per capita). Figure 1.4 shows the increase in GDP over several years, while Table 1.2 compares a number of economic indicators for a sampling of countries.

Another important indicator of a nation's economic health is the relationship between its spending and income (from taxes). When a nation spends more than it takes in from taxes, it has a **budget deficit.** In the 1990s, the U.S. government eliminated its long-standing budget deficit by balancing the money spent for social, defense, and other programs with the amount of money taken in from taxes.

In recent years, however, the budget deficit has reemerged and grown to record levels, partly due to defense spending in the aftermath of the terrorist attacks of September 11, 2001. Because Americans do not want their taxes increased, it is difficult for the federal government to bring in more revenue and reduce the deficit. Like consumers and businesses, when the government needs money, it borrows from the public, banks, and other institutions. The national debt (the amount of money the nation owes its lenders) recently exceeded $11 trillion due largely to increased spending by the government.[17] This figure is especially worrisome because, to reduce the debt to a manageable level, the government either has to increase its revenues (raise taxes) or reduce spending on social, defense, and legal programs, neither of which is politically popular. The national debt figure changes daily and can be seen at the Department of the Treasury, Bureau of the Public Debt, Web site. Table 1.3 describes some of the other ways we evaluate our nation's economy.

Lowe's vs. Home Depot: Location, Location, Location

Which do you prefer, Lowe's or Home Depot? It may not seem that important, but your answer is critical to both companies. Fifty-three percent of the respondents surveyed preferred Lowe's, versus 47 percent for Home Depot. Those preferring Lowe's cited better product selection and customer service. Prices are comparable at both stores. So what accounts for the fact that recently Home Depot netted $4.395 billion while Lowe's netted $2.809 billion? In a word . . . location!

Lowe's boasts over 1,650 stores, while Home Depot has 2,278 retail stores. Although consumers regularly shop in both stores, those preferring Lowe's still spent an average of $454 at Home Depot during a six-month period. Those preferring Home Depot spent well over $100 less at Lowe's in the same time frame. On average, Home Depot caters more to men, contractors, and serious do-it-yourselfers, whereas Lowe's caters more to women and those looking to put the finishing touches on decorating projects.

Although Home Depot gets more traffic, consumers are not committed to either store. This forces each store to fight for sales. Due to the recession, store expansion is no longer so feasible. Hence, both companies have sought to increase customer satisfaction in their existing stores. Home Depot wants to increase its customer service, including working on its product line and creating a better shopping environment (the factors that caused Lowe's to score higher in the survey cited above). Lowe's desires to increase store efficiency for its customers during this difficult time. Each store is trying to improve on the other, which can only lead to better shopping experiences for consumers all around.[18] ❖

Q: **Discussion Questions**

1. Why is there so much competition between Lowe's and Home Depot in the home improvement market?

2. How have Lowe's and Home Depot differentiated their stores in the minds of consumers?

3. Which home improvement company do you feel has the better competitive image? Lowe's or Home Depot?

FIGURE 1.4 Growth in U.S. Gross Domestic Product

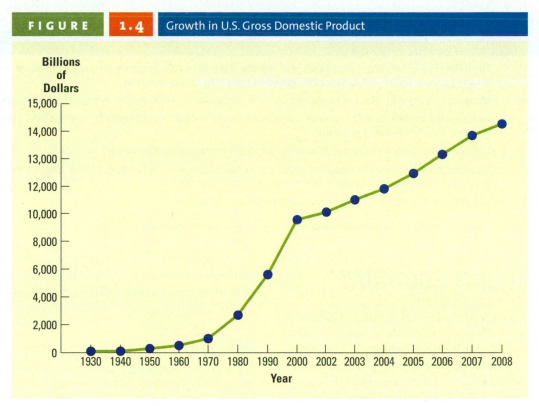

Sources: "Gross Domestic product or Expenditure, 1930–2007," *InfoPlease* (n.d.), www.infoplease.com/ipa/A0104575.html (accessed March 9, 2009); "Table 1.1.5, Gross Domestic Product," Bureau of Economic Analysis National Income and Product Accounts Table, www.bea.gov/national/nipaweb/TableView.asp?SelectedTable=5&FirstYear=2007&LastYear=2008&Freq=Qtr (accessed March 9, 2009).

TABLE 1.2   A Comparative Analysis of a Sampling of Countries

Country	GDP (in billions of U.S. dollars)	GDP per capita (in U.S. dollars)	Unemployment Rate (%)	Inflation Rate (%)
Argentina	$585	14,500	7.8	22
Australia	824.9	39,300	4.5	4.7
Brazil	2.03 (trillion)	10,300	8	5.8
Canada	1.336 (t)	40,200	6.1	3
China	7.8 (t)	6,100	4[*]	6
France	2.097 (t)	32,700	7.4	1
Germany	2.863 (t)	34,800	7.9	2.8
India	3.319 (t)	2,900	6.8	7.8
Israel	205.7	28,900	6.1	4.7
Japan	4.487 (t)	35,300	4.2	1.8
Mexico	1.578 (t)	14,400	4.1	6.2
Russia	2.225 (t)	15,800	6.2	13.9
South Africa	566.1	10,400	21.7	11.3
United Kingdom	2.281 (t)	37,400	5.5	3.8
United States	14.58 (t)	48,000	7.2	4.2

[*]Estimated for urban areas; unemployment rates in rural areas may be higher.

Source: "Country Listing," *The World Fact Book 2008* (n.d.), www.cia.gov/library/publications/the-world-factbook/index.html (accessed March 9, 2009).

TABLE 1.3   How Do We Evaluate Our Nation's Economy?

Unit of Measure	Description
Trade balance	The difference between our exports and our imports. If the balance is negative, as it has been since the mid-1980s, it is called a trade deficit and is generally viewed as unhealthy for our economy.
Consumer Price Index	Measures changes in prices of goods and services purchased for consumption by typical urban households.
Per capita income	Indicates the income level of "average" Americans. Useful in determing how much "average" consumers spend and how much money Americans are earning.
Unemployment rate	Indicates how many working-age Americans are not working who otherwise want to work.*
Inflation	Monitors price increases in consumer goods and services over specified periods of time. Used to determine if costs of goods and services are exceeding worker compensation over time.
Worker productivity	The amount of goods and services produced for each hour worked.

*Americans who do not want to work in a traditional sense, such as househusbands/housewives, are not counted as unemployed.

THE AMERICAN ECONOMY

As we said previously, the United States is a mixed economy based on capitalism. The answers to the three basic economic issues are determined primarily by competition and the forces of supply and demand, although the federal government does intervene in economic decisions to a certain extent. To understand the current state of the American economy and its effect on business practices, it is helpful to examine its history and the roles of the entrepreneur and the government.

●● L06

Trace the evolution of the American economy, and discuss the role of the entrepreneur in the economy.

A Brief History of the American Economy

the early economy Before the colonization of North America, Native Americans lived as hunter/gatherers and farmers, with some trade among tribes. The colonists who came later operated primarily as an *agricultural economy.* People were self-sufficient and produced everything they needed at home, including food, clothing, and furniture. Abundant natural resources and a moderate climate nourished industries such as farming, fishing, shipping, and fur trading. A few manufactured goods and money for the colonies' burgeoning industries came from England and other countries.

As the nation expanded slowly toward the West, people found natural resources such as coal, copper, and iron ore and used them to produce goods such as horseshoes, farm implements, and kitchen utensils. Farm families that produced surplus goods sold or traded them for things they could not produce themselves, such as fine furniture and window glass. Some families also spent time turning raw materials into clothes and household goods. Because these goods were produced at home, this system was called the domestic system.

the industrial revolution The 19th century and the Industrial Revolution brought the development of new technology and factories. The factory brought together all the resources needed to make a product—materials, machines,

The founders of Vineyard Vines reveal the success of entrepreneurship and benefits of creating a winning business model.

and workers. Work in factories became specialized as workers focused on one or two tasks. As work became more efficient, productivity increased, making more goods available at lower prices. Railroads brought major changes, allowing farmers to send their surplus crops and goods all over the nation for barter or for sale.

Factories began to spring up along the railways to manufacture farm equipment and a variety of other goods to be shipped by rail. Samuel Slater set up the first American textile factory after he memorized the plans for an English factory and emigrated to the United States. Eli Whitney revolutionized the cotton industry with his cotton gin. Francis Cabot Lowell's factory organized all the steps in manufacturing cotton cloth for maximum efficiency and productivity. John Deere's farm equipment increased farm production and reduced the number of farmers required to feed the young nation. Farmers began to move to cities to find jobs in factories and a higher standard of living. Henry Ford developed the assembly-line system to produce automobiles. Workers focused on one part of an automobile and then pushed it to the next stage until it rolled off the assembly line as a finished automobile. Ford's assembly line could manufacture many automobiles efficiently, and the price of his cars was $200, making them affordable to many Americans.

the manufacturing and marketing economies
Industrialization brought increased prosperity, and the United States gradually became a *manufacturing economy*—one devoted to manufacturing goods and providing services rather than producing agricultural products. The assembly line was applied to more industries, increasing the variety of goods available to the consumer. Businesses became more concerned with the needs of the consumer and entered the *marketing economy*. Expensive goods such as cars and appliances could be purchased on a time-payment plan. Companies conducted research to find out what products consumers needed and wanted. Advertising made consumers aware of differences in products and prices.

Because these developments occurred in a free-enterprise system, consumers determined what goods and services were produced. They did this by purchasing the products they liked at prices they were willing to pay. The United States prospered, and American citizens had one of the highest standards of living in the world.

the service and internet-based economy
After World War II, with the increased standard of living, Americans had more money and more time. They began to pay others to perform services that made their lives easier.

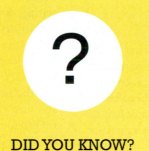

DID YOU KNOW?

60 percent of adult women work.[19]

Beginning in the 1960s, more and more women entered the workforce. The profile of the family changed: Today there are more single-parent families and individuals living alone, and in two-parent families, both parents often work. One result of this trend is that time-pressed Americans are increasingly paying others to do tasks they used to do at home, like cooking, laundry, landscaping, and child care. These trends have gradually changed the United States to a *service economy*—one devoted to the production of services that make life easier for busy consumers. Service industries such as restaurants, banking, medicine, child care, auto repair, leisure-related industries, and even education are growing rapidly and may account for as much as 80 percent of the U.S. economy. These trends continue with advanced technology contributing to new service products such as overnight mail, electronic banking, and shopping through cable television networks and the Internet. Table 1.4 provides an overview of e-commerce in the United States. More about the Internet and e-commerce can be found in Chapter 4.

The Role of the Entrepreneur

An **entrepreneur** is an individual who risks his or her wealth, time, and effort to develop for profit an innovative product or way of doing something. Emeterio Ortiz was making homemade salsa in 1918 during the Mexican

● **ENTREPRENEUR** an individual who risks his or her wealth, time, and effort to develop for profit an innovative product or way of doing something

Designer Beck Hickey found a way to turn used skateboards into a business opportunity by transforming them into Sk8bags—a line of handbag-related products. Hickey's products are sold at sports shops across the United States as well as abroad.

TABLE 1.4   U.S. E-Commerce Overview

Total retail sales of all types	$4,572 billion
Total e-commerce sales	$145.6 billion
Total travel sales online	$105 billion
Online advertising	$23.6 billion
Number of VOIP subscribers, U.S.	$23.3 million
Active home Internet users in the U.S.	220.1 million
Number of high-speed Internet connections	145 million
Number of Web logs	133 million
Percent of U.S. adults online	72

Source: "E-Commerce & Internet Industry Overview," Plunkett Research, Ltd., www.plunkettresearch.com/Industries/ECommerceInternet/ECommerceInternetStatistics/tabid/167/Default.aspx (accessed March 9, 2009).

Revolution. Nearly a century later Juanita Carmack, her great-granddaughter started sharing the recipe with friends and when her children left home, she started her own business, Taco Chic Salsa. The salsa, from the secret family recipe, has been enormously successful—it is available in over 60 stores and plans to seek a distributor are under way. The successful entrepreneur started her business in Rathdrum Idaho.[20]

The free-enterprise system provides the conditions necessary for entrepreneurs to succeed. In the past, entrepreneurs were often inventors who brought all the factors of production together to produce a new product. Thomas Edison, whose inventions include the record player and lightbulb, was an early American entrepreneur. Henry Ford was one of the first persons to develop mass assembly methods in the automobile industry. Other entrepreneurs, so-called captains of industry, invested in the country's growth. John D. Rockefeller built Standard Oil out of the fledgling oil industry, and Andrew Carnegie invested in railroads and founded the United States Steel Corporation. Andrew Mellon built the Aluminum Company of America and Gulf Oil. J. P. Morgan started financial institutions to fund the business activities of other entrepreneurs. Although these entrepreneurs were born in another century, their legacy to the American economy lives on in the companies they started, many of which still operate today. Milton Hershey began producing chocolate in 1894 in Lancaster, Pennsylvania. In 1900, the company was mass producing chocolate in many forms, lowering the cost of chocolate and making it more affordable to the masses whereas it has once been a high-priced, luxury good. Early advertising touted chocolate as "a palatable confection and most nourishing food." Today, the Hershey Company employs almost 13,000 employees and sells almost $5 billion in chocolates and candies throughout the world.[21]

Entrepreneurs are constantly changing American business practices with new technology and innovative management techniques. Bill Gates, for example, built Microsoft, a software company whose products include MS-DOS (a disk operating system), Word, and Windows, into a multibillion-dollar enterprise. Frederick Smith had an idea to deliver packages overnight, and now his FedEx Company plays an important role in getting documents and packages delivered all over the world for businesses and individuals. Entrepreneurs have been associated with such uniquely American concepts as Dell Computers, Ben & Jerry's, Levi's, Holiday Inns, McDonald's, Dr Pepper, and Wal-Mart. Wal-Mart, founded by entrepreneur Sam Walton, was the first retailer to reach $100 billion in sales in one year and now routinely passes that mark. Wal-Mart has more than 1.9 million employees and operates more than 6,700 stores in the United States, Canada, Mexico, Asia, Europe, and South America. San Walton's heirs own about 40 percent of the company.[22] We will examine the importance of entrepreneurship further in Chapter 6.

The Role of Government in the American Economy

The American economic system is best described as modified capitalism because the government regulates business to preserve competition and protect consumers and employees. Federal, state, and local governments intervene in the economy with laws and regulations designed to promote competition and to protect consumers, employees, and the environment. Many of these laws are discussed in Appendix A.

Additionally, government agencies such as the U.S. Department of Commerce measure the health of the economy

An Encyclopedia of Information with a Mouse Click

Almost everyone uses Wikipedia, the multilingual, Web-based free content encyclopedia project launched in 2001 as a nonprofit financed by user donations. Volunteers from around the world write it collaboratively, and almost all of its articles can be edited by anyone with access to the Internet. Since its creation, Wikipedia has grown rapidly into one of the largest reference Web sites in the world. It has over 8.2 million articles in 253 languages, and the English Wikipedia edition has more than 2 million articles. Since its creation it has been rising in popularity and currently ranks among the top ten most-visited Web sites worldwide. Wikipedia has more than 160 million unique visitors monthly, and this number continues to increase. Jimmy Wales, Wikipedia's founder, has enjoyed success as an entrepreneur based on his understanding of rapid changes in the marketing environment and utilizing emerging technologies to develop new products. He has made transparency a core principle; his collaborative products capture social networking and the desire to have information accessible in an efficient and inexpensive way.[23] ❖

> # BUSINESS ETHICS GENERALLY REFERS TO THE STANDARDS AND PRINCIPLES USED BY SOCIETY TO DEFINE APPROPRIATE AND INAPPROPRIATE CONDUCT IN THE WORKPLACE.

(GDP, productivity, etc.) and, when necessary, take steps to minimize the disruptive effects of economic fluctuations and reduce unemployment. When the economy is contracting and unemployment is rising, the federal government through the Federal Reserve Board (see Chapter 14) tries to spur growth so that consumers will spend more money and businesses will hire more employees. To accomplish this, it may reduce interest rates or increase its own spending for goods and services. When the economy expands so fast that inflation results, the government may intervene to reduce inflation by slowing down economic growth. This can be accomplished by raising interest rates to discourage spending by businesses and consumers. Techniques used to control the economy are discussed in Chapter 14.

The Role of Ethics and Social Responsibility in Business

In the last few years, you may have read about a number of scandals at a number of well-known corporations, including Enron, WorldCom, Tyco, and Arthur Andersen. In many cases, misconduct by individuals within these firms had an adverse effect on current and retired employees, investors, and others associated with these firms. In some cases, individuals went to jail for their actions. Top executives at General Re, an insurance division of Berkshire Hathaway, were convicted of fraud stemming from transactions between AIG and General Re Corporation. The convicted former employees faced prison sentences up to 230 years and fines up to $46 million for the fraudulent misrepresentation of assets.[24] These scandals undermined public confidence in Corporate America and sparked a new debate about ethics in business. Business ethics generally refers to the standards and principles used by society to define appropriate and inappropriate conduct in the workplace. In many cases, these standards have been codified as laws prohibiting actions deemed unacceptable.

Society is increasingly demanding that businesspeople behave ethically and socially responsibly toward not only their customers but also their employees, investors, government regulators, communities, and the natural environment. "Intel helped establish a goal for PFCs (perfluorocompounds) that

the entire industry could support," Intel President and CEO Paul Otellini told *CRO*. "It came together before Kyoto and was the first worldwide, industry-wide goal to address climate change. We view our environmental strategies as integral to the way we do business. We strive to lead by example, and to be trusted stakeholders to governments worldwide."[25] Green business strategies create long-run relationships with all stakeholders by maintaining, supporting, and enhancing the natural environment.

One of the primary lessons of the scandals of the early 2000s has been that the reputation of business organizations depends not just on bottom-line profits but also on ethical conduct and concern for the welfare of others. Consider that in the aftermath of these scandals, the reputations of every U.S. company suffered regardless of their association with the scandals.[26] While progress is being made in business ethics, as employees become more sensitive to ethical issues, reporting of ethical misconduct has increased over the past few years. The fact that employees continue to report observing misconduct and experiencing pressure to engage in unethical or illegal acts remains troubling and suggests that companies need to continue their efforts to raise ethical standards. We take a closer look at ethics and social responsibility in business in Chapter 2.

CAN YOU LEARN BUSINESS IN A CLASSROOM?

Obviously, the answer is yes, or there would be no purpose for this textbook! To be successful in business, you need knowledge, skills, experience, and good judgment. The topics covered in this chapter and throughout this book provide some of the knowledge you need to understand the world of business. The boxes and examples within each chapter describe experiences to help you develop good business judgment. The interactive exercises and assignments found in our Web site at www.mhhe.com/inbus will help you develop skills that may be useful in your future career. However, good judgment is based on knowledge and experience plus personal insight and

SO YOU WANT A JOB IN THE BUSINESS WORLD

When most people think of a career in business, they see themselves entering the door to large companies and multinationals that they read about in the news and discussed in class. In a national survey, students indicated they would like to work for Google, Walt Disney, Apple, and Ernst & Young. In fact, most jobs are not with large corporations, but are in small companies, nonprofit organizations, government, and even self-employed individuals. There are 20 million individuals the Small Business Administration says own their businesses and have no employees. In addition, there are nearly 5 million small businesses which employ 10 or fewer workers. With over 75 percent of the economy based on services, there are jobs available in industries such as health care, finance, education, hospitality, entertainment, and transportation. The world is changing quickly, and large corporations replace the equivalent of their entire workforce every four years.

The fast pace of technology today means that you have to be prepared to take advantage of emerging job opportunities and markets. You must also become adaptive and recognize that business is becoming more global, with job opportunities around the world. If you may want to obtain such a job, you shouldn't miss a chance to spend some time overseas. As get you started on the path to thinking about job opportunities, consider all the changes in business today that might affect your possible long-term track and that could bring you lots of success. You may want to stay completely out of large organizations and corporations and put yourself in a position for an entrepreneurial role as a self-employed contractor or small-business owner. However, many people feel that experience in larger businesses is helpful to your success later as an entrepreneur.

You're on the road to learning the key knowledge, skills, and trends that you can use to be a star in business. Businesses' impact on our society, especially in the area of sustainability and improvement of the environment, is a growing challenge and opportunity. Green businesses and green jobs in the business world are provided to give you a glimpse at the possibilities. Along the way, we will introduce you to some specific careers and offer advice on developing your own job opportunities. Research indicates that you won't be that happy with your job unless you enjoy your work and feel that it has a purpose. Since you spend most of your waking hours every day at work, you need to seriously think about what is important to you in a job.[27]

FIGURE 1.5 The Organization of This Book

Economy (Chapter 1)

Finance (Chapters 14, 15, 16)

Owners

Competition (Chapter 1)

(Chapters 7, 8, 9, 10, 11) Management

Employees

Customers

Information Technology (Chapter 4)

(Chapters 12, 13) Marketing

Legal and Regulatory Forces (Appendix A)

Business Ethics and Social Responsibility (Chapter 2)

Special Topics:
Global Business (Chapter 3)
Forms of Ownership (Chapter 5)
Small Business, Entrepreneurship, and Franchising (Chapter 6)

understanding. Therefore, you need more courses in business, along with some practical experience in the business world, to help you develop the special insight necessary to put your personal stamp on knowledge as you apply it. The challenge in business is in the area of judgment, and judgment does not develop from memorizing an introductory business textbook. If you are observant in your daily experiences as an employee, as a student, and as a consumer, you will improve your ability to make good business judgments.

Figure 1.5 is an overview of how the chapters in this book are linked together and how the chapters relate to the participants, the activities, and the environmental factors found in the business world. The topics presented in the chapters that follow are those that will give you the best opportunity to begin the process of understanding the world of business. ■

Team Exercise

Major economic systems, including capitalism, socialism, and communism, as well as mixed economies, were discussed in this chapter. Assuming that you want an economic system that is best for the majority, not just a few members of society, defend one of the economic systems as the best system. Form groups and try to reach agreement on one economic system. Defend why you support the system you prefer.

CHECK OUT www.mhhe.com/FerrellM2e

for study materials including Interactive Exercises, Quizzes, iPod downloads, and video.

● ● learning OBJECTIVES

LO1 Define business ethics and social responsibility, and examine their importance.

LO2 Detect some of the ethical issues that may arise in business.

LO3 Specify how businesses can promote ethical behavior.

LO4 Explain the four dimensions of social responsibility.

LO5 Debate an organization's social responsibilities to owners, employees, consumers, the environment, and the community.

BUSINESS ETHICS AND SOCIAL RESPONSIBILITY

introduction Auto manufacturers that make hybrid cars have taken on the challenge of contributing to society through their business activities. At the other extreme, wrongdoing by some businesses has focused public attention and government involvement to encourage more acceptable business conduct. Any business decision may be judged as right or wrong, ethical or unethical, legal or illegal.

In this chapter, we take a look at the role of ethics and social responsibility in business decision making. First we define business ethics and examine why it is important to understand ethics' role in business. Next we explore a number of business ethics issues to help you learn to recognize such issues when they arise. Finally, we consider steps businesses can take to improve ethical behavior in their organizations. The second half of the chapter focuses on social responsibility. We survey some important responsibility issues and detail how companies have responded to them.

LO1

Define business ethics and social responsibility, and examine their importance.

BUSINESS ETHICS AND SOCIAL RESPONSIBILITY

In this chapter, we define **business ethics** as the principles and standards that determine acceptable conduct in business organizations. The acceptability of behavior in business is determined by customers, competitors, government regulators, interest groups, and the public, as well as each individual's personal moral principles and values. Enron is an example of one of the largest ethical disasters in the 21st century. Two former Enron CEOs, Ken Lay and Jeff Skilling, were found guilty on all counts of conspiring to hide the company's financial condition. The judge in

Many consumers and social advocates believe that businesses should not only make a profit but also consider the social implications of their activities. We define **social responsibility** as a business's obligation to maximize its positive impact and minimize its negative impact on society. Although many people use the terms *social responsibility* and *ethics* interchangeably, they do not mean the same thing. Business ethics relates to an *individual's* or a *work group's* decisions that society evaluates as right or wrong, whereas social responsibility is a broader concept that concerns the impact of the *entire business's* activities on society. From an ethical perspective, for example, we may be concerned about a health care organization overcharging the government for Medicare services. From a social responsibility perspective, we might be concerned about the impact that this overcharging will have on the ability of the health care system to provide adequate services for all citizens.

The most basic ethical and social responsibility concerns have been codified as laws and regulations that encourage businesses to conform to society's standards, values, and attitudes. For example, after accounting scandals at a number of well-known firms in the early 2000s shook public confidence in the integrity of Corporate America, the reputations of every U.S. company suffered regardless of their association with the scandals.[2] To help restore confidence in corporations and mar-

> **"Many consumers and social advocates believe that businesses should not only make a profit but also consider the social implications of their activities."**

the case said the defendants could be found guilty of consciously avoiding knowing about wrongdoing at the company. Many other top executives, including Andy Fastow, the chief financial officer, were found guilty of misconduct and are serving time in prison. The fall of Enron took many layers of management pushing the envelope and a great deal of complacency on the part of employees who saw wrongdoing and ignored it. Most unethical activities within organizations are supported by an organizational culture that encourages employees to bend the rules.[1]

kets, Congress passed the Sarbanes-Oxley Act, which criminalized securities fraud and stiffened penalties for corporate fraud. At a minimum, managers are expected to obey all laws and regulations. Most legal issues arise as choices that society deems unethical, irresponsible, or otherwise unacceptable. However, all actions deemed unethical by society are not necessarily illegal, and both legal and ethical concerns change over time (see Table 2.1). Business law refers to the laws and regulations that govern the conduct of business. Many problems and

TABLE 2.1 A Timeline of Ethical and Socially Responsible Concerns

1960s	1970s	1980s	1990s	2000s
• Environmental issues	• Employee militancy	• Bribes and illegal contracting practices	• Sweatshops and unsafe working conditions in third-world countries	• Employee benefits
• Civil rights issues	• Human rights issues	• Influence peddling		• Privacy issues
• Increased employee-employer tension	• Covering up rather than correcting issues	• Deceptive advertising	• Rising corporate liability for personal damages (e.g., cigarette companies)	• Financial misconduct
• Honesty	• Discrimination	• Financial fraud (e.g., savings and loan scandal)		• Sustainability
• Changing work ethic	• Harassment	• Transparency issues	• Financial mismanagement and fraud	• Cyber crime
• Rising drug use				• Intellectual property theft

Source: Adapted from "Business Ethics Timeline," Copyright © 2008, *Ethics Resource Center* (n.d.), www.ethics.org, updated 2008. Used with permission.

conflicts in business can be avoided if owners, managers, and employees know more about business law and the legal system. Business ethics, social responsibility, and laws together act as a compliance system requiring that businesses and employees act responsibly in society. In this chapter, we explore ethics and social responsibility; Appendix A addresses business law, including the Sarbanes-Oxley Act.

THE ROLE OF ETHICS IN BUSINESS

You have only to pick up *The Wall Street Journal* or *USA Today* to see examples of the growing concern about legal and ethical issues in business. HealthSouth, for example, has joined the growing list of companies tarnished by accounting improprieties and securities fraud. Former CEO Richard Scrushy was indicted for allegedly conspiring to inflate the health care firm's reported revenues by $2.7 billion to meet shareholder expectations. Although Scrushy pleaded "not guilty" to the 85 criminal charges, 15 former HealthSouth executives have admitted to participating in the deception. Scrushy was acquitted by a jury trial in the first attempt to hold a chief executive accountable under the Sarbanes-Oxley Act. The defense called the star witness, former HealthSouth finance chief William T. Owens, a big rat.[3] In 2006, Scrushy was found guilty on six counts of bribery and mail fraud by an Alabama court for making payments to an Alabama governor to be on the state hospital regulatory board. He plans to appeal the conviction. Regardless of what an individual believes about a particular action, if society judges it to be unethical or wrong, whether correctly or not, that judgment directly affects the organization's ability to achieve its business goals.[4]

Well-publicized incidents of unethical and illegal activity—ranging from accounting fraud to using the Internet to steal another person's credit-card number, from deceptive advertising of food and diet products to unfair competitive practices in the computer software industry—strengthen the public's perceptions that ethical standards and the level of trust in business need to be raised. Author David Callahan has commented, "Americans who wouldn't so much as shoplift a pack of chewing gum are committing felonies at tax time, betraying the trust of their patients, misleading investors, ripping off their insurance companies, lying to their clients, and much more."[5] Often, such charges start as ethical conflicts but evolve into legal disputes when cooperative conflict resolution cannot be accomplished. For example, in Germany the President of Deutsche Post AG,

parent of DHL, had to resign after being accused of tax evasion. In the U.S., Charles O. Prince III, former CEO of Citigroup; Stanley O'Neal, former CEO of Merrill Lynch; and Angela Mozilo, founder and CEO of Countrywide Financial, rejected suggestions that they reaped lavish compensation packages while engaging in highly risky subprime lending associated with an international financial crisis. While Mr. O'Neal was fired for Merrill Lynch's poor performance, he was given $161 million severance package on top of the $70 million he earned during four years as CEO.[6]

However, it is important to understand that business ethics goes beyond legal issues. Ethical conduct builds trust among individuals and in business relationships, which validates and promotes confidence in business relationships. Establishing trust and confidence is much more difficult in organizations that have established reputations for acting unethically. If you were to discover, for example, that a manager had misled you about company benefits when you were hired, your trust and confidence in that company would probably

In 2009, Wall Street financier Bernie Madoff pleaded guilty to defrauding hundreds of investors out of more than $50 billion. How did he and his employees manage to deceive so many investors for so many years? And why did they do it?

diminish. And if you learned that a colleague had lied to you about something, you probably would not trust or rely on that person in the future.

Ethical issues are not limited to for-profit organizations. In government, several politicians and some high-ranking officials have been forced to resign in disgrace over ethical indiscretions. Irv Lewis "Scooter" Libby, a White House advisor, was indicted on five counts of criminal charges: one count of obstruction of justice, two counts of perjury, and two counts of making false statements. He was convicted on four of those counts.[7] President Bush Commuted Libby's 30-month sentence, keeping him from going to jail. While serving as attorney general of New York, Eliot Spitzer had a reputation for fighting crime. He too has stumbled into an ethical mess of his own making. The New York Governor appeared in a federal complaint charging others with managing an international prostitution ring. Mr. Spitzer was named as a client of the crime ring, having hired a prostitute in Washington D.C. for $4,300. During his race for Governor of New York, Mr. Spitzer spoke of his duties as attorney general, saying: "I had a simple rule. I never asked if a case was popular or unpopular. I never asked if it was big or small, hard or easy. I simply asked if it was right or wrong." Mr. Spitzer resigned as Governor of New York, his career destroyed by his misconduct.[8] Even sports can be subject to ethical lapses. At many universities, for example, coaches and athletic administrators have been put on administrative leave after allegations of improper recruiting practices by team members came to light.[9] Jimmy Johnson's crew chief, Chad Knaus, was thrown out of the Daytona 500 for illegal modifications made to Johnson's car during NASCAR pole qualifying. Although Johnson finished fifth in qualifying, he had to start from the rear of the field and then went on to win the 2006 Daytona 500.[10] Thus, whether made in science, politics, sports, or business, most decisions are judged as right or wrong, ethical or unethical. Negative judgments can affect an organization's ability to build relationships with customers and suppliers, attract investors, and retain employees.[11]

such a choice often involves weighing monetary profit against what a person considers appropriate conduct. The best way to judge the ethics of a decision is to look at a situation from a customer's or competitor's viewpoint: Should liquid-diet manufacturers make unsubstantiated claims about their products? Should an engineer agree to divulge her former employer's trade secrets to ensure that she gets a better job with a competitor? Should a salesperson omit facts about a product's poor safety record in his presentation to a customer? Such questions require the decision maker to evaluate the ethics of his or her choice.

Many business issues may seem straightforward and easy to resolve, but in reality, it helps to have several years of experience in business when making ethical decisions on complex issues. For example, if you are a salesperson, when does offering a gift—such as season basketball tickets—to a customer become a bribe rather than just a sales practice? Clearly, there are no easy answers to such a question. But the size of the transaction, the history of personal relationships within the particular company, as well as many other factors may determine whether an action will be judged as right or wrong by others.

> **Many business issues may seem straightforward and easy to resolve, but in reality, it helps to have several years of experience in business when making ethical decisions on complex issues.**

Although we will not tell you in this chapter what you ought to do, others—your superiors, co-workers, and family—will make judgments about the ethics of your actions and decisions. Learning how to recognize and resolve ethical issues is an important step in evaluating ethical decisions in business.

 LO2

Detect some of the ethical issues that may arise in business.

Recognizing Ethical Issues in Business

Learning to recognize ethical issues is the most important step in understanding business ethics. An **ethical issue** is an identifiable problem, situation, or opportunity that requires a person to choose from among several actions that may be evaluated as right or wrong, ethical or unethical. In business,

Ethics is also related to the culture in which a business operates. In the United States, for example, it would be inappropriate for a businessperson to bring an elaborately wrapped gift to a prospective client on their first meeting—the gift could be viewed as a bribe. In Japan, however, it is considered impolite *not* to bring a gift. Experience with the culture in which a business operates is critical to understanding what is ethical or unethical.

To help you understand ethical issues that perplex businesspeople today, we will take a brief look at some of them in this section. The vast number of news-format investigative programs has increased consumer and employee awareness of organizational misconduct. In addition, the multitude of cable channels and Internet resources has improved the awareness of ethical problems among the general public. The National Business Ethics Survey of more than 3,400 U.S. employees found that workers witness many instances of ethical misconduct in their organizations (see Table 2.2). The most common types of observed misconduct were abusive/intimidating behavior, lying, and placing employee interests over organizational interests.[12]

> # ONE OF THE PRINCIPAL CAUSES OF UNETHICAL BEHAVIOR IN ORGANIZATIONS IS OVERLY AGGRESSIVE FINANCIAL OR BUSINESS OBJECTIVES.

Many of these issues relate to decisions and concerns that managers have to deal with daily. It is not possible to discuss every issue, of course. However, a discussion of a few issues can help you begin to recognize the ethical problems with which businesspersons must deal. Many ethical issues in business can be categorized in the context of their relation with abusive and intimidating behavior, conflicts of interest, fairness and honesty, communications, and business associations.

abusive and intimidating behavior Abusive or intimidating behavior is the most common ethical problem for employees. The concepts can mean anything from physical threats, false accusations, being annoying, profanity, insults, yelling, harshness, or ignoring someone, to unreasonableness, and the meaning of these words can differ by person—you probably have some ideas of your own. Abusive behavior can be placed on a continuum from a minor distraction to disrupting the workplace. For example, what one person may define as yelling might be another's definition of normal speech. Civility in our society has been a concern, and the workplace is no exception. The productivity level of many organizations has been damaged by the time spent unraveling abusive relationships.

Abusive behavior is difficult to assess and manage because of diversity in culture and lifestyle. What does it mean to speak profanely? Is profanity only related to specific words or other such terms that are common in today's business world? If you are using words that are normal in your language but others

consider profanity, have you just insulted, abused, or disrespected them?

Within the concept of abusive behavior, intent should be a consideration. If the employee was trying to convey a compliment but the comment was considered abusive, then it was probably a mistake. The way a word is said (voice inflection) can be important. Add to this the fact that we now live in a multicultural environment—doing business and working with many different cultural groups—and the businessperson soon realizes the depth of the ethical and legal issues that may arise. There are problems of word meanings by age and within cultures. For example an expression such as "Did you guys hook up last night?" can have various meanings, including some that could be considered offensive in a work environment.

Bullying is associated with a hostile workplace when someone considered a target (or a group) is threatened, harassed, belittled, or verbally abused or overly criticized. While bullying may create what some may call a hostile environment, this term is generally associated with sexual harassment. Although sexual harassment has legal recourse, bullying has little legal recourse at this time. Bullying is a widespread problem in the United States, and can cause psychological damage that can result in health-endangering consequences to the target. The Workplace Bullying Institute's latest survey found that "37% of U.S. workers have been bullied, that is 54 million Americans."[13] Another 12% of workers have witnessed bullying. As Table 2.3 indicates, bullying can use a mix of verbal, nonverbal, and manipulative threatening expressions to damage workplace productivity. One may wonder why workers tolerate such activities, the problem

TABLE 2.2 Types and Incidences of Observed Misconduct

Type of Conduct Observed	Employees Observing It
Putting own interests ahead of organization	22%
Abusive behavior	21
Lying to employees	20
Misreporting hours worked	17
Internet abuse	16
Safety violations	15
Lying to stakeholders	14
Discrimination	13
Stealing	11

Source: "National Business Ethics Survey 2007: An inside View of Private Sector Ethics," *Ethics Resource Center,* www.ethics.org/research/NBESOffers.asp (accessed March 9, 2009).

TABLE 2.3 Actions Associated with Bullies

1. Spreading rumors to damage others
2. Blocking others' communication in the workplace
3. Flaunting status or authority to take advantage of others
4. Discrediting others' ideas and opinions
5. Use of e-mails to demean others
6. Failing to communicate or return communication
7. Insults, yelling, and shouting
8. Using terminology to discriminate by gender, race, or age
9. Using eye or body language to hurt others or their reputation
10. Taking credit for others' work or ideas

Source: © O. C. Ferrell, 2006.

● **BRIBES** payments, gifts, or special favors intended to influence the outcome of a decision

is that 81 percent of workplace bullies are supervisors. A top officer at Boeing cited an employee survey indicating 26 percent had observed abusive or intimidating behavior by management.[14]

conflict of interest

A conflict of interest exists when a person must choose whether to advance his or her own personal interests or those of others. For example, a manager in a corporation is supposed to ensure that the company is profitable so that its stockholder-owners receive a return on their investment. In other words, the manager has a responsibility to investors. If she instead makes decisions that give her more power or money but do not help the company, then she has a conflict of interest—she is acting to benefit herself at the expense of her company and is not fulfilling her responsibilities. To avoid conflicts of interest, employees must be able to separate their personal financial interests from their business dealings. For example, a $1 million donation by Citigroup to the 92nd Street Y nursery school represents a possible conflict of interest. Jack Grubman, an analyst for Salomon Smith Barney, upgraded his rating for AT&T stock after Sanford Weill, the CEO of Citigroup (the parent company of Salomon Smith Barney), agreed to use his influence to help Grubman's twins gain admission to the elite Manhattan nursery school. During the late 1990s, Weill, an AT&T board member, had been upset that Citigroup wasn't getting any of AT&T's business. Grubman changed his AT&T rating to buy. A year later he bragged in an e-mail that he had made the switch to placate Weill in exchange for Weill's help in getting Grubman's children into the exclusive 92nd Street Y nursery school. Grubman has denied elevating his rating for AT&T's stock to gain admission to the school, but his children were enrolled. Industry leaders still avoid him, publicly anyway, but on the fringes of telecom, Grubman has had no trouble finding people who are willing to overlook his past or are simply unaware of it. According to a *Fortune* article, although Grubman was "banned from Wall Street, the former Telecom King wants to prove that he wasn't a huckster."[15]

As mentioned earlier, it is considered improper to give or accept **bribes**—payments, gifts, or special favors intended to influence the outcome of a decision. A bribe is a conflict of interest because it benefits an individual at the expense of an organization or society. Companies that do business overseas should be aware that bribes are a significant ethical issue and are in fact illegal in many countries. For example, three former executives of IBM Korea went to jail in Seoul after being convicted of using bribes to win orders for computer parts.[16] Bribery is more prevalent in some countries than in others. Transparency International has developed a corruption perceptions index (Table 2.4). Note there are numerous countries perceived as less corrupt than the United States.[17]

fairness and honesty

Fairness and honesty are at the heart of business ethics and relate to the general values of decision makers. At a minimum, businesspersons are expected

TABLE 2.4   Countries Perceived to be Least Corrupt

Rank	Country	2008 CPI Score*
1	Denmark/New Zealand/Sweden	9.3
4	Singapore	9.2
5	Finland/Switzerland	9.0
7	Iceland/Netherlands	8.9
9	Australia/Canada	8.7
11	Luxembourg	8.3
12	Austria/Hong Kong	8.1
14	Germany/Norway	7.9
16	Ireland/United Kingdom	7.7
18	Belgium/Japan/United States	7.3
21	Saint Lucia	7.1

*CPI score relates to perceptions of the degree of corruption as seen by businesspeople and country analysts and ranges between 10 (highly clean) and 0 (highly corrupt).

Source: "Transparency International 2008 Corruption Perception Index," Transparency International, (n.d.), www.transparency.org/policy_research/surveys_indices/cpi/2008 (accessed March 9, 2009).

to follow all applicable laws and regulations. But beyond obeying the law, they are expected not to harm customers, employees, clients, or competitors knowingly through deception, misrepresentation, coercion, or discrimination. Honesty and fairness can relate to how the employees uses the resources of the organization. Vault.com found that 67 percent of employees have taken office supplies from work to use for matters unrelated to their job. Most employees do not view taking office supplies as stealing or dishonest, with 97 percent saying they have never gotten caught and it would not matter if they were found out. In addition, only 3.7 percent say they have taken items like keyboards, software, and memory sticks. Still, an employee should be aware of policies on taking items and recognize how these decisions relate to ethical behavior.[18] Figure 2.1 on the next page provides an overview of the most pilfered office supplies.

One aspect of fairness relates to competition. Although numerous laws have been passed to foster competition and make monopolistic practices illegal, companies sometimes gain control over markets by using questionable practices that harm competition. Bullying can also occur between companies that are in intense competition. Even respected companies such as Intel have been accused of monopolistic bullying. A competitor, Advanced Micro Devices (AMD), claimed in a lawsuit that 38 companies, including Dell and Sony, were strong-arming customers (such as Apple) into buying Intel chips rather than those marketed by AMD. The AMD lawsuit seeks billions of dollars and will take years to litigate. In many cases, the alleged misconduct not only can have monetary and legal implications but can threaten reputation, investor confidence, and customer loyalty. A front-cover *Forbes* headline stated, "Intel to ADM: Drop Dead." An example of the intense competition and Intel's ability to use its large size won it the high-profile Apple account, displacing IBM and Freescale. ADM said it had no opportunity to

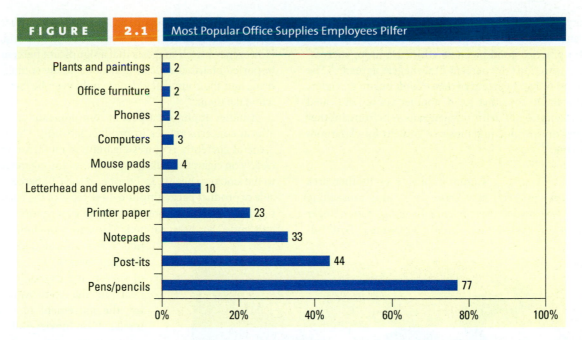

FIGURE 2.1 Most Popular Office Supplies Employees Pilfer

Item	Percent
Plants and paintings	2
Office furniture	2
Phones	2
Computers	3
Mouse pads	4
Letterhead and envelopes	10
Printer paper	23
Notepads	33
Post-its	44
Pens/pencils	77

Source: "More Employees Taking Supplies," *The (Wilmington, Del.) News Journal,* using data from Lawyers.com, April 1, 2007, http://www.usatoday.com/money/industries/retail/2007-03-30-supply_N.htm (accessed March 9, 2009).

bid because Intel offered to deploy 600 Indian engineers to help Apple software run more smoothly on Intel chips.[19]

Another aspect of fairness and honesty relates to disclosure of potential harm caused by product use. Mitsubishi Motors, Japan's number-four automaker, faced criminal charges and negative publicity after executives admitted that the company had systematically covered up customer complaints about tens of thousands of defective automobiles over a 20-year period to avoid expensive and embarrassing product recalls.[20]

Dishonesty has become a significant problem in the United States. As reported earlier in this chapter, lying was the second most observed form of misconduct in the National Business Ethics Survey. Dishonesty is not found only in business, however.

A survey of nearly 25,000 high school students revealed that 62 percent of the students admitted to cheating on an exam at least once, 35 percent confessed to copying documents from the Internet, 27 percent admitted to shoplifting, and 23 percent owned up to cheating to win in sports.[21] If today's students are tomorrow's leaders, there is likely to be a correlation between acceptable behavior today and tomorrow, adding to the argument that the leaders of today must be prepared for the ethical

Bernard Madoff Pulls Off the Largest Ponzi Scheme Ever

In 2009, billionaire Bernie Madoff exchanged his $7 million penthouse for a tiny prison cell. This scheming genius was guilty of operating a $65 billion Ponzi scheme that fooled even the Securities and Exchange Commission (SEC) for decades. Madoff promised over 9,000 investors steady returns of 10 to 12 percent on their investments, no matter how the market was faring. Madoff invested none of the money. He used new clients' deposits to pay off older investors asking for withdrawals as well as to fund a second legitimate company and his family's lavish lifestyle. This worked fine as long as he continually attracted new investors. However, once new money stops flowing in, Ponzi schemes are revealed for what they are.

What is remarkable is that Madoff kept the scam going for nearly two decades. He con-vinced people with his air of respectability and prestige, and many wealthy persons were eager to invest with him. Madoff brought in billions, and was able to live the high life for a time.

Then the inevitable happened: New inves-tors began dwindling. The situation quickly deteriorated with the worsening economic situation in late 2008. On December 11 Madoff admitted his guilt to his two sons, who worked for their father but were not involved in the fraud. The results were catastrophic. Some investors, many of them retirees or chari-table institutions, had placed all their money in the company. In all, Madoff's scam resulted in the loss of $65 billion, and 9,000 claims for losses were filed. Many questioned why the SEC had not caught on in spite of numerous red flags. The organization had investigated Madoff many times over the years, but never uncovered any wrongdoing. As a result, some investors sued the SEC for negligence, the first time investors have sued a regulatory agency. Many say that new safeguards are necessary to prevent similar crimes in the future.[22] ❖

Q: Discussion Questions

1. Why did Bernard Madoff engage in such purposeful misconduct?

2. How would you describe how a Ponzi scheme works?

3. How can an individual avoid being a victim of a Ponzi scheme?

risks associated with this downward trend. According to a poll by Deloitte and Touche of teenagers age 13 to 18, when asked if people who practice good business ethics are more successful than those who don't, 69 percent of teenagers agreed.[23] The same poll found only 12 percent of teens think business leaders today are ethical. On the other hand, another survey indicated that many students do not define copying answers from another students' paper or downloading music or content for classroom work as cheating.[24]

communications Communications is another area in which ethical concerns may arise. False and misleading advertising, as well as deceptive personal-selling tactics, anger consumers and can lead to the failure of a business. Truthful-

Some surveys have shown that ethical lapses are becoming more common among American youth.

ness about product safety and quality is also important to consumers. Claims about dietary supplements and weight-loss products can be particularly problematic. For example, the Fountain of Youth Group, LLC, and its founder, Edita Kaye, settled charges brought by the Federal Trade Commission that the company made unsubstantiated claims about its weight-loss products. Under the settlement, the firm agreed to stop making specific weight-loss and health claims about its products without competent scientific proof. It was also fined $6 million, but that fine was suspended because the firm lacked the resources to pay it.[25]

Some companies fail to provide enough information for consumers about differences or similarities between products. For example, driven by high prices for medicines, many consum-

ers are turning to Canadian, Mexican, and overseas Internet sources for drugs to treat a variety of illnesses and conditions. However, research suggests that a significant percentage of these imported pharmaceuticals may not actually contain the labeled drug, and the counterfeit drugs could even be harmful to those who take them.[26]

Another important aspect of communications that may raise ethical concerns relates to product labeling. The U.S. Surgeon General currently requires cigarette manufacturers to indicate clearly on cigarette packaging that smoking cigarettes is harmful to the smoker's health. In Europe, at least 30 percent of the front side of product packaging and 40 percent of the back needs to be taken up by the warning. The use of descriptors such as "light" and "mild" has been banned.[27] However, labeling of other products raises ethical questions when it threatens basic rights, such as freedom of speech and expression. This is the heart of the controversy surrounding the movement to require warning labels on movies and video games, rating their content, language, and appropriate audience age. Although people in the entertainment industry believe that such labeling violates their First Amendment right to freedom of expression, other consumers—particularly parents—believe that such labeling is needed to protect children from harmful influences. Similarly, alcoholic beverage and cigarette manufacturers have argued that a total ban on cigarette and alcohol advertisements violates the First Amendment. Internet regulation, particularly that designed to protect children and the elderly, is on the forefront in consumer protection legislation. Because of the debate surrounding the acceptability of these business activities, they remain major ethical issues.

business relationships The behavior of businesspersons toward customers, suppliers, and others in their workplace may also generate ethical concerns. Ethical behavior within a business involves keeping company secrets, meeting obligations and responsibilities, and avoiding undue pressure that may force others to act unethically.

Managers, in particular, because of the authority of their position, have the opportunity to influence employees' actions. For example, a manager can influence employees to use pirated computer software to save costs. The use of illegal software puts the employee and the company at legal risk, but employees may feel pressured to do so by their superior's authority. The National Business Ethics Survey found that employees who feel pressure to compromise ethical standards view top and middle managers as the greatest source of such pressure.[28]

It is the responsibility of managers to create a work environment that helps the organization achieve its objectives and fulfill its responsibilities. However, the methods that managers use to enforce these responsibilities should not compromise employee rights. Organizational pressures may encourage a person to engage in activities that he or she might otherwise view as unethical, such as invading others' privacy or stealing a competitor's secrets. For example, Betty Vinson, an accounting executive at WorldCom, protested when her superiors asked her to make improper accounting entries to cover up the company's deteriorating financial condition. She acquiesced only after being told that it was the only way to save the troubled company. She, along with several other WorldCom accountants, pleaded guilty to conspiracy and fraud charges related to WorldCom's bankruptcy after the accounting improprieties came to light.[29] Or the firm may provide only vague or lax supervision on ethical issues, providing the opportunity for misconduct. Managers who offer no ethical direction to employees create many opportunities for manipulation, dishonesty, and conflicts of interest.

Plagiarism—taking someone else's work and presenting it as your own without mentioning the source—is another ethical issue. As a student, you may be familiar with plagiarism in school; for example, copying someone else's term paper or quoting from a published work or Internet source without acknowledging it. In business, an ethical issue arises when an employee copies reports or takes the work or ideas of others and presents it as his or her own. At *USA Today,* for example, an internal investigation into the work of veteran reporter Jack Kelley identified dozens of stories in which Kelley appeared to have plagiarized material from competing newspapers. The investigation also uncovered evidence Kelley fabricated significant portions of at least eight major stories and conspired to cover up his lapses in judgment. The newspaper later apologized to its readers, and Kelley resigned.[30] A manager attempting to take credit for a subordinate's ideas is engaging in another type of plagiarism.

  Many employees utilize different ethical standards at work than they do at home.

Making Decisions about Ethical Issues

Although we've presented a variety of ethical issues that may arise in business, it can be difficult to recognize specific ethical issues in practice. Whether a decision maker recognizes an issue as an ethical one often depends on the issue itself. Managers, for example, tend to be more concerned about issues that affect those close to them, as well as issues that have immediate rather than long-term consequences. Thus, the perceived importance of an ethical issue substantially affects choices, and only a few issues receive scrutiny, while most receive no attention at all.[31]

Table 2.5 lists some questions you may want to ask yourself and others when trying to determine whether an action is ethical. Open discussion of ethical issues does not eliminate ethical problems, but it does promote both trust and learning in an organization.[32] When people feel that they cannot discuss what they are doing with their co-workers or superiors, there is a good chance that an ethical issue exists. Once a person has recognized an ethical issue and can openly discuss it with others, he or she has begun the process of resolving an ethical issue.

● ● LO3

Specify how businesses can promote ethical behavior.

Improving Ethical Behavior in Business

Understanding how people make ethical choices and what prompts a person to act unethically may reverse the current trend toward unethical behavior in business. Ethical decisions in an organization are influenced by three key factors: individual moral standards, the influence of managers and co-workers, and the opportunity to engage in misconduct (Figure 2.2). While you have great control over your personal ethics outside the workplace, your co-workers and superiors exert significant control over your choices at work through authority and example. In fact, the activities and examples set by co-workers, along with rules and policies established by the firm, are critical in gaining consistent ethical compliance in an organization. If the company fails to provide good examples and direction for appropriate conduct, confusion and conflict will develop and result in the opportunity for

TABLE 2.5 Questions to Consider in Determining Whether an Action Is Ethical

Are there any potential legal restrictions or violations that could result from the action?
Does your company have a specific code of ethics or policy on the action?
Is this activity customary in your industry? Are there any industry trade groups that provide guidelines or codes of conduct that address this issue?
Would this activity be accepted by your co-workers? Will your decision or action withstand open discussion with co-workers and managers and survive untarnished?
How does this activity fit with your own beliefs and values?

FIGURE 2.2   Three Factors That Influence Business Ethics

Individual Standards and Values **+** Managers' and Co-workers' Influence **+** Opportunity: Codes and Compliance Requirements **=** Ethical/Unethical Choices in Business

activities are acceptable and which are not, and they limit the opportunity for misconduct by providing punishments for violations of the rules and standards. According to the National Business Ethics Survey (NBES), employees in organizations that have written standards of conduct, ethics training, ethics offices or hotlines, and systems for anonymous reporting of misconduct are more likely to report misconduct when they observe it. The survey also found that such programs are associated with higher employee perceptions that they will be held accountable for ethical infractions.[34] The enforcement of such codes and policies through rewards and punishments increases the acceptance of ethical standards by employees.

One of the most important components of an ethics program is a means through which employees can report observed misconduct anonymously. The NBES found that although employees are increasingly reporting illegal and unethical activities they observe in the workplace, 54 percent of surveyed employees indicated they are unwilling to report misconduct because they fear that no corrective action will be taken or that their report will not remain confidential.[35] The lack of anonymous reporting mechanisms may encourage **whistleblowing,** which occurs when an employee exposes an employer's wrongdoing to outsiders, such as the media or government regulatory agencies. However, more companies are establishing programs to encourage employees to report illegal or unethical practices internally so that they can take steps to remedy problems before they result in legal action or generate negative publicity. In recent years, whistleblowers have provided crucial evidence documenting illegal actions at a number of companies. At Enron, for example, Sherron Watkins, a vice president, warned the firm's CEO, Ken Lay, that the energy company was using improper accounting procedures. Lay forwarded Watkins's concerns to Vinson and Elkins, Enron's outside lawyers, and they provided opinion letters approving the questionable transactions. Watkins also took her concerns to senior accountants at Arthur Andersen, and it is unclear if any action was taken. Watkins sold some of her Enron stock based on her knowledge, but was not indicted for

misconduct. If your boss or co-workers leave work early, you may be tempted to do so as well. If you see co-workers engaged in personal activities such as shopping online and watching YouTube, you may be more likely to do so also. In addition, having sound personal values contributes to an ethical workplace.

Because ethical issues often emerge from conflict, it is useful to examine the causes of ethical conflict. Business managers and employees often experience some tension between their own ethical beliefs and their obligations to the organizations in which they work. Many employees utilize different ethical standards at work than they do at home. This conflict increases when employees feel that their company is encouraging unethical conduct or exerting pressure on them to engage in it.

It is difficult for employees to determine what conduct is acceptable within a company if the firm does not have ethics policies and standards. And without such policies and standards, employees may base decisions on how their peers and superiors behave. Professional **codes of ethics** are formalized rules and standards that describe what a company expects of its employees. Codes of ethics do not have to be so detailed that they take into account every situation, but they should provide guidelines and principles that can help employees achieve organizational objectives and address risks in an acceptable and ethical way. The development of a code of ethics should include not only a firm's executives and board of directors, but also legal staff and employees from all areas of a firm.[33] Table 2.6 lists some key things to consider when developing a code of ethics.

Codes of ethics, policies on ethics, and ethics training programs advance ethical behavior because they prescribe which

TABLE 2.6   Key Things to Consider in Developing a Code of Ethics

- Create a team to assist with the process of developing the code (include management and nonmanagement employees from across departments and functions).
- Solicit input from employees from different departments, functions, and regions to compile a list of common questions and answers to include in the code document.
- Make certain that the headings of the code sections can be easily understood by all employees.
- Avoid referencing specific U.S. laws and regulations or those of specific countries, particularly for codes that will be distributed to employees in multiple regions.
- Hold employee group meetings on a complete draft version (including graphics and pictures) of the text using language that everyone can understand.
- Inform employees that they will receive a copy of the code during an introduction session.
- Let all employees know that they will receive future ethics training which will, in part, cover the important information contained in the code document.

Source: Adapted from William Miller, "Implementing an Organizational Code of Ethics," *International Business Ethics Review* 7 (Winter 2004), pp. 1, 6–10.

insider trading. Soon after, Watkins testified before Congress that Enron had concealed billions of dollars in debt through a complex scheme of off-balance-sheet partnerships.[36] Enron ultimately went bankrupt when its improprieties and high levels of debt were exposed. Unfortunately, whistleblowers are often treated negatively in organizations. The government is rewarding firms that encourage employees to report misconduct—with reduced fines and penalties when violations occur.

The current trend is to move away from legally based ethical initiatives in organizations to cultural- or integrity-based initiatives that make ethics a part of core organizational values. Organizations recognize that effective business ethics programs

ties will probably be legal. (We looked at ethical responsibilities in the first half of this chapter.) Finally, voluntary responsibilities are additional activities that may not be required but which promote human welfare or goodwill. Legal and economic concerns have long been acknowledged in business, but voluntary and ethical issues are more recent concerns.

Corporate citizenship is the extent to which businesses meet the legal, ethical, economic, and voluntary responsibilities placed on them by their various stakeholders. It involves the

> ["The current trend is to move away from legally based ethical initiatives in organizations to cultural- or integrity-based initiatives that make ethics a part of core organizational values."]

are good for business performance. Firms that develop higher levels of trust function more efficiently and effectively and avoid damaged company reputations and product images. Organizational ethics initiatives have been supportive of many positive and diverse organizational objectives, such as profitability, hiring, employee satisfaction, and customer loyalty.[37] Conversely, lack of organizational ethics initiatives and the absence of workplace values such as honesty, trust, and integrity can have a negative impact on organizational objectives. According to one report on employee loyalty and work practices, 79 percent of employees who questioned their bosses' integrity indicated that they felt uncommitted or were likely to quit soon.[38]

activities and organizational processes adopted by businesses to meet their social responsibilities. A commitment to corporate citizenship by a firm indicates a strategic focus on fulfilling the social responsibilities expected of it by its stakeholders. Corporate citizenship involves action and measurement of the extent to which a firm embraces the corporate citizenship philosophy and then follows through by implementing citizenship and

● ● **LO4**

Explain the four dimensions of social responsibility.

THE NATURE OF SOCIAL RESPONSIBILITY

There are four dimensions of social responsibility: economic, legal, ethical, and voluntary (including philanthropic) (Figure 2.3).[39] Earning profits is the economic foundation of the pyramid in Figure 2.3, and complying with the law is the next step. However a business whose *sole* objective is to maximize profits is not likely to consider its social responsibility, although its activi-

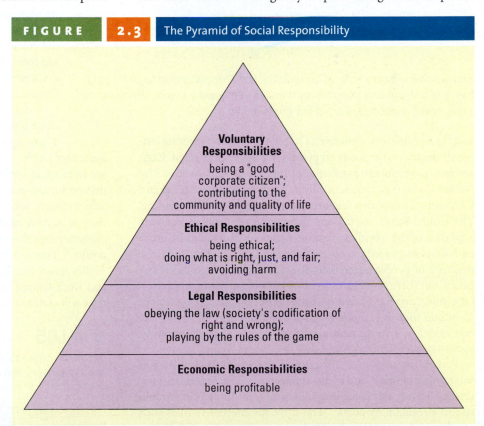

FIGURE 2.3 The Pyramid of Social Responsibility

Source: Reprinted with permission from A. B. Carroll, "The Pyramid of Corporate Social Responsibility: Toward the Moral Management of Organizational Stakeholders," *Business Horizons,* July/August 1991. Copyright © 1991 by the Board of Trustees at Indiana University, Kelley School of Business.

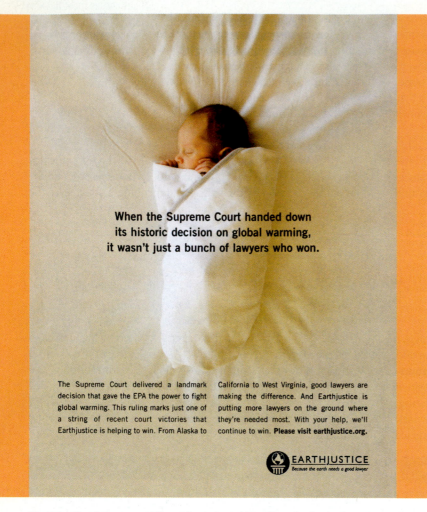

When the Supreme Court handed down
its historic decision on global warming,
it wasn't just a bunch of lawyers who won.

The Supreme Court delivered a landmark decision that gave the EPA the power to fight global warming. This ruling marks just one of a string of recent court victories that Earthjustice is helping to win. From Alaska to California to West Virginia, good lawyers are making the difference. And Earthjustice is putting more lawyers on the ground where they're needed most. With your help, we'll continue to win. **Please visit earthjustice.org.**

EARTHJUSTICE
Because the earth needs a good lawyer

Earthjustice is a nonprofit environmental law firm dedicated to protecting the environment and people's right to live in a healthy world. "Because the earth needs a good lawyer" is the firm's motto.

social responsibility initiatives. One of the major corporate citizenship issues is the focus on preserving the environment. Consumers, governments, and special interest groups such as The Nature Conservancy are concerned about greenhouse gases and CO_2 carbon emissions that are contributing to global warming. The United States was the number-one CO_2 producer, at nearly a quarter of the world's greenhouse gas emissions, until China's emissions surpassed the country sometime in 2006 or 2007. The majority of people agree that climate change is a global emergency, but there is no agreement on how to solve the problem.[40] One study done at Princeton University calls for a reduction of 25 billion tons of carbon emissions over the next 50 years—the equivalent of erasing nearly four years of global emissions at today's rates.[41]

Part of the answer to this crisis is alternative energy such as solar, wind, biofuels, and hydro applications. The American Solar Energy Society estimates that the number of "green" jobs could rise to 40 million by 2030.[42] The drive for alternative fuels such as ethanol from corn has added new issues such as food price increases and food shortages. Over 2 billion consumers earn less than $2 a day in wages. Sharply increased food costs has led to

riots and government policies to restrict trade in basic commodities such as rice, corn, and soybeans.[43]

To respond to these developments, most companies are introducing eco-friendly products and marketing efforts. Americans as consumers are generally concerned about the environment, but only 47 percent trust companies to tell them the truth in environmental marketing.[44] This is because most businesses are promoting themselves as green-conscious and concerned about the environment without actually making the necessary commitments to environmental health. Even employees feel their employers aren't doing enough to protect the environment, with nearly 60 percent feeling that more needs to be to done to reduce, recycle and support green policies.[45] *Corporate Responsibility Officer* magazine publishes an annual list of the 100 best American corporate citizens based on service to seven stakeholder groups: stockholders, local communities, minorities, employees, global stakeholders, customers, and the environment. Table 2.7 shows the top 20 from that list.

Although the concept of social responsibility is receiving more and more attention, it is still not universally accepted. Table 2.8 lists some of the arguments for and against social responsibility.

Social Responsibility Issues

As with ethics, managers consider social responsibility on a daily basis as they deal with real issues. Among the many social issues that managers must consider are their firms' relations with owners and stockholders, employees, consumers, the environment, and the community.

Social responsibility is a dynamic area with issues changing constantly in response to society's desires. There is much evidence that social responsibility is associated with improved business performance. Consumers are refusing to buy from businesses that receive publicity about misconduct. A number of studies have found a direct relationship between social responsibility and profitability, as well as that social responsibility is linked to employee commitment and customer loyalty—major concerns of any firm trying to increase profits.[46] This section highlights a few of the many social responsibility issues that managers face; as managers become aware of and work toward the solution of current social problems, new ones will certainly emerge.

● ● **L05**

Debate an organization's social responsibilities to owners, employees, consumers, the environment, and the community.

relations with owners and stockholders

Businesses must first be responsible to their owners, who are primarily concerned with earning a profit or a return on their investment in a company. In a small business, this responsibility

TABLE 2.7 Best Corporate Citizens

1	Intel Corp.
2	Eaton Corp.
3	Nike Inc.
4	Deere and Co.
5	Genentech Inc.
6	Corning Inc.
7	Humana Inc.
8	Bank of America Corp.
9	ITT Corp.
10	PG&E Corp.
11	Dominion Resources Inc.
12	State Street Corp.
13	Dow Chemical Co.
14	Cisco Systems Inc.
15	Wisconsin Energy Corp.
16	Progress Energy Inc.
17	Entergy Corp.
18	Norfolk Southern Corp.
19	Sun Microsystems Inc.
20	Public Service Enterprise Group Inc.

Source: Dennis Schaal, "100 Best Corporate Citizens 2008," *Corporate Responsibility Officer,* www.thecro.com/files/100best-JanFeb08-Listing.pdf (accessed March 9, 2009).

proper accounting procedures, providing all relevant information to investors about the current and projected performance of the firm, and protecting the owners' rights and investments. In short, the business must maximize the owners' investment in the firm.

employee relations   Another issue of importance to a business is its responsibilities to employees, for without employees a business cannot carry out its goals. Employees expect businesses to provide a safe workplace, pay them adequately for their work, and tell them what is happening in their company. They want employers to listen to their grievances and treat them fairly. When employees at Ramtech Building Systems Inc. approached management with their concerns about cursing used in the company's manufacturing facilities, a Language Code of Ethics was instituted. Many employees indicate that obscene language is common in the workplace, particularly in high-stress jobs. For example, 43 percent of the 12,000 U.S. Postal Service employees surveyed recently reported being cursed at in the workplace.[47] Companies are adjusting their policies and offering training to clean up employee language.

Of a more serious nature, a growing employee-relations concern for multinational companies is the spread of AIDS and its effect on the workforce. Daimler-Chrysler South Africa (DCSA), for example, provides HIV/AIDS testing, free anti-AIDS drugs, and additional treatment and support for its 6,000 South African employees and their families in an effort to combat the disease, which has infected about 9 percent of

TABLE 2.8 The Arguments for and against Social Responsibility

For:

1. Business helped to create many of the social problems that exist today, so it should play a significant role in solving them, especially in the areas of pollution reduction and cleanup.

2. Businesses should be more responsible because they have the financial and technical resources to help solve social problems.

3. As members of society, businesses should do their fair share to help others.

4. Socially responsible decision making by businesses can prevent increased government regulation.

5. Social responsibility is necessary to ensure economic survival: If businesses want educated and healthy employees, customers with money to spend, and suppliers with quality goods and services in years to come, they must take steps to help solve the social and environmental problems that exist today.

Against:

1. It sidetracks managers from the primary goal of business—earning profits. Every dollar donated to social causes or otherwise spent on society's problems is a dollar less for owners and investors.

2. Participation in social programs gives businesses greater power, perhaps at the expense of particular segments of society.

3. Some people question whether business has the expertise needed to assess and make decisions about social problems.

4. Many people believe that social problems are the responsibility of government agencies and officials, who can be held accountable by voters.

is fairly easy to fulfill because the owner(s) personally manages the business or knows the managers well. In larger businesses, particularly corporations owned by thousands of stockholders, assuring responsibility to the owners becomes a more difficult task.

A business's responsibilities to its owners and investors, as well as to the financial community at large, include maintaining

DCSA's employees there. The company spends an estimated $420,000 a year on antiretroviral drugs. Other German automakers, including Volkswagen and BMW, have launched similar programs to cover their employees in South Africa, where 600 people die every day from the disease. Many U.S. companies have set up AIDS prevention and treatment programs for their employees in Africa as well. Companies as diverse as Coca-Cola

The Coca-Cola Africa Foundation provides millions of dollars each year to reduce the impact of HIV/AIDS on Coca-Cola's employees and independent bottlers in Africa.

(the largest private employer on the African continent), MTV, American Express, Nike, and ExxonMobil have also joined the Global Business Coalition to help fight the epidemic.[48]

Congress has passed several laws regulating safety in the workplace, many of which are enforced by OSHA. Labor unions have also made significant contributions to achieving safety in the workplace and improving wages and benefits. Most organizations now recognize that the safety and satisfaction of their employees are a critical ingredient in their success, and many strive to go beyond what is expected of them by the law. Healthy, satisfied employees supply more than just labor to their employers, however. Employers are beginning to realize the importance of

obtaining input from even the lowest-level employees to help the company reach its objectives.

A major social responsibility for business is providing equal opportunities for all employees regardless of their sex, age, race, religion, or nationality. Women and minorities have been slighted in the past in terms of education, employment, and advancement opportunities; additionally, many of their needs have not been addressed by business. For example, as many as 1.6 million current and former female Wal-Mart employees filed a class-action discrimination lawsuit accusing the giant retailer of paying them lower wages and salaries than it does men in comparable positions. Pretrial proceedings not only uncovered discrepancies between the pay of men and women but also the fact that men dominate higher-paying store manager positions while women occupy more than 90 percent of cashier jobs, most of which pay about $14,000 a year. Wal-Mart faces fines and penalties in the millions of dollars if found guilty of sexual discrimination.[49] Women, who continue to bear most child-rearing responsibilities, often experience conflict between those responsibilities and their duties as employees. Consequently, day care has become a major employment issue for women, and more companies are providing day care facilities as part of their effort to recruit and advance women in the workforce. In addition, companies are considering alternative scheduling such as flex-time and job sharing to accommodate employee concerns. Telecommuting has grown significantly over the past 5 to 10 years, as well. Many Americans today believe business has a social obligation to provide special opportunities for women and minorities to improve their standing in society.

EarthCraft Helps More People Bring the Eco-Friendly Message Home

These days, going green is big. People purchase local organic produce, buy chemical-free household products, and sometimes drive hybrid cars. However, if you want to take your green commitment further, EarthCraft House can help. Founded in 1999 by the Atlanta Home Builders Association and Southface, EarthCraft is a residential green building program focused on building energy-efficient, healthy, and comfortable homes.

So what is an EarthCraft house? It can be newly constructed or renovated. To become EarthCraft-certified, a house must meet guidelines for energy efficiency, durability, indoor air quality, resource efficiency, waste management, and water conservation. New homes must meet ENERGY STAR certification criteria and score at least 150 points on an EarthCraft scoring sheet.

How does an EarthCraft house benefit the environment and the homeowner? Home energy sources may contribute to global warming and other environmental issues. To counteract this, EarthCraft houses are energy-efficient, reducing greenhouse gases up to 1,100 pounds annually. Construction materials for the average house often deplete natural resources, yet EarthCraft homes are often built using recycled and renewable materials. An EarthCraft house also conserves water and reduces storm water pollution.

Homeowner benefits are twofold. First, EarthCraft aims to create a healthier home. For example, an EarthCraft home does away with mold and mildew and reduces dust. In addition, an EarthCraft home comes with two types of mortgage incentives. The Energy Efficient Mortgage increases the buyer's purchasing power due to the lower operating costs of an energy-efficient home. The Energy Improvement Mortgage can be used to finance energy-efficient upgrades on an existing home. All in all, it's a win-win![50] ❖

Q: Discussion Questions

1. In addition to reducing carbon dioxide emissions, what are other reasons to build an energy-efficient, "green" house?

2. Would an improved mortgage be incentive enough for you to pay extra for an energy-efficient house?

3. What additional incentives might convince people to go green when building or remodeling their homes?

consumer relations A critical issue in business today is business's responsibility to customers, who look to business to provide them with satisfying, safe products and to respect their rights as consumers. The activities that independent individuals, groups, and organizations undertake to protect their rights as consumers are known as **consumerism.** To achieve their objectives, consumers and their advocates write letters to companies, lobby government agencies, make public service announcements, and boycott companies whose activities they deem irresponsible.

Many of the desires of those involved in the consumer movement have a foundation in John F. Kennedy's 1962 consumer bill of rights, which highlighted four rights. The *right to safety* means that a business must not knowingly sell anything that could result in personal injury or harm to consumers. Defective or dangerous products erode public confidence in the ability of business to serve society. They also result in expensive litigation that ultimately increases the cost of products for all consumers. The right to safety also means businesses must provide a safe place for consumers to shop. In recent years, many large retailers have been under increasing pressure to improve safety in their large warehouse-type stores. At Home Depot, for example, three consumer deaths and numerous serious injuries have been caused by falling merchandise. One lawsuit brought against the company over injuries received in one of its stores resulted in a $1.5 million judgment. To help prevent further deaths, injuries, and litigation, Home Depot now has a corporate safety officer and has hired 130 safety managers to monitor store compliance with new safety measures.[51]

The *right to be informed* gives consumers the freedom to review complete information about a product before they buy it. This means that detailed information about ingredients, risks, and instructions for use are to be printed on labels and packages. The *right to choose* ensures that consumers have access to a variety of products and services at competitive prices. The assurance of both satisfactory quality and service at a fair price is also a part of the consumer's right to choose. Some consumers are not being given the right to choose. Many are being billed for products and services they never ordered. According to the Federal Trade Commission, complaints about unordered merchandise and services jumped 169 percent over a two-year period. Burdine's, a department store chain, was investigated for failing to notify customers it was enrolling them in a company buying club. Fleet Mortgage was sued for adding fees for unrequested insurance to customers' mortgage bills, and HCI Direct was sued by 11 states for charging customers for panty hose samples they had never ordered.[52] The *right to be heard* assures consumers that their interests will receive full and sympathetic consideration when the government formulates policy. It also assures the fair treatment of consumers who voice complaints about a purchased product.

The role of the Federal Trade Commission's Bureau of Consumer Protection is to protect consumers against unfair, deceptive,

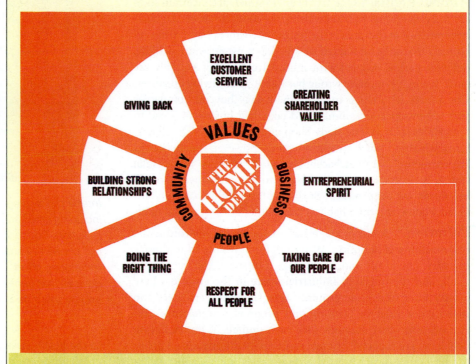

EXCELLENT CUSTOMER SERVICE
CREATING SHAREHOLDER VALUE
GIVING BACK
VALUES
COMMUNITY
BUSINESS
BUILDING STRONG RELATIONSHIPS
ENTREPRENEURIAL SPIRIT
PEOPLE
DOING THE RIGHT THING
TAKING CARE OF OUR PEOPLE
RESPECT FOR ALL PEOPLE

EXCELLENT CUSTOMER SERVICE
Along with our quality products, service, price and selection, we must go the extra mile to give customers knowledgeable advice about merchandise and to help them use those products to their maximum benefit.

CREATING SHAREHOLDER VALUE
The investors who provide the capital necessary to allow our Company to grow need and expect a return on their investment. We are committed to providing it.

ENTREPRENEURIAL SPIRIT
The Home Depot associates are encouraged to initiate creative and innovative ways of serving our customers and improving the business, as well as to adopt good ideas from others.

TAKING CARE OF OUR PEOPLE
The key to our success is treating people well. We do this by encouraging associates to speak up and take risks, by recognizing and rewarding good performance and by leading and developing people so they may grow.

RESPECT FOR ALL PEOPLE
In order to remain successful, our associates must work in an environment of mutual respect where each associate is regarded as part of The Home Depot team.

DOING THE RIGHT THING
We exercise good judgment by "doing the right thing" instead of just "doing things right." We strive to understand the impact of our decisions, and we accept responsibility for our actions.

BUILDING STRONG RELATIONSHIPS
Strong relationships are built on trust, honesty and integrity. We listen and respond to the needs of customers, associates, communities and vendors, treating them as partners.

GIVING BACK
An important part of the fabric of The Home Depot is in giving our time, talents, energy and resources to worthwhile causes in our communities and society.

Home Depot acknowledges the importance of all stakeholders in operating its business.

or fraudulent practices. The bureau, which enforces a variety of consumer protection laws, is divided into five divisions. The Division of Enforcement monitors compliance with and investigates violations of laws, including unfulfilled holiday delivery promises by online shopping sites, employment opportunities fraud, scholarship scams, misleading advertising for health care products, and more.

environmental issues Environmental responsibility has become a leading issue as both business and the public acknowledge the damage done to the environment in the past. Today's consumers are increasingly demanding that businesses take a greater responsibility for their actions and how they affect the environment.

Animal Rights. One area of environmental concern in society today is animal rights. Probably the most controversial business practice in this area is the testing of cosmetics and drugs on animals that may be injured or killed as a result. Animal-rights activists, such as People for the Ethical Treatment of Animals, say such research is morally wrong because it harms living creatures. Consumers who share this sentiment may boycott companies that test products on animals and take their business instead to companies such as The Body Shop and John Paul Mitchell Systems, which do not use animal testing. However, researchers in the cosmetics and pharmaceutical industries argue that animal testing is necessary to prevent harm to human beings who will eventually use the products. Business practices that harm endangered wildlife and their habitats are another environmental issue.

Pollution. Another major issue in the area of environmental responsibility is pollution. Water pollution results from dumping toxic chemicals and raw sewage into rivers and oceans, oil spills, and the burial of industrial waste in the ground where it may filter into underground water supplies. Fertilizers and insecticides used in farming and grounds maintenance also run off into water supplies with each rainfall. Water pollution problems are especially notable in heavily industrialized areas. Medical waste—such as used syringes, vials of blood, and AIDS-contaminated materials—has turned up on beaches in New York, New Jersey, and Massachusetts, as well as other places. Society is demanding that water supplies be clean and healthful to reduce the potential danger from these substances.

Air pollution is usually the result of smoke and other pollutants emitted by manufacturing facilities, as well as carbon monoxide and hydrocarbons emitted by motor vehicles. In addition

Intel is developing a number of tiny eco-friendly devices, including small sensors that can continuously analyze pollution. Conceivably, the sensors could be put into people's cell phones all around the world as part of a mass pollution-monitoring effort. The company also is developing small devices that generate energy from sources such as the sun and people's body heat and motion.

to the health risks posed by air pollution, when some chemical compounds emitted by manufacturing facilities react with air and rain, acid rain results. Acid rain has contributed to the deaths of many valuable forests and lakes in North America as well as in Europe. Air pollution may also contribute to global warming, in which carbon dioxide collects in the earth's atmosphere, trapping the sun's heat and preventing the earth's surface from cooling. It is indisputable that the global surface temperature has been increasing over the past 35 years. Worldwide passenger vehicle

From Oil Man to Pickens Plan

Texas billionaire T. Boone Pickens's transformation from oil man to wind farm advocate has captured the nation's attention. In 1956, Pickens formed the Mesa Petroleum Company, which became the nation's largest independently owned oil company. In 1997 Pickens formed BP Management Hedge Fund, which invests in energy stock and commodities. After earning his wealth through oil, Pickens has moved on to the energy source he thinks will replace it. Launched in July 2008, the Pickens Plan proposes a three-pronged approach to phasing out oil dependency. First, the plan calls for installing thousands of wind turbines across the Great Plains to provide 20 percent of the nation's electricity. Second, the government must install smart grids to distribute the wind power. Third, natural gas would become a fuel for automobiles, reducing foreign oil importation by an estimated 38 percent. Unfortunately, wind power installation and electricity grid overhaul will cost an estimated $185 billion. Pickens has so much faith in his plan that he invested $58 million in a multimedia campaign and has lobbied government officials to support him. The Pickens Plan could have a significant effect on how the United States powers the country, potentially placing Pickens as the major innovator behind a new energy source for America.[53] ❖

ownership has been growing due to rapid industrialization and consumer purchasing power in China, India, and other developing countries with large populations. The most important way to contain climate change is to control carbon emissions. The move to green buildings, higher-mileage cars, and other emissions reductions resulting from better efficiency has the potential to generate up to 50% of the reductions needed to keep warming at no more than 2°C above present temperatures—considered the "safe" level.[54] The 2007 U.S. Federal Energy bill raised average fuel economy (CAFÉ) standards to 35 mpg for cars by 2020, while Europe has the goal of a 40 mpg standard by the same deadline. Since buildings create half of U.S. greenhouse emissions, there is tremendous opportunity to develop conservation measures. For example, some utilities charge more for electricity in peak demand periods, which encourages behavioral changes that reduce consumption.[55] There are more than 100 million bicycles produced worldwide, more than double the passenger vehicles produced annually.[56]

Land pollution is tied directly to water pollution because many of the chemicals and toxic wastes that are dumped on the land eventually work their way into the water supply. Land pollution results from the dumping of residential and industrial waste, strip mining, forest fires, and poor forest conservation. In Brazil and other South American countries, rain forests are being destroyed—at a rate of one acre per minute—to make way for farms and ranches, at a cost of the extinction of the many animals and plants (some endangered species) that call the rain forest home. Large-scale deforestation also depletes the oxygen supply available to humans and other animals.

Related to the problem of land pollution is the larger issue of how to dispose of waste in an environmentally responsible manner. Americans are producing more trash, with the average person producing about 5 pounds of trash every day up from about 3.3 pounds in 1970. At the same time, more than 30 percent of Americans recycle, up from 8 percent in 1970.[57] Americans use 100 billion plastic bags each year, which is between 10 and 20 percent of the total global usage (estimated at 500 billion to 1 trillion bags).[58] It takes 1,000 years for the bags to decompose. San Francisco has banned plastic bags; Ireland is now charging a nationwide tax of 15 cents on all supermarket shopping bags; and Australia and China are planning a similar program.[59] Whole Foods, the nation's leading natural and organic supermarket, ended its use of plastic bags on Earth Day 2008.[60] Whole Foods estimates that this move will keep 150 million new plastic grocery bags out of the environment each year.

DID YOU KNOW?

In one year, Americans generated 230 million tons of trash and recycled 23.5 percent of it.[64]

Response to Environmental Issues. Partly in response to federal legislation such as the National Environmental Policy Act of 1969 and partly due to consumer concerns, businesses are responding to environmental issues. Many small and large companies, including Walt Disney Company, Chevron, and Scott Paper, have created a new executive position—a vice president of environmental affairs—to help them achieve their business goals in an environmentally responsible manner. A survey indicated that 83.5 percent of *Fortune* 500 companies have a written environmental policy, 74.7 percent engage in recycling efforts, and 69.7 percent have made investments in waste-reduction efforts.[61] Many companies, including Alcoa, Dow Chemical, Phillips Petroleum, and Raytheon, now link executive pay to environmental performance.[62] Some companies are finding that environmental consciousness can save them money. DuPont saved more than $3 billion through energy conservation by replacing natural gas with methane in its industrial boilers in many of its plants.[63]

Many firms are trying to eliminate wasteful practices, the emission of pollutants, and/or the use of harmful chemicals from their manufacturing processes. Other companies are seeking ways to improve their products. Utility providers, for example, are increasingly supplementing their services with alternative energy sources, including solar, wind, and geothermal power. In many places, local utility customers can even elect to purchase electricity from green sources—primarily wind power—for a few extra dollars a month. The Austin, Texas, city-owned utility's award-winning GreenChoice program includes many small and large businesses among its customers.[65] Indeed, a growing number of businesses and consumers are choosing "green power" sources where available. New Belgium Brewing, the third largest craft brewer, is the first all-wind-powered brewery in the United States. Many businesses have turned to *recycling*, the reprocessing of materials—aluminum, paper, glass, and some plastic—for reuse. Such efforts to make products, packaging, and processes more environmentally friendly have been labeled "green" business or marketing by the public and media. Lumber products at Home Depot may carry a seal from the Forest Stewardship Council to indicate that they were harvested from sustainable forests using environmentally friendly methods.[66] Likewise, most Chiquita bananas are certified through the Better Banana Project as having been grown with more environmentally and labor-friendly practices.[67]

It is important to recognize that, with current technology, environmental responsibility requires trade-offs (costs versus benefits). Society must weigh the huge costs of limiting or

[**"It is important to recognize that, with current technology, environmental responsibility requires trade-offs (costs versus benefits)."**]

eliminating pollution against the health threat posed by the pollution. Environmental responsibility imposes costs on both business and the public. Although people certainly do not want oil fouling beautiful waterways and killing wildlife, they insist on low-cost, readily available gasoline and heating oil. People do not want to contribute to the growing garbage-disposal problem, but they often refuse to pay more for "green" products packaged in an environmentally friendly manner, to recycle as much of their own waste as possible, or to permit the building of additional waste-disposal facilities (the "not in my backyard," or NIMBY, syndrome). Managers must coordinate environmental goals with other social and economic ones.

community relations

A final, yet very significant, issue for businesses concerns their responsibilities to the general welfare of the communities and societies in which they operate. Many businesses simply want to make their communities better places for everyone to live and work. The most common way that businesses exercise their community responsibility is through donations to local and national charitable organizations. Corporations contributed more than $12 billion to environmental and social causes last year.[68] For example, Safeway, the nation's fourth-largest

MooShoes, Inc., is a vegan-owned business that sells an assortment of cruelty-free bags, T-shirts, wallets, books, and the "vegetarian shoes" shown here. The company, which was the first of its kind in New York City, also has an online outlet.

> ["Business is also beginning to take more responsibility for the hard-core unemployed."]

grocer, has donated millions of dollars to organizations involved in medical research, such as Easter Seals and the Juvenile Diabetes Research Foundation International. The company's employees have also raised funds to support social causes of interest.[69] Avon's Breast Cancer Awareness Crusade has helped raise $300 million to fund community-based breast cancer education and early detection services. Avon, a marketer of women's cosmetics, is also known for employing a large number of women and promoting them to top management; the firm has more female top managers (86 percent) than any other *Fortune* 500 company.[70] Even small companies participate in philanthropy through donations and volunteer support of local causes and national charities, such as the Red Cross and the United Way.

After realizing that the current pool of prospective employees lacks many basic skills necessary to work, many companies have become concerned about the quality of education in the United States. Recognizing that today's students are tomorrow's employees and customers, firms such as Kroger, Campbell's Soup, Kodak, American Express, Apple Computer, Xerox, and Coca-Cola are donating money, equipment, and employee time to help improve schools in their communities and around the nation. They provide scholarship money, support for teachers, and computers for students, and they send employees out to tutor and motivate young students to stay in school and succeed. Target, for example, contributes significant resources to education, including direct donations of $100 million to schools

as well as fund-raising and scholarship programs that assist teachers and students. Through the retailer's Take Charge of Education program, customers using a Target Guest Card can designate a specific school to which Target donates 1 percent of their total purchase. This program is designed to make customers feel that their purchases are benefiting their community while increasing the use of Target Guest Cards.[71]

Another tactic taken by some companies is to let consumers decide whether they want to contribute to socially responsible activities. What if Dell sold one notebook computer for $1,000 and the same computer for $1,150, with the understanding that the purchase of *this* computer would support the fight against AIDs around the world? Dell and Microsoft recently created products for the Product(Red) campaign, joining other large corporations such as The Gap, Apple, and Motorola in support of The Global Fund, an international organization fighting AIDs, tuberculosis, and malaria. The Product(Red) computer sold by Dell is significant to consumers and communicates their support to others.[72]

Business is also beginning to take more responsibility for the hard-core unemployed. Some are mentally or physically handicapped; some are homeless. Organizations such as the National Alliance of Businessmen fund programs to train the hard-core unemployed so that they can find jobs and support themselves. In addition to fostering self-support, such opportunities enhance self-esteem and help people become productive members of society. ■

SO YOU WANT A JOB IN BUSINESS ETHICS AND SOCIAL RESPONSIBILITY

In the words of Kermit the Frog, "It's not easy being green." Maybe it is not easy, but green business opportunities abound. A popular catchphrase, "Green is the new black," indicates how fashionable green business is becoming. Consumers are more in tune with and concerned about green products, policies, and behaviors by companies than ever before. Companies are looking for new hires to help them see their business creatively and bring insights to all aspects of business operations. The American Solar Energy Society estimates that the number of green jobs could rise to 40 million in the United States by 2030. Green business strategies not only give a firm a commercial advantage in the marketplace but help lead the way toward a greener world. The fight to reduce our carbon footprint in an attempt to slow climate change has opened up opportunities for renewable energy, recycling, conservation, and an increase in overall efficiency in the way resources are used. New businesses that focus on hydro, wind, and solar power are on the rise and will need talented businesspeople to lead them. Carbon emissions trading is gaining popularity as large corporations and individuals alike seek to lower their footprints. A job in this growing field could be similar to that of a stock trader, or you could lead the search for carbon-efficient companies in which to invest.

In the ethics arena, current trends in business governance strongly support the development of ethics and compliance departments to help guide organizational integrity. This alone is a billion-dollar business, and there are jobs in developing organizational ethics programs, developing company policies, and training employees and manage-

ment. An entry-level position might be as a communication specialist or trainer for programs in a business ethics department. Eventually there's an opportunity to become an ethics officer who would have the responsibilities of meeting with employees, the board of directors, and top management to discuss and provide advice about ethics issues in the industry; developing and distributing a code of ethics; creating and maintaining an anonymous, confidential service to answer questions about ethical issues; taking actions on possible ethics code violations; and reviewing and modifying the code of ethics of the organization.

There are also opportunities to work on initiatives to help companies relate social responsibility to stakeholder interests and needs. These jobs could involve coordinating and implementing philanthropic programs that give back to others who are important to the organization or developing a community volunteering program for employees. In addition to the human relations function, most companies develop programs to help employees and their families improve their quality of life. Companies have found that the healthier and happier employees are, the more productive they will be in the workforce.

Social responsibility, ethics, and sustainable business practices are not a trend; they are good for business and the bottom line. Just ask Toyota, which sold well over 1 million hybrid cars worldwide in 10 years. New industries are being created and old ones are adapting to the new market demands, opening up many varied job opportunities that will lead not just to a paycheck but to the satisfaction of making the world a better place.[73]

Team Exercise

Sam Walton, the founder of Wal-Mart, had an early strategy for growing his business related to pricing. The "Opening Price Point" strategy used by Walton involved offering the introductory product in a product line at the lowest point in the market. For example, the minimally equipped microwave oven would sell for less than anyone else in town could sell the same unit. The strategy was that if consumers saw a product, such as the microwave, and saw it as a good value, they would assume that all the microwaves were good values. Walton noted that most people don't buy the entry-level product; they want more features and capabilities and trade up. Form teams and assign the role of defending this strategy or casting it as an unethical act. Have teams present their thoughts on either side of the issue.

CHECK OUT www.mhhe.com/FerrellM2e

for study materials including Interactive Exercises, Quizzes, iPod downloads, and video.

APPENDIX A

THE LEGAL AND REGULATORY ENVIRONMENT

Business law refers to the rules and regulations that govern the conduct of business. Problems in this area come from the failure to keep promises, misunderstandings, disagreements about expectations, or, in some cases, attempts to take advantage of others. The regulatory environment offers a framework and enforcement system in order to provide a fair playing field for all businesses. The regulatory environment is created based on inputs from competitors, customers, employees, special interest groups, and the public's elected representatives. Lobbying by pressure groups that try to influence legislation often shapes the legal and regulatory environment.

SOURCES OF LAW

Laws are classified as either criminal or civil. *Criminal law* not only prohibits a specific kind of action, such as unfair competition or mail fraud, but also imposes a fine or imprisonment as punishment for violating the law. A violation of a criminal law is thus called a crime. *Civil law* defines all the laws not classified as criminal, and it specifies the rights and duties of individuals and organizations (including businesses). Violations of civil law may result in fines but not imprisonment. The primary difference between criminal law and civil law is that criminal laws are enforced by the state or nation, whereas civil laws are enforced through the court system by individuals or organizations.

> "The primary method of resolving conflicts and business disputes is through lawsuits, where one individual or organization takes another to court using civil laws."

Criminal and civil laws are derived from four sources: the Constitution (constitutional law), precedents established by judges (common law), federal and state statutes (statutory law), and federal and state administrative agencies (administrative law). Federal administrative agencies established by Congress control and influence business by enforcing laws and regulations to encourage competition and protect consumers, workers, and the environment. The Supreme Court is the ultimate authority on legal and regulatory decisions for appropriate conduct in business.

COURTS AND THE RESOLUTION OF DISPUTES

The primary method of resolving conflicts and business disputes is through **lawsuits,** where one individual or organization takes another to court using civil laws. The legal system, therefore, provides a forum for businesspeople to resolve disputes based on our legal foundations. The courts may decide when harm or damage results from the actions of others.

Because lawsuits are so common in the world of business, it is important to understand more about the court system where such disputes are resolved. Both financial restitution and specific actions to undo wrongdoing can result from going before a court to resolve a conflict. All decisions made in the courts are based on criminal and civil laws derived from the legal and regulatory system.

A businessperson may win a lawsuit in court and receive a judgment, or court order, requiring the loser of the suit to pay monetary damages. However, this does not guarantee the victor will be able to collect those damages. If the loser of the suit lacks the financial resources to pay the judgment—for example, if the loser is a bankrupt business—the winner of the suit may not be able to collect the award. Most business lawsuits involve a request for a sum of money, but some lawsuits request that a court specifically order a person or organization to do or to refrain from doing a certain act, such as slamming telephone customers.

The Court System

Jurisdiction is the legal power of a court, through a judge, to interpret and apply the law and make a binding decision in a particular case. In some instances, other courts will not enforce the decision of a prior court because it lacked jurisdiction. Federal courts are granted jurisdiction by the Constitution or by Congress. State legislatures and constitutions determine which state courts hear certain types of cases. Courts of general jurisdiction hear all types of cases; those of limited jurisdiction hear only specific types of cases. The Federal Bankruptcy Court, for example, hears only cases involving bankruptcy. There is some combination of limited and general jurisdiction courts in every state.

In a **trial court** (whether in a court of general or limited jurisdiction and whether in the state or the federal system), two tasks must be completed. First, the court (acting through the judge or a jury) must determine the facts of the case. In other words, if there is conflicting evidence, the judge or jury must decide who to believe. Second, the judge must decide which law or set of laws is pertinent to the case and must then apply those laws to resolve the dispute.

An **appellate court,** on the other hand, deals solely with appeals relating to the interpretation of law. Thus, when you hear about a case being appealed, it is not retried, but rather reevaluated. Appellate judges do not hear witnesses but instead base their decisions on a written transcript of the original trial. Moreover, appellate courts do not draw factual conclusions; the appellate judge is limited to deciding whether the trial judge made a mistake in interpreting the law that probably affected the outcome of the trial. If the trial judge made no mistake (or if mistakes would not have changed the result of the trial), the appellate court will let the trial court's decision stand. If the appellate court finds a mistake, it usually sends the case back to

Marcia and Bill Baker found Heinz was underfilling their 20-oz. ketchup bottles by 1.5 oz. Heinz paid civil penalties and costs of $180,000 and had to overfill all ketchup bottles in California by 1/8 oz. for a year.

the trial court so that the mistake can be corrected. Correction may involve the granting of a new trial. On occasion, appellate courts modify the verdict of the trial court without sending the case back to the trial court.

Alternative Dispute Resolution Methods

Although the main remedy for business disputes is a lawsuit, other dispute resolution methods are becoming popular. The schedules of state and federal trial courts are often crowded; long delays between the filing of a case and the trial date are common. Further, complex cases can become quite expensive to pursue. As a result, many businesspeople are turning to alternative methods of resolving business arguments: mediation and arbitration, the mini-trial, and litigation in a private court.

Mediation is a form of negotiation to resolve a dispute by bringing in one or more third-party mediators, usually chosen by the disputing parties, to help reach a settlement. The mediator suggests different ways to resolve a dispute between the parties. The mediator's resolution is nonbinding—that is, the parties do not have to accept the mediator's suggestions; they are strictly voluntary.

Arbitration involves submission of a dispute to one or more third-party arbitrators, usually chosen by the disputing parties, whose decision usually is final. Arbitration differs from mediation in that an arbitrator's decision must be followed, whereas a mediator merely offers suggestions and facilitates negotiations. Cases may be submitted to arbitration because a contract—such as a labor contract—requires it or because the parties agree to do so. Some consumers are barred from taking claims to court by agreements drafted by banks, brokers, health plans, and others. Instead, they are required to take complaints to mandatory arbitration. Arbitration can be an attractive alternative to a lawsuit because it is often cheaper and quicker, and the parties frequently can choose arbitrators who are knowledgeable about the particular area of business at issue.

A method of dispute resolution that may become increasingly important in settling complex disputes is the **mini-trial,** in which both parties agree to present a summarized version of their case to an independent third party. That person then advises them of his or her impression of the probable outcome if the case were to be tried. Representatives of both sides then attempt to negotiate a settlement based on the advisor's recommendations. For example, employees in a large corporation who believe they have muscular or skeletal stress injuries caused by the strain of repetitive motion in using a computer could agree to a mini-trial to address a dispute related to damages. Although the mini-trial itself does not resolve the dispute, it can help the parties resolve the case before going to court. Because the mini-trial is not subject to formal court rules, it can save companies a great deal of money, allowing them to recognize the weaknesses in a particular case.

In some areas of the country, disputes can be submitted to a private nongovernmental court for resolution. In a sense, a **private court system** is similar to arbitration in that an independent third party resolves the case after hearing both sides of the story. Trials in private courts may be either informal or highly formal, depending on the people involved. Businesses typically agree to have their disputes decided in private courts to save time and money.

REGULATORY ADMINISTRATIVE AGENCIES

Federal and state administrative agencies (listed in Table A.1) also have some judicial powers. Many administrative agencies, such as the Federal Trade Commission, decide disputes that involve their regulations. In such disputes, the resolution process is usually called a "hearing" rather than a trial. In these cases, an administrative law judge decides all issues.

Federal regulatory agencies influence many business activities and cover product liability, safety, and the regulation or deregulation of public utilities. Usually, these bodies have the power to enforce specific laws, such as the Federal Trade Commission Act, and have some discretion in establishing operating rules and regulations to guide certain types of industry practices. Because of this discretion and overlapping areas of responsibility, confusion or conflict regarding which agencies have jurisdiction over which activities is common.

Of all the federal regulatory units, the **Federal Trade Commission (FTC)** most influences business activities related to questionable practices that create disputes between businesses and their customers. Although the FTC regulates a variety of business practices, it allocates a large portion of resources to curbing false advertising, misleading pricing, and deceptive packaging and labeling. When it receives a complaint or otherwise has reason to believe that a firm is violating a law, the FTC issues a complaint stating that the business is in violation.

If a company continues the questionable practice, the FTC can issue a cease-and-desist order, which is an order for the business to stop doing whatever has caused the complaint. In such cases, the charged firm can appeal to the federal courts to have the order rescinded. However, the FTC can seek civil penalties in court—up to a maximum penalty of $10,000 a day for each infraction—if a cease-and-desist order is violated. In its battle against unfair pricing, the FTC has issued consent decrees alleging that corporate attempts to engage in price fixing or invitations to competitors to collude are violations even when the competitors in question refuse the invitations. The commission can also require companies to run corrective advertising in response to previous ads considered misleading.

Pfizer—Puffery or Deception?

Pfizer, Inc., is a pharmaceutical company that produces the drug Lipitor, which has been proved to lower cholesterol. However, increased competition prompted Pfizer to rethink its advertising strategy. The company hired Dr. Robert Jarvik, inventor of an artificial heart, to star in new ads for the drug. Jarvik is not a practicing physician, and this called into question the validity and morality of the endorsement. The company abruptly pulled the ads in 2008 in the wake of a federal investigation into the matter.

The accusations do not call into question the importance of Jarvik's accomplishments or the effectiveness of the medication. They do, however, question Jarvik's credentials, as he is not a practicing physician. They also question whether the ads fraudulently mislead consumers.

Exaggerated marketing claims are known as *puffery*. Advertising moves beyond puffery into deceptive, or false, advertising if it gives consumers untrue or unrealistic ideas about the product. False advertising can range from misrepresenting a product, to advertising the best features rather than the standard ones, to using fillers or oversized packaging to make the consumer think that he or she is buying more. Deceptive advertising is considered fraud. The House Committee on Energy and Commerce has called into question the validity of the claims asserted by Jarvik in the ad and is considering whether the ads are deceptive or merely puffery. This distinction can be difficult to determine. Some believe that the best approach for Pfizer would be to move toward advertising that utilizes scientific data instead of emotional appeals.[74] ❖

Q: Discussion Questions

1. If the information conveyed in the ads is truthful, should it matter that Dr. Jarvik is associated with the development of an artificial heart but is not a practicing physician?

2. What advertising approaches do you think that Pfizer should take in the future to avoid the kind of scrutiny and criticism engendered by the Jarvik Lipitor ads?

3. How might one determine when a company has crossed the line between puffery and outright deception?

"OF ALL THE FEDERAL REGULATORY UNITS, THE FEDERAL TRADE COMMISSION (FTC) MOST INFLUENCES BUSINESS ACTIVITIES RELATED TO QUESTIONABLE PRACTICES THAT CREATE DISPUTES BETWEEN BUSINESSES AND THEIR CUSTOMERS."

TABLE A.1 The Major Regulatory Agencies

Agency	Major Areas of Responsibility
Federal Trade Commission (FTC)	Enforces laws and guidelines regarding business practices; takes action to stop false and deceptive advertising and labeling.
Food and Drug Administration (FDA)	Enforces laws and regulations to prevent distribution of adulterated or misbranded foods, drugs, medical devices, cosmetics, veterinary products, and particularly hazardous consumer products.
Consumer Product Safety Commission (CPSC)	Ensures compliance with the Consumer Product Safety Act; protects the public from unreasonable risk of injury from any consumer product not covered by other regulatory agencies.
Interstate Commerce Commission (ICC)	Regulates franchises, rates, and finances of interstate rail, bus, truck, and water carriers.
Federal Communications Commission (FCC)	Regulates communication by wire, radio, and television in interstate and foreign commerce.
Environmental Protection Agency (EPA)	Develops and enforces environmental protection standards and conducts research into the adverse effects of pollution.
Federal Energy Regulatory Commission (FERC)	Regulates rates and sales of natural gas products, thereby affecting the supply and price of gas available to consumers; also regulates wholesale rates for electricity and gas, pipeline construction, and U.S. imports and exports of natural gas and electricity.
Equal Employment Opportunity Commission (EEOC)	Investigates and resolves discrimination in employment practices.
Federal Aviation Administration (FAA)	Oversees the policies and regulations of the airline industry.
Federal Highway Administration (FHA)	Regulates vehicle safety requirements.
Occupational Safety and Health Administration (OSHA)	Develops policy to promote worker safety and health and investigates infractions.
Securities and Exchange Commission (SEC)	Regulates corporate securities trading and develops protection from fraud and other abuses; provides an accounting oversight board.

The FTC also assists businesses in complying with laws. New marketing methods are evaluated every year. When general sets of guidelines are needed to improve business practices in a particular industry, the FTC sometimes encourages firms within that industry to establish a set of trade practices voluntarily. The FTC may even sponsor a conference bringing together industry leaders and consumers for the purpose of establishing acceptable trade practices.

Unlike the FTC, other regulatory units are limited to dealing with specific products, services, or business activities. The Food and Drug Administration (FDA) enforces regulations prohibiting the sale and distribution of adulterated, misbranded, or hazardous food and drug products. For example, the FDA outlawed the sale and distribution of most over-the-counter hair-loss remedies after research indicated that few of the products were effective in restoring hair growth.

The Environmental Protection Agency (EPA) develops and enforces environmental protection standards and conducts research into the adverse effects of pollution. The Consumer Product Safety Commission recalls about 300 products a year, ranging from small, inexpensive toys to major appliances. The Consumer Product Safety Commission's Web site provides details regarding current recalls.

IMPORTANT ELEMENTS OF BUSINESS LAW

To avoid violating criminal and civil laws, as well as discouraging lawsuits from consumers, employees, suppliers, and others, businesspeople need to be familiar with laws that address business practices.

The Uniform Commercial Code

At one time, states had their own specific laws governing various business practices, and transacting business across state lines was difficult because of the variation in the laws from state to state. To simplify commerce, every state—except Louisiana—has enacted the Uniform Commercial Code (Louisiana has enacted portions of the code). The **Uniform Commercial Code (UCC)** is a set of statutory laws covering several business law topics. Article II of the Uniform Commercial Code, which is discussed in the following paragraphs, has a significant impact on business.

Sales Agreements.
Article II of the Uniform Commercial Code covers sales agreements for goods and services such as installation but does not cover stocks, bonds, or real estate, or personal services. Among its many provisions, Article II stipulates that a sales agreement can be enforced even though it does not specify the selling price or the time or place of delivery. It also requires that a buyer pay a reasonable price for goods at the time of delivery if the buyer and seller have not reached an agreement on price. Specifically, Article II addresses the rights of buyers and sellers, transfers of ownership, warranties, and the legal placement of risk during manufacture and delivery.

Article II also deals with express and implied warranties. An **express warranty** stipulates the specific terms the seller will honor. Many automobile manufacturers, for example, provide three-year or 36,000-mile warranties on their vehicles, during which period they will fix any and all defects specified in the warranty. An **implied warranty** is imposed on the producer or seller by law, although it may not be a written document provided at the time of sale. Under Article II, a consumer may assume that the product for sale has a clear title (in other words, that it is not stolen) and that the product will both serve the purpose for which it was made and sold as well as function as advertised.

The Law of Torts and Fraud

A **tort** is a private or civil wrong other than breach of contract. For example, a tort can result if the driver of a Domino's Pizza delivery car loses control of the vehicle and damages property or injures a person. In the case of the delivery car accident, the injured persons might sue the driver and the owner of the company—Domino's in this case—for damages resulting from the accident.

Fraud is a purposeful unlawful act to deceive or manipulate in order to damage others. Thus, in some cases, a tort may also represent a violation of criminal law. Health care fraud has become a major issue in the courts.

An important aspect of tort law involves **product liability**—businesses' legal responsibility for any negligence in the design, production, sale, and consumption of products. Product liability laws have evolved from both common and statutory law. Some states have expanded the concept of product liability to include injuries by products whether or not the producer is proved negligent. Under this strict product liability, a consumer who files suit because of an injury has to prove only that the product was defective, that the defect caused the injury, and that the defect made the product unreasonably dangerous. For example, a carving knife is expected to be sharp and is not considered defective if you cut your finger using it. But an electric knife could be considered defective and unreasonably dangerous if it continued to operate after being switched off.

Reforming tort law, particularly in regard to product liability, has become a hot political issue as businesses look for relief from huge judgments in lawsuits. Although many lawsuits are warranted—few would disagree that a wrong has occurred when a patient dies because of negligence during a medical procedure or when a child is seriously injured by a defective toy, and that the families deserve some compensation—many suits are not. Because of multimillion-dollar judgments, companies are trying to minimize their liability, and sometimes they pass on the costs of the damage awards to their customers in the form of higher prices. Some states have passed laws limiting damage awards, and some tort reform is occurring at the federal level. Table A.2 lists the state court systems the Institute for Legal Reform has identified as being "best" and "worst" to business in terms of juries' fairness, judges' competence and impartiality, and other factors.

The Law of Contracts

Virtually every business transaction is carried out by means of a **contract,** a mutual agreement between two or more parties that can be enforced in a court if one party chooses not to comply with the terms of the contract. If you rent an apartment or house, for example, your lease is a contract. If you have borrowed money under a student loan program, you have a contractual agreement to repay the money. Many aspects of contract law are covered under the Uniform Commercial Code.

A "handshake deal" is in most cases as fully and completely binding as a written, signed contract agreement. Indeed, many oil-drilling and construction contractors have for years agreed to take on projects on the basis of such handshake deals. However, individual states require that some contracts be in writing to be enforceable. Most states require that at least some of the following contracts be in writing:

- Contracts involving the sale of land or an interest in land.
- Contracts to pay somebody else's debt.
- Contracts that cannot be fulfilled within one year.
- Contracts for the sale of goods that cost more than $500 (required by the Uniform Commercial Code).

Only those contracts that meet certain requirements—called *elements*—are enforceable by the courts. A person or business

TABLE A.2 Lawsuit Climate for Businesses

Best	Worst
Delaware	West Virginia
Nebraska	Louisiana
Maine	Mississippi
Indiana	Alabama
Utah	Illinois
Virginia	Hawaii
Iowa	California
Vermont	South Carolina
Colorado	Florida
Kansas	Texas
Minnesota	Nevada
South Dakota	Rhode Island

Source: Institute for Legal Reform, 2008 Lawsuit Climate Report, www.instituteforlegalreform.com/component/ilr_harris_poll/30/all.html?year=2008 (accessed March 9, 2009).

New car buyers receive express warranties stating what is covered for repair or replacement over a specific period of time.

seeking to enforce a contract must show that it contains the following elements: voluntary agreement, consideration, contractual capacity of the parties, and legality.

For any agreement to be considered a legal contract, all persons involved must agree to be bound by the terms of the contract. *Voluntary agreement* typically comes about when one party makes an offer and the other accepts. If both the offer and the acceptance are freely, voluntarily, and knowingly made, the acceptance forms the basis for the contract. If, however, either the offer or the acceptance is the result of fraud or force, the individual or organization subject to the fraud or force can void, or invalidate, the resulting agreement or receive compensation for damages.

The second requirement for enforcement of a contract is that it must be supported by *consideration*—that is, money or something of value must be given in return for fulfilling a contract. As a general rule, a person cannot be forced to abide by the terms of a promise unless that person receives a consideration. The something-of-value could be money, goods, services, or even a promise to do or not to do something.

Contractual capacity is the legal ability to enter into a contract. As a general rule, a court cannot enforce a contract if either party to the agreement lacks contractual capacity. A person's contractual capacity may be limited or nonexistent if he or she is a minor (under the age of 18), mentally unstable, retarded, insane, or intoxicated.

Legality is the state or condition of being lawful. For an otherwise binding contract to be enforceable, both the purpose of and the consideration for the contract must be legal. A contract in which a bank loans money at a rate of interest prohibited by

> ● ● An agency is a common business relationship created when one person acts on behalf of another and under that person's control.

law, a practice known as usury, would be an illegal contract, for example. The fact that one of the parties may commit an illegal act while performing a contract does not render the contract itself illegal, however.

Breach of contract is the failure or refusal of a party to a contract to live up to his or her promises. In the case of an apartment lease, failure to pay rent would be considered breach of contract. The breaching party—the one who fails to comply—may be liable for monetary damages that he or she causes the other person.

The Law of Agency

An **agency** is a common business relationship created when one person acts on behalf of another and under that person's control. Two parties are involved in an agency relationship: The **principal** is the one who wishes to have a specific task accomplished; the **agent** is the one who acts on behalf of the principal to accomplish the task. Authors, movie stars, and athletes often employ agents to help them obtain the best contract terms.

An agency relationship is created by the mutual agreement of the principal and the agent. It is usually not necessary that such an agreement be in writing, although putting it in writing is certainly advisable. An agency relationship continues as long as both the principal and the agent so desire. It can be terminated by mutual agreement, by fulfillment of the purpose of the agency, by the refusal of either party to continue in the relationship, or by the death of either the principal or the agent. In most cases, a principal grants authority to the agent through a formal *power of attorney*, which is a legal document authorizing a person to act as someone else's agent. The power of attorney can be used for any agency relationship, and its use is not limited to lawyers. For instance, in real estate transactions, often a lawyer or real estate agent is given power of attorney with the authority to purchase real estate for the buyer. Accounting firms often give employees agency relationships in making financial transactions.

Both officers and directors of corporations are fiduciaries, or people of trust, who use due care and loyalty as an agent in making decisions on behalf of the organization. This relationship creates a duty of care, also called duty of diligence, to make informed decisions. These agents of the corporation are not held responsible for negative outcomes if they are informed and diligent in their decisions. The duty of loyalty means that all decisions should be in the interests of the corporation and its stakeholders. Scandals at Enron, Tyco, and WorldCom are associated with officers and directors who failed to carry out their fiduciary duties. Lawsuits from shareholders called for the officers and directors to pay large sums of money from their own pockets.

The Law of Property

Property law is extremely broad in scope because it covers the ownership and transfer of all kinds of real, personal, and intellectual property. **Real property** consists of real estate and everything permanently attached to it; **personal property** basically is everything else. Personal property can be further subdivided into tangible and intangible property. *Tangible property* refers to items that have a physical existence, such as automobiles, business inventory, and clothing. *Intangible property* consists of rights and duties; its existence may be represented by a document or by some other tangible item. For example, accounts receivable, stock in a corporation, goodwill, and trademarks are all examples of intangible personal property. **Intellectual property** refers to property, such as musical works, artwork, books, and computer software, that is generated by a person's creative activities.

Copyrights, patents, and trademarks provide protection to the owners of property by giving them the exclusive right to use it. *Copyrights* protect the ownership rights on material (often intellectual property) such as books, music, videos, photos, and computer software. The creators of such works, or their heirs, generally have exclusive rights to the published or unpublished works for the creator's lifetime, plus 50 years. *Patents* give inventors exclusive rights to their inventions for 17 years. The most intense competition for patents is in the pharmaceutical industry. Most patents take a minimum of 18 months to secure.

A *trademark* is a brand (name, mark, or symbol) that is registered with the U.S. Patent and Trademark Office and is thus legally protected from use by any other firm. Among the symbols that have been so protected are McDonald's golden arches and Coca-Cola's distinctive bottle shape. It is estimated that large multinational firms may have as many as 15,000 conflicts related to trademarks. Companies are diligent about protecting their trademarks both to avoid confusion in consumers' minds and because a term that becomes part of everyday language can no longer be trademarked. The names *aspirin* and *nylon,* for example, were once the exclusive property of their creators but became so widely used as product names (rather than brand names) that now anyone can use them.

As the trend toward globalization of trade continues, and more and more businesses trade across national boundaries, protecting property rights, particularly intellectual property such as computer software, has become an increasing challenge. While a company may be able to register as a trademark a brand name or symbol in its home country, it may not be able to secure that protection abroad. Some countries have copyright and patent laws that are less strict than those of the United States; some countries will not enforce U.S. laws. China, for example, has often been criticized for permitting U.S. goods to be counterfeited there. Such counterfeiting harms not only the sales of U.S. companies but also their reputations if the knockoffs are of poor quality. Thus, businesses engaging in foreign trade may have to take extra steps to protect their property because local laws may be insufficient to protect them.

The Law of Bankruptcy

Although few businesses and individuals intentionally fail to repay (or default on) their debts, sometimes they cannot fulfill their financial obligations. Individuals may charge goods and services beyond their ability to pay for them. Businesses may take on too much debt in order to finance growth or business events such as an increase in the cost of commodities can bankrupt a company. An option of last resort in these cases is bankruptcy, or legal insolvency. In May and June 2009 both GM and Chrysler filed for Chapter 11 bankruptcy. Most of Chrysler's assets were sold to the Italian automaker Fiat with the hope that the company would emerge leaner and more competitive as a result. As part of the restructuring, GM shuttered many of its faltering plants, and the United States government became a principal shareholder of the once-powerful automotive company. The bankruptcy filings of two major automakers were unprecedented in U.S. history, and so was the government response of nationalization.

Individuals or companies may ask a bankruptcy court to declare them unable to pay their debts and thus release them from the obligation of repaying those debts. The debtor's assets may then be sold to pay off as much of the debt as possible. In the case of a personal bankruptcy, although the individual is released from repaying debts and can start over with a clean slate, obtaining credit after bankruptcy proceedings is very difficult. About 2 million households in the United States filed for bankruptcy in 2005, the most ever. However, a new, more restrictive law went into effect in late 2005, and fewer consumers were using bankruptcy to eliminate their debts. The 2008–2009 recession spiked the number of bankruptcy proceedings even though it was more difficult to declare bankruptcy. The law makes it harder for consumers to prove that they should be allowed to clear their debts for what is called a "fresh start" or Chapter 7 bankruptcy. In 2008, Aloha Airlines took the drastic step of filing for Chapter 7 bankruptcy. After filing, the carrier quickly closed for business, while United Airlines and Hawaiian Airlines stepped in to honor Aloha's tickets and reservations. Although the person or company in debt usually initiates bankruptcy proceedings, creditors may also initiate them. Table A.3 describes the various levels of bankruptcy protection a business or individual may seek.

"OUR USE AND DEPENDENCE ON THE INTERNET ARE INCREASINGLY CREATING A POTENTIAL LEGAL PROBLEM FOR BUSINESSES."

TABLE A.3 Types of Bankruptcy

Chapter 7	Requires that the business be dissolved and its assets liquidated, or sold, to pay off the debts. Individuals declaring Chapter 7 retain a limited amount of exempt assets, the amount of which may be determined by state or federal law, at the debtor's option. Although the type and value of exempt assets varies from state to state, most states' laws allow a bankrupt individual to keep an automobile, some household goods, clothing, furnishings, and at least some of the value of the debtor's residence. All nonexempt assets must be sold to pay debts.
Chapter 11	Temporarily frees a business from its financial obligations while it reorganizes and works out a payment plan with its creditors. The indebted company continues to operate its business during bankruptcy proceedings. Often, the business sells off assets and less-profitable subsidiaries to raise cash to pay off its immediate obligations.
Chapter 13	Similar to Chapter 11 but limited to individuals. This proceeding allows an individual to establish a three- to five-year plan for repaying his or her debt. Under this plan, an individual ultimately may repay as little as 10 percent of his or her debt.

LAWS AFFECTING BUSINESS PRACTICES

One of the government's many roles is to act as a watchdog to ensure that businesses behave in accordance with the wishes of society. Congress has enacted a number of laws that affect business practices; some of the most important of these are summarized in Table A.4. Many state legislatures have enacted similar laws governing business within specific states.

The **Sherman Antitrust Act,** passed in 1890 to prevent businesses from restraining trade and monopolizing markets, condemns "every contract, combination, or conspiracy in restraint of trade." For example, a request that a competitor agree to fix prices or divide markets would, if accepted, result in a violation of the Sherman Act. Proof of intent plays an important role in attempted monopolization cases under the Sherman Act. Enforced by the Antitrust Division of the Department of Justice, the Sherman Antitrust Act applies to firms operating in interstate commerce and to U.S. firms operating in foreign commerce. The Sherman Antitrust Act, still highly relevant 100 years after its passage, is being copied throughout the world as the basis for regulating fair competition.

Because the provisions of the Sherman Antitrust Act are rather vague, courts have not always interpreted it as its creators intended. The Clayton Act was passed in 1914 to limit specific activities that can reduce competition. The **Clayton Act** prohibits price discrimination, tying and exclusive agreements, and the acquisition of stock in another corporation where the effect may be to lessen competition substantially or tend to create a monopoly. In addition, the Clayton Act prohibits members of one company's board of directors from holding seats on the boards of competing corporations. The act also exempts farm cooperatives and labor organizations from antitrust laws.

In spite of these laws regulating business practices, there are still many questions about the regulation of business. For instance, it is difficult to determine what constitutes an accept-able degree of competition and whether a monopoly is harmful to a particular market. Many mergers were permitted in the 1990s that resulted in less competition in the banking, publishing, and automobile industries. In some industries, such as utilities, it is not cost effective to have too many competitors. For this reason, the government permits utility monopolies, although recently, the telephone, electricity, and communications industries have been deregulated. Furthermore, the antitrust laws are often rather vague and require interpretation, which may vary from judge to judge and court to court. Thus, what one judge defines as a monopoly or trust today may be permitted by another judge a few years from now. Businesspeople need to understand what the law says on these issues and try to conduct their affairs within the bounds of these laws.

THE INTERNET: LEGAL AND REGULATORY ISSUES

Our use and dependence on the Internet are increasingly creating a potential legal problem for businesses. With this growing use come questions of maintaining an acceptable level of privacy for consumers and proper competitive use of the medium. Some might consider that tracking individuals who visit or "hit" their Web site by attaching a "cookie" (identifying you as a Web site visitor for potential recontact and tracking your movement throughout the site) is an improper use of the Internet for business purposes. Others may find such practices acceptable and similar to the practices of non-Internet retailers who copy information from checks or ask customers for their name, address, or phone number before they will process a transaction. There are few specific laws that regulate business on the Internet, but the standards for acceptable behavior that are reflected in the basic laws and regulations designed for traditional businesses can be applied to business on the Internet as well.

TABLE A.4 Major Federal Laws Affecting Business Practices

Act (Date Enacted)	Purpose
Sherman Antitrust Act (1890)	Prohibits contracts, combinations, or conspiracies to restrain trade; establishes as a misdemeanor monopolizing or attempting to monopolize.
Clayton Act (1914)	Prohibits specific practices such as price discrimination, exclusive dealer arrangements, and stock acquisitions in which the effect may notably lessen competition or tend to create a monopoly.
Federal Trade Commission Act (1914)	Created the Federal Trade Commission; also gives the FTC investigatory powers to be used in preventing unfair methods of competition.
Robinson-Patman Act (1936)	Prohibits price discrimination that lessens competition among wholesalers or retailers; prohibits producers from giving disproportionate services or facilities to large buyers.
Wheeler-Lea Act (1938)	Prohibits unfair and deceptive acts and practices regardless of whether competition is injured; places advertising of foods and drugs under the jurisdiction of the FTC.
Lanham Act (1946)	Provides protections and regulation of brand names, brand marks, trade names, and trademarks.
Celler-Kefauver Act (1950)	Prohibits any corporation engaged in commerce from acquiring the whole or any part of the stock or other share of the capital assets of another corporation when the effect substantially lessens competition or tends to create a monopoly.
Fair Packaging and Labeling Act (1966)	Makes illegal the unfair or deceptive packaging or labeling of consumer products.
Magnuson-Moss Warranty (FTC) Act (1975)	Provides for minimum disclosure standards for written consumer product warranties; defines minimum consent standards for written warranties; allows the FTC to prescribe interpretive rules in policy statements regarding unfair or deceptive practices.
Consumer Goods Pricing Act (1975)	Prohibits the use of price maintenance agreements among manufacturers and resellers in interstate commerce.
Antitrust Improvements Act (1976)	Requires large corporations to inform federal regulators of prospective mergers or acquisitions so that they can be studied for any possible violations of the law.
Trademark Counterfeiting Act (1980)	Provides civil and criminal penalties against those who deal in counterfeit consumer goods or any counterfeit goods that can threaten health or safety.
Trademark Law Revision Act (1988)	Amends the Lanham Act to allow brands not yet introduced to be protected through registration with the Patent and Trademark Office.
Nutrition Labeling and Education Act (1990)	Prohibits exaggerated health claims and requires all processed foods to contain labels with nutritional information.
Telephone Consumer Protection Act (1991)	Establishes procedures to avoid unwanted telephone solicitations; prohibits marketers from using automated telephone dialing system or an artificial or prerecorded voice to certain telephone lines.
Federal Trademark Dilution Act (1995)	Provides trademark owners the right to protect trademarks and requires relinquishment of names that match or parallel existing trademarks.
Digital Millennium Copyright Act (1998)	Refined copyright laws to protect digital versions of copyrighted materials, including music and movies.
Children's Online Privacy Protection Act (2000)	Regulates the collection of personally identifiable information (name, address, e-mail address, hobbies, interests, or information collected through cookies) online from children under age 13.
Sarbanes-Oxley Act (2002)	Made securities fraud a criminal offense; stiffened penalties for corporate fraud; created an accounting oversight board; and instituted numerous other provisions designed to increase corporate transparency and compliance.
Do Not Call Implementation Act (2003)	Directs FCC and FTC to coordinate so their rules are consistent regarding telemarketing call practices, including the Do Not Call Registry.
Troubled Asset Relief Program (2008)	Allows the government to purchase up to $700 billion of troubled assets. The government took majority ownership of AIG and General Motors and a minority interest in many financial institutions.

The central focus for future legislation of business conducted on the Internet is the protection of personal privacy. The present basis of personal privacy protection is the U.S. Constitution, various Supreme Court rulings, and laws such as the 1971 Fair Credit Reporting Act, the 1978 Right to Financial Privacy Act, and the 1974 Privacy Act, which deals with the release of government records. With few regulations on the use of information by businesses, companies legally buy and sell information on customers to gain competitive advantage. It has been suggested that the treatment of personal data as property will ensure privacy rights by recognizing that customers have a right to control the use of their personal data.

Whether you like it or not, in 2009 Google, like Yahoo! and AOL, began tracking people's Web browsing patterns. By tracking the sites you visit, the companies' advertisers can aim ads targeted closer to your interests.

Internet use is different from traditional interaction with businesses in that it is readily accessible, and most online businesses are able to develop databases of information on customers. Congress has restricted the development of databases on children using the Internet. The Children's Online Privacy Protection Act of 2000 prohibits Web sites and Internet providers from seeking personal information from children under age 13 without parental consent.

The Internet has also created a copyright dilemma for some organizations that have found that the Web addresses of other online firms either match or are very similar to their company trademark. "Cybersquatters" attempt to sell back the registration of these matching sites to the trademark owner. Companies such as Taco Bell, MTC, and KFC have paid thousands of dollars to gain control of domain names that match or parallel company trademarks. The Federal Trademark Dilution Act of 1995 helps companies address this conflict. The act provides

LEGAL PRESSURE FOR RESPONSIBLE BUSINESS CONDUCT

To ensure greater compliance with society's desires, both federal and state governments are moving toward increased organizational accountability for misconduct. Before 1991, laws mainly punished those employees directly responsible for an offense. Under new guidelines established by the Federal Sentencing Guidelines for Organizations (FSGO), however, both the responsible employees and the firms that employ them are held accountable for violations of federal law. Thus, the government now places responsibility for controlling and preventing misconduct squarely on the shoulders of top management. The main objectives of the federal guidelines are to train employees, self-monitor and supervise employee conduct, deter unethical acts, and punish those organizational members who engage in illegal acts.

"To ensure greater compliance with society's desires, both federal and state governments are moving toward increased organizational accountability for misconduct."

trademark owners the right to protect trademarks, prevents the use of trademark-protected entities, and requires the relinquishment of names that match or closely parallel company trademarks. The reduction of geographic barriers, speed of response, and memory capability of the Internet will continue to create new challenges for the legal and regulatory environment in the future.

A 2004 amendment to the FSGO requires that a business's governing authority be well informed about its ethics program with respect to content, implementation, and effectiveness. This places the responsibility squarely on the shoulders of the firm's leadership, usually the board of directors. The board must ensure that there is a high-ranking manager accountable for the day-to-day operational oversight of the ethics program. The board must provide for adequate authority, resources, and

TABLE A.5 Seven Steps to Compliance

1. Develop standards and procedures to reduce the propensity for criminal conduct.
2. Designate a high-level compliance manager or ethics officer to oversee the compliance program.
3. Avoid delegating authority to people known to have a propensity to engage in misconduct.
4. Communicate standards and procedures to employees, other agents, and independent contractors through training programs and publications.
5. Establish systems to monitor and audit misconduct and to allow employees and agents to report criminal activity.
6. Enforce standards and punishments consistently across all employees in the organization.
7. Respond immediately to misconduct and take reasonable steps to prevent further criminal conduct.

Source: United States Sentencing Commission, *Federal Sentencing Guidelines for Organizations,* 1991.

access to the board or an appropriate subcommittee of the board. The board must ensure that there are confidential mechanisms available so that the organization's employees and agents may report or seek guidance about potential or actual misconduct without fear of retaliation. Finally, the board is required to oversee the discovery of risks and to design, implement, and modify approaches to deal with those risks.

If an organization's culture and policies reward or provide opportunities to engage in misconduct through lack of managerial concern or failure to comply with the seven minimum requirements of the FSGO (provided in Table A.5), the organization may incur not only penalties but also the loss of customer trust, public confidence, and other intangible assets. For this reason, organizations cannot succeed solely through a legalistic approach to compliance with the sentencing guidelines; top management must cultivate high ethical standards that will serve as barriers to illegal conduct. The organization must want to be a good citizen and recognize the importance of compliance to successful workplace activities and relationships.

The federal guidelines also require businesses to develop programs that can detect—and that will deter employees from engaging in— misconduct. To be considered effective, such compliance programs must include disclosure of any wrongdoing, cooperation with the government, and acceptance of responsibility for the misconduct. Codes of ethics, employee ethics training, hotlines (direct 800 phone numbers), compliance directors, newsletters, brochures, and other communication methods are typical components of a compliance program. The ethics component, discussed in Chapter 2, acts as a buffer, keeping firms away from the thin line that separates unethical and illegal conduct.

 Sarbanes-Oxley Act . . . criminalized securities fraud and strengthened penalties for corporate fraud.

Despite the existing legislation, a number of ethics scandals in the early 2000s led Congress to pass—almost unanimously—the **Sarbanes-Oxley Act,** which criminalized securities fraud and strengthened penalties for corporate fraud. It also created an accounting oversight board that requires corporations to establish codes of ethics for financial reporting and to develop greater transparency in financial reports to investors and other interested parties. Additionally, the law requires top corporate executives to sign off on their firms' financial reports, and they risk fines and jail sentences if they misrepresent their companies' financial position. Table A.6 summarizes the major provisions of the Sarbanes-Oxley Act.

The Sarbanes-Oxley Act has created a number of concerns and is considered burdensome and expensive to corporations. Large corporations report spending more than $4 million each year to comply with the Act according to Financial Executives International. The Act has caused more than 500 public companies a year to report problems in their accounting systems. More than 1,000 businesspersons have been convicted of corporate crimes since the law was passed in 2002. This means that the overwhelming majority of businesses are in compliance with the law.

On the other hand, there are many benefits, including greater accountability of top managers and boards of directors, that improve investor confidence and protect employees, especially their retirement plans. It is believed that the law has more benefits than drawbacks—with the greatest benefit being that boards of directors and top managers are better informed. Some companies, such as Cisco and Pitney Bowes, report improved efficiency and cost savings from better financial information. ■

TABLE A.6   Major Provisions of the Sarbanes-Oxley Act

1. Requires the establishment of a Public Company Accounting Oversight Board in charge of regulations administered by the Securities and Exchange Commission.

2. Requires CEOs and CFOs to certify that their companies' financial statements are true and without misleading statements.

3. Requires that corporate boards of directors' audit committees consist of independent members who have no material interests in the company.

4. Prohibits corporations from making or offering loans to officers and board members.

5. Requires codes of ethics for senior financial officers; code must be registered with the SEC.

6. Prohibits accounting firms from providing both auditing and consulting services to the same client without the approval of the client firm's audit committee.

7. Requires company attorneys to report wrongdoing to top managers and, if necessary, to the board of directors; if managers and directors fail to respond to reports of wrongdoing, the attorney should stop representing the company.

8. Mandates "whistleblower protection" for persons who disclose wrongdoing to authorities.

9. Requires financial securities analysts to certify that their recommendations are based on objective reports.

10. Requires mutual fund managers to disclose how they vote shareholder proxies, giving investors information about how their shares influence decisions.

11. Establishes a 10-year penalty for mail/wire fraud.

12. Prohibits the two senior auditors from working on a corporation's account for more than five years; other auditors are prohibited from working on an account for more than seven years. In other words, accounting firms must rotate individual auditors from one account to another from time to time.

Source: O. C. Ferrell, John Fraedrich, and Linda Ferrell, *Business Ethics: Ethical Decision Making and Cases,* 6th ed. (Boston: Houghton Mifflin, 2005), p. 63.

business *in a* borderless world

introduction Consumers around the world can drink Coca-Cola and Pepsi; eat at McDonald's and Pizza Hut; see movies from Mexico, England, France, Australia, and China; and watch CNN and MTV on Toshiba and Sony televisions. The products you consume today are just as likely to have been made in China, Korea, or Germany as in the United States. Likewise, consumers in other countries buy Western electrical equipment, clothing, rock music, cosmetics, and toiletries, as well as computers, robots, and earth-moving equipment.

Many U.S. firms are finding that international markets provide tremendous opportunities for growth. Accessing these markets can promote innovation, while intensifying global competition spurs companies to market better and less expensive products. Today, the 6.7 billion people that inhabit the earth create one tremendous marketplace.

chapter three

● ● learning **OBJECTIVES**

LO1 Explore some of the factors within the international trade environment that influence business.

LO2 Investigate some of the economic, legal-political, social, cultural, and technological barriers to international business.

LO3 Specify some of the agreements, alliances, and organizations that may encourage trade across international boundaries.

LO4 Summarize the different levels of organizational involvement in international trade.

LO5 Contrast two basic strategies used in international business.

In this chapter, we explore business in this exciting global marketplace. First, we'll look at the nature of international business, including barriers to and promoters of trade across international boundaries. Next, we consider the levels of organizational involvement in international business. Finally, we briefly discuss strategies for trading across national borders.

LO1

Explore some of the factors within the international trade environment that influence business.

THE ROLE OF INTERNATIONAL BUSINESS

International business refers to the buying, selling, and trading of goods and services across national boundaries. Falling political barriers and new technology are making it possible for more and more companies to sell their products overseas as well as at home. And as differences among nations continue to narrow, the trend toward the globalization of business is becoming increasingly important. Starbucks, for example, serves 20 million customers a week at more than 15,750 coffee shops in 44 countries.[2] Amazon .com, an online retailer, has distribution centers

DID YOU KNOW?

McDonald's serves 50 million customers a day at 31,000 restaurants in 118 countries.[1]

Tide, Crest, and Oil of Olay, and it regularly relies on groups that live in the countryside for consumer information.[3] Indeed, most of the world's population and two-thirds of its total purchasing power are outside the United States.

When McDonald's sells a Big Mac in Moscow, Sony sells a stereo in Detroit, or a small Swiss medical supply company sells a shipment of orthopedic devices to a hospital in Monterrey, Mexico, the sale affects the economies of the countries involved. To begin our study of international business, we must first consider some economic issues: why nations trade, exporting and importing, and the balance of trade.

Why Nations Trade

Nations and businesses engage in international trade to obtain raw materials and goods that are otherwise unavailable to them or are available elsewhere at a lower price than that at which they themselves can produce. A nation, or individuals and organizations from a nation, sells surplus materials and goods to acquire funds to buy the goods, services, and ideas its people need. Poland and Hungary, for example, want to trade with Western nations so that they can acquire new technology and techniques to revitalize their formerly communist economies. Which goods and services a nation sells depends on what resources it has available.

Some nations have a monopoly on the production of a particular resource or product. Such a monopoly, or **absolute advantage,** exists when a country is the only source of an item, the only producer of an item, or the most efficient producer of an item. Because South Africa has the largest deposits of diamonds in the world, one company, De Beers Consolidated Mines, Ltd., controls a major portion of the

> ❝ **Falling political barriers and new technology are making it possible for more and more companies to sell their products overseas as well as at home.** ❞

from Nevada to Germany that fill millions of orders a day and ship them to customers in every corner of the world. In China, Procter & Gamble has developed bargain-priced versions of

world's diamond trade and uses its control to maintain high prices for gem-quality diamonds. The United States, until recently, held an absolute advantage in oil-drilling equipment.

*Laws and regulations in other countries can trip up companies
that are trying to expand internationally. Some companies,
such as the insurer Zurich, have set up programs to take the
headaches out of going global.*

Until recently, the United States had a comparative advantage in manufacturing automobiles, heavy machinery, airplanes, and weapons; other countries now hold the comparative advantage for many of these products. Other countries, particularly India and Ireland, are also gaining a comparative advantage over the United States in the provision of some services, such as call-center operations, engineering, and software programming. As a result, U.S. companies are increasingly **outsourcing**, or transferring manufacturing and other tasks to countries where labor and supplies are less expensive. Outsourcing has become a controversial practice in the United States because many jobs have moved overseas, where those tasks can be accomplished for lower costs. For example, India is a popular choice for call centers for U.S. firms. As call centers are the first job choice for millions of young Indians, employers are getting choosier about the people they hire, and it is difficult to train Indians to speak the kind of colloquial English, French, Spanish, German, or Dutch that customers want, although there are estimates that more than 160,000 workers with excellent English and foreign-language skills are needed. Many foreigners are beginning to see India and the call-center jobs as a way to travel the world. They typically earn about $350 a month and work the phones for six months or a year before chilling on the beaches of Goa or trekking the Himalayas. There are more than 30,000 foreigners working at Indian info tech and outsourcing companies, which is triple the number of two years ago.[4]

Trade between Countries

To obtain needed goods and services and the funds to pay for them, nations trade by exporting and importing. **Exporting** is

> "Outsourcing has become a controversial practice in the United States because many jobs have moved overseas, where tasks can be accomplished for lower costs."

But an absolute advantage not based on the availability of natural resources rarely lasts, and Japan and Russia are now challenging the United States in the production of oil-drilling equipment.

Most international trade is based on **comparative advantage,** which occurs when a country specializes in products that it can supply more efficiently or at a lower cost than it can produce other items. The United States has a comparative advantage in producing agricultural commodities such as corn and wheat.

the sale of goods and services to foreign markets. The United States exported more than *$1.8 trillion in goods and services* in 2008.[5] In China, General Motors is targeting wealthier customers with the Cadillac, middle management with the Buick Excelle, office workers with the Chevrolet Spark, and rural consumers with the Wuling minivan.[6] U.S. businesses export many goods and services, particularly agricultural, entertainment (movies, television shows, etc.), and technological products. **Importing** is the purchase of goods and services from foreign sources. Many of the goods you buy in the United States are likely to be imports or to have some imported components. Sometimes, you may not even realize they are imports. The United States imported more than *$2.5 trillion* in goods and services in 2008.[7]

Balance of Trade

You have probably read or heard about the fact that the United States has a trade deficit, but what is a trade deficit? A nation's **balance of trade** is the difference in value between its exports and imports. Because the United States (and some other nations as well) imports more products than it exports, it has a negative balance of trade, or **trade deficit.** In 2008, the United States had a $677 billion trade deficit. Total U.S. imports reached over $2.5 trillion, while exports totalled only $1.84 trillion (see Table 3.1).[8] The trade deficit fluctuates accord-

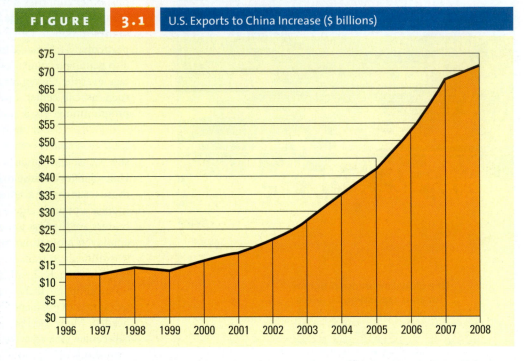

FIGURE 3.1 U.S. Exports to China Increase ($ billions)

Source: David J. Lynch, "Building Explosion in China Pumps Up Exports from USA," *USA Today*, April 20, 2006. P. B1.s; "U.S. Domestic Exports for Selected World Areas and the Top Fifteen Countries—2008," U.S. Census Bureau, Foreign Trade Statistics, www.census.gov/foreign-trade/statistics/highlights/top/top0812yr.html (accessed March 10, 2009).

ing to such factors as the health of the United States and other economies, productivity, perceived quality, and exchange rates. As Figure 3.1 indicates, U.S. exports to China have been rapidly increasing but not fast enough to offset the imports from China. Trade deficits are harmful because they can mean the failure of businesses, the loss of jobs, and a lowered standard of living.

Of course, when a nation exports more goods than it imports, it has a favorable balance of trade, or trade surplus. Until about 1970, the United States had a trade surplus due to an abundance of natural resources and the relative efficiency of its manufacturing systems. Table 3.2 shows the top 10 countries with which the United States has a trade deficit and a trade surplus.

The difference between the flow of money into and out of a country is called its **balance of payments.** A country's balance of trade, foreign investments, foreign aid, loans, military expenditures, and money spent by tourists constitute its balance of payments. As you might expect, a country with a trade surplus generally has a favorable balance of payments because it is receiving more money from trade with foreign countries than it is paying out. When a country has a trade deficit, more money flows out of the country than into it. If more money flows out of the country than into it from tourism and other sources, the country may experience declining production and higher unemployment, because there is less money available for spending.

TABLE 3.1 U.S. Trade Deficit, 1980–2008 (in billions of dollars)

	1980	1990	2000	2006	2008
Exports	$333	$576	$1,133	$1,437.8	$1,843
Imports	326	632	1,532	2,201.4	2,520.1
Trade Surplus/ Deficit	7	−57	−399	−763.6	−677.1

Sources: Department of Commerce and Rober E. Scoot, "International Picture," The Economic Policy Institute, February 10, 2008, www.epi.org/publications/entry/indicators_intlpict_20080215/ (accessed March 10, 2009); "2008 Annual Trade Highlights, Dollar Change from Prior Year," U.S. Census Bureau, Foreign Trade Statistics (n.d.), www.census.gov/foreign-trade/statistics/highlights/annual.html (accessed March 10, 2009).

 LO2

Investigate some of the economic, legal-political, social, cultural, and technological barriers to international business.

TABLE 3.2 Top 10 Countries Maintaining Trade Deficits/Surpluses with the United States

Trade Deficit	Trade Surplus
1. China	Netherlands
2. Japan	United Arab Emirates
3. Mexico	Hong Kong
4. Federal Republic of Germany	Belgium
5. Canada	Singapore
6. Ireland	Australia
7. Italy	Brazil
8. South Korea	Qatar
9. Saudi Arabia	Turkey
10. Taiwan	Egypt

Sources: "Top Ten Countries with Which the U.S. has a Trade Deficit," www.census.gov/foreign-trade/top/dst/current/deficit.html (accessed March 10, 2009); "Top Ten Countries with Which the U.S. Has a Trade Surplus," www.census.gov/foreign-trade/top/dst/current/surplus.html (accessed March 10, 2009).

the same things that are found in *industrialized nations*—economically advanced countries such as the United States, Japan, Great Britain, and Canada. Many countries in Africa, Asia, and South America, for example, are in general poorer and less economically advanced than those in North America and Europe; they are often called *less-developed countries* (LDCs). LDCs are characterized by low per-capita income (income generated by the nation's production of goods and services divided by the population), which means that consumers are less likely to purchase nonessential products. Nonetheless, LDCs represent a potentially huge and profitable market for many businesses because they may be buying technology to improve their infrastructures, and much of the population may desire consumer products. For example, cellular and wireless phone technology is reaching many countries at less expense than traditional hard-wired telephone systems. Consequently, opportunities for growth in the cell phone market remain strong in Southeast Asia, Africa, and the Middle East. Haier, China's top appliance maker, makes larger washing machines for Chinese cities, but has also developed a smaller model costing just $37 for poorer areas.[9]

"Devaluation decreases the value of currency in relation to other currencies."

INTERNATIONAL TRADE BARRIERS

Completely free trade seldom exists. When a company decides to do business outside its own country, it will encounter a number of barriers to international trade. Any firm considering international business must research the other country's economic, legal, political, social, cultural, and technological background. Such research will help the company choose an appropriate level of involvement and operating strategies, as we will see later in this chapter.

Economic Barriers

When looking at doing business in another country, managers must consider a number of basic economic factors, such as economic development, infrastructure, and exchange rates.

economic development When considering doing business abroad, U.S. businesspeople need to recognize that they cannot take for granted that other countries offer

The infrastructure of countries—their transportation, communication, and other systems—differs around the world. AT&T took the opportunity to make inroads with consumers who don't want their cell phones to stop working when they go abroad.

A country's level of development is determined in part by its **infrastructure,** the physical facilities that support its economic activities, such as railroads, highways, ports, airfields, utilities and power plants, schools, hospitals, communication systems, and commercial distribution systems. When doing business in LDCs, for example, a business may need to compensate for rudimentary distribution and communication systems, or even a lack of technology.

exchange rates The ratio at which one nation's currency can be exchanged for another nation's currency is the **exchange rate.** Exchange rates vary daily and can be found in newspapers and on many sites on the Internet. Familiarity with exchange rates is important because they affect the cost of imports and exports.

Occasionally, a government may alter the value of its national currency. Devaluation decreases the value of currency in relation to other currencies. If the U.S. government were to devalue the dollar, it would lower the cost of American goods abroad and make trips to the United States less expensive for foreign tourists. Thus, devaluation encourages the sale of domestic goods and tourism. Mexico has repeatedly devalued the peso for this reason. Revaluation, which increases the value of a currency in relation to other currencies, occurs rarely.

Legal and Political Barriers

A company that decides to enter the international marketplace must contend with potentially complex relationships among the different laws of its own nation, international laws, and the laws of the nation with which it will be trading; various trade restrictions imposed on international trade; and changing political climates. Many companies provide assistance in this area. MyCustoms.com helps companies comply with local trade rules, and NextLinx Corp. provides business advice about international commerce laws.[10]

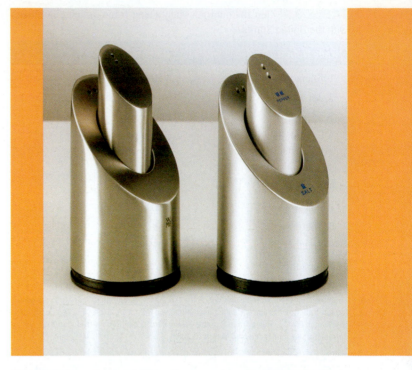

Plagiarus Awards are dubious honors given to companies that steal product designs. The goal is to shame the makers of those products. The salt and pepper shakers on the right won a Plagiarus Award. They are a Chinese knockoff of the salt and pepper shakers on the right, made by a German company.

Japanese and Americans Swap Food

The Japanese are known for their longevity and slender physiques, a result of their healthy diets. However, things have begun to change as the Japanese, particularly the younger generations, have become interested in all things American—including American foods. Creeping into the Japanese diet is a taste for sweets, and who better to capitalize on this than American fast-food chains?

Among the American fast-food chains booming in Japan are Krispy Kreme and McDonald's. Krispy Kreme opened its doors in Japan in December 2006. In the first three days, over 10,000 people flocked to one location. Some wait in lines for over two hours for a doughnut. Why is Krispy Kreme doing so well? According to researcher Hikaru Hakuhodo, the Japanese are interested in what is considered new and cool, and American products fit the bill. However, things do not stay cool forever. Doughnut Planet and Dunkin' Donuts had their day in Japan and are long gone. Will Krispy Kreme be able to hang on?

And how will the Japanese fare by continuing to indulge like Americans? In the past two decades, Japanese obesity has grown by over 10 percent and illnesses such as diabetes have increased by almost 50 percent. Japanese women are now an average of 26.5 pounds heavier than Japanese women of the 1950s. Meanwhile, Americans have embraced Japanese-style food in an effort to become healthier. So which culture is cooler, Japan or the United States? Will Krispy Kreme and the like survive, or will the Japanese realize that they have been the cool ones all along?[11] ❖

 Discussion Questions

1. What is going to happen to Japanese consumers if they start consuming much more American fast food?

2. Why is Krispy Kreme doing so well in Japan?

3. What is the possibility that the Japanese will recognize that their increasingly Western diet is not as healthy as their previous diet?

laws and regulations The United States has a number of laws and regulations that govern the activities of U.S. firms engaged in international trade. For example, the Webb-Pomerene Export Trade Act of 1918 exempts American firms from antitrust laws if those firms are acting together to enter international trade. This law allows selected U.S. firms to form monopolies to compete with foreign monopolistic organizations, although they are not allowed to limit free trade and competition within the United States or to use unfair methods of competition in international trade. The United States also has a variety of friendship, commerce, and navigation treaties with other nations. These treaties allow business to be transacted between citizens of the specified countries.

Once outside U.S. borders, businesspeople are likely to find that the laws of other nations differ from those of the United States. Many of the legal rights that Americans take for granted do not exist in other countries, and a firm doing business abroad must understand and obey the laws of the host country. Many countries forbid foreigners from owning real property outright; others have strict laws limiting the amount of local currency that can be taken out of the country and the amount of foreign currency that can be brought in.

Some countries have copyright and patent laws that are less strict than those of the United States, and some countries fail to honor U.S. laws. Because copying is a tradition in China and Vietnam and laws protecting copyrights and intellectual property are weak and minimally enforced, those countries are flooded with counterfeit videos, movies, CDs, computer software, furniture, and clothing. Companies are angry because the counterfeits harm not only their sales, but also their reputations if the knockoffs are of poor quality. Such counterfeiting is not limited to China or Vietnam. In recent years 35 percent of the packaged software installed on personal computers worldwide has been illegal, amounting to $40 billion in global losses due to software piracy. However, some improvements in a number of markets indicate education, enforcement, and policy efforts are beginning to pay off in emerging economies such as China, Russia, and India and in Central/Eastern Europe and in the Middle East and Africa.[12] In countries where these activities occur, laws against them may not be sufficiently enforced, if counterfeiting is in fact deemed illegal. Thus, businesses engaging in foreign trade may have to take extra steps to protect their products because local laws may be insufficient to do so.

tariffs and trade restrictions Tariffs and other trade restrictions are part of a country's legal structure but may be established or removed for political reasons. An **import tariff** is a tax levied by a nation on goods imported into the country. A *fixed tariff* is a specific amount of money levied on each unit of a product brought into the country, while an *ad valorem tariff* is based on the value of the item. Most countries allow citizens traveling abroad to bring home a certain amount of merchandise without paying an import tariff. A U.S. citizen may bring $200 worth of merchandise into the United States

duty free. After that, U.S. citizens must pay an ad valorem tariff based on the cost of the item and the country of origin. Thus, identical items purchased in different countries might have different tariffs.

Countries sometimes levy tariffs for political reasons, as when they impose sanctions against other countries to protest their actions. However, import tariffs are more commonly imposed to protect domestic products by raising the price of imported ones. Such protective tariffs have become controversial, as Americans become increasingly concerned over the U.S. trade deficit. Protective tariffs allow more expensive domestic goods to compete with foreign ones. In early 2008, food shortages required that countries in the developing world cut import taxes and restrict exports to keep more affordable food in country. Saudi Arabia, for example, cut wheat tariffs from 25 percent to zero and reduced tariffs on poultry, dairy and vegetable oils to forestall rising food prices.[13]

Critics of protective tariffs argue that their use inhibits free trade and competition. Supporters of protective tariffs say they insulate domestic industries, particularly new ones, against well-established foreign competitors. Once an industry matures, however, its advocates may be reluctant to let go of the tariff that protected it. Tariffs also help when, because of low labor costs and other advantages, foreign competitors can afford to sell their products at prices lower than those charged by domestic companies. Some Americans argue that tariffs should be used to keep domestic wages high and unemployment low.

Exchange controls restrict the amount of currency that can be bought or sold. Some countries control their foreign trade by forcing businesspeople to buy and sell foreign products through a central bank. If John Deere, for example, receives payments for its tractors in a foreign currency, it may be required to sell the currency to that nation's central bank. When foreign currency is in short supply, as it is in many Third World and Eastern European countries, the government uses foreign currency to purchase necessities and capital goods and produces other products locally, thus limiting its need for foreign imports.

A **quota** limits the number of units of a particular product that can be imported into a country. A quota may be established by voluntary agreement or by government decree. After U.S. yarn suppliers complained that cotton yarn (used in underwear, socks, and T-shirts) from Pakistan was flooding the market, a quota was imposed. Pakistan complained, and a textile-monitoring panel recommended that the United States lift the restrictions. The United States refused. However, in 2001, the quota was ruled a violation of global trade rules, and the United States was ordered to remove it.[14]

● **IMPORT TARIFF** a tax levied by a nation on goods imported into the country

● **EXCHANGE CONTROLS** regulations that restrict the amount of currency that can be bought or sold

● **QUOTA** a restriction on the number of units of a particular product that can be imported into a country

An **embargo** prohibits trade in a particular product. Embargoes are generally directed at specific goods or countries and may be established for political, economic, health, or religious reasons. The United States forbids the importation of cigars from Cuba for political reasons. Health embargoes prevent the importing of various pharmaceuticals, animals, plants, and agricultural products. Muslim nations forbid the importation of alcoholic beverages on religious grounds.

One common reason for setting quotas or tariffs is to prohibit **dumping,** which occurs when a country or business sells products at less than what it costs to produce them. The United States, for example, levied extra import duties against some types of Canadian lumber after the U.S. International Trade Commission found evidence that lower prices on the partially subsidized Canadian lumber threatened to harm the domestic lumber industry. However, some of the antidumping tariffs were later found to be in violation of global trade rules, and the United States was ordered to rescind them.[15] A company may dump its products for several reasons. Dumping permits quick entry into a market. Sometimes dumping occurs when the domestic market for a firm's product is too small to support an efficient level of production. In other cases, technologically obsolete products that are no longer salable in the country of origin are dumped overseas. Dumping is relatively difficult to prove, but even the suspicion of dumping can lead to the imposition of quotas or tariffs.

political barriers Unlike legal issues, political considerations are seldom written down and often change rapidly. Nations that have been subject to economic sanctions for political reasons in recent years include Cuba, Iran, Syria, and North Korea. While these were dramatic events, political considerations affect international business daily as governments enact tariffs, embargoes, or other types of trade restrictions in response to political events.

Businesses engaged in international trade must consider the relative instability of countries such as Colombia, Haiti, and Honduras. Political unrest in countries such as Peru, Somalia, and Russia may create a hostile or even dangerous environment for foreign businesses. Civil war, as in Chechnya and Bosnia, may disrupt business activities and place lives in danger. And, a sudden change in power can result in a regime that is hostile to foreign investment. Some businesses have been forced out of a country altogether, as they were when Fidel Castro closed Cuba to American business. The current administration seems more positive about loosening trade and travel restrictions with Cuba. Whether they like it or not, companies are often involved directly or indirectly in international politics.

Political concerns may lead a group of nations to form a **cartel,** a group of firms or nations that agrees to act as a monopoly and not compete with each other, to generate a competitive advantage in world markets. Probably the most famous cartel is OPEC, the Organization of Petroleum Exporting Countries, founded in the 1960s to increase the price of petroleum throughout the world and to maintain high prices. By working to ensure stable oil prices, OPEC hopes to enhance the economies of its member nations.

Social and Cultural Barriers

Most businesspeople engaged in international trade underestimate the importance of social and cultural differences; but these differences can derail an important transaction. For example, when Big Boy opened a restaurant in Bangkok, it quickly became popular with European and American tourists, but the local Thais refused to eat there. Instead, they placed gifts of rice and incense at the feet of the Big Boy statue (a chubby boy holding a hamburger) because it reminded them of Buddha. In Japan, customers were forced to tiptoe around a logo painted on the floor at the entrance to an Athlete's Foot store because in Japan, it is considered taboo to step on a crest.[16] And in Russia, consumers found the American-style energetic happiness of McDonald's employees insincere and offensive when the company opened its first stores there.[17] Unfortunately, cultural norms are rarely written down, and what is written down may well be inaccurate.

Sometimes companies face a political backlash not of their own making. In 2008, Chinese citizens boycotted Carrefour, a major French retailer. The boycott was in response to France's efforts to use the 2008 Beijing Olympics to pressure China to improve its human rights record in Tibet.

TABLE 3.3 Cultural Behavioral Differences

Region	Gestures Viewed as Rude or Unacceptable
Japan, Hong Kong, Middle East	Summoning with the index finger
Middle and Far East	Pointing with index finger
Thailand, Japan, France	Sitting with soles of shoes showing
Brazil, Germany	Forming a circle with fingers (e.g., the "O.K." sign in the United States)
Japan	Winking means "I love you"
Buddhist countries	Patting someone on the head

Source: Adapted from Judie Haynes, "Communicating with Gestures," *EverythingESL* (n.d.), www.everythingesl.net/inservices/body_language.php (accessed April 28, 2009).

Cultural differences include differences in spoken and written language. Although it is certainly possible to translate words from one language to another, the true meaning is sometimes misinterpreted or lost. Consider some translations that went awry in foreign markets:

- A Scandinavian vacuum manufacturer Electrolux used the following in an American campaign: "Nothing sucks like an Electrolux."

- The Coca-Cola name in China was first read as "Ke-kou-ke-la," meaning "bite the wax tadpole."

- In Italy, a campaign for Schweppes Tonic Water translated the name into Schweppes Toilet Water.[18]

Translators cannot just translate slogans, advertising campaigns, and Web site language; they must know the cultural differences that could affect a company's success.

Differences in body language and personal space also affect international trade. Body language is nonverbal, usually unconscious communication through gestures, posture, and facial expression. Personal space is the distance at which one person feels comfortable talking to another. Americans tend to stand a moderate distance away from the person with whom they are speaking. Arab businessmen tend to stand face-to-face with the object of their conversation. Additionally, gestures vary from culture to culture, and gestures considered acceptable in American society—pointing, for example—may be considered rude in others. Table 3.3 shows some of the behaviors considered rude or unacceptable in other countries. Such cultural differences may generate uncomfortable feelings or misunderstandings when business people of different countries negotiate with each other.

Family roles also influence marketing activities. Many countries do not allow children to be used in advertising, for example. Advertising that features people in nontraditional social roles may or may not be successful. The California Milk Processor Board aired a commercial in which a father and his young daughter shop at a supermarket for sugar, flour, cinnamon, and milk for a cake to be baked when they get home. The ad does not seem unusual except that when it was aired on Spanish-language television, the concept was striking. It is rare for Latino men to appear along with their daughters in Spanish-language ads and even rarer for the commercials to be set outside the home. The Hispanic culture typically reinforces how little boys need their fathers, not how little girls do.[19]

Plumpy'nut Fights Malnutrition in the Developing World

Michel Lescanne, a Frenchman who did aid work in Africa, founded Nutriset in 1986 to combat hunger and malnutrition. Currently, close to 1 billion people live hungry in the world. Malnutrition kills more people annually than do AIDS, malaria, and tuberculosis combined. Most malnourished people live in developing regions such as India and sub-Saharan Africa. In 1998, Nutriset invented the "Plumpy'nut" packet. One three-ounce packet delivers 500 calories, and severely malnourished children can thrive on three or four packets daily. Plumpy'nut's thick brown paste is made from ground peanuts, sugar, and powdered milk and fortified with vitamins. It does not require clean water for dilution and can be eaten easily by a small child without assistance. Plumpy'nut is not perishable and does not require refrigeration, and its small size and low weight make transportation simple.

A dose of Plumpy'nut costs about $1. Nutriset partners with entrepreneurs to produce it locally, using local ingredients when possible. Doctors Without Borders helps distribute the product, usually giving a week's supply to mothers who treat their children at home. Each week the children are weighed to track success, which has been immense, but Plumpy'nut can help only when children begin early in life, before developmental disorders set in. According to Dr. Tectonidis of Doctors Without Borders, if the United States and the European Union would spend food aid funds on Plumpy'nut, production would increase; minimal spending would have a huge impact.

Nutriset reinvests 80 percent of its profit into developing new products. The company partners with small producers in Ethiopia, the Caribbean, Latin America, Malawi, Niger, Republic of Congo, and Uganda to produce Plumpy'nut locally. Nutriset has combined entrepreneurship, social responsibility, and the opportunity to help millions of children thrive.[20] ❖

Q: Discussion Questions

1. Why is Plumpy'nut considered a socially responsible food product for Africa?

2. How can this company contribute to environmental causes?

3. Can you think of other uses for Plumpy'nut to help feed hungry people around the world?

The people of other nations quite often have a different perception of time as well. Americans value promptness; a business meeting scheduled for a specific time seldom starts more than a few minutes late. In Mexico and Spain, however, it is not unusual for a meeting to be delayed half an hour or more. Such a late start might produce resentment in an American negotiating in Spain for the first time.

Companies engaged in foreign trade must observe the national and religious holidays and local customs of the host country. In many Islamic countries, for example, workers expect to take a break at certain times of the day to observe religious rites. Companies also must monitor their advertising to guard against offending customers. In Thailand and many other countries, public displays of affection between the sexes are unacceptable in advertising messages; in many Middle Eastern nations, it is unacceptable to show the soles of one's feet. In the Muslim world, exposure of a woman's skin, even her arms, is considered offensive.[21]

With the exception of the United States, most nations use the metric system. This lack of uniformity creates problems for both buyers and sellers in the international marketplace. American sellers, for instance, must package goods destined for foreign markets in liters or meters, and Japanese sellers must convert to the English system if they plan to sell a product in the United States. Tools also must be calibrated in the correct system if they are to function correctly. Hyundai and Honda service technicians need metric tools to make repairs on those cars.

The literature dealing with international business is filled with accounts of sometimes humorous but often costly mistakes that occurred because of a lack of understanding of the social and cultural differences between buyers and sellers. Such problems cannot always be avoided, but they can be minimized through research on the cultural and social differences of the host country.

Technological Barriers

Many countries lack the technological infrastructure found in the United States, and some marketers are viewing such barriers as opportunities. For instance, marketers are targeting many countries, such as India and China and some African countries, where there are few private phone lines. Citizens of these countries are turning instead to wireless communication through cell phones. Technological advances, such as the Internet, are creating additional global marketing opportunities. In some countries, broadband access to the Internet is spreading much faster than in the United States. In fact, 10 nations, including South Korea, Hong Kong, and Canada, outrank the United States in terms of subscribers to broadband Internet access. The growth of high-speed Internet access should facilitate online commerce.[22]

 L03

Specify some of the agreements, alliances, and organizations that may encourage trade across international boundaries.

TRADE AGREEMENTS, ALLIANCES, AND ORGANIZATIONS

Although these economic, political, legal, and sociocultural issues may seem like daunting barriers to international trade, there are also organizations and agreements—such as the General Agreement on Tariffs and Trade, the World Bank, and the International Monetary Fund—that foster international trade and can help companies get involved in and succeed in global markets. Various regional trade agreements, such as the North American Free Trade Agreement and the European Union, also promote trade among member nations by eliminating tariffs and trade restrictions. In this section, we'll look briefly at these agreements and organizations.

General Agreement on Tariffs and Trade (GATT)

During the Great Depression of the 1930s, nations established so many protective tariffs covering so many products that international trade became virtually impossible. By the end of World War II, there was considerable international momentum to liberalize trade and minimize the effects of tariffs. The **General Agreement on Tariffs and Trade (GATT),** originally signed by 23 nations in 1947, provided a forum for tariff negotiations and a place where international trade problems could be discussed and resolved. More than 100 nations abided by its rules. GATT sponsored rounds of negotiations aimed at reducing trade restrictions. The most recent round, the Uruguay Round (1988–1994), further reduced trade barriers for most products and provided new rules to prevent dumping.

The **World Trade Organization (WTO),** an international organization dealing with the rules of trade between nations, was created in 1995 by the Uruguay Round. Key to the World Trade Organization are the WTO agreements, which are the legal ground rules for international commerce. The agreements were negotiated and signed by most of the world's trading nations and ratified by their parliaments. The goal is to help producers of goods and services and exporters and importers conduct their business. In addition to administering the WTO trade agreements, the WTO presents a forum for trade negotiations, monitors national trade policies, provides technical assistance and training for developing countries, and cooperates with other international organizations. Based in Geneva, Switzerland, the WTO has also adopted a leadership role in negotiating trade disputes among nations.[23] For example, the WTO investigated complaints from the European Union and seven countries about a U.S. tariff on imported steel and ultimately ruled the U.S. duties illegal under international trade rules. The United States had imposed the tariffs to protect domestic steel producers from less expensive imported steel, but the WTO found that the United States had failed to prove that its steel industry had been harmed by dumping.[24] Facing the prospect of retaliatory sanctions against American goods, the United States dropped the tariffs 16 months early after the ruling.[25]

The North American Free Trade Agreement (NAFTA)

The **North American Free Trade Agreement** (**NAFTA**), which went into effect on January 1, 1994, effectively merged Canada, the United States, and Mexico into one market of over 445 million consumers.[26] By 2009, NAFTA had eliminated virtually all tariffs on goods produced and traded among the three member nations. The estimated annual output of this trade alliance is nearly $17 trillion U.S.[27] NAFTA makes it easier for U.S. businesses to invest in the other two North American countries; provides intellectual property protection (of special interest to the high-technology and entertainment industries); expands trade by requiring equal treatment of U.S. firms in both countries; and simplifies country-of-origin rules. Although most

Many U.S. companies have taken advantage of Mexico's comparatively low labor costs and proximity to the United States to set up production facilities, sometimes called *maquiladoras*. Aerospace companies, for example, have been attracted to Mexico's lower wages and government promotions. With wages around $3.50 per hour for skill laborers, Mexico's aerospace industry boomed with the loosening of trade barriers.[33] With the *maquiladoras* accounting for roughly half of Mexico's exports, Mexico rose to become the world's 12th largest economy.[34]

One of the hopes of NAFTA was that Mexico's membership would help link the United States and Canada to other Latin American countries as well, providing additional opportunities to integrate trade among all nations in the Western Hemisphere into a Free Trade Area of the Americas (FTAA) with nearly 1 billion consumers.[35] However, talks to implement the Free Trade Area of the Americas faltered and the idea was basically dead by 2005. However, other regional trading blocs have formed in Central America though the Central American Free Trade Americas (CAFTA) and among the major economies of South America with the Mercado Común del Sur (Mercosur).

Despite its benefits, NAFTA has been controversial and disputes have continued throughout its history. Archer Daniels Midland, for example, filed a claim against the Mexican government for losses resulting from a tax on soft drinks sweetened

● **NORTH AMERICAN FREE TRADE AGREEMENT (NAFTA)** agreement that eliminates most tariffs and trade restrictions on agricultural and manufactured products to encourage trade among Canada, the United States, and Mexico

"NAFTA makes it easier for U.S. businesses to invest in Mexico and Canada."

tariffs on products were lifted almost immediately, duties on more sensitive products such as household glassware, footwear, and some fruits and vegetables were phased out over a 15-year period.

Canada's 33.8 million consumers are relatively affluent, with a per capita GDP of just over $39,000.[28] Exports to Canada support over 1.5 million U.S. jobs. Canadian investments in the U.S. have increased in recent years, and various markets, like air travel, have opened up as regulatory barriers dissolved.[29] In fact, Canada remains the single largest trading partner of the United States.[30]

With a per-capita GDP of $14,200 Mexico's 111 million consumers are less affluent than Canada's.[31] However, they purchase $150 billion in U.S. products annually. In addition, there are 28.3 million Mexican Americans living in the United States, with an average household income of nearly $39,000.[32] Some of these individuals send remittances to relatives in Mexico, assisting in U.S.-Mexico development and trade.

with high-fructose corn syrup, which the company believed violated the provisions of NAFTA.[36] While many Americans feared the agreement would erase jobs in the United States, it has been the Mexicans who have been most disappointed that NAFTA has not created more jobs for them. Moreover, Mexico's increased standard of living has increased the cost of doing business there, driving some U.S. companies to outsource to Asia instead. Indeed, China is now the United States' second largest trading partner.[37]

Although NAFTA has been controversial, it has been largely a positive factor for U.S. firms wishing to engage in international marketing. Because licensing requirements have been relaxed under the pact, smaller businesses that previously could not afford to invest in Mexico and Canada have been able to do business in those markets without having to locate there. NAFTA's long phase-in period allowed ample time for businesses to adjust to reduced tariffs. Furthermore, increased competition has led to a more efficient North American market.

The European Union (EU)

The **European Union (EU),** also called the *European Community* or *Common Market,* was established in 1958 to promote trade among its members, which initially included Belgium, France, Italy, West Germany, Luxembourg, and the Netherlands. East and West Germany united in 1991, and by 1995 the United Kingdom, Spain, Denmark, Greece, Portugal, Ireland, Austria, Finland, and Sweden had joined as well. The Czech Republic, Estonia, Hungary, Latvia, Lithuania, Poland, Slovakia, and Slovenia joined in 2004. In 2007 Bulgaria and Romania also became members, and Cyprus and Malta joined in 2008, which brought total membership to 27. Croatia, the former Yugoslav Republic of Macedonia, and Turkey are candidate countries that hope to join the European Union soon.[38] Until 1993 each nation functioned as a separate market, but at that time the members officially unified into one of the largest single world markets, which today includes 395 million consumers.

To facilitate free trade among members, the EU is working toward standardization of business regulations and requirements, import duties, and value-added taxes; the elimination of

completely free trade remain. Consequently, it may take many years before the EU is truly one deregulated market.

The EU has enacted some of the world's strictest laws concerning antitrust issues, which have had unexpected consequences for some non-European firms. For example, after a five-year investigation, the union fined U.S.-based Microsoft a record 497 million euros ($750 million U.S.) for exploiting its "near-monopoly" in computer operating systems in Europe by including a free media player with Windows to the detriment of software offered by European makers. Microsoft denied the charges and appealed. Microsoft lost its appeal in the courts. In addition to the fine, the European Commission insisted that Microsoft release its programming codes to European rivals to allow them to make their competing products compatible with computers relying on Microsoft's Windows operating system.[40]

Asia-Pacific Economic Cooperation (APEC)

The **Asia-Pacific Economic Cooperation (APEC),** established in 1989, promotes open trade and economic and technical cooperation among member nations, which initially included Australia, Brunei Darussalam, Canada, Indonesia, Japan, Korea, Malaysia, New Zealand, the Philippines, Singapore, Thailand, and the United States. Since then the alliance has grown to include China, Hong Kong, Chinese Taipei, Mexico, Papua New Guinea, Chile, Peru, Russia, and Vietnam. The

> ## "The IMF is the closest thing the world has to an international central bank."

customs checks; and the creation of a standardized currency for use by all members. Many European nations (Austria, Belgium, Finland, France, Germany, Ireland, Italy, Luxembourg, the Netherlands, Portugal, and Spain) link their exchange rates together to a common currency, the *euro;* however, several EU members have rejected use of the euro in their countries. Although the common currency requires many marketers to modify their pricing strategies and will subject them to increased competition, the use of a single currency frees companies that sell goods among European countries from the nuisance of dealing with complex exchange rates.[39] The long-term goals are to eliminate all trade barriers within the EU, improve the economic efficiency of the EU nations, and stimulate economic growth, thus making the union's economy more competitive in global markets, particularly against Japan and other Pacific Rim nations, and North America. However, several disputes and debates still divide the member nations, and many barriers to

21-member alliance represents approximately 41 percent of the world's population, 49 percent of world trade, and 55 percent of world GDP. APEC differs from other international trade alliances in its commitment to facilitating business and its practice of allowing the business/private sector to participate in a wide range of APEC activities.[41]

Despite economic turmoil and a recession in Asia in recent years, companies of the APEC have become increasingly competitive and sophisticated in global business in the last three decades. The Japanese and South Koreans in particular have made tremendous inroads into world markets for automobiles, motorcycles, watches, cameras, and audio and video equipment. Products from Samsung, Sony, Sanyo, Toyota, Daewoo, Mitsubishi, Suzuki, and Toshiba are sold all over the world and have set standards of quality by which other products are often judged. The People's Republic of China, a country of more than 1.3 billion people (approximately one-fifth of the world's population), has launched a program of economic reform to stimulate its economy by privatizing many industries, restructuring its banking system, and increasing public spending on infrastructure (including railways and telecommunications).[42] As a result, China has become a manufacturing powerhouse with an economy growing at a rate of more than 10 percent a year.[43] Less visible and sometimes less stable Pacific Rim regions, such as Thailand, Singapore, Taiwan, Vietnam, and Hong Kong, have also become major manufacturing and financial centers.

World Bank

The **World Bank,** more formally known as the International Bank for Reconstruction and Development, was established by the industrialized nations, including the United States, in 1946 to loan money to underdeveloped and developing countries.

It loans its own funds or borrows funds from member countries to finance projects ranging from road and factory construction to the building of medical and educational facilities. The World Bank and other multilateral development banks (banks with international support that provide loans to developing countries) are the largest source of advice and assistance for developing nations. The International Development Association and the International Finance Corporation are associated with the World Bank and provide loans to private businesses and member countries.

International Monetary Fund

The **International Monetary Fund (IMF)** was established in 1947 to promote trade among member nations by eliminating trade barriers and fostering financial cooperation. It also makes short-term loans to member countries that have balance-of-payment deficits and provides foreign currencies to member nations. The International Monetary Fund also tries to avoid financial crises and panics by alerting the international community about countries that will not be able to repay their debts. The IMF's Internet site provides additional information about the organization, including news releases, frequently asked questions, and members.

The IMF is the closest thing the world has to an international central bank. If countries get into financial trouble, they can borrow from the World Bank. The IMF has bailed out Thailand, Russia, and Argentina and, in recent years, has focused on loans to developing countries. The usefulness of the IMF for developed countries is limited because these countries use private markets as a major source of capital.[44]

⬤ ⬤ L04

Summarize the different levels of organizational involvement in international trade.

GETTING INVOLVED IN INTERNATIONAL BUSINESS

Businesses may get involved in international trade at many levels—from a small Kenyan firm that occasionally exports African crafts to a huge multinational corporation such as Shell Oil that sells products around the globe. The degree of commitment of resources and effort required increases according to the level at which a business involves itself in international trade. This section examines exporting and importing, trading companies, licensing and franchising, contract manufacturing, joint ventures, direct investment, and multinational corporations.

Exporting and Importing

Many companies first get involved in international trade when they import goods from other countries for resale in their own businesses. For example, a grocery store chain may import bananas from Honduras and coffee from Colombia. A business may get involved in exporting when it is called upon to supply

The key difference between the IMF and the World Bank is that the IMF focuses primarily on maintaining the international monetary system, whereas the World Bank concentrates on poverty reduction through low-interest loans and other programs. In this photo, outgoing World Bank President James D. Wolfensohn (right); Development Committee Chairman Trevor Manuel, the Finance Minister of South Africa (center); and IMF Managing Director Rodrigo de Rato (far left) speak with reporters at the IMF headquarters in Washington.

Although a company may export its wares overseas directly or import goods directly from their manufacturer, many choose to deal with an intermediary, commonly called an *export agent*. Export agents seldom produce goods themselves; instead, they usually handle international transactions for other firms. Export agents either purchase products outright or take them on consignment. If they purchase them outright, they generally mark up the price they have paid and attempt to sell the product in the international marketplace. They are also responsible for storage and transportation.

An advantage of trading through an agent instead of directly is that the company does not have to deal with foreign currencies or the red tape (paying tariffs and handling paperwork) of international business. A major disadvantage is that because the export agent must make a profit, either the price of the product must be increased or the domestic company must provide a larger discount than it would in a domestic transaction.

TABLE 3.4 U.S. Exporters and Value by Company Size

	Number of Exporters	%	Value (Dollars and Billions)	%
Small (<100 employees)	223,071	90.7	182.9	20.1
Medium (100–499 employees)	16,216	6.6	80.1	8.8
Large (500+ employees)	6,658	2.7	647.5	71.1

Source: "Profile of U.S. Exporting Companies, 2005–2006," U.S. Census Bureau, press release, January 11, 2008, www.census.gov/foreign-trade/Press-Release/edb/2006/ (accessed March 10, 2009).

a foreign company with a particular product. Such exporting enables enterprises of all sizes to participate in international business. Table 3.4 shows the number of U.S. exporters and the export value by company size, while Figure 3.2 shows the major export markets for U.S. companies.

Exporting sometimes takes place through **countertrade agreements,** which involve bartering products for other products instead of for currency. Such arrangements are fairly common in international trade, especially between Western companies and Eastern European nations. An estimated 40 percent or more of all international trade agreements contain countertrade provisions.

Trading Companies

A **trading company** buys goods in one country and sells them to buyers in another country. Trading companies handle all activities required to move products from one country to another, including consulting, marketing research, advertising, insurance, product research and design, warehousing, and foreign exchange services to companies interested in selling their products in foreign markets. Trading companies are similar to export agents, but their role in international trade is larger. By linking sellers and buyers of goods in different countries, trading companies promote international trade. The best known U.S. trading company is Sears World Trade, which specializes in consumer goods, light industrial items, and processed foods.

Licensing and Franchising

Licensing is a trade arrangement in which one company—the *licensor*—allows another company—the *licensee*—to use its company name, products, patents, brands, trademarks, raw materials, and/or production processes in exchange for a fee or royalty. The Coca-Cola Company and PepsiCo frequently use licensing as a means to market their soft drinks, apparel, and other merchandise in other countries. Licensing is an attractive alternative to direct investment when the political stability of a foreign country is in doubt or when resources are unavailable

FIGURE 3.2 U.S. Exporters and Value by Country

Country	Number of Exporters
Canada	87,554
Mexico	44,204
United Kingdom	39,684
Japan	26,648
China	25,873

Number of Exporters

Source: "Profile of U.S. Exporting Companies, 2005–2006," U.S. Census Bureau, press release, January 11, 2008, www.census.gov/foreign-trade/Press-Release/edb/2006/ (accessed March 10, 2009).

TABLE 3.5 Top 10 Global Franchise Operations

1. Subway
2. KFC Corp.
3. McDonald's
4. Dunkin' Donuts
5. Domino's Pizza LLC
6. Curves
7. RE/MAX Int'l. Inc.
8. Sonic Drive In Restaurants
9. Pizza Hut
10. The UPS Store/Mail Boxes Etc.

Source: "Top 10 Global Franchises for 2008," *Entrepreneur* (n.d.), www.entrepreneur.com/franchises/rankings/globalfranchises-115388/2008,-1.html (accessed March 10, 2009).

for direct investment. Licensing is especially advantageous for small manufacturers wanting to launch a well-known brand internationally. Yoplait is a French yogurt that is licensed for production in the United States.

Franchising is a form of licensing in which a company—the *franchiser*—agrees to provide a *franchisee* a name, logo, methods of operation, advertising, products, and other elements associated with the franchiser's business, in return for a financial commitment and the agreement to conduct business in accordance with the franchiser's standard of operations. Wendy's, McDonald's, Pizza Hut, and Holiday Inn are well-known franchisers with international visibility. Twenty percent of all U.S. franchise systems have foreign operations. The majority of these were located in developed markets such as Canada, Japan, Europe, and Australia.[45] Table 3.5 lists the top 10 global franchises as ranked by *Entrepreneur* magazine.

Licensing and franchising enable a company to enter the international marketplace without spending large sums of money abroad or hiring or transferring personnel to handle overseas affairs. They also minimize problems associated with shipping costs, tariffs, and trade restrictions. And they allow the firm to establish goodwill for its products in a foreign market, which will help the company if it decides to produce or market its products directly in the foreign country at some future date. However, if the licensee (or franchisee) does not maintain high standards of quality, the product's image may be hurt; therefore, it is important for the licensor to monitor its products overseas and to enforce its quality standards.

Contract Manufacturing

Contract manufacturing occurs when a company hires a foreign company to produce a specified volume of the firm's product to specification; the final product carries the domestic firm's name. Spalding, for example, relies on contract manufacturing for its sports equipment; Reebok uses Korean contract manufacturers to manufacture many of its athletic shoes.

Outsourcing

Earlier, we defined outsourcing as transferring manufacturing or other tasks (such as information technology operations) to companies in countries where labor and supplies are less expensive. Many U.S. firms have outsourced tasks to India, Ireland, Mexico, and the Philippines, where there are many well-educated workers and significantly lower labor costs. Experts estimate that 80 percent of *Fortune* 500 companies have some relationship with an offshore company. Bank of America, for example, set up a subsidiary in India to outsource 1,000 back-office support jobs. The bank also contracts with several Indian firms to provide software services.[46] Experts believe that two-thirds of U.S. banks outsource services to China, India, and Russia.[47] Even small firms can outsource. For example, Avalon, an Irish manufacturer of high-end guitars played by musicians like Eric Clapton, contracted with Cort Musical Instruments Company in South Korea to augment the firm's production and help it build a global brand. The outsourcing arrangement helped the small business boost output from 1,500 guitars a year to 8,000 annually, helping it become more competitive with larger manufacturers.[48]

Although outsourcing has become politically controversial in recent years amid concerns over jobs lost to overseas workers, foreign companies transfer tasks and jobs to U.S. companies—sometimes called *insourcing*—far more often than U.S. companies outsource tasks and jobs abroad.[49] For example, Indian-based Bharti TeleVentures, a cell-phone operator, signed a 10-year contract to insource its software, hardware, and other information-technology tasks to IBM in the United States.[50] However, some firms are bringing their outsourced jobs back after concerns that foreign workers were not adding enough value.

Joint Ventures and Alliances

Many countries, particularly LDCs, do not permit direct investment by foreign companies or individuals. Or a company may lack sufficient resources or expertise to operate in another country. In such cases, a company that wants to do business in another country may set up a joint venture by finding a local partner (occasionally, the host nation itself) to share the costs and operation of the business. General Motors, for

● **FRANCHISING** a form of licensing in which a company—the franchiser—agrees to provide a franchisee a name, logo, methods of operation, advertising, products, and other elements associated with a franchiser's business, in return for a financial commitment and the agreement to conduct business in accordance with the franchiser's standard of operations

● **CONTRACT MANUFACTURING** the hiring of a foreign company to produce a specified volume of the initiating company's product to specification; the final product carries the domestic firm's name

● **JOINT VENTURE** the sharing of the costs and operation of a business between a foreign company and a local partner

well as the Toyota Corolla, the Pontiac Vibe, and a right-hand drive Toyota Voltz for sale in Japan.[52]

Direct Investment

Companies that want more control and are willing to invest considerable resources in international business may consider **direct investment,** the ownership of overseas facilities. Direct investment may involve the development and operation of new facilities—such as when Starbucks opens a new coffee shop in Japan—or the purchase of all or part of an existing operation in a foreign country. India's Tata Motors purchased Jaguar and Land Rover from Ford Motor Company. Tata, a maker of cars and trucks, is attempting to broaden its global presence, including manufacturing these vehicles in the United Kingdom.[53]

The highest level of international business involvement is the **multinational corporation (MNC),** a corporation, such as IBM or ExxonMobil, that operates on a worldwide scale, without significant ties to any one nation or region. Table 3.6 lists the 10 largest multinational corporations. MNCs are more than simple corporations. They often have greater assets than some of the countries in which they do business. General Motors, ExxonMobil, Ford Motors, and General Electric,

Direct investments don't always go as planned. When Coke attempted to extend its reach in China by purchasing that country's biggest juice maker, it faced fierce opposition from the Chinese. Eventually it abandoned the effort. The Dutch company InBev faced similar opposition in the United States before acquiring Anheuser Busch.

example, has a joint venture with Russian automaker Avtovaz in Togliatti, which manufactures four-wheel-drive Chevrolet Nivas and Opel Astras for the Russian market. Demand for the relatively pricey Astra has grown along with Russian household incomes.[51]

In some industries, such as automobiles and computers, strategic alliances are becoming the predominant means of competing. A **strategic alliance** is a partnership formed to create competitive advantage on a worldwide basis. In such industries, international competition is so fierce and the costs of competing on a global basis are so high that few firms have the resources to go it alone, so they collaborate with other companies. An example of such an alliance is New United Motor Manufacturing Inc. (NUMMI), formed by Toyota and General Motors in 1984 to make automobiles for both firms. This alliance joined the quality engineering of Japanese cars with the marketing expertise and market access of General Motors. Today, NUMMI manufactures the popular Toyota Tacoma compact pick-up truck as

TABLE 3.6 The 10 Largest Global Corporations

Rank	Company	Revenues (in millions)
1	Wal-Mart Stores	$351,139
2	ExxonMobil	347,254
3	Royal Dutch Shell	318,845
4	BP	274,316
5	General Motors	207,349
6	Toyota Motor	230,000
7	Chevron	200,567
8	DaimlerChrysler	190,191
9	ConocoPhillips	172,451
10	Total	168,357

Source: "Global 500: Fortune's Annual Ranking of the World's Largest Corporations," *Fortune,* http://money.cnn.com/magazines/fortune/global500/2008/ (accessed March 10, 2009).

for example, have sales higher than the GDP of many of the countries in which they operate. Nestlé, with headquarters in Switzerland, operates more than 300 plants around the world and receives revenues from Europe; North, Central, and South America; Africa; and Asia. The Royal Dutch/Shell Group, one of the world's major oil producers, is another MNC. Its main offices are located in The Hague and London. Other MNCs include BASF, British Petroleum, Cadbury Schweppes, Matsushita, Mitsubishi, Siemens, Texaco, Toyota, and Unilever. Many MNCs have been targeted by antiglobalization activists at global business forums, and some protests have turned violent. The activists contend that MNCs increase the gap between rich and poor nations, misuse and misallocate scarce resources, exploit the labor markets in LDCs, and harm their natural environments.[54]

 L05

Contrast two basic strategies used in international business.

INTERNATIONAL BUSINESS STRATEGIES

Planning in a global economy requires businesspeople to understand the economic, legal, political, and sociocultural realities of the countries in which they will operate. These factors will affect the strategy a business chooses to use outside its own borders.

Developing Strategies

Companies doing business internationally have traditionally used a **multinational strategy**, customizing their products, promotion, and distribution according to cultural, technological, regional, and national differences. In France, for example, South Korean–owned AmorePacific Corporation marketed its Lolita Lempicka perfume, with a decidedly French accent. Named for

a French fashion designer, the fifth-best-selling fragrance in France was formulated by French experts and marketed in a bottle designed by a French artist. Indeed, few French consumers realize the popular perfume is owned by a Korean firm.[55] Many soap and detergent manufacturers have adapted their products to local water conditions, washing equipment, and washing habits. For customers in some less-developed countries, Colgate-Palmolive Co. has developed an inexpensive, plastic, hand-powered washing machine for use in households that have no electricity. Even when products are standardized, advertising often has to be modified to adapt to language and cultural differences. Also, celebrities used in advertising in the United States may be unfamiliar to foreign consumers and thus would not be effective in advertising products in other countries.

More and more companies are moving from this customization strategy to a **global strategy (globalization)**, which involves standardizing products (and, as much as possible, their promotion and distribution) for the whole world, as if it were a single entity. Examples of globalized products are American clothing, movies, music, and cosmetics. ExxonMobil launched a $150 million marketing effort to promote its brands: Exxon, Esso, Mobil, and General. The ads have the same look and feel regardless of the country in which they appear. The ad's message was the same for all countries except the story was told in one of 25 languages.[56]

Before moving outside their own borders, companies must conduct environmental analyses to evaluate the potential of and problems associated with various markets and to determine what strategy is best for doing business in those markets. Failure to do so may result in losses and even negative publicity. Some companies rely on local managers to gain greater insights into and faster response to changes within

Business in a Borderless World

Eric Brewer is no stranger to working with the Internet. In 1996, he cofounded Inktomi Corporation, an Internet search company that was sold to Yahoo! in 2003 for $235 million. In 2000, he worked with the Clinton administration to help make it possible to search federal documents. He is widely respected in his field, having become a tenured professor of computer science at the age of 32. However, after achieving notable accomplishments nationally, Brewer began looking at ways in which

he could use his knowledge to make a global impact and truly help people. These days, Brewer, now 40, and his graduate students are deep into the creation and implementation of an affordable and effective way to provide poor villages throughout the world with wireless Internet access. Their creation, Wildnet, uses publicly available radio spectrum and Linux (a free operating system) along with Intel computer boards and store-bought Wi-Fi radio chips to create affordable transmitters

that work as quickly as a typical cable modem, transmitting data up to 60 miles. As of April 2007, Wildnets had been constructed in the Philippines, Ghana, Guinea-Bissau, and India. Wildnet has had an important impact in these areas, particularly in India, where poor villagers are actually receiving improved eye care thanks to Wildnet. The development of Wildnet technology now takes up the bulk of Brewer's time as director of the Intel Research Berkeley Lab.[57] ❖

SO YOU WANT A JOB IN GLOBAL BUSINESS

Have you always dreamed of traveling the world? Whether backpacking through Central America or sipping espressos at five-star European restaurants is your style, the increasing globalization of business might just give you your chance to see what the world has to offer. Most new jobs will have at least some global component, even if they are located within the United States, so being globally aware and keeping an open mind to different cultures are vital in today's business world. Think about the 1.3 billion consumers in China who already have purchased 500 million mobile phones. In the future, some of the largest markets will be in Asia.

Many jobs discussed in chapters throughout this book tend to have strong international components. For example, product management and distribution management are discussed as marketing careers in Chapter 13. As more and more companies sell products around the globe, their function, design, packaging, and promotion need to be culturally relevant to many different people in many different places. Products very often cross multiple borders before reaching the final consumer, both in their distribution and through the supply chain to produce the products.

Jobs exist in export and import management, product and pricing management, distribution and transportation, and advertising. Many "born global" companies such as Google operate virtually and consider all countries their market. Many companies sell their products through eBay and other Internet sites and never leave the United States. Today communication and transportation facilitate selling and buying products worldwide with delivery in a few days. You may have sold or purchased a product on eBay outside the United States without thinking about how easy and accessible international markets are to business. If you have, welcome to the world of global business.

To be successful you must have an idea not only of differing regulations from country to country, but of different language, ethics, and communication styles and the varying needs and wants of international markets. From the regulatory side, you may need to be aware of laws related to intellectual property, copyrights, antitrust, advertising, and pricing in every country. Translating is never only about translating the language. Perhaps even more important is ensuring that your message gets through. Whether on a product label or in advertising or promotional materials, the use of images and words varies widely across the globe.

a country. Astute businesspeople today "think globally, act locally." That is, while constantly being aware of the total picture, they adjust their firms' strategies to conform to local needs and tastes.

Managing the Challenges of Global Business

As we've pointed out in this chapter, many past political barriers to trade have fallen or been minimized, expanding and opening new market opportunities. Managers who can meet the challenges of creating and implementing effective and sensitive business strategies for the global marketplace can help lead their companies to success. For example, the Commercial Service is the global business solutions unit of the U.S. Department of Commerce that offers U.S. firms wide and deep practical knowledge of international markets and industries,

a unique global network, inventive use of information technology, and a focus on small and medium-sized businesses. Another example is the benchmarking of best international practices that benefits U.S. firms, which is conducted by the network of CIBERs (Centers for International Business Education and Research) at leading business schools in the United States. These 30 CIBERs are funded by the U.S. government to help U.S. firms become more competitive globally. A major element of the assistance that these governmental organizations can provide firms (especially for small and medium-sized firms) is knowledge of the internationalization process.[58] Small businesses, too, can succeed in foreign markets when their managers have carefully studied those markets and prepared and implemented appropriate strategies. Being globally aware is therefore an important quality for today's managers and will become a critical attribute for managers of the 21st century. ∎

Team Exercise

Visit Transparency International's Country Corruption Index: Web site at http://transparency.org/policy_research/surveys_indices/cpi. Select two countries, and each team should research some of the economic, ethical, legal, regulatory, and political barriers that would have an impact on international trade. Each team should pair a fairly ethical country with a fairly unethical country (i.e., Sweden with Myanmar, Ireland with Haiti). Each team should then report its findings.

CHECK OUT www.mhhe.com/FerrellM2e

for study materials including Interactive Exercises, Quizzes, iPod downloads, and video.

Managing Information Technology & E-Business

4

learning **OBJECTIVES**

LO1 Summarize the role and impact of technology in the global economy.

LO2 Specify how information is managed, and explain a management information system.

LO3 Describe the Internet and explore its main uses.

LO4 Define e-business, and discuss the e-business models.

LO5 Identify the legal and social issues of information technology and e-business.

Introduction

The technology behind computers, the Internet, and their applications has changed the face of business over the past few decades. **Information technology (IT)** relates to processes and applications that create new methods to solve problems, perform tasks, and manage communication. Information technology has been associated with using computers to obtain and process information as well as using application software and the Internet to organize and communicate information. Information technology's impact on the economy is very powerful, especially with regard to productivity, employment, and working environments. Technology has resulted in social issues related to privacy, intellectual property, quality of life, and the ability of the legal system to respond to this environment. Most businesses are using information technology to develop new strategies, enhance employee productivity, and improve services to customers.

In this chapter we first examine the role and impact of technology in our information-driven economy. Next, we discuss the need to manage information. We then analyze management information systems and take a look at information technology applications. Then we provide an overview of the Internet and examine e-business as a strategy to improve business performance and create competitive advantage. Finally, we examine the legal and social issues associated with information technology and e-business.

LO1

Summarize the role and impact of technology in the global economy.

THE IMPACT OF TECHNOLOGY ON OUR LIVES

Technology relates to the application of knowledge, including the processes and procedures to solve problems, perform tasks, and create new methods to obtain desired outcomes. IT includes intellectual knowledge as well as the computer systems

order is received, there is a flow of information to achieve this one-to-one fulfillment strategy. A similar company, Reflect. com, was launched by Procter & Gamble to provide customized beauty products. The company is no longer in business.[2] Keeping pace with new information technology is a challenge for businesses adjusting to new competitive environments.

Information technology has improved global access by linking people in businesses through telecommunications. Satellites permit instant visual and electronic voice connections almost anywhere in the world. The self-sustaining nature of technology acts as a catalyst to spur even faster development. As new innovations are introduced, they stimulate the need for more technology to facilitate further development. Technologies begin a process that creates new opportunities in every industry segment or customer area that is affected.

Productivity, the amount of output per hour of work, is a key ingredient in determining the standard of living. For the past eight years, the United States has enjoyed significantly faster productivity growth than it did over the preceding two decades. Some analysts believe that the potential gains in productivity

> ## "Technology has been a driving force in the advancement of economic systems and the quality of life."

devised to achieve business objectives. Technology has been a driving force in the advancement of economic systems and the quality of life. Today, our economic productivity is based more on technology than on any other advance. Information technology is important because our economy is service based. Technology has changed the way consumers take vacations, make purchases, drive cars, and obtain entertainment. Consider the encyclopedia. Thanks to the ever-growing amount of information available on the Internet, sales of traditional hard-bound encyclopedias have plummeted as more people turn to Internet search engines to help them with research for school, work, or fun. Sales of *Encyclopedia Britannica,* first published in 1768, have declined rapidly over the last decade, while other publishers went out of business. The firms that survived did so by adapting and providing computerized encyclopedia or online access to encyclopedia content. In the workplace, technology has improved productivity and efficiency, reduced costs, and enhanced customer service. The Web site Wikipedia.org was created in 2001 as a free online encyclopedia that anyone can use. Users across the globe may access and edit the contents of the more than 10 million articles in more than 260 languages.[1] The economy of the 21st century is based on these dynamic changes in our society.

Information technology also is changing many traditional products. AFE Cosmetics and Skincare operates www.cosmetics.com, which provides customized cosmetics and skin care products. Lip gloss can be customized to match a specific outfit. Foundation can be matched to skin tone. From the time an

from technological advances associated with the computer revolution are far from over.[3] In recent years, economic and productivity growth has resulted in the annual addition of 2 million jobs.[4] For example, the ability to access information in "real time" through the electronic data interface between retailers, wholesalers, and manufacturers has reduced delivery lead times, as well as the hours required to produce and deliver products. The process of releasing an album with a major record label is arduous, with the input and consent of lawyers, marketers, promoters, CD manufacturers and retail conglomerates. In 2003, the five-member band Radiohead decided to use the expiration of its contract with record label EMI to reinvent the launch of an album. Their next album, *In Rainbows,* was released electronically on Radiohead.com, with no set price. Downloaders were free to choose their own fee for the 10-song album.[5]

 LO2

Specify how information is managed, and explain a management information system.

MANAGING INFORMATION

Data refers to numerical or verbal descriptions related to statistics or other items that have not been analyzed or summarized. Data can exist in a variety of forms—as patterns of numbers or letters printed on paper, stored in electronic memory, or accumulated as facts in a person's mind.[6] **Knowledge** is usually referred to as an understanding of data gained through study or experience. **Information** then includes meaningful and useful interpretation of data and knowledge that can be used in making decisions. The less information available, the more risk associated with a decision. For example, when a manager purchases a new computer without conducting any research, the risk of a poor decision is great. A more informed decision could be made after determining existing, and likely, computing needs and the price, capability, and quality of available computers from a number of sources. Information is necessary for good decision making. When information is properly understood, guidelines can be developed that help simplify and improve decisions in future similar circumstances. Therefore, effective information management is crucial.

Businesses often engage in data processing efforts to improve data flow and the usefulness of information. Often, computers are communicating this data without the direct interface or help of an individual. Goods can be ordered when inventories drop or a previous customer can be notified automatically when new product information is available. All of this depends on software and equipment that has been put in place to make data more useful based on established decision criteria.

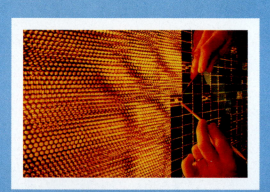

Despite outsourcing, U.S. workers remain at the top of the heap in terms of productivity, in large part because they have access to better technology.

Management Information Systems

Because information is a major business resource, it should be viewed as an asset that must be developed and distributed to managers. Technology has been used to develop systems that provide managers with the information needed to make decisions. A **management information system (MIS)** is used for organizing and transmitting data into information that can be used for decision making. The purpose of the MIS is to obtain data from both internal and external sources to create information that is easily accessible and structured for user-friendly communication to managers. The MIS can range from a simple system in which information is delivered through e-mail to a complex system of records and data that is delivered through sophisticated communications software. At Anheuser-Busch, for example, a system called BudNet compiles information about

Protesters Use the Internet to Organize

Workers, students, organizations, and individuals worldwide are using the Internet to stage large protests to fight for what they believe in. There are a number of positive reasons to consider virtual protests beyond the obvious goal of achieving change. For workers, the Internet provides an easier way to protest without losing work time or pay. These online protests also benefit companies by opening an avenue for dissent that creates little or no disruption in productivity. For example, 2,000 Italian IBM employees staged a protest in Second Life. As a result, their union renegotiated a pay settlement.

Again using Second Life, the fashion designer Stella McCartney and People for the Ethical Treatment of Animals (PETA) staged an antifur protest. Second Life avatars dressed in T-shirts stating "I'd Rather be Pixelated Than Wear Fur." PETA also held a competition to replace its famous slogan, "I'd Rather Go Naked Than Wear Fur." Because millions of users frequent Second Life, this was a novel and low-cost way to reach a huge audience. In Hong Kong, students staged a Facebook protest when their bank, HSBC, threatened to ax free overdraft protection on checking accounts. As a result, the bank maintained the program and abolished interest fees.

While they are a worldwide phenomenon, virtual protests are especially widely used in the United States. For example, visit stopglobalwarming.org and you can join an online protest with over 1 million members which boasts luminaries such as Nobel Peace Prize laureate Wangari Maathal. MoveOn.org is famous for its virtual protests, which are often environmentally or politically based. Virtual protests have a lot of advantages. They are easier to organize, are safer for protesters, can reach a much wider audience, and can be more efficient. And they can be environmentally beneficial—virtual protests can save energy, paper, and much more.[7] ❖

Q: Discussion Questions

1. What are the advantages for groups that use the Internet as a method to stage protests about their concerns?

2. How may a virtual protest have limitations compared with a personal, onsite protest?

3. Because virtual protests are environmentally friendly, is it possible that this green method of communication will become much more popular?

requests for directions, or connect with an online concierge for entertainment, restaurant, and shopping information. When an airbag deploys in a vehicle equipped with OnStar, the system automatically alerts an adviser, who calls immediately to discern the nature of the emergency.[9]

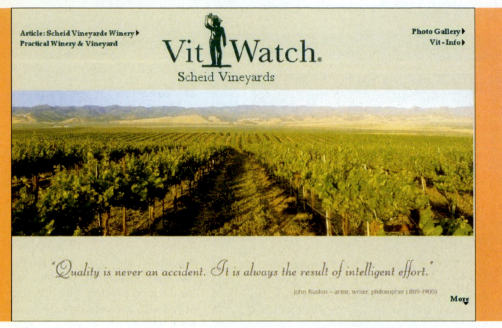

Article: Scheid Vineyards Winery ▶
Practical Winery & Vineyard

Photo Gallery ▶
Vit-Info ▶

Vit Watch.
Scheid Vineyards

"Quality is never an accident. It is always the result of intelligent effort."

John Ruskin – artist, writer, philosopher (1819-1900)

More ▾

Scheid Vineyards produces premium wine grapes and operates approximately 5,700 acres of vineyards, primarily in Monterey County, California. The company sells most of its grapes to wineries that produce high-quality table wines. Scheid's clients can get real-time information about the specific grape blocks they're purchasing via the company's "Vit Watch" information system, accessible on the Web. Vit Watch allows both Scheid and its client to keep abreast of what is happening "in the field"—literally.

past sales at individual stores, inventory, competitors' displays and prices, and a host of other information collected by distributors' sales representatives on handheld computers. The system allows company executives to respond quickly to changes in demographic or social trends or competitors' strategies with an appropriate promotional message, package, display, or discount. The system also helps the company pinpoint demographic consumption trends, craft promotional messages, and even develop new products such as Tilt, an innovative malt beverage with caffeine, guarana, and ginseng.[8]

The MIS breaks down time and location barriers, making information available when and where it is needed to solve problems. An effective MIS can make information available around the globe in seconds, and with wireless communications, it is possible for users to carry the system in a briefcase or pocket. Wireless devices in use today include computers, personal data assistants, cell phones, pagers, and GPS positioning devices found in cars. For example, General Motors provides OnStar Telematics that provide advanced satellite-based communication to pinpoint a car's location. The system can put the car's driver in touch with an adviser for emergency assistance or

Collecting Data

To be effective, an MIS must be able to collect data, store and update data, and process and present information. Much of the data that is useful for managers typically comes from sources inside the organization. Such internal data can be obtained from company records, reports, and operations. The data may relate to customers, suppliers, expenses, and sales. Information about employees such as salaries, benefits, and turnover can be of great value and is usually incorporated into the system. External sources of data include customers, suppliers, industry publications, the mass media, and firms that gather data for sale.

A **database** is a collection of data stored in one place and accessible throughout the network. A database management program permits participants to electronically store information and organize the data into usable categories that are arranged by decision requirements. For example, if management needs to know the 20 top customers by sales volume, the system can quickly access the database and print a list of the customers in a matter of moments. The same type of information retrieval can occur throughout the functional areas of the business with the appropriate database management software.

Databases developed by Information Resources Inc. (IRI) allow businesses to tap into an abundance of information on sales, pricing, and promotion for hundreds of consumer product categories using data from scanners at the checkouts in stores. IRI can track new products to assess their performance and gauge competitors' reactions. Once new products are on store shelves, IRI monitors related information, including the prices and market share of competing products. IRI also can help companies assess customers' reactions to changes in a product's price, packaging, and display. When a product's sales in relation to promotional efforts are tracked, the effect of a company's advertising as well as that of competitors can be known.[10] Nearly all of the consumer package goods firms in the *Fortune Global 500* use Information Resources Inc.'s services.[11]

THE INTERNET

The **Internet,** the global information system that links many computer networks together, has profoundly altered the way people communicate, learn, do business, and find entertainment. Although many people believe the Internet began in the early 1990s, its origins can actually be traced to the late 1950s (see Table 4.1). Over the past four decades, the network evolved from a system for government and university researchers into a tool used by millions around the globe for communication, information, entertainment, and e-business. With the development of the **World Wide Web,** a collection of interconnected Web sites or "pages" of text, graphics, audio, and video within the Internet, use of the Internet exploded in the early 1990s.

An **intranet** is a network of computers similar to the Internet that is available only to people inside an organization. Businesses establish intranets to make the MIS available for employees and to create interactive communication about data. The intranet allows employees to participate in creating information useful throughout the organization. The development of an intranet saves money and time because paper is eliminated and data becomes available on an almost instantaneous basis. More than half of all businesses are running some type of intranet. Even universities are capturing the benefits of intranets. Duke University has introduced an intranet system to help students manage their on-campus recruiting work. With this system, Duke MBA students can

● **INTERNET** global information system that links many computer networks together

● **WORLD WIDE WEB** a collection of interconnected Web sites or pages of text, graphics, audio, and video within the Internet

● **INTRANET** a network of computers similar to the Internet that is available only to people inside an organization

TABLE 4.1 History of Information Technology

Year	Event	Significance
1836	Telegraph	The telegraph revolutionized human (tele)communications with Morse code, a series of dots and dashes used to communicate between humans.
1858–1866	Transatlantic cable	Transatlantic cable allowed direct instantaneous communication across the Atlantic Ocean.
1876	Telephone	The telephone created voice communication, and telephone exchanges provide the backbone of Internet connections today.
1957	USSR launches Sputnik	Sputnik was the first artificial earth satellite and the start of global communications.
1962–1968	Packet switching networks developed	The Internet relies on packet switching networks, which split data into tiny packets that may take different routes to a destination.
1971	Beginning of the Internet	People communicate over the Internet with a program to send messages across a distributed network.
1973	Global networking becomes a reality	Ethernet outlined—this is how local networks are basically connected today, and gateways define how large networks (maybe of different architecture) can be connected together.
1991	World Wide Web established	User-friendly interface to World Wide Web established with text-based, menu-driven interface to access Internet resources.
1992	Multimedia changes the face of the Internet	The term "surfing the Internet" is coined.
1993	World Wide Web revolution begins	Mosaic, user-friendly Graphical Front End to the World Wide Web, makes the Internet more accessible and evolves into Netscape.
1995	Internet service providers advance	Online dial-up systems (CompuServe, America Online, Prodigy) begin to provide Internet access.
2000	Broadband connections to the Internet emerge	Provides fast access to multimedia and large text files.
2002	Advances in wireless	Mobile phones, handheld computers, and personal data assistants provide wireless access to the Internet.
2004	Wireless technology expands	Use of radio waves to send e-mail, Web pages, and other information through the air (Wi-Fi).
2006	Wireless expands globally	Worldwide expansion of smart phones and Wi-Fi in developing countries.
2009	WiMax Network	Faster and covers North America, creating one big hot spot. Internet appliance options are advanced.

apply for jobs, sign up for career counseling, bid on interview slots, post job leads, and network with other students.[12]

Some businesses open up their intranets to other selected individuals or companies through an **extranet,** a network of computers that permits selected companies and other organizations to access the same information and may allow different managers in various organizations to collaborate and communicate about the information. For example, one of the most common uses of an extranet is for a company such as Wal-Mart to permit suppliers such as Procter & Gamble and Kraft to access the Wal-Mart MIS to determine inventory levels and product availability. An extranet allows users to share data, process orders, and manage information.

In the next few pages, we will take a brief look at wireless technologies that are making the Internet easier to use.

Wireless Technologies

Future wireless technologies are driving us beyond PCs toward an array of Internet appliances such as personal digital assistants (PDAs), smart phones, and other digital devices. The BlackBerry and the Palm Pilot are established PDAs with millions of users. Livescribe's new Pulse is

a smart pen that can store audio along with written notes to be downloaded to a Windows PC, which then can be sent or accessed by other wireless devices.[13] When it was launched in 2007, the Apple iPhone was named *Time* magazine's Invention of the Year for its integrated wireless multimedia features, including e-mail, Web browsing, an iPod-like media player, and a camera.[14]

Internet browsing by a mobile phone is growing throughout the world as cell phone penetration has increased. In South Korea, Japan, and urban China, at least 90 percent of house-

"Much of the world growth in Internet use is coming from countries such as China, India, Brazil, Russia, and Indonesia."

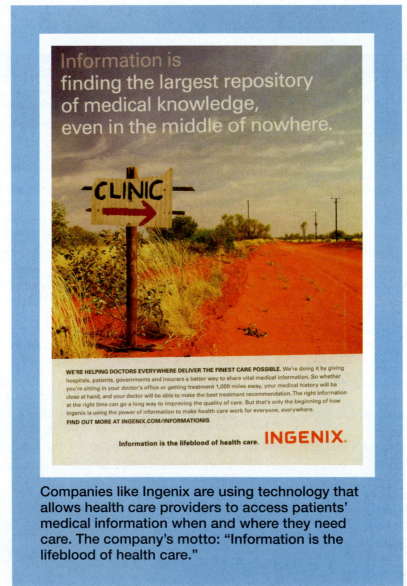

Information is finding the largest repository of medical knowledge, even in the middle of nowhere.

CLINIC

WE'RE HELPING DOCTORS EVERYWHERE DELIVER THE FINEST CARE POSSIBLE. We're doing it by giving hospitals, patients, governments and insurers a better way to share vital medical information. So whether you're sitting in your doctor's office or getting treatment 1,000 miles away, your medical history will be close at hand, and your doctor will be able to make the best treatment recommendation. The right information at the right time can go a long way to improving the quality of care. But that's only the beginning of how Ingenix is using the power of information to make health care work for everyone, everywhere.
FIND OUT MORE AT INGENIX.COM/INFORMATIONIS

Information is the lifeblood of health care. **INGENIX.**

Companies like Ingenix are using technology that allows health care providers to access patients' medical information when and where they need care. The company's motto: "Information is the lifeblood of health care."

holds have at least one mobile phone, and the total number of Chinese mobile phones users is over 600 million.[15] In the United States, 75 percent of households own a mobile phone. Globally, around one-fourth of cell phone owners have used their phones to browse the Web. In China, almost 118 million people accessed the Internet through their mobile phones in 2008, a 133 percent increase from the previous year.[16]

Wireless fidelity (Wi-Fi) networks are changing the way individuals and businesses use the Internet. Wi-Fi sends Web pages and other information to a laptop computer or another electronic device by using radio waves. In the not too distant future, experts expect Wi-Fi to link all sorts of devices—not just computers but lamps, stereos, appliances, and more—and fully integrate the Internet into our lives. Cooks using wireless notebook computers can take advantage of the Epicurious Web site, which allows access to "how to" videos that can be watched while one is cooking in the kitchen. Wi-Fi also is transforming the way companies use the internet. Some firms use Wi-Fi to replace expensive wired

a computer, others allow you to use your traditional phone line with an adapter. Companies operating in this market include Vonage, Skype, Sunrocket, Time Warner Cable, and Net Zero, to name a few.[19]

> # "Internet browsing by a mobile phone is growing throughout the world as cell phone penetration has increased."

networks or to maintain communications even in hard to reach places such as warehouses. Thus, investments in Wi-Fi can boost productivity and improve the ease of use and connectivity of multiple devices. Bluetooth technology allows mobile phones, computers, and personal digital assistantes, as well as other devices, to be interconnected using a short-range wireless connection. With this technology, users can have all mobile and fixed computer devices in sync with one another. Bluetooth wireless technology is installed on more than 5 million units every week as well as some automobiles, such as select BMWs.[17]

WiMax is a new technology that is used to move beyond Wi-Fi by covering a much larger area. In fact, this new technology is intended to turn North America into one big hot spot. Leading information technology companies such as Sprint, Google, Comcast, and Time Warner are creating a new company to utilize this technology, Clearwire, which has the potential to give the United States an opportunity to be the leader in wireless broadband. WiMax offers download speeds three times faster than the current average mobile download speed. The technology works through WiMax transmitters on cell phone towers.[18]

Internet Voice, also known as Voice over Internet Protocol (VOIP), allows users to make telephone calls using broadband Internet connections instead of traditional hard-wired land lines. While some services work only through

RFID chips aren't just for tracking products anymore. They're for people, too. VeriChip Corporation, a Florida-based firm, has begun making tiny implantable radio frequency identification chips to protect infants, to identify unconscious people, or to prevent people with dementia from wandering off and never being found. The roots of VeriChip trace back to the events of September 11, 2001, when New York firemen were writing their badge ID numbers on their chests in case they were found injured or unconscious.

Another emerging technology of great importance to business is radio frequency identification (RFID) systems, which use radio waves to identify and track resources and products within the distribution channel. Goods tagged with an RFID tag can be tracked electronically from supplier to factory floor, from warehouse to retail store. Companies also are increasingly employing global positioning systems (GPS) to facilitate shipping and inventory management tasks. Wal-Mart is a leader in the use of RFID technology, getting its suppliers to use RFID chips in the pallets and cases shipped to stores. This helps minimize one of the most costly problems in retailing—empty shelves with replacement products hiding in the storeroom. In a study by the University of Arkansas, stores using this technology and process saw a 165 percent reduction in product missing from shelves.[20]

The growth of wireless voice communications and their increasing integration with Internet technologies are generating opportunities for further innovations and applications. For example, location-based wireless technologies already aid police and parents in protecting children from kidnapping and other crimes. Multimedia messaging services (MMS) and streaming mobile video raise exciting possibilities for more person-to-person services and even personalized entertainment. However, these possibilities also raise privacy questions, as we shall see later in this chapter.[21]

●● **LO4**

Define e-business, and discuss the e-business models.

E-BUSINESS

Because the phenomenal growth of the Internet and the World Wide Web has provided the opportunity for e-business to grow faster than any other innovation in recent years, we have devoted an entire section to this subject. E-business growth has not been without some setbacks as businesses have experimented with new approaches to utilizing information technology and the Internet. Because e-business is based on an interactive model to conduct business, it has expanded the methods for maintaining business relationships. The nature of the Internet has created tremendous opportunities for businesses to forge relationships with consumers and business customers, target markets more precisely, and even reach previously inaccessible markets. The Internet also facilitates business transactions, allowing companies to network with manufacturers, wholesalers, retailers, suppliers, and outsource firms to serve customers more efficiently. Traditional methods included conducting business personally, through the mail (package document delivery service), and via telephone. The telecommunication opportunities created by the Internet have set the stage for e-business development and growth.

The Nature of E-Business

In general, e-business has the same goal as traditional business. All businesses try to earn a profit by providing products that satisfy people's needs. **E-business** can be distinguished from traditional business as carrying out the goals of business through utilization of the Internet. There are many different areas of e-business that use familiar terms. For example, e-commerce uses the Internet to carry out marketing activities, including buying and selling activities conducted online. These activities include communicating and fostering exchanges and relationships with customers, suppliers, and the public. Amazon.com is the most successful e-business, with $14.8 billion in revenue, and is ranked as the 171st largest U.S. company on the 2008 *Fortune* 500 list ranked by revenue. Amazon now accounts for 6 percent of the $136 billion online retail market in the United States Retail sales are Amazon's biggest business, but now one-third of the company's sales are between businesses, including small stores and retailers as large as Target. Amazon takes a commission or charges a fee to fill such orders. Amazon is a true global e-business, with 50% of its revenue from international sales. The United Kingdom, Japan, and Germany each account for 10 percent of Amazon sales.[22]

E-commerce includes activities such as conducting marketing research, providing and obtaining price and product information, and advertising, as well as online selling. Even the U.S. government engages in e-commerce activities—marketing everything from bonds and other financial instruments to oil-drilling leases and wild horses. Procter & Gamble uses the Internet as a fast, cost-effective means for marketing research, judging consumer demand for potential new products by inviting online consumers to sample new prototype products and provide feedback. If a product gets rave reviews from the samplers, the company may decide to introduce it. Procter & Gamble already conducts nearly 100 percent of its concept testing and 40 percent of its 6,000 product tests and other studies online,

Jeff Bezos, founder, CEO, and chairman of Amazon.com, holds the company's first sign, quickly spray-painted prior to an interview with a Japanese television station in 1995.

saving the company significant time and money in getting new products to market.[23]

E-business has changed our economy with companies that could not exist without the technology available through the Internet. The top independent U.S. video Web site, Veoh, for example, is trying to give consumers the broadest collection of video available anywhere on the Internet. Veoh gives users easy access to full-length TV shows and other video, often hosted elsewhere on the Web. A key feature differentiating the site from

customers need or want, not merely developing a brand name or reducing the costs associated with online transactions.

Instead of e-business changing all industries, it has had much more impact in certain industries where the cost of business and customer transactions is very high. For example, investment trading is less expensive online because customers can buy and sell investments, such as stocks and mutual funds, on

● **E-BUSINESS** carrying out the goals of business through utilization of the Internet

> ## e-commerce uses the Internet to carry out marketing activities, including buying and selling activities conducted online.

others such as YouTube and Yahoo is the ability to download shows for later viewing.[24]

Many companies that attempted to transact business on the Internet, often called dot-coms, had problems making a profit. Most of the early dot-coms, such as eToys.com, Pets.com, Garden.com, Hardware.com, and BigWords.com, found that no single technology could completely change the nature of busi-

their own. Firms such as E* Trade and Charles Schwab Corp, the biggest online brokerage firm, have been innovators in online trading. Traditional brokers such as Merrill Lynch have had to follow these companies and provide online trading for their customers.

E-business can use many benefits of the Internet to reduce the cost of both customer and business transactions. Because

> ## "E-business can use many benefits of the Internet to reduce the cost of both customer and business transactions."

ness, and many failed.[25] Some dot-coms failed because they thought the only thing that mattered was the brand awareness they created through advertising. The reality, however, is that Internet markets are more similar to traditional markets than they are different. Thus, successful e-business strategies, like traditional business strategies, depend on creating products that

the Internet lowers the cost of communication, it can contribute significantly in any industry or activity that depends on the flow of information. Opportunities exist for information-intensive industries such as entertainment, health care, government services, education, and computer services such as software.[26] For example, some insurance companies now pay for

Business.com is a Valuable B2B Search Engine

In 1999, Jake Winebaum and Sky Dayton spent $7.5 million to buy the Internet domain name Business.com. This is the third largest price ever paid for a domain name. Although Winebaum and Dayton were widely ridiculed at the time, their "wild" purchase turns out to have been a wise one. Why buy the domain name in the first place? It seems that a site such as Business.com can generate a good deal of its traffic not from people who are searching for the site specifically but from people typing in a generic name as part of a search. There-

fore, people looking for information on business in general would be likely to end up at Business.com. What is Business.com? It is a business-to-business search engine, directory, and pay-per-click advertising network. Advertisers include companies such as The Wall Street Journal, Entrepreneur.com, and Hoovers. The site currently generates about 6 million unique visitors per month, and in its wake, the company has launched Business.com Network (distribution partnerships with top-tier online business properties, includ-

ing BusinessWeek.com and Forbes.com) and Work.com (a business-oriented community site). Eight years after their original purchase, Winebaum and Dayton decided to put the company up for auction. It was snatched up by R.H. Donnelly Corporation (a Yellow Pages and online local commercial search company) for a reported $350 million and deferred purchase consideration—about 24 times Business.com's 2007 cash flow. Who knew![27] ❖

BUSINESS-TO-BUSINESS (B2B) use of the Internet for transactions and communications between organizations

doctor–patient e-visits. Computer-literate patients can now consult their doctors through many Web sites, including Superior Health Medical Group. Patients of Superior Health can access e-Visit to obtain diagnoses, advice, and prescriptions without ever leaving their homes. Visitors can expect a response within 24 hours, and the approximate cost is $35 versus $63 for an office visit. During the first four months the service was offered, there was no charge for using e-Visit to familiarize consumers with the service and to encourage use.[28]

A recent trend to help companies control the rising labor costs associated with providing customer service and support is the practice of outsourcing service jobs. The federal government does not keep track of how many U.S. jobs have moved to companies overseas, but there are estimates that 300,000 to 400,000 jobs have gone to places like China, Russia, and India in the last three years. Whether U.S. citizens are aware of it or not, they may be talking to an employee in India whenever they call the technical support number for Delta Airlines, American Express, Sprint, CitiBank, IBM, or Hewlett-Packard; even McDonald's is outsourcing drive-through orders.

In the future, most benefits and significant gains will come from restructuring the way work is done within businesses. While e-business can reduce the cost of both customer and business transactions, it can also improve coordination within and across businesses. E-business systems can become the communications backbone linking traditional relationships and storing employee knowledge in management information systems so that co-workers can access this knowledge instead of starting from the ground up. Leading experts suggest that most e-business benefits will come from changes in business practices and the way organizations function. With the crucial role of communication and information in business, the long-term impact of e-business on economic growth could be substantial.[29] Figure 4.1 shows the increase in advertising revenue for the top four Internet portals.

One area where e-business may have promised too much is in manufacturing. Intranets can be important in reducing inventories and eliminating costs in purchasing and other supply-chain activities, as well as in eliminating unnecessary transactions. The Internet can be useful in determining the cost of components and other supplies and detailed information on customers to help customize products. Still the Internet mainly helps in moving information, while most manufacturing involves making things and motivating employees to maintain quality. Manufacturers still need to move truckloads of materials through congested highways and maintain a labor force that can get the job done. E-business can help manage manufacturing operations but is only one component that can provide quality and productivity.

E-Business Models

There are three major e-business models or markets with unique challenges and opportunities that represent areas with shared characteristics and decisions related to organizational structure, job requirements, and financial needs. The models are based on e-business customer profiles and the way the Internet is used to maintain relationships.

busines-to-business Business-to-business (B2B) e-business, sometimes called collaborative commerce, is the use of the Internet for transactions and communications between organizations. B2B activities are the largest and fastest growing area of e-business, with one-fourth of all B2B transactions taking place on the Internet. Typical ways that a company might join the B2B world range from the easiest—going online with an electronic catalog—to the more complex—creating a private trading network, using collaborative design, engaging in supply chain management, and creating a public exchange.[30]

Many B2B companies combine these to be successful. For example, Internet infrastructure maker Cisco Systems receives 68 percent of its orders online, and 70 percent of its service calls are resolved online. Cisco is in the process of linking all of its contract manufacturers and key suppliers into an advanced Web supply-chain management system called the e-HUB. This advanced Internet communication system speeds up the information about demand

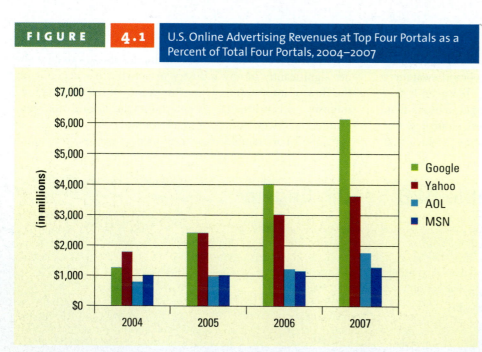

FIGURE 4.1 U.S. Online Advertising Revenues at Top Four Portals as a Percent of Total Four Portals, 2004–2007

Source: eMarketer, Andrew Corn, "Google, Yahoo, AOL, MSN: Big on Internet Advertising," *Seeking Alpha,* http://seekingalpha.com/article/30421-google-yahoo-aol-msn-big-on-internet-advertising (accessed March 10, 2009).

and is distributed to suppliers.[31] Ford Motor Company links 30,000 auto parts suppliers and its 6,900-member dealer network for transactions. Ford expects to save $8.9 billion a year on costs and earn approximately $3 million a year from fees it charges for the use of its supplier network.[32]

The forces unleashed by the Internet are particularly important in B2B relationships, where uncertainties are being reduced by improving the quantity, reliability, and timeliness of information. General Motors, IBM, and Procter & Gamble are learning to consolidate and rationalize their supply chains by using the Internet. Covisint is a leading provider of services that provide linkages between partners, customers, and suppliers. One Web site seeks to give small businesses and inventors a place on the Internet. Eureka! Ranch Technology Ltd.'s USA National Innovations Marketplace is an online registry for inventors and researchers to post their ideas. Small and large businesses can search the ideas and develop partnerships. This allows big business access to outside help, and small businesses and inventors get a chance to land a big partner.[33]

business-to-consumer Business-to-consumer (B2C) e-business means delivering products and services directly to individual consumers through the Internet. The Internet provides an opportunity for mass customization,

e-services include MapQuest's driving direction service and travel services provided by Travelocity.com and Expedia.com. A majority of travelers use the Internet for booking travel. Nearly 80 percent use the Internet for travel information or planning.[35] Web sites such as RetailMeNot.com and CouponCabin.com provide e-services by allowing online shoppers to access coupon codes and locate the best deals on the Internet.[36] The key to the success of e-service sites is creating and nurturing one-to-one relationships with consumers. For example, some e-service travel sites also sell books/maps, apparel, insurance, and bags/luggage.[37]

consumer-to-consumer One market that is sometimes overlooked is the **consumer-to-consumer (C2C)** market, where consumers market goods and services to each other through the Internet. C2C e-business has become very popular thanks to eBay and other online auctions through which consumers can sell goods, often for higher prices than they might receive through newspaper classified ads or garage sales. Some consumers have even turned their passion for trad-

"Services provided in e-business relationships are often referred to as e-services."

meaning that individuals can communicate electronically over the Internet and receive responses that satisfy their individual needs. If products and communication can be customized to fit the individual, long-term relationships can be nurtured. For example, after a consumer makes a purchase at Amazon.com, the site provides recommendations for books, music, DVD, and toys as well as electronics and software on future site visits by that consumer. Dell Computer is a leading B2C e-business that not only custom-builds computers for consumers but also provides customer service online.

U.S. e-tailers generated more than $136 billion in sales in 2007. Experts believe the escalation of online retail sales will come primarily from first-time Internet buyers and that the online buying population will continue to grow to include one-half the adult population by 2008.[34]

Services provided in e-business relationships are often referred to as e-services. E-services are efforts to enhance the value of products through an experience that is created for the consumer. While traditional retailers provide many services, e-business companies have discovered that the unique characteristics of the Internet provide additional opportunities for enhancing the value to the consumer. Some examples of

ing online into successful businesses. For example, a collector of vintage guitars might find items in local markets, such as pawnshops or flea markets, and then sell them for a higher price on eBay. Others use Zshops at Amazon.com for selling used items. The growing C2C market may threaten some traditional businesses if consumers find it more efficient to sell their books, CDs, and other used items through online auctions or other C2C venues.[38]

Customer Relationship Management (CRM)[39]

One characteristic of companies engaged in e-business is a renewed focus on building customer loyalty and retaining customers. **Customer relationship management (CRM)** focuses on using information about customers to create strategies that develop and sustain desirable long-term customer relationships. This focus is possible because today's technology helps companies target customers more precisely and accurately than ever before. CRM technology allows businesses to identify specific customers, establish interactive dialogs with them to learn about their needs, and combine this information with their purchase histories to customize products to meet those needs. Procter & Gamble, for example, encourages Oil of Olay customers to join their Club Olay. Members receive special offers, free samples, and skin type/product pairings. In addition, Procter & Gamble is able to collect information on products registrants use as well as reactions to P&G products.[40]

Advances in technology and data collection techniques now permit firms to profile customers in real time. The goal is to assess

Sales automation software can link a firm's sales force to applications that facilitate selling and providing service to customers. Often these applications enable customers to assist themselves instead of using traditional sales and service organizations. Salesforce.com provides sales force automation for clients such as Accenture, Cisco, Deloitte, and Intel. Systems such as Salesforce make tracking and forecasting sales more efficient and effective.[42] In addition, CRM systems can provide sales managers with information that helps provide the best product solution for customers and thus maximize service. Dell Computer, for example, employs CRM data to identify those customers with the greatest needs for computer hardware and

> ## "Companies are increasingly automating and managing customer relationships through technology."

the worth of individual customers and thus estimate their lifetime value (LTV) to the firm. Some customers—those who require considerable coddling or who return products frequently—may simply be too expensive to retain given the low level of profits they generate. Companies can discourage these unprofitable customers by requiring them to pay higher fees for additional services. For example, many banks and brokerages charge sizable maintenance fees on small accounts. Such practices allow firms to focus their resources on developing and managing long-term relationships with more profitable customers.[41]

CRM focuses on building satisfying relationships with customers by gathering useful data at all customer-contact points—telephone, fax, online, and personal—and analyzing those data to better understand customers' needs and desires. Companies are increasingly automating and managing customer relationships through technology. Indeed, one fast-growing area of CRM is customer-support and call-center software, which helps companies capture information about all interactions with customers and provides a profile of the most important aspects of the customer experience on the Web and on the phone. Customer-support and call-center software can focus on those aspects of customer interaction that are most relevant to performance, such as how long customers have to wait on the phone to ask a question of a service representative or how long they must wait to receive a response from an online request. This technology can also help marketers determine whether call-center personnel are missing opportunities to promote additional products or to provide better service. For example, after buying a new Saab automobile, the customer is supposed to meet a service mechanic who can answer any technical questions about the new car during the first service visit. Saab follows up this visit with a telephone survey to determine whether the new car buyer met the Saab mechanic and to learn about the buyer's experience with the first service call.

then provides these select customers with additional value in the form of free, secure, customized Web sites. These "premier pages" allow customers—typically large companies—to check their order status, arrange deliveries, and troubleshoot problems. Although Dell collects considerable data about its customers from its online sales transactions, the company avoids selling customer lists to outside vendors.[43]

 LO5

Identify the legal and social issues of information technology and e-business.

LEGAL AND SOCIAL ISSUES

The extraordinary growth of information technology, the Internet, and e-business has generated many legal and social issues for consumers and businesses. These issues include privacy concerns, identity theft, and protection of intellectual property and copyrights. Each of these is discussed in this section, as well as steps taken by individuals, companies, and the government to address the issues.

Privacy

Businesses have long tracked consumers' shopping habits with little controversy. However, observing the contents of a consumer's shopping cart or the process a consumer goes through when choosing a box of cereal generally does not result in specific, personally identifying data. Although consumers' use of credit cards, shopping cards, and coupons involves giving up a certain degree of anonymity in the traditional shopping process, consumers can still choose to remain anonymous by paying cash.

Shopping on the Internet, however, allows businesses to track consumers on a far more personal level, from their online purchases to the Web sites they favor.[44] Current technology has made it possible to amass vast quantities of personal information, often without consumers' knowledge, and allows for the collection, sharing, and selling of this information to interested third parties. Privacy has, therefore, become one of Web users' biggest concerns.

How is personal information collected on the Web? Many sites follow users' online "tracks" by storing a "cookie," or identifying string of text, on their computers. Cookies permit Web site operators to track how often a user visits the site, what he or she looks at while there, and in what sequence. Cookies allow Web site visitors to customize services, such as virtual shopping carts, as well as the particular content they see when they

Fashion designers for Zara, the Spain-based fashion retailer, collect purchase information and research customer trends to determine what their customers will want to wear in the next few weeks. They share this information with other departments to forecast sales and coordinate deliveries.

> ## The extraordinary growth of information technology, the Internet, and e-business has generated many legal and social issues for consumers and businesses.

log on to a Web page, but the potential for misuse has left many consumers uncomfortable with this technology.

Some measure of protection of personal privacy is provided by the U.S. Constitution, as well as Supreme Court rulings and federal laws (see Table 4.2). Some of these laws relate specifically to Internet privacy, while others protect privacy both on and off the Internet. The U.S. Federal Trade Commission (FTC) also regulates and enforces privacy standards and monitors Web sites to ensure compliance.

Businesses are beginning to recognize that the only way to circumvent further government regulation with respect to privacy is to develop systems and policies to protect consumers' interests. Several nonprofit organizations have also stepped in to help companies develop privacy policies. Among the best known of these are TRUSTe and the Better Business Bureau Online. TRUSTe is a nonprofit organization devoted to promoting global trust in Internet technology. Companies that agree to abide by TRUSTe's privacy standards may display a "trustmark" on their Web sites. Almost 2,000 Web sites display the trustmark seal of approval from TRUSTe.[45] The BBBOnLine program provides verification, monitoring and review, consumer dispute resolution, a compliance seal, enforcement mechanisms, and an educational component. It is managed by the Council of Better Business Bureaus, an organization with considerable experience in conducting self-regulation and dispute-resolution programs, and it employs guidelines and requirements outlined by the Federal Trade Commission and the U.S. Department of Commerce.[46]

Spam

Spam, or unsolicited commercial e-mail (UCE), has become a major source of discontent with the Internet. Many Internet users believe spam violates their privacy and steals their resources. Many companies despise spam because it costs them $50 billion

"SOME MEASURE OF PROTECTION OF PERSONAL PRIVACY IS PROVIDED BY THE U.S. CONSTITUTION, AS WELL AS SUPREME COURT RULINGS AND FEDERAL LAWS."

a year in lost productivity, new equipment, antispam filters, and manpower. By some estimates, spam accounts for 94 percent of all e-mail. However, it is not just the rising volume of spam that is a problem, but also the size of the spam messages. To defeat content filters, spammers are increasingly using images, which means that unsolicited bulk e-mail is getting bulkier.[47] Spam has been likened to receiving a direct-mail promotional piece with postage due. Some angry recipients of spam have even organized boycotts against companies that advertise in this manner. Other recipients, however, appreciate the opportunity to learn about new products. Table 4.3 shows how spam volume has changed in personal and corporate e-mail accounts.

Most commercial online services and Internet service providers offer their subscribers the option to filter out e-mail from certain Internet addresses that generate a large volume of spam. Google, for instance, employs "spam-fighting scientists" to decrease the amount of spam received in Gmail accounts and has successfully diverted 99 percent of spam from Gmail inboxes.[48] Businesses are installing software to filter out spam from outside their networks. Some companies have filed suit against spammers under the Controlling the Assault of Non-Solicited Pornography and Marketing (CAN-SPAM) Law, which went into effect in 2004 and bans fraudulent or deceptive unsolicited commercial e-mail and requires senders to provide information on how

TABLE 4.2 Privacy Laws

Act (Date Enacted)	Purpose
Privacy Act (1974)	Requires federal agencies to adopt minimum standards for collecting and processing personal information; limits the disclosure of such records to other public or private parties; requires agencies to make records on individuals available to them on request, subject to certain conditions.
Right to Financial Privacy Act (1978)	Protects the rights of financial-institution customers to keep their financial records private and free from unjust government investigation.
Computer Security Act (1987)	Brought greater confidentiality and integrity to the regulation of information in the public realm by assigning responsibility for standardization of communication protocols, data structures, and interfaces in telecommunications and computer systems to the National Institute of Standards and Technology (NIST), which also announces security and privacy guidelines for federal computer systems.
Computer Matching and Privacy Protection Act (1988)	Amended the Privacy Act by adding provisions regulating the use of computer matching, the computerized comparison of individual information for purposes of determining eligibility for federal benefits programs.
Video Privacy Protection Act (1988)	Specifies the circumstances under which a business that rents or sells videos can disclose personally identifiable information about a consumer or reveal an individual's video rental or sales records.
Telephone Consumer Protection Act (1991)	Regulates the activities of telemarketers by limiting the hours during which they can solicit residential subscribers, outlawing the use of artificial or prerecorded voice messages to residences without prior consent, prohibiting unsolicited advertisements by telephone facsimile machines, and requiring telemarketers to maintain a "do not call list" of any consumers who request not to receive further solicitation.
Driver Privacy Protection Act (1993)	Restricts the circumstances under which state departments of motor vehicles may disclose personal information about any individual obtained by the department in connection with a motor vehicle record.
Fair Credit Reporting Act (amended in 1997)	Promotes accuracy, fairness, and privacy of information in the files of consumer reporting agencies (e.g., credit bureaus); grants consumers the right to see their personal credit reports, to find out who has requested access to their reports, to dispute any inaccurate information with the consumer reporting agency, and to have inaccurate information corrected or deleted.
Children's Online Privacy Protection Act (2000)	Regulates the online collection of personally identifiable information (name, address, e-mail address, hobbies, interests, or information collected through cookies) from children under age 13 by specifying what a Web site operator must include in a privacy policy, when and how to seek consent from a parent, and what responsibilities an operator has to protect children's privacy and safety online.
Do Not Call Implementation Act (2003)	Directs the FCC and FTC to coordinate so that their rules are consistent regarding telemarketing call practices, including the Do Not Call Registry and other lists, as well as call abandonment.
CAN-SPAM Act (2004)	Bans unsolicited commercial e-mail and requires special labeling and procedures to opt out to prevent future e-mails.

TABLE 4.3   How Spam Volume Has Changed

How Spam Volume Changed?	Users (%)
Getting more spam in personal e-mail account	37
Getting less spam in personal e-mail account	10
Have not noticed a change	51
Getting more spam in work e-mail account	29
Getting less spam in work e-mail account	8
Have not noticed a change	55

Source: Enid Burnes, "Computer Users More Savvy About E-mail Spam," *ClickZ Stats*, May 25, 2007, www.clickz.com/3625976 (accessed March 10, 2009).

recipients can opt out of receiving additional messages. However, spammers appear to be ignoring the law and finding creative ways to get around spam filters.[49] Although North America is believed to be the source of 80 percent of spam, the European Union ordered eight member nations to enact antispam and privacy-protection legislation. The EU already has strict regulations concerning electronic communications and bans all unsolicited commercial e-mail, but not all member nations have ratified the regulations.[50] Figure 4.2 shows the volume of spam by country.

Identity Theft

Another area of growing concern is identity theft, which occurs when criminals obtain personal information that allows them to impersonate someone else in order to use a person's credit to obtain financial accounts and make purchases. The Federal Trade Commission reported 258,427 consumer complaints about identity theft in 2007, up from 86,212 in 2001. The most common complaints related to credit-card fraud, as well as utility fraud, bank fraud, employment-related fraud, government document fraud, and loan fraud.[51] Because of the Internet's relative anonymity and speed, it fosters legal and illegal access to databases containing Social Security numbers, drivers' license numbers, dates of birth, mothers' maiden names, and other information that can be used to establish a credit card or bank account in another person's name in order to make transactions. One growing scam used to initiate identity theft fraud is the practice of *phishing*, whereby con artists counterfeit a genuine well-known Web site and send out e-mails directing victims to the fake Web site, where they find instructions to reveal sensitive information such as credit card numbers. Phishing scams have faked Web sites for PayPal, AOL, and the Federal Deposit Insurance Corporation.[52]

> "Another area of growing concern is identity theft, which occurs when criminals obtain personal information that allows them to impersonate someone else in order to use a person's credit to obtain financial accounts and make purchases."

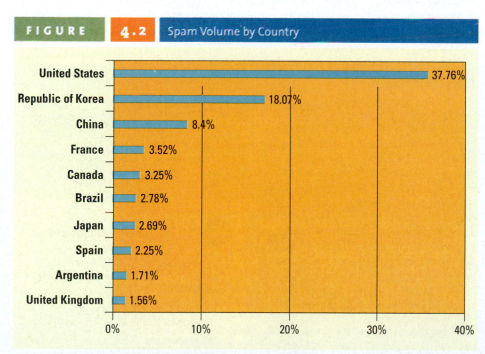

FIGURE 4.2   Spam Volume by Country

- United States — 37.76%
- Republic of Korea — 18.07%
- China — 8.4%
- France — 3.52%
- Canada — 3.25%
- Brazil — 2.78%
- Japan — 2.69%
- Spain — 2.25%
- Argentina — 1.71%
- United Kingdom — 1.56%

Source: "Messaging Security Resources: Percentage of Total Spam Volumes by Country," *Secure Computing* (n.d.), www.ciphertrust.com/resources/statistics/spam_sources.php (accessed March 10, 2009).

Typically, it takes 14 months before a victim discovers identity theft, and in 45 percent of the cases, it took nearly two years to resolve the theft.[53] The Javelin Strategy and Research 2007 Identity Fraud Survey Report indicated that 8.4 million U.S. adults were a victim of identity theft in 2007, totaling $49.3 billion in fraud.[54] To deter identity theft, the National Fraud Center wants financial institutions to implement new technologies, such as digital certificates, digital signatures, and biometrics—the use of fingerprinting or retina scanning.[55]

Intellectual Property and Copyrights

In addition to protecting personal privacy, Internet users and others are concerned about protecting their rights to property they may create, including songs, movies, books, and software. Such intellectual property consists of the ideas and creative materials developed to solve problems, carry out applications, and educate and entertain others. Intellectual property is generally protected via patents and copyrights. The American Society for Industrial Security estimates that intellectual property and proprietary information losses in the United States total tens of billions of dollars per year.[56] This issue has become a global concern because of disparities in enforcement of laws throughout the world. In fact, the Business Software Alliance estimates that global losses from software piracy amount to $48 billion a year, including movies, music, and software downloaded from the Internet.[57]

U.S. copyright laws protect original works in text form, pictures, movies, computer software, musical multimedia, and audiovisual work. Owners of copyrights have the right to reproduce, derive from, distribute and publicly display, and perform the copyrighted works. Copyright infringement is the unauthorized execution of the rights reserved by a copyright holder. Congress passed the Digital Millennium Copyright Act (DMCA) in 1998 to protect copyrighted materials on the Internet and limit the liability of online service providers.

Taxing the Internet?

An increasingly controversial issue in e-business is whether states should be able to levy a sales tax on Internet sales. The issue of collecting taxes on online purchases had been subject to a moratorium that went into effect in 2001. However, many states—facing huge budget deficits—have been lobbying for the right to charge a sales tax on Internet sales originating within their states. In 2005, the Sales Tax Simplification Agreement passed with the support of 18 states. The purpose of the agreement is to simplify the nation's varying state tax laws. Under this system, it is expected that companies that are not required by law to remit sales tax on Internet sales may voluntarily collect taxes.[58]

The Dynamic Nature of Information Technology and E-Business

As we have pointed out in this chapter, information technology and e-business are having a major effect on the business world and thus your future career. Future leaders of businesses will need more than just a technical understanding of information technology; they will need a strategic understanding of how information technology and e-business can help make business more efficient and productive. Companies that depend on information technology as their core focus provide examples of how savvy managers can adapt to using our knowledge in this area. Companies such as UPS have found that information systems make their "bricks, mortar, and trucks" world come alive to provide service to customers. Charles Schwab has made stock trading and obtaining securities information more efficient while providing significant savings to customers. Dell Computer and Cisco have found it possible to sell over half their products online. Many medium-size and large companies are changing

Second Life: When One Isn't Enough!

Second Life allows people to live alternative lives in a virtual world. The three-dimensional world is constructed and owned by those "living" there. The people inhabiting Second Life interact with each other, purchase land, build houses, and run businesses. They can buy, sell, and trade products with Linden dollars, which have real-world value, and exchange 270 Linden dollars for one U.S. dollar. Owed by Linden Labs, Second Life went public in 2003 and is populated by almost 13 million residents, who create avatars to represent themselves within the virtual world. Residents can fly, walk underwater, and make their avatars look like humans, animals, and more.

Recently, corporate marketers have begun to use Second Life to test products and entice customers. This has caused concern among Second Life residents, many of whom run the profitable businesses that are part of the virtual world. But Linden Labs is not concerned, claiming that businesses in Second Life must learn to operate under rules different from those used in the real world.

Despite the objections from residents, corporations are eager to try out Second Life. Some, like Toyota, have found Second Life to be productive. IBM uses Second Life to conduct "in-world" meetings and training and to maintain a 24-hour business center populated by avatars. Recently, CNN established a news center in Second Life, allowing residents to gather information, report on what is happening in Second Life, and offer journalistic training from the likes of Larry King.

Although Second Life has experienced some problems as the virtual world meets the real world, many argue that the entire Web is headed in the direction of Second Life. Time will tell whether Second Life's population and corporate participation will continue to grow.[59] ❖

Q: Discussion Questions

1. Why do you think that Second Life has become so popular?

2. Why do some people view Second Life as not a game but as a real-life experience?

3. What are some of the opportunities for companies to promote their products on Second Life?

SO YOU WANT A JOB IN INFORMATION TECHNOLOGY

The business world is increasingly dependent on information technologies to conduct daily business activities. It is becoming more and more important to pair your IT skills with appropriate business knowledge. A wide variety of jobs in information technology (IT) are available, from technical support specialists and network administrators to Internet technology strategists and chief information officers. Many types of firms employ IT professionals, including large corporations and technology service providers as well as smaller businesses and even nonprofit organizations.

Employers have a higher demand for certain skills, such as network security, software development, and programming in Java and XML. Certain industries present a more dynamic market for IT professionals, including entertainment, health care, biotechnology, food and beverages and pharmaceuticals.

Offshoring remains an issue in searching for many types of IT jobs. Jobs such as technical or customer support specialists are frequently outsourced. Even so, hiring managers in IT expect jobs to be difficult to fill due to a lack of skilled workers. For people with the right combination of IT skills and business understanding, this field is still a vibrant source of jobs. IT job titles in growing demand include project manager, business analyst, program manager, and security analyst. Executive-level titles such as chief technology officer and chief information officer are becoming more common in Corporate America. Salaries for IT jobs range widely, depending on the type and level of job. Technical support specialists earn around $44,000, information security officers make about $80,000, and chief information officers often earn salaries around $125,000; a help desk support specialist makes about $45,000.

E-business requires not only IT skills, but also knowledge about all the functional areas of business. E-business uses the Internet to carry out marketing, finance, management, and operations activities. These activities include communicating and creating relationships with customers, suppliers, and the public. Amazon.com is the world's number one retailer, but most other retailers have an online element to their business. Customer relationship management is based on information systems but also requires marketing knowledge to determine how to target and satisfy customers.

If you are interested in an IT job, you need to be flexible, adapt, and keep yourself up to date on current and expected changes in information technology. Preparing yourself to create and manage databases, make and distribute podcasts, set up Web sites, and manage information systems can position you for a job in almost an organization of almost any size. Businesses, nonprofits, and government need IT assistance, and once you have developed the right skill set and knowledge, there are many different types of positions available.

the way they do business in response to the availability of new technologies that facilitate business in a changing world. Small businesses, too, can succeed by using information technology as leverage to implement appropriate strategies. In the future, manufacturing, retailing, health care, and even government will continue to adapt and use information technologies that will improve business operations. Today, technology presents a tremendous range of potential applications that can improve the efficiency of employees and companies while providing better service to customers. With technology changing on an almost daily basis, it is impossible to predict the long-term effect on the global world of business. ∎

Team Exercise

Develop a new business idea based on e-business. This chapter provides examples of successful e-businesses. Each team should develop an e-business idea and explain why this new business could be successful in reaching customers using the e-business model. Students should indicate which industries are best for developing e-business relationships.

CHECK OUT www.mhhe.com/FerrellM2e

for study materials including Interactive Exercises, Quizzes, iPod downloads, and video.

Options FOR Organizing Business

introduction

The legal form of ownership taken by a business is seldom of great concern to you as a customer. When you eat at a restaurant, you probably don't care whether the restaurant is owned by one person (a sole proprietorship), has two or more owners who share the business (a partnership), or is an entity owned by many stockholders (a corporation); all you want is good food. If you buy a foreign car, you probably don't care whether the company that made it has laws governing its form of organization that are different from those for businesses in the United States. You are buying the car because it is well made, fits your price range, or appeals to your sense of style. Nonetheless, a business's legal form of ownership affects how it operates, how much tax it pays, and how much control its owners have.

This chapter examines three primary forms of business ownership—sole proprietorship, partnership, and corporation—and weighs the advantages and disadvantages of each. These forms are the most often used whether the business is a traditional "bricks and mortar" company, an online-only one, or a combination of both. We also take a look at S corporations, limited liability companies, and cooperatives and discuss some trends in business ownership.

chapter 5

You may wish to refer to Table 5.1 to compare the various forms of business ownership mentioned in the chapter.

● ● **LO1**

Define and examine the advantages and disadvantages of the sole proprietorship form of organization.

SOLE PROPRIETORSHIPS

Sole proprietorships, businesses owned and operated by one individual, are the most common form of business organization in the United States. Common examples include many restaurants, barbershops, flower shops, dog kennels, and independent grocery stores. In 1962, Gordon Segal and his wife, Carole, opened a flatware and china store in Chicago with a $17,000 loan. They never could have guessed that the store would become Crate and Barrel and would eventually operate in over 165 locations. Segal ran the company until 2008, when he stepped down as CEO at the age 69. Crate and Barrel is an unusual example of a proprietorship growing very large.[1] Indeed, many sole proprietors focus on services—small retail stores, financial counseling, appliance repair, child care, and the like—rather than on the manufacture of goods, which often requires large amounts of money not available to small businesses.

Sole proprietorships are typically small businesses employing fewer than 50 people. (We'll look at small businesses in greater detail in Chapter 6.) There are 15 to 20 million sole proprietorships in the United

● ● **Common examples include many restaurants, barbershops, flower shops, dog kennels, and independent grocery stores.**

States, constituting more than 80 percent of all U.S. businesses. It is interesting to note that men are twice as likely as women to start their own business (see Figure 5.1).[2]

Advantages of Sole Proprietorships

Sole proprietorships are generally managed by their owners. Because of this simple management structure, the owner/manager can make decisions quickly. This is just one of many advantages of the sole proprietorship form of business.

ease and cost of formation Forming a sole proprietorship is relatively easy and inexpensive. In some states, creating a sole proprietorship involves merely announcing the new business in the local newspaper. Other proprietorships, such as barbershops and restaurants, may require state and local licenses and permits because of the nature of the business. The cost of these permits may run from $25 to $100. No lawyer is needed to create such enterprises, and the owner can usually take care of the required paperwork.

Of course, an entrepreneur starting a new sole proprietorship must find a suitable site from which to operate the business. Some sole proprietors look no farther than their garage or a spare bedroom that they can convert into a workshop or office. Among the more famous businesses that sprang to life in their founders' homes are Google, Walt Disney, Dell, eBay, Hewlett-Packard, Apple Computer, and Mattel.[3] Computers, personal copiers, fax machines, and other high-tech gadgets have been a boon for home-based businesses, permitting them to interact quickly with customers, suppliers, and others. Many independent salespersons and contractors can perform their work using a notebook computer as they travel. E-mail and cell phones have made it possible for many proprietorships to develop in the

TABLE 5.1 Various Forms of Business Ownership

Structure	Ownership	Taxation	Liability	Use
Sole Proprietorship	1 owner	Individual income taxed	Unlimited	Individual starting a business and easiest way to conduct business
Partnership	2 or more owners	Individual owners' income taxed	Somewhat limited	Easy way for two individuals to conduct business
Corporation	Any number of shareholders	Corporate and shareholder taxed	Limited	A legal entity with shareholders or stakeholders
S Corporation	Up to 75 shareholders	Taxed as a partnership	Limited	A legal entity with tax advantages for restricted number of shareholders
Limited Liability Company	Unlimited number of shareholders	Taxed as a partnership	Limited	Avoid personal lawsuits

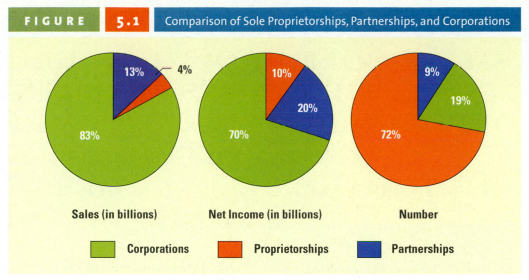

Source: U.S. Bureau the Census, *Statistical Abstract of the U.S. 2009,* www.census.gov/compendia/statab/cats/business_
enterprise/sole_proprietorships_partnerships_corporations.html (accessed March 10, 2009).

> ## Sole proprietorships have the most freedom from government regulation.

services area. Internet connections also allow small businesses to establish Web sites to promote their products and even to make low-cost long-distance phone calls with voice over Internet protocol (VOIP) technology.

secrecy
Sole proprietorships make possible the greatest degree of secrecy. The proprietor, unlike the owners of a partnership or corporation, does not have to discuss publicly his or her operating plans, minimizing the possibility that competitors can obtain trade secrets. Financial reports need not be disclosed, as do the financial reports of publicly owned corporations.

distribution and use of profits
All profits from a sole proprietorship belong exclusively to the owner. He or she does not have to share them with any partners or stockholders. The owner decides how to use the profits—for expansion of the business, for salary increases, or for travel to purchase additional inventory or find new customers.

flexibility and control of the business
The sole proprietor has complete control over the business and can make decisions on the spot without anyone else's approval. This control allows the owner to respond quickly to competitive business conditions or to changes in the economy.

government regulation
Sole proprietorships have the most freedom from government regulation. Many government regulations—federal, state, and local—apply only to businesses that have a certain number of employees, and securities laws apply only to corporations that issue stock. Nonetheless, sole proprietors must ensure that they follow all laws that do apply to their business.

Customer relationships are important to the success of sole proprietorships.

> ## "IT IS USUALLY DIFFICULT FOR A SMALL SOLE PROPRIETORSHIP TO MATCH THE WAGES AND BENEFITS OFFERED BY A LARGE COMPETING CORPORATION BECAUSE THE PROPRIETORSHIP'S LEVEL OF PROFITS MAY NOT BE AS HIGH."

taxation Profits from the business are considered personal income to the sole proprietor and are taxed at individual tax rates. The owner pays one income tax. Another tax benefit is that a sole proprietor is allowed to establish a tax-exempt retirement account or a tax-exempt profit-sharing account. Such accounts are exempt from current income tax, but payments taken after retirement are taxed when they are received.

closing the business A sole proprietorship can be dissolved easily. No approval of co-owners or partners is necessary. The only legal condition is that all loans must be paid off.

Disadvantages of Sole Proprietorships

What may be seen as an advantage by one person may turn out to be a disadvantage to another. The goals and talents of the individual owner are the deciding factors. For profitable businesses managed by capable owners, many of the following factors do not cause problems. On the other hand, proprietors starting out with little management experience and little money are likely to encounter many of the disadvantages.

unlimited liability The sole proprietor has unlimited liability in meeting the debts of the business. In other words, if the business cannot pay its creditors, the owner may be forced to use personal, nonbusiness holdings such as a car or a home to pay off the debts. In a few states, however, houses and homesteads cannot be taken by creditors even if the proprietor declares bankruptcy. The more wealth an individual has, the greater is the disadvantage of unlimited liability.

limited sources of funds Among the relatively few sources of money available to the sole proprietorship are a bank, friends, family, the Small Business Administration, and his or her own funds. The owner's personal financial condition determines his or her credit standing. Additionally, sole proprietorships may have to pay higher interest rates on funds borrowed from banks than do large corporations because they

E-Bikes Offer Exercise and Environmental Consciousness

We have heard of electric cars, but electric bikes? The bicycle industry is finding new ways to be environmentally friendly with the introduction of bikes that allow riders to travel without releasing carbon emissions or even breaking a sweat. Electric bikes (e-bikes) are equipped with a motor and battery. With each pedal stroke, the motor provides additional power, allowing riders to pedal without expending as much energy as they do with conventional bicycles. Typical e-bikes have a maximum speed of 25 mph and cost from $500 to $3,000.

E-bikes are more common in bicycle cultures like Asia and Europe, but they are also breaking into America. Americans bought 170,000 e-bikes in 2008 and around 200,000 in 2009, and sales are expected to continue to increase. Best Buy even introduced e-bikes in some of its stores. Schwinn has come out with the motto "Save the world without killing your knees" to advertise its line of e-bikes, playing up the e-bike's environmental friendliness and ease of use. Schwinn offers the high-end Tailwind, with batteries that charge in under 30 minutes.

Other companies are focusing on e-bikes specifically. One such company is Ultra Motor Company Limited, a private corporation and developer of light electric vehicles. Its product, the A2B Metro, can go for 20 miles on a charge. This 100 percent electric vehicle resembles a mix of a scooter and a bicycle. Unlike motorcycles, this e-bike's motor is quiet, allowing for peaceful commutes. The e-bike could very well be the answer urban commuters are looking for. Its zero carbon emissions make it a good deal for those who care about the environment, those who have a hard time finding parking, and those who simply want to get more exercise.[4] ❖

 Discussion Questions

1. Ultra Motor Company Limited is a private corporation. What are the advantages of being private and not being traded on a stock exchange?

2. Schwinn is a division of a public corporation and publicly traded company, Dorel Industries. What advantages are there in being part of a public corporation?

3. What could be a disadvantage of operating an electric bike firm as a sole proprietorship?

are considered greater risks. Often the only way a sole proprietor can borrow for business purposes is to pledge a car, a house, other real estate, or other personal assets to guarantee the loan. And if the business fails, the owner may lose the personal assets as well as the business. Publicly owned corporations, in contrast, not only can obtain funds from commercial banks but can sell stocks and bonds to the public to raise money. If a public company goes out of business, the owners do not lose personal assets.

limited skills

The sole proprietor must be able to perform many functions and possess skills in diverse fields such as management, marketing, finance, accounting, bookkeeping, and personnel. Business owners can rely on specialized professions for advice and services, such as accountants and attorneys. Musicians, for example, can turn to agents for assistance in navigating through the complex maze of the recording business. One startup firm specializing in this type of assistance for online musicians and bands is the Digital Artists Agency, which researches, markets, and cultivates online music talent in exchange for a commission on their online sales of music, tickets, and merchandise.[5] In the end, however, it is up to the business owner to make the final decision in all areas of the business.

lack of continuity

The life expectancy of a sole proprietorship is directly related to that of the owner and his or her ability to work. The serious illness of the owner could result in failure if competent help cannot be found.

It is difficult to arrange for the sale of a proprietorship and at the same time assure customers that the business will continue to meet their needs. For instance, how does one sell a veterinary practice? A veterinarian's major asset is patients. If the vet dies suddenly, the equipment can be sold but the patients will not necessarily remain loyal to the office. On the other hand, a veterinarian who wants to retire could take in a younger partner and sell the practice to the partner over time. And one advantage to the partnership is that not all the patients are likely to look for a new vet.

lack of qualified employees

It is usually difficult for a small sole proprietorship to match the wages and benefits offered by a large competing corporation because the proprietorship's level of profits may not be as high. In addition, there is little room for advancement within a sole proprietorship, so the owner may have difficulty attracting and retaining qualified employees. On the other hand, the trend of large corporations to downsize and outsource tasks has created opportunities for small business to acquire well-trained employees.

taxation

Although we listed taxation as an advantage for sole proprietorships, it can also be a disadvantage, depending on the proprietor's income. Under current tax rates, sole proprietors pay a higher marginal tax rate than do small corporations

on income of less than $75,000. The tax effect often determines whether a sole proprietor chooses to incorporate his or her business.

 L02

Identify two types of partnership, and evaluate the advantages and disadvantages of the partnership form of organization.

PARTNERSHIPS

One way to minimize the disadvantages of a sole proprietorship and maximize its advantages is to have more than one owner. Most states have a model law governing partnerships based on the Uniform Partnership Act. This law defines a **partnership** as "an association of two or more persons who carry on as co-owners of a business for profit." Partnerships are the least used form of business (see Figure 5.1). Moreover, partnerships account for only 10 percent of sales and 19 percent of income. They are typically larger than sole proprietorships but smaller than corporations.

Types of Partnership

There are two basic types of partnership: general partnership and limited partnership. A **general partnership** involves a complete sharing in the management of a business. In a general partnership, each partner has unlimited liability for the debts of the business. For example, Cirque du Soleil grew from a group of Quebec street performers, who acted as partners, into a half-billion-dollar global company.[6] Professionals such as lawyers, accountants, and architects often join together in general partnerships.

A **limited partnership** has at least one general partner, who assumes unlimited liability, and at least one limited partner, whose liability is limited to his or her investment in the business. Limited partnerships exist for risky investment projects where the chance of loss is great. The general partners accept the risk of loss; the limited partners' losses are limited to their initial investment. Limited partners do not participate in the management of the business but share in the profits in accordance with the terms of a partnership agreement. Usually the general partner receives a larger share of the profits after the limited partners have received their initial investment back. Popular examples are oil-drilling partnerships and real estate partnerships.

Friends since junior high, Ben Cohen and Jerry Greenfield began Ben & Jerry's Homemade Ice Cream as a partnership in 1978. The pair took a correspondence course in ice-cream making before founding the company in a renovated Vermont gas station.

Articles of Partnership

Articles of partnership are legal documents that set forth the basic agreement between partners. Most states require articles of partnership, but even if they are not required, it makes good sense for partners to draw them up. Articles of partnership usually list the money or assets that each partner has contributed (called *partnership capital*), state each partner's individual management role or duty, specify how the profits and losses of the partnership will be divided among the partners, and describe how a partner may leave the partnership as well as any other restrictions that might apply to the agreement. Table 5.2 lists some of the issues and provisions that should be included in articles of partnership.

Advantages of Partnerships

Law firms, accounting firms, and investment firms with several hundred partners have partnership agreements that are quite complicated in comparison with the partnership agreement

among two or three people owning a computer repair shop. The advantages must be compared with those offered by other forms of business organization, and not all apply to every partnership.

ease of organization Starting a partnership requires little more than drawing up articles of partnership. No legal charters have to be granted, but the name of the business should be registered with the state.

availability of capital and credit When a business has several partners, it has the benefit of a combination of talents and skills and pooled financial resources. Partnerships tend to be larger than sole proprietorships and therefore have greater earning power and better credit ratings. Because many limited partnerships have been formed for tax purposes rather than for economic profits, the combined income of all U.S. partnerships is quite low, as shown in Figure 5.1. Nevertheless, the professional partnerships of many lawyers, accountants, and investment banking firms make quite large profits. Goldman Sachs, a large New York investment banking partnership, earns several hundred million dollars in an average year.

combined knowledge and skills Partners in the most successful partnerships acknowledge each other's talents and avoid confusion and conflict by specializing in a particular area of expertise such as marketing, production, accounting, or service. The diversity of skills in a partnership

TABLE 5.2 Issues and Provisions in Articles of Partnership

1. Name, purpose, location
2. Duration of the agreement
3. Authority and responsibility of each partner
4. Character of partners (i.e., general or limited, active or silent)
5. Amount of contribution from each partner
6. Division of profits or losses
7. Salaries of each partner
8. How much each partner is allowed to withdraw
9. Death of partner
10. Sale of partnership interest
11. Arbitration of disputes
12. Required and prohibited actions
13. Absence and disability
14. Restrictive covenants
15. Buying and selling agreements

Source: Adapted from "Partnership Agreement Sample," State of New Jersey, www.state.nj.us/njbusiness/starting/basies/partnership_agreement_sample.shtml (accessed March 10, 2009).

● **ARTICLES OF PARTNER-SHIP** legal documents that set forth the basic agreement between partners

makes it possible for the business to be run by a management team of specialists instead of by a generalist sole proprietor. Service-oriented partnerships in fields such as law, financial planning, and accounting may attract customers because clients may think that the service offered by a diverse team is of higher quality than that provided by one person. Larger law firms, for example, often have individual partners who specialize in certain areas of the law—such as family, bankruptcy, corporate, entertainment, and criminal law.

decision making Small partnerships can react more quickly to changes in the business environment than can large partnerships and corporations. Such fast reactions are possible because the partners are involved in day-to-day operations and can make decisions quickly after consultation. Large partnerships with hundreds of partners in many states are not common. In those that do exist, decision making is likely to be slow.

regulatory controls Like a sole proprietorship, a partnership has fewer regulatory controls affecting its activities than does a corporation. A partnership does not have to file

committed by BP's employees. The partners also accused BP's CEO, Robert Dudley, of acting in BP's interest and not taking into account Russian shareholders' concerns. Because of this dispute, the company is considering selling the Russian-owned THK half of the business to the Russian government-run oil company Gazprom.[7] In such cases, the ultimate solution may be dissolving the partnership. Major disadvantages of partnerships include the following.

unlimited liability In general partnerships, the general partners have unlimited liability for the debts incurred by the business, just as the sole proprietor has unlimited liability for his or her business. Such unlimited liability can be a distinct disadvantage to one partner if his or her personal financial resources are greater than those of the others. A potential partner should check to make sure that all partners have comparable resources to help the business in times of trouble. This disadvantage is eliminated for limited partners, who can lose only their initial investment.

"All partners are responsible for the business actions of all others."

public financial statements with government agencies or send out quarterly financial statements to several thousand owners, as do corporations such as Apple and Ford Motor Co. A partnership does, however, have to abide by all laws relevant to the industry or profession in which it operates as well as state and federal laws relating to hiring and firing, food handling, and so on, just as the sole proprietorship does.

Disadvantages of Partnerships

Partnerships have many advantages compared to sole proprietorships and corporations, but they also have some disadvantages. Limited partners have no voice in the management of the partnership, and they may bear most of the risk of the business while the general partner reaps a larger share of the benefits. There may be a change in the goals and objectives of one partner but not the other, particularly when the partners are multinational organizations. This can cause friction, giving rise to an enterprise that fails to satisfy both parties or even forcing an end to the partnership. Many partnership disputes wind up in court or require outside mediation. For example, in early 2008, Russian partners of the 50/50 oil partnership THK-BP began demanding the ouster of some of BP's upper-level management. The Russians expressed concern over potentially unethical behavior, with accusations ranging from spying to tax evasion,

business responsibility All partners are responsible for the business actions of all others. Partners may have the ability to commit the partnership to a contract without approval of the other partners. A bad decision by one partner may put the other partners' personal resources in jeopardy. Personal problems such as a divorce can eliminate a significant portion of one partner's financial resources and weaken the financial structure of the whole partnership.

life of the partnership A partnership is terminated when a partner dies or withdraws. In a two-person partnership, if one partner withdraws, the firm's liabilities would be paid off and the assets divided between the partners. Obviously, the partner who wishes to continue in the business would be at a serious disadvantage. The business could be disrupted, financing would be reduced, and the management skills of the departing partner would be lost. The remaining partner would have to find another or reorganize the business as a sole proprietorship. In very large partnerships such as those found in law firms and investment banks, the continuation of the partnership may be provided for in the articles of partnership. The provision may simply state the terms for a new partnership agreement among the remaining partners. In such cases, the disadvantage to the other partners is minimal.

Selling a partnership interest has the same effect as the death or withdrawal of a partner. It is difficult to place a value on a partner's share of the partnership. No public value is placed on the partnership, as there is on publicly owned corporations. What is a law firm worth? What is the local hardware store worth? Coming up with a fair value that all partners can agree to is not easy. Selling a partnership interest is easier if the articles of partnership specify a method of valuation. Even if there is not a procedure for selling one partner's interest, the old partnership must still be dissolved and a new one created. In contrast, in the corporate form of business, the departure of owners has little effect on the financial resources of the business, and the loss of managers does not cause long-term changes in the structure of the organization.

distribution of profits Profits earned by the partnership are distributed to the partners in the proportions specified in the articles of partnership. This may be a disadvantage if the division of the profits does not reflect the work each partner puts into the business. You may have encountered this disadvantage while working on a student group project: You may have felt that you did most of the work and that the other students in the group received grades based on your efforts. Even the perception of an unfair profit-sharing agreement may cause tension between the partners, and unhappy partners can have a negative effect on the profitability of the business.

limited sources of funds As with a sole proprietorship, the sources of funds available to a partnership are limited. Because no public value is placed on the business (such as the current trading price of a corporation's stock), potential partners do not know what one partnership share is worth. Moreover, because partnership shares cannot be bought and sold easily in public markets, potential owners may not want to tie up their money in assets that cannot be readily sold on short notice. Accumulating enough funds to operate a national business, especially a business requiring intensive investments in facilities and equipment, can be difficult. Partnerships also may have to pay higher interest rates on funds borrowed from banks than do large corporations because partnerships may be considered greater risks.

Taxation of Partnerships

Partnerships are quasi-taxable organizations. This means that partnerships do not pay taxes when submitting the partnership tax return to the Internal Revenue Service. The tax return simply provides information about the profitability of the organization and the distribution of profits among the partners. Partners must report their share of profits on their individual tax returns and pay taxes at the income tax rate for individuals.

● ● **LO3**

Describe the corporate form of organization, and cite the advantages and disadvantages of corporations.

 Corporations account for 83 percent of all U.S. sales and 70 percent of all income.

CORPORATIONS

When you think of a business, you probably think of a huge corporation such as General Electric, Procter & Gamble, or Sony because most of your consumer dollars go to such corporations. A **corporation** is a legal entity, created by the state, whose assets and liabilities are separate from its owners. As a legal entity, a corporation has many of the rights, duties, and powers of a person, such as the right to receive, own, and transfer property. Corporations can enter into contracts with individuals or with other legal entities, and they can sue and be sued in court.

Corporations account for the majority of all U.S. sales and income. Thus, most of the dollars you spend as a consumer probably go to incorporated businesses (see Figure 5.1). Most corporations are not mega-companies like General Mills or Ford Motor; even small businesses can incorporate. As we shall

Carpinteros Focuses on Quality and Tradition

Keith Gorges and Kurt and Eric Faust bought Taos Furniture of Santa Fe in 2000 for $60,000, giving those investors the company name and the machinery; many of the company's craftsmen remained as well. To distinguish the company from other Southwest furniture companies, and to recover from a business slowdown after 9/11, the partners rebranded the company *Carpinteros*, which means "carpenters" in Spanish. In 2006, sales topped $1 million for the first time.

The company has been successful because of its high quality hand-hewn products and the attention to detail that goes into every piece. The highly trained woodworkers, often local artisans, at Carpinteros use a hand planer to smooth every surface.

Because of the time and care that go into their products, it would be impossible for Gorges and the Fausts to compete with manufactured furniture companies, and therefore they do not. They market to the high-end customer; the fact that the business is a partnership and that try to the craftsmen are local adds to the small-business, boutique feel of the company. Through differentiating their product, and fostering an intimate feel for their company, the partners have been successful in their endeavors.[8] ❖

see later in the chapter, many smaller firms elect to incorporate as "S corporations," which operate under slightly different rules and have greater flexibility than do traditional "C corporations" like General Mills.[9]

Corporations are typically owned by many individuals and organizations who own shares of the business, called **stock** (thus, corporate owners are often called *shareholders* or *stockholders*). Stockholders can buy, sell, give or receive as gifts, or inherit their shares of stock. As owners, the stockholders are entitled to all profits that are left after all the corporation's other obligations have been paid. These profits may be distributed in the form of cash payments called **dividends.** For example, if a corporation earns $100 million after expenses and taxes and decides to pay the owners $40 million in dividends, the stockholders receive 40 percent of the profits in cash dividends. However, not all after-tax profits are paid to stockholders in dividends. In this example, the corporation retained $60 million of profits to finance expansion.

1. Name and address of the corporation.
2. Objectives of the corporation.
3. Classes of stock (common, preferred, voting, nonvoting) and the number of shares for each class of stock to be issued.
4. Expected life of the corporation (corporations are usually created to last forever).
5. Financial capital required at the time of incorporation.
6. Provisions for transferring shares of stock between owners.
7. Provisions for the regulation of internal corporate affairs.
8. Address of the business office registered with the state of incorporation.
9. Names and addresses of the initial board of directors.
10. Names and addresses of the incorporators.

Based on the information in the articles of incorporation, the state issues a **corporate charter** to the company. After securing this charter, the owners hold an organizational

A corporation may be privately or publicly owned.

Creating a Corporation

A corporation is created, or incorporated, under the laws of the state in which it incorporates. The individuals creating the corporation are known as *incorporators.* Each state has a specific procedure, sometimes called *chartering the corporation,* for incorporating a business. Most states require a minimum of three incorporators; thus, many small businesses can be and are incorporated. Another requirement is that the new corporation's name cannot be similar to that of another business. In most states, a corporation's name must end in "company," "corporation," "incorporated," or "limited" to show that the owners have limited liability. (In this text, however, the word *company* means any organization engaged in a commercial enterprise and can refer to a sole proprietorship, a partnership, or a corporation.)

The incorporators must file legal documents generally referred to as *articles of incorporation* with the appropriate state office (often the secretary of state). The articles of incorporation contain basic information about the business. The following 10 items are found in the Model Business Corporation Act, issued by the American Bar Association, which is followed by most states:

meeting at which they establish the corporation's bylaws and elect a board of directors. The bylaws might set up committees of the board of directors and describe the rules and procedures for their operation.

Types of Corporations

If the corporation does business in the state in which it is chartered, it is known as a *domestic corporation.* In other states where the corporation does business, it is known as a *foreign corporation.* If a corporation does business outside the nation in which it incorporated, it is called an *alien corporation.* A corporation may be privately or publicly owned.

A **private corporation** is owned by just one person or a few people who are closely involved in managing the business. These people, often a family, own all the corporation's stock, and no stock is sold to the public. Many corporations are quite large, yet remain private, including Koch, an energy and natural resource business. It is the nation's largest private corporation. By acquiring Georgia-Pacific, Charles Koch turned his family business into the world's largest private corporation. The fifth largest privately held company in the United States is Mars, founded by Forrest Mars, Sr., who spent time in Switzerland learning to

create chocolate confectionaries. Mars recently grew significantly through the acquisition of the Wm. Wrigley Jr. Company. Mars was founded in Tacoma Washington in 1911. The business was successful early on because it paid employees three times the normal wage for the time. The company remains successful to this day, largely because of its established brands, such as M&Ms, and healthy snack lines for kids, like Generation Max.[10] Other well-known privately held companies include Cargill, Publix Supermarkets, Dollar General, and MGM Entertainment.[11] Privately owned corporations are not required to disclose financial information publicly, but they must, of course, pay taxes.

A **public corporation** is one whose stock anyone may buy, sell, or trade. Table 5.3 lists the largest U.S. corporations by revenues. Thousands

The candy maker Mars, which sells its products in more than 100 countries, is privately owned by the Mars family. Forrest Mars, Sr., founded the company after creating the recipe for M&Ms.

TABLE 5.3 The Largest U.S. Corporations, Arranged by Revenues

Rank	Company	Revenues ($ millions)	Profits ($ millions)
1.	Wal-Mart Stores	378,799	12,731
2.	Exxon Mobil	372,824	40,610
3.	Royal Dutch Shell	355,782	31,331
4.	BP	291,438	20,845
5.	Toyota Motor	230,201	15,042
6.	Chevron	210,783	18,688
7.	ING Group	201,516	12,649
8.	Total	187,280	18,042
9.	General Motors	182,347	−38,732
10.	ConocoPhillips	178,558	11,891
11.	Daimler	177,167	5,446
12.	General Electric	176,656	22,208
13.	Ford Motor	172,468	−2,723
14.	Fortis	164,877	5,467
15.	AXA	162,762	7,755
16.	Sinopec	159,260	4,166
17.	Citigroup	159,229	3,617
18.	Volkswagen	149,054	5,639
19.	Dexia Group	147,648	3,467
20.	HSBC Holdings	146,500	19,133

Source: "*Fortune* 500: *Fortune*'s Annual Ranking of America's Largest Corporations," *Fortune,* http://money.cnn.com/magazines/fortune/global500/2008/full_list/ (accessed March 10, 2009).

● **PUBLIC CORPORA-TION** a corporation whose stock anyone may buy, sell, or trade

● **INITIAL PUBLIC OFFER-ING (IPO)** selling a corporation's stock on public markets for the first time

● **QUASI-PUBLIC COR-PORATIONS** corporations owned and operated by the federal, state, or local government

of smaller public corporations in the United States have sales under $10 million. In large public corporations such as AT&T, the stockholders are often far removed from the management of the company. In other public corporations, the managers are often the founders and the major shareholders. Ford Motor Company, for example, was founded by Henry Ford; his great grandson William Clay Ford Jr. is chairman of the board of directors.[12] Publicly owned corporations must disclose financial information to the public under specific laws that regulate the trade of stocks and other securities.

A private corporation that needs more money to expand or take advantage of opportunities may have to obtain financing by "going public" through an **initial public offering (IPO),** that is, becoming a public corporation by selling its

of public disclosure of future activities for competitive reasons. Taking a corporation private is also one technique for avoiding a takeover by another corporation.

Two other types of corporations are quasi-public corporations and nonprofit corporations. **Quasi-public corporations** are owned and operated by the federal, state, or local government. The focus of these corporations is providing a service to citizens, such as mail delivery, rather than earning a profit. Indeed, many quasi-public corporations operate at a loss. Examples of quasi-public corporations include the National Aeronautics and Space Administration (NASA) and the U.S. Postal Service.

> **Privately owned corporations are not required to disclose financial information publicly, but they must, of course, pay taxes.**

stock so that it can be traded in public markets. For example, Intrepid Potash, a mining company headquartered in Denver with mines in New Mexico and Utah, is this country's largest producer of potash, serving nearly 10 percent of the market. Potash is a substance that is used as a fertilizer in crop and plant production. The stock initially sold for $32 per share when the company went public in 2008. The value immediately skyrocketed, with stocks soon selling for more than $51 per share. Although this type of price jump is not common for IPOs, it does occur.[13] Also, privately owned firms are occasionally forced to go public with stock offerings when a major owner dies and the heirs have enormous estate taxes to pay. The tax payment becomes possible only with the proceeds of the sale of stock. This happened to the brewer Adolph Coors Inc. When Adolph Coors died, his business went public and his family sold shares of stock to the public to pay the estate taxes.

On the other hand, public corporations can be "taken private" when one or a few individuals (perhaps the management of the firm) purchase all the firm's stock so that it can no longer be sold publicly. For example, Chrysler was split from Daimler when Cerberus, a private equity investment firm, bought a controlling interest in Chrysler from DaimlerChrysler.[14] Taking a corporation private may be desirable when new owners want to exert more control over the firm or want to avoid the necessity

Google founders Larry Page and Sergey Brin were able to raise a whopping $1.66 billion via an initial public offering of the company's stock in 2004. The Google IPO was one of the largest in stock market history.

Like quasi-public corporations, **nonprofit corporations** focus on providing a service rather than earning a profit, but they are not owned by a government entity. Organizations such as the Children's Television Workshop, the Elks Clubs, misuse of funds. An important duty of the board of directors is to hire corporate officers, such as the president and the chief executive officer (CEO), who are responsible to the directors for the management and daily operations of the

"Taking a corporation private is also one technique for avoiding a takeover by another corporation."

The sharp rise of CEO pay in the United States has called into question how independent firms' board members are, given the fact that many of them are CEOs themselves.

the American Lung Association, the American Red Cross, museums, and private schools provide services without a profit motive. To fund their operations and services, nonprofit organizations solicit donations from individuals and companies and grants from the government and other charitable foundations.

Elements of a Corporation

the board of directors
A **board of directors,** elected by the stockholders to oversee the general operation of the corporation, sets the long-range objectives of the corporation. It is the board's responsibility to ensure that the objectives are achieved on schedule. Board members are legally liable for the mismanagement of the firm or for any

firm. The role and expectations of the board of directors took on greater significance after the accounting scandals of the early 2000s and the passage of the Sarbanes-Oxley Act.[15] As a result, most corporations have restructured how they compensate directors for their time and expertise in serving on a board.

Directors can be employees of the company (*inside directors*) or people unaffiliated with the company (*outside directors*). Inside directors are usually the officers responsible for running the company. Outside directors are often top executives from other companies, lawyers, bankers, even professors. Directors today are increasingly chosen for their expertise, competence, and ability to bring diverse perspectives to strategic discussions. Outside directors are also thought to bring more independence to the monitoring function because they are not bound by past allegiances, friendships, a current role in the company, or some other issue that may create a conflict of interest. Many of the corporate scandals uncovered in recent years might have been prevented if each of the companies' boards of directors had been better qualified, more knowledgeable, and more independent. There is a growing shortage of available and qualified board members. Boards are increasingly telling their own CEOs that they should be focused on serving the company, not serving on outside boards. Because of this, the average CEO sits on less than one outside board. This represents a decline from a decade ago, when the average was two. As many CEOs are turning down outside positions, many companies have taken steps to ensure that boards have experienced directors. Most firms have increased the mandatory retirement age to 72 or older, and 11 percent have raised it to 75 or even older. Minimizing the amount of overlap between directors sitting on different boards helps limit conflicts of interest and provides for independence in decision-making.[16]

"OF ALL THE FORMS OF BUSINESS ORGANIZATION, THE PUBLIC CORPORATION FINDS IT EASIEST TO RAISE MONEY."

stock ownership Corporations issue two types of stock: preferred and common. Owners of **preferred stock** are a special class of owners because although they generally do not have any say in running the company, they have a claim to any profits before any other stockholders do. Other stockholders do not receive any dividends unless the preferred stockholders have been paid. Dividend payments on preferred stock are usually a fixed percentage of the initial issuing price (set by the board of directors). For example, if a share of preferred stock originally cost $100 and the dividend rate was stated at 7.5 percent, the dividend payment will be $7.50 per share per year. Dividends are usually paid quarterly. Most preferred stock carries a cumulative claim to dividends. This means that if the company does not pay preferred-stock dividends in one year because of losses, the dividends accumulate to the next year. Such dividends unpaid from previous years must also be paid to preferred stockholders before other stockholders can receive any dividends.

Although owners of **common stock** do not get such preferential treatment with regard to dividends, they do get some say in the operation of the corporation. Their ownership gives them the right to vote for members of the board of directors and on other important issues. Common stock dividends may vary according to the profitability of the business, and some corporations do not issue dividends at all, but instead plow their profits back into the company to fund expansion.

Common stockholders are the voting owners of a corporation. They are usually entitled to one vote per share of common stock. During an annual stockholders' meeting,

DID YOU KNOW?

The first corporation with a net income of more than $1 billion in one year was General Motors, with a net income in 1955 of $1,189,477,082.[17]

may vote by *proxy,* which is a written authorization by which stockholders assign their voting privilege to someone else, who then votes for his or her choice at the stockholders' meeting. It is a normal practice for management to request proxy statements from shareholders who are not planning to attend the annual meeting. Most owners do not attend annual meetings of the very large companies, such as Westinghouse or Boeing, unless they live in the city where the meeting is held.

Common stockholders have another advantage over preferred shareholders. In most states, when the corporation decides to sell new shares of common stock in the marketplace, common stockholders have the first right, called a *preemptive right,* to purchase new shares of the stock from the corporation. A preemptive right is often included in the articles of incorporation. This right is important because it allows stockholders to purchase new shares to maintain their original positions. For example, if a stockholder owns 10 percent of a corporation that decides to issue new shares, that stockholder has the right to buy enough of the new shares to retain the 10 percent ownership.

Advantages of Corporations

Because a corporation is a separate legal entity, it has some very specific advantages over other forms of ownership. The biggest advantage may be the limited liability of the owners.

limited liability Because the corporation's assets (money and resources) and liabilities (debts and other obligations) are separate from its owners', in most cases

---

"Common stockholders are the voting owners of a corporation."

---

common stockholders elect a board of directors. Because they can choose the board of directors, common stockholders have some say in how the company will operate. Common stockholders

the stockholders are not held responsible for the firm's debts if it fails. Their liability or potential loss is limited to the amount of their original investment. Although a creditor can sue a corporation for not paying its debts, even forcing the corporation into bankruptcy, it cannot make the stockholders pay the corporation's debts out of their personal assets. Occasionally, the owners of a private corporation may pledge personal assets to secure a loan for the corporation; this would be most unusual for a public corporation.

ease of transfer of ownership Stockholders can sell or trade shares of stock to other people without causing the termination of the corporation, and they can do this without the prior approval of other shareholders. The transfer of ownership (unless it is a majority position) does not affect the daily or long-term operations of the corporation.

The shareholders of common stock aren't liable for a firm's debts if it goes bankrupt. However, the value of their shares can be "diluted" if the firm issues additional shares to raise money—or the government buys newly issued shares to take an ownership stake in the firm in order to prop it up.

perpetual life A corporation usually is chartered to last forever unless its articles of incorporation stipulate otherwise. The existence of the corporation is unaffected by the death or withdrawal of any of its stockholders. It survives until the owners sell it or liquidate its assets. However, in some cases, bankruptcy ends a corporation's life. Bankruptcies occur when companies are unable to compete and earn profits. Eventually, uncompetitive businesses must close or seek protection from creditors in bankruptcy court while the business tries to reorganize.

external sources of funds Of all the forms of business organization, the public corporation finds it easiest to raise money. When a corporation needs to raise more money, it can sell more stock shares or issue bonds (corporate "IOUs," which pledge to repay debt), attracting funds from anywhere in the United States and even overseas. The larger a corporation becomes, the more sources of financing are available to it. We take a closer look at some of these in Chapter 16.

expansion potential Because large public corporations can find long-term financing readily, they can easily expand into national and international markets. And as a legal entity, a corporation can enter into contracts without as much difficulty as a partnership.

Disadvantages of Corporations

Corporations have some distinct disadvantages resulting from tax laws and government regulation.

double taxation As a legal entity, the corporation must pay taxes on its income just as you do. When after-tax corporate profits are paid out as dividends to the stockholders, the dividends are taxed a second time as part of the individual owner's income. This process creates double taxation for the stockholders of dividend-paying corporations. Double taxation does not occur with the other forms of business organization.

forming a corporation The formation of a corporation can be costly. A charter must be obtained, and this usually requires the services of an attorney and payment of legal fees. Filing fees ranging from $25 to $150 must be paid to the state that awards the corporate charter, and certain states require that an annual fee be paid to maintain the charter.

disclosure of information Corporations must make information available to their owners, usually through an annual report to shareholders. The annual report contains financial information about the firm's profits, sales, facilities and equipment, and debts, as well as descriptions of the company's operations, products, and plans for the future. Public corporations must also file reports with the Securities and Exchange Commission (SEC), the government regulatory agency that regulates securities such as stocks and bonds. The larger the firm, the more data the SEC requires. Because all reports filed with the SEC are available to the public, competitors can access them. Additionally, complying with securities laws takes time.

employee-owner separation Many employees are not stockholders of the company for which they work. This separation of owners and employees may cause employees to feel that their work benefits only the owners. Employees without an ownership stake do not always see how they fit into the corporate picture and may not understand the importance of profits to the health of the organization. If managers are part owners but other employees are not, management–labor relations take on a different, sometimes difficult, aspect from those in partnerships and sole proprietorships. However, this situation is changing as more corporations establish employee stock ownership plans (ESOPs), which give shares of the company's stock to its employees. Such plans build a partnership between employee and employer and can boost productivity because they motivate employees to work harder so that they can earn dividends from their hard work as well as from their regular wages. In 2009, 14 percent of the 100 best corporates to work for were employee-owned. Employee-owned corporates strive hard to create positive work environments.[18]

OTHER TYPES OF OWNERSHIP

In this section we will take a brief look at joint ventures, S corporations, limited liability companies, and cooperatives—businesses formed for special purposes.

Joint Ventures

A **joint venture** is a partnership established for a specific project or for a limited time. The partners in a joint venture may be individuals or organizations, as in the case of the international joint ventures discussed in Chapter 3. Control of a joint venture may be shared equally, or one partner may control decision making. Joint ventures are especially popular in situations that call for large investments, such as extraction of natural resources and the development of new products. Audi and Volkswagen entered into a joint venture to share a manufacturing plant in the United States. Through this arrangement, Audi hopes to eliminate some of the risk associated with U.S. dollar fluctuations. Audi's hope is that this arrangement will allow the company to sell 200,000 vehicles annually in the United States.[19]

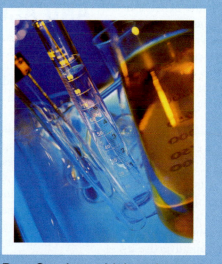

Dow Corning, which makes over 7,000 silicon-based products, began as a joint venture between Corning Glass Works and Dow Chemical in 1943.

S Corporations

An **S corporation** is a form of business ownership that is taxed as though it were a partnership. Net profits or losses of the corporation pass to the owners, thus eliminating double taxation. The benefit of limited liability is retained. Formally known as Subchapter S Corporations, they have become a popular form of business ownership for entrepreneurs and represent almost half of all corporate filings.[20] Accounting Systems, a Fort Collins, Colorado, accounting software firm, elected to incorporate as an S corporation to gain credibility from being incorporated, tax advantages, and limited liability. Advantages of S corporations include the simple method of taxation, the limited liability of shareholders, perpetual life, and the ability to shift income and appreciation to others. Disadvantages include restrictions on the number (75) and types (individuals, estates, and certain trusts) of shareholders and the difficulty of formation and operation.

Limited Liability Companies

A **limited liability company (LLC)** is a form of business ownership that provides limited liability, as in a corporation, but is taxed like a partnership. Although relatively new in the United States, LLCs have existed for many years abroad. Professionals such as lawyers, doctors, and engineers often use the LLC form of ownership. Many consider the LLC a blend of the best characteristics of corporations, partnerships, and sole proprietorships. One of the major reasons for the LLC form of ownership is to protect the members' personal assets in case of lawsuits. LLCs are flexible and simple to run and do not require the members to hold meetings, keep minutes, or make resolutions, all of which are necessary in corporations. For example, Segway, which markets the Segway Human Transporter, is a limited liability company.

> **Companies large and small achieve growth and improve profitability by expanding their operations, often by developing and selling new products or selling current products to new groups of customers in different geographic areas.**

Cooperatives

Another form of organization in business is the **cooperative or co-op,** an organization composed of individuals or small businesses that have banded together to reap the benefits of belonging to a larger organization. Blue Diamond Growers, for example, is a cooperative of California almond growers; Ocean Spray is a cooperative of cranberry farmers. A co-op is set up not to make money as an entity but so that its members can become more profitable or save money. Co-ops are generally expected to operate without profit or to create only enough profit to maintain the co-op organization.

Many cooperatives exist in small farming communities. The co-op stores and markets grain; orders large quantities of fertilizer, seed, and other supplies at discounted prices; and reduces costs and increases efficiency with good management. A co-op can purchase supplies in large quantities and pass the savings on to its members. It also can help distribute the products of its members more efficiently than each could on an individual basis. A cooperative can advertise its members' products and thus generate demand. Ace Hardware, a cooperative of independent hardware store owners, allows its members to share in the savings that result from buying supplies in large quantities; it also provides advertising, which individual members might not be able to afford on their own.

 L04

Define and debate the advantages and disadvantages of mergers, acquisitions, and leveraged buyouts.

TRENDS IN BUSINESS OWNERSHIP: MERGERS AND ACQUISITIONS

Companies large and small achieve growth and improve profitability by expanding their operations, often by developing and selling new products or selling current products to new groups of customers in different geographic areas. Such growth, when carefully planned and controlled, is usually beneficial to the firm and ultimately helps it reach its goal of enhanced profitability. But companies also grow by merging with or purchasing other companies.

A **merger** occurs when two companies (usually corporations) combine to form a new company. An **acquisition** occurs when one company purchases another, generally by buying most of its stock. The acquired company may become a subsidiary of the buyer, or its operations and assets may be merged with those of the buyer. For example, the decision to authorize Whole Foods' acquisition of Wild Oats was carefully analyzed, as was the merger of Sirius and XM Satellite Radio. One of the largest acquisitions of 2008 was the Mars candy company buyout of the Wrigley confectionary company. Mars acquired the popular chewing gum and mints company for $23 billion, creating one of the world's largest confectionary companies and putting pressure on smaller competitors like Cadbury and Hershey.[21] Acquisitions sometimes involve the purchase of a division or some other part of a company rather than the entire company. The late 1990s saw a merger and acquisition frenzy, which is slowing in the 21st century (see Table 5.4).[22]

When firms that make and sell similar products to the same customers merge, it is known as a *horizontal merger,* as when Martin Marietta and Lockheed, both defense contractors, merged to form Martin Lockheed. Horizontal mergers, however, reduce the number of corporations competing within an industry, and for this reason they are usually reviewed carefully by federal regulators before the merger is allowed to proceed.

When companies operating at different but related levels of an industry merge, it is known as a *vertical merger.* In many instances, a vertical merger results when one corporation merges with one of its customers or suppliers. For example, if Burger King were to purchase a large Idaho potato farm—to ensure a ready supply of potatoes for its french fries—a vertical merger would result.

A *conglomerate merger* results when two firms in unrelated industries merge. For example, the purchase of Sterling Drug, a pharmaceutical firm, by Eastman Kodak, best known for its films and cameras, represents a conglomerate merger because the two companies are in different industries.

When a company (or an individual), sometimes called a *corporate raider,* wants to acquire or take over another company, it first offers to buy some or all of the other company's stock at a premium over its current price in a *tender offer.* Most such offers are "friendly," with both groups agreeing to the proposed deal, but some are "hostile," when the second company does not want to be taken over. The Belgian brewing giant InBev recently sought to acquire Anheuser Busch—an offer that was not welcomed by Anheuser. InBev offered Anheuser $46.3 billion in cash to acquire the American lager company, a move that would help the European brewer shore up business in a region where it does not have a strong presence. Anheuser expressed strong opposition to the proposal, going so far as to team up with Mexico's Grupo Modelo and seeking the aid of Warren Buffet to keep it from happening. August Busch IV, CEO of Anheuser, has expressed strong public opposition to the buyout.[23] InBev was successful in acquiring Anheuser Busch for $52 billion. The deal was criticized for the loss of another American business icon.

To head off a hostile takeover attempt, a threatened company's managers may use one or more of several techniques. They may ask stockholders not to sell to the raider; file a lawsuit in an effort to abort the takeover; institute a *poison pill* (in which the firm allows stockholders to buy more shares of stock at prices lower than the current market value) or *shark repellent* (in which management requires a large majority of stock holders to approve the takeover); or seek a *white knight* (a more acceptable firm that is willing to acquire the threatened company). In some cases, management may take the company private or even take on more debt so that the heavy debt obligation will "scare off" the raider.

In a **leveraged buyout (LBO),** a group of investors borrows money from banks and other institutions to acquire a company (or a division of one), using the assets of the purchased company to guarantee repayment of the loan. In some LBOs, as much as 95 percent of the buyout price is paid with borrowed money, which eventually must be repaid.

With the explosion of mergers, acquisitions, and leveraged buyouts in the 1980s and 1990s, some financial journalists coined the term *merger mania.* Many companies joined the merger mania simply to enhance their own operations by consolidating them with the operations of other firms. Mergers and acquisitions enabled these companies to gain a larger market share in their industries, acquire valuable assets such as new products or plants and equipment, and lower their costs. Mergers also represent a means of making profits quickly, as was the case during the 1980s when many companies' stock was undervalued. Quite simply, such companies represent a bargain to other companies that can afford to buy them. Additionally, deregulation of some industries has permitted consolidation of firms within those industries for the first time, as is the case in the banking and airline industries.

TABLE 5.4 Major Mergers and Acquisitions Worldwide 2000–2006

Rank	Year	Acquirer*	Target	Transaction Value (in millions of US dollars)
1.	2000	America Online Inc. (AOL) *(Merger)*	Time Warner	$164,747
2.	2000	Glaxo Wellcome Plc.	SmithKline Beecham Plc.	75,961
3.	2004	Royal Dutch Petroleum Co.	Shell Transport & Trading Co.	74,559
4.	2006	AT&T Inc.	BellSouth Corporation	72,671
5.	2001	Comcast Corporation	AT&T Broadband & Internet Svcs.	72,041
6.	2004	Sanofi-Synthelabo SA	Aventis SA	60,243
7.	2000	Nortel Networks Corporation *(spinoff)*		59,974
8.	2002	Pfizer Inc.	Pharmacia Corporation	59,515
9.	2004	JPMorgan Chase & Co.	Bank One Corporation	58,761
10.	2006	E.on AG *(pending)*	Endesa SA	56,266

*Unless noted, deal was an acquisition.

Source: www.manda-institute.org/en/statistics-top-m&a-deals-transactions.htm (accessed March 10, 2009).

SO YOU'D LIKE TO START A BUSINESS

If you have a good idea and want to turn it into a business, you are not alone. Small businesses are popping up all over the United States, and the concept of entrepreneurship is hot. Entrepreneurs seek opportunities and creative ways to make profits. Business emerges in a number of different organizational forms, each with its own advantages and disadvantages. Sole proprietorships are the most common form of business organization in the United States. They tend to be small businesses and can take pretty much any form—anything from a hair salon to a scuba shop and from an organic produce provider to a financial advisor. Proprietorships are everywhere, serving consumers' wants and needs. Proprietorships have a big advantage in that they tend to be simple to manage—decisions get made quickly when the owner and the manager are the same person—and are fairly simple and inexpensive to set up. Rules vary by state, but at most all you will need is a license from the state.

Many people have been part of a partnership at some point in their lives. Group work in school is an example of a partnership. If you ever worked as a DJ on the weekend with your friend and split the profits, you have experienced a partnership. General and limited are the two main types of partnerships. General partners have unlimited liability and share completely in the management, debts, profits of the business. Limited partners, in contrast, consist of at least one general partner and one or more limited partners who do not participate in the management of the company but share in the profits. This form of partnership is used more often in risky investments where the limited partner stands only to lose his or her initial investment. Real estate limited partnerships are an example of how investors can minimize their financial exposure, given the poor performance of the real estate market in recent years. Although it has its advantages, partnership is the least utilized form of business. Part of the reason is that all the partners are responsible for the actions and decisions of all the other partners, whether or not all the partners were involved. Usually, the partners have to write up an articles of partnership that outlines their respective responsibilities in the business. Even in states where it is not required, it is a good idea to draw up this document as a way to cement each partner's role and, one hopes, minimize conflict. Unlike a corporation, proprietorships and partnerships both expire upon the death of one or more of those involved.

Corporations tend to be larger businesses, but do not need to be. A corporation can consist of nothing more than a small group of family members. To become a corporation you will have to file in the state in which you wish to incorporate. Each state has its own procedure for incorporation, meaning there are no general guidelines to follow. You can make your corporation private or public, meaning the company issues stocks and the shareholders are the owners. While incorporating is a popular form of organization because it gives the company an unlimited life span and limited liability (meaning that if your business fails, you cannot lose personal funds to make up for the losses), there is a downside. You will be taxed as a corporation and as an individual, resulting in double taxation. No matter what form of organization suits your business idea best, there is a world of options out there for you if you want to be or experiment with being an entrepreneur.

Some people view mergers and acquisitions favorably, pointing out that they boost corporations' stock prices and market value, to the benefit of their stockholders. In many instances, mergers enhance a company's ability to meet foreign competition in an increasingly global marketplace. And companies that are victims of hostile takeovers generally streamline their operations, reduce unnecessary staff, cut costs, and otherwise become more efficient with their operations, which benefits their stockholders whether or not the takeover succeeds.

Community Supported Agriculture Supports Farmers and Communities

These days, *sustainable* and *local* are terms that are heard frequently. Individuals want to care for the land and control their own health. To this end, community supported agriculture (CSA) is a popular alternative to shopping at a big chain grocery store. CSAs originated in Japan over 30 years ago. The first U.S. CSA was Indian Line Farm, founded in 1985. Today there are close to 2,500 CSAs around the country.

A CSA allows local farmers to conduct business directly with consumers. A CSA farmer creates a growing season budget that includes costs such as land payments, seeds, salaries, equipment, and more. The farmer then divides this budget by a certain number of shares of crops; people purchase the shares and receive a portion of local, often organic, produce each week during the growing season. The CSA relationship between farmers and members creates a sustainable situation in which members receive quality produce and farmers have a reliable method for distributing their crops.

How does the CSA benefit the environment and contribute to health? CSA farms often are dedicated to ecological farming practices. Farmers, knowing that their costs are met, are able to focus on growing high-quality produce rather than searching for distributors. Because the cost of distribution is lower, members receive produce at prices competitive with those of conventionally grown produce sold in stores. In addition, because deliveries are made locally, produce is fresher and delivery creates less pollution. Some of these farms also produce free-range meats and other products known for health benefits that are said to cut down on overall environmental pollution. In a world where people are looking to take better care of themselves and the environment, the CSA fits right in.[24] ❖

Q: Discussion Questions

1. What are some of the benefits gained by farmers from switching to the CSA model?

2. Why are people opting to use CSAs instead of shopping at traditional grocery stores?

3. Can you think of any drawbacks to the CSA model?

Critics, however, argue that mergers hurt companies because they force managers to focus their efforts on avoiding takeovers rather than managing effectively and profitably. Some companies have taken on a heavy debt burden to stave off a takeover, later to be forced into bankruptcy when economic downturns left them unable to handle the debt. Mergers and acquisitions also can damage employee morale and productivity, as well as the quality of the companies' products.

Many mergers have been beneficial for all involved; others have had damaging effects for the companies, their employees, and customers. No one can say if mergers will continue to slow, but many experts say the utilities, telecommunications, financial services, natural resources, computer hardware and software, gaming, managed health care, and technology industries are likely targets. ■

Team Exercise

Form groups and have them find examples of mergers and acquisitions. Mergers can be broken down into traditional mergers, horizontal mergers, and conglomerate mergers. When companies are found, note how long the merger or acquisition took, whether there were any requirements by the government before approval of the merger or acquisition, and whether you found any failed mergers or acquisitions which did not achieve government approval. Report your findings to the class and explain what the companies hoped to gain from the merger or acquisition.

CHECK OUT www.mhhe.com/FerrellM2e

for study materials including Interactive Exercises, Quizzes, iPod downloads, and video.

small business, entrepreneurship, and franchising

6

learning OBJECTIVES

LO1 Define entrepreneurship and small business.

LO2 Investigate the importance of small business in the U.S. economy and why certain fields attract small business.

LO3 Specify the advantages of small-business ownership.

LO4 Summarize the disadvantages of small-business ownership, and analyze why many small businesses fail.

LO5 Describe how you go about starting a small business and what resources are needed.

LO6 Evaluate the demographic, technological, and economic trends that are affecting the future of small business.

LO7 Explain why many large businesses are trying to "think small."

Introduction

Although many business students go to work for large corporations upon graduation, others may choose to start their own business or find employment opportunities in small businesses with 500 or fewer employees. There are almost 24 million small businesses operating in the United States today.[1] Each small business represents the vision of its entrepreneurial owners to succeed by providing new or better products. Small businesses are the heart of the U.S. economic and social system because they offer opportunities and express the freedom of people to make their own destinies. Today, the entrepreneurial spirit is growing around the world, from Russia and China to Germany, Brazil, and Mexico.

This chapter surveys the world of entrepreneurship and small business. First we define entrepreneurship and small business and examine the role of small business in the American economy. Then we explore the advantages and disadvantages of small-business ownership and analyze why small businesses succeed or fail. Next, we discuss how an entrepreneur goes about starting a small business and the challenges facing small business today. Finally, we look at entrepreneurship in larger businesses.

  ## LO1

Define entrepreneurship and small business.

THE NATURE OF ENTREPRENEURSHIP AND SMALL BUSINESS

In Chapter 1, we defined an entrepreneur as a person who risks his or her wealth, time, and effort to develop for profit an innovative product or way of doing something. **Entrepreneurship** is the process of creating and managing a business to achieve desired objectives. Many large businesses you may recognize, including Levi Strauss and Co., Procter & Gamble, McDonald's, Dell Computers, Microsoft, and Federal Express, all began as small businesses based on the entrepreneurial visions of their founders. Some entrepreneurs who start small businesses have the ability to see emerging trends; in response, they create a company to provide a product that serves customer needs. For example, rather than inventing a major new technology, an innovative company may take advantage of a new technology to create markets that did not exist before, such as Amazon.com. Or they may offer something familiar but improved or repackaged, such as Starbucks did with its coffee shops. They may innovate by focusing on a particular market segment and delivering a combination of features that consumers in that segment could not find anywhere else (e.g. Patagonia, a company that uses many organic materials in its clothing, has pledged 1 percent of sales to the preservation and restoration of the natural environment. Customers can return their worn-out Capilene Performance Baselayers for recycling.)[2]

Of course, smaller businesses do not have to evolve into such highly visible companies to be successful, but those entrepreneurial efforts that result in rapidly growing businesses become more visible with their success. Entrepreneurs who have achieved success, like Michael Dell and Bill Gates (Microsoft), are the most visible.

The entrepreneurship movement is accelerating with many new, smaller businesses emerging. Technology once available only to the largest firms can now be acquired by a small business. Printers, fax machines, copiers, voice-mail, computer bulletin boards and networks, cellular phones, and even overnight delivery services enable small businesses to be more competitive with today's giant corporations. Small businesses can also form alliances with other companies to produce and sell products in domestic and global markets.

What Is a Small Business?

This question is difficult to answer because smallness is relative. In this book, we will define a **small business** as any independently owned and operated business that is not dominant in its competitive area and does not employ more than 500 people. A local Mexican restaurant may be the most patronized Mexican restaurant in your community, but because it does not dominate the restaurant industry as a whole, the restaurant can be considered a small business. This definition is similar to the one used by the **Small Business Administration (SBA),** an independent agency of the federal government that offers managerial and financial assistance to small businesses. On its Web site, the SBA outlines the first steps in starting a small business and offers a wealth of information to current and potential small business owners.

  ## LO2

Investigate the importance of small business in the U.S. economy and why certain fields attract small business.

The Role of Small Business in the American Economy

No matter how you define small business, one fact is clear: Small businesses are vital to the soundness of the American economy. As you can see in Table 6.1, more than 99 percent of

TABLE 6.1 Facts About Small Businesses

- Represent 99.7% of all employer firms.
- Employ more than half of all private sector employees.
- About 6–7% of the U.S. population is in the process of starting a business at any given time.
- 53% of new small businesses begin in the home with less than $10,000.
- Are responsible for 39% of GNP.
- Contribute 44% of all sales in the country.
- Are twice as innovative per employee as larger firms.

Sources: www.nfib.com/object/smallBusinessFacts (accessed March 10, 2009); www.ntia.doc.gov/opadhome/mtdpweb/sbfacts.htm (accessed March 10, 2009).

all U.S. firms are classified as small businesses, and they employ 50 percent of private workers. Small firms are also important as exporters, representing 97 percent of U.S. exporters of goods and contributing 29 percent of the value of exported goods.[3] In addition, small businesses are largely responsible for fueling job creation and innovation. Small businesses also provide opportunities for minorities and women to succeed in business. Women-owned businesses total nearly 10.5 million—with over 50 percent employing more than 12.8 million people—and generate $1.9 trillion in sales. Over the past 20 years, the number of women-owned businesses has grown at a rate twice that of the average rate of 10 percent for firms overall. In addition, women-owned firms account for 41 percent of all privately held firms.[4] Minority-owned businesses have been growing faster than other classifiable firms as well, representing 17.6 percent of all small businesses. The number of minority-owned businesses is increasing at a rate of 30 percent, even higher than for women-owned firms. Hispanics own the most small businesses (7 percent) followed by African Americans (5.3 percent) Asians (4.9 percent), American Indians and Native Alaskans (0.9 percent), and Native Hawaiians and other Pacific Islanders (0.1 percent).[5] For example, Cuban born Jose M. Ledon decided it was time to start his own business after running various trenching and excavating companies in and around Las Vegas. Starting out with only $30,000, he hired 17 employees and was able to secure credit to purchase some equipment. By the business' second year, sales were $46 million, a dramatic increase over his first year, which was $3.8 million. Jose now has 212 employees and has added a division installing curbs, gutters, and sidewalks.[6]

job creation   The energy, creativity, and innovative abilities of small-business owners have resulted in jobs for other people. In fact, in the last decade, 60 to 80 percent of net new jobs annually were created by small businesses.[7] Table 6.2 indicates that 99.7 percent of all businesses employ fewer than 500 people.[8]

Many small businesses today are being started because of encouragement from larger ones. Many jobs are being created by big-company/small-company alliances. Whether through formal joint ventures, supplier relationships, or product or marketing cooperative projects, the rewards of collaborative relationships are creating many jobs for small-business owners and their

TABLE 6.2   Number of Firms by Employment Size

Firm Size	Number of Firms	Percentage of All Firms
0–19 employees	5,377,631	89
20–99 employees	535,865	9
100–499 employees	90,560	2
500 or more employees	18,071	0.3

Source: U.S. Census Bureau, "U.S. Business Statistics by Employment Size of Enterprise," www.census.gov/econ/susb (accessed March 10, 2009).

employees. Some publishing companies, for example, contract out almost all their editing and production to small businesses. Elm Street Publishing Services is a small editing/production house in Hinsdale, Illinois, that provides most services required to turn a manuscript into a bound book.

innovation   Perhaps one of the most significant strengths of small businesses is their ability to innovate and bring significant changes and benefits to customers. Small firms produce 55 percent of innovations. Among the important 20th-century

Most of America's new jobs aren't created by big corporations. They are created by small businesses such as this dry-cleaning firm.

innovations by U.S. small firms are the airplane, the audio tape recorder, double-knit fabric, fiber-optic examining equipment, the heart valve, the optical scanner, the pacemaker, the personal computer, soft contact lenses, and the zipper. Paul Moller, an entrepreneur and inventor, may be working on one of the most important 21st-century innovations: a flying car. Although currently still in the testing phase, Moller's SkyCar may one day help commuters avoid congested freeways. The car is currently being tested at Stanford University, tethered to a large Crane.[9]

The innovation of successful firms takes many forms. Small businessman Ray Kroc found a new way to sell hamburgers and turned his ideas into one of the most successful fast-food franchises in the world—McDonald's. Small businesses have become an integral part of our lives. James Dyson's name is synonymous with high quality vacuum cleaners. Today, his $1 billion company produces a bagless vacuum cleaner that commands 25% of the U.S. market. However, it took a lot of work to achieve such success. Dyson developed 5,127 prototypes before he got the design and function right. He recently created a successful hand dryer and is working to develop other innovative appliances. Similarly, Bikram Choudhury's name is associated

SERVICES INCLUDE BUSINESSES THAT WORK FOR OTHERS BUT DO NOT ACTUALLY PRODUCE TANGIBLE GOODS

with yoga. Bikram Yoga uses a sequence of 26 signature poses, and the business has expanded to training courses, books, CDs, clothing, and numerous franchises. Choudhury is credited with popularizing yoga in the U.S., and with turning "his particular brand of yoga into the McDonald's of a $3 billion industry."[10] They provide fresh ideas and usually have greater flexibility to change than do large companies.

Industries That Attract Small Business

Small businesses are found in nearly every industry, but retailing and wholesaling, services, manufacturing, and high technology are especially attractive to entrepreneurs because they are relatively easy to enter and require low initial financing. Small-business owners also find it easier to focus on a specific group of consumers in these fields than in others, and new firms in these industries suffer less from heavy competition, at least in the early stages, than do established firms.

retailing and wholesaling Retailers acquire goods from producers or wholesalers and sell them to consumers. Main streets, shopping strips, and shopping malls are lined with independent music stores, sporting-goods shops, dry cleaners, boutiques, drugstores, restaurants, caterers, service stations, and hardware stores that sell directly to consumers. Retailing attracts entrepreneurs because gaining experience and exposure in retailing is relatively easy. Additionally, an entrepreneur opening a new retailing store does not have to spend the large sums of money for the equipment and distribution systems that a manufacturing business requires. All that a new retailer needs is a lease on store space, merchandise, enough money to sustain the business, knowledge about prospective customers' needs and desires, the ability to use promotion to generate awareness, and basic management skills. Some small retailers are taking their businesses online. For example, Susan Brown invented a donut shaped pillow with an opening in one side called the "Boppy." The product is sold online at **www.boppy.com,** and in Babies R Us and Pottery Barn Kids stores. Although approached by Wal-Mart, Brown declined the offer in a desire to keep a more upscale feel. The Boppy has annual sales around $50 million and was provided start up capital through a microloan of $25,000 from the Colorado Enterprise Fund, a nonprofit community-development institution.[11] In 2007 it was the number-one baby product in the nation, according to *American Baby Magazine.*

Wholesalers supply products to industrial, retail, and institutional users for resale or for use in making other products. Wholesaling activities range from planning and negotiating for supplies, promoting, and distributing (warehousing and transporting) to providing management and merchandising assistance to clients. Wholesalers are extremely important for many products, especially consumer goods, because of the marketing activities they perform. Although it is true that wholesalers themselves can be eliminated, their functions must be passed on to some other organization such as the producer, or another intermediary, often a small business. Frequently, small businesses are closer to the final customers and know what it takes to keep them satisfied. Some smaller businesses start out manufacturing but find their real niche as a supplier or distributor of larger firms' products.

services Services include businesses that work for others but do not actually produce tangible goods. They represent one of the fastest growing sectors of the U.S. economy, accounting for 66 percent of the U.S. economy and employing roughly 70 percent of the workforce.[12] Real estate, insurance, and personnel agencies, barbershops, banks, television and computer repair shops, copy centers, dry cleaners, and accounting firms are all service businesses. Services also attract individuals—such as beauticians, morticians, jewelers, doctors, and veterinarians—whose skills are not usually required by large firms. Many of these service providers are also retailers because they provide their services to ultimate consumers.

manufacturing Manufacturing goods can provide unique opportunities for small businesses. Started in 1988, the Malcolm Baldrige Award recognizes achievements in quality and performance in businesses of all sizes. It is designed to spur competitive business practices in American industry, but it has been rare for small businesses (with 500 or fewer employees) to win the award. However, the winner in the Small Business category in 2007 was Pro-Tec Coating Company in Leipsic, Ohio. Pro-Tec provides coated sheet metal to the automotive industry. Pro-Tec's product helps improve vehicle crashworthiness and fuel economy through innovations in weight reduction.[13] Small businesses can often customize products to meet specific customer needs and wants. Such products include custom artwork, jewelry, clothing, and furniture.

high technology High technology is a broad term used to describe businesses that depend heavily on advanced scientific and engineering knowledge. People who have been able to innovate or identify new markets in the fields of computers, biotechnology, genetic engineering, robotics, and other markets have become today's high-tech giants. Mark Zuckerberg, the 24-year-old CEO of Facebook (a social networking Web site), for instance, has created a company that is one of the fastest growing dot-coms in history. With international expansion in 2007, the number of Web site visitors tripled. In early 2008, users spent 20 billion total minutes on the site versus 6.4 billion minutes the previous year. In 2007 Microsoft paid $240 million for 1.6 percent of Facebook, bringing its valuation to roughly $15 billion. The company continues to grow, and Zuckerberg has hired Google's Sheryl Sandberg as COO in order to "impose some corporate discipline on an undergraduate flip-flops-and-Red-Bull vibe." Other successful young entrepreneurs in high-tech companies include the founders of Google, Myspace, and Yahoo![14] Many of them, nonetheless, started out in garages, basements, kitchens, and dorm rooms.

 L03

Specify the advantages of small-business ownership.

Geek Squad employees vow to "fix any PC problem anytime, anywhere." The Geek Squad began as a one-man service firm in Minnesota in 1994. Founder Robert Stephens initially traveled by bicycle to and from service calls. Best Buy owns the firm today.

ADVANTAGES OF SMALL-BUSINESS OWNERSHIP

There are many advantages to establishing and running a small business. These can be categorized as personal advantages and business advantages. Table 6.3 lists some of the traits that can help entrepreneurs succeed.

Independence

Independence is probably one of the leading reasons that entrepreneurs choose to go into business for themselves. Being a small-business owner means being your own boss. Many people start their own businesses because they believe they will do better for themselves than they could do by remaining with their current employer or by changing jobs. They may feel stuck on the corpo-

?

DID YOU KNOW?

39 percent of high-tech jobs are in small businesses.[15]

rate ladder and think that no business would take them seriously enough to fund their ideas. Sometimes people who venture forth to start their own small business are those who simply cannot work for someone else. Such people may say that they just do not fit the "corporate mold."

More often, small-business owners just want the freedom to choose whom they work with, the flexibility to pick where and when to work, and the option of working in a family setting. The availability of the computer, copy machine, business telephone, and fax machine has permitted many people to work at home. Only a few

Recycled Toothbrushes Make Sense

Many eco-responsible entrepreneurial companies create recycled products, but a recycled toothbrush might sound a bit far-fetched. Not so. Eric Hudson and his company, Recycline, make Preserve toothbrushes, tongue cleaners, razors, and more from recycled materials. Committed to sustainable, eco-friendly practices, including a zero waste initiative and offsetting electricity use with wind power credits, Hudson believed Recycline products could make a difference and set out to find his niche. After sending product samples to movie companies, Hudson learned that Will Ferrell's character in *Stranger Than Fiction* would be using a Recycline toothbrush. His marketing organization took the film appearance and used it to acquire greater sales at select Target stores that carried the Preserve line. Recycline offered free toothbrushes and movie tickets to volunteers willing to pass

out postcards reading "Meet Harold Crick's [Ferrell's character] toothbrush." The cards directed moviegoers to the nearest Target store to purchase the toothbrush. The company also used articles in newspapers and trade publications to promote the product.

To create its toothbrushes and the handles of its razors sustainably, Recycline entered into a partnership with yogurt maker Stonyfield Farm. Recycline reuses Stonyfield's discarded yogurt containers, which are not otherwise recyclable. To make it easier for Recycline to collect the containers, Whole Foods has started the Gimme 5 program. At select stores around the nation consumers can drop off their no. 5 plastic containers so that Recycline can collect them to produce other things. Because consumers are interested in green products and concerned about the way the country is using its limited resources, a toothbrush made

from recycled materials isn't so far out. The company hopes to become the brand consumers turn to for high-quality, innovative, environmentally friendly, and stylish personal care products.[16] ❖

Q: **Discussion Questions**

1. What are the advantages for Recycline in partnering with Stonyfield Farm?

2. List some additional ways Hudson could market his recycled-plastic toothbrushes and shavers.

3. How will the company have to change as it grows larger?

TABLE 6.3 Traits Needed to Succeed in Entrepreneurship

Neuroticism—helps entrepreneurs focus on details

Extroversion—facilitates network building

Conscientiousness—facilitates planning

Agreeableness—facilitates networking

Openness to new ideas

Source: Alex de Noble in Joshua Kurlantzick, "About Face," *Entrepreneur,* January 2004, www.entrepreneur.com/article/0,4621,312260,00.html.

years ago, most of them would have needed the support that an office provides.

Costs

As already mentioned, small businesses often require less money to start and maintain than do large ones. Obviously, a firm with just 25 people in a small factory spends less money on wages and salaries, rent, utilities, and other expenses than does a firm employing tens of thousands of people in several large facilities. And rather than maintain the expense and staff of keeping separate departments for accounting, advertising, and legal counseling, small businesses can hire other firms (often small businesses themselves) to supply these services as they are needed. Additionally, small-business owners sometimes can rely on friends and family members who volunteer to work to get out a difficult project in order to save money.

Flexibility

With small size comes the flexibility to adapt to changing market demands. Small businesses usually have only one layer of management—the owners. Decisions therefore can be made and carried out quickly. In larger firms, decisions about even routine matters can take weeks because they must pass through two or more levels of management before action is authorized. When McDonald's introduces a new product, for example, it must first research what consumers want, then develop the product and test it carefully before introducing it nationwide, a process that sometimes takes years. An independent snack shop, however,

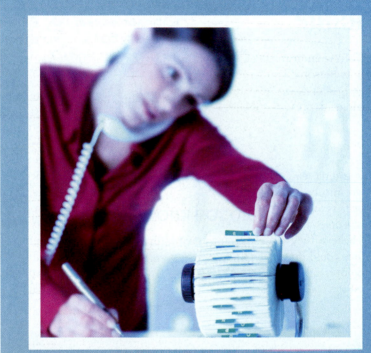

Entrepreneurs have a great deal of independence but also experience a great deal of stress.

can develop and introduce a new product (perhaps to meet a customer's request) in a much shorter time.

Focus

Small firms can focus their efforts on a few key customers or on a precisely defined market niche—that is, a specific group of customers. Many large corporations must compete in the mass market or for large market segments. Smaller firms can develop products for particular groups of customers or to satisfy a need that other companies have not addressed. For example, launched in 2006 in Indianapolis, Fatheadz focuses on producing sunglasses for people with big heads. To be an official "fathead" you need a ball cap size of at least 7⅝ and a head circumference above the ear of at least 23.5 inches. The idea arose when Rico Elmore was walking down the Las Vegas Strip with his brother and realized that he had lost his sunglasses. He went to a nearby sunglass shop, and out of 300 pairs of glasses, he could not find one that fit. Customers include the entire starting line of the Indianapolis Colts, Rupert Boneham (of *Survivor* fame), and Tim Sylvia, former heavyweight title holder of Ultimate Fighting Championship.[17] By targeting small niches or product needs, small businesses sometimes can avoid fierce competition from larger firms, helping them grow into stronger companies.

Reputation

Small firms, because of their capacity to focus on narrow niches, can develop enviable reputations for quality and service. A good example of a small business with a formidable reputation is W. Atlee Burpee and Co., which has the country's premier bulb and seed catalog. Burpee has an unqualified returns policy (complete satisfaction or your money back) that demonstrates a strong commitment to customer satisfaction.

 L04

Summarize the disadvantages of small-business ownership, and analyze why many small businesses fail.

DISADVANTAGES OF SMALL-BUSINESS OWNERSHIP

The rewards associated with running a small business are so enticing that it's no wonder many people dream of it. However, as with any undertaking, small-business ownership has its disadvantages.

High Stress Level

A small business is likely to provide a living for its owner, but not much more (although there are exceptions as some examples in this chapter have shown). There are always worries about competition, employee problems, new equipment, expanding inventory, rent increases, or changing market demand. In addition to other stresses, small-business owners tend to be victims of physical and psychological stress. The small-business person is often the owner, manager, sales force, shipping and receiving clerk, bookkeeper, and custodian. Figure 6.1 shows the five biggest challenges and goals of small and medium-sized businesses. Many creative persons fail, not because of their business concepts, but rather because of difficulties in managing their business.

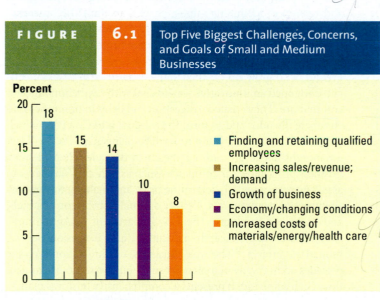

| FIGURE | 6.1 | Top Five Biggest Challenges, Concerns, and Goals of Small and Medium Businesses |

Percent

- 18 — Finding and retaining qualified employees
- 15 — Increasing sales/revenue; demand
- 14 — Growth of business
- 10 — Economy/changing conditions
- 8 — Increased costs of materials/energy/health care

Source: "Entrepreneurial Challenges Survey Results," *Entrepreneur,* www.entrepreneur.com/encyclopedia/businessstatistics/article81812.html (accessed March 10, 2009).

High Failure Rate

Despite the importance of small businesses to our economy, there is no guarantee of small-business success. Roughly 70 percent of all new businesses fail within the first ten years.[18] Neighborhood restaurants are a case in point. Look around your own neighborhood, and you can probably spot the locations of several restaurants that are no longer in business.

Small businesses fail for many reasons. A poor business concept—such as insecticides for garbage cans (research found that consumers are not concerned with insects in their garbage)—will produce disaster nearly every time. Expanding a hobby into a business may work if a genuine market niche exists, but all too often people start such a business without identifying a real need for the goods or services. Other notable causes of small-business failure include the burdens imposed by government regulation, insufficient funds to withstand slow sales, and vulnerability to competition from larger companies. However, three major causes of small-business failure deserve a close look: undercapitalization, managerial inexperience or incompetence, and inability to cope with growth; roughly 90 percent of small business failures can be attributed to these faults.[19]

undercapitalization The shortest path to failure in business is **undercapitalization,** the lack of funds to operate a business normally. Too many entrepreneurs think that all they need is enough money to get started, that the business can survive on cash generated from sales soon thereafter. But almost all businesses suffer from seasonal variations in sales, which make cash tight, and few businesses make money from the start. Many small rural operations cannot obtain financing within their own communities because small rural banks often lack the necessary financing expertise or assets sizable enough to counter the risks involved with small-business loans. Without sufficient funds, the best small-business idea in the world will fail.

managerial inexperience or incompetence Poor management is the cause of many business failures. The fact that an entrepreneur has a brilliant vision for a small business does not mean he or she has the knowledge or experience to manage a growing business effectively. A person who is good at creating great product ideas and marketing them may lack the skills and experience

Entrepreneur Dennis Albaugh Is a Pesticide Prince

Dennis Albaugh experienced some ups and downs along the way, but he is a success story now. After selling fertilizers and chemicals for various companies for years, Albaugh decided to start his own company. He invested his $2,000 of savings in the weed killer 2,4-D and started out with a single customer. After some years of reselling 2,4-D Albaugh began to manufacture it himself. In 1990, one of his competitors, Agrolinz, decided to sell its factory. Albaugh bought the factory, raising the money through inventory liquidation. His sales more than doubled. In 1995, Albaugh purchased Atanor, one of his suppliers. Finally, in 1999, he purchased a glyphosate factory. Glyphosate is the active ingredient in Roundup. In 2000, glyphosate lost its Monsanto (the company producing it) patent, and Albaugh began to make it. Today Albaugh is the second largest producer of glyphosate—a $3 billion market.[20] ❖

Franson Nwaeze and Paula Merrell wanted to open a restaurant, but most lenders were skeptical because of their lack of restaurant experience and money. When the husband-and-wife team learned that banks were much more willing to loan them money to buy a gas station, they purchased a Conoco station in Watauga, Texas, and opened up a successful restaurant in one-half of it. The business's motto is "fill'er-up outside, fill'er-up inside."

to make good management decisions in hiring, negotiating, finance, and control. Moreover, entrepreneurs may neglect those areas of management they know little about or find tedious, at the expense of the business's success.

inability to cope with growth

Sometimes, the very factors that are advantages turn into serious disadvantages when the time comes for a small business to grow. Growth often requires the owner to give up a certain amount of direct authority, and it is frequently hard for someone who has called all the shots to give up control. Similarly, growth requires specialized management skills in areas such as credit analysis and promotion—skills that the founder may lack or not have time to apply. The founders of many small businesses, including those of Gateway and Dell Computers, found that they needed to bring in more experienced managers to help manage their companies through intense growing pains.

Poorly managed growth probably affects a company's reputation more than anything else, at least initially. And products that do not arrive on time or goods that are poorly made can quickly reverse a company's success. The biggest, immediate threats to small and medium-sized businesses include rising inflation, trade deficit and collapse of the dollar's value, energy and other supply shortages, excessive household and/or corporate debt, and the growing federal deficit.[21]

L05

Describe how you go about starting a small business and what resources are needed.

STARTING A SMALL BUSINESS

We've told you how important small businesses are, and why they succeed and fail, but *how do you go about* starting your own business? To start any business, large or small, you must first have an idea. Sam Walton, founder of Wal-Mart stores, had an idea for a discount retailing enterprise and spawned the world's largest retailing empire, and that changed the way traditional companies look at their business. Next, you need to devise a business plan to guide planning and development in the business. Finally, you must make decisions about form of ownership, the financial resources needed, and whether to buy an existing business, start a new one, or buy a franchise.

The Business Plan

A key element of business success is a **business plan**—a precise statement of the rationale for the business and a step-by-step explanation of how it will achieve its goals. The business plan should include an explanation of the business, an analysis of the competition, estimates of income and expenses, and other information. It should establish a strategy for acquiring sufficient funds to keep the business going. Indeed, many financial institutions decide whether to loan a small business money based on its business plan. However, the business plan should act as a guide and reference document—not a shackle to limit the business's flexibility and decision making. Finally, the business plan should be revised periodically to ensure that the firm's goals and strategies can adapt to changes in the environment. Ben and Matthew Freund, who grew up on their father's dairy farm in Connecticut, developed an innovative way to deal with their abundance of cow manure. They created a digestion and dehydration process to eliminate the odor and to form the product into CowPots, which can be buried in the ground to fertilize plants. CowPots will last for months above ground, but begin to degrade when planted. Business plans allow for companies such as Ben and Matthew's to assess market potential, determine price and manufacturing possibilities and requirements, identify optimal distribution channels, and brand the products. The U.S. Department of Agriculture's Cooperative State Research, Education, and Extension Service funded this project.[22] The Small Business Administration Web site provides an overview of a plan for small businesses to use to gain financing. Appendix B presents a comprehensive business plan.

Forms of Business Ownership

After developing a business plan, the entrepreneur has to decide on an appropriate legal form of business ownership—whether it is best to operate as a sole proprietorship, partnership, or corporation—and examine the many factors that affect that decision, which we explored in Chapter 5.

Financial Resources

The old adage "it takes money to make money" holds true in developing a business enterprise. To make money from a small business, the owner must first provide or obtain money (capital) to start the business and keep it running smoothly. Even a small retail store will probably need at least $50,000 in initial financing to rent space, purchase or lease necessary equipment and furnishings, buy the initial inventory of merchandise, and provide working capital. Often, the small-business owner has to put up a significant percentage of the necessary capital. Few new business owners have the entire amount, however, and must look to other sources for additional financing.

equity financing
The most important source of funds for any new business is the owner. Many owners include among their personal resources ownership of a home or the accumulated value in a life-insurance policy or a savings account. A new business owner may sell or borrow against the value of such assets to obtain funds to operate a business. Additionally, the owner may bring useful personal assets—such as a computer, desks and other furniture, a car or truck—as part of his or her ownership interest in the firm. Such financing is referred to as *equity financing* because the owner uses real personal assets rather than borrowing funds from outside sources to get started in a new business. The owner can also provide working capital by reinvesting profits into the business or simply by not drawing a full salary.

Small businesses can also obtain equity financing by finding investors for their operations. They may sell stock in the business to family members, friends, employees, or other investors. When Tony Volk developed the pop-up turkey timer, he probably had no idea that he would one day sell around $100 million and be the only maker of the small plastic gadget that pops out of the turkey at 180 degrees. The Volk pop-ups are embedded in 30 million of the 46 million turkeys consumed for Thanksgiving. To support the company's early growth, Tony had to convince his brother Henry to quit his job as an auditor and join the company. For more than 40 years, this family-run business has been a leader in innovative packaging and products.[23] **Venture capitalists** are persons or organizations that agree to provide some funds for a new business in exchange for an ownership interest or stock. Venture capitalists hope to purchase the stock of a small business at a low price and then sell the stock for a profit after the business has grown successful. The renewable energy industry has recently become a popular investment option among venture capitalists, whose funding for 'cleantech,' or renewable energy technology, increased 70 percent in 2007. Cleantech represented almost 10 percent of all venture capital funding with most of the money going to solar companies.[24] Individual venture capitalists are sometimes called *angels*. Increasingly, angels are banding together and pooling resources to reduce risk and increase the odds of finding the next Google or Amazon.com.[25] Although these forms of equity financing have helped many small businesses, they require that the small-

The most important source of funds for any new business is the owner.

business owner share the profits of the business—and sometimes control, as well—with the investors.

debt financing
New businesses sometimes borrow over half of their financial resources. Banks are the main suppliers of external financing to small businesses. On the federal level, the Small Business Administration offers financial assistance to qualifying businesses. More detail on the SBA's loan programs can be found at the SBA Web site. They can also look to family and friends as sources for loans of long-term funds or other assets, such as a computer or an automobile, that are exchanged for an ownership interest in a business. In such cases, the business owner can usually structure a favorable repayment schedule and sometimes negotiate an interest rate below current bank rates. If the business goes bad, however, the emotional losses for all concerned may greatly exceed the money involved. Anyone lending a friend or family member money for a venture should state the agreement clearly in writing.

The amount a bank or another institution is willing to loan depends on its assessment of the venture's likelihood of success and of the entrepreneur's ability to repay the loan. The bank will often require the entrepreneur to put up *collateral,* a financial interest in the property or fixtures of the business, to guarantee payment of the debt. Additionally, the small-business owner may have to offer some personal property as collateral, such as his or her home, in which case the loan is called a *mortgage.* If the small business fails to repay the loan, the lending institution may eventually claim and sell the collateral (or the owner's home, in the case of a mortgage) to recover its loss.

Banks and other financial institutions can also grant a small business a *line of credit*—an agreement by which a financial institution promises to lend a business a predetermined sum on demand. A line of credit permits an entrepreneur to take quick advantage of opportunities that require a bank loan. Small businesses may obtain funding from their suppliers in the form of a *trade credit*—that is, suppliers allow the business to take possession of the needed goods and services and pay for them at a later date or in installments. Occasionally, small businesses engage in *bartering*—trading their own products for the goods and services offered by other businesses. For example, an accountant may offer accounting services to an office supply firm in exchange for computer paper and diskettes.

Additionally, some community groups sponsor loan funds to encourage the development of particular types of businesses. State and local agencies may guarantee loans, especially to minority businesspeople or for development in certain areas.

name recognition. Visit the Web site of the International Franchise Association to learn more on this topic.

The practice of franchising first began in the United States when Singer used it to sell sewing machines in the 19th century. It soon became commonplace in the distribution of goods in the automobile, gasoline, soft drink, and hotel industries. The concept of franchising grew especially rapidly during the 1960s, when it expanded to more diverse industries. Table 6.4 shows the 10 fastest growing franchises and the top 10 new franchises.

There are both advantages and disadvantages to franchising for the entrepreneur. Franchising allows a franchisee the opportunity to set up a small business relatively quickly, and because of its association with an established brand, a franchise outlet often reaches the break-even point faster than an independent business would. Franchisees often report the following advantages:

- Management training and support.
- Brand-name appeal.
- Standardized quality of goods and services.
- National advertising programs.
- Financial assistance.

Approaches to Starting a Small Business

starting from scratch versus buying an existing business Although entrepreneurs often start new small businesses from scratch much the way we have discussed in this section, they may elect instead to buy an already existing business. This has the advantage of providing a network of existing customers, suppliers, and distributors and reducing some of the guesswork inherent in starting a new business from scratch. However, an entrepreneur buying an existing business must also deal with whatever problems the business already has.

franchising Many small-business owners find entry into the business world through franchising. A license to sell another's products or to use another's name in business, or both, is a **franchise.** The company that sells a franchise is the **franchiser.** Dunkin' Donuts, McDonald's, and Jiffy Lube are

> ## "Many small-business owners find entry into the business world through franchising."

well-known franchisers with national visibility. The purchaser of a franchise is called a **franchisee.**

The franchisee acquires the rights to a name, logo, methods of operation, national advertising, products, and other elements associated with the franchiser's business in return for a financial commitment and the agreement to conduct business in accordance with the franchiser's standard of operations. Depending on the franchise, the initial fee to join a system varies. In addition, franchisees buy equipment, pay for training, and obtain a mortgage or lease. The franchisee also pays the franchiser a monthly or annual fee based on a percentage of sales or profits. In return, the franchisee often receives building specifications and designs, site recommendations, management and accounting support, and, perhaps most important, immediate

- Proven products and business formats.
- Centralized buying power.

TABLE 6.4 Fastest Growing and Hottest New Franchises

Top 10 Fastest Growing Franchises	Top 10 New Franchises
1. Jan-Pro Franchising Int'l. Inc.	1. Instant Tax Service
2. Subway	2. Snap Fitness Inc.
3. Instant Tax Service	3. Stratus Building Solutions
4. Stratus Building Solutions	4. Chester's Int'l.
5. Snap Fitness Inc.	5. HealthSource Chiropractic and Progressive Rehab
6. Dunkin' Donuts	6. Goin' Postal
7. Jazzercise Inc.	7. Senior Helpers
8. Bonus Building Care	8. Oreck Clean Home Center
9. Anytime Fitness	9. Fast-teks On-site Computer Services
10. Vanguard Cleaning Systems	10. Murphy Business & Financial Corp.

Source: "Top 10 New and Fastest Growing Franchises, 2009 Rankings," *Entrepreneur,* www.entrepreneur.com/franchises/toptenlists/index.html (accessed March 10, 2009).

- Site selection and territorial protection.
- Greater chance for success.[26]

However, the franchisee must sacrifice some freedom to the franchiser. Some shortcomings experienced by some franchisees include:

- Franchise fees and profit sharing with the franchiser.
- Strict adherence to standardized operations.
- Restrictions on purchasing.
- Limited product line.
- Possible market saturation.
- Less freedom in business decisions.[27]

Strict uniformity is the rule rather than the exception. Entrepreneurs who want to be their own bosses are often frustrated with a franchise.

Help for Small-Business Managers

Because of the crucial role that small business and entrepreneurs play in the U.S. economy, a number of organizations offer programs to improve the small-business owner's ability to compete. These include entrepreneurial training programs and programs sponsored by the Small Business Administration. Such programs provide small-business owners with invaluable assistance in managing their businesses, often at little or no cost to the owner.

Entrepreneurs can learn critical marketing, management, and finance skills in seminars and college courses. In addition, knowledge, experience, and judgment are necessary for success in a new business. While knowledge can be communicated and some experiences can be simulated in the classroom, good judgment must be developed by the entrepreneur. Local chambers of commerce and the U.S. Department of Commerce offer information and assistance helpful in operating a small business. National publications such as *Inc.* and *Entrepreneur* share statistics, advice, tips, and success/failure stories. Additionally, many urban areas—including Chicago; Jacksonville, Florida; Portland, Oregon; St. Louis; and Nashville—have weekly business journal/newspapers that provide stories on local businesses as well as on business techniques that a manager or small business can use.

The Small Business Administration offers many types of management assistance to small businesses, including counseling for firms in difficulty, consulting on improving operations, and training for owner/managers and their employees. Among its many programs, the SBA funds Small Business Development Centers (SBDCs). These are business clinics, usually located on college campuses, that provide counseling at no charge and training at only a nominal charge. SBDCs are often the SBA's principal means of providing direct management assistance.

The Service Corps of Retired Executives (SCORE) and the Active Corps of Executives (ACE) are volunteer agencies funded by the SBA to provide advice for owners of small firms. Both are

1-800-Got-Junk will haul away what your garbage collector won't. The company has more than 300 franchises, most of which are in the United States and Canada.

staffed by experienced managers whose talents and experience the small firms could not ordinarily afford. SCORE has 10,500 volunteers at nearly 400 U.S. locations and has served 7.9 million small businesses since 1964.[28] The SBA also has organized Small Business Institutes (SBIs) on almost 500 university and college campuses in the United States. Seniors, graduate students, and faculty at each SBI provide onsite management counseling.

Finally, the small-business owner can obtain advice from other small-business owners, suppliers, and even customers. A customer may approach a small business it frequents with a request for a new product, for example, or a supplier may offer suggestions for improving a manufacturing process. Networking—building relationships and sharing information with colleagues—is vital for any businessperson, whether you work for a huge corporation or run your own small business. Communicating with other business owners is a great way to find ideas for dealing with employees and government regulation, improving processes, or solving problems. New technology is making it easier to network. For example, some states are setting up computer bulletin boards for the use of their businesses to network and share ideas.

 LO6

Evaluate the demographic, technological, and economic trends that are affecting the future of small business.

THE FUTURE FOR SMALL BUSINESS[29]

Although small businesses are crucial to the economy, they can be more vulnerable to turbulence and change in the marketplace than large businesses. Next, we take a brief look at the

> ## COMMUNICATING WITH OTHER BUSINESS OWNERS IS A GREAT WAY TO FIND IDEAS FOR DEALING WITH EMPLOYEES AND GOVERNMENT REGULATION, IMPROVING PROCESSES, OR SOLVING PROBLEMS.

demographic, technological, and economic trends that will have the most impact on small business in the future.

Demographic Trends

America's baby boom started in 1946 and ended in 1964. The earliest boomers are already past 50, and in the next few years, millions more will pass that mark. The boomer generation numbers about 76 million, or 28 percent of U.S. citizens.[30] This segment of the population is probably the wealthiest, but most small businesses do not actively pursue it. Some exceptions, however, include Gold Violin, which sells designer canes and other products online and through a catalog, and LifeSpring, which delivers nutritional meals and snacks directly to the customer. Industries such as travel, financial planning, and health care will continue to grow as boomers age. Many experts think that the boomer demographic is the market of the future.

Another market with huge potential for small business is the echo boomers, also called millennials or Generation Y. Millennials number around 75 million and possess a number of unique characteristics. Born between 1977 and 1994, this cohort is not solely concerned about money. Those who fall into this group are also concerned with advancement, recognition, and improved capabilities. They need direct, timely feedback and frequent encouragement and recognition. Millennials do well when training sessions combine entertainment with learning. Working remotely is more acceptable to this group than to previous generations, and virtual communication may become as important as face-to-face meetings.[31]

Yet another trend is the growing number of immigrants living in the United States, who now represent about one-eighth, or 12 percent, of the population.[32] This vast number of people provides still another greatly untapped market for small businesses. Retailers who specialize in ethnic products, and service providers who offer bi- or multilingual employees, can find vast potential in this market. Table 6.5 ranks top cities in the United States for entrepreneurs.

Technological and Economic Trends

Advances in technology have opened up many new markets to small businesses. Although thousands of small dot-coms have failed, experts predict that Internet usage will continue to increase, and one of the hot areas will be the Internet infrastruc-

Dinosaur Fossils Incite Controversy and Enterprise

Entrepreneurs are known for wild ideas, but most probably would not consider dinosaur fossil hunting a viable venture. Yet it is a growing industry in the West, with many ranchers and farmers entering the business as they make discoveries on their land or purposely pursue it as a more lucrative market than ranching or farming. Larry Tuss, owner of 6,000 acres of Montana farmland, has unearthed five dinosaur skeletons on his property since 2001. To help with the technical aspects of excavation, Tuss enlisted a fossil company to help prepare the fossils for sale. With a Triceratops skull going for $250,000 and a Tyrannosaurus rex skeleton selling for $1.8 million, Tuss's land could yield him much cash.

Another fossil hunter, rancher and rodeo rider Bucky Derflinger, discovered a juvenile Tyrannosaurus rex skeleton on his father's ranch in 1998. Derflinger made enough profit on the sale to finance a down payment on a 4,000-acre ranch. Since then, Derflinger has located many dinosaur fossils on the family's land. Although the fossils bring in a good income, Bucky and his father do not plan to give up ranching.

While Tuss and Derflinger enjoy fossil hunting's rewards, some people are infuriated by this practice. Paleontologists are concerned that unskilled fossil hunters could damage or destroy fossils through inadequate precautions during excavations; they are also concerned about selling fossils to private collectors, who will not allow them to be used in research. However, with dinosaur fossils selling for thousands of dollars, people have strong financial incentives to fossil hunt, against researchers' recommendations. Many doubt that scientists and profit-seeking fossil hunters will ever reach an agreement.[33] ❖

 Discussion Questions

1. Why might ranchers continue their businesses as fossil hunters even after they have heard scientists' reasons for being concerned about fossil hunting?

2. How could the fossil hunters gain more control over their businesses and more market share?

3. Could incentives ever be aligned enough that fossil hunters and scientists both get what they want?

TABLE 6.5 Top U.S. Cities for Small-Business Entrepreneurs in 2009

1. Raleigh, NC
2. Charlotte, NC
3. Seattle, WA
4. Austin, TX
5. Boise, Idaho
6. Salt Lake City, UT
7. Orlando, FL
8. Oklahoma City, OK
9. Denver, CO
10. Portland, ME

Source: G. Scott Thomas, "The Best Places to Start a Small Business," *Bizjournals*, February 2, 2009, www.bizjournals.com/edit_special/75.html (accessed March 10, 2009).

markets small wind turbines for producing electric power for homes, sailboats, and telecommunications. Solar Attic Inc. has developed a process to recover heat from home attics to use in heating hot water or swimming pools. As entrepreneurs begin to realize that worldwide energy markets are valued in the hundreds of billions of dollars, the number of innovative companies entering this market will increase. In addition, many small businesses have the desire and employee commitment to purchase such environmentally friendly products. New Belgium Brewing Company received the U.S. Environmental Protection Agency and Department of Energy Award for leadership in conservation for making a 10-year commitment to purchase wind energy. The company's employees unanimously agreed to cover the increased costs of wind-generated electricity from the employee profit-sharing program.

ture area that enables companies to improve communications with employees, suppliers, and customers.

Technological advances and an increase in service exports have created new opportunities for small companies to expand their operations abroad. Changes in communications and technology can allow small companies to customize their services quickly for international customers. Also, free trade agreements and trade alliances are helping to create an environment in which small businesses have fewer regulatory and legal barriers.

In recent years, economic turbulence has provided both opportunities and threats for small businesses. As large information technology companies such as Cisco, Oracle, and Sun Microsystems had to recover from an economic slowdown and an oversupply of Internet infrastructure products, some smaller firms found new niche markets. Smaller companies can react quickly to change and can stay close to their customers. While many well-funded dot-coms were failing, many small businesses were learning how to use the Internet to promote their businesses and sell products online. For example, many arts and crafts dealers and makers of specialty products found they could sell their wares on existing Web sites such as eBay. Service providers related to tourism, real estate, and construction also found they could reach customers through their own or existing Web sites.

Deregulation of the energy market and interest in alternative fuels and in fuel conservation have spawned many small businesses. Earth First Technologies Inc. produces clean-burning fuel from contaminated water or sewage. Southwest Windpower Inc. manufactures and

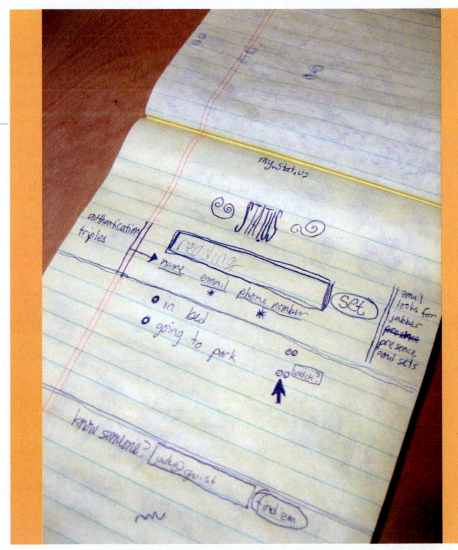

Jack Dorsey founded the idea for Twitter on a sketch pad. Dorsey says the idea was based on the way dispatched vehicles, such as cabs, communicate with one another. Via radio, they are constantly squawking to each other about where they are and what they are doing.

The future for small business remains promising. The opportunities to apply creativity and entrepreneurship to serve customers are unlimited. While large organizations such as Wal-Mart, which has more than 1.8 million employees, typically must adapt to change slowly, a small business can adapt to customer and community needs and changing trends immediately. This flexibility provides small businesses with a definite advantage over large companies. The Internet is helping many small businesses gain a competitive advantage without a lot of additional costs. Table 6.6 shows that most consumers will use the Internet to seek out local businesses, and that many businesses have a marketing budget weighted toward online advertising in order to take advantage of this trend.

TABLE 6.6 Small Business Web Strategy

Sixty-three percent of consumers turn to the Internet first to find a local business.	
Percentage of Small-Business Owners	**Percentage of Marketing Budget Dedicated to Online Advertising**
Less than 10%	80
11 to 20%	8
21 to 30%	3
More than 31%	9

Source: Nielsen Online/Web Visible survey of 261 small-business owners. *USA Today,* March 5, 2009, p. B-1.

"Intrapreneurs" are employees within firms who "think outside the box" to come up with great new products, services, and procedures. Some companies do a better job of listening to and fostering their intrapreneurs than others.

●● **LO7**

Explain why many large businesses are trying to "think small."

MAKING BIG BUSINESSES ACT "SMALL"

The continuing success and competitiveness of small businesses through rapidly changing conditions in the business world have led many large corporations to take a closer look at what makes their smaller rivals tick. More and more firms are emulating small businesses in an effort to improve their own bottom line. Beginning in the 1980s and continuing through the present, the buzzword in business has been to *downsize,* or the even newer term is *right-size* to reduce management layers, corporate staff, and work tasks in order to make the firm more

flexible, resourceful, and innovative like a smaller business. Many well-known U.S. companies, including IBM, Ford, Apple Computer, General Electric, Xerox, and 3M, have downsized to improve their competitiveness, as have German, British, and Japanese firms. Other firms have sought to make their businesses "smaller" by making their operating units function more like independent small businesses, each responsible for its profits, losses, and resources. Of course, some large corporations, such as Southwest Airlines, have acted like small businesses from their inception, with great success.

Trying to capitalize on small-business success in introducing innovative new products, more and more companies are attempting to instill a spirit of entrepreneurship into even

CHECK OUT

www.mhhe.com/FerrellM2e

for study materials including Interactive Exercises, Quizzes, iPod downloads, and video.

SO YOU WANT TO BE AN ENTREPRENEUR OR SMALL-BUSINESS OWNER

In times when jobs are scarce many people turn to entrepreneurship as a way to find employment. As long as there continue to be new niches and unfulfilled needs of consumers, there will be a demand for entrepreneurs and small businesses. Entrepreneurs and small-business owners have been, and will continue to be a vital part of the U.S. economy, whether in retailing, wholesaling, manufacturing, technology, or even services. There are a lot of advantages to forming a business around your idea. Independence is perhaps the biggest one for a lot of people, especially those who do not work well in a corporate setting and like to call their own shots. Smaller businesses are also clearly cheaper to start up than large ones in terms of salaries that must be paid, infrastructure, and equipment. Smallness also gives you a lot of flexibility to change with the times. If consumers suddenly start demanding new and different products or services, a small business is more likely to deliver them quickly.

Starting your own business is not easy, however, especially in slow economic times. Even in good times, taking an idea and turning it into a business has a very high failure rate. This situation can be even worse when money is tight. Reduced revenues and expensive materials can hurt a small business more than a large one because a small business has fewer resources to begin with. When people are feeling the pinch from rising food and fuel prices, they tend to cut back on other expenditures, potentially harming your small business or entrepreneurship. Increased costs of materials also will cut into your bottom line. There are a number of things you can do to help keep your company afloat, however:

- Set clear payment schedules for all clients. Small businesses tend to be worse about collecting payments than are large ones, especially if the clients are acquaintances. However, you need to keep cash flowing into the company to keep business going.

- Take the time to learn about tax breaks. A lot of people do not realize all the deductions they can claim for items such as equipment and health insurance, among others.

- Focus on the customers you have, not on spending a lot of time looking for new ones—this idea plays into relationship management. It is far less expensive for a company to keep its existing customers happy than it is attract new ones.

- Although entrepreneurs and small-business owners are more likely to be friends with their customers, do not let this tempt you to give things away for free. Make it clear to your customers what the basic price is for what you are selling, and charge for extra features, extra service, and so on.

- Make sure the office has the conveniences employees need, like a good coffee maker and other drinks and snacks. This will help keep employees happy, but it also will help keep productivity up by keeping employees closer to their desks.

- A really important consideration is how a manager/owner's actions set an example. If money is tight, show your commitment to cutting costs and making the business work by doing simple things like taking the bus to work or bringing a sack lunch (in a cheap reusable bag) every day.

- Don't be so focused on cost cutting that you don't try to increase sales while keeping costs the same. Do not forget to increase productivity—do not look only at cutting costs.

In unsure economic times, these measures should help new entrepreneurs and small-business owners sustain their businesses. Learning how to run a business on a shoestring is a great way to cut fat and establish lean, efficient operations.[34]

the largest firms. In major corporations, **intrapreneurs,** like entrepreneurs, take responsibility for, or "champion," the development of innovations of any kind *within* the larger organization.[35] Often they use company resources and time to develop a new product for the company. ∎

Team Exercise

Explore successful global franchises. Go to the companies' Web sites and find the requirements for applying for three franchises. The chapter provides examples of successful franchises. What do the companies provide, and what is expected to be provided by the franchisor? Compare and contrast each group's findings for the franchises researched. For example, at Subway, the franchisee is responsible for the initial franchise fee, finding locations, leasehold improvements and equipment, hiring employees and operating restaurants, and paying an 8 percent royalty to the company and a fee into the advertising fund. The company provides access to formulas and operational systems, store design and equipment ordering guidance, a training program, an operations manual, a representative onsite during the opening, periodic evaluations and ongoing support, and informative publications.

7

THE NATURE of MANAGEMENT

Introduction

For any organization—small or large, for profit or nonprofit—to achieve its objectives, it must have equipment and raw materials to turn into products to market, employees to make and sell the products, and financial resources to purchase additional goods and services, pay employees, and generally operate the business. To accomplish this, it must also have one or more managers to plan, organize, staff, direct, and control the work that goes on.

This chapter introduces the field of management. It examines and surveys the various functions, levels, and areas of management in business. The skills that managers need for success and the steps that lead to effective decision making also are discussed.

LO1

Define management, and explain its role in the achievement of organizational objectives.

THE IMPORTANCE OF MANAGEMENT

Management is a process designed to achieve an organization's objectives by using its resources effectively and efficiently in a changing environment. *Effectively* means having the intended result; *efficiently* means accomplishing the objectives with a minimum of resources. **Managers** make decisions about the use of the organization's resources and are concerned with planning, organizing, staffing, directing, and controlling the organization's activities so as to reach its objectives. For example, in an effort to reclaim its title as overall sales leader among commercial jet companies, Boeing launched the 787 Dreamliner. Dreamliner sold nearly 900 units of the $162 million aircraft before the model ever flew, making it Boeing's hottest selling commercial aircraft ever with nearly $15 billion in sales. However, the project was plagued with problems from the start and even late in 2009 not a single plane had been deemed fit to fly. In spite of the many setbacks, the openness and honesty of the company when communicating its problems have allowed Boeing to continue to be a profitable company.[1] Management is universal. It takes place not only in businesses of all sizes, but also in government, the military, labor unions, hospitals, schools, and religious groups—any organization requiring the coordination of resources.

Every organization, in the pursuit of its objectives, must acquire resources (people, raw materials and equipment, money, and information) and coordinate their use to turn out a final good or service. Employees are one of the most important resources in helping a business attain its objectives. Successful companies such as Starbucks recruit, train, compensate, and provide benefits (such as shares of stock and health insurance) to foster employee loyalty. Acquiring suppliers is another important part of managing resources and ensuring that products are made available to customers. As firms reach global markets, companies such as General Motors, Union Pacific, and Cargill enlist hundreds of diverse suppliers that provide goods and services to support operations. A good supplier maximizes efficiencies and provides creative solutions to help the company reduce expenses and reach its objectives.[2] Finally, the manager needs adequate financial resources to pay for the essential activities; the primary source of funding is the money generated from sales of tickets and snacks. All these resources and activities must be coordinated and controlled if the business is to earn a profit. Organizations must have adequate resources of all types, and managers must carefully coordinate the use of these resources if they are to achieve the organization's objectives.

LO2

Describe the major functions of management.

MANAGEMENT FUNCTIONS

To coordinate the use of resources so that the business can develop, make, and sell products, managers engage in a series of activities: planning, organizing, staffing, directing, and controlling (Figure 7.1). Although we describe each separately, these five functions are interrelated, and managers may perform two or more of them at the same time.

Planning

Planning, the process of determining the organization's objectives and deciding how to accomplish them, is the first function of management. Planning is a crucial activity, for it designs the map that lays the groundwork for the other functions. It involves forecasting events and determining the best course of action from a set of options or choices. The plan itself specifies what should be done, by whom, where, when, and how. Ford is struggling to find the right strategy in an atmosphere of global competition. The company lost its focus

FIGURE 7.1 The Functions of Management

Managers

Planning	Organizing	Staffing	Directing	Controlling
activities to achieve the organization's objectives	resources and activities to achieve the organization's objectives	the organization with qualified people	employees' activities toward achievement of objectives	the organization's activities to keep it on course

over the past decade or so, and now it is seeking to sharpen its image. Ford is attempting to associate itself with smaller cars to appeal to an international market. The Fiesta is the model Ford hopes will catch on abroad. It is rolling out in Europe first, it enters North American markets in 2010. If the global market accepts the new Fiesta, all the management and planning that went into it will have paid off.[3] All businesses—from the smallest restaurant to the largest multinational corporation—need to develop plans for achieving success. But before an organization can plan a course of action, it must first determine what it wants to achieve.

objectives Objectives, the ends or results desired by the organization, derive from the organization's **mission,** which describes its fundamental purpose and basic philosophy. A photo lab, for example, might say that its mission is to provide customers with memories. To carry out its mission, the photo lab sets specific objectives relating to its mission, such as reducing development defects to less than 2 percent, introducing a selection of photo albums and frames for customers' use in displaying their photos, providing customers' proofs or negatives over the Internet, providing technical assistance, and so on. Herbal tea marketer Celestial Seasonings says that its mission is "To create and sell healthful, naturally oriented products that nurture people's bodies and uplift their souls."[4]

A business's objectives may be elaborate or simple. Common objectives relate to profit, competitive advantage, efficiency, and growth. Organizations with profit as a goal want to have money and assets left over after paying off business expenses. Objectives regarding competitive advantage generally are stated in terms of percentage of sales increase and market share, with the goal of increasing those figures.

○ ● **Objectives, the ends or results desired by the organization**

Efficiency objectives involve making the best use of the organization's resources. The photo lab's objective of holding defects to less than 2 percent is an example of an efficiency objective. Growth objectives relate to an organization's ability to adapt and to get new products to the marketplace in a timely fashion. The mission of Procter & Gamble is to continue to improve customers' quality of life through meaningful product research, development, and innovation. It took more than eight years and 180 researchers to develop the polymer that helps prevent diaper rash, resulting in happier and healthier babies. P&G spends nearly $2 billion on product research and development.[5] Other organizational objectives include service, ethical, and community goals. Deloitte, a top professional services organization, was honored with the Points of Light Institute's Corporate Engagement Award for Excellence for its commitment to volunteerism. Deloitte has a 3-year $50 million commitment to pro bono work, as well as IMPACT Day, a companywide commitment to volunteering in which 40,000 employees are encouraged to leave the office and volunteer in their communities.[6] Objectives provide direction for all managerial decisions; additionally, they establish criteria by which performance can be evaluated.

plans There are three general types of plans for meeting objectives—strategic, tactical, and operational. A firm's highest managers develop its **strategic plans,** which establish the long-range objectives and overall strategy or course of action by which the firm fulfills its mission. Strategic

● **MISSION** the statement of an organization's fundamental purpose and basic philosophy

● **STRATEGIC PLANS** those plans that establish the long-range objectives and overall strategy or course of action by which a firm fulfills its mission

TCP and Compact Fluorescent Light Bulbs Are Lighting the Way Toward Sustainability

Compact fluorescent lights (CFLs) use 75 percent less energy than traditional incandescent bulbs, making them eco-friendly. TCP (Technical Consumer Products), Inc., is the largest provider of CFLs in the United States. The man behind TCP is Ellis Yan. Yan owns factories in Shanghai and produces over 1 million CFLs daily. Many of TCP's bulbs are sold to Home Depot and Wal-Mart.

Although CFLs cost more to buy than standard incandescent bulbs, CFL users save money by saving energy. For example, if a CFL bulb has 10,000 hours of life, a user saves 550 kilowatt-hours. Using the figure of 10 cents per kilowatt-hour, a user saves $55 in energy costs per bulb. In addition, one would use 10 to 13 incandescent bulbs to match the life of a CFL bulb. According

to the TCP Web site, if every home in the United States replaced one incandescent bulb with a CFL, the country would save enough energy to light over 3 million homes annually, save more than $600 million in annual energy costs, and prevent greenhouse gases equivalent to the emissions of over 800,000 cars.

Ellis Yan is passionate about both his business and the opportunity to make a positive impact by reducing energy consumption. Although other companies, such as GE and Sylvania, are involved in the CFL market, TCP has a head start and a powerful reputation. Voted 2009 ENERGY STAR Partner of the Year by the U.S. Environmental Protection Agency and the Department of Energy, TCP is making a difference.[7] ❖

Q: Discussion Questions

1. Based on the types of leaders described in the text, what kind of leader do you think Yan is?

2. What reasons does TCP have for being confident about the continued success of the company?

3. What are the advantages of switching to CFLs, and how should this help boost business for TCP?

plans generally cover periods ranging from 2 to 10 years or even longer. They include plans to add products, purchase companies, sell unprofitable segments of the business, issue stock, and move into international markets. Faced with stiff competition, rising costs, and slowing sales, many companies are closing U.S. plants and moving production to factories abroad. For example, Converse Inc. (sneaker maker), Lionel LLC (producer of model trains), and Zebco (fishing reel manufacturer) all stopped U.S. production in favor of Asian factories.[8] Strategic plans must take into account the organization's capabilities and resources, the changing business environment, and organizational objectives. Plans should be market-driven, matching customers' desire for value with operational capabilities, processes, and human resources.[9]

Tactical plans are short-range plans designed to implement the activities and objectives specified in the strategic plan. These plans, which usually cover a period of one year or less, help keep the organization on the course established in the strategic plan. Because tactical plans permit the organization to react to changes in the environment while continuing to focus on the company's overall strategy, management must periodi-

cally review and update them. Declining performance or failure to meet objectives set out in tactical plans may be one reason for revising them. For example, when fuel prices rose rapidly in 2008, airlines and other transportation firms such as FedEx and UPS had to add surcharges to maintain control over expenses. By 2009, fuel prices fell significantly from a high of $147 a barrel to a mere $30 a barrel. When oil prices are low, other groups are hurt by falling revenues, such as oil producers and investors, although many businesses find it easier to turn a profit when oil prices are lower.[10] When public concern emerged over Americans' high level of plastic bag consumption, which stands at over 110 billion bags a year, the grocery chain Whole Foods stopped offering plastic bags altogether. Wal-Mart and Kroger began to offer reusable canvas and nylon bags in response to this problem.[11] These situations required companies to develop short-run or tactical plans to deal with stakeholder concerns.

A retailing organization with a five-year strategic plan to invest $5 billion in 500 new retail stores may develop five tactical plans (each covering one year) specifying how much to spend to set up each new store, where to locate each new store, and when to open each new store. Tactical plans are designed to execute the overall strategic plan. Because of their short-term nature, they are easier to adjust or abandon if changes in the environment or the company's performance so warrant.

Operational plans are very short term and specify what actions specific individuals, work groups, or departments need to accomplish to achieve the tactical plan and ultimately the strategic plan. They may apply to just one month, week, or even day. For example, a work group may be assigned a weekly production quota to ensure there are sufficient products available to elevate market share (tactical goal) and ultimately help the firm be number one in its product category (strategic goal). Returning to our retail store example, operational plans may specify the schedule for opening one new store, hiring new employees, obtaining merchandise, training new employees, and opening for actual business.

Another element in planning is the idea of **crisis management or contingency planning,** which deals with potential disasters such as product tampering, oil spills, fire, earthquake, computer virus, or even a reputation crisis due to unethical or illegal conduct by one or more employees. Investment bank Bear Stearns found itself on the brink of

Firms need to develop contingency plans—sometimes quickly. To prevent disaster, the investment banking firm Merrill Lynch hastily arranged to sell itself to Bank of America in 2008. The move saved Merrill. However, Bank of America's stock price dropped sharply because its investors feared it had paid too much.

collapse in 2008. Its problems were largely due to the credit crisis and subprime lending disasters. Within minutes, Bear Stearns lost half of its market value. The bank's financial condition deteriorated to the point of failure within 24 hours, which could have brought down the U.S. stock market. To save the company and prevent widespread financial panic, another bank, JP Morgan Chase, joined with the U.S. Federal Reserve to provide loans and create a merger between Bear Stearns and JP Morgan Chase. Businesses that have contingency plans tend to respond more effectively when problems occur than do businesses that lack such plans; this may lead to the avoidance of a Bear Stearns–level disaster.

Many companies, including Ashland Oil, H. J. Heinz, and Johnson & Johnson, have crisis management teams to deal specifically with problems, permitting other managers to continue to focus on their regular duties. Some companies even hold regular disaster drills to ensure that their employees know how to respond when a crisis does occur. Crisis management plans generally cover maintaining business operations throughout a crisis and communicating with the public, employees, and officials about the nature of and the company's response to the problem. Communication is especially important to minimize panic and damaging rumors; it also demonstrates that the company is aware of the problem and plans to respond. In 2005, major hurricanes hitting the Gulf Coast region disrupted many business activities. The airlines were especially damaged when many Americans were reluctant to travel. Incidents such as this highlight the importance of tactical planning for crises and the need to respond publicly and quickly when a disaster occurs.

Organizing

Rarely are individuals in an organization able to achieve common goals without some form of structure. Organizing is the structuring of resources and activities to accomplish objectives in an efficient and effective manner. Managers organize by reviewing plans and determining what activities are necessary to implement them; then they divide the work into small units and assign it to specific individuals, groups, or departments. As companies reorganize for greater efficiency, more often than not, they are organizing work into teams to handle core processes such as new-product development instead of organizing around traditional departments such as marketing and production.

Many firms were forced to downsize their workforces when the economy slipped into a recession in 2008.

Organizing is important for several reasons. It helps create synergy, whereby the effect of a whole system equals more than that of its parts. It also establishes lines of authority, improves communication, helps avoid duplication of resources, and can improve competitiveness by speeding up decision making. In an effort to reduce costs and improve efficiency, media giant Reuters Group PLC reorganized its product-based divisions into four key customer segments. The new business units are part of the company's strategy to get closer to clients by using Internet technologies. The units focus on clients involved in financial products (sales and trading, enterprise solutions and research, and asset management), corporate products, and media products.[12] Because organizing is so important, we'll take a closer look at it in Chapter 8.

Staffing

Once managers have determined what work is to be done and how it is to be organized, they must ensure that the organization has enough employees with appropriate skills to do the work. Hiring people to carry out the work of the organization is known as staffing. Beyond recruiting people for positions within the firm, managers must determine what skills are needed for specific jobs, how to motivate and train employees to do their assigned jobs, how much to pay employees, what benefits to provide, and how to prepare employees for higher-level jobs in the firm at a later date. These elements of staffing will be explored in detail in Chapters 10 and 11.

Another aspect of staffing is downsizing, the elimination of significant numbers of employees from an organization, which has been a pervasive and much-talked-about trend. Whether it is called downsizing, rightsizing, trimming the fat, or the new reality in business, the implications of downsizing have been dramatic. After filing for Chapter 11 bankruptcy, General Motors was forced to downsize as part of its restructuring. The company eliminated over 1,100 dealerships, laid off employees, cut pay, and closed over a dozen plants. While many people have lost their jobs at GM, the ultimate goal is to make the company solvent and competitive again.[13] Many firms downsize by outsourcing production, sales, and technical positions to companies in other countries with lower labor costs. Downsizing has helped numerous firms reduce costs quickly and become more profitable (or become profitable after lengthy losses) in a short period of time.

Downsizing and outsourcing, however, have painful consequences. Obviously, the biggest casualty is those who lose their jobs, along with their incomes, insurance, and pensions. Some find

attitude and need to be led. Ten to 15 percent will be openly hostile or try to sabotage change in an effort to return to the way things were before. The remaining 10 to 15 percent will be the leaders who will try proactively to help make the situation work.[14] A survey of workers who remained after a downsizing found that many felt their jobs demanded more time and energy.[15]

After a downsizing situation, an effective manager will promote optimism and positive thinking and minimize criticism and fault-finding. Management should also build teamwork and encourage positive group discussions. Honest communication is important during a time of change and will lead to trust. Truthfulness about what has happened and also about future expectations is essential.

"Participation makes workers feel important, and the company benefits."

new jobs quickly; others do not. Another victim is the morale of the employees at downsized firms who get to keep their jobs. The employees left behind in a downsizing often feel more insecure, angry, and sad, and their productivity may decline as a result, the opposite of the effect sought. Managers can expect that 70 to 80 percent of those surviving a downsize will take a "wait-and-see"

Risk-management departments are a type of control mechanism that some firms use. The departments prevent firms such as banks from taking on too many risky endeavors, such as risky loans.

Directing

Once the organization has been staffed, management must direct the employees. **Directing** is motivating and leading employees to achieve organizational objectives. All managers are involved in directing, but it is especially important for lower-level managers who interact daily with the employees operating the organization. For example, an assembly-line supervisor for Frito-Lay must ensure that her workers know how to use their equipment properly and have the resources needed to carry out their jobs, and she must motivate her workers to achieve their expected output of packaged snacks.

Managers may motivate employees by providing incentives—such as the promise of a raise or promotion—for them to do a good job. But most workers want more than money from their jobs: They need to know that their employer values their ideas and input. Smart managers, therefore, ask workers to contribute ideas for reducing costs, making equipment more efficient, improving customer service, or even developing new products. This participation makes workers feel important, and the company benefits. Recognition and appreciation are often the best motivators for employees. Employees who understand more about their effect on the financial success of the company may be motivated to work harder for that success, and managers who understand the needs and desires of workers can motivate their employees to work harder and more productively. The motivation of employees is discussed in detail in Chapter 10.

Controlling

Planning, organizing, staffing, and directing are all important to the success of an organization, whether its objective is earning a profit or something else. But what happens when a firm fails to reach its goals despite a strong planning effort? **Controlling** is the process of evaluating and correcting activities to keep the organization on course. Control involves five activities: (1) measuring performance, (2) comparing present performance with standards or objectives, (3) identifying deviations from the standards, (4) investigating the causes of deviations, and (5) taking corrective action when necessary.

Controlling and planning are closely linked. Planning establishes goals and standards for performance. By monitoring performance and comparing it with standards, managers can determine whether performance is on target. When performance is substandard, management must determine why and take appropriate actions to get the firm back on course. In short, the control function helps managers assess the success of their plans. When plans have not been successful, the control process facilitates revision of the plans. ExxonMobil has run ads indicating that peak oil demand is decades away. This message conflicts with ads that Chevron is running, indicating that the world consumes two barrels of oil for every one that it finds. A strategy for dealing with concerns about depleting energy resources is for oil companies to invest in finding and developing new supplies of petroleum.[16]

The control process also helps managers deal with problems arising outside the firm. For example, if a firm is the subject of negative publicity, management should use the control process to determine why and to guide the firm's response.

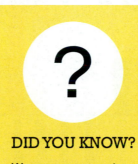

DID YOU KNOW?

Women represent only 15.7 percent of corporate officers and just 6.2 percent of all top earners.[17]

TYPES OF MANAGEMENT

All managers—whether the sole proprietor of a small video store or the hundreds of managers of a large company such as Paramount Pictures—perform the five functions just discussed. In the case of the video store, the owner handles all the functions, but in a large company with more than one manager, responsibilities must be divided and delegated. This division of responsibility is generally achieved by establishing levels of management and areas of specialization—finance, marketing, and so on.

Levels of Management

As we have hinted, many organizations have multiple levels of management—top management, middle management, and first-line, or supervisory management. These levels form a pyramid, as shown in Figure 7.2. As the pyramid shape implies, there are generally more middle managers than top managers, and still more first-line managers. Very small organizations may have only one manager (typically, the owner), who assumes the responsibilities of all three levels. Large businesses have many managers at each level to coordinate the use of the organization's resources. Managers at all three levels perform all five management functions, but the amount of time they spend on each function varies, as we shall see (Figure 7.3).

top management In businesses, **top managers** include the president and other top executives, such as the chief executive officer (CEO), chief financial officer (CFO), and chief operations officer (COO), who have overall responsibility for

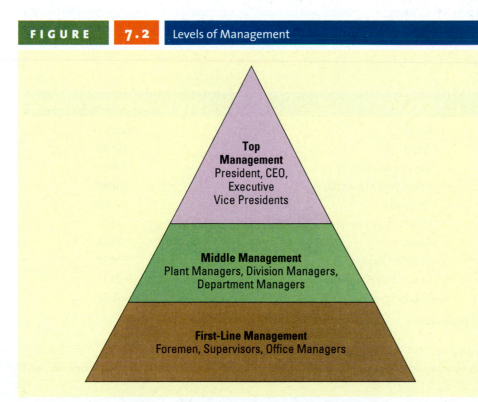

FIGURE 7.2 Levels of Management

Top Management
President, CEO, Executive Vice Presidents

Middle Management
Plant Managers, Division Managers, Department Managers

First-Line Management
Foremen, Supervisors, Office Managers

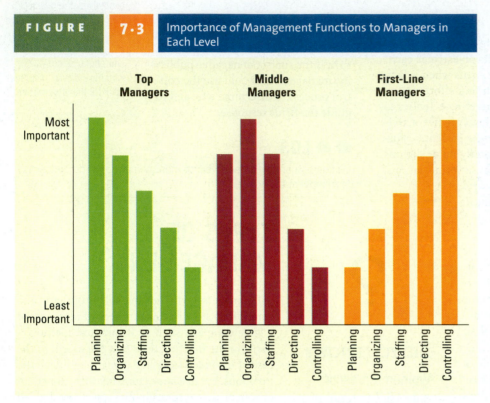

FIGURE 7.3 Importance of Management Functions to Managers in Each Level

Top Managers | Middle Managers | First-Line Managers

Most Important — Least Important

Planning, Organizing, Staffing, Directing, Controlling

global trends.[18] In public corporations, even chief executive officers have a boss—the firm's board of directors. With technological advances continuing and privacy concerns increasing, some companies are adding a new top management position—chief privacy officer (CPO). There are currently an estimated 2,000 CPOs in U.S. corporations, and that number is expected to rise over the next few years in response to growing concerns about privacy as well as new legislation such as the Sarbanes-Oxley Act. Among the companies that have appointed CPOs are American Express, Citigroup, Hewlett-Packard, Microsoft, and the U.S. Postal Service.[19] In government, top management refers to the president, a governor, or a mayor or city manager; in education, a chancellor of a university or a county superintendent of education.

Top-level managers spend most of their time planning. They make the organization's strategic decisions, decisions that focus on an overall scheme or key idea for using resources to take advantage of opportunities. They decide whether to add products, acquire companies, sell unprofitable business segments, and move into foreign markets. Top managers also represent their company to the public and to government regulators.

the organization. For example, Carlos Ghosn, CEO of both Renault and Nissan, utilizes quick decision making to adapt to changing tastes in global markets. His joint ventures for Nissan and Renault include electric car projects in Denmark, creating a $3,000 car for India, and orchestrating the exit strategy for the full-size Nissan Titan in the United States. The Titan plant in Mississippi is being converted to light commercial truck production. In addition, Ghosn agreed to supply small cars to Chrysler. In emerging markets he is focused on local tastes and export designs in order to ride

Given the importance and range of top management's decisions, top managers generally have many years of varied experience and command top salaries. In addition to salaries, top managers' compensation packages typically include bonuses, long-term incentive awards, stock, and stock options. Table 7.1 lists the

TABLE 7.1 The 10 Highest Paid CEOs

Rank	CEO	Company	Total Compensation[a] ($ in millions)
1.	Lawrence J. Ellison	Oracle	$192.92
2.	Frederic M. Poses	Trane	127.10
3.	Aubrey K. McClendon	Chesapeake Energy	116.89[b]
4.	Angelo R. Mozilo	Countrywide Financial	102.84[b]
5.	Howard D. Schultz	Starbucks	98.60[c]
6.	Nabeel Gareeb	MEMC Electronic Mats	79.56
7.	Daniel P. Amos	Aflac	75.16
8.	Lloyd C. Blankfein	Goldman Sachs Group	73.72
9.	Richard D. Fairbank	Capital One Financial	73.17
10.	Bob R. Simpson	XTO Energy	72.27[b]

[a]2007 compensation includes salary, bonuses, other compensation, and stock gains.

[b]Prior-year data.

[c]New chief executive; compensation may be for another executive office.

Source: Scott DeCarlo, "Top Paid CEOs," *Forbes,* April 30, 2008, www.forbes.com/2008/04/30/ceo-pay-compensation-lead-bestbosses08-cx-sd_0430ceo_intro.html?boxes=custom (accessed March 10, 2009).

10 highest paid CEOs including bonuses, stock options and other compensation.

Compensation committees are increasingly working with boards of directors and CEOs to attempt to keep pay in line with performance in order to benefit stockholders and key stakeholders. The majority of major companies cite their concern about attracting capable leadership for the CEO and other top executive positions in their organizations. Sixty-seven percent are concerned about their ability to attract and retain the most competent leadership. A new trend in shareholder activism supports shareholders voting on executives' compensation packages. Aflac Chairman and CEO Dan Amos accepted this process, and in early 2008, stockholders voted on his 2009 compensation package. Aflac stock had soared 38 percent the previous year. More than 93 percent of shareholders approved Amos's compensation of $14.8 million. Amos is the eighth longest-tenured CEO in the United States, having served 18 years on the job and the return to shareholders had been a compound growth of 22 percent. Successful management translates into happy stockholders who are willing to compensate their top executives fairly and in line with performance.[20]

Workforce diversity is an important issue in today's corporations. Effective managers at enlightened corporations have found that diversity is good for workers and for the bottom line. Putting together different kinds of people to solve problems often results in better solutions. Betsy Holden, CEO of Kraft Foods, said, "When we look at the composition of teams within our company, we have found that those with a variety of perspectives are simply the most creative."[21] Managers from companies devoted to workforce diversity devised six rules that make diversity work (see Table 7.2). Diversity is explored in greater detail in Chapter 11.

middle management   Rather than making strategic decisions about the whole

organization, **middle managers** are responsible for tactical planning that will implement the general guidelines established by top management. Thus, their responsibility is more narrowly focused than that of top managers. Middle managers are involved in the specific operations of the organization and spend more time organizing than do other managers. In business, plant managers, division managers, and department managers make up middle management. The product manager for laundry detergent at a consumer products manufacturer, the department chairperson in a university, and the head of a state public health department are all middle managers. The

Larry Ellison, of the software firm Oracle, is among the best paid CEOs in the United States, if not the world. Ellison frequently earns more than $500 million annually, mostly in the form of exercised stock options.

TABLE 7.2   Six Rules That Make Diversity Work

Rule	Action
1. Search for the best	Invest time and money in "affirmative recruiting."
2. Help newcomers fit in	Emphasize cooperation and teamwork.
3. Educate everyone	Address employees' fears of change and discomfort with people from diverse backgrounds; encourage minority employees to express their views; encourage others to listen.
4. Keep score	Hold managers accountable for diversity goals and progress.
5. Sweat the details	Pay attention to the smaller differences in diverse employees and address concerns.
6. See the future	Invest in potential employees of the future (e.g., develop programs that target minority groups in middle and high schools).

Source: Annie Finnigan, "Different Strokes," *Working Woman,* April 2001, pp. 42–48.

may be asked to analyze the costs and revenues of a new sandwich product to determine its contribution to Subway's profitability. All organizations must have adequate financial resources to acquire the physical and human resources that are necessary to create goods and services. Consequently, financial resource management is of the utmost importance.

ranks of middle managers have been shrinking as more and more companies downsize to be more productive.

first-line management.

Most people get their first managerial experience as **first-line managers,** those who supervise workers and the daily operations of the organization. They are responsible for implementing the plans established by middle management and directing workers' daily performance on the job. They spend most of their time directing and controlling. Common titles for first-line managers are foreman, supervisor, and office manager.

Areas of Management

At each level, there are managers who specialize in the basic functional areas of business: finance, production and operations, human resources (personnel), marketing, and administration.

financial management

Financial managers focus on obtaining the money needed for the successful operation of the organization and using that money in accordance with organizational goals. Among the responsibilities of financial managers are projecting income and expenses over a specified period, determining short- and long-term financing needs and finding sources of financing to fill those needs, identifying and selecting appropriate ways to invest extra funds, monitoring the flow of financial resources, and protecting the financial resources of the organization. A financial manager at Subway, for example,

> **Most people get their first managerial experience as first-line managers**

production and operations management

Production and operations managers develop and administer the activities involved in transforming resources into goods, services, and ideas ready for the marketplace. Production and operations managers are typically involved in planning and designing production facilities, purchasing raw materials and supplies, managing inventory, scheduling processes to meet demand, and ensuring that products meet quality standards.

Because no business can exist without the production of goods and services, production and operations managers are vital to an organization's success. At Pfizer Global Research, for example, Robert Swanson works as an associate director of logistics and supply chain management, which makes him responsible for transporting and caring for lab equipment, protective gear, chemicals, and maintenance and office supplies and shipping scientific documents, materials, and other equipment to other Pfizer facilities around the world.[22]

human resources management

Human resources managers handle the staffing function and deal with employees in a formalized manner. Once known as personnel managers, they determine an organization's human resource needs; recruit and hire new employees; develop and administer employee benefits, training, and performance appraisal programs; and deal with government regulations concerning employment practices. For example, some companies recognize that their employees' health affects their health care costs. Therefore, more progressive companies provide health care facilities and outside health club memberships, encourage proper nutrition, and discourage smoking in an effort to improve employee health and lower the costs of providing health care benefits. Pfizer of Canada and DaimlerChrysler's Windsor, Canada, Assembly Plant, launched a program called "Turn Up Your Heart." The goal of the program is to assess and reduce the risks of heart disease among both employees and retirees and to increase quality of life and productivity while reducing health care costs. The results of the program after one year were dramatic. Almost half of the participants lost an average of 16 pounds, there was a 36 percent reduction in smoking (among those with high cardiovascular risks), and participants reduced their 10-year cardiovascular risk from "moderate" at the beginning of the program to "low risk" at its end. Business analysts

Production managers oversee the activities that need to be done to transform the company's resources into quality goods and services in a timely manner.

indicate that DaimlerChrysler Canada could save more than $2 million in 10 years if this program were implemented across Canada.[23]

marketingmanagement
Marketing managers are responsible for planning, pricing, and promoting products and making them available to customers through distribution. The marketing manager who oversees Sony televisions, for example, must make decisions regarding a new television's size, features, name, price, and packaging, as well as plan what type of stores to distribute the television through and the advertising campaign that will introduce the new television to consumers. Within the realm of marketing, there are several areas of specialization: product development and management, pricing, promotion, and distribution. Specific jobs are found in areas such as marketing research, advertising, personal selling, retailing, telemarketing, and Internet marketing.

information technology (IT) management
Information technology (IT) managers are responsible for implementing, maintaining, and controlling technology applications in business, such as computer networks. Google, the online search engine, is one of the five most popular sites on the Internet and employs more than 5,500 employees, many of whom are IT managers. Google is the world's largest search engine as a result of partnerships with America Online, Netscape, and others. To maintain its creative and productive culture, Google employees have access to workout rooms, and roller hockey is played in the parking lot twice a week. The Google Café provides healthy lunches and dinners for all staff members.[24] One major task in IT management is securing computer systems from unauthorized users while making the system easy to use for employees, suppliers, and others who have legitimate reason to access the system. Another crucial task is protecting the systems' data, even during a disaster such as a fire. IT managers are also responsible for teaching and helping employees use technology resources efficiently through training and support. At many companies, some aspects of IT management are outsourced to third-party firms that can perform this function expertly and efficiently.

administrative management
Administrative managers are not specialists; rather, they manage an entire business or a major segment of a business, such as the Cadillac Division of General Motors. Such managers coordinate the activities of specialized managers, which in the GM Cadillac Division would include marketing managers, production managers, and financial managers. Because of the broad nature of their responsibilities, administrative managers are often called general managers. However, this does not mean that administrative managers lack expertise in any particular area. Many top executives have risen through the ranks of financial management, production and operations management, or marketing management; but most top managers are actually administrative managers, employing skills in all areas of management.

 L04

Specify the skills managers need to be successful.

SKILLS NEEDED BY MANAGERS

Managers are typically evaluated as to how effective and efficient they are. Managing effectively and efficiently requires certain skills—leadership, technical expertise, conceptual skills, analytical skills, and human relations skills. Table 7.3 describes some of the roles managers may fulfill.

> ## "Strong leaders manage and pay attention to the culture of their organizations and the needs of their customers."

Leadership

Leadership is the ability to influence employees to work toward organizational goals. Strong leaders manage and pay attention to the culture of their organizations and the needs of their customers. Table 7.4 offers some tips for successful leadership while Table 7.5 lists the world's 10 most admired companies and their CEOs. The list is compiled for *Fortune* magazine by executives and analysts who grade companies according to nine attributes, including quality of management. A survey of 150 senior executives indicated that 89 percent believe it is more challenging today to be a leader compared with five years ago.[25]

TABLE 7.3 Managerial Roles

Type of Role	Specific Role	Examples of Role Activities
Decisional	Entrepreneur	Commit organizational resources to develop innovative goods and services; decide to expand internationally to obtain new customers for the organization's products
	Disturbance handler	Move quickly to take corrective action to deal with unexpected problems facing the organization from the external environment, such as a crisis like an oil spill, or from the internal environment, such as producing faulty goods or services
	Resource allocator	Allocate organizational resources among different functions and departments of the organization; set budgets and salaries of middle and first-level managers
	Negotiator	Work with suppliers, distributors, and labor unions to reach agreements about the quality and price of input, technical, and human resources; work with other organizations to establish agreements to pool resources to work on joint projects
Informational	Monitor	Evaluate the performance of managers in different functions and take corrective action to improve their performance; watch for changes occurring in the external and internal environment that may affect the organization in the future
	Disseminator	Inform employees about changes taking place in the external and internal environment that will affect them and the organization; communicate to employees the organization's vision and purpose
	Spokesperson	Launch a national advertising campaign to promote new goods and services; give a speech to inform the local community about the organization's future intentions
Interpersonal	Figurehead	Outline future organizational goals to employees at company meetings; open a new corporate headquarters building; state the organization's ethical guidelines and the principles of behavior employees are to follow in their dealings with customers and suppliers
	Leader	Provide an example for employees to follow; give direct commands and orders to subordinates; make decisions concerning the use of human and technical resources; mobilize employee support for specific organizational goals
	Liaison	Coordinate the work of managers in different departments; establish alliances between different organizations to share resources to produce new goods and services

Source: Gareth R. Jones and Jennifer M. George, *Essentials of Contemporary Management* (Burr Ridge, IL: McGraw-Hill/Irwin, 2004), p. 14.

Managers often can be classified into three types based on their leadership style. *Autocratic leaders* make all the decisions and then tell employees what must be done and how to do it. They generally use their authority and economic rewards to get employees to comply with their directions. *Democratic leaders* involve their employees in decisions. The manager presents a situation and encourages his or her subordinates to express opinions and contribute ideas. The manager then considers the employees' points of view and makes the decision. *Free-rein leaders* let their employees work without much interference.

The manager sets performance standards and allows employees to find their own ways to meet them. For this style to be effective, employees must know what the standards are, and they must be motivated to attain the standards. The free-rein style of leadership can be a powerful motivator because it demonstrates a great deal of trust and confidence in the employee.

TABLE 7.4 Seven Tips for Successful Leadership

- Build effective and responsive interpersonal relationships.
- Communicate effectively—in person, print, e-mail, etc.
- Build the team and enable employees to collaborate effectively.
- Understand the financial aspects of the business.
- Know how to create an environment in which people experience positive morale and recognition.
- Lead by example.
- Help people grow and develop.

Source: Susan M. Heathfield, "Seven Tips About Successful Management," What You Need to Know About.com (n.d.), http://humanresources.about.com/cs/managementissues/qt/mgmtsuccess.htm (accessed March 9, 2009).

TABLE 7.5 World's Most Admired Companies and Their CEOs

Company	Chief Executive Officer
Apple	Steve Jobs
Berkshire Hathaway	Warren Buffet
Toyota Motor	Katsuaki Watanabe
Google	Eric Schmidt
Johnson & Johnson	William Weldon
Proctor & Gamble	Alan Lafley
FedEx	Frederick Smith
Southwest Airlines	Gary Kelly
General Electric	Jeffrey R. Immelt
Microsoft	Steve Ballmer

Source: Adapted from "World's Most Admired Companies 2009," *Fortune,* http://money.cnn.com/magazines/fortune/mostadmired/2009/index.html (accessed March 11, 2009).

> ## "EMPLOYEES WHO HAVE BEEN INVOLVED IN DECISION MAKING GENERALLY REQUIRE LESS SUPERVISION THAN THOSE NOT SIMILARLY INVOLVED."

The effectiveness of the autocratic, democratic, and free-rein styles depends on several factors. One consideration is the type of employee. An autocratic style of leadership is generally needed to stimulate unskilled, unmotivated employees; highly skilled, trained, and motivated employees may respond better to democratic or free-rein leaders. On the other hand, employees who have been involved in decision making generally require less supervision than those not similarly involved. Other considerations are the manager's abilities and the situation itself. When a situation requires quick decisions, an autocratic style of leadership may be best because the manager does not have to consider input from a lot of people. If a special task force must be set up to solve a quality-control problem, a normally democratic manager may give free rein to the task force. Many managers, however, are unable to use more than one style of leadership. Some are unable to allow their subordinates to participate in decision making, let alone make any decisions. Thus, what leadership style is "best" depends on specific circumstances, and effective managers strive to adapt their leadership style as circumstances warrant. Many organizations offer programs to develop leadership. For example, banking giant Citigroup's CFO Charles Prince resigned after the subprime credit meltdown forced Citigroup to write down billions of dollars. While at Citigroup, Prince had focused on improving ethics. He also supported a corporate creed that leaders should "accept accountability for our failures."[26]

Technical Expertise

Managers need **technical expertise,** the specialized knowledge and training needed to perform jobs that are related to their area of management. Accounting managers need to be able to perform accounting jobs, and production managers need to be able to perform production jobs. Although a production manager may not actually perform a job, he or she needs technical expertise to train employees, answer questions, provide guidance, and solve problems. Technical skills are most needed by first-line managers and least critical to top-level managers.

Today, most organizations rely on computers to perform routine data processing, simplify complex calculations, organize and maintain vast amounts of information to communicate, and help managers make sound decisions. For this reason, most managers have found computer expertise to be an essential skill.

Conceptual Skills

Conceptual skills, the ability to think in abstract terms and to see how parts fit together to form the whole, are needed by all managers, particularly top-level managers. Top management must be able to evaluate continually where the company will be in the future. Conceptual skills also involve the ability to think creatively. Recent scientific research has revealed that creative thinking, which is behind the development of many innovative products and ideas, including fiber optics and compact disks,

Countrywide Financial: Instigators of the Financial Crisis

Countrywide Financial was the largest provider of home loans in the country before becoming involved in the subprime scandal. At first, Countrywide's offering of subprime loans looked like a good way to help lower-income individuals achieve the American dream of owning a house. Yet due to the decisions of reckless company officials, Countrywide is now thought to be a major instigator of the 2008–2009 financial crisis. Much of its culpability stems from risky, and downright deceptive, business practices. Numerous liar loans have been traced back to the company. Liar loans were created when consumers overstated their income on home loan applications, some by over 50 percent. They were a major factor in the chain reaction that led to the financial crisis, and experts estimate

that losses from them could total about $100 billion. Many believe the company knowingly issued the liar loans in exchange for quick profits. It was learned later that Countrywide officials, including CEO Angelo Mozilo, also were selling hundreds of millions in stock and stock options, possibly due to insider information. Mozilo himself is accused of taking $10 million more than what was disclosed in reports; if true, this would make the company guilty of inaccurate financial reporting. These unethical actions make it more likely that company officials knew Countrywide was engaging in dishonest mortgage practices. As a result of its major losses, the company started to founder. In 2008, Bank of America agreed to purchase it for $4 billion, a fraction of what the company was worth. It has yet to

be seen whether Countrywide's reputation can be restored.[27] ❖

 Q: Discussion Questions

1. Which management functions did Countrywide fail to implement properly (planning, organizing, staffing, directing, or controlling)?

2. How could top management better manage risks to prevent a Countrywide-type scandal?

3. What went wrong with decision making at Countrywide?

Human Relations Skills

People skills, or **human relations skills,** are the ability to deal with people, both inside and outside the organization. Those who can relate to others, communicate well with others, understand the needs of others, and show a true appreciation for others are generally more successful than managers who lack human relations skills. People skills are especially important in hospitals, airline companies, banks, and other organizations that provide services. For example, at Southwest Airlines, every new employee attends "You, Southwest and Success," a day-long class designed to teach employees about the airline and its reputation for impeccable customer service. All employees in management positions at

Although 6 of 10 college graduates today are women, women are still grossly underrepresented as board members, corporate officers, and CEOs in America.

> **Promoting people within the organization into management positions tends to increase motivation by showing employees that those who work hard and are competent can advance in the company.**

can be learned. As a result, IBM, AT&T, GE, Hewlett-Packard, Intel, and other top U.S. firms hire creative consultants to teach their managers how to think creatively.

Analytical Skills

Analytical skills refer to the ability to identify relevant issues and recognize their importance, understand the relationships between them, and perceive the underlying causes of a situation. When managers have identified critical factors and causes, they can take appropriate action. All managers need to think logically, but this skill is probably most important to the success of top-level managers.

Southwest take mandatory leadership classes that address skills related to listening, staying in touch with employees, and handling change without compromising values.

WHERE DO MANAGERS COME FROM?

Good managers are not born; they are made. An organization acquires managers in three ways: promoting employees from within, hiring managers from other organizations, and hiring managers graduating from colleges.

Promoting people within the organization into management positions tends to increase motivation by showing employees that those who work hard and are competent can advance in the company. Internal promotion also provides managers who are already familiar with the company's goals and problems. Procter & Gamble prefers to promote managers from within, which creates managers who are familiar with the company's products and policies and builds company loyalty. Promoting from within, however, can lead to problems: It may limit innovation. The new manager may continue the practices and policies of previous managers. Thus it is vital for companies—even companies committed to promotion from within—to hire outside people from time to time to bring new ideas into the organization.

Finding managers with the skills, knowledge, and experience required to run an organization or department is sometimes difficult. At Coca-Cola, for example, the board of directors agonized for months over the best choice to replace former CEO and chairman Douglas Daft upon his retirement. Their search marked the first time in the firm's history that it had sought new leadership from outside the company, although the board concentrated its search among executives experienced with well-known consumer brands.[28] Their ultimate choice wasn't exactly an outsider: E. Neville Isdell had risen through the ranks of Coca-Cola for more than 30 years before leaving to take the reins of another company.[29] For the first time in more than two decades, Americans drank fewer soft drinks than the previous year. Coca-Cola Classic sales fell 2 percent from the previous year, and strong leadership is needed to grow the core business and improve stock performance.[30] Specialized executive employment agencies—sometimes called headhunters, recruiting managers, or executive search firms—can help locate candidates from other companies. The downside is that even though outside people can bring fresh ideas to a company, hiring them may cause resentment among existing employees as well as involve greater expense in relocating an individual to another city or state.

Schools and universities provide a large pool of potential managers, and entry-level applicants can be screened for their developmental potential. People with specialized management skills, such as those with an M.B.A. (Master of Business Administration) degree, may be good candidates.

Some companies offer special training programs for future potential managers. For example, Lehman Brothers Holdings Inc. financed a one-day run-through at the Marine Corps base at Quantico, Virginia, for M.B.A. candidates from the University of Pennsylvania's Wharton School of Business. In an effort to acquire leadership skills, student volunteers faced physically

Flight attendant David Holmes became a YouTube sensation by rapping passenger instructions on Southwest Airlines flights. Southwest Airlines is known for excellent human relations and knowing how to keep the workplace fun.

daunting tasks, including climbing an 18-foot wall with an 18-degree incline, crossing a rope 20 feet above the ground, crawling facedown under barbed wire through mud, and wading through a four-foot-deep stretch of 50-degree swampy water. The course challenged the students to stay composed in stressful situations, such as rescuing an "injured hostage" in an allotted time and carrying a 20-pound can of "ammunition" across a stream before advancing enemy troops arrived. According to the commanding officer, "The course is designed to take you beyond your self-imposed limits." Top business schools compete to produce the most sought-after graduates. The course at Quantico is designed to develop leadership skills, decisiveness, and teamwork, and Wharton hopes the "taste of life in the trenches" was a valuable experience for the students who participated.[31]

 L05

Summarize the systematic approach to decision making used by many business managers.

DECISION MAKING

Managers make many different kinds of decisions, such as hours of work, which employees to hire, what products to introduce, and what price to charge for a product. Decision making is important in all management functions and levels, whether the decisions are on a strategic, tactical, or operational level. A systematic approach using these six steps usually leads to more effective decision making: (1) recognizing and defining the decision situation, (2) developing options to resolve the situation, (3) analyzing the options, (4) selecting the best option, (5) implementing the decision, and (6) monitoring the consequences of the decision (Figure 7.4).

Recognizing and Defining the Decision Situation

The first step in decision making is recognizing and defining the situation. The situation may be negative—for example, huge losses on a particular product—or positive—for example, an opportunity to increase sales.

Situations calling for small-scale decisions often occur without warning. Situations requiring large-scale decisions, however, generally occur after some warning signals. Effective managers pay attention to such signals. Declining profits, small-scale losses in previous years, inventory buildup, and retailers' unwillingness to stock a product are signals that may warn of huge losses to come. If managers pay attention to such signals, problems can be contained.

Once a situation has been recognized, management must define it. Huge losses reveal a problem—for example, a failing product. One manager may define the situation as a product quality problem; another may define it as a change in consumer preference. These two definitions may lead to vastly different solutions to the problem. The first manager, for example, may seek new sources of raw materials of better quality. The second manager may believe that the product has reached the end of its life span and decide to discontinue it. This example emphasizes the importance of carefully defining the problem rather than jumping to conclusions.

Developing Options

Once the decision situation has been recognized and defined, the next step is to develop a list of possible courses of action. The best lists include both standard courses of action and creative ones. As a general rule, more time and expertise are devoted to the development stage of decision making when the decision is of major importance. When the decision is of lesser importance, less time and expertise will be spent on this stage. Options may be developed individually, by teams, or through analysis of similar situations in comparable organizations. Creativity is a very important part of selecting the best option. Creativity depends on new and useful ideas, regardless of where an idea originates or the method used to create the ideas. The best option can range from a required solution to an identified problem to a volunteered solution to an observed problem by an outside work group member.[32]

Analyzing Options

After developing a list of possible courses of action, management should analyze the practicality and appropriateness of each option. An option may be deemed impractical because of a lack of financial resources to implement it, legal restrictions, ethical and social responsibility considerations, authority constraints, technological constraints, economic limitations, or simply a lack of information and expertise to implement the option. For example, a small computer manufacturer may recognize an opportunity to introduce a new type of computer but lack the financial resources to do so. Other options may be more practical for the computer company: It may consider selling its technology to another computer company that has adequate resources or it may allow itself to be purchased by a larger company that can introduce the new technology.

When assessing appropriateness, the decision maker should consider whether the proposed option adequately addresses the situation. When analyzing the consequences of an option, managers should consider the impact the option will have on the situation and on the organization as a whole. For example, when considering a price cut to boost sales, management must consider the consequences of the

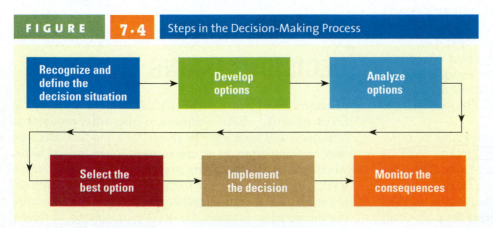

FIGURE 7.4 Steps in the Decision-Making Process

- Recognize and define the decision situation
- Develop options
- Analyze options
- Select the best option
- Implement the decision
- Monitor the consequences

action on the organization's cash flow and consumers' reaction to the price change.

Selecting the Best Option

When all courses of action have been analyzed, management must select the best one. Selection is often a subjective procedure because many situations do not lend themselves to mathematical analysis. Of course, it is not always necessary to select only one option and reject all others; it may be possible to select and use a combination of several options.

Implementing the Decision

To deal with the situation at hand, the selected option or options must be put into action. Implementation can be fairly simple or very complex, depending on the nature of the decision. Effective implementation of a decision to abandon a product, close a plant, purchase a new business, or something similar requires planning. For example, when a product is dropped, managers must decide how to handle distributors and customers and what to do with the idle production facility. Additionally, they should anticipate resistance from people within the organization (people tend to resist change because they fear the unknown). Finally, management should be ready to deal with the unexpected consequences. No matter how well planned implementation is, unforseen problems will arise. Management must be ready to address these situations when they occur.

Monitoring the Consequences

After managers have implemented the decision, they must determine whether the decision has accomplished the desired result. Without proper monitoring, the consequences of decisions may not be known quickly enough to make efficient changes. If the desired result is achieved, management can reasonably conclude that it made a good decision. If the desired result is not achieved, further analysis is warranted. Was the decision simply wrong, or did the situation change? Should some other option have been implemented?

If the desired result is not achieved, management may discover that the situation was incorrectly defined from the beginning. That may require starting the decision-making process all over again. Finally, management may determine that the decision was good even though the desired results have not yet shown up or it may determine a flaw in the decision's implementation. In the latter case, management would not change the decision but would change the way in which it was implemented.

THE REALITY OF MANAGEMENT

Management is not a cut-and-dried process. There is no mathematical formula for managing an organization, although many managers passionately wish for one! Management is a widely varying process for achieving organizational goals. Managers plan, organize, staff, direct, and control, but management expert John P. Kotter says even these functions can be boiled down to two basic activities:

1. Figuring out what to do despite uncertainty, great diversity, and an enormous amount of potentially relevant information, and

2. Getting things done through a large and diverse set of people despite having little direct control over most of them.[33]

Managers spend as much as 75 percent of their time working with others—not only with subordinates but with bosses, people outside their hierarchy at work, and people outside the organization itself. In these interactions they discuss anything and everything remotely connected with their business.

Managers spend a lot of time establishing and updating an agenda of goals and plans for carrying out their responsibilities. An **agenda** contains both specific and vague items, covering short-term goals and long-term objectives. Like a calendar, an agenda helps the manager figure out what must be done and how to get it done to meet the objectives set by the organization. Technology tools such as personal digital assistants (PDAs) can help managers manage their agendas, contacts, and time.

Dennie Ibbotson Makes Art out of Fallen Trees

The mountain pine beetle plagues pine forests throughout the United States and has contributed to their rapid die-off. However, Evergreen, Colorado–based Dennie Ibbotson has managed to find a silver lining to this scourge. The beetle leaves a blue stain, caused by a fungus, on wood that it attacks. It is this pigment that helps give Ibbotson's works uniqueness. He uses pine beetle–felled trees to fashion decorative and functional objects and often personalizes his pieces with images of Colorado wildlife and Native American motifs. Using a mallet and chisel to carve the images onto wood can take hundreds of hours, and his pieces sell for around $20,000. A secondary benefit of Ibbotson's work is clearing the forest floor of dead timber, which reduces the risk of forest fires. Ibbotson's art, therefore, not only is an homage to the forest and to the Colorado lifestyle but also helps preserve these things for the future.[34] ❖

Managers also spend a lot of time **networking**—building relationships and sharing information with colleagues who can help them achieve the items on their agendas. Managers spend much of their time communicating with a variety of people and participating in activities that on the surface do not seem to have much to do with the goals of their organization. Nevertheless, these activities are crucial to getting the job done. Networks are not limited to immediate subordinates and bosses; they include other people in the company as well as customers,

how many people you know, but how many you have helped and who know you well enough to recommend you that really count. Opportunity can knock almost anywhere with such extensive networking. grateful for numerous referrals to her friends; her Nierenberg's dentist introduced her to a Wall Street executive who happened to be in the dentist's office at the same time as Nierenberg. She followed up on the meeting and later landed four consulting projects at the executive's firm.[35] Her clients include Citigroup, Time Inc., TIAA–CREF, Food Network, Coach, and Tiffany.[36]

Finally, managers spend a great deal of time confronting the complex and difficult challenges of the business world today. Some of these challenges relate to rapidly changing technology (especially in production and information processing),

> ❝ **Managers also spend a lot of time networking—building relationships and sharing information with colleagues who can help them achieve the items on their agendas.** ❞

suppliers, and friends. These contacts provide managers with information and advice on diverse topics. Managers ask, persuade, and even intimidate members of their network in order to get information and to get things done. Networking helps managers carry out their responsibilities. Andrea Nierenberg, independent business consultant and founder of Nierenberg Group Inc., has been called a "networking success story" by *The Wall Street Journal*. She writes three notes a day: one to a client, one to a friend, and one to a prospective client. She maintains a database of 3,000 contacts. However, she believes that it isn't

increased scrutiny of individual and corporate ethics and social responsibility, the changing nature of the workforce, new laws and regulations, increased global competition and more challenging foreign markets, declining educational standards (which may limit the skills and knowledge of the future labor and customer pool), and time itself—that is, making the best use of it. But such diverse issues cannot simply be plugged into a computer program that supplies correct, easy-to-apply solutions. It is only through creativity and imagination that managers can make effective decisions that benefit their organizations. ■

SO YOU WANT TO BE A MANAGER: WHAT KIND OF MANAGER DO YOU WANT TO BE?

Managers are needed in a wide variety of organizations. Experts suggest that employment will increase by millions of jobs by 2016. But the requirements for jobs become more demanding with every passing year with the speed of technology and communication increasing by the day and the stress of global commerce adding to the pressures to perform. However, if you like a challenge and have the right kind of personality, management remains a viable field. Even as companies are forced to restructure, management remains a vital role in business. In fact, the Bureau of Labor Statistics predicts that management positions in public relations, marketing, and advertising are set to increase around 12 percent overall between 2006 and 2016. Financial managers will be in even more demand, with those jobs increasing 13 percent in that time period. Computer and IT managers will continue to be in strong demand, with the number of jobs increasing 16 percent between 2006 and 2016.

Salaries for managerial positions remain strong overall. While pay can vary significantly depending on your level of experience, the firm where you work, and the region of the country where you live, below is a list of the nationwide average incomes for a variety of different managers:

Chief executives: $151,370

Computer and information systems managers: $113, 880

Financial managers: $106,200

Marketing managers: $113,400

Human resource managers: $99,810

Operations managers: $103,780

Medical/health services managers: $84,980

Administrative managers: $76,370

Sales managers: $106,790

In short, if you want to be a manager, there are opportunities in almost every field. There may be fewer middle management positions available in firms, but managers remain a vital part of most industries and will continue to be long into the future—especially as navigating global business becomes ever more complex.[37]

Team Exercise

Form groups and assign the responsibility for locating examples of crisis management implementation for companies dealing with natural disasters (explosions, fires, earthquakes, etc.), technology disasters (viruses, plane crashes, compromised customer data, etc.), or ethical or legal disasters. How did these companies communicate with key stakeholders? What measures did each company take to provide support to those involved in the crisis? Report your findings to the class.

CHECK OUT www.mhhe.com/FerrellM2e

for study materials including Interactive Exercises, Quizzes, iPod downloads, and video.

organization, teamwork, and communication

Introduction An organization's structure determines how well it makes decisions and responds to problems, and it influences employees' attitudes toward their work. A suitable structure can minimize a business's costs and maximize its efficiency. For these reasons, many businesses, such as Motorola, Apple Computer, and Hewlett-Packard, have changed their organizational structures in recent years in an effort to enhance their profits and competitive edge.

Because a business's structure can so profoundly affect its success, this chapter will examine organizational structure in detail. First, we discuss how an organization's culture affects its operations. Then we consider the development of structure, including how tasks and responsibilities are organized through specialization and departmentalization. Next, we explore some of the forms organizational structure may take. Finally, we consider communications within business.

chapter eight

ORGANIZATIONAL CULTURE

One of the most important aspects of organizing a business is determining its **organizational culture,** a firm's shared values, beliefs, traditions, philosophies, rules, and role models for behavior. Also called corporate culture, an organizational culture exists in every organization, regardless of size, organizational type, product, or profit objective. For example, the organizational culture of the Marine Corps focuses on teamwork, often splitting into buddy teams and not working alone. The Marines drill into recruits to do the right thing whether it's good for you or not, whether it is easy or hard.[1] A firm's culture may be expressed formally through its mission statement, codes of ethics, memos, manuals, and ceremonies, but it is more commonly expressed informally. Examples of informal expressions of culture include dress codes (or the lack thereof), work habits, extracurricular activities, and stories. Employees often learn the accepted standards through discussions with co-workers.

At Southwest Airlines, for example, new employees watch videotapes and attend training sessions that extol the company's policies, philosophies, and culture. This training encourages employees to have fun and to make flying exciting for their passengers. Such activities mark Southwest's culture as fun, casual, and friendly. Disneyland/Disney World and McDonald's have organizational cultures focused on cleanliness, value, and service. At Matsushita, employees sing a company song every morning that translates, "As individuals we will work to improve life and contribute to human progress." The company's president, Kunio Nakamura, also believes the highest paid employee should earn no more than 10 times the lowest paid employee. The effort to hire younger employees and more women is also affecting the Japanese firm's culture.[2] When such values and philosophies are shared by all members of an organization, they will be expressed in its relationships with stakeholders. However, organizational cultures that lack such positive values may result in employees who are unproductive and indifferent and have poor attitudes, which will be reflected externally to customers. Unethical cultures may have contributed to the misconduct at a number of well-known companies, such as Enron and WorldCom, at the turn of the century. Merck & Company agreed to pay $58 million to settle Vioxx advertising claims in 2008 with 29 states and the District of Columbia. Many agree that Merck operated with an aggressive and very competitive organizational culture in the late 1990s. Pennsylvania Attorney General Tom Corbett said that in 1999, Merck ran "an aggressive and deceptive advertising campaign which misrepresented the safety and improperly concealed the increased risks associated with Vioxx." Those ads continued to run until 2004. In addition, Merck has agreed to stop ghostwriting articles in medical journals to promote its interests.[3]

Organizational culture helps ensure that all members of a company share values and suggests rules for how to behave and deal with problems within the organization. The key to success in any organization is satisfying stakeholders, especially customers. Establishing a positive organizational culture sets the tone for all other decisions, including building an efficient organizational structure.

●● LO1

Define organizational structure, and relate how organizational structures develop.

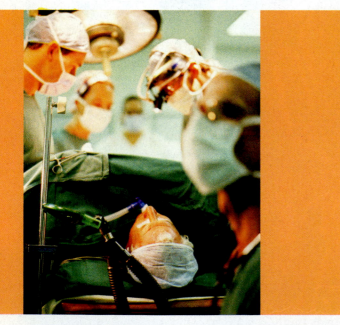

At W. L. Gore & Associates, which makes Gore-Tex fabric as well as surgical, aerospace, and other products, there are no bosses. Employees are hired as "associates" and assigned to "sponsors" in the functional groups in which they work. This structure has helped create a culture of innovation within the company.

DEVELOPING ORGANIZATIONAL STRUCTURE

Structure is the arrangement or relationship of positions within an organization. Rarely is an organization, or any group of individuals working together, able to achieve common objectives without some form of structure, whether that structure is explicitly defined or only implied. A professional baseball team such as the Colorado Rockies is a business organization with an explicit formal structure that guides the team's activities so that it can increase game attendance, win games, and sell souvenirs such as T-shirts. But even an informal group playing softball for fun has an organization that specifies who will pitch, catch, bat, coach, and so on. Governments and nonprofit organizations also have formal organizational structures to facilitate the achievement of their objectives. Getting people to work together efficiently and coordinating the skills of diverse individuals require careful planning. Developing appropriate organizational structures is therefore a major challenge for managers in both large and small organizations.

An organization's structure develops when managers assign work tasks and activities to specific individuals or work groups and coordinate the diverse activities required to reach the firm's objectives. When Macy's, for example, has a sale, the store manager must work with the advertising department to make the public aware of the sale, with department managers to ensure that extra salespeople are scheduled to handle the increased customer traffic, and with merchandise buyers to ensure that enough sale merchandise is available to meet expected consumer demand. All the people occupying these positions must work together to achieve the store's objectives.

The best way to begin to understand how organizational structure develops is to consider the evolution of a new business such as a clothing store. At first, the business is a sole proprietorship in which the owner does everything—buys, prices, and displays the merchandise; does the accounting and tax records; and assists customers. As the business grows, the owner hires a

Growth requires organizing— the structuring of human, physical, and financial resources to achieve objectives in an effective and efficient manner.

salesperson and perhaps a merchandise buyer to help run the store. As the business continues to grow, the owner hires more salespeople. The growth and success of the business now require the owner to be away from the store frequently, meeting with suppliers, engaging in public relations, and attending trade shows. Thus, the owner must designate someone to manage the salespeople and maintain the accounting, payroll, and tax functions. If the owner decides to expand by opening more stores, still more managers will be needed. Figure 8.1 shows these stages of growth with three **organizational charts** (visual displays of organizational structure, chain of command, and other relationships).

Growth requires organizing—the structuring of human, physical, and financial resources to achieve objectives in an effective and efficient manner. Growth necessitates hiring people who have specialized skills. With more people and greater specialization, the organization needs to develop a formal structure to function efficiently. Endangered Species Chocolate moved from Oregon to Indianapolis and has seen its sales explode in three years from $3 million to $17 million, with a goal of reaching $30 million by 2013. The company's success can be attributed to a major reorganization and focus on the triple bottom line (financial, environmental, and the social side of the business). The company has nearly grown its workforce from 18 employees to 50 and gives 10% of profits to support "species, habitat, and humanity."[4] As we shall see, structuring an organization requires that management assign work tasks

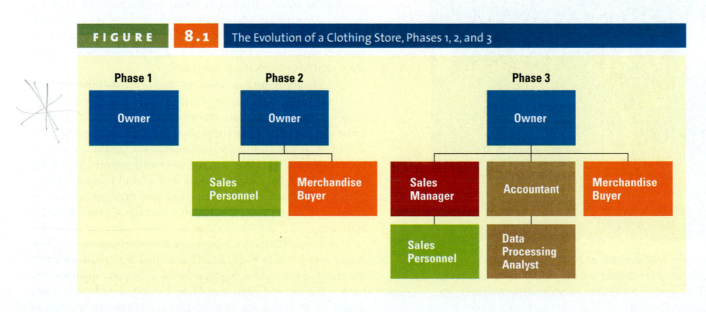

FIGURE 8.1 The Evolution of a Clothing Store, Phases 1, 2, and 3

to specific individuals and departments and assign responsibility for the achievement of specific organizational objectives.

●● **L02**

Describe how specialization and departmentalization help an organization achieve its goals.

ASSIGNING TASKS

For a business to earn profits from the sale of its products, its managers must first determine what activities are required to achieve its objectives. At Celestial Seasonings, for example, employees must purchase herbs from suppliers, dry the herbs and place them in tea bags, package and label the tea, and then ship the packages to grocery stores around the country. Other necessary activities include negotiating with supermarkets and other retailers for display space, developing new products, planning advertising, managing finances, and managing employees. All these activities must be coordinated, assigned to work groups, and controlled. Two important aspects of assigning these work activities are specialization and departmentalization.

Specialization

After identifying all activities that must be accomplished, managers then break these activities down into specific tasks that can be handled by individual employees. This division of labor into small, specific tasks and the assignment of employees to do a single task is called **specialization.**

The rationale for specialization is efficiency. People can perform more efficiently if they master just one task rather than

> ## Specialization means workers don't waste time shifting from one job to another, and training is easier.

Henry Ford, the founder of Ford Motor Company, revolutionized the transportation industry by creating assembly lines like this one to specialize the tasks his workers performed.

all tasks. In *The Wealth of Nations*, 18th-century economist Adam Smith discussed specialization, using the manufacture of straight pins as an example. Individually, workers could produce 20 pins a day when each employee produced complete pins. Thus, 10 employees working independently of each other could produce 200 pins a day. However, when one worker drew the wire, another straightened it, a third cut it, and a fourth ground the point, 10 workers could produce 48,000 pins per day.[5] To save money and achieve the benefits of specialization, some companies outsource and hire temporary workers to provide key skills. Many highly skilled, diverse experience workers are available through temp agencies.[6]

Specialization means workers don't waste time shifting from one job to another, and training is easier. However, efficiency is not the only motivation for specialization. Specialization also occurs when the activities that must be performed within an organization are too numerous for one person to handle. Recall the example of the clothing store. When the business was young and small, the owner could do everything; but when the business grew, the owner needed help waiting on customers, keeping the books, and managing other business activities.

Overspecialization can have negative consequences. Employees may become bored and dissatisfied with their jobs, and the result of their unhappiness is likely to be poor-quality work, more injuries, and high employee turnover. Although some degree of specialization is necessary for efficiency, because of differences in skills, abilities, and interests, all people are not equally suited for all jobs. We examine some strategies to overcome these issues in Chapter 10.

Departmentalization

After assigning specialized tasks to individuals, managers next organize workers doing similar jobs into groups to make them easier to manage. **Departmentalization** is the grouping of jobs into working units usually called departments, units, groups, or divisions. As we shall see, departments are commonly organized by function, product, geographic region, or customer (Figure 8.2). Most companies use more than one departmentalization plan to enhance productivity. For instance,

many consumer goods manufacturers have departments for specific product lines (beverages, frozen dinners, canned goods, and so on) as well as departments dealing with legal, purchasing, finance, human resources, and other business functions. For smaller companies, accounting can be set up online, almost as an automated department. Accounting software can handle electronic transfers so you never have to worry about a late bill.[7] Many city governments also have departments for specific services (e.g., police, fire, waste disposal) as well as departments for legal, human resources, and other business functions. Figure 8.3 on page 154 depicts the organizational chart for the city of Corpus Christi, Texas, showing these departments.

● **DEPARTMENTALIZA-TION** the grouping of jobs into working units usually called departments, units, groups, or divisions

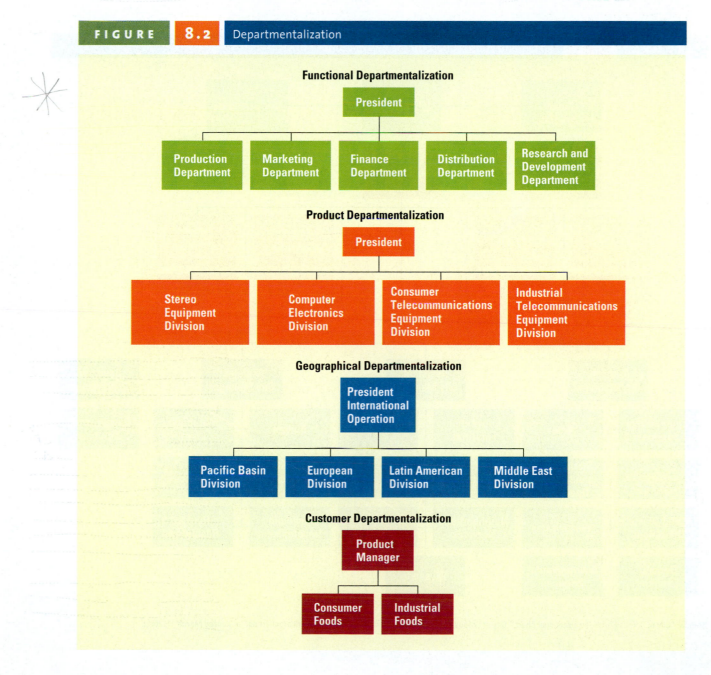

FIGURE 8.2 Departmentalization

Functional Departmentalization

President

- Production Department
- Marketing Department
- Finance Department
- Distribution Department
- Research and Development Department

Product Departmentalization

President

- Stereo Equipment Division
- Computer Electronics Division
- Consumer Telecommunications Equipment Division
- Industrial Telecommunications Equipment Division

Geographical Departmentalization

President International Operation

- Pacific Basin Division
- European Division
- Latin American Division
- Middle East Division

Customer Departmentalization

Product Manager

- Consumer Foods
- Industrial Foods

supervises the finance department. This approach is common in small organizations. A weakness of functional departmentalization is that because it tends to emphasize departmental units rather than the organization as a whole, decision making that involves more than one department may be slow, and it requires greater coordination. Thus, as business grow, they tend to adopt other approaches to organizing jobs.

functional departmentalization Functional departmentalization groups jobs that perform similar functional activities, such as finance, manufacturing, marketing, and human resources. Each of these functions is managed by an expert in the work done by the department—an engineer supervises the production department; a financial executive

product departmentalization Product departmentalization, as you might guess, organizes jobs around the products of the firm. Procter & Gamble has global units, such as laundry and cleaning products, paper products, and health care products. Each division develops and implements its own product plans, monitors the results, and

FIGURE 8.3 An Organizational Chart for the City of Corpus Christi

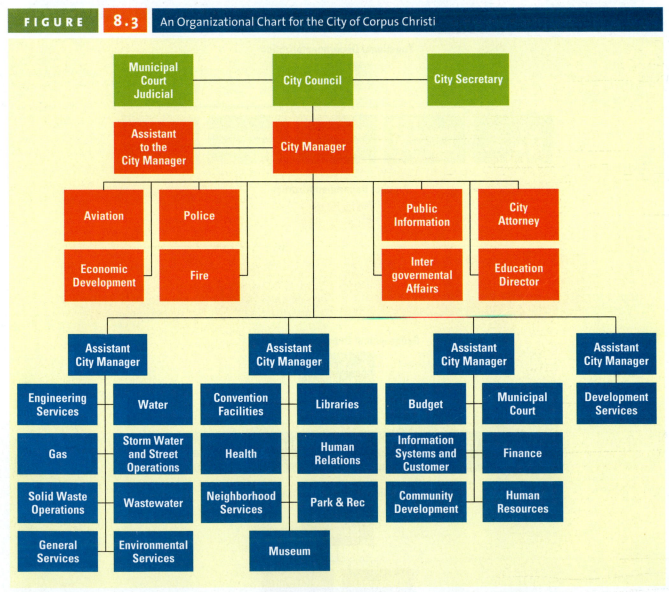

Source: "City of Corpus Christi Organizational Chart," City of Corpus Christi (n.d), http://cctexas.com/files/g5/cityorgchart.pdf (accessed March 11, 2009).

takes corrective action as necessary. Functional activities—production, finance, marketing, and others—are located within each product division. Consequently, organizing by products duplicates functions and resources and emphasizes the product rather than achievement of the organization's overall objectives. However, it simplifies decision making and helps coordinate all activities related to a product or product group. Kodak, for example, reorganized into special product groups devoted to digital business (Consumer Digital Imaging Group and Graphic Communications Group) and the Film Producers Group. President and COO Philip J. Faraci hopes this structure will support continued profitable growth in digital markets.[8]

geographical departmentalization Geographical departmentalization groups jobs according to geographic location, such as a state, region, country, or continent. FritoLay, for example, is organized into four regional divisions, allowing the company to get closer to its customers and respond more quickly and efficiently to regional competitors. Multinational corporations often use a geographical approach because of vast differences between different regions. Coca-Cola, General Motors, and Caterpillar are organized by region. However, organizing by region requires a large administrative staff and control system to coordinate operations, and tasks are duplicated among the different regions.

customer departmentalization Customer departmentalization arranges jobs around the needs of various types of customers. Banks, for example, typically have separate departments for commercial banking activities and for consumer or retail banking. This permits the bank to address the unique requirements of each group. Airlines, such as British Airways and Delta, provide prices and services customized for either business/frequent travelers or infrequent/vacationing customers. Customer departmentalization, like geographical departmentalization, does not focus on the organization as a whole and therefore requires a large administrative staff to coordinate the operations of the various groups.

 LO3

Determine how organizations assign responsibility for tasks and delegate authority.

ASSIGNING RESPONSIBILITY

After all workers and work groups have been assigned their tasks, they must be given the responsibility to carry them out. Management must determine to what extent it will delegate responsibility throughout the organization and how many employees will report to each manager.

Delegation of Authority

Delegation of authority means not only giving tasks to employees but also empowering them to make commitments, use resources, and take whatever actions are necessary to carry out those tasks. Let's say a marketing manager at Nestlé has assigned an employee to design a new package that is less wasteful (more environmentally responsible) than the current package for one of the company's frozen dinner lines. To carry out the assignment, the employee needs access to information and the authority to make certain decisions on packaging materials, costs, and so on. Without the authority to carry out the assigned task, the employee would have to get the approval of others for every decision and every request for materials.

As a business grows, so do the number and complexity of decisions that must be made; no one manager can handle them all. Hotels such as Westin Hotels and Resorts and the Ritz-Carlton give authority to service providers, including front desk personnel, to make service decisions such as moving a guest to another room or providing a discount to guests who experience a problem at the hotel. Delegation of authority frees a manager to concentrate on larger issues, such as planning and dealing with problems and opportunities.

Delegation also gives a **responsibility,** or obligation, to employees to carry out assigned tasks satisfactorily and holds them accountable for the proper execution of their assigned work. The principle of **accountability** means that employees who accept an assignment and the authority to carry it out are answerable to a superior for the outcome. Returning to the Nestlé example, if the packaging design prepared by the employee is unacceptable or late, the employee must accept the blame. If the new design is innovative, attractive, and cost-efficient, as well as environmentally responsible, or is completed ahead of schedule, the employee will accept the credit.

The process of delegating authority establishes a pattern of relationships and accountability between a superior and his or her subordinates. The president of a firm delegates responsibility for all marketing activities to the vice president of marketing. The vice president accepts this responsibility and has the authority to obtain all relevant information, make certain decisions, and delegate any or all activities to his or her subordinates. The vice president, in turn, delegates all advertising activities to the advertising manager, all sales activities to the sales manager, and so on. These managers then delegate specific tasks to their subordinates. However, the act of delegating authority to a subordinate does not relieve the superior of accountability for the delegated job. Even though the vice president of marketing delegates work to subordinates, he or she is still ultimately accountable to the president for all marketing activities.

Degree of Centralization

The extent to which authority is delegated throughout an organization determines its degree of centralization.

centralized organizations In a **centralized organization,** authority is concentrated at the top, and very little decision-making authority is delegated to lower levels. Although decision-making authority in centralized organizations rests with top levels of management, a vast amount of responsibility for carrying out daily and routine procedures is delegated to even the lowest levels of the organization. Many government organizations, including the U.S. Army, the Postal Service, and the IRS, are centralized.

Businesses tend to be more centralized when the decisions to be made are risky and when low-level managers are not highly skilled in decision making. In the banking industry, for example, authority to make routine car loans is given to all loan managers, while the authority to make high-risk loans, such as for a large residential development, may be restricted to upper-level loan officers.

Overcentralization can cause serious problems for a company, in part because it may take longer for the organization as a whole to implement decisions and to respond to changes and problems on a regional scale. McDonald's, for example, was one of the last chains to introduce a chicken sandwich because of the amount of research, development, test marketing, and layers of approval the product had to go through.

decentralized organizations A **decentralized organization** is one in which decision-making authority is delegated as far down the chain of command as possible. Decentralization is characteristic of organizations that operate in complex, unpredictable environments. Businesses that face intense competition often decentralize to improve responsiveness and enhance creativity. Lower-level managers who interact with the external environment often develop a good understanding of it and thus are able to react quickly to changes.

Delegating authority to lower levels of managers may increase the organization's productivity. Decentralization requires that lower-level managers have strong decision-making skills. In recent years the trend has been toward more decentralized organizations, and some of the largest and most successful companies, including GE, Sears, IBM, and JCPenney, have decentralized decision-making authority. McDonald's, which is realizing most of its growth outside the United States, is becoming increasingly decentralized and 'glo-cal' varying products in specific markets to better meet consumer needs. This change in organizational structure for McDonald's is fostering

Bed, Bath & Beyond empowers its store managers, who know their customers better than anyone else. Each manager selects about 70 percent of his or her store's merchandise, including linens, appliances, picture frames, and imported olive oil, to ensure they match that store's customers.

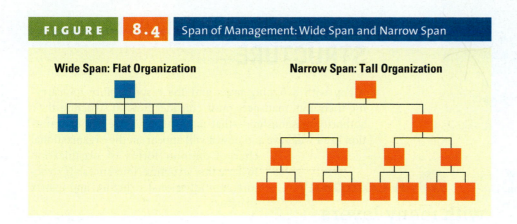

FIGURE **8.4** Span of Management: Wide Span and Narrow Span

Wide Span: Flat Organization

Narrow Span: Tall Organization

● **SPAN OF MANAGE-MENT** the number of subordinates who report to a particular manager

● **ORGANIZATIONAL LAYERS** the levels of management in an organization.

greater innovation and local market success. In Brazil, Italy, or Portugal, you can order a 'Big Tasty'. The 'Big Tasty' is a giant burger (5.5 oz.) smothered in barbecue sauce, topped with square cut lettuce, tomatoes, 3 slices of cheese, and providing 840 calories. Try to find this sandwich in the United States, and you will not. The sandwich was concocted in a test kitchen in Germany and tested and launched in Sweden it has been a success in other parts of Europe, Latin American, and Australia. Diversity and decentralization seem to be McDonald's keys to being better, not just bigger.[9] Nonprofit organizations benefit from decentralization as well.

Span of Management

How many subordinates should a manager manage? There is no simple answer. Experts generally agree, however, that top managers should not directly supervise more than four to eight people, while lower-level managers who supervise routine tasks are capable of managing a much larger number of subordinates. For example, the manager of the finance department may supervise 25 employees, whereas the vice president of finance may supervise only five managers. **Span of management** refers to the number of subordinates who report to a particular manager. A *wide span of management* exists when a manager directly supervises a very large number of employees. A *narrow span of management* exists when a manager directly supervises only a few subordinates (Figure 8.4). At Whole Foods, each store consists of eight teams that oversee departments (seafood, produce, checkout, etc). After training, teams vote on whether

a new hire will be a productive member, and a two-thirds vote is required to win a full-time position. These teams are responsible for all key operational decisions from pricing, ordering and staffing to in-store promotions. Compared with centralized department stores, this combination of a small span of control with decentralization allows Whole Foods to uniquely appeal to local markets' needs.[10]

Should the span of management be wide or narrow? To answer this question, several factors need to be considered. A narrow span of management is appropriate when superiors and subordinates are not in close proximity, the manager has many responsibilities in addition to the supervision, the interaction between superiors and subordinates is frequent, and problems are common. However, when superiors and subordinates are located close to one another, the manager has few responsibilities other than supervision, the level of interaction between superiors and subordinates is low, few problems arise, subordinates are highly competent, and a set of specific operating procedures governs the activities of managers and their subordinates, a wide span of management will be more appropriate. Narrow spans of management are typical in centralized organizations, while wide spans of management are more common in decentralized firms.

Organizational Layers

Complementing the concept of span of management are **organizational layers,** the levels of management in an organization.

Gourmet Country Farm Popularizes Green Garlic in the United States

Green garlic, the kind used by Dilip Naik's grandmother in India, is not common in the United States. Naik resolved to grow it for himself, combating its short growing season with hydroponics. Through his company Gourmet Country Farm, Naik sold his green garlic to Whole Foods, Central Market, and specialty stores. His secret to success was developing the technology to harvest the product year-round through the use of special growing beds and irrigation methods. Since labor is a big issue in agriculture, he made his daughter-in-law the business development manager and hired three employees to harvest the product. He also contracted with a local food distributor to deliver to area stores. His son also works in the operation. Naik is building a business culture focused on execution, family involvement, and the delivery of a high-quality unique product.[11] ❖

FORMS OF ORGANIZATIONAL STRUCTURE

Along with assigning tasks and the responsibility for carrying them out, managers must consider how to structure their authority relationships—that is, what structure the organization itself will have and how it will appear on the organizational chart. Common forms of organization include line structure, line-and-staff structure, multidivisional structure, and matrix structure.

A company with many layers of managers is considered tall; in a tall organization, the span of management is narrow (see Figure 8.4). Because each manager supervises only a few subordinates, many layers of management are necessary to carry out the operations of the business. McDonald's, for example, has a tall organization with many layers, including store managers, district managers, regional managers, and functional managers (finance, marketing, and so on), as well as a chief executive officer and many vice presidents. Because there are more managers in tall organizations than in flat organizations, administrative costs are usually higher. Communication is slower because information must pass through many layers.

Organizations with few layers are flat and have wide spans of management. When managers supervise a large number of employees, fewer management layers are needed to conduct the organization's activities. Managers in flat organizations typically perform more administrative duties than managers in tall organizations because there are fewer of them. They also spend more time supervising and working with subordinates.

Many of the companies that decentralized during the 1980s and 1990s also flattened their structures and widened their spans of management, often by eliminating layers of middle management. Many corporations, including Avon, AT&T, and Ford Motor Company, did so to reduce costs, speed decision making, and boost overall productivity.

🟡 🔵 **A company with many layers of managers is considered tall**

Line Structure

The simplest organizational structure, **line structure,** has direct lines of authority that extend from the top manager to employees at the lowest level of the organization. For example, a convenience store employee may report to an assistant manager, who reports to the store manager, who reports to a regional manager or, in an independent store, directly to the owner (Figure 8.5). This structure has a clear chain of command, which enables managers to make decisions quickly. A mid-level manager facing a decision must consult only one person, his or her immediate supervisor. However, this structure requires that managers possess a wide range of knowledge and skills. They are responsible for a variety of activities and must be knowledgeable about them all. Line structures are most common in small businesses.

Line-and-Staff Structure

The **line-and-staff structure** has a traditional line relationship between superiors and subordinates, and specialized managers—called staff managers—are available to assist line managers (Figure 8.6). Line managers can focus on their area of expertise in the operation of the business, while staff managers provide advice and support to line departments on specialized matters such as finance, engineering, human resources, and the law. In the city of Corpus Christi (refer back to Figure 8.3), for example, assistant city managers are line managers who oversee groups of related departments. However, the city attorney, police chief, and fire chief are effectively staff managers who

 LO4

Compare and contrast some common forms of organizational structure.

FIGURE	8.5	Line Structure

Convenience Store

Owner — Manager — Assistant Manager — Hourly Employee

MULTIDIVISIONAL STRUCTURE a structure that organizes departments into larger groups called divisions

MATRIX STRUCTURE a structure that sets up teams from different departments, thereby creating two or more intersecting lines of authority; also called a project-management structure

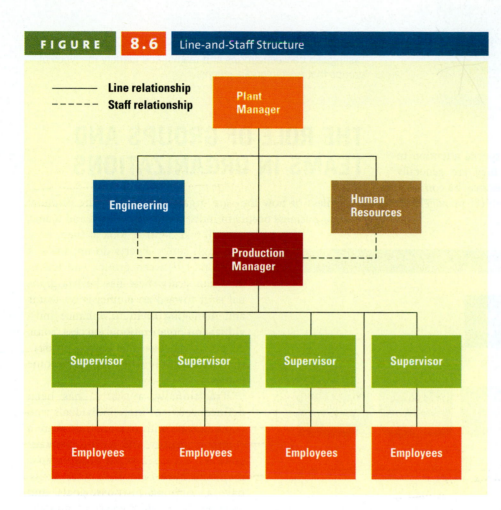

FIGURE 8.6 Line-and-Staff Structure

Line relationship
Staff relationship

Plant Manager

Engineering

Human Resources

Production Manager

Supervisor | Supervisor | Supervisor | Supervisor

Employees | Employees | Employees | Employees

Multidivisional structures permit delegation of decision-making authority, allowing divisional and department managers to specialize. They allow those closest to the action to make the decisions that will affect them. Delegation of authority and divisionalized work also mean that better decisions are made faster, and they tend to be more innovative. Most importantly, by focusing each division on a common region, product, or customer, each is more likely to provide products that meet the needs of its particular customers. However, the divisional structure inevitably creates work duplication, which makes it more difficult to realize the economies of scale that result from grouping functions together.

report directly to the city manager (the city equivalent of a business chief executive officer). Staff managers do not have direct authority over line managers or over the line manager's subordinates, but they do have direct authority over subordinates in their own departments. However, line-and-staff organizations may experience problems with overstaffing and ambiguous lines of communication. Additionally, employees may become frustrated because they lack the authority to carry out certain decisions.

Multidivisional Structure

As companies grow and diversify, traditional line structures become difficult to coordinate, making communication difficult and decision making slow. When the weaknesses of the structure—the "turf wars," miscommunication, and working at cross-purposes—exceed the benefits, growing firms tend to restructure, often into the divisionalized form. A **multidivisional structure** organizes departments into larger groups called divisions. Just as departments might be formed on the basis of geography, customer, product, or a combination of these, so too divisions can be formed based on any of these methods of organizing. Within each of these divisions, departments may be organized by product, geographic region, function, or some combination of all three.

Matrix Structure

Another structure that attempts to address issues that arise with growth, diversification, productivity, and competitiveness, is the matrix. A **matrix structure,** also called a project-management structure, sets up teams from different departments, thereby creating two or more intersecting lines of authority (see Figure 8.7). The matrix structure superimposes project-based departments on the more traditional, function-based departments. Project teams bring together specialists from a variety of areas to work together on a single project, such as developing a new fighter jet. In this arrangement, employees are responsible to two managers—functional managers and project managers. Matrix structures are usually temporary: Team members typically go back to their functional or line department after a project is finished. However, more firms are becoming permanent matrix structures, creating and dissolving project teams as needed to meet customer needs. The aerospace industry was one of the first to apply the matrix structure, but today it is used by universities and schools, accounting firms, banks, and organizations in other industries.

Matrix structures provide flexibility, enhanced cooperation, and creativity, and they enable the company to respond quickly

L05

Distinguish between groups and teams, and identify the types of groups that exist in organizations.

THE ROLE OF GROUPS AND TEAMS IN ORGANIZATIONS

to changes in the environment by giving special attention to specific projects or problems. However, they are generally expensive and quite complex, and employees may be confused about whose authority has priority—the project manager's or the immediate supervisor's.

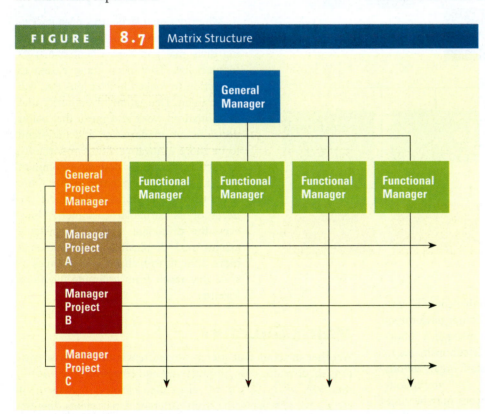

| FIGURE | 8.7 | Matrix Structure |

Regardless of how they are organized, most of the essential work of business occurs in individual work groups and teams, so we'll take a closer look at them now. Although some experts do not make a distinction between groups and teams, in recent years there has been a gradual shift toward an emphasis on teams and managing them to enhance individual and organizational success. Some experts now believe that highest productivity results only when groups become teams.[12]

Traditionally, a **group** has been defined as two or more individuals who communicate with one another, share a common identity, and have a common goal. A **team** is a small group whose members have complementary skills; have a common purpose, goals, and approach; and hold themselves mutually accountable.[13] All teams are groups, but not all groups are teams. Table 8.1 points out some important differences between them. Work groups emphasize individual work products, individual accountability, and even individual leadership. Salespeople working independently for the same

TABLE 8.1 Differences between Groups and Teams

Working Group	Team
Has strong, clearly focused leader	Has shared leadership roles
Has individual accountability	Has individual and group accountability
Has the same purpose as the broader organizational mission	Has a specific purpose that the team itself delivers
Creates individual work products	Creates collective work products
Runs efficient meetings	Encourages open-ended discussion and active problem-solving meetings
Measures its effectiveness indirectly by its effects on others (e.g., financial performance of the business)	Measures performance directly by assessing collective work products
Discusses, decides, and delegates	Discusses, decides, and does real work together

Source: Robert Gatewood, Robert Taylor, and O. C. Ferrell, *Management: Comprehension Analysis and Application,* 1995, p. 427. Copyright © 1995 Richard D. Irwin, a Times Mirror Higher Education Group, Inc., company. Reproduced with permission of the McGraw-Hill Companies.

● COMMITTEE a perma-
nent, formal group that
performs a specific task

● TASK FORCE a tempo-
rary group of employees
responsible for bringing
about a particular change

● PROJECT TEAMS
groups similar to task
forces which normally run
their operation and have
total control of a specific
work project

company could be a work group. In contrast, work teams share leadership roles, have both individual and mutual accountability, and create collective work products. In other words, a work group's performance depends on what its members do as individuals, while a team's performance is based on creating a knowledge center and a competency to work together to accomplish a goal. When CEO Joe Albanese had to leave his CEO position at Commodore Builders for active duty in the Army, his team rebalanced his workload and continued its projects. Albanese had established teams that focused on collaboration. A core team was prepared to lead the company in his absence. Albanese simply unplugged himself, leaving the team to perform his duties including day-to-day leadership.[14]

The types of groups an organization establishes depends on the tasks it needs to accomplish and the situation it faces. Some specific kinds of groups and teams include committees, task forces, project teams, product-development teams, quality-assurance teams, and self-directed work teams. All of these can be *virtual teams*—employees in different locations who rely on e-mail, audio conferencing, fax, Internet, videoconferencing, or other technological tools to accomplish their goals. One survey found that almost 48 percent of workers have participated in virtual teams.[15]

selected by the Coca-Cola Company and the class representatives in a discrimination lawsuit filed against the company. Creation of the seven-member independent task force was one of the key elements in the settlement between the two parties. The task force will ensure the company's compliance with the settlement agreement and provide oversight of its diversity efforts.[16]

Teams

Teams are becoming far more common in the U.S. workplace as businesses strive to enhance productivity and global competitiveness. In general, teams have the benefit of being able to pool members' knowledge and skills and make greater use of them than can individuals working alone. Team building is becoming increasingly popular in organizations, with 48 percent of executives indicating their companies had team-building training.[17] Teams require harmony, cooperation, synchronized effort, and flexibility to maximize their contribution.[18] Teams can also create more solutions to problems than

> ## "Teams are becoming far more common in the U.S. workplace as businesses strive to enhance productivity and global competitiveness."

Committees

A **committee** is usually a permanent, formal group that does some specific task. For example, many firms have a compensation or finance committee to examine the effectiveness of these areas of operation as well as the need for possible changes. Ethics committees are formed to develop and revise codes of ethics, suggest methods for implementing ethical standards, and review specific issues and concerns.

Task Forces

A **task force** is a temporary group of employees responsible for bringing about a particular change. They typically come from across all departments and levels of an organization. Task force membership is usually based on expertise rather than organizational position. Occasionally, a task force may be formed from individuals outside a company. Such was the case in the task force

can individuals. Furthermore, team participation enhances employee acceptance of, understanding of, and commitment to team goals. Teams motivate workers by providing internal rewards in the form of an enhanced sense of accomplishment for employees as they achieve more, and external rewards in the form of praise and certain perks. Consequently, they can help get workers more involved. They can help companies be more innovative, and they can boost productivity and cut costs.

According to psychologist Ivan Steiner, team productivity peaks at about five team members. People become less motivated and group coordination becomes more difficult after this size. Jeff Bezos, Amazon.com CEO, says that he has a "two-pizza rule": If a team cannot be fed by two pizzas, it is too large. Keep teams small enough where everyone gets a piece of the action.[19]

project teams Project teams are similar to task forces, but normally they run their operation and have

quality-assurance teams

Quality-assurance teams, sometimes called **quality circles,** are fairly small groups of workers brought together from throughout the organization to solve specific quality, productivity, or service problems. Although the *quality circle* term is not as popular as it once was, the concern about quality is stronger than ever. The use of teams to address quality issues will no doubt continue to increase throughout the business world.

self-directed work teams

A **self-directed work team (SDWT)** is a group of employees responsible for an entire work process or segment that delivers a product to an internal or external customer.[21] Sometimes called self-managed teams or autonomous work groups, SDWTs reduce the need for extra layers of management and thus can help control costs. For example, MySQL, a $40 million software maker, operates a worldwide workforce with no office. At MySQL people are matched with the technology task. The company relies on phone contact via Skype Internet voice communication. Voice communication is considered better than e-mail and helpful in building real contacts and understanding of tasks. One problem, though, is that a self-directed team does not end at the end of the day. It is always 8 a.m. somewhere for MySQL employees.[22]

SDWTs permit the flexibility to change rapidly to meet the competition or respond to customer needs. The defining characteristic of an SDWT is the extent to which it is empowered or given authority to make and implement work decisions. Thus, SDWTs are designed to give employees a feeling of "ownership" of a whole job. With shared team responsibility for work outcomes, team members often have broader job assignments and cross-train to master other jobs, thus permitting greater team flexibility.

The software company My SQL has a worldwide workforce but no offices. Employees work virtually in self-directed work teams.

total control of a specific work project. Like task forces, their membership is likely to cut across the firm's hierarchy and be composed of people from different functional areas. They are almost always temporary, although a large project, such as designing and building a new airplane at Boeing Corporation, may last for years.

Product-development teams are a special type of project team formed to devise, design, and implement a new product. Sometimes product-development teams exist within a functional area—research and development—but now they more frequently include people from numerous functional areas and may even include customers to help ensure that the end product meets the customers' needs. Students at the University of Wisconsin-Madison formed a product-development team to compete in the Institute of Food Technologists' annual competition, creating new food products with high potential for grocery store sales. The team is diverse, made up of undergraduates, graduate students, food chemists, food engineers, and bacteriologists. Some are research-oriented, while others focus on business. Additionally, members hail from all corners of the globe. This has proved successful, with the team winning multiple awards for such food items as Handicotti, a hand-held snack featuring cheese, pasta sauce, and vegetables enclosed by a large pasta shell and Healthy sTarts, a breakfast item featuring a yogurt-filled granola cup topped with blueberries and strawberries.[20]

DID YOU KNOW?

People spend an average of one to one-and-a-half days per week in meetings.[23]

● ● **LO6**

Describe how communication occurs in organizations.

COMMUNICATING IN ORGANIZATIONS

Communication within an organization can flow in a variety of directions and from a number of sources, each using both oral and written forms of communication. The success of

Online software products such as Wikis are allowing work groups to share information and work collaboratively on documents. The best-known Wiki is the online encyclopedia Wikipedia.

communication systems within the organization has a tremendous effect on the overall success of the firm. Communication mistakes can lower productivity and morale.

Alternatives to face-to-face communications—such as meetings—are growing thanks to technology such as voice-mail, e-mail, and online newsletters. At Matsushita, for example, company executives are required to file reports to president Kunio Nakamura by mobile e-mail and are provided an Internet-equipped mobile phone for that purpose.[24] Companies use intranets or internal computer networks to share information and to increase collaboration. Intranets help employees quickly find or view information, any time, subject to security provisions. Advanced Micro Devices, Deloitte Touche and L. L. Bean are among those recognized for having the best corporate intranets in the United States.[25] At many companies, however, such communications technology has contributed to a state of information overload for employees, who spend more and more time managing e-mail. A growing problem is employees

A Screenwriter Saves Trees and the Environment with Rubbersidewalks

In 2001, screenwriter Lindsay Smith discovered that 26 perfectly healthy trees in her neighborhood were about to be uprooted and destroyed because their roots had damaged the surrounding sidewalks. Driven to save the trees, Smith was granted 48 hours to come up with an alternative solution. During that time, Smith located Richard Valeriano, who helped her access a prototype of a sidewalk paver composed of recycled tires. County officials agreed to leave the trees in place and consider the rubber alternative. Smith was motivated to improve the prototype, and her company, Rubbersidewalks, was born.

Using a $250,000 matching grant from the California Integrated Waste Management Board and her own credit, Smith worked to improve the look and durability of the prototype. In 2004, she received another $100,000. This allowed Smith to launch the sales portion of her business.

Although recycled pavers sound great, one might ask how they could be useful to cities facing root damage problems. Rubber sidewalk pavers have spaces between them, and this allows water to permeate to the tree roots. As a result, the roots do not press up through sidewalks, searching for moisture. It is also a much easier product to maintain, since pavers can be removed individually. Although these pavers initially can cost a city more than concrete, the city can save a substantial amount on root pruning and easements. Rubbersidewalks sales have increased 300 percent, and Smith has clients in 95 cities in 28 states and in Canada. The Rubbersidewalks product uses recycled tires and saves trees, making it doubly beneficial environmentally.[26] ❖

Q: **Discussion Questions**

1. Why was communication so important to Lindsay Smith in developing her company Rubbersidewalks?

2. How was communication used not only to save trees but also to get various business partners to participate in the new company?

3. Do you think that companies focused on the importance of green business have an advantage in reaching out to community stakeholders for support?

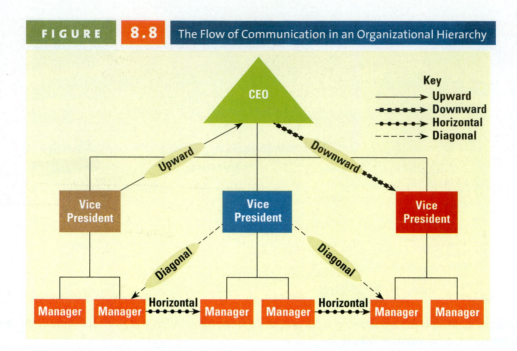

FIGURE 8.8 The Flow of Communication in an Organizational Hierarchy

abusing e-mail. Only 9.3 percent of employees surveyed say that they never check personal email at work, with 13 percent admitting that they send and receive personal e-mails constantly, and 31 percent saying they do occasionally.[27]

Experts say that managers must (1) plan how they will share important news, (2) repeat important information, and (3) rehearse key presentations. According to one study, 62 percent of executives think employees and companies benefit from fun and humor in communications and management style.[28]

Formal Communication

Formal channels of communication are intentionally defined and designed by the organization. They represent the flow of communication within the formal organizational structure, as shown on organizational charts. Traditionally, formal communication patterns were classified as vertical and horizontal, but with the increased use of teams and matrix structures, formal communication may occur in a number of patterns (Figure 8.8).

Wal-Mart and Dell: A Match You Can "Bargain" On

After years of Dell being the leader in the PC market, its rival Hewlett-Packard has overtaken it. Since its foundation, Dell has succeeded by selling PCs and computer-related products through direct phone or Internet sales, helping it retain a cost advantage over its competitors. However, companies that sell products through a combination of retail and direct sales are gaining ground. Hewlett-Packard now holds the number one slot, and competition is climbing. With Dell's market share dropping to 15 percent, things needed to change.

In response, founder Michael Dell has returned to helm the company. Michael Dell had created the company's model of building computers to order at a time when the concept was innovative. The most notable change under Dell's second stint at the helm is the company's new affiliation with Wal-Mart.

Although Dell has forayed into the retail sector before, its partnership with Wal-Mart takes a different approach. Wal-Mart is the largest retail chain around, with approximately 200 million American customers. Because of Wal-Mart's popularity, Dell is approaching retail on a huge scale.

Currently, Dell markets several products at Wal-Mart stores throughout the United States, Canada, and Puerto Rico, including laptops, desktops, and printers. An advantage of the partnership is that Wal-Mart does not require Dell to create extensive displays or commit for a long period. Therefore, Dell's partnership with Wal-Mart is less risky. The marriage of Dell and Wal-Mart should provide Dell with much-needed experience. To sell retail, the company must make changes in areas like the supply chain and advertising. This relationship also will provide Dell with

valuable information as it continues to expand to other retailers and develops a retail track record.[29] ❖

Q: Discussion Questions

1. Why was Michael Dell the ideal person to change the corporate culture to become more competitive?

2. Why does changing the marketing and operations of a company require a new organizational culture?

3. How will the information gained from retail partners such as Wal-Mart and Costco change the corporate culture at Dell?

Upward communication flows from lower to higher levels of the organization and includes information such as progress reports, suggestions for improvement, inquiries, and grievances. *Downward communication* refers to the traditional flow of information from upper organizational levels to lower levels. This type of communication typically involves directions, the assignment of tasks and responsibilities, performance feedback, and certain details about the organization's strategies and goals. Speeches, policy and procedures manuals, employee handbooks, company leaflets, telecommunications, and job descriptions are examples of downward communication.

Horizontal communication involves the exchange of information among colleagues and peers on the same organizational level, such as across or within departments. Horizontal information informs, supports, and coordinates activities both within the department and with other departments. At times, the business will formally require horizontal communication among

as well. Communication between friends, for instance, cuts across department, division, and even management–subordinate boundaries. Such friendships and other nonwork social relationships constitute the *informal organization* of a firm, and their impact can be great.

● **GRAPEVINE** an informal channel of communication, separate from management's formal, official communication channels

The most significant informal communication occurs through the **grapevine,** an informal channel of communication, separate from management's formal, official communication channels. Grapevines exist in all organizations. Information passed along the grapevine may relate to the job or organization, or it may be gossip and rumors unrelated to either. The accuracy of grapevine information has been of great concern to managers.

Additionally, managers can turn the grapevine to their advantage. Using it as a "sounding device" for possible new policies is one example. Managers can obtain valuable information

> **"Grapevines exist in all organizations. Information passed along the grapevine may relate to the job or organization, or it may be gossip and rumors unrelated to either."**

particular organizational members, as is the case with task forces or project teams.

With more and more companies downsizing and increasing the use of self-managed work teams, many workers are being required to communicate with others in different departments and on different levels to solve problems and coordinate work. When these individuals from different units and organizational levels communicate, it is *diagonal communication.* At OpenAir.com Inc., all staff members meet every day at 9:30 a.m. to share information and anecdotes about customer calls from the previous day. No chairs are allowed, and everyone is encouraged to participate. COO Morris Panner says that the communication style "reemphasizes the fact that our company is based on collaboration."[30]

Informal Communication Channels

Along with the formal channels of communication shown on an organizational chart, all firms communicate informally

Some surveys show that the majority of companies monitor their workers' Internet use and other communications.

from the grapevine that could improve decision making. Some organizations use the grapevine to their advantage by floating ideas, soliciting feedback, and reacting accordingly. People love to gossip, and managers need to be aware that grapevines exist in every organization. Managers who understand how the grapevine works also can use it to their advantage by feeding it facts to squelch rumors and incorrect information.

Monitoring Communications

Technological advances and the increased use of electronic communication in the workplace have made monitoring its use necessary for most companies. Failing to monitor employee's use of e-mail and the Internet can be costly. Chevron Corp. agreed to pay $2 million to employees who claimed that unmonitored, sexually harassing e-mail created a threatening environment for them.[31] Instituting practices that show respect for employee privacy but do not abdicate employer responsibility is increasingly necessary in today's workplace. Several Web sites provide model policies and detailed guidelines for conducting electronic monitoring, including the Model Electronic Privacy Act on the American Civil Liberties Union site. ■

SO YOU WANT A JOB IN MANAGING ORGANIZATIONAL CULTURE, TEAMWORK, AND COMMUNICATION

Jobs dealing with organizational culture and structure are usually at the top of the organization. If you want to be a CEO or high-level manager, you will help shape these areas of business. By contrast, if you are an entrepreneur or small businessperson, you will need to make decisions about assigning tasks, departmentalization, and assigning responsibility. Even managers in small organizations have to make decisions about decentralization, span of management, and forms of organizational structure. While these decisions may be part of your job, there are usually no job titles for these specific areas. Specific jobs that attempt to improve organizational culture could include ethics and compliance positions as well as those who are in charge of communicating memos, manuals, and policies that help establish the culture. These jobs will be in communications, human resources, and positions that assist top organizational managers.

Teams are becoming more common in the workplace, and it is possible to become a member of a product development group or quality assurance team. There are also human resource positions that encourage teamwork through training activities. The area of corporate communications provides lots of opportunities for specific jobs that facilitate communication systems. Thanks to technology, there are job positions to help disseminate information through online newsletters, intranets, or internal computer networks to share information to increase collaboration. In addition to the many advances involving electronic communications, there are technology concerns that create new job opportunities. Monitoring workplace communications such as the use of e-mail and the Internet has created new industries. There have to be internal controls in the organization to make sure the organization does not engage in copyright infringement. If this is an area of interest, there are specific jobs that provide an opportunity to use your technological skills to assist in maintaining appropriate standards in communicating and using technology.

If you go to work for a large company with many divisions, you can expect a number of positions dealing with the tasks discussed here. If you go to work for a small company, you probably will engage in most of these tasks as a part of your position. Organizational flexibility requires individual flexibility, and those employees willing to take on new domains and challenges will be the employees who survive and prosper in the future.

Team Exercise

Assign the responsibility for providing the organizational structure of a company for which one of your team members has worked. Was the organization centralized or decentralized in terms of decision making? Would you consider the span of control to be wide or narrow? Were any types of teams, committees, or task forces utilized in the organization? Report your work to the class.

CHECK OUT www.mhhe.com/FerrellM2e

for study materials including Interactive Exercises, Quizzes, iPod downloads, and video.

LO1 Define operations management, and differentiate between operations and manufacturing.

LO2 Explain how operations management differs in manufacturing and service firms.

LO3 Describe the elements involved in planning and designing an operations system.

LO4 Specify some techniques managers may use to manage the logistics of transforming inputs into finished products.

LO5 Assess the importance of quality in operations management.

MANAGING SERVICE & MANUFACTURING OPERATIONS

CHAPTER NINE

Introduction

All organizations create products—goods, services, or ideas—for customers. Thus, organizations as diverse as Dell Computer, Campbell Soup, UPS, and a public hospital have a number of similarities relating to how they transform resources into the products we consume. Most hospitals use similar admission procedures, while Burger King and Dairy Queen use similar food preparation methods to make hamburgers. Such similarities are to be expected. But even organizations in unrelated industries take similar steps in creating goods or services. The check-in procedures of hotels and commercial airlines are comparable, for example.

The way Subway assembles a sandwich and the way GMC assembles a truck are similar (both use automation and an assembly line). These similarities are the result of operations management, the focus of this chapter.

Here, we discuss the role of production or operations management in acquiring and managing the resources necessary to create goods and services. Production and operations management involves planning and designing the processes that will transform those resources into finished products, managing the movement of those resources through the transformation process, and ensuring that the products are of the quality expected by customers.

LO1

Define operations management, and differentiate between operations and manufacturing.

THE NATURE OF OPERATIONS MANAGEMENT

Operations management (OM), the development and administration of the activities involved in transforming resources into goods and services, is of critical importance. Operations managers oversee the transformation process and the planning and designing of operations systems, managing logistics, quality, and productivity. Quality and productivity have become fundamental aspects of operations management because a company that cannot make products of the quality desired by consumers, using resources efficiently and effectively, will not be able to remain in business. OM is the "core" of most organizations because it is responsible for the creation of the organization's goods or services.

Historically, operations management has been called "production" or "manufacturing" primarily because of the view that it was limited to the manufacture of physical goods. Its focus was on methods and techniques required to operate a factory efficiently. The change from "production" to "operations" recognizes the increasing importance of organizations that provide services and ideas. Additionally, the term *operations* represents an interest in viewing the operations function as a whole rather than simply as an analysis of inputs and outputs.

Today, OM includes a wide range of organizational activities and situations outside of manufacturing, such as health care, food service, banking, entertainment, education, transportation, and charity. Thus, we use the terms **manufacturing** and **production** interchangeably to represent the activities and processes used in making *tangible* products, whereas we use the broader term **operations** to describe those processes used in the making of *both tangible and intangible products*. Manufacturing provides tangible products such as Hewlett-Packard's latest printer, and operations provides intangibles such as a stay at Wyndham Hotels and Resorts.

The Transformation Process

At the heart of operations management is the transformation process through which **inputs** (resources such as labor, money, materials, and energy) are converted into **outputs** (goods, services, and ideas). The transformation process combines inputs in predetermined ways by using different equipment, administrative procedures, and technology to create a product (Figure 9.1). To ensure that this process generates quality products efficiently, operations managers control the process by taking measurements (feedback) at various points in the transformation process and comparing them to previously established standards. If there is any deviation between the actual and desired outputs, the manager may take some sort of corrective action. All adjustments made to create a satisfying product are a part of the transformation process.

This transformation may take place through one or more processes. In a business that manufactures oak furniture, for example, inputs pass through several processes before being turned into the final outputs—furniture that has been designed to meet the desires of customers (Figure 9.2). The furniture maker must first strip the oak trees of their bark and saw them into appropriate sizes—one step in the transformation process. Next, the firm dries the strips of oak lumber, a second form of transformation. Third, the

| FIGURE | 9.1 | The Transformation Process of Operations Management |

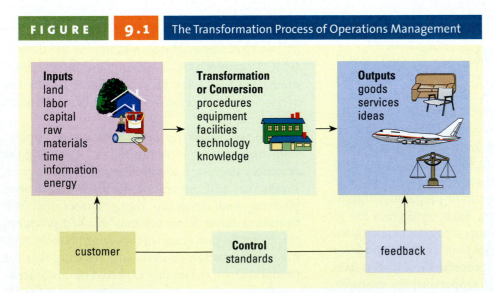

dried wood is routed into its appropriate shape and made smooth. Fourth, workers assemble and treat the wood pieces, then stain or varnish the piece of assembled furniture. Finally, the completed piece of furniture is stored until it can be shipped to customers at the appropriate time. Of course, many businesses choose to eliminate some of these stages by purchasing already processed materials—lumber, for example—or outsourcing some tasks to third-party firms with greater expertise.

 L02

Explain how operations management differs in manufacturing and service firms.

Operations Management in Service Businesses

Different types of transformation processes take place in organizations that provide services, such as airlines, colleges, and most nonprofit organizations. An airline transforms inputs such as employees, time, money, and equipment through processes such as booking flights, flying airplanes, maintaining equipment, and training crews. The output of these processes is flying passengers and/or packages to their destinations. In a nonprofit organization like Habitat for Humanity, inputs such as money, materials, information, and volunteer time and labor are used to transform raw materials into homes for needy families. In this setting, transformation processes include fund-raising and promoting the cause in order to gain new volunteers and donations of supplies, as well as pouring concrete, raising walls,

| FIGURE | 9.2 | Inputs, Outputs, and Transformation Processes in the Manufacture of Oak Furniture |

Inputs
oak trees
labor
information/
knowledge
stain or varnish
router/saw
warehouse space/
time

Transformation
cutting or
sawing
routing
measuring
assembling
staining/varnishing
storing

Outputs
oak furniture

and setting roofs. Transformation processes occur in all organizations, regardless of what they produce or their objectives. For most organizations, the ultimate objective is for the produced outputs to be worth more than the combined costs of the inputs. The service sector represents approximately 80 percent of all employment in the United States, and the fastest growth of jobs is in service industries.[1]

Unlike tangible goods, services are effectively actions or performances that must be directed toward the consumers who use them. Consider Whole Foods, an all-natural grocery chain. By creating a fun shopping experience, Whole Foods turns the drudgery of grocery shopping into entertainment and pleasure.[2] Thus, there is a significant customer-contact component to most services. Examples of high-contact services include health care, real estate, tax preparation, and food service. At the world-renowned Inn at Little Washington, for example, food servers are critical to delivering the perfect dining experience expected by the most discriminating diners. Wait staff are expected not only to be courteous but also to demonstrate a detailed knowledge of the restaurant's offerings, and even to assess the mood of

JetBlue Recovers and Excels in Service

Founded in 2000, JetBlue Airways gathered loyal customers thanks to its customer service and unique offerings. In 2003, the company garnered $103 million in profits. At first, JetBlue tried delaying rather than canceling flights, but that policy placed JetBlue at the bottom of the list of airlines able to meet their flight schedules and cut profits to $46 million by 2004. A year later, the company lost $20 million. Then, on Valentine's Day, 2007, disaster struck.

On that day, a huge storm hit. JetBlue had an insufficient response time due to a lack of manpower and poor decision making. Over 1,000 travelers were stranded in their planes for over six hours. Thousands were also stuck inside JetBlue terminals for up to four days. By the time JetBlue tackled the issue, the company had canceled 1,200 flights. It lost

$41 million because of forgone revenue and reimbursement.

Despite negative publicity, JetBlue honored the elements that originally made it a customer favorite. The company immediately apologized, acknowledging its faults. Refunds and free rebooking were offered to travelers affected by February's storm. The company also improved its weather forecasting ability. Consequently, when another ice storm hit the company's hub on March 16, 2007, JetBlue completed 98 percent of its flights by the next day—a vast improvement in one month.

JetBlue also created a Flier's Bill of Rights—the first of its kind in the airline industry. Due to this bill, customers who are delayed receive vouchers ranging from $25 to the full ticket price, depending on the length of the delay. Thanks to

its Bill of Rights and customer dedication, analysts believe JetBlue will survive.[3] ❖

Q: Discussion Questions

1. How did JetBlue implement service recovery to restore the confidence of consumers?

2. How can a company such as JetBlue plan in advance to prevent major failures in customer service?

3. Why do you think JetBlue is now one of the most highly ranked airlines in terms of quality service?

guests in order to respond to diners appropriately.[4] Low-contact services, such as online auction services like eBay, often have a strong high-tech component.

Regardless of the level of customer contact, service businesses strive to provide a standardized process, and technology offers an interface that creates an automatic and structured response. The ideal service provider will be high-tech and high-touch. JetBlue, for example, strives to maintain an excellent Web site; friendly, helpful customer contact; and satellite TV service at every seat on each plane. Thus, service organizations must build their operations around good execution, which comes from hiring and training excellent employees, developing flexible systems, customizing services, and maintaining adjustable capacity to deal with fluctuating demand.[5]

Another challenge related to service operations is that the output is generally intangible and even perishable. Few services can be saved, stored, resold, or returned.[6] A seat on an airline or a table in a restaurant, for example, cannot be sold or used at a later date. Because of the perishability of services, it can be extremely difficult for service providers to estimate the demand accurately to match the right supply of a service. If an airline overestimates demand, for example, it will still have to fly each plane even with empty seats. The flight costs the same regardless of whether it is 50 percent full or 100 percent full, but the former will result in much higher costs per passenger. If the airline underestimates demand, the result can be long lines of annoyed customers or even the necessity of bumping some customers off an overbooked flight.

Businesses that manufacture tangible goods and those that provide services or ideas are similar yet different. For example, both types of organizations must make design and operating decisions. Most goods are manufactured prior to purchase, but most services are performed after purchase. Flight attendants at Southwest Airlines, hotel service personnel, and even the Tennessee Titans football team engage in performances that are a part of the total product. Though manufacturers and service providers often perform similar activities, they also differ in several respects. We can classify these differences in five basic ways.

nature and consumption of output First, manufacturers and service providers differ in the nature and consumption of their output. For example, the term *manufacturer* implies a firm that makes tangible products. A service provider, in contrast, produces more intangible outputs such as U.S. Postal Service delivery of priority mail or a business stay in a Hyatt hotel. As mentioned earlier, the very nature of the service provider's product requires a higher degree of customer contact. Moreover, the actual performance of the service typically occurs at the point of consumption. At the Hyatt, the business traveler may evaluate in-room communications and the restaurant. Toyota and other automakers, in contrast, can separate the production of a car from its actual use. Manufacturing, then, can occur in an isolated environment, away from the customer. However, service providers, because of their need for customer contact, are often more limited than manufacturers in selecting work methods, assigning jobs, scheduling work, and exercising control over operations. At Toyota, for example, any employee who observes a problem can pull a cord and bring the assembly line to a stop to address the issue.[7] The quality of the service experience often is controlled by a service contact employee. However, some hospitals are studying the manufacturing processes and quality control mechanisms applied in the automotive industry in an effort to improve their service quality. By analyzing work processes to find unnecessary steps to eliminate and using teams to identify and address problems as soon as they occur, these hospitals are slashing patient waiting times, decreasing inventories of wheelchairs, readying operating rooms sooner, and generally moving patients through their hospital visit more quickly, with fewer errors, and at a lower cost.[8]

Because services are perishable, service providers like ski areas offer less expensive tickets at night to stimulate demand.

uniformity of inputs A second way to classify differences between manufacturers and service providers has to do with the uniformity of inputs. Manufacturers typically have more control over the amount of variability of the resources they use than do service providers. For example, each customer calling Fidelity Investments is likely to require different services due to differing needs, whereas many of the tasks required to manufacture a Lincoln Navigator sport utility vehicle are the same across each unit of output. Consequently, the products of service organizations tend to be more "customized" than those of their manufacturing counterparts. Consider, for example, a haircut versus a bottle of shampoo. The haircut is much more likely to incorporate your specific desires (customization) than is the bottle of shampoo.

uniformity of output Manufacturers and service providers also differ in the uniformity of their output, the final product. Because of the human element inherent in providing services, each service tends to be performed differently. Not all grocery checkers, for example, wait on customers in the same way. If a barber or stylist performs 15 haircuts in a day, it is unlikely that any two of them will be exactly the same. Consequently, human and technological elements associated with a service can result in a different day-to-day or even hour-to-hour performance of that service. The service experience can vary even at McDonald's or Burger King despite the fact that the two chains employ very similar procedures and processes. Moreover, no two customers are exactly alike in their perception of the service experience. Health care offers another excellent example of this challenge. Every diagnosis, treatment, and surgery varies because every individual is different. In manufacturing, the high degree of automation available allows manufacturers to generate uniform outputs, and thus, the operations are more

effective and efficient. For example, we would expect every TAG Heuer or Rolex watch to maintain very high standards of quality and performance.

labor required A fourth point of difference is the amount of labor required to produce an output. Service providers are generally more labor-intensive (require more labor) because of the high level of customer contact, perishability of the output (must be consumed immediately), and high degree of variation of inputs and outputs (customization). For example, Adecco provides temporary support personnel. Each temporary worker's performance determines Adecco's product quality. A manufacturer, in contrast, is likely to be more capital-intensive because of the machinery and technology used in the mass production of highly similar goods. For instance, it would take a considerable investment for Nokia to make a digital phone that has a battery with longer life.

measurement of productivity The final distinction between service providers and manufacturers involves the measurement of productivity for each output produced. For manufacturers, measuring productivity is fairly straightforward because of the tangibility of the output and its high degree of uniformity. For a service provider, variations in demand (e.g., higher demand for air travel in some seasons than in others), variations in service requirements from job to job, and the intangibility of the product make productivity measurement more difficult. Consider, for example, how much easier it is to measure the productivity of employees involved in the production of Intel computer processors as opposed to serving the needs of Prudential Securities' clients.

It is convenient and simple to think of organizations as being either manufacturers or service providers as in the preceding discussion. In reality, however, most organizations are a combination of the two, with both tangible

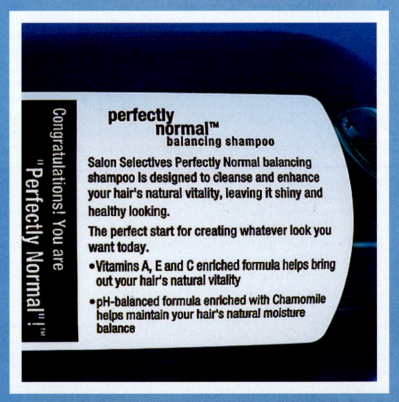

perfectly normal™ balancing shampoo

Salon Selectives Perfectly Normal balancing shampoo is designed to cleanse and enhance your hair's natural vitality, leaving it shiny and healthy looking.

The perfect start for creating whatever look you want today.

• Vitamins A, E and C enriched formula helps bring out your hair's natural vitality

• pH-balanced formula enriched with Chamomile helps maintain your hair's natural moisture balance

Congratulations! You are "Perfectly Normal"!™

The products produced by manufacturers are more likely to be standardized than the products produced by service organizations. For example, the shampoo you use daily is more standardized than the haircut you get on any given day.

and intangible qualities embodied in what they produce. For example, Porsche provides customer services such as toll-free hotlines and warranty protection, while banks may sell checks and other tangible products that complement their primarily intangible product offering. Thus, we consider "products" to include both tangible physical goods as well as intangible service offerings. It is the level of tangibility of its principal product that tends to classify a company as either a manufacturer or a service provider. From an OM standpoint, this level of tangibility greatly influences the nature of the company's operational processes and procedures.

 L03

Describe the elements involved in planning and designing an operations system.

PLANNING AND DESIGNING OPERATIONS SYSTEMS

Before a company can produce any product, it must first decide what it will produce and for what group of customers. It must then determine what processes it will use to make these products as well as the facilities it needs to produce them. These decisions constitute operations planning. Although planning was once the sole realm of the production and operations department, today's successful companies involve all departments within an organization, particularly marketing and research and development, in these decisions.

Planning the Product

Before making any product, a company first must determine what consumers want and then design a product to satisfy that want. Most companies use marketing research (discussed in Chapter 12) to determine the kinds of goods and services to provide and the features they must possess. Nissan, for example, conducted intensive market research before launching its first full-size pickup truck, the Titan. The company interviewed truck buyers about their likes and dislikes and sent researchers to drive competing trucks for a month to learn firsthand about how the large vehicles handle in a variety of situations.[9] Marketing research can also help gauge the demand for a product and how much consumers are willing to pay for it.

Developing a product can be a lengthy, expensive process. For example, in the automobile industry, developing the new technology for night vision, bumper-mounted sonar systems that make parking easier, and a satellite service that locates and analyzes car problems has been a lengthy, expensive process. Most companies work to reduce development time and costs. For example, through Web collaboration, faucet manufacturer Moen has reduced the time required to take an idea to a finished product in stores to just 16 months, a drop of 33 percent.[10] Once management has developed an idea for a product that customers will buy, it must then plan how to produce the product.

Within a company, the engineering or research and development department is charged with turning a product idea into a workable design that can be produced economically. In smaller companies, a single individual (perhaps the owner) may be solely responsible for this crucial activity. Regardless of who is responsible for product design, planning does not stop with a blueprint for a product or a description of a service; it must also work out efficient production of the product to ensure that enough is available to satisfy consumer demand. How does a lawn mower company transform steel, aluminum, and other materials into a mower design that satisfies consumer and environmental requirements? Operations managers must plan for the types and quantities of materials needed to produce the product, the skills and quantity of people needed to make the product, and the actual processes through which the inputs must pass in their transformation to outputs.

Designing the Operations Processes

Before a firm can begin production, it must first determine the appropriate method of transforming resources into the desired product. Often, consumers' specific needs and desires dictate a process. Customer needs, for example, require that all 3/4-inch bolts have the same basic thread size, function, and quality; if they did not, engineers and builders could not rely on 3/4-inch bolts in their construction projects. A bolt manufacturer, then, will probably use a standardized process so that every 3/4-inch bolt produced is like every other one. In contrast, a bridge often must be customized so that it is appropriate for the site and expected load; furthermore, the bridge must be constructed on site rather than in a factory. Typically, products are designed to be manufactured by one of three processes: standardization, modular design, or customization.

standardization Most firms that manufacture products in large quantities for many customers have found that they can make them cheaper and faster by standardizing designs. **Standardization** is making identical, interchangeable components or even complete products. With standardization, a customer may not get exactly what he or she wants, but the product generally costs less than a custom-designed product. Television sets, ballpoint pens, and tortilla chips are standardized products; most are manufactured on an assembly line. Standardization speeds up production and quality control and reduces production costs. And, as in the example of the 3/4-inch bolts, standardization provides consistency so that customers who need certain products to function uniformly all the time will get a product that meets their expectations. As a result of its entry into the World Trade Organization, China promoted the standardization of agricultural production across the country; the nation saw a large increase in agricultural productivity as a result.[11]

modular design

Modular design involves building an item in self-contained units, or modules, that can be combined or interchanged to create different products. Personal computers, for example, are generally composed of a number of components—CPU case, motherboard, RAM chips, hard drives, graphics card, etc.—that can be installed in different configurations to meet the customer's needs. Because many modular components are produced as integrated units, the failure of any portion of a modular component usually means replacing the entire component. Modular design allows products to be repaired quickly, thus reducing the cost of labor, but the component itself is expensive, raising the cost of repair materials. Many automobile manufacturers use modular design in the production process. Manufactured homes are built on a modular design and cost $58,000, on average, compared with $267,000 for new site–built houses, including the land.[12]

Clayton Homes, a manufactured-home company, has begun building eco-friendly modular "ihomes" like the one shown here. Home buyers can choose the components they want in a home and have them configured the way they like.

customization

Customization is making products to meet a particular customer's needs or wants. Products produced in this way are generally unique. Such products include repair services, photocopy services, custom artwork, jewelry, and furniture, as well as large-scale products such as bridges, ships, and computer software. Although there may be similarities among ships, for example, builders generally design and build each ship to meet the needs of the customer who will use it. Delta Marine Industries, for example, custom-builds each luxury yacht to the customer's exact specifications and preferences for things like helicopter garages, golf courses, and swimming pools. The Seattle-based company has delivered 22 yachts longer than 100 feet since 1990.[13] Likewise, when you go to a printing shop to order business cards, the company must customize the cards with your name, address, and title.

Planning Capacity

Planning the operational processes for the organization involves two important areas: capacity planning and facilities planning. The term **capacity** basically refers to the maximum load that an organizational unit can carry or operate. The unit of measurement may be a worker or machine, a department, a branch, or even an entire plant. Maximum capacity can be stated in terms of the inputs or outputs provided. For example, an electric plant might state plant capacity in terms of the

MINK Shoes Make Veganism Fashionable

Vegan stylist Rebecca Brough started to explore the idea of creating a line of high-fashion vegan shoes in 2000. She took a chance and brought her designs to the Lineapelle Fair shoe convention in Italy. Sixteen cobblers turned her down before Brough met Marco Gambassi, who agreed in 2002 to collaborate on MINK shoes. Because Brough's designs are constructed by hand using eco-friendly and recycled materials, they are time-consuming, and not many cobblers felt the idea was worthwhile. Gambassi was interested in the process and created a resin from a rubber tree plant to replace the traditional nonvegan glue used in shoemaking. Distributing the shoes was another matter. Many high-end retailers were skeptical that vegan shoes would sell. After visiting 287 stores, Brough still had no takers and decided to use her contacts as a former stylist to promote the product. Brough convinced celebrities such as Paris Hilton and Natalie Portman to wear her designs. That exposure set things in motion, and by 2006 Brough had sold 740 pairs of shoes and made a gross profit of $75,000.[14] ❖

maximum number of kilowatt-hours that can be produced without causing a power outage, while a restaurant might state capacity in terms of the maximum number of customers who can be effectively—comfortably and courteously—served at any one particular time. Honda Motor Company's Marysville, Ohio, plant, which produces the Accord sedan, Accord coupe, and Acura TL, has an annual production capacity of 440,000 vehicles.[15]

Efficiently planning the organization's capacity needs is an important process for the operations manager. Capacity levels that fall short can result in unmet demand and, consequently, lost customers. In contrast, when there is more capacity available than needed, operating costs are driven up needlessly due to unused and often expensive resources. To avoid such situations, organizations must accurately forecast demand and then plan capacity based on these forecasts. Another reason for the importance of efficient capacity planning has to do with long-term commitment of resources. Often, once a capacity decision—such as factory size—has been implemented, it is very difficult to change the decision without incurring substantial costs.

DID YOU KNOW?

Hershey's makes more than 80 million of its kisses chocolates per day in its Hershey, Pennsylvania and Virginia plants.[16]

Planning Facilities

Once a company knows what process it will use to create its products, it can design and build an appropriate facility in which to make them. Many products are manufactured in factories, but others are produced in stores, at home, or where the product ultimately will be used. Companies must decide where to locate their operations facilities, what layout is best for producing their particular product, and even what technology to apply to the transformation process.

Many firms are developing both a traditional organization for customer contact as well as a virtual organization. Charles Schwab Corporation, a securities brokerage and investment company, maintains traditional offices and has developed complete telephone and Internet services for customers. Through its Web site, investors can obtain personal investment information and trade securities over the Internet without leaving their home or office.[17]

facility location Where to locate a firm's facilities is a significant question because once the decision has been made and implemented, the firm must live with it due to the high costs involved. When a company decides to relocate or open a facility at a new location, it must pay careful attention to factors such as proximity to market, availability of raw materials, availability of transportation, availability of power, climatic influences, availability of labor, community characteristics (quality of life), and taxes and inducements. Inducements and tax reductions have become an increasingly important criterion in recent years. In deciding where to locate a new plant, Tesla Motors found itself in a bidding war between Albuquerque, New Mexico and San Carlos, California. Ultimately, the company chose California because the state provided Tesla with $100 million in tax-free financing for manufacturing equipment, along with an addition $1 million for employment

Nintendo's Wii consoles were a smash hit when they first hit the market—to the point where the game maker reportedly lacked the production capacity to produce all the machines consumers demanded.

training.[18] According to the Institute for Local Self-Reliance, Wal-Mart often receives millions of dollars in free roads, land, sewers, and tax abatements from local governments as incentives to locate new stores or distribution centers in certain areas.[19] The facility-location decision is complex because it involves the evaluation of many factors, some of which cannot be measured with precision. Because of the long-term impact of the decision, however, it is one that cannot be taken lightly.

facility layout Arranging the physical layout of a facility is a complex, highly technical task. Some industrial architects specialize in the design and layout of certain types of businesses. There are three basic layouts: fixed-position, process, and product.

A company using a **fixed-position layout** brings all resources required to create the product to a central location. The product—perhaps an office building, house, hydroelectric plant, or bridge—does not move. A company using a fixed-position layout may be called a **project organization** because it is typically involved in large, complex projects such as construction or exploration. Project organizations generally make a unique product, rely on highly skilled labor, produce very few units, and have high production costs per unit.

Firms that use a **process layout** organize the transformation process into departments that group related processes. A metal fabrication plant, for example, may have a cutting department, a drilling department, and a polishing department. A

continuous manufacturing organizations, so named because once they are set up, they run continuously, creating products with many similar characteristics. Examples of products produced on assembly lines are automobiles, television sets, vacuum cleaners, toothpaste, and meals from a cafeteria. Continuous manufacturing organizations using a product layout are characterized by the standardized product they produce, the large number of units produced, and the relatively low unit cost of production.

Many companies actually use a combination of layout designs. For example, an automobile manufacturer may rely on an assembly line (product layout) but may also use a process layout to manufacture parts.

technology Every industry has a basic, underlying technology that dictates the nature of its transformation process. The steel industry continually tries to improve steelmaking techniques. The health care industry performs research into medical technologies and pharmaceuticals to improve the qual-

> ## Every industry has a basic, underlying technology that dictates the nature of its transformation process.

hospital may have an X-ray unit, an obstetrics unit, and so on. These types of organizations are sometimes called **intermittent organizations,** which deal with products of a lesser magnitude than do project organizations, and their products are not necessarily unique but possess a significant number of differences. Doctors, makers of custom-made cabinets, commercial printers, and advertising agencies are intermittent organizations because they tend to create products to customers' specifications and produce relatively few units of each product. Because of the low level of output, the cost per unit of product is generally high.

The **product layout** requires that production be broken down into relatively simple tasks assigned to workers, who are usually positioned along an assembly line. Workers remain in one location, and the product moves from one worker to another. Each person in turn performs his or her required tasks or activities. Companies that use assembly lines are usually known as

ity of health care service. Two developments that have strongly influenced the operations of many businesses are computers and robotics.

Computers have been used for decades and on a relatively large scale since IBM introduced its 650 series in the late 1950s. The operations function makes great use of computers in all phases of the transformation process. **Computer-assisted design (CAD),** for example, helps engineers design components, products, and processes on the computer instead of on paper. **Computer-assisted manufacturing (CAM)** goes a step further, employing specialized computer systems to actually guide and control the transformation processes. Such systems can monitor the transformation process, gathering information about the equipment used to produce the products and about the product itself as it goes from one stage of the transformation process to the next. The computer provides information to an operator who may, if necessary, take corrective action. In some highly automated systems, the computer itself can take corrective action.

Using **flexible manufacturing,** computers can direct machinery to adapt to different versions of similar operations. For example, with instructions from a computer, one machine can be programmed to carry out its function for several different versions of an engine without shutting down the production line for refitting.

Robots are also becoming increasingly useful in the transformation process. These "steel-collar" workers have become particularly important in industries such as nuclear power, hazardous-waste disposal, ocean research, and space construction and maintenance, in which human lives would otherwise be at risk. Robots are used in numerous applications by companies around the world. Many assembly operations—cars, television sets, telephones, stereo equipment, and numerous other products—depend on industrial robots. The Robotics Industries Association estimates that there are 190,000 robots currently being used in the United States, placing the United States second behind Japan in terms of robot usage. The RIA estimates that worldwide 1 million robots are in use.[20] Researchers continue to make more sophisticated robots, and some speculate that in the future robots will not be limited to space programs and production and operations, but will also be able to engage in farming, laboratory research, and even household activities. Moreover, robotics are increasingly being used in the medical field. Voice-activated robotic arms operate video cameras for surgeons. Similar technology assists with biopsies, as well as heart, spine, and nervous system procedures. A heart surgeon at London Health Science Centre in Ontario uses a surgical robot to perform bypass operations on patients without opening their chests, except for five tiny incisions, while their hearts continue beating. There are over 800 surgical robots installed in the United States alone, and the industry is expected to continue to grow rapidly. The advantages include less blood loss and fewer postoperative complications.[21]

When all these technologies—CAD/CAM, flexible manufacturing, robotics, computer systems, and more—are integrated, the result is **computer-integrated manufacturing (CIM),** a complete system that designs products, manages machines and materials, and controls the operations function. Companies adopt CIM to boost productivity and quality and reduce costs. Such technology, and computers in

Autodesk

CREATE
Industrial designers create initial sketches of the guitar's interchangeable body

INTEGRATE
Engineers design the mechanical structure in Autodesk® Inventor™ using data from the original sketch.

COLLABORATE
The digital prototype is shared among designers, engineers and even customers, so the design can be refined earlier in the process.

HOW DIGITAL PROTOTYPING GETS THIS CUSTOM ELECTRIC GUITAR ON STAGE FASTER.

autodesk.com/digitalprototyping

Image courtesy of RKS Guitars LLC

Autodesk Inc.'s computer-assisted design (CAD) software helps architects and engineers design, draft, and model buildings and products, including custom guitars like this one.

particular, will continue to make strong inroads into operations on two fronts—one dealing with the technology involved in manufacturing and one dealing with the administrative functions and processes used by operations managers. The operations manager must be willing to work with computers and other forms of technology and to develop a high degree of computer literacy.

 L04

Specify some techniques managers may use to manage the logistics of transforming inputs into finished products.

MANAGING THE SUPPLY CHAIN

A major function of operations is **supply chain management,** which refers to connecting and integrating all parties or members of the distribution system to satisfy customers.[22] Also called logistics, supply chain management includes all the

department aims to obtain items of the desired quality in the right quantities at the lowest possible cost. Rushing Water Canoes, for example, must procure not only aluminum and other raw materials, and various canoe parts and components, but also machines and equipment, manufacturing supplies (oil, electricity, and so on), and office supplies to make its canoes. People in the purchasing department locate and evaluate suppliers of these items. They must constantly be on the lookout for new materials or parts that will do a better job or cost less than those currently being used. The purchasing function can be quite complex and is one area made much easier and more efficient by technological advances.

Not all companies purchase all the materials needed to create their products. Often, they can make some components

● **PURCHASING** the buying of all the materials needed by the organization; also called procurement

● **INVENTORY** all raw materials, components, completed or partially completed products, and pieces of equipment a firm uses

● **INVENTORY CONTROL** the process of determining how many supplies and goods are needed and keeping track of quantities on hand, where each item is, and who is responsible for it

> **"A major function of operations is supply chain management, which refers to connecting and integrating all parties or members of the distribution system to satisfy customers."**

activities involved in obtaining and managing raw materials and component parts, managing finished products, packaging them, and getting them to customers. Sunny Delight had to quickly recreate its supply chain after spinning off from Procter & Gamble. This means it had to develop ordering, shipping, and billing, as well as warehouse management systems and transportation, so it could focus on growing and managing the Sunny Delight brand.[23] The supply chain integrates firms such as raw material suppliers, manufacturers, retailers, and ultimate consumers into a seamless flow of information and products.[24] Some aspects of logistics (warehousing, packaging, distributing) are so closely linked with marketing that we will discuss them in Chapter 13. In this section, we look at purchasing, managing inventory, outsourcing, and scheduling, which are vital tasks in the transformation of raw materials into finished goods. To illustrate logistics, consider a hypothetical small business—we'll call it Rushing Water Canoes Inc.—that manufactures aluminum canoes, which it sells primarily to sporting goods stores and river-rafting expeditions. Our company also makes paddles and helmets, but the focus of the following discussion is the manufacture of the company's quality canoes as they proceed through the logistics process.

Purchasing

Purchasing, also known as procurement, is the buying of all the materials needed by the organization. The purchasing

more economically and efficiently than can an outside supplier. Coors, for example, manufactures its own cans at a subsidiary plant. However, firms sometimes find that it is uneconomical to make or purchase an item, and instead arrange to lease it from another organization. Some airlines, for example, lease airplanes rather than buy them. Whether to purchase, make, or lease a needed item generally depends on cost, as well as on product availability and supplier reliability.

Managing Inventory

Once the items needed to create a product have been procured, some provision has to be made for storing them until they are needed. Every raw material, component, completed or partially completed product, and piece of equipment a firm uses—its **inventory**—must be accounted for, or controlled. There are three basic types of inventory. *Finished-goods inventory* includes those products that are ready for sale, such as a fully assembled automobile ready to ship to a dealer. *Work-in-process inventory* consists of those products that are partly completed or are in some stage of the transformation process. At McDonald's, a cooking hamburger represents work-in-process inventory because it must go through several more stages before it can be sold to a customer. *Raw materials inventory* includes all the materials that have been purchased to be used as inputs for making other products. Nuts and bolts are raw materials for an automobile manufacturer, while hamburger patties, vegetables, and buns are raw materials for a fast-food restaurant. Our fictional Rushing Water Canoes has an inventory of materials for making canoes, paddles, and helmets, as well as its inventory of finished products for sale to consumers.

We won't let your chicken go bad.

FAC Food Service Logistics helps manage the supply chain and inventory of food companies in the United States so that their products—chicken included—arrive on time and unspoiled.

Inventory control is the process of determining how many supplies and goods are needed and keeping track of quantities on hand, where each item is, and who is responsible for it.

Operations management must be closely coordinated with inventory control. The production of televisions, for example, cannot be planned without some knowledge of the availability of all the necessary materials—the chassis, picture tubes, color guns, and so forth. Also, each item held in inventory—any type of inventory—carries with it a cost. For example, storing fully assembled televisions in a warehouse to sell to a dealer at a future date requires not only the use of space, but also the purchase of insurance to cover any losses that might occur due to fire or other unforeseen events.

Inventory managers spend a great deal of time trying to determine the proper inventory level for each item. The answer to the question of how many units to hold in inventory depends on variables such as the usage rate of the item, the cost of maintaining the item in inventory, the cost of paperwork and other procedures associated with ordering or making the item, and the cost of the item itself. Several approaches may be used to determine how many units of a given item should be procured at one time and when that procurement should take place.

the economic order quantity model To control the number of items maintained in inventory, managers need to determine how much of any given item they should order. One popular approach is the **economic order quantity (EOQ) model,** which identifies the optimum number of items to order to minimize the costs of managing (ordering, storing, and using) them.

just-in-time inventory management An increasingly popular technique is **just-in-time (JIT) inventory management,** which eliminates waste by using smaller quantities of materials that arrive "just in time" for use in the transformation process and therefore require less storage space and other inventory management expense. JIT minimizes inventory by providing an almost continuous flow of items from suppliers to the production facility. Many U.S. companies, including General Motors, Hewlett-Packard, IBM, and Harley Davidson, have adopted JIT to reduce costs and boost efficiency.

Let's say that Rushing Water Canoes uses 20 units of aluminum from a supplier per day.

Traditionally, its inventory manager might order enough for one month at a time: 440 units per order (20 units per day times 22 workdays per month). The expense of such a large inventory could be considerable because of the cost of insurance coverage, recordkeeping, rented storage space, and so on. The just-in-time approach would reduce these costs because aluminum would be purchased in smaller quantities, perhaps in lot sizes of 20, which the supplier would deliver once a day. Of course, for such an approach to be effective, the supplier must be extremely reliable and relatively close to the production facility.

material-requirements planning Another inventory management technique is **material-requirements planning (MRP),** a planning system that schedules the precise quantity of materials needed to make the product. The basic components of MRP are a master production schedule, a bill of materials, and an inventory status file. At Rushing Water Canoes, for example, the inventory-control manager will look at the production schedule to determine how many canoes the company plans to make. He or she will then prepare a bill of materials—a list of all the materials needed to make that quantity of canoes. Next, the manager will determine the quantity of these items that RWC already holds in inventory (to avoid ordering excess materials) and then develop a schedule for ordering and accepting delivery of the right quantity of materials to satisfy the firm's needs. Because of the large number of parts and materials that go into a typical production process, MRP must be done on a computer. It can be, and often is, used in conjunction with just-in-time inventory management.

Outsourcing

Increasingly, outsourcing has become a component of supply chain management in operations. As we mentioned in Chapter 3, outsourcing refers to the contracting of manufacturing or other tasks to independent companies, often overseas. Many companies elect to outsource some aspects of their operations to companies that can provide these products more efficiently, at a lower cost, and with greater customer satisfaction. Globalization has put pressure on supply chain managers to improve speed and balance resources against competitive pressures. Companies outsourcing to China, in particular, face heavy regulation, high transportation costs, inadequate facilities, and unpredictable supply chain execution. Therefore, suppliers need to provide useful, timely, and accurate information about every aspect of the quality requirements, schedules, and solutions to dealing with problems. For example, Chinese suppliers took responsibility for the lead paint on children's toys crisis in the United States, but it was an overall management and supply chain system failure that permitted these toxic toys to be sold in U.S. stores.[25] Many high-tech firms have outsourced the production of memory chips, computers, and telecom equipment to Asian companies.[26] The hourly labor costs in countries such as China and India are far less than in the United States, Europe, or even Mexico. These developing countries have improved their manufacturing capabilities, infrastructure, and techni-

By tracking its sales in real time, 7-11 Japan manages its inventory on a minute-by-minute basis at each of its thousands of stores. Multiple times each day the stores receive fresh inventory, and employees rearrange the shelves, depending on what's selling well.

cal and business skills, making them more attractive regions for global sourcing. However, the cost of outsourcing halfway around the world must be considered in decisions.[27] While information technology is often outsourced today, transportation, human resources, services, and even marketing functions can be outsourced. Our hypothetical Rushing Water Canoes might contract with a local janitorial service to clean its offices and with a local accountant to handle routine bookkeeping and tax-preparation functions.

Outsourcing, once used primarily as a cost-cutting tactic, has increasingly been linked with the development of competitive advantage through improved product quality, speeding up the time it takes products to get to the customer, and overall supply-chain efficiencies. Table 9.1 provides the world's top five outsourcing providers that assist mainly in information technology. Outsourcing allows companies to free up time and resources to focus on what they do best and to create better opportunities to focus on customer satisfaction. Many executives view outsourcing as an innovative way to boost productivity and

programs. One popular method is the *Program Evaluation and Review Technique (PERT)*, which identifies all the major activities or events required to complete a project, arranges them in a sequence or path, determines the critical path, and estimates the time required for each event. Producing a McDonald's Big Mac, for example, involves removing meat, cheese, sauce, and vegetables from the refrigerator; grilling the hamburger patties; assembling the ingredients; placing the completed Big Mac in its package; and serving it to the customer (Figure 9.3). The cheese,

> ## " Many executives view outsourcing as an innovative way to boost productivity and remain competitive against low-wage offshore factories. "

remain competitive against low-wage offshore factories. However, outsourcing may create conflict with labor and negative public opinion when it results in U.S. workers being replaced by lower-cost workers in other countries. According to a survey by Opinion Research Corporation, 69 percent of respondents believed that boycotting products and services from companies that actively send jobs overseas would influence companies.[28]

Routing and Scheduling

After all materials have been procured and their use determined, managers must then consider the **routing,** or sequence of operations through which the product must pass. For example, before employees at Rushing Water Canoes can form aluminum sheets into a canoe, the aluminum must be cut to size. Likewise, the canoe's flotation material must be installed before workers can secure the wood seats. The sequence depends on the product specifications developed by the engineering department of the company.

Once management knows the routing, the actual work can be scheduled. **Scheduling** assigns the tasks to be done to departments or even specific machines, workers, or teams. At Rushing Water, cutting aluminum for the company's canoes might be scheduled to be done by the "cutting and finishing" department on machines designed especially for that purpose.

Many approaches to scheduling have been developed, ranging from simple trial and error to highly sophisticated computer

pickles, onions, and sauce cannot be put on before the hamburger patty is completely grilled and placed on the bun. The path that requires the longest time from start to finish is called the *critical path* because it determines the minimum amount of time in which the process can be completed. If any of the activities on the critical path for production of the Big Mac fall behind schedule, the sandwich will not be completed on time, causing customers to wait longer than they usually would.

 L05

Assess the importance of quality in operations management.

MANAGING QUALITY

Quality, like cost and efficiency, is a critical element of operations management, for defective products can quickly ruin a firm. Quality reflects the degree to which a good or service meets the demands and requirements of customers. Customers are increasingly dissatisfied with the quality of service provided

TABLE 9.1 The World's Top Five Outsourcing Providers

Company	Services *
Accenture	Human resource management; information and communication technology management; financial management
IBM	Customer relationship management, human resource management; information and communication technology management
Infosys Technologies	Information and communication technology management; transaction processes, information technology, and strategic consulting
Sodexo	Real estate and asset management; facility services; service vouchers and cards
Capgemini	Customer relationship management; information and communication technology management; financial management

*The services section was provided by the authors.

Source: "The 2008 Global Outsourcing 100™," International Association of Outsourcing Professionals™ www.outsourcingprofessional.org/content/23/152/1197/ (accessed March 11, 2009).

FIGURE **9.3** A Hypothetical PERT Diagram for a McDonald's Big Mac

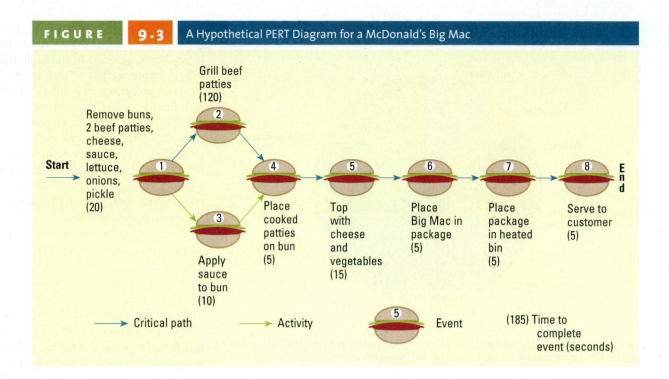

by many airlines. Consumers file thousands of air travel complaints each year.[29] Determining quality can be difficult because it depends on customers' perceptions of how well the product meets or exceeds their expectations. For example, the fuel economy of an automobile or its reliability (defined in terms of frequency of repairs) can be measured with some degree of precision. Although automakers rely on their own measures of vehicle quality, they also look to independent sources such as the J. D. Power & Associates annual initial quality survey (see Figure 9.5) for confirmation of their quality assessment as well as consumer perceptions of quality. Many people were surprised when J. D. Power ranked Hyundai second behind only Toyota in

terms of quality in 2004; for Hyundai executives, the news only substantiated the company's assessment of its long-running initiative to improve quality. However, it is more difficult to measure psychological characteristics such as design, color, and status. It is especially difficult to measure these characteristics when the product is a service. A company has to decide exactly which quality characteristics it considers important and then define those characteristics in terms that can be measured.

The Malcolm Baldrige National Quality Award is given each year to companies that meet rigorous standards of quality. The Baldrige criteria are (1) leadership, (2) information and analysis, (3) strategic planning, (4) human resource development and

Smart Cars Make Sense

With gas prices fluctuating and environmental concerns growing, the automobile market has seen a global decline in sales, and people are looking to save more and pollute less. A possible solution: get Smart. The Smart car is the brainchild of Nicholas Hayek (known for Swatch watches) and is built by Mercedes-Benz. Futuristic in design, the Smart measures just over 106 inches in length. Over 770,000 of the original Smart fortwo have been sold in 36 countries since 2001, and the current Smart model is doing well in the United States, with many customers on waiting lists.

So what makes the manufacturers of Smart think that a country full of individuals interested in the fastest or biggest (Hummer come to mind, anyone?) cars would consider this tiny package? For one thing, gas prices are an ongoing

concern. The Smart fortwo gets 33 mpg in the city and 40 mpg on the highway. For those looking to go green, the fortwo has earned the Ultra Low Emission Vehicle designation due to its low exhaust emissions. In addition, as U.S. cities become more crowded, parking becomes more of a challenge. The Smart is ideal for city driving and even more for city parking. It's true that the Smart car does not get the best gas mileage out there, is not quite as environmentally friendly as a hybrid, and may not speed down the highway (although it can achieve a maximum speed of 84 mph—over any U.S. speed limit). However, when you combine all that the Smart does offer with its price tag—$11,590 to $16,590—it may be worth considering. Perhaps it is wise to take a cue from the car's moniker—buying tiny may display a high level of intelligence.[30] ❖

Q: **Discussion Questions**

1. Since Mercedes-Benz is known for quality cars, should the Smart car maintain the same quality as other Mercedes?

2. Will American consumers be able to accept and pay the appropriate price for a small car that is also very high quality?

3. How is the Smart car contributing to the reduction of greenhouse gases and educating consumers to go green?

FIGURE 9.4 Types and Percentages of Air Travel Complaints in 2009

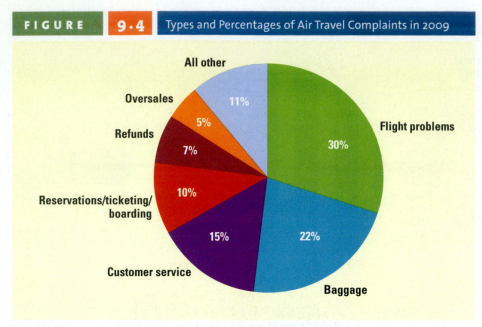

Source: Office of Aviation Enforcement and Proceedings "Air Travel Consumer Reports for 2009," June 2009. *Aviation Consumer Protection Division,* http://airconsumer.ost.dot.gov/reports/atc.htm (accessed March 23, 2009).

Total quality management (TQM) is a philosophy that uniform commitment to quality in all areas of the organization will promote a culture that meets customers' perceptions of quality. It involves coordinating efforts to improve customer satisfaction, increase employee participation and empowerment, form and strengthen supplier partnerships, and foster an organizational culture of continuous quality improvement. TQM requires continuous quality improvement and employee empowerment.

Continuous improvement of an organization's goods and services is built around the notion that quality is free; by contrast, *not* having high-quality goods and services can be very expensive, especially in terms of dissatisfied customers.[33] A primary tool of the continuous improvement process is *benchmarking,* the measuring and evaluating of the quality of the organization's goods, services, or processes compared with the quality produced by the best-performing companies in the industry.[34] Benchmarking lets the organization know where it stands competitively in its industry, thus giving it a goal to aim for over time.

Companies employing total quality management programs know that quality control should be incorporated throughout the transformation process, from the initial plans to develop a specific product through the product and production facility design processes to the actual manufacture of the product.

management, (5) process management, (6) business results, and (7) customer focus and satisfaction. The criteria have become a worldwide framework for driving business improvement.

Quality is so important that we need to examine it in the context of operations management. **Quality control** refers to the processes an organization uses to maintain its established quality standards. Consumers bring back 11 to 20 percent of all the electronic products they purchase, with wireless phones, GPS units, MP3 players, and wireless networking gear having the highest return rates. When the returned products are analyzed, 68 percent had no problems ("consumer operating error"), 27 percent were returned because of buyers' remorse ("spouse didn't like it"), and only 5 percent were defective.[31] Best Buy's Geek Squad helps reduce returns of PCs by 40 percent when they deliver and set up a computer. This demonstrates that measuring perceived quality relates to more than just technical defects of a product, but also to other characteristics.[32]

Quality has become a major concern in many organizations, particularly in light of intense foreign competition and increasingly demanding customers. To regain a competitive edge, a number of firms have adopted a total quality management approach.

FIGURE 9.5 J. D. Power & Associates Initial Automobile Quality Study

Source: J. D. Power and Associates Report, 2008 Initial Quality Study, www.jdpower.com/corporate/news/releases/pressrelease.aspx?ID=2008063 (accessed March 11, 2009).

● **QUALITY CONTROL** the processes an organization uses to maintain its established quality standards

● **TOTAL QUALITY MANAGEMENT (TQM)** a philosophy that uniform commitment to quality in all areas of an organization will promote a culture that meets customers' perceptions of quality

● **STATISTICAL PROCESS CONTROL** a system in which management collects and analyzes information about the production process to pinpoint quality problems in the production system

● **ISO 9000** a series of quality assurance standards designed by the International Organization for Standardization (ISO) to ensure consistent product quality under many conditions

In other words, they view quality control as an element of the product itself, rather than as simply a function of the operations process. When a company makes the product correctly from the outset, it eliminates the need to rework defective products, expedites the transformation process itself, and allows employees to make better use of their time and materials. One method through which many companies have tried to improve quality is **statistical process control,** a system in which management collects and analyzes information about the production process to pinpoint quality problems in the production system.

Establishing Standards—ISO 9000

Regardless of whether a company has a TQM program for quality control, it must first determine what standard of quality it desires and then assess whether its products meet that standard. Product specifications and quality standards must be set so the company can create a product that will compete in the marketplace. Rushing Water Canoes, for example, may specify that each of its canoes has aluminum walls of a specified uniform thickness, that the front and back of each canoe be reinforced with a specified level of steel, and that each canoe contain a specified amount of flotation material for safety. Production facilities must be designed that can produce products with the desired specifications.

Quality standards can be incorporated into service businesses as well. A hamburger chain, for example, may establish standards relating to how long it takes to cook an order and serve it to customers, how many fries are in each order, how thick the burgers are, or how many customer complaints might be acceptable. Once the desired quality characteristics, specifications, and standards have been stated in measurable terms, the next step is inspection.

The International Organization for Standardization (ISO) has created a series of quality management standards—**ISO 9000**—designed to ensure the customer's quality standards are met. The standards provide a framework for documenting how a certified business keeps records, trains employees, tests products, and fixes defects. To grant ISO 9000 certification, an independent auditor must verify that a business's factory, laboratory, or office meets the quality standards spelled out by the International Organization for Standardization. The certification process can require significant investment, but for many companies, the process is essential to being able to compete. Thousands of U.S. firms have been certified, and many more are working to meet the standards. Certification has become a virtual necessity for doing business in Europe in some high-technology businesses. ISO 9002 certification was established for service providers.

Inspection

Inspection reveals whether a product meets quality standards. Some product characteristics may be discerned by fairly simple inspection techniques—weighing the contents of cereal boxes or measuring the time it takes for a customer to receive his or her hamburger. As part of the ongoing quality assurance program at Hershey Foods, all wrapped Hershey Kisses are checked, and all imperfectly wrapped kisses are rejected.[35] Other inspection techniques are more elaborate. Automobile manufacturers use automated machines to open and close car doors to test the durability of latches and hinges. The food-processing and pharmaceutical industries use various chemical tests to determine the quality of their output. Rushing Water Canoes might use a special device that can precisely measure the thickness of each canoe wall to ensure that it meets the company's specifications.

Organizations normally inspect purchased items, work-in-process, and finished items. The inspection of purchased items and finished items takes place after the fact; the inspection of work-in-process is preventive. In other words, the purpose of inspection of purchased items and finished items is to determine what the quality level is. For items that are being worked on—an automobile moving down the assembly line or a canoe being assembled—the purpose of the inspection is to find defects before the product is completed so that necessary corrections can be made.

ISO 9000 standards relate to quality management. ISO14000 standards relate to environmental management—managing businesses to minimize any harmful effects to the environment. (From www.iso.org/iso/iso_catalogue/management_standards/ iso_9000_iso_14000/qmp.htm.)

Sampling

An important question relating to inspection is how many items should be inspected. Should all canoes produced by Rushing Water be inspected or just some of them? Whether to inspect 100 percent of the output or only part of it is related to the cost of the inspection process, the destructiveness of the inspection process (some tests last until the product fails), and the potential cost of product flaws in terms of human lives and safety.

Some inspection procedures are quite expensive, use elaborate testing equipment, destroy products, and/or require a significant number of hours to complete. In such cases, it is usually desirable to test only a sample of the output. If the sample passes inspection, the inspector may assume that all the items in the lot from which the sample was drawn would also pass inspection. By using principles of statistical inference, management can employ sampling techniques that assure a relatively high probability of reaching the right conclusion—that is, rejecting a lot that does not meet standards and accepting a lot that does. Nevertheless, there will always be a risk of making an incorrect conclusion—accepting a population that *does not* meet standards (because the sample was satisfactory) or rejecting a population that *does* meet standards (because the sample contained too many defective items).

Sampling is likely to be used when inspection tests are destructive. Determining the life expectancy of lightbulbs by turning them on and recording how long they last would be foolish: There is no market for burned-out lightbulbs. Instead, a generalization based on the quality of a sample would be applied to the entire population of lightbulbs from which the sample was drawn. However, human life and safety often depend on the proper functioning of specific items, such as the navigational systems installed in commercial airliners. For such items, even though the inspection process is costly, the potential cost of flawed systems—in human lives and safety—is too great not to inspect 100 percent of the output. ■

Team Exercise

Form groups and assign the responsibility for finding companies that outsource their production to other countries. What are the key advantages of the outsourcing decision? Do you see any drawbacks or weaknesses in this approach? Why would a company not outsource when that tactic can be undertaken to cut manufacturing cost? Report your findings to the class.

CHECK OUT www.mhhe.com/FerrellM2e

for study materials including Interactive Exercises, Quizzes, iPod downloads, and video.

● ● learning **OBJECTIVES**

LO1   Define human relations, and determine why its study is important.

LO2   Summarize early studies that laid the groundwork for understanding employee motivation.

LO3   Compare and contrast the human-relations theories of Abraham Maslow and Frederick Herzberg.

LO4   Investigate various theories of motivation, including theories X, Y, and Z; equity theory; and expectancy theory.

LO5   Describe some of the strategies that managers use to motivate employees.

MOTIVATING THE WORKFORCE

Introduction Successful programs teach some important lessons about how to interact with and motivate employees to do their best. Because employees do the actual work of the business and influence whether the firm achieves its objectives, most top managers agree that employees are an organization's most valuable resource. To achieve organizational objectives, employees must have the motivation, ability (appropriate knowledge and skills), and tools (proper training and equipment) to perform their jobs. Ensuring that employees have the appropriate knowledge and skills and the proper training is the subject of Chapter 11; this chapter focuses on employee motivation.

We examine employees' needs and motivation, managers' views of workers, and several strategies for motivating employees. Managers who understand the needs of their employees can help them reach higher levels of productivity and thus contribute to the achievement of organizational goals.

LO1

Define human relations, and determine why its study is important.

NATURE OF HUMAN RELATIONS

What motivates employees to perform on the job is the focus of **human relations,** the study of the behavior of individuals and groups in organizational settings. In business, human relations involves motivating employees to achieve organizational objectives efficiently and effectively. The field of human relations has become increasingly important over the years as businesses strive to understand how to boost workplace morale, maximize employees' productivity and creativity, and motivate their ever more diverse employees to be more effective.

Motivation is an inner drive that directs a person's behavior toward goals. A goal is the satisfaction of some need, and a need is the dif-

ference between a desired state and an actual state. Both needs and goals can be motivating. Motivation explains why people behave as they do; similarly, a lack of motivation explains, at times, why people avoid doing what they should do. A person who recognizes or feels a need is motivated to take action to satisfy the need and achieve a goal (Figure 10.1). Consider a person who feels cold. Because of the difference between the actual temperature and the desired temperature, the person recognizes a need. To satisfy the need and achieve the goal of being warm, the person may adjust the thermostat, put on a sweater, reach for a blanket, start a fire, or hug a friend. Human relations is concerned with the needs of employees, their goals and how they try to achieve them, and the impact of those needs and goals on job performance.

One prominent aspect of human relations is **morale**—an employee's attitude toward his or her job, employer, and colleagues. High morale contributes to high levels of productivity, high returns to stakeholders, and employee loyalty. Conversely, low morale may cause high rates of absenteeism and turnover (when employees quit or are fired and must be replaced by new employees). Table 10.1 outlines some of the direct and indirect expenses associated with low employee morale and turnover. The turnover cost for a fast-food employee is estimated at $500, whereas the turnover cost for professional positions can be up to 2.4 times the employee's annual salary. The highest cost to an organization for low morale comes from disgruntled or dissatisfied CEOs. CEO turnover has grown nearly 60 percent over the past decade.[1]

Respect, involvement, appreciation, adequate compensation, promotions, a pleasant work environment, and a positive organizational culture are all morale boosters. Nike seeks to provide a comprehensive compensation and benefits package that includes traditional elements such as Medical, Dental, Vision, Life & Disability Insurance, paid holidays and time off as well as sabbaticals, and team as well as individual compensation plans. More comprehensive benefits include: employee discounts on Nike products, health care and family care reimbursement accounts, scholarships for children of employees, employee assistance plans, work/life balance resources and referrals, adoption assistance, tuition assistance, a group legal plan, a group long term care plan, and matching gift programs. At the Beaverton, Oregon, world headquarters, employees may take advantage of onsite day care; onsite fitness centers, cafés,

DID YOU KNOW?

Employee absences cost companies nearly 15 percent of their payroll.[2]

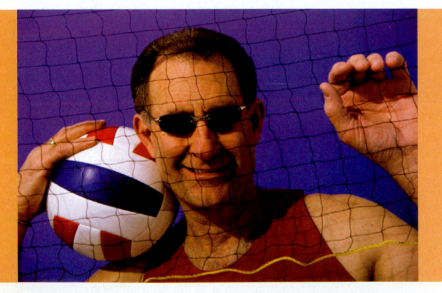

On its Web site, Google advertises the "benefits beyond the basics" it uses to attract and motivate top-notch employees. At the company's Mountain View, California, headquarters employees can see an onsite doctor and get their oil changed, their cars washed, their bikes repaired, and their dry cleaning done. The company also offers onsite massage therapy, a gym and volleyball court, hairstyling, and fitness classes.

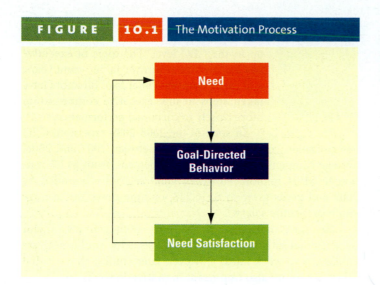

FIGURE 10.1 The Motivation Process

Need → Goal-Directed Behavior → Need Satisfaction

TABLE 10.1 Negative Morale Results in Significant Turnover Costs

Direct Expenses	Indirect Expenses
Severance package	Managers/co-workers' time to engage in first and second interviews
Recruitment fees	Human resource management's time advising management and engaging in appropriate background checks
Advertising expenses	Management's time to recruit and train the new employee
Cost of screening/ pre-employment tests	Lost knowledge, skills, contacts, and possibly employees
Travel expenses	Exit interview cost

Source: John Bishop, "The High Cost of Turnover," Ezine @rticles, March 13, 2007, http://ezinearticles.com/?The-High-Cost-of-Turnover&id=486954, accessed August 12, 2009.

and restaurants; convenience store; onsite hair and nail salon; an annual TriMet transit pass ($20 annual fee versus $600); chances to test products under development; and an opportunity to become a headquarters tour guide.[3]

Many companies offer a diverse array of benefits designed to improve the quality of employees' lives and increase their morale and satisfaction. As mentioned earlier, many companies offer reward programs to improve morale, lower turnover, and motivate employees. Some of the "best companies to work for" offer onsite day care, concierge services (e.g., dry cleaning, shoe repair, prescription renewal), domestic partner benefits to same-sex couples, and fully paid sabbaticals. Figure 10.2 shows the most preferred forms of employee recognition.

FIGURE 10.2 Most Preferred Forms of Recognition at the Workplace

Verbal Recognition: 42%
Cash Bonuses: 19%
Additional Time Off: 9%
Training or Seminars: 7%
Cards or Notes: 6%

Source: OfficeArrow survey of 388 administrative professionals; "Most Preferred Forms of Recognition at Workplace," *USA Today Snapshots,* May 4, 2009, p. B1.

LO2

Summarize early studies that laid the groundwork for understanding employee motivation.

HISTORICAL PERSPECTIVES ON EMPLOYEE MOTIVATION

Throughout the 20th century, researchers conducted numerous studies to try to identify ways to motivate workers and increase productivity. From these studies have come theories that have been applied to workers with varying degrees of success. A brief discussion of two of these theories—the classical theory of motivation and the Hawthorne Studies—provides a background for understanding the present state of human relations.

Classical Theory of Motivation

The birth of the study of human relations can be traced to time and motion studies conducted at the turn of the century by Frederick W. Taylor and Frank and Lillian Gilbreth. Their studies analyzed how workers perform specific work tasks in an effort to improve the employees' productivity. These efforts led to the application of scientific principles to management.

According to the **classical theory of motivation,** money is the sole motivator for workers. Taylor suggested that workers who were paid more would produce more, an idea that would benefit both companies and workers. To improve productivity, Taylor thought that managers should break down each job into its component tasks (specialization), determine the best way to perform each task, and specify the output to be achieved by a worker performing the task. Taylor also believed that incentives would motivate employees to be more productive. Thus, he suggested that managers link workers' pay directly to their output. He developed the piece-rate system, under which employees were paid a certain amount for each unit they produced; those who exceeded their quota were paid a higher rate per unit for all the units they produced.

More and more corporations are tying pay to performance in order to motivate—even up to the CEO level. The topic of executive pay has become controversial in recent years, and many corporate boards of directors have taken steps to link executive compensation more closely to corporate performance.

In spite of the 2008-2009 recession, CEO compensation continued to be high. Between 2007 and 2008, average compensation declined by 6 percent, from $11.7 million to $10.4 million. However, CEO salaries rebounded by 2009 and perks grew to $336,248, or nine times the average employee's entire salary.[5]

Like most managers of the early 20th century, Taylor believed that satisfactory pay and job security would motivate employees to work hard. However, later studies showed that other factors are also important in motivating workers.

The Hawthorne Studies

Elton Mayo and a team of researchers from Harvard University wanted to determine what physical conditions in the

> "Taylor believed that satisfactory pay and job security would motivate employees to work hard. However, later studies showed that other factors are also important in motivating workers."

We can still see Taylor's ideas in practice today in the use of mathematical models, statistics, and incentives. Moreover, companies are increasingly striving to relate pay to performance at both the hourly and the managerial level. According to Marriott Hotels, roughly 40 percent of incentive planners choose an individual incentive to motivate and reward their employees. In contrast, team incentives are used to generate partnership and working together to accomplish organizational goals. The state of Washington offers teams 25 percent of the revenue generated (not to exceed $10,000 per member) as the result of a continuous improvement or total quality process.[4]

workplace—such as light and noise levels—would stimulate employees to be most productive. From 1924 to 1932, they studied a group of workers at the Hawthorne Works Plant of the Western Electric Company and measured their productivity under various physical conditions.

What the researchers discovered was quite unexpected and very puzzling: Productivity increased regardless of the physical conditions. This phenomenon has been labeled the Hawthorne Effect. When questioned about their behavior, the employees expressed satisfaction because their co-workers in the experiments were friendly and, more important, because

HireWorkers Helps Immigrants Find Jobs

Immigrant job seekers looking for low-wage jobs such as janitor, housekeeper, and dishwasher often lack access to the Internet and frequently have trouble finding work. As a Mexican immigrant himself, Eli Portnoy understood the problems immigrant job seekers face and saw how HireWorkers could help low-wage job seekers and their employers. Job seekers fill out HireWorkers postcards with their job experience and background information. Portnoy's company distributes the postcards to a large number of retail locations (a form is available online for those who have Internet access). The HireWorkers service is free for job seekers, and employers pay $69 to $99 to search the company's database. Once job seekers and employers submit their information, the company's system goes to work, using patent-pending technology to match employers' requests with appropriate job seekers. Once matches are found, the company automatically calls the job seekers.[6] ❖

their supervisors had asked for their help and cooperation in the study. In other words, they were responding to the attention they received, not the changing physical work conditions. The researchers concluded that social and psychological factors could significantly affect productivity and morale. Medtronic, often called the "Microsoft of the medical-device industry," has a built-in psychological factor that influences employee morale. The company makes life-saving medical devices, such as pacemakers, neurostimulators, and stents. New hires at Medtronic receive medallions inscribed with a portion of the firm's mission statement, "alleviate pain, restore health, and extend life." There is an annual party where people whose bodies function thanks to Medtronic devices give testimonials. Obviously, Medtronic employees feel a sense of satisfaction in their jobs. However, in a more recent study investigating the impact of office temperature, when the office temperature dropped from 77 degrees to 68 degrees (a less comfortable temperature), typing mistakes increased by 74 percent and output dropped 46 percent.[7]

The Hawthorne experiments marked the beginning of a concern for human relations in the workplace. They revealed that human factors do influence workers' behavior and that managers who understand the needs, beliefs, and expectations of people have the greatest success in motivating their workers. Figure 10-3 shows that work/life balance is important to employees and that many will choose a job based on that criterion.

 LO3

Compare and contrast the human-relations theories of Abraham Maslow and Frederick Herzberg.

Working conditions are important. However, the Hawthorne Studies, which were carried out at the electric company shown here beginning in the 1920s, uncovered a more human element: Researchers found that the workers became more productive due to the attention they received—regardless of their working conditions.

THEORIES OF EMPLOYEE MOTIVATION

The research of Taylor, Mayo, and many others has led to the development of a number of theories that attempt to describe what motivates employees to perform. In this section, we will discuss some of the most important of these theories. The successful implementation of ideas based on these theories will vary, of course, depending on the company, its management, and its employees. It should be noted, too, that what worked in the past may no longer work today. Good managers must have the ability to adapt their ideas to an ever-changing, diverse group of employees.

Maslow's Hierarchy of Needs

Psychologist Abraham Maslow theorized that people have five basic needs: physiological, security, social, esteem, and self-actualization. **Maslow's hierarchy** arranges these needs into the order in which people strive to satisfy them (Figure 10.4).[8]

Physiological needs, the most basic and first needs to be satisfied, are the essentials for living—water, food, shelter, and clothing. According to Maslow, humans devote all their efforts to satisfying physiological needs until

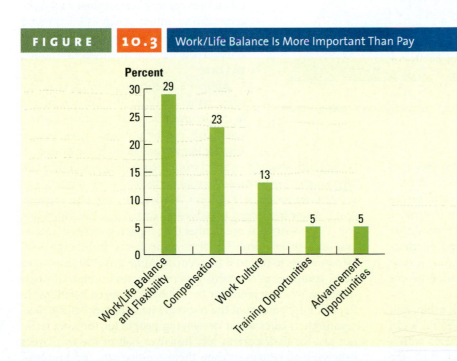

| FIGURE | 10.3 | Work/Life Balance Is More Important Than Pay |

Percent

A bar chart showing: Work/Life Balance and Flexibility: 29; Compensation: 23; Work Culture: 13; Training Opportunities: 5; Advancement Opportunities: 5.

Source: "Work-life Balance Tops Pay," *USA Today Snapshots,* March 13, 2008, p. B1.

FIGURE **10.4** Maslow's Hierarchy of Needs

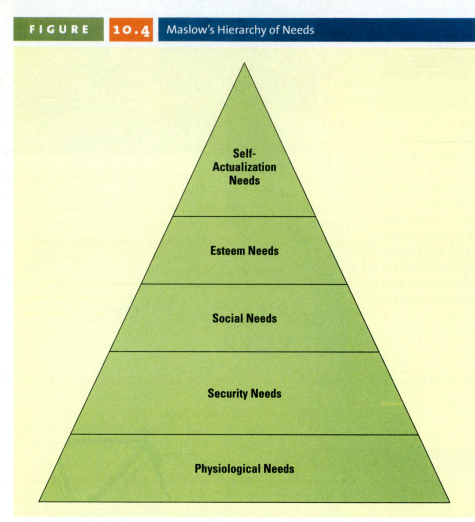

Source: Adapted from Abraham H. Maslow, "A Theory of Human Motivation," *Psychology Review* 50 (1943), pp. 370–396. American Psychology Association.

a party. Once their social needs have been satisfied, people attempt to satisfy their need for esteem.

Esteem needs relate to respect—both self-respect and respect from others. One aspect of esteem needs is competition—the need to feel that you can do something better than anyone else. Competition often motivates people to increase their productivity. Esteem needs are not as easily satisfied as the needs at lower levels in Maslow's hierarchy because they do not always provide tangible evidence of success. However, these needs can be realized through rewards and increased involvement in organizational activities. Until esteem needs are met, people focus their attention on achieving respect. When they feel they have achieved some measure of respect, self-actualization becomes the major goal of life.

Self-actualization needs, at the top of Maslow's hierarchy, mean being the best you can be. Self-actualization involves maximizing your potential. A self-actualized person feels that she or he is living life to its fullest in every way. For Stephen King, self-actualization might mean being praised as the best fiction writer in the world; for actress Halle Berry, it might mean winning an Oscar.

Maslow's theory maintains that the more basic needs at the bottom of the hierarchy must be satisfied before higher-level goals can be pursued. Thus, people who are hungry and homeless are not concerned with obtaining respect from their colleagues. Only when physiological, security, and social needs have been more or less satisfied do people seek esteem. Maslow's theory also suggests that if a low-level need is suddenly reactivated, the individual will try to satisfy that need rather than higher-level needs. Many laid-off workers probably shift their focus from high-level esteem needs to the need for security. Almost 10,000 employees in 32 countries in business, government, and nonprofit organizations were surveyed for the Global Employee Relationship Report. Fifty percent of the respondents said they believe their organization cares about developing people for the long term, not just for their current job. Just over half of the employees believed their employers show them genuine care and concern.[9]

they are met. Only when these needs are met can people focus their attention on satisfying the next level of needs—security.

Security needs relate to protecting oneself from physical and economic harm. Actions that may be taken to achieve security include reporting a dangerous workplace condition to management, maintaining safety equipment, and purchasing insurance with income protection in the event you become unable to work. Once security needs have been satisfied, people may strive for social goals.

Social needs are the need for love, companionship, and friendship—the desire for acceptance by others. To fulfill social needs, a person may try many things: making friends with a co-worker, joining a group, volunteering at a hospital, throwing

Managers should learn from Maslow's hierarchy that employees will be motivated to contribute to organizational goals only if they are able to first satisfy their physiological, security, and social needs through their work.

Herzberg's Two-Factor Theory

In the 1950s psychologist Frederick Herzberg proposed a theory of motivation that focuses on the job and on the environment where work is done. Herzberg studied various factors relating to the job and their relation to employee motivation and concluded that they can be divided into hygiene factors and motivational factors (Table 10.2).

Hygiene factors, which relate to the work setting and not to the content of the work, include adequate wages, comfortable and safe working conditions, fair company policies, and job security. These factors do not necessarily motivate employees to

responsibility, and advancement. The absence of motivational factors may not result in dissatisfaction, but their presence is likely to motivate employees to excel. Many companies are beginning to employ methods to give employees more responsibility and control and to involve them more in their work, which serves to motivate them to higher levels of productivity and quality. L. L. Bean employees have tremendous latitude to satisfy customers' needs. One employee drove 500 miles from Maine to New York to deliver a canoe to a customer who was leaving on a trip. Disney

> ❝ **Maslow's theory maintains that the more basic needs at the bottom of the hierarchy must be satisfied before higher-level goals can be pursued.** ❞

excel, but their absence may be a potential source of dissatisfaction and high turnover. Employee safety and comfort are clearly hygiene factors.

Many people feel that a good salary is one of the most important job factors, even more important than job security and the chance to use one's mind and abilities. Salary and security, two of the hygiene factors identified by Herzberg, make it possible for employees to satisfy the physiological and security needs identified by Maslow. However, the presence of hygiene factors is unlikely to motivate employees to work harder.

Motivational factors, which relate to the content of the work itself, include achievement, recognition, involvement,

has a similar commitment to empowering customers and making customers happy.[10]

Herzberg's motivational factors and Maslow's esteem and self-actualization needs are similar. Workers' low-level needs (physiological and security) have largely been satisfied by minimum-wage laws and occupational-safety standards set by various government agencies and are therefore not motivators. Consequently, to improve productivity, management should focus on satisfying workers' higher-level needs (motivational factors) by providing opportunities for achievement, involvement, and advancement and by recognizing good performance.

● ● **LO4**

Investigate various theories of motivation, including theories X, Y, and Z; equity theory; and expectancy theory.

TABLE 10.2 Herzberg's Hygiene and Motivational Factors

Hygiene Factors	Motivational Factors
Company policies	Achievement
Supervision	Recognition
Working conditions	Work itself
Relationships with peers, supervisors, and subordinates	Responsibility
Salary	Advancement
Security	Personal growth

McGregor's Theory X and Theory Y

In *The Human Side of Enterprise*, Douglas McGregor related Maslow's ideas about personal needs to management. McGregor contrasted two views of management: the traditional view, which he called Theory X, and a humanistic view, which he called Theory Y.

According to McGregor, managers who adopt **Theory X** assume that workers generally dislike work and must be forced to do their jobs. They believe that the following statements are true of workers: *more of autocratic mgr.*

1. The average person naturally dislikes work and will avoid it when possible.

2. Most workers must be coerced, controlled, directed, or threatened with punishment to get them to work toward the achievement of organizational objectives.

3. The average worker prefers to be directed and to avoid responsibility, has relatively little ambition, and wants security.[11]

Managers who subscribe to the Theory X view maintain tight control over workers, provide almost constant supervision, try to motivate through fear, and make decisions in an autocratic fashion, eliciting little or no input from their subordinates. The Theory X style of management focuses on physiological and security needs and virtually ignores the higher needs discussed by Maslow.

The Theory X view of management does not take into account people's needs for companionship, esteem, and personal growth, whereas Theory Y, the contrasting view of management, does. Managers subscribing to the **Theory Y** view assume that workers like to work and that under proper conditions employees will seek out responsibility in an attempt to satisfy their social, esteem, and self-actualization needs. McGregor describes the assumptions behind Theory Y in the following way:

1. The expenditure of physical and mental effort in work is as natural as play or rest.

2. People will exercise self-direction and self-control to achieve objectives to which they are committed.

3. People will commit to objectives when they realize that the achievement of those goals will bring them personal reward.

4. The average person will accept and seek responsibility.

5. Imagination, ingenuity, and creativity can help solve organizational problems, but most organizations do not make adequate use of these characteristics in their employees.

6. Organizations today do not make full use of workers' intellectual potential.[12]

> " **According to McGregor, managers who adopt Theory X assume that workers generally dislike work and must be forced to do their jobs.** "

Interface Makes It a Mission to Have Zero Emissions

Ray Anderson founded Interface, Inc., the largest U.S. modular tile carpet maker, in 1973. Today, it is a leader in sustainable and environmentally sound practices. In 1994, Anderson read *The Ecology of Commerce* by Paul Hawken, and it transformed his life. The book led Anderson to reformulate his company and made him a strong advocate for conservation. Anderson has been featured in environmental documentaries and has received awards such as Civic Venture's Purpose Prize and Auburn University's International Quality of Life award.

What makes Interface so green? Simply put, it's the company's Mission Zero—a plan to reduce its environmental footprint to zero by 2020. Interface recycles old carpet to avoid filling up landfills, created Cool Carpet to offset emissions, uses 100 percent recycled carpet tile backing on its Cool Blue line, and is partially powering the Cool Blue line with landfill gas. Interface also has reduced its greenhouse gas emissions by 60 percent in absolute tonnage and runs many of its operations on wind and solar power.

Interface relies on its dedicated employees, who are passionate about Mission Zero. To motivate them Interface invented the Fast Forward training program, which makes every employee a Mission Zero ambassador. The company also has begun using the Gallup Organization's strength-based management development program, focusing on employee strengths rather than weaknesses. Employees also have been encouraged to become environmental stewards. For example, a night shift factory worker helped suggest what has become the Cool CO_2mmute program for offsetting commuting emissions.

Interface has received numerous accolades for its green practices, recycling efforts, and high-quality design. It is also considered one of the top sustainable stocks by sustainablebusiness.com. There is no arguing that businesses and individuals would do well to take note of Ray Anderson and Interface.[13] ❖

Q: Discussion Questions

1. How does Ray Anderson set an example as the CEO to motivate employees toward green business practices?

2. How does being green motivate employees in their everyday jobs?

3. What does Interface do to involve employees in its decisions about running a green business?

Obviously, managers subscribing to the Theory Y philosophy have a management style very different from that of managers subscribing to the Theory X philosophy. Theory Y managers maintain less control and supervision, do not use fear as the primary motivator, and are more democratic in decision making, allowing subordinates to participate in the process. Theory Y managers address the high-level needs in Maslow's hierarchy as well as physiological and security needs. Today, Theory Y enjoys widespread support and may have displaced Theory X.

Theory Z

Theory Z is a management philosophy that stresses employee participation in all aspects of company decision making. It was first described by William Ouchi in his book *Theory Z—How American Business Can Meet the Japanese Challenge*. Theory Z incorporates many elements associated with the Japanese approach to management, such as trust and intimacy, but Japanese ideas have been adapted for use in the United States. In a Theory Z organization, managers and workers share responsibilities; the management style is participative; and employment is long term and often lifelong. Theory Z results in employees feeling organizational ownership. Research has found that such feelings of ownership may produce positive attitudinal and behavioral effects for employees.[14] In a Theory Y organization, managers focus on assumptions about the nature of the worker. The two theories can be seen as complementary. Table 10.3 compares the traditional American management style, the Japanese management style, and Theory Z (the modified Japanese management style).

Variations on Theory Z

Theory Z has been adapted and modified for use in a number of U.S. companies. One adaptation involves workers in decisions through quality circles. Quality circles (also called quality-assurance teams) are small, usually having five to eight members who discuss ways to reduce waste, eliminate problems, and improve quality, communication, and work satisfaction. Such quality teams are a common technique for harnessing the knowledge and creativity of hourly employees to solve problems in companies.

Even more involved than quality circles are programs that operate under names such as *participative management, employee involvement,* and *self-directed work teams.* Regardless of the term used to describe such programs, they strive to give employees more control over their jobs while making them more responsible for the outcome of their efforts. Such programs often organize employees into work teams of 5 to 15 members

Some management theorists believe that employees who don't feel that they have been treated equitably by their employers are more inclined to "even the score" by stealing or embezzling money from them.

TABLE 10.3 Comparison of American, Japanese, and Theory Z Management Styles

	American	Japanese	Theory Z
Duration of employment	Relatively short term; workers subject to layoffs when business slows	Lifelong; no layoffs	Long term; layoffs rare
Rate of promotion	Rapid	Slow	Slow
Amount of specialization	Considerable; worker develops expertise in one area only	Minimal; worker develops expertise in all aspects of the organization	Moderate; worker learns all aspects of the organization
Decision making	Individual	Consensual; input from all concerned parties is considered	Consensual; emphasis on quality
Responsibility	Assigned to the individual	Shared by the group	Assigned to the individual
Control	Explicit and formal	Less explicit and less formal	Informal but with explicit performance measures
Concern for workers	Focus is on work only	Focus extends to worker's whole life	Focus includes worker's life and family

Source: Adapted from William Ouchi, *Theory Z—How American Business Can Meet the Japanese Challenge*, p. 58. © 1981 by Addison-Wesley Publishing Company, Inc. Reprinted by permission of Perseus Books Publishers, a member of Perseus Books, L.L.C.

● **EQUITY THEORY** an assumption that how much people are willing to contribute to an organization depends on their assessment of the fairness, or equity, of the rewards they will receive in exchange

● **EXPECTANCY THEORY** the assumption that motivation depends not only on how much a person wants something but also on that person's perception on how likely he or she is to get it

who are responsible for producing an entire product item. Team members are cross-trained and can therefore move from job to job within the team. Each team essentially manages itself and is responsible for its quality, scheduling, ordering and use of materials, and problem solving. Many firms have successfully employed work teams to boost morale, productivity, quality, and competitiveness.

Equity Theory

According to **equity theory,** how much people are willing to contribute to an organization depends on their assessment of the fairness, or equity, of the rewards they will receive in exchange. In a fair situation, a person receives rewards proportional to the contribution he or she makes to the organization. However, in practice, equity is a subjective notion. Each worker regularly develops a personal input–output ratio by taking stock of his or her contribution (inputs) to the organization in time, effort, skills, and experience and assessing the rewards (outputs) offered by the organization in pay, benefits, recognition, and promotions. The worker compares his or her ratio to the input–output ratio of some other person—a "comparison other," who may be a co-worker, a friend working in another organization, or an "average" of several people working in the organization. If the two ratios are close, the individual will feel that he or she is being treated equitably.

Let's say you have a high-school education and earn $25,000 a year. When you compare your input–output ratio with that of a co-worker who has a college degree and makes $35,000 a year, you will probably feel that you are being paid fairly. However, if you perceive that your personal input–output ratio is lower than that of your college-educated co-worker, you may feel that you are being treated unfairly and be motivated to seek change. But if you learn that a co-worker who makes $35,000 has only a high-school diploma, you may feel cheated by your employer. To achieve equity, you could try to increase your outputs by asking for a raise or promotion. You could also try to have your co-worker's inputs increased or his or her outputs decreased. Failing to achieve equity, you may be motivated to look for a job at a different company. Table 10.4 shows how your income would need to vary by market to have the same quality of life. Inequity in real income can result in enormous dissatisfaction and employee turnover. You would need more than $200,000 to have the same quality of life in New York that you could have with an income of almost $89,000 in Houston.[15]

Because almost all the issues involved in equity theory are subjective, they can be problematic. Author David Callahan has

TABLE 10.4 Gross Salary Needed to Replicate $100,000 after Adjusting for Cost of Living

City	Salary
New York	$205,426
San Francisco	179,034
Los Angeles	156,106
San Diego	149,384
Washington, D.C.	141,894
Boston	137,649
Chicago	126,929
Seattle	117,037
Atlanta	102,805
Denver	102,348
Cleveland	101,986
Milwaukee	101,478
Phoenix	97,976
Dallas	93,665
Charlotte	92,991
Houston	88,977

Source: Jeanne Sahadi, "Where the (Best) 6-Figure Jobs Are," CNNMoney. com, http://money.cnn.com/2006/07/13/pf/six_fig_farthest/index.htm (accessed March 23, 2009).

argued that feelings of inequity may underlie some unethical or illegal behavior in business, such as the $600 billion a year stolen from companies by their own employees. Shoplifting alone is the cause of more than $10 billion a year in company losses.[16] Callahan believes that employees who do not feel they are being treated equitably may be motivated to equalize the situation by lying, cheating, or otherwise "improving" their pay, perhaps by stealing.[17] Managers should try to avoid equity problems by ensuring that rewards are distributed on the basis of performance and that all employees clearly understand the basis for their pay and benefits.

Expectancy Theory

Psychologist Victor Vroom described **expectancy theory,** which states that motivation depends not only on how much a person wants something but also on the person's perception of how likely he or she is to get it. A person who wants something and has reason to be optimistic will be strongly motivated. For example, say you really want a promotion. And let's say because you have taken some night classes to improve your skills and, moreover, have just made a large, significant sale, you feel confident that you are qualified and able to handle the new position. Therefore, you are motivated to try to get the promotion. In contrast, if you do not believe you are likely to get what you want, you may not be motivated to try to get it, even though you really want it.

● ● LO5

Describe some of the strategies that managers use to motivate employees.

STRATEGIES FOR MOTIVATING EMPLOYEES

Based on the various theories that attempt to explain what motivates employees, businesses have developed several strategies for motivating their employees and boosting morale and productivity. Some of these techniques include behavior modification and job design, as well as the already described employee involvement programs and work teams.

Behavior Modification

Behavior modification involves changing behavior and encouraging appropriate actions by relating the consequences of behavior to the behavior itself. The concept of behavior modification was developed by psychologist B. F. Skinner, who showed that there are two types of consequences that can modify behavior—reward and punishment. Skinner found that behavior that is rewarded will tend to be repeated, while behavior that is punished will tend to be eliminated. For example, employees who know that they will receive a bonus, such as an expensive restaurant meal, for making a sale over $2,000 may be more motivated to make sales. Workers who know they will be punished for being tardy are likely to make a greater effort to get to work on time.

However, the two strategies may not be equally effective. Punishing unacceptable behavior may provide quick results but may lead to undesirable long-term side effects, such as employee dissatisfaction and increased turnover. In general, rewarding appropriate behavior is a more effective way to modify behavior.

Job Design

Herzberg identified the job itself as a motivational factor. Managers have several strategies that they can use to design jobs to help improve employee motivation. These include job rotation, job enlargement, job enrichment, and flexible scheduling strategies.

job rotation

Job rotation allows employees to move from one job to another in an effort to relieve the boredom that is often associated with job specialization. Businesses often turn to specialization in hopes of increasing productivity, but there is a negative side effect to this type of job design: Employees become bored and dissatisfied, and productivity declines. Job rotation reduces this boredom by allowing workers to undertake a greater variety of tasks and giving them the opportunity to learn new skills. With job rotation, an employee spends a specified amount of time performing one job and then moves on to another, different job. The worker eventually returns to the initial job and begins the cycle again.

Job rotation is a good idea, but it has one major drawback. Because employees may eventually become bored with all the jobs in the cycle, job rotation does not totally eliminate the problem of boredom. Job rotation is extremely useful, however, in situations where a person is being trained for a position that requires an understanding of various units in an organization. Eli Lilly is a strong believer in the benefits of job

● **BEHAVIOR MODIFICATION** changing behavior and encouraging appropriate actions by relating the consequences of behavior to the behavior itself

● **JOB ROTATION** movement of employees from one job to another in an effort to relieve the boredom often associated with job specialization

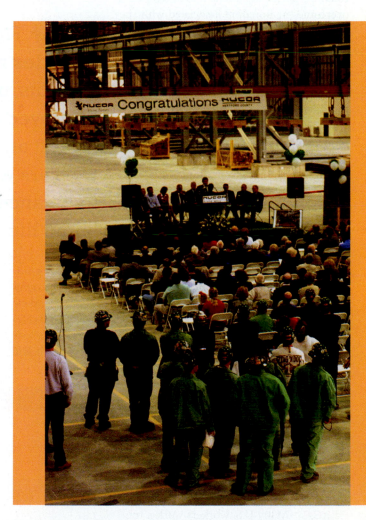

Nucor Corporation's 22,000-plus nonunion employees don't see themselves as ordinary steel workers. There are no special benefits or compensation plans for executives at Nucor. The company's flat organizational structure encourages employees to adopt the mind-set of owner-operators.

rotation. The company leaves employees in their current jobs and asks them to take on additional assignments outside their field of expertise or interest. The results of the process have been positive, and Nokia is trying the same process with similar outcomes.[18] Many executive training programs require trainees to spend time learning a variety of specialized jobs. Job rotation is also used to cross-train today's self-directed work teams.

job enlargement

Job enlargement adds more tasks to a job instead of treating each task as separate. Like job rotation, job enlargement was developed to overcome the boredom associated with specialization. The rationale behind this strategy is that jobs are more satisfying as the number of tasks performed by an individual increases. Employees sometimes enlarge, or craft, their jobs by noticing what needs to be done and then changing tasks and relationship boundaries to adjust. Individual orientation and motivation shape opportunities to craft new jobs and job relationships.[19] Job enlargement strategies have been more successful in increasing job satisfaction than have job rotation strategies. IBM, AT&T, and Maytag are among the many companies that have used job enlargement to motivate employees.

job enrichment

Job enrichment incorporates motivational factors, such as opportunity for achievement, recognition, responsibility, and advancement, into a job. It gives workers not only more tasks within the job but more control and authority over the job. Job enrichment programs enhance a worker's feeling of responsibility and provide opportunities for growth and advancement when the worker is able to take on the more challenging tasks. Hyatt Hotels Corporation and General Foods use job enrichment to improve the quality of work life for their employees. The potential benefits of job enrichment are great, but it requires careful planning and execution.

flexible scheduling strategies

Many U.S. workers work a traditional 40-hour workweek consisting of five 8-hour days with fixed starting and ending times. Facing problems of poor morale and high absenteeism as well as a diverse workforce with changing needs, many managers have turned to flexible

Flextime provides many benefits, including improved ability to recruit and retain workers who wish to balance work and home life.

scheduling strategies such as flextime, compressed workweeks, job sharing, part-time work, and telecommuting. Retention is critical in jobs such as information technology. A survey by CareerBuilder.com showed that 40 percent of working fathers were offered flexible work schedules versus 53 percent of working mothers.[20]

Flextime is a program that allows employees to choose their starting and ending times, as long as they are at work during a specified core period (Figure 10.5). It does not reduce the total number of hours that employees work; instead, it gives employees more flexibility in choosing which hours they work. A firm may specify that employees must be present from 10:00 a.m. to 3:00 p m. One employee may choose to come in at 7:00 a.m. and leave at the end of the core time, perhaps to attend classes at a nearby college after work. Another employee, a mother who lives in the suburbs, may come in at 9:00 a.m. to have time to drop off her children at a day care center and commute by public transportation to her job. Flextime provides many benefits, including improved ability to recruit and retain workers who wish to balance work and home life. Customers can be better served by allowing more coverage of customers over longer hours. Workstations and facilities can be better utilized by staggering employee use. Communities experience reduced traffic at traditional "rush hours."

Related to flextime are the scheduling strategies of the compressed workweek and job sharing. The **compressed workweek** is a four-day (or shorter) period in which an employee works 40 hours. Under such a plan, employees typically work

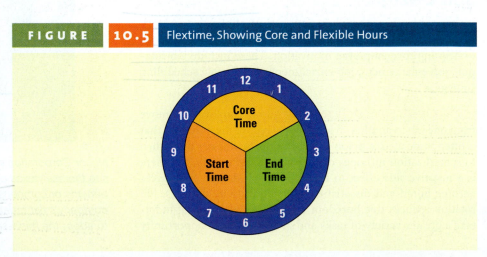

FIGURE 10.5 Flextime, Showing Core and Flexible Hours

● JOB SHARING per-
formance of one full-time
job by two people on part-
time hours

10 hours per day for four days and have a three-day weekend. The compressed workweek reduces the company's operating expenses because its actual hours of operation are reduced. It is also sometimes used by parents who want to have more days off to spend with their families.

Job sharing occurs when two people do one job. One person may work from 8:00 a.m. to 12:30 p.m.; the second person comes in at 12:30 p.m. and works until 5:00 p.m. Job sharing gives both people the opportunity to work as well as time to fulfill other obligations, such as parenting or school. Thirty percent of companies allow job sharing.[21] With job sharing, the company has the benefit of the skills of two people for one job, often at a lower total cost for salaries and benefits than one person working eight hours a day would be paid.

Two other flexible scheduling strategies attaining wider use include allowing full-time workers to work part time for a certain period and allowing workers to work at home either full or part time. Employees at some firms may be permitted to work part time for several months in order to care for a new baby or an elderly parent or just to slow down for a little while to "recharge their batteries." By 2020, 40 percent of U.S. workers will be caring for an aging parent, and employees are expected to demand benefits that reflect this major shift.[22] When the employees return to full-time work, they are usually given a position comparable to their original full-time position. Other firms are allowing employees to telecommute or telework (work at home a few days of the week), staying connected via computers, modems, and telephones. More than 45 million Americans work from home. Of those who work "at home," the average number of places these individuals work is 3.4, and these places can include home, car, and restaurant or coffee bar.[23] Although many employees ask for the option of working at home to ease the responsibilities of caring for family members, some have discovered that they are more productive at home without the distractions of the workplace. An assessment of 12 company telecommuting programs, including Apple, AT&T, and the state of California, found that positive productivity changes occurred. Traveler's Insurance Company reports its telecommuters to be 20 percent more productive than its traditional employees.[24] Other employees, however, have discovered that they are not suited for working at home. Human resource management executives are split as to whether telecommuting helps or hurts employees' careers. Thirty percent feel telecommuting helps their careers, while 25 percent feel that it hurts, whereas 39 percent feel it does neither.[25] Still, work-at-home programs do help reduce overhead costs for businesses. For example, some companies used to maintain a surplus of office space but have reduced the surplus through employee telecommuting, "hoteling" (being assigned to a desk through a reservation system), and "hot-desking" (several people using the same desk but at different times).

Companies are turning to flexible work schedules to provide more options to employees who are trying to juggle their work duties with other responsibilities and needs. Preliminary results indicated that flexible scheduling plans increase job satisfaction, which, in turn, leads to increases in productivity. Some recent research, however, has indicated there are potential problems with telecommuting. Some managers are reluctant to adopt the practice because the pace of change in today's workplace is faster than ever, and telecommuters may be left behind or actually cause managers more work in helping them stay abreast of changes. Some employers also worry that telecommuting workers create a security risk by creating more opportunities for computer hackers or equipment thieves. Some employees have found that working outside the office may hurt career advancement opportunities, and some report that instead of helping them balance work and family responsibilities, telecommuting increases the strain by blurring the barriers between the office and home. Co-workers call at all hours, and telecommuters are apt to continue to work when they are not supposed to (after regular business hours or during vacation time).[26]

Companies today are finding out that dads are just as interested in flextime as moms are. At Xerox, not only are some dads (and moms) allowed to work from home to care for children, some take unpaid leave during the summer months to spend time with their kids.

Importance of Motivational Strategies

Motivation is more than a tool that managers can use to foster employee loyalty and boost productivity. It is a process that affects all the relationships within an organization and influences many areas, such as pay, promotion, job design, training

SO YOU THINK YOU MAY BE GOOD AT MOTIVATING A WORKFORCE

If you are good at mediation, know how to smooth conflict, and have a good understanding of motivation and human relations theories, you might be a good leader, human resources manager, or training expert. Most organizations, especially as they grow, will need to implement human relations programs. These programs are necessary to teach employees about sensitivity to other cultures, religions, and beliefs, as well as for teaching the workforce about the organization so that they understand how they fit into the larger picture. Employees need to appreciate the benefits of working together to make the firm run smoothly, and they also need to understand how their contributions help the firm. To stay motivated, most employees need to feel that what they do each day contributes something of value to the firm. Disclosing information and including employees in decision-making processes also will help employees feel valuable and wanted within the firm.

There are a lot of different ways employers can reward and encourage employees. However, employers must be careful when considering what kinds of incentives to use. Different cultures value different kinds of incentives more highly than do others. For example, a Japanese worker probably would not like it if she were singled out from the group and given a large cash bonus as a reward for her work. Japanese workers tend to be more group-oriented, and therefore anything that singles out individuals would not be an effective way of rewarding and motivating. American workers, in contrast, are very individualistic, and a raise and public praise might be more effective. However, what might motivate a younger employee (bonuses, raises, and perks) may not be the same as what motivates a more seasoned, experienced, and financially successful employee (recognition, opportunity for greater influence, and increased training). Motivation is not an easy thing to understand, especially as firms become more global and more diverse.

Another important part of motivation is enjoying where you work and your career opportunities. Below is a list of the best places to do business and start careers in the United States, according to *Forbes* magazine. Chances are, workers who live in these places have encountered fewer frustrations than have workers in places at the bottom of the list and therefore probably are more content with where they work.

Best Places for Business and Careers

Rank	Metro Area	Job Growth Rank	Metro Area Population (in 1,000s)
1.	Raleigh, NC	21	1,034
2.	Boise, ID	13	585
3.	Fort Collins, CO	80	281
4.	Des Moines, IA	60	543
5.	Lexington, KY	110	443
6.	Atlanta, GA	69	5,266
7.	Richmond, VA	75	1,211
8.	Olympia, WA	22	240
9.	Spokane, WA	36	452
10.	Knoxville, TN	84	673

Source: "The Best Places for Business and Careers," *Forbes,* March 19, 2008, www .forbes.com/lists/2008/1/bestplaces08_Best-Places-For-Business-And-Careers_Rank.html (accessed March 23, 2008).

Best Buy Brings Diversity to the Geek Squad

Best Buy is using powerful methods to motivate its managers to support diversity. Since 2004, Best Buy has conducted management diversity training at the Lorraine Motel, made famous by the assassination of Dr. Martin Luther King, Jr., in 1968. The motel has been converted into the National Civil Rights Museum, and those who enter it are given a history lesson on the civil rights movement.

Best Buy believes that immersion is the best way to educate its managers about the need for diversity, hence the trip to Memphis. The company says it is dedicated to inclusion and wants managers to personalize this message and take it back with them to their stores to share with employees. Through diversity training, those at Best Buy say they hope to encourage employees to be themselves.

Best Buy is also increasing its female employee ratios. In 2003, the company started its Women's Leadership Forum, which aims to improve the experiences of female employees and customers. As of fiscal 2007, Best Buy in the United States had increased the number of female general managers by 40 percent, female sales managers by 100 percent, and female district managers by 200 percent. Female employees working in home theater departments increased by 100 percent, and female Geek Squad employees (Best Buy computer whizzes) increased by 284 percent. This focus on women seems to be working. Company data indicate that in about four years, female customer revenue has increased by $4.4 billion.

Those at Best Buy say that these methods for increasing diversity have helped the company create a more family-like atmosphere along with increasing the company's bottom line.[27] ❖

Q: Discussion Questions

1. Why is racial and gender diversity important in motivating employees?

2. How does Best Buy's trip to Memphis encourage racial diversity among managers and employees?

3. Why does a diverse workforce help increase the bottom line in a retail company such as Best Buy?

opportunities, and reporting relationships. Employees are motivated by the nature of the relationships they have with their supervisors, by the nature of their jobs, and by characteristics of the organization. Motivation tools, then, must be varied as well. Managers can further nurture motivation by being honest, supportive, empathetic, accessible, fair, and open. Motivating employees to increase satisfaction and productivity is an important concern for organizations seeking to remain competitive in the global marketplace. ■

CHECK OUT

www.mhhe.com/FerrellM2e

for study materials including Interactive Exercises, Quizzes, iPod downloads, and video.

managing human resources

11

introduction Recruiting loyal and motivated employees is a vital task in any organization. If a business is to achieve success, it must have sufficient numbers of employees who are qualified and motivated to perform the required duties. Thus, managing the quantity (from hiring to firing) and quality (through training, compensating, and so on) of employees is an important business function. Meeting the challenge of managing increasingly diverse human resources effectively can give a company a competitive edge in a global marketplace.

This chapter focuses on the quantity and quality of human resources. First we look at how human resources managers plan for, recruit, and select qualified employees. Next we look at training, appraising, and compensating employees, aspects of human resources management designed to retain valued employees. Along the way, we'll also consider the challenges of managing unionized and diverse employees.

LO1

Define human resources management, and explain its significance.

THE NATURE OF HUMAN RESOURCES MANAGEMENT

Chapter 1 defined human resources as labor, the physical and mental abilities that people use to produce goods and services. **Human resources management (HRM)** refers to all the activities involved in determining an organization's human resources needs, as well as acquiring, training, and compensating people to fill those needs. Human resources managers are concerned with maximizing the satisfaction of employees and motivating them to meet organizational objectives productively. In some companies, this function is called personnel management.

HRM has increased in importance over the last few decades, in part because managers have developed a better understanding of human relations through the work of Maslow, Herzberg, and others. Moreover, the human resources themselves are changing. Employees today are concerned not only about how much a job pays; they are concerned also with job satisfaction, personal performance, leisure, the environment, and the future. Once dominated by white men, today's workforce includes significantly more women, African Americans, Hispanics, and other minorities, as well as disabled and older workers. Human resources managers must be aware of these changes and make the best of them to increase the productivity of their employees. Every manager practices some of the functions of human resources management at all times.

PLANNING FOR HUMAN RESOURCES NEEDS

When planning and developing strategies for reaching the organization's overall objectives, a company must consider whether it will have the human resources necessary to carry out its plans. After determining how many employees and what skills are needed to satisfy the overall plans, the human resources department (which may range from the owner in a small business to hundreds of people in a large corporation) ascertains how many employees the company currently has and how many will be

retiring or otherwise leaving the organization during the planning period. With this information, the human resources manager can then forecast how many more employees the company will need to hire and what qualifications they must have. HRM planning also requires forecasting the availability of people in the workforce who will have the necessary qualifications to meet the organization's future needs. The human resources manager then develops a strategy for satisfying the organization's human resources needs.

Next, managers analyze the jobs within the organization so that they can match the human resources to the available assignments. **Job analysis** determines, through observation and study, pertinent information about a job—the specific tasks that constitute it; the knowledge, skills, and abilities necessary to perform it; and the environment in which it will be performed. Managers use the information obtained through a job analysis to develop job descriptions and job specifications.

A **job description** is a formal, written explanation of a specific job that usually includes job title, tasks to be performed (for instance, waiting on customers), relationship with other jobs, physical and mental skills required (such as lifting heavy boxes or calculating data), duties, responsibilities, and working conditions. A **job specification** describes the qualifications necessary for a specific job in terms of education (some jobs require a college degree), experience, personal characteristics (newspaper ads frequently request outgoing, hardworking persons), and physical characteristics. Both the job description and the job specification are used to develop recruiting materials such as newspaper and online advertisements.

 LO2

Summarize the processes of recruiting and selecting human resources for a company.

RECRUITING AND SELECTING NEW EMPLOYEES

After forecasting the firm's human resources needs and comparing them to existing human resources, the human resources manager should have a general idea of how many new employees the firm needs to hire. With the aid of job analyses, management can then recruit and select employees who are qualified to fill specific job openings.

Recruiting

Recruiting means forming a pool of qualified applicants from which management can select employees. There are two sources from which to develop this pool of applicants: internal and external.

Internal sources of applicants include the organization's current employees. Many firms have a policy of giving first consideration to their own employees—or promoting from within. The cost of hiring current employees to fill job openings is inexpensive when compared with the cost of hiring from external sources, and it is good for employee morale.

External sources consist of advertisements in newspapers and professional journals, employment agencies, colleges, vocational schools, recommendations from current employees, competing firms, unsolicited applications, and online. There are hundreds of Web sites where employers can post job openings and job seekers can post their résumés, including Monster.com, Hotjobs.com, and CareerBuilder.com. Employers looking for employees for specialized jobs can use more focused sites such as computerwork.com. Increasingly, companies can turn to their own Web sites for potential candidates: Nearly all the *Fortune* 500 firms provide career Web sites where they recruit, provide employment information, and take applications. Using these sources of applicants is generally more expensive than hiring from within, but it may be necessary if there are no current employees who meet the job specifications or there are better-qualified people outside the organization. Recruiting for entry-level managerial and professional positions is often carried out on college and university campuses. For managerial or professional positions above the entry level, companies sometimes depend on employment agencies or executive search firms, sometimes called *headhunters,* which specialize in luring qualified people away from other companies.

Selection

Selection is the process of collecting information about applicants and using that information to decide which ones to hire. It includes the application itself, as well as interviewing, testing, and reference checking. This process can be quite lengthy and expensive. At Procter & Gamble, for example, the steps include the application, screening and comprehensive interviews, day visits/site visits, and for those outside the United States, a problem-solving test. P&G attracts and retains high-quality employees.[1] Such rigorous scrutiny is necessary to find applicants who can do the work expected and fit into the firm's structure and culture. If an organization finds the "right" employees through its recruiting and selection process, it will not have to spend as much money later in recruiting, selecting, and training replacement employees.

the application In the first stage of the selection process, the individual fills out an application form and perhaps has a brief interview. The application form asks for the applicant's name, address, telephone number, education, and previous work experience. The goal of this stage of the selection process is to get acquainted with the applicants and weed out those who are obviously not qualified for the job. Most companies ask for the following information before contacting a potential candidate: current salary, reason for seeking a new job, years of experience, availability, and level of interest in the position. In addition to identifying obvious qualifications, the application can provide subtle clues about whether a person is appropriate for a particular job. For instance, an applicant who gives unusually creative answers may be perfect for a position at an advertising agency; a person who turns in a sloppy, hurriedly scrawled application probably would not be appropriate for a technical job requiring precise adjustments. Many companies now accept online applications. The online application at Procter & Gamble is designed not only to collect biographical data but to create a picture of the applicant and how that person might contribute within the company. The Web site states that there are no right or wrong answers and indicates that completion takes about

Some recruiters and firms use special software to "troll" social networking sites such as Linked In to find outstanding employees—employees who may not be looking for a job but who could be recruited successfully.

"ABILITY AND PERFORMANCE TESTS ARE USED TO DETERMINE WHETHER AN APPLICANT HAS THE SKILLS NECESSARY FOR THE JOB."

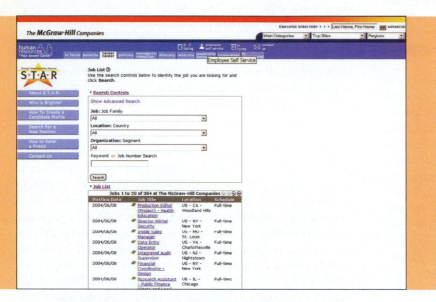

The McGraw-Hill Companies has an online database of job offerings called "Strategic Talent Acquisition Resources," or STAR. STAR helps employees manage their careers by alerting them about future opportunities that match their experiences, captures all résumés in a common database so that they can be shared nationwide, allows for electronic approvals, and eliminates all paper résumés.

30 to 45 minutes. Applicants also must submit an electronic copy of their résumés.[2]

the interview The next phase of the selection process involves interviewing applicants. Interviews allow management to obtain detailed information about an applicant's experience and skills, reasons for changing jobs, and attitudes toward the job and an idea of whether the person would fit in with the company. Furthermore, the interviewer can answer the applicant's questions about the requirements for the job, compensation, working conditions, company policies, organizational culture, and so on. A potential employee's questions may be just as revealing as his or her answers. Table 11.1 provides some insights on finding the right work environment. Table 11.2 lists some of the most common questions asked by interviewers, while Table 11.3 reveals mistakes candidates make in interviewing.

testing Another step in the selection process is testing. Ability and performance tests are used to determine whether an applicant has the skills necessary for the job. Aptitude, IQ, or personality tests may be used to assess an applicant's potential for a certain kind of work and his or her ability to fit into the organization's culture. One of

AT&T Achieves Supplier Diversity

According to revenue, AT&T, Inc., is the largest communications holding company in the world. Headquartered in Dallas, Texas, the company employs 302,660 people globally and provides IP-based communications, wireless, high-speed Internet, and home phone services. For over 40 years, AT&T has retained a commitment to supplier diversity, which is important for many reasons. For example, promoting supplier diversity can improve the communities in which businesses operate. Working with diverse suppliers also offers AT&T a wider variety of resources.

AT&T developed its Supplier Diversity Programs to promote, increase, and improve the quality of the overall participation in its supply chain of businesses owned by minorities, women, and disabled veterans. In 10 years, AT&T has spent over $27 billion on this focus and increased its spending with diverse sup-

pliers by 288 percent. AT&T is part of the Billion Dollar Roundtable, a supplier diversity think tank of corporations spending over $1 billion annually with diverse companies. Only 13 companies qualify at this level. AT&T eventually wants to acquire 21.5 percent of its total procurement from diversity-owned enterprises.

One of those companies is Georgia-based Metasys Technologies. The Asian-American company provides IT staffing solutions, services procurement management, and business process outsourcing. Partnerships like this are critical. The United States population is one-third minorities, and within a couple of generations the United States may be a majority minority country, but only 15 percent of all businesses are minority-owned. One supplier diversity goal is to increase this number. AT&T has received awards for its supplier diversity

programs, including the DiversityBusiness.com Top 50 award, which diverse business owners select. As AT&T evolves, its commitment to working with and assisting diverse business owners appears to be a constant.[3] ❖

Q: Discussion Questions

1. Why should large companies such as AT&T invest valuable resources in increasing the diversity of their suppliers?

2. How does a diverse supplier base help a company's bottom line?

3. What else could AT&T do to ensure diversity?

TABLE 11.1 Interviewing Tips

1. Evaluate the work environment. Do employees seem to get along and work well in teams?
2. Evaluate the attitude of employees. Are employees happy, tense, or overworked?
3. Are employees enthusiastic and excited about their work?
4. What is the organizational culture, and would you feel comfortable working there?

Source: "What to Look for During Office Visits," Texas A&M Career Center, http:// career center.tamu.edu/guides/interviews/lookforinoffice.html (accessed March 23, 2009).

TABLE 11.2 Top 10 Interview Questions

1. What are your weaknesses?
2. Why should we hire you?
3. Why do you want to work here?
4. What are your goals?
5. Why did you leave (or why are you leaving) your job?
6. When were you most satisfied with your job?
7. What can you do for us that the other candidate can't?
8. What are three positive things your last boss would say about you?
9. What salary are you seeking?
10. If you were an animal, which one would you want to be?

Source: Carole Martin, "Prep for the Top 10 Interview Questions," http://content.monster .com/articles/3479/17512/1/home.aspx (accessed March 23, 2009).

TABLE 11.3
MOST COMMON INTERVIEW MISTAKES

Dressing inappropriately	51%
Negative comments regarding previous employer	49%
Arrogance	44%
Insufficient answers	30%
Not asking good questions	29%
Keys to Interview Success	
Do research	
Don't lie	
Be professional	
Be prepared	
Be positive	

Source: Rosemary Haefner, "Top 10 Interview Mistakes," May 12, 2008, www.cnn .com/2008/LIVING/worklife/05/12/cb.interview.misakes/index.html (accessed June 2, 2009).

the most commonly used tests is the Myers-Briggs Type Indicator. The Myers-Briggs Type Indicator Test is used more than 2.5 million times each year according to a survey by *Workforce Management*. Although polygraph ("lie detector") tests were once a common technique for evaluating the honesty of applicants, in 1988 their use was restricted to specific government jobs and jobs involving security or access to drugs. Applicants

may also undergo physical examinations to determine their suitability for some jobs, and many companies require applicants to be screened for illegal drug use. There are more than 11 million heavy drinkers and 16 million illegal drug users in the United States. Among this group, 75 percent are employed full time and around half work for small businesses. On average in small businesses, 1 of 10 employees are either alcohol or drug abusers. Small businesses may have a higher percentage of these employees because they do not engage in systematic drug testing. If you employ a drug or alcohol abuser, you can expect a 33 percent loss in productivity from this employee, which costs the employer roughly $7,000 annually. Overall, substance abuse costs American employers $160 billion each year through high employee turnover and absenteeism, workplace accidents, higher workers' compensation costs, higher medical costs, and workplace theft and violence.[4] Like the application form and the interview, testing serves to eliminate those who do not meet the job specifications.

reference checking Before making a job offer, the company should always check an applicant's references. Reference checking usually involves verifying educational background and previous work experience. Background checking is important because applicants may misrepresent themselves on their applications or résumés. The star of *Dinner Impossible* on the Food Network fabricated portions of his résumé, including the claim that he cooked for Britain's royal family. The Food Network, upon learning of these errors, did not renew Robert Irvine's contract, indicating that viewers place trust in the network and the accuracy of information that it provides and that Irvine "challenged that trust."[5] Reference checking is a vital, albeit often overlooked, stage in the selection process. Managers charged with hiring should be aware, however, that many organizations will confirm only that an applicant is a former employee, perhaps with beginning and ending work dates, and will not release details about the quality of the employee's work.

Legal Issues in Recruiting and Selecting

Legal constraints and regulations are present in almost every phase of the recruitment and selection process, and a violation of these regulations can result in lawsuits and fines. Therefore, managers should be aware of these restrictions to avoid legal problems. Some of the laws affecting human resources management are discussed here.

Because one law pervades all areas of human resources management, we'll take a quick look at it now. **Title VII of the Civil Rights Act** of 1964 prohibits discrimination in employment. It also created the Equal Employment Opportunity Commission (EEOC), a federal agency dedicated to increasing job opportunities for women and minorities and eliminating job discrimination based on race, religion, color, sex, national origin, or handicap. As a result of Title VII, employers must not impose sex distinctions in job specifications, job descriptions, or newspaper advertisements. Between 75,000 and 95,000 charges of discrimination are filed each year with the EEOC.[6] Sexual harassment cases make up the largest number of claims the EEOC sees each day. The Civil Rights Act of 1964 also outlaws the use of discriminatory tests for applicants. Aptitude tests and other indirect tests must be validated; in other words, employers must be able to demonstrate that scores on such tests are related to job performance so that no one race has an advantage in taking the tests. Although many hope for improvements in organizational diversity, in a survey of 357 global senior executives, 76 percent have one or no minorities among their top executives. Minorities make up 17 percent of the U.S. workforce, and that number should hit 20 percent by 2016. In spite of a lack of diversity, many of these companies indicate they have an initiative to support workplace diversity.[7]

Other laws affecting HRM include the Americans with Disabilities Act (ADA), which prevents discrimination against disabled persons. It also classifies people with AIDS as handicapped and, consequently, prohibits using a positive AIDS test as reason to deny an applicant employment. The Age Discrimination in Employment Act specifically outlaws discrimination based on age. Its focus is banning hiring practices that discriminate against people between the ages of 49 and 69, but it also outlaws policies that require employees to retire before age 70. Generally, however, when companies need employees, recruiters head to college campuses, and when downsizing is necessary, many older workers are offered early retirement. However, there are many benefits that companies are realizing in hiring older workers. Some of these benefits include that they are more dedicated, punctual, honest, and detail-oriented; are good listeners; take pride in their work; exhibit good organizational skills; are efficient and confident; are mature; can be seen as role models; have good communication skills; and offer an opportunity for reduced labor cost because they already have insurance plans.[8] The Equal Pay Act mandates that men and women who do equal work must receive the same wage. Wage differences are acceptable only if they are attributed to seniority, performance, or qualifications. Despite these laws, one year out of college, women earn 80 percent of what men earn. A decade later, women earn only 69 percent as much as men. There is significant variation based on the job: for example, in education generally, women earn 95 percent as much as males; however, in the area of math, women earn 76 percent as much as men.[9]

● ● **LO3**

Discuss how workers are trained and their performance appraised.

DEVELOPING THE WORKFORCE

Once the most qualified applicants have been selected and offered positions and have accepted their offers, they must be formally introduced to the organization and trained so that they can begin to be productive members of the workforce. **Orientation** familiarizes the newly hired employees with fellow workers, company procedures, and the physical properties of the company. It generally includes a tour of the building; introductions to supervisors, co-workers, and subordinates; and the distribution of organizational manuals describing the organization's policy on vacations, absenteeism, lunch breaks, company benefits, and so on. Orientation also involves socializing the new employee into the ethics and culture of the new company. Many larger companies now show videotapes of procedures, facilities, and key personnel in the organization to help speed the adjustment process.

Training and Development

Although recruiting and selection are designed to find employees who have the knowledge, skills, and abilities the company needs, new employees still must undergo **training**

The investment firm Merrill Lynch considers diversity within its organization not just a legal requirement but a business imperative.

to learn how to do their specific job tasks. *On-the-job training* allows workers to learn by actually performing the tasks of the job, while *classroom training* teaches employees with lectures, conferences, videotapes, case studies, and Web-based materials. While the perception is that employee training costs are expensive and the temptation during recessionary times is to cut training programs, reducing training can actually hurt employee morale and make workers less prepared to do their jobs. Consumers may end up dissatisfied as well if customer service suffers due to inadequately trained employees.[10] **Development** is training that augments the skills and knowledge of managers and professionals. Training and development are also used to improve the skills of employees in their present positions and prepare them for increased responsibility and job promotions. Training is therefore a vital function of human resources management. Training and development plans are tailored to meet each employee's needs at Procter & Gamble. In addition to on-the-job training, the company offers one-on-one coaching from managers, peer mentoring, individualized work plans that outline key projects and highlight skills to sharpen, and formal classroom training conducted at the company's "Learning Center" in Cincinnati.[11]

Assessing Performance

Assessing an employee's performance—his or her strengths and weaknesses on the job—is one of the most difficult tasks for managers. However, performance appraisal is crucial because it gives employees feedback on how they are doing and what they need to do to improve their performance. It also provides a basis for determining how to compensate and reward employees, and it generates information about the quality of the firm's selection, training, and development activities. Table 11.4 identifies 20 characteristics that may be assessed in a performance review.

Performance appraisals may be objective or subjective. An objective assessment is quantifiable. For example, a Westinghouse employee may be judged by how many circuit boards he typically produces in one day or by how many of his boards have defects. A Century 21 real estate agent may be judged by the number of houses she has shown or the number of sales she has closed. A company can also use tests as an objective method of assessment. Whatever method they use, managers must take into account the work environment when they appraise performance objectively.

DID YOU KNOW?

The most important benefit of an internship is experiencing different work environments. (See Figure 11.1.)[12]

When jobs do not lend themselves to objective appraisal, the manager must relate the employee's performance to some other standard. One popular tool used in subjective assessment is the ranking system, which lists various performance factors on which the manager ranks employees against each other. Although used by many large companies, ranking systems are unpopular with many employees. Qualitative criteria, such as teamwork and communication skills, used to evaluate employees are generally hard to gauge. Such grading systems have triggered employee lawsuits that allege discrimination in grade/ranking assignments. Best Buy settled an age discrimination lawsuit with 44 former information technology (IT) employees aged 40 to 71 (average age 51), which required the company to reinstate the employees or pay them salaries and benefits until they reached retirement age.[13]

Another performance appraisal method used by many companies is the 360-degree feedback system, which provides feedback from a panel that typically includes superiors, peers, and subordinates. Because of the tensions it may cause, peer appraisal appears to be difficult for many. However, companies that have success with 360-degree feedback tend to be open to learning and willing to experiment and are led by executives who are direct about the expected benefits as well as the challenges.[14] Managers and leaders with high emotional intelligence (sensitivity to their own as well as others' emotions) assess and reflect upon their interactions with colleagues on a daily basis. In addition, they conduct follow-up analysis on their projects,

● **TRAINING** teaching employees to do specific job tasks through either classroom development or on-the-job experience

● **DEVELOPMENT** training that augments the skills and knowledge of managers and professionals

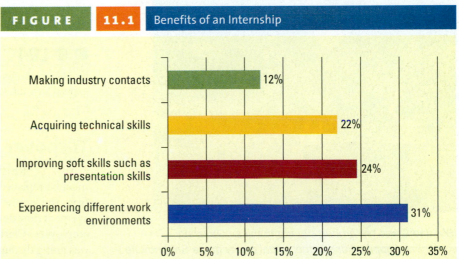

FIGURE 11.1 Benefits of an Internship

- Making industry contacts — 12%
- Acquiring technical skills — 22%
- Improving soft skills such as presentation skills — 24%
- Experiencing different work environments — 31%

TABLE 11.4   General Performance Characteristics

Communication ability—effectiveness with which the employee presents accurate information both verbally and in writing.

Relationships with others—extent to which the employee establishes positive relationships with co-workers.

Ability to work without supervision—extent to which the employee can work by himself/herself; requiring very little supervision and being self-sufficient.

Accuracy of work—degree to which the employee makes mistakes or errors that require correction.

Appearance—physical appearance of the employee at work; cleanliness, grooming, neatness, and appropriateness of dress for the job.

Cooperation—extent to which the employee cooperates with supervisors, associates, and those for which work is performed.

Dependability—extent to which the employee can be relied upon to meet work schedules and fulfill job responsibilities and commitments.

Use of work time—how effectively and efficiently the employee uses his/her time to accomplish his/her job tasks (e.g., does not wait until the last minute to work on important projects).

Meeting schedules—extent to which the employee efficiently completes his/her work and effectively meets deadlines.

Punctuality—extent to which the employee is prompt in reporting for work and assignments/appointments at the specified time.

Adaptability—extent to which the employee can adapt to job or organizational changes.

Willingness to learn—extent to which the employee wants to learn about his/her job and asks intelligent questions about the job.

Safety—extent to which the employee follows established safety practices and corrects unsafe work practices on the job.

Favorable job attitude—extent to which the employee displays interest and enthusiasm for his/her work and takes pride in a job well done.

Job knowledge—extent to which the employee knows the details of the job and follows the job procedures.

Quantity of work—extent to which the employee produces an amount of acceptable work to meet schedules over which he/she has control.

Quality of work—extent to which the employee neatly, thoroughly, and accurately completes job assignments according to established standards of quality.

Attendance—concerns whether the employee is at work each day.

Relationship with the public—extent to which the employee establishes good relationships with the public (e.g., being courteous and helpful).

Judgment—quality of work-related decisions made by the employee.

Source: University of South Carolina, Division of Human Resources-Employee Relations Office, Employee Performance Management System, http://hr.sc.edu/relations/epms.html (accessed June 16, 2007).

asking the right questions and listening carefully to responses without getting defensive about their actions.[15]

Whether the assessment is objective or subjective, it is vital that the manager discuss the results with the employee so that the employee knows how well he or she is doing the job. The results of a performance appraisal become useful only when they are communicated, tactfully, to the employee and presented as a tool to allow the employee to grow and improve in his or her position and beyond. Performance appraisals also are used to determine whether an employee should be promoted, transferred, or terminated from the organization.

 L04

Identify the types of turnover companies may experience, and explain why turnover is an important issue.

IBM and Cisco are among the companies now using customized applications in the virtual reality game Second Life to train and develop their employees.

Turnover

Turnover, which occurs when employees quit or are fired and must be replaced by new employees, results in lost productivity from the vacancy, fees to recruit replacement employees, management time devoted to interviewing, and training costs for new employees. Clarkston Consulting in Durham, North Carolina, was going through a phase in which employees were dissatisfied and were working more than the industry norm of 56 hours per week (not including travel) and turnover was increasing. The company engaged in intense training to improve skills and understand competitive and best practices, and it introduced a truncated travel schedule. The travel program allowed employees to leave home on Monday, stay in a hotel and work at the client's site for four days, and return to work at home on Friday. Removing large amounts of travel from evenings and weekends significantly improved morale, productivity, and satisfaction.[16] Part of the reason for worker dissatisfaction may be overworked employees as a result of downsizing and a lack of training and advancement opportunities.[17] Of course, turnover is not always an unhappy occasion when it takes the form of a promotion or transfer.

A **promotion** is an advancement to a higher-level job with increased authority, responsibility, and pay. In some companies and most labor unions, seniority—the length of time a person has been with the company or at a particular job classification—

a union organizer. However, recent legislation and court decisions now require that companies fire employees fairly, for just cause only. Managers must take care, then, to warn employees when their performance is unacceptable and may lead to dismissal. They should also document all problems and warnings in employees' work records. To avoid the possibility of lawsuits from individuals who may feel they have been fired unfairly, employers should provide clear, business-related reasons for any firing, supported by written documentation if possible. Employee disciplinary procedures should be explained carefully to all employees and should be set forth in employee handbooks.

Many companies have downsized in recent years, laying off tens of thousands of employees in an effort to become more productive and competitive. General Motors, in light of declining demand for large fuel-inefficient vehicles, launched plans to close truck and SUV plants as well as cutting its dealer

> ## The results of a performance appraisal become useful only when they are communicated, tactfully, to the employee and presented as a tool to allow the employee to grow and improve in his or her position and beyond.

is the key issue in determining who should be promoted. Most managers base promotions on seniority only when they have candidates with equal qualifications: Managers prefer to base promotions on merit.

A **transfer** is a move to another job within the company at essentially the same level and wage. Transfers allow workers to obtain new skills or to find a new position within an organization when the old position has been eliminated because of automation or downsizing.

Separations occur when employees resign, retire, are terminated, or are laid off. Table 11.5 lists some guidelines for employees leaving the organization. Employees may be terminated, or fired, for poor performance, violation of work rules, absenteeism, and so on. Businesses traditionally have been able to fire employees *at will,* that is, for any reason other than for race, religion, sex, or age or because an employee is

TABLE 11.5 What to Avoid When Leaving Your Job

1. Don't use this as an opportunity to get emotional and say negative things about your boss or co-workers.
2. Don't damage or steal any company property, physical or intellectual.
3. Make sure that you secure the appropriate references before leaving.
4. Don't share negative sentiments with your replacement.
5. When interviewing for your next job, be careful not to be negative toward your previous employer.

Source: Adapted from Dawn Rosenberg McKay, "Five Things Not to Do When You Leave Your Job," http://careerplanning.about.com/od/jobseparation/a/leave_mistakes.htm (accessed March 23, 2009).

network 40 percent and laying off thousands of employees in the United States, Canada, and Mexico. After emerging from bankruptcy, general Motors continued to shed employees and downsize the company in an effort to become profitable again.[18] Layoffs are sometimes temporary; employees may be brought back when business conditions improve. When layoffs are to be permanent, employers often help employees find other jobs and may extend benefits while the employees search for new employment. Such actions help lessen the trauma of the layoffs.

A well-organized human resources department strives to minimize losses due to separations and transfers because recruiting and training new employees is very expensive. Note that a high turnover rate in a company may signal problems with the selection and training process, the compensation program, or even the type of company. To help reduce turnover, companies have tried a number of strategies. Levi Strauss & Company, for example, provides emergency grants or loans of up to $1,000 to help employees confronted with a car that won't start, a sick child, or another unexpected financial hardship. Kraft Foods allows U.S. workers to share jobs, swap shifts, or take annual vacations in one-hour increments to help them deal with family emergencies. CVS offers simulated work experience to support new employees coming off welfare who have never held a traditional job.[19] Table 11.6 shows considerations for owners and managers in retaining and motivating their employees.

  L05

Specify the various ways a worker may be compensated.

COMPENSATING THE WORKFORCE

People don't work for free, and how much they are paid for their work is a complicated issue. Also, designing a fair compensation plan is an important task because pay and benefits represent a substantial portion of an organization's expenses. Wages that are too high may result in the company's products being priced too high, making them uncompetitive in the market. Wages that are too low may damage employee morale and result in costly turnover. Remember that compensation is one of the hygiene factors identified by Herzberg.

Goldman Sachs is among many financial firms that have looked for ways other than higher compensation and bonuses to motivate their workers after the most recent economic downturn.

TABLE 11.6 Retention Considerations for Employers

1. Treat your employees as valued clients or customers
2. Keep your employees informed about the strategy and vision of the organization.
3. Strong retention strategies become strong recruiting advantages.
4. Retention is much more effective when you put the right person into the right job. Know the job, and try to understand your employees' motivation.
5. Money is important, but it is not the only reason people stay with an organization.
6. Employee committees to help develop retention strategies can be a valuable way to focus on key and relevant issues.
7. Management must believe in the value of retention strategies.
8. Recognition, in various forms, is a powerful retention strategy.
9. Remember, fun in the workplace is very important to many employees.
10. Know your competitors' benefit packages. Keep current and ahead of the pack to retain the best employees.

Source: Adapted from L. John Mason, "Retaining Your Best Employees Plus: Top 10 Retention Tips," www.dstress.com/articles/retaining_key.html (accessed March 23, 2009).

Designing a fair compensation plan is a difficult task because it involves evaluating the relative worth of all jobs within the business while allowing for individual efforts. Compensation for a specific job is typically determined through a **wage/salary survey,** which tells the company how much compensation comparable firms are paying for specific jobs that the firms have in common. Compensation for individuals within a specific job category depends on both the compensation for that job and the individual's productivity. Therefore, two employees with identical jobs may not receive exactly the same pay because of individual differences in performance.

Financial Compensation

Financial compensation falls into two general categories—wages and salaries. **Wages** are financial rewards based on the number of hours the employee works or the level of output achieved. Wages based on the number of hours worked are called time wages. The federal minimum wage increased to $6.55 per hour in 2008. Many states also mandate minimum wages; in a case in which the two wages are in conflict, the higher of the two wages prevails. There may even be differences between city and state minimum wages. In New Mexico, the minimum wage is $7.50, whereas in the state capital of Santa Fe, the minimum wage is $10.50, due to a higher cost of living.[20] Roughly one-fourth of the U.S. workforce earns an income below the weighted poverty line for a family of four.[21] Table 11.7 compares wage and other information for Costco and Wal-Mart, two well-known discount chains. Time wages are appropriate when employees are continually interrupted and when quality is more important than quantity. Assembly-line workers, clerks, and maintenance personnel are commonly paid on a time-wage basis. The advantage of time wages is the ease of computation. The disadvantage is that time wages provide no incentive to increase productivity. In fact, time wages may encourage employees to do less than a full day's work.

To overcome these disadvantages, many companies pay on an incentive system, using piece wages or commissions. Piece wages are based on the level of output achieved. A major advantage of piece wages is that they motivate employees to supervise their own activities and increase output. Skilled craftworkers are often paid on a piece-wage basis. At Longaberger, the

● **WAGE/SALARY SURVEY** a study that tells a company how much compensation comparable firms are paying for specific jobs that the firms have in common

● **WAGES** financial rewards based on the number of hours the employee works or the level of output achieved

Starbucks Works Hard to Stay Green

These days Starbucks is everywhere, with 15,000 stores globally. Of course, thousands of stores employ many thousands of employees. So how do these employees, known as "partners," fare at Starbucks? Compared to competitors, pretty well. All eligible full-time and part-time partners receive health care benefits, and Starbucks frequently updates its pay packages to stay competitive.

Starbucks is also taking part in the green trend. For example, the company purchases about 4 percent certified Fair Trade coffee and plans to increase that proportion. Lately, Starbucks has been researching how to reduce its carbon emissions footprint. In 2005, Starbucks teamed up with the World Research Institute's Green Power Market Development Group, which assists compa-

nies in purchasing renewable energy at better prices. The company has been increasing its use of wind power to reduce its carbon dioxide emissions. It has recycling programs in place and has introduced the first paper cup made with 10 percent postconsumer recycled fiber.

Starbucks encourages its partners and customers to go green too. It has run prominent campaigns, such as planetgreengame.com, and is tracking how much energy is used by specific equipment throughout its stores. Although some argue that this large company is not doing enough, others feel that any step in the right direction is a positive thing. We can certainly hope, thanks to the security and support that Starbucks offers its partners, that they feel motivated to go out and do their

part to help both their communities and the environment.[22] ❖

Q: Discussion Questions

1. How does Starbucks compensate its employees in ways that encourage lower turnover and a more productive workforce?

2. How do Starbucks' green initiatives affect employees?

3. What might encouraging volunteerism do for employee morale and company loyalty?

world's largest maker of handmade baskets, weavers are paid per piece. The 2,500 workers produced 40,000 baskets a day, but productivity varied by as much as 400 percent among the weavers. A team of basket makers was assembled to try to improve productivity and reduce weaver downtime and the amount of leftover materials. After studying the basket makers for 19 days, the team's suggestions were implemented. The changes resulted in $3 million in annual savings for the company.[23]

The other incentive system, **commission,** pays a fixed amount or a percentage of the employee's sales. Kele & Co Jewelers in Plainfield, Illinois, makes sterling silver jewelry and offers semiprecious and gemstones at affordable prices. Its handcrafted jewelry is sold on the Internet (www.keleonline.com) and through independent sales representatives (ISRs) all over the country. The unique aspect of Kele's sales process is its innovative sales and commission structure. ISRs have no minimum sales quotas, sales are shared among team members during training and after being promoted, and there is no requirement to purchase inventory as jewelry is shipped from Kele headquarters. ISRs receive a 30 percent commission on sales. Kele also pays for the design, development, and maintenance of a Web site to support ISRs. The goal is to increase the profit margin and earning potential of the salespeople. The company's goal is to become the largest direct sales company in the industry.[24] This method motivates employees to sell as much as they can. Some companies combine payment based on commission with time wages or salaries.

A **salary** is a financial reward calculated on a weekly, monthly, or annual basis. Salaries are associated with white-collar workers such as office personnel, executives, and professional employees. Although a salary provides a stable stream of income, salaried workers may be required to work beyond the usual hours without additional financial compensation.

In addition to the basic wages or salaries paid to employees, a company may offer **bonuses** for exceptional performance as an incentive to increase productivity further. Many workers receive a bonus as a "thank you" for good work and an incentive to continue working hard. Many owners and managers are recognizing that simple bonuses and perks foster happier employees and reduce turnover. For example, the owner of Ticketcity.com, a small business in Austin, Texas, offers employees tickets to major events like the Super Bowl and the Master's golf tournament and even management retreats. The owner of a DreamMaker remodeling franchise in Peoria, Illinois, provides employees money to use toward new vehicles, takes them on staff outings to sporting games, and funds their retirement plans.[25]

Another form of compensation is **profit sharing,** which distributes a percentage of company profits to the employees whose work helped to generate those profits. Some profit-sharing plans involve distributing shares of company stock to employees. Usually referred to as *ESOPs*—employee stock ownership plans—they have been gaining popularity in recent years. One reason for the popularity of ESOPs is the sense of partnership that they create between the organization and employees. Profit sharing can also motivate employees to work hard, because increased productivity and sales mean that the profits or the stock dividends will increase. Many organizations offer employees a stake in the company through stock purchase plans, ESOPs, or stock investments through 401(k) plans. Employees below senior management levels rarely received stock options, until recently. Companies are adopting broad-based stock option plans to build a stronger link between employees' interests and the organization's interests. A study by professors at the Wharton School of the University of Pennsylvania found that companies that paid middle managers 20 percent more in options than comparable companies saw increased performance and stock prices that rose an average 5 percent faster a year. Similar results were seen in companies that paid technical specialists at least 20 percent more in options.[26] Table 11.8 provides the salary of college basketball coaches. The University of Florida college basketball team, coached by the top earning coach Billy Donovan, is consistently one of the strongest in the country. Roy Wil-

TABLE 11.7 Managing the Workforce: Costco versus Wal-Mart

	Costco	Wal-Mart
Number of employees	86,900—U.S.	1.3 million—U.S.
	118,800—international	1.9 million—international
Sales	$72.5 billion	$374.5 billion
Average hourly wage	$16.00	$9.68
Percent of employees covered by health plans	82%	48%
Turnover (per year)	20%	50%
Profits per employee	$13,467	$11,039

Sources: "Costco Employment," www.priceviewer.com/costco/costco_employment.htm (accessed March 23, 2009); Wal-Mart Annual Report 2008, http://walmartstores.com/sites/AnnualReport/2008/index.html (accessed March 23, 2009); a workforce management blog, www.benefitsbuzz.net/2008/10/why-wal-mart-doesnt-treat-employees-as-well-as-costco-and-why-you-dont-see-a-difference-in-service-anyway.html (accessed March 23, 2009); Costco profile, http://investing.businessweek.com/research/stocks/earnings/earnings.asp?symbol=COST.O (accessed March 23, 2009).

liams, another top earning coach, led North Carolina to the NCAA Championship in 2009.

Benefits

Benefits are nonfinancial forms of compensation provided to employees, such as pension plans for retirement; health, disability, and life insurance; holidays and paid days off for vacation or illness; credit union membership; health programs; child care; elder care; assistance with adoption; and more. According to the Bureau of Labor Statistics, employer costs for employee compensation for civilian workers in the United States average $28.11 per hour worked. Wages and salaries account for approximately 69.8 percent of

> ● **BENEFITS** nonfinancial forms of compensation provided to employees, such as pension plans, health insurance, paid vacation and holidays

TABLE 11.8 Salary of 15 College Basketball Coaches and Their Performance

School	Coach	Guaranteed Salary (millions)	Winning Percentage at Current School
University of Florida	Billy Donovan	$3.3	71.2
University of Kansas	Bill Self	3.0	81.8
University of Memphis (accepted at Kentucky)	John Calipari	2.5	78.4
Ohio State University	Thad Matta	2.5	73.3
University of Louisville	Rick Pitino	2.25	72.9
Duke University	Mike Krzyzaweski	2.2	78.0
University of North Carolina	Roy Williams	2.0	82.4
University of Texas	Rick Barnes	2.0	72.2
UCLA	Ben Howland	1.97	74.1
Michigan State University	Tom Izzo	1.74	71.0

Source: "Do Millionaire Coaches Earn Their Money?" March 12, 2009, http://online.wsj.com/public/resources/documents/st_CoachesNCAAA_20090312.html (accessed June 2, 2009).

TABLE 11.9 Google's Employees' Benefits

- Health insurance:
  - Employee medical insurance (spouse and domestic-partner insurance also available)
  - Dental insurance
  - Vision insurance
- Vacation (15 days per year for one–three years' employment; 20 days off for four–five years' employment; 25 days for more than six years' employment)
- Twelve paid holidays/year
- Savings plans
  - 401(k) retirement plan, matched by Google up to $2,500/year
  - Flexible spending accounts
- Disability and life insurance
- Employee Assistance Program
- Free lunches, breakfast foods, and snacks
- Massages, gym membership, hair stylist, fitness class, and bike repair
- Weekly activities
- Maternity and parental leave
- Adoption assistance
- Tuition reimbursement
- Employee referral plan
- On-site doctor
- Google child care center and backup child care
- Ski trip, company movie day, summar picnic, health fair, credit union, sauna, roller hockey, discounts for local attractions

Source: "Google Benefits," www.google.com/support/jobs/bin/static.py?page=benefits.html (accessed March 23, 2009).

those costs, while benefits account for 30.2 percent. Legally required benefits (Social Security, Medicare, federal and state employment insurance, and workers' compensation) account for 7.9 percent of total compensation.[27] Such benefits increase employee security and, to a certain extent, their morale and motivation.

The Survey of Unit Employment Practices (SULEP) People Report found that among 75 restaurant industry companies, the average rate of employee turnover in companies that offer basic health, dental, or retirement benefits is 109 percent, compared with 136 percent for companies that do not offer any benefits to their employees.[28] Table 11.9 lists some of the benefits the Internet search engine Google offers its employees. Although health insurance is a common benefit for full-time employees, rising health care costs have forced a growing number of employers to trim this benefit. While still considered one of the best companies to work for, Microsoft was forced to cut benefits in order to trim costs. While prescrip-

In recent years, some single workers have felt that co-workers with spouses and children seem to get "special breaks" and extra time off to deal with family issues. Some companies use flexible benefit programs to allow employees to choose the benefits they would like, up to a specified amount. Over the last two decades, the list of fringe benefits has grown dramatically, and new benefits are being added every year.

 LO6

Discuss some of the issues associated with unionized employees, including collective bargaining and dispute resolution.

MANAGING UNIONIZED EMPLOYEES

Employees who are dissatisfied with their working conditions or compensation have to negotiate with management to bring about change. Dealing with management on an individual basis

> ❝ **The most common counseling services offered include drug and alcohol-abuse treatment programs, fitness programs, smoking cessation clinics, stress-management clinics, financial counseling, family counseling, and career counseling.** ❞

tion drug costs have gone up at Microsoft, the company still retains other such perks as subsidized gym memberships and free beverages on the job.[29]

A benefit increasingly offered is the employee assistance program (EAP). Each company's EAP is different, but most offer counseling for and assistance with employees' personal problems that might hurt their job performance if not addressed. The most common counseling services offered include drug and alcohol-abuse treatment programs, fitness programs, smoking cessation clinics, stress-management clinics, financial counseling, family counseling, and career counseling. EAPs help reduce costs associated with poor productivity, absenteeism, and other workplace issues by helping employees deal with personal problems that contribute to these issues. For example, exercise and fitness programs reduce health insurance costs by helping employees stay healthy. Family counseling may help workers trying to cope with a divorce or other personal problems better focus on their jobs.

Companies try to provide the benefits they believe their employees want, but different people may want different things.

is not always effective, however, so employees may organize themselves into **labor unions** to deal with employers and to achieve better pay, hours, and working conditions. Organized employees are backed by the power of a large group that can hire specialists to represent the entire union in its dealings with management. Union workers make significantly more than nonunion employees. Roughly 12 percent of the workforce is unionized. The national weekly median average income for a non-union service worker is $404, or $10 per hour, versus a union worker's wages of $629 per week, or $15 per hour. One of the more dramatic differences can be found in the construction industry, where unionized workers make nearly $10 per hour more.[30]

However, union growth has slowed in recent years, and prospects for growth do not look good. One reason is that most blue-collar workers, the traditional members of unions, have already been organized. Factories have become more automated and need fewer blue-collar workers. The United States has shifted from a manufacturing to a service economy, further reducing the demand for blue-collar workers.

Moreover, in response to foreign competition, U.S. companies are scrambling to find ways to become more productive and cost efficient. Job enrichment programs and participative management have blurred the line between management and workers. Because workers' say in the way plants are run is increasing, their need for union protection is decreasing.

Nonetheless, labor unions have been successful in organizing blue-collar manufacturing, government, and health care workers, as well as smaller percentages of employees in other industries. Consequently, significant aspects of HRM, particularly compensation, are dictated to a large degree by union contracts at many companies. Therefore, we'll take a brief look at collective bargaining and dispute resolution in this section.

● **COLLECTIVE BAR-GAINING** the negotiation process through which management and unions reach an agreement about compensation, working hours, and working conditions for the bargaining unit

● **LABOR CONTRACT** the formal, written document that spells out the relationship between the union and management for a specified period of time—usually two or three years

● **PICKETING** a public protest against management practices that involves union members marching and carrying antimanagement signs at the employer's plant

Collective Bargaining

Collective bargaining is the negotiation process through which management and unions reach an agreement about compensation, working hours, and working conditions for the bargaining unit (Figure 11.2). The objective of negotiations is to reach agreement about a **labor contract,** the formal, written document that spells out the relationship between the union and management for a specified period, usually two or three years.

In collective bargaining, each side tries to negotiate an agreement that meets its demands; compromise is frequently necessary. Management tries to negotiate a labor contract that permits the company to retain control over things like work schedules; the hiring and firing of workers; production standards; promotions, transfers, and separations; the span of management in each department; and discipline. Unions tend to focus on contract issues such as magnitude of wages; better pay rates for overtime, holidays, and undesirable shifts; scheduling of pay increases; and benefits. These issues will be spelled out in the labor contract, which union members will vote to either accept (and abide by) or reject.

Many labor contracts contain a *cost-of-living escalator clause (COLA),* which calls for automatic wage increases during periods of inflation to protect the "real" income of the employees. During tough economic times, unions may be forced to accept *givebacks*—wage and benefit concessions made to employers to allow them to remain competitive or, in some cases, to survive and continue to provide jobs for union workers.

Resolving Disputes

Sometimes management and labor simply cannot agree on a contract. Most labor disputes are handled through collective bargaining or through grievance procedures. When these processes break down, however, either side may resort to more drastic measures to achieve its objectives.

labor tactics Picketing is a public protest against management practices

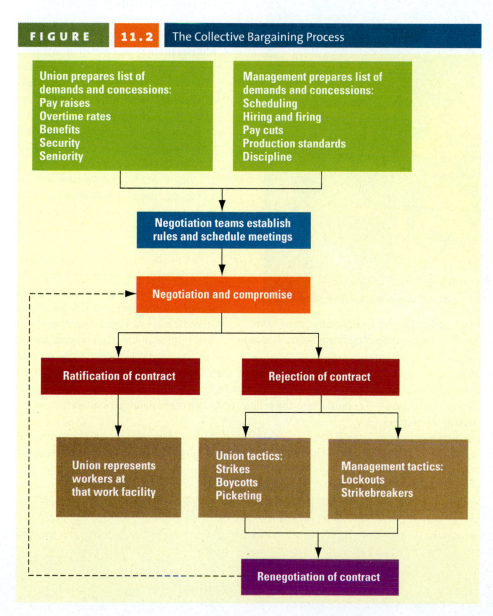

FIGURE 11.2 The Collective Bargaining Process

Union prepares list of demands and concessions:
Pay raises
Overtime rates
Benefits
Security
Seniority

Management prepares list of demands and concessions:
Scheduling
Hiring and firing
Pay cuts
Production standards
Discipline

Negotiation teams establish rules and schedule meetings

Negotiation and compromise

Ratification of contract

Rejection of contract

Union represents workers at that work facility

Union tactics:
Strikes
Boycotts
Picketing

Management tactics:
Lockouts
Strikebreakers

Renegotiation of contract

and involves union members marching (often waving antimanagement signs and placards) at the employer's plant. Picketing workers hope that their signs will arouse sympathy for their demands from the public and from other unions. Picketing may occur as a protest or in conjunction with a strike.

Strikes (employee walkouts) are one of the most effective weapons labor has. By striking, a union makes carrying out the normal operations of a business difficult at best and impossible at worst. Strikes receive widespread publicity, but they remain a weapon of last resort. In California, members of the United Food

for health insurance for the first time.[31] The threat of a strike is often enough to get management to back down. In fact, the number of worker-days actually lost to strikes is less than the amount lost to the common cold.

A boycott is an attempt to keep people from purchasing the products of a company. In a boycott, union members are asked not to do business with the boycotted organization. Some unions may even impose fines on members who ignore the boycott. To gain further support for their objectives, a union involved in a boycott may also ask the public—through picketing and advertising—not to purchase the products of the picketed firm.

management tactics

Management's version of a strike is the lockout; management actually closes a work site so that employees cannot go to work. Lockouts are used, as a general rule, only when a union strike has partially shut down a plant and it seems less expensive for the plant to close completely. In 2008, 15 major work stoppages involving 1,000 or more employees participating in strikes and lockouts idled 189,000 workers, with 1.27 million lost workdays.[32]

Strikebreakers, called "scabs" by striking union members, are people hired by management to replace striking employees. Managers hire strikebreakers to continue operations and reduce the losses associated with strikes—and to show the unions that

Employees have been known to do more than just strike. During an economic downturn, some French workers angered by job losses went so far as to hold their managers hostage.

and Commercial Workers (UFCW) went on strike against Albertson's, Ralph's, and Von's supermarkets after they failed to reach agreement on a new contract. The strike, which cost the companies millions of dollars in lost sales and the striking employees significant lost wages, ended when members agreed to ratify a new contract that gave them bonuses but required them to pay

they will not bow to their demands. Strikebreaking is generally a last-resort measure for management because it does great damage to the relationship between management and labor.

outside resolution
Management and union members normally reach mutually agreeable decisions without

Hon Hai Precision Industry Co. Inspires Loyalty in China

Terry Gou is a self-made billionaire thanks to his company, Hon Hai Precision Industry Co. in Taiwan, which produces plastic parts for black and white televisions. In 1988, Gou moved his factory to China and expanded into making parts for PCs as well as Apple's iPod and iPhone products, Hewlett-Packard computers, Motorola phones, and Wii consoles. Gou's factory in Shenzhen, China, has 270,000 employees and is the largest exporter in China, with revenues of over $55 billion. Gou has chosen to keep production in China, although it would be cheaper to move elsewhere. Gou is a leader inspiring loyalty, and Hon Hai has a good reputation for quality control and competitive pricing.[33] ❖

outside assistance. Sometimes though, even after lengthy negotiations, strikes, lockouts, and other tactics, management and labor still cannot resolve a contract dispute. In such cases, they have three choices: conciliation, mediation, and arbitration. **Conciliation** brings in a neutral third party to keep labor and management talking. The conciliator has no formal power over union representatives or over management. The conciliator's goal is to get both parties to focus on the issues and to prevent negotiations from breaking down. Like conciliation, **mediation** involves bringing in a neutral third party, but the mediator's role is to suggest or propose a solution to the problem. Mediators have no formal power over either labor or management. With **arbitration,** a neutral third party is brought in to settle the dispute, but the arbitrator's solution is legally binding and enforceable. Generally, arbitration takes place on a voluntary basis—management and labor must agree to it, and they usually split the cost (the arbitrator's fee and expenses) between them. Occasionally, management and labor submit to *compulsory arbitration,* in which an outside party (usually the federal government) requests arbitration as a means of eliminating a prolonged strike that threatens to disrupt the economy.

● ● **LO7**

Describe the importance of diversity in the workforce.

tation represent *primary characteristics* of diversity which are inborn and cannot be changed. In the upper section of Figure 11.3 are eight *secondary characteristics* of diversity—work background, income, marital status, military experience, religious beliefs, geographic location, parental status, and education—which *can* be changed. We acquire, change, and discard them as we progress through our lives.

Defining characteristics of diversity as either primary or secondary enhances our understanding, but we must remember that each person is defined by the interrelation of all characteristics. In dealing with diversity in the workforce, managers must consider the complete person—not one or a few of a person's differences.

Why Is Diversity Important?

The U.S. workforce is becoming increasingly diverse. Once dominated by white men, today's workforce includes significantly more women, African Americans, Hispanics, and other

● **MEDIATION** a method of outside resolution of labor and management differences in which the third party's role is to suggest or propose a solution to the problem

● **ARBITRATION** settlement of a labor/management dispute by a third party whose solution is legally binding and enforceable

● **DIVERSITY** the participation of different ages, genders, races, ethnicities, nationalities, and abilities in the workplace

THE IMPORTANCE OF WORKFORCE DIVERSITY

Customers, employees, suppliers—all the participants in the world of business—come in different ages, genders, races, ethnicities, nationalities, and abilities, a truth that business has come to label **diversity.** Understanding this diversity means recognizing and accepting differences as well as valuing the unique perspectives such differences can bring to the workplace.

The Characteristics of Diversity

When managers speak of diverse workforces, they typically mean differences in gender and race. While gender and race are important characteristics of diversity, others are also important. We can divide these differences into primary and secondary characteristics of diversity. In the lower segment of Figure 11.3, age, gender, race, ethnicity, abilities, and sexual orien-

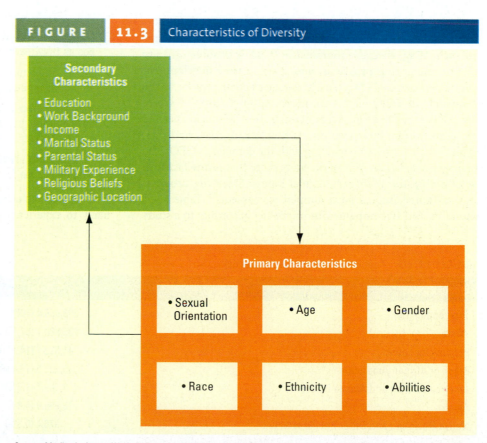

FIGURE 11.3 Characteristics of Diversity

Secondary Characteristics
- Education
- Work Background
- Income
- Marital Status
- Parental Status
- Military Experience
- Religious Beliefs
- Geographic Location

Primary Characteristics
- Sexual Orientation
- Age
- Gender
- Race
- Ethnicity
- Abilities

Source: Marilyn Loden and Judy B. Rosener, *Workforce America! Managing Employee Diversity as a Vital Resource,* 1991, p. 20. Used with permission. Copyright © 1991 The McGraw-Hill Companies.

minorities, as well as disabled and older workers. Women now make up 49.83% of the non-farm workforce, the closest ratio between men and women in history. However, women's wage remain lower than men and they are not proportionally represented among managers.[34] Table 11.10 presents some of the population data from the Census Bureau. It is estimated that within the next 50 years, Hispanics will represent 24 percent of the population, while African Americans and Asians/Pacific Islanders will account for 15 percent and 9 percent, respectively.[35] These groups have traditionally faced discrimination and higher unemployment rates and have been denied opportunities to assume leadership roles in corporate America. Consequently, more and more companies are trying to improve HRM programs to recruit, develop, and retain more diverse

by *Fortune*. Effectively managing diversity in the workforce involves cultivating and valuing its benefits and minimizing its problems.

The Benefits of Workforce Diversity

There are a number of benefits to fostering and valuing workforce diversity, including the following:

1. More productive use of a company's human resources.

2. Reduced conflict among employees of different ethnicities, races, religions, and sexual orientations as they learn to respect each other's differences.

> ## "Once dominated by white men, today's workforce includes significantly more women, African Americans, Hispanics, and other minorities, as well as disabled and older workers.

employees to better serve their diverse customers. Some firms are providing special programs such as sponsored affinity groups, mentoring programs, and special career development opportunities. At US West, each manager's contributions to the company's diversity efforts are measured by a 16-point scorecard called the Diversity Accountability Tool. Managers use the scorecard to rate their own efforts to foster diversity and then explain their scores in a meeting with the company's CEO. The manager receives an official diversity score that is one factor in determining the manager's annual bonus. Since the program was instituted, scores have jumped 60 percent.[36] Table 11.11 shows the top 10 companies for minorities according to a study

3. More productive working relationships among diverse employees as they learn more about and accept each other.

4. Increased commitment to and sharing of organizational goals among diverse employees at all organizational levels.

5. Increased innovation and creativity as diverse employees bring new, unique perspectives to decision-making and problem-solving tasks.

6. Increased ability to serve the needs of an increasingly diverse customer base.[37]

Companies that do not value their diverse employees are likely to experience greater conflict, as well as prejudice and

TABLE 11.10   Population by Race (in thousands)

Ethnic Group	Total	Increase from 2000 to 2004
Total population	293,655.4 (100%)	4.3%
White	239,880.1 (81.7%)	3.6
Hispanic or Latino	41,322.1 (14.1%)	17.0
Black or African American	39,232.5 (13.4%)	5.7
American Indian and Alaska Native	4,409.4 (1.5%)	7.7
Asian	13,956.6 (4.8%)	16.2
Native Hawaiian and Other Pacific Islander	976.4 (0.3%)	7.7

Source: "Population by Race and Hispanic Origin: 2000 and 2004," U.S. Census Bureau, Population Estimates Program, April 1, 2000, and July 1, 2004, www.census.gov/population/pop-profile/dynamic/RACEHO.pdf (updated February 2007, accessed March 23, 2009).

● **AFFIRMATIVE ACTION PROGRAMS** legally mandated plans that try to increase job opportunities for minority groups by analyzing the current pool of workers, identifying areas where women and minorities are underrepresented, and establishing specific hiring and promotion goals, with target dates, for addressing the discrepancy

discrimination. Among individual employees, for example, racial slurs and gestures, sexist comments, and other behaviors by co-workers harm the individuals at whom such behavior is directed. The victims of such behavior may feel hurt, depressed, or even threatened and suffer from lowered self-esteem, all of which harm their productivity and morale. In such cases, women and minority employees may simply leave the firm, wasting the time, money, and other resources spent on hiring and training them. When discrimination comes from a supervisor, employees may also fear for their jobs. A discriminatory atmosphere not only can harm productivity and increase turnover but also may subject a firm to costly lawsuits and negative publicity.

Astute businesses recognize that they need to modify their human resources management programs to target the needs of *all* their diverse employees as well as the needs of the firm itself. They realize that the benefits of diversity are long term in nature and come only to those organizations willing to make the commitment. Most important, as workforce diversity becomes a val-

ued organizational asset, companies spend less time managing conflict and more time accomplishing tasks and satisfying customers, which is, after all, the purpose of business.

Affirmative Action

Many companies strive to improve their working environment through **affirmative action programs,** legally mandated plans that try to increase job opportunities for minority groups by analyzing the current pool of workers, identifying areas where women and minorities are underrepresented, and establishing specific hiring and promotion goals along with target dates for meeting those goals to resolve the discrepancy. Affirmative action began in 1965 as Lyndon B. Johnson issued the first of a series of presidential directives. It was designed to make up for past hiring

> **"Astute businesses recognize that they need to modify their human resources management programs to target the needs of *all* their diverse employees as well as the needs of the firm itself."**

TABLE 11.11 Top 20 Companies for Diversity

1. Johnson & Johnson
2. AT&T
3. Ernst & Young
4. Marriott International
5. PricewaterhouseCoopers
6. Sodexo
7. Kaiser Permanente
8. Merck & Co.
9. Coca-Cola Co.
10. IBM Corp.
11. Procter & Gamble
12. Verizon Communications
13. American Express Co.
14. Bank of America
15. JPMorgan Chase
16. Abbot
17. Cox Communications
18. Pepsi Bottling Group
19. MGM MIRAGE
20. Novartis Pharmaceuticals Corp.

Source: "2009 DiversityInc Top 50 Companies for Diversity," www.diversityinc.com/public/department289.cfm (accessed March 24, 2009).

Managing human resources is a challenging and creative facet of a business. This is the department that handles the recruiting, hiring, training, and firing of employees. Because of the diligence and detail required in hiring and the sensitivity required in firing, human resources managers must have a broad skill set. Human resources therefore is vital to the overall functioning of the business because without the right staff a firm will not be able to carry out its plans effectively. As in basketball, a team is only as strong as its individual players, and those players must be able to work together to enhance strengths and downplay weaknesses. In addition, a good human resources manager can anticipate upcoming needs and changes in the business, hiring in line with the dynamics of the market and the organization.

Once a good workforce is in place, human resources managers must ensure that employees are properly trained and oriented and clearly understand some elements of what the organization expects. Since hiring new people is expensive, time-consuming, and turbulent, it is imperative that all employees be carefully selected, trained, and motivated so that they will remain committed and loyal to the company. This is not an easy task, but it is one of the responsibilities of a human resources manager. Because even with references, a résumé, background checks, and an interview it can be hard to tell how a person will fit in the organization, the HR manager needs to have the ability to anticipate how every individual will "fit in." Human resources jobs include compensation, labor relations, benefits, training, ethics, and compliance managers. All the tasks associated with the interface with hiring, developing, and maintaining employee motivation come into play in human resources management. Jobs are diverse, and salaries depend on responsibilities, education, and experience.

One of the major considerations for an HR manager is workforce diversity. A multicultural, multiethnic workforce consisting of men and women will help bring a variety of viewpoints and improve the quality and creativity of organizational decision making. Diversity is an asset and can help a company avoid having blind spots or too much harmony in thought, background, and perspective, which stifles good team decisions. However, a diverse workforce can present some management challenges. Human resources management is often responsible for managing diversity training and compliance to make sure employees do not violate the ethical culture of the organization or break the law. Different people have different goals, motivations, and ways of thinking about issues that are informed by their culture, their religion, and the people closest to them. No one way of thinking is more right or more wrong than others, and they are all valuable. A human resources manager's job can become very complicated, however, because of diversity. To be good at human resources, you should be aware the value of differences, strive to be culturally sensitive, and ideally have a strong understanding and appreciation of different cultures and religions. The ability to manage diversity and those differences will affect your overall career success.

and promotion prejudices, overcome workplace discrimination, and provide equal employment opportunities for blacks and whites. Since then, minorities have made solid gains.

Legislation passed in 1991 reinforces affirmative action but prohibits organizations from setting hiring quotas that might result in reverse discrimination. Reverse discrimination occurs when a company's policies force it to consider only minorities or women instead of concentrating on hiring the person who is best qualified. More companies are arguing that affirmative action stifles their ability to hire the best employees, regardless of their minority status. Because of these problems, affirmative action became politically questionable in the mid-1990s. ∎

Team Exercise

Form groups and go to monster.com to look up job descriptions for positions in business (account executive in advertising, marketing manager, human resources director, production supervisor, financial analyst, bank teller, etc.). What are the key requirements for the position you have been assigned (education, work experience, language/computer skills, etc.)? Does the position announcement provide a thorough understanding of the job? Was any key information that you would have expected omitted? Report your findings to the class.

CHECK OUT www.mhhe.com/FerrellM2e

for study materials including Interactive Exercises, Quizzes, iPod downloads, and video.

CUSTOMER-DRIVEN MARKETING

CHAPTER TWELVE

Introduction Marketing involves planning and executing the development, pricing, promotion, and distribution of ideas, goods, and services to create exchanges that satisfy individual and organizational goals. These activities ensure that the products consumers want to buy are available at a price they are willing to pay and that consumers are provided with information about product features and availability. Organizations of all sizes and objectives engage in these activities.

In this chapter, we focus on the basic principles of marketing. First we define and examine the nature of marketing. Then we look at how marketers develop marketing strategies to satisfy the needs and wants of their customers. Next we discuss buying behavior and how marketers use research to determine what consumers want to buy and why. Finally we explore the impact of the environment on marketing activities.

● **MARKETING** a group of activities designed to expedite transactions by creating, distributing, pricing, and promoting goods, services, and ideas

● **EXCHANGE** the act of giving up one thing (money, credit, labor, goods) in return for something else (goods, services, or ideas)

LO1

Define marketing and describe the exchange process.

NATURE OF MARKETING

A vital part of any business undertaking, **marketing** is a group of activities designed to expedite transactions by creating, distributing, pricing, and promoting goods, services, and ideas. These activities create value by allowing individuals and organizations to obtain what they need and want. A business cannot achieve its objectives unless it provides something that customers value. Nike, for example, has created the Nike Plus system, which combines Nike's popular footwear with Apple's extremely successful iPod. For $29, users can buy the Nike Plus iPod kit, which includes a sensor that can be inserted in the bottom of a Nike Plus–equipped shoe, along with a receiver that is attached to an iPod Nano. When installed, the kit measures a runner's speed, Calories burned, and distance run.[1] But just creating an innovative product that meets many users' needs isn't sufficient in today's volatile global marketplace. Products must be conveniently available, competitively priced, and uniquely promoted.

Of all the business concepts covered in this text, marketing may be the hardest for organizations to master. Businesses try to respond to consumer wants and needs and to anticipate changes in the environment. Unfortunately, it is difficult to understand and predict what consumers want: Motives are often unclear; few principles can be applied consistently; and markets tend to fragment, desiring customized products, new value, or better service.

It is important to note what marketing is not: It is not manipulating consumers to get them to buy products they don't want. It is not just selling and advertising; it is a systematic approach to satisfying consumers. Marketing focuses on the many activities—planning, pricing, promoting, and distributing products—that foster exchanges.

> **A business cannot achieve its objectives unless it provides something that customers value.**

The Exchange Relationship

At the heart of all business is the **exchange,** the act of giving up one thing (money, credit, labor, goods) in return for something else (goods, services, or ideas). Businesses exchange their goods, services, or ideas for money or credit supplied by customers in a voluntary *exchange relationship,* as illustrated in Figure 12.1. The buyer must feel good about the purchase, or the exchange will not continue. If your local dry cleaner cleans your nice suit properly, on time, and without damage, you will probably feel good about using its services. But if your suit is damaged or isn't ready on time, you probably will use another dry cleaner next time.

For an exchange to occur, certain conditions are required. As indicated by the arrows in Figure 12.1, buyers and sellers must be able to communicate about the "something of value" available to each. An exchange does not necessarily take place just because buyers and sellers have something of value to exchange. Each participant must be willing to give up his or her respective "something of value" to receive the "something" held by the other. You are willing to exchange your "something of value"— your money or credit—for compact discs, soft drinks, football tickets, or new shoes because you consider those products more valuable or more important than holding on to your cash or credit potential.

When you think of marketing products, you may think of tangible things—cars, stereo systems, or books, for example. What most consumers want, however, is a way to get a job done, solve a problem, or gain some enjoyment. You may purchase a Hoover vacuum cleaner not because you want a vacuum cleaner

Martha Stewart tries to facilitate the "exchange relationship" with hundreds of thousands of her customers by tweeting them daily about her company's products and promotional events, such as her book signings.

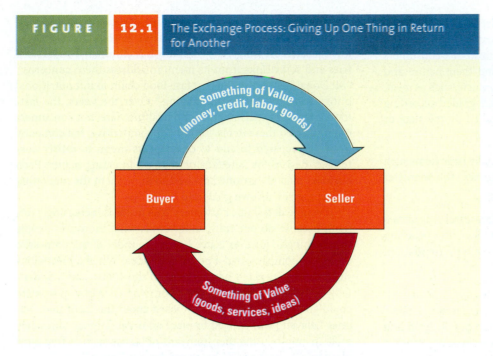

Functions of Marketing

Marketing focuses on a complex set of activities that must be performed to accomplish objectives and generate exchanges. These activities include buying, selling, transporting, storing, grading, financing, marketing research, and risk taking.

buying Everyone who shops for products (consumers, stores, businesses, governments) decides whether and what to buy. A marketer must understand buyers' needs and desires to determine what products to make available.

selling The exchange process is expedited through selling. Marketers usually view selling as a persuasive activity that is accomplished through promotion (advertising, personal selling, sales promotion, publicity, and packaging).

but because you want clean carpets. Starbucks provides coffee drinks at a premium price, providing convenience, quality, and an inviting environment. Therefore, the tangible product itself may not be as important as the image or the benefits associated with the product. This intangible "something of value" may be capability gained from using a product or the image evoked by it, such as "7 For all Mankind" jeans, which can sell for over $200 a pair.

 L02

Specify the functions of marketing.

transporting Transporting is the process of moving products from the seller to the buyer. Marketers focus on transportation costs and services.

storing Like transporting, storing is part of the physical distribution of products and includes warehousing goods. Warehouses hold some products for lengthy periods in order to create time utility. Consumers want frozen orange juice year-round, for example, although the production season for oranges is only a few months out of the year. This means that sellers must arrange cold storage for frozen orange juice concentrate all year.

Recycling Plastic Bags for Fashion

Every year 500 billion to 1 trillion plastic bags are consumed globally. The United States alone consumes around 88 billion plastic bags a year, with the average family using 1,460, the production of which takes 12 million barrels of oil. Less than 1 percent of these bags are recycled. Plastic bags take over 1,000 years to photodegrade fully, and as they break down, harmful gases are released into the environment. This disregard for plastic bag recycling represents a pollution crisis of global magnitude.

As a response, many fashionable and environmentally conscious people are promoting high-style reusable totes made from plastic bags. Anita Ahuja, known as "the bag lady," heads an organization that takes plastic bags and recycles them into stylish, low-priced handbags. Based in Delhi, India, Ahuja employs hundreds of garbage pickers, who give her material for her bags along with cleaning up Delhi's streets. Anita donates some of her profits to charities, such as starting a school for her employees' children, as she tries to break out into the fashion world.

Plastic bags also are being made into other fashion accessories. One artist in Australia uses plastic bags and other plastic containers to make jewelry such as rings and brooches. Another idea some designers have had is to use plastic shopping bags to create a synthetic fabric. In this way, raincoats, purses, and even dresses have been created from reused plastic shopping bags. Designers are lending an air of exclusivity and desirability to being eco-friendly, causing used plastic bag accessories to be a new fashion statement.[2] ❖

Q: **Discussion Questions**

1. What kinds of consumers are the designers discussed above targeting?

2. What might be some good marketing strategies to encourage the use of reusable bags?

3. What other green fashion movements could benefit from the promotional efforts of these canvas bag designers?

grading   Grading refers to standardizing products and displaying and labeling them so that consumers clearly understand their nature and quality. Many products, such as meat, steel, and fruit, are graded according to a set of standards that often are established by the state or federal government.

financing   For many products, especially large items such as automobiles, refrigerators, and new homes, the marketer arranges credit to expedite the purchase.

marketing research   Through research, marketers ascertain the need for new goods and services. By gathering information regularly, marketers can detect new trends and changes in consumer tastes.

risk taking   Risk is the chance of loss associated with marketing decisions. Developing a new product creates a chance of loss if consumers do not like it enough to buy it. Spending money to hire a sales force or to conduct marketing research also involves risk. The implication of risk is that most marketing decisions result in either success or failure.

  LO3

Explain the marketing concept and its implications for developing marketing strategies.

The Marketing Concept

A basic philosophy that guides all marketing activities is the **marketing concept,** the idea that an organization should try to satisfy customers' needs through coordinated activities that

choices; in addition to offering grilled chicken, fruit and walnut salads, reduced-fat ice cream, fruit 'n yogurt parfait, and low-fat salad dressings, the company has eliminated supersized fries and soft drinks from its menu to address these concerns.[3] "McDonald's was also the first fast-food chain to put nutritional information on its food packaging.[4] Over the years, the fast-food giant has experimented with healthier fare, but consumers often rejected these items. To remain competitive, the company must be prepared to add to or adapt its menu to satisfy customers' desires for new fads or changes in eating habits. Each business must determine how best to implement the marketing concept, given its own goals and resources.

Trying to determine customers' true needs is increasingly difficult because no one fully understands what motivates people to buy things. However, Estée Lauder, founder of her namesake cosmetics company, had a pretty good idea. When a prestigious store in Paris rejected her perfume in the 1960s, she "accidentally" dropped a bottle on the floor, where nearby customers could get a whiff of it. So many asked about the scent that Galeries Lafayette was obliged to place an order. Lauder ultimately built an empire using then-unheard-of tactics such as free samples and gifts with purchases to market her "jars of hope."

Although customer satisfaction is the goal of the marketing concept, a business also must achieve its own objectives, such as boosting productivity, reducing costs, or achieving a percentage of a specific market. If it does not, it will not survive. For example, Dell could sell computers for $100 and give customers a lifetime guarantee, which would be great for customers but not so great for Dell. Obviously, the company must strike a balance between achieving organizational objectives and satisfying customer needs and wants.

To implement the marketing concept, a firm must have good information about what consumers want, adopt a consumer orientation, and coordinate its efforts throughout the organization; otherwise, it may be awash with goods, services, and ideas that

> ❝ **According to the marketing concept, a business must find out what consumers need and want and then develop the good, service, or idea that fulfills their needs or wants.** ❞

also allow it to achieve its own goals. According to the marketing concept, a business must find out what consumers need and want and then develop the good, service, or idea that fulfills their needs or wants. The business then must get the product to the customer. In addition, the business must continually alter, adapt, and develop products to keep pace with changing consumer needs and wants. McDonald's, as already mentioned, faces increasing pressure to provide more healthful fast-food

consumers do not want or need. Successfully implementing the marketing concept requires that a business view customer value as the ultimate measure of work performance and improving value, and the rate at which this is done, as the measure of success.[5] Everyone in the organization who interacts with customers—*all* customer-contact employees—must know what customers want. They are selling ideas, benefits, philosophies, and experiences—not just goods and services.

Someone once said that if you build a better mousetrap, the world will beat a path to your door. Suppose you do build a better mousetrap. What will happen? Actually, consumers are not likely to beat a path to your door because the market is too competitive. A coordinated effort by everyone involved with the mousetrap is needed to sell the product. Your company must reach out to customers and tell them about your mousetrap, especially how your mousetrap works better than those offered by competitors. If you do not make the benefits of your product widely known, in most cases, it will not be successful. Consider Apple's 208 national and international retail stores, which market computers and electronics in a way unlike any other computer manufacturer or retail store. The upscale stores, located in high-rent shopping districts, show off Apple's products in sparse, stylish settings to encourage consumers to try new things—like making a movie on a computer. The stores also offer special events such as concerts and classes to give customers ideas on how to maximize their use of Apple's products. You must also find—or create—stores willing to sell your mousetrap to consumers. You must implement the marketing concept by making a product with satisfying benefits and making it available and visible.

Wrigley's originally gave gum away to promote its baking powder. The company continues to reorient and reinvent itself. In 2008, it merged with the candy maker Mars.

However, businesspeople are not always focused on customers when they create and operate businesses. Many companies fail to grasp the importance of customer relationships and fail to implement customer strategies. A survey indicated that only 46 percent of executives believe that their firm is committed to

> ## "Our society and economic system have changed over time, and marketing has become more important as markets have become more competitive."

Orville Wright said that an airplane is "a group of separate parts flying in close formation." This is what most companies are trying to accomplish: They are striving for a team effort to deliver the right good or service to customers. A breakdown at any point in the organization—whether in production, purchasing, sales, distribution, or advertising—can result in lost sales, lost revenue, and dissatisfied customers.

Evolution of the Marketing Concept

The marketing concept may seem like the obvious approach to running a business and building relationships with customers.

customers, but 67 percent of executives frequently meet with customers.[6] Our society and economic system have changed over time, and marketing has become more important as markets have become more competitive.

the production orientation During the second half of the 19th century, the Industrial Revolution was well under way in the United States. New technologies such as electricity, railroads, internal combustion engines, and mass-production techniques made it possible to manufacture goods with ever-increasing efficiency. Together with new management ideas and ways of using labor, products poured into the marketplace, where demand for manufactured goods was strong.

Samantha Daniels Is Matchmaker to the Wealthy

Originally a divorce attorney from Pennsylvania, Samantha Daniels changed course to become a matchmaker for Los Angeles and New York's wealthy singles. While Daniels remains single, she has had great success finding love for some of the country's richest and most influential individuals. She takes a very hands-on approach and says that her number one concern is finding the right match for her clients. She strategically matches individuals and brings them together over drinks, at exclusive events, or in trendy venues. In case you're wondering how this setup works, a potential client pays around $500 for a two-hour initial consultation. She likes to conduct the initial meetings in public to observe her clients' behavioral patterns. Each client is asked to supply information about ex-spouses, homes, and finances and to fill out a prepared questionnaire. If the deal goes further, Daniels charges anywhere from $25,000 to $50,000 to provide dates, coaching, personal shopping, and styling advice. Although this might sound like a strange way to find love, Daniels says that business is booming, with around 200 requests for help daily.[7] ❖

the sales orientation

By the early part of the 20th century, supply caught up with and then exceeded demand, and businesspeople began to realize they would have to "sell" products to buyers. During the first half of the 20th century, businesspeople viewed sales as the major means of increasing profits, and this period came to have a sales orientation. They believed the most important marketing activities were personal selling and advertising. Today some people still inaccurately equate marketing with a sales orientation.

the marketing orientation

By the 1950s, some businesspeople began to recognize that even efficient production and extensive promotion did not guarantee sales. These businesses, and many others since, found that they must first determine what customers want and then produce it rather than making the products first and then trying to persuade customers that they need them. Managers at General Electric first suggested that the marketing concept was a companywide philosophy of doing business. As more organizations realized the importance of satisfying customers' needs, U.S. businesses entered the marketing era, one with a marketing orientation.

A **marketing orientation** requires organizations to gather information about customer needs, share that information throughout the firm, and use that information to help build long-term relationships with customers. Top executives, marketing managers, nonmarketing managers (those in production, finance, human resources, and so on), and customers all become mutually dependent and cooperate in developing and carrying out a marketing orientation. Nonmarketing managers must communicate with marketing managers to share information important to understanding the customer. Consider the 118-year history of Wrigley's gum. In 1891 it was given away to promote sales of baking powder. Gum was launched as a product in 1893, and after four generations of Wrigley family CEOs, the company continues to reinvent itself and focus on consumers. The family sold the company to Mars. Wrigley now functions as a stand-alone subsidiary of Mars. The deal combined such popular brands as Wrigley's gums and Life Savers with Mars's M&Ms, Snickers and Skittles to form the world's largest confectionary company.[8]

Trying to assess what customers want, which is difficult to begin with, is further complicated by the rate at which trends, fashions, and tastes can change. Businesses today want to satisfy customers and build meaningful long-term relationships with them. It is more efficient to retain existing customers and even increase the amount of business each customer provides the organization than to find new customers. Most companies' success depends on increasing the amount of repeat business. As we saw in Chapter 4, many companies are turning to technologies associated with customer relationship management to help build relationships and boost business with existing customers.

Communication remains a major element of any strategy to develop and manage long-term customer relationships. By providing multiple points of interactions with customers—that is, Web sites, telephone, fax, e-mail, and personal contact—companies can personalize customer relationships. Like many online retailers, Amazon.com stores and analyzes purchase data to understand each customer's interests. This information helps the retailer improve its ability to satisfy individual customers and thereby increase sales of books, music, movies, and other products to each customer. The ability to identify individual customers allows marketers to shift their focus from targeting groups of similar customers to increasing their share of an individual customer's purchases. Regardless of the medium through which communication occurs, customers ultimately should be the drivers of marketing strategy because they understand what they want. Customer relationship management systems should ensure that marketers listen to customers to respond to their needs and concerns and build long-term relationships.

 L04

Examine the development of a marketing strategy, including market segmentation and marketing mix.

DEVELOPING A MARKETING STRATEGY

To implement the marketing concept and customer relationship management, a business needs to develop and maintain a **marketing strategy,** a plan of action for developing, pricing, distributing, and promoting products that meet the needs of specific customers. This definition has two major components: selecting a target market and developing an appropriate marketing mix to satisfy that target market.

Selecting a Target Market

A **market** is a group of people who have a need, purchasing power, and the desire and authority to spend money on goods, services, and ideas. A **target market** is a more specific group of consumers on whose needs and wants a company focuses its marketing efforts. Dell targets kindergarten to eighth-grade students with its notebook computers, which sell at very low prices. The computers are brightly colored with a grippable rubber surface. A light on the lid of the computer informs teachers if students are online.[9]

Marketing managers may define a target market as a relatively small number of people, or they may define it as the total market (Figure 12.2). Ferrari, for example, targets its products at a small, very exclusive, high-income market—people who want the ultimate in prestige in an automobile. General Motors, by contrast, manufactures vehicles ranging from the Aveo to Cadillac to GMC trucks in an attempt to appeal to varied tastes, needs, and desires. Likewise, the Gap, Inc., owns the Gap, Old Navy, Banana Republic, and Piperlime.

Some firms use a **total-market approach** in which they try to appeal to everyone and assume that all buyers have similar needs and wants. Sellers of salt, sugar, and many agricultural products use a total-market approach because everyone is a potential consumer of these products. Most firms, though, use **market segmentation** and divide the total market into groups of people who have relatively similar product needs. A **market segment** is a collection of individuals, groups, or organizations that share one or more characteristics and thus have relatively similar product needs and desires. Women over age 55 are the fastest-growing demographic or segment on Facebook. Woman overall are the largest market segment in the United States.[10] At the household level, segmentation can unlock each consumer's social, cultural, and stage in life to determine preferences and needs. One market segment that many marketers are focusing on is the growing Hispanic population. Staples gained a footing in the Hispanic market with a program called Exito Empressarial (Business Success) for small business owners. It is a seminar program to learn about accounting, taxes, and running a small business.[11] Table 12.1 shows the buying power and market share

● **MARKET SEGMENTATION** a strategy whereby a firm divides the total market into groups of people who have relatively similar product needs

● **MARKET SEGMENT** a collection of individuals, groups, or organizations that share one or more characteristics and thus have relatively similar product needs and desires

● **CONCENTRATION APPROACH** a market segmentation approach whereby a company develops one marketing strategy for a single market segment

percentages of four market segments. Companies use market segmentation to focus their efforts and resources on specific target markets so that they can develop a productive marketing strategy. Two common approaches to segmenting markets are the concentration approach and the multisegment approach.

market segmentation approaches In the **concentration approach,** a company develops one marketing strategy for a single market segment. The concentration approach allows a firm to specialize, focusing all its efforts on the one market segment. Porsche, for example, focuses all its marketing efforts on high-income individuals who want to

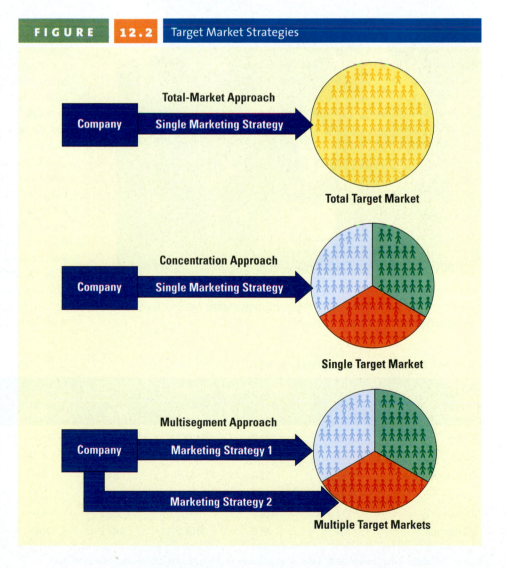

FIGURE 12.2 Target Market Strategies

Total-Market Approach

Company — Single Marketing Strategy → Total Target Market

Concentration Approach

Company — Single Marketing Strategy → Single Target Market

Multisegment Approach

Company — Marketing Strategy 1 / Marketing Strategy 2 → Multiple Target Markets own high-performance vehicles. A firm can generate a large sales volume by penetrating a single market segment deeply. The concentration approach may be especially effective when a firm can identify and develop products for a particular segment ignored by other companies in the industry.

In the **multisegment approach,** the marketer aims its marketing efforts at two or more segments, developing a marketing strategy for each. Many firms use a multisegment approach that includes different advertising messages for different segments. The U.S. Post Office, for example, offers personalized stamps; clothing company J. Crew sells jeans customization kits; various on-demand television services ensure that consumers watch only what they want to watch; and the LEGO toy company offers a service through its Web site by which children can design their own sets.[12] Companies also develop product variations to appeal to different market segments. For example, Samsung has widened its range of smartphones to appeal to the high-end and lower-end consumer. The company offers models for those who want a smartphone with the maximum capabilities. However,

> ## "A firm can generate a large sales volume by penetrating a single market segment deeply."

J&D Foods caters to the niche group of bacon lovers. Started as a lark by a couple of tech employees, the company makes bacon-flavored mayonnaise, salt, and even lip balm.

Samsung has also developed an ultra cheap model targeted at developing countries, where consumers have not traditionally been able to afford smartphones.[13] Many other firms also attempt to use a multisegment approach to market segmentation. The manufacturer of Raleigh bicycles uses a multisegment approach and has designed separate marketing strategies for racers, tourers, commuters, and children.

Niche marketing is a narrow market segment focus when efforts are on one small, well-defined segment that has a unique, specific set of needs. Catering to ice cream "addicts" and people who crave new, exotic flavors, several companies are selling ice cream on the Internet. This niche represents only a fraction of the $20.3 billion a year ice cream business, but online sales at some of the biggest makers increased 30 percent in just one year. Some of the firms focusing on this market are IceCreamSource.com, Nuts About Ice Cream, and Graeter's.[14]

TABLE 12.1 Minority Buying Power by Race

Category	Buying Power (billions)				% Market Share			
	1990	2000	2008	2013	1990	2000	2008	2013
White	3,816.2	6,231.2	9,135.7	11,796.0	89.4	86.7	85.2	84.2
Black	318.1	590.2	913.1	1,239.5	7.4	8.2	8.5	8.8
American Indian	19.7	39.0	61.8	84.6	0.5	0.5	0.6	0.6
Asian	116.5	268.8	509.1	752.3	2.7	3.7	4.7	5.4
Hispanic	211.9	489.5	951.0	1,386.2	5.0	6.8	8.9	9.9
Multiracial	NA	58.3	101.2	141.2	NA	0.8	0.9	1.0

Source: "The Multicultural Economy 2008," www.selig.uga.edu/BuyingPower/BuyPwr.pdf (accessed March 24, 2009).

For a firm to use a concentration or multisegment approach to market segmentation successfully, several requirements must be met:

1. Consumers' needs for the product must be heterogeneous.
2. The segments must be identifiable and divisible.
3. The total market must be divided in a way that allows the estimated sales potential, cost, and profits of the segments to be compared.
4. At least one segment must have enough profit potential to justify developing and maintaining a special marketing strategy.
5. The firm must be able to reach the chosen market segment with a particular market strategy.

bases for segmenting markets

Companies segment markets on the basis of several variables:

1. *Demographic*—age, sex, race, ethnicity, income, education, occupation, family size, religion, social class. These characteristics are often closely related to customers' product needs and purchasing behavior, and they can be readily measured. For example, deodorants are often segmented by sex: Secret and Soft n' Dry for women; Old Spice and Mennen for men.
2. *Geographic*—climate, terrain, natural resources, population density, subcultural values. These influence consumers' needs and product usage. Climate, for example, influences consumers' purchases of clothing, automobiles, heating and air-conditioning equipment, and leisure activity equipment.
3. *Psychographic*—personality characteristics, motives, lifestyles. Soft-drink marketers provide their products in several types of packaging, including two-liter bottles and cases of cans, to satisfy different lifestyles and motives.
4. *Behavioristic*—some characteristic of the consumer's behavior toward the product. These characteristics commonly involve some aspect of product use.

Developing a Marketing Mix

The second step in developing a marketing strategy is to create and maintain a satisfying marketing mix. The **marketing mix** refers to four marketing activities—product, price, distribution, and promotion—that the firm can control to achieve specific goals within a dynamic marketing environment. (Figure 12.3) The buyer or the target market is the central focus of all marketing activities.

product

A product—whether a good, a service, an idea, or some combination—is a complex mix of tangible and intangible attributes that provide satisfaction and benefits. A *good* is a physical entity you can touch. A Porsche Cayenne, an iPhone, a Hewlett-Packard printer, and a kitten available for adoption at an animal shelter are examples of goods. A *service* is the application of human and mechanical efforts to people or objects to provide intangible benefits to customers. Air travel, dry cleaning, haircuts, banking, insurance, medical care, and day care are examples of services. *Ideas* include concepts, philosophies, images, and issues. For instance, an attorney, for a fee, may advise you about what rights you have if the IRS decides to audit your tax return. Other marketers of ideas include political parties, churches, and schools.

A product has emotional and psychological as well as physical characteristics and includes everything that the buyer receives from an exchange. This definition includes supporting services such as installation, guarantees, product information, and promises of repair. Products usually have both favorable and unfavorable attributes; therefore, almost every purchase or exchange involves trade-offs as consumers try to maximize their benefits and satisfaction and minimize unfavorable attributes.

● **MARKETING MIX** the four marketing activites—product, price, promotion, and distribution—that the firm can control to achieve specific goals within a dynamic marketing environment

Apple and Phinnaeus or Julie and David: What's in a Name?

With celebrities naming their children Tallulah Belle, Apple, and Phinnaeus, many expectant parents feel pressure to come up with interesting names for their kids. Maryanna Korwitts has developed a business around the national concern for picking the right name. She believes that a name can endow people with certain personality traits. Korwitts is a self-designated nameologist. She studies names and how they may affect people's lives. She even changed her own name from Mary Ann, which she thought caused her to be a procrastinator overly concerned with others' opinions of her, to Maryanna, a name she says has helped her become more balanced.

Korwitts started off as a schoolteacher. Over time, she noticed similarities among students who had the same name. For example, Julies tended to lose things and Davids tended to be studious. Intrigued, Korwitts began studying naming practices in ancient and traditional cultures. She found that many cultures gave great thought to naming individuals. They even changed names to bring about improvements in a person's life. Korwitts ended up starting Name Structures. Today, she writes books, lectures, makes television appearances, and provides consultations.

Parents who feel stressed about finding the perfect names for their children can pay $399 for a copy of Korwitts's book *Name Power 101*, five online *BABYtalk* profiles of top name choices, three 30-minute phone consultations, and a personalized *Name Owner's Manual* for the baby. During the consultations, Korwitts discusses possible first and middle names on the basis of the positive or negative influences they may have on a child's personality, life, and family dynamic. For believers in nameology, Korwitts is there to help fill their naming needs.[15] ❖

Q: Discussion Questions

1. What business opportunity has Maryanna Korwitts identified and taken advantage of, and was the founding of her business customer-driven?
2. What is Korwitts's target market?
3. What kinds of companies or products would represent competitive threats to Korwitts's business?

FIGURE 12.3 The Marketing Mix: Product, Price, Promotion, and Distribution

Product

Customer

Promotion

Price

Distribution

Marketing Environment

Products are among a firm's most visible contacts with consumers. If they do not meet consumer needs and expectations, sales will be difficult and product life spans will be brief. The product is an important variable—often the central focus—of the marketing mix; the other variables (price, promotion, and distribution) must be coordinated with product decisions.

price Almost anything can be assessed by a **price,** a value placed on an object exchanged between a buyer and a seller. Although the seller usually establishes the price, it may be negotiated between buyer and seller. The buyer usually exchanges purchasing power—income, credit, wealth—for the satisfaction or utility associated with a product. Because financial price is the measure of value commonly used in an exchange, it quantifies value and is the basis of most market exchanges.

Marketers view price as much more than a way of assessing value, however. It is a key element of the marketing mix because it relates directly to the generation of revenue and profits. Prices can also be changed quickly to stimulate demand or respond to competitors' actions. Sudden increases or decreases in the price of commodities can have strong impact on the consumer demand for goods and services. For example, when the cost of oil increases, consumers tend to alter their gas consumption habits by driving and flying less, or even purchasing a more fuel efficient vehicle. However, when fuel prices drop people are less concerned about their consumption of gas and tend to drive more. Demand for fuel-efficient vehicles like the Ford Focus or

DID YOU KNOW?

During its first year of operation, sales of Coca-Cola averaged just nine drinks per day for total first-year sales of $50. Today, Coca-Cola products are consumed at the rate of 1.6 billion servings per day.[16]

Chevy Aveo are affected by these fluctuations in the price of the commodity petroleum.

distribution **Distribution** (sometimes referred to as "place" because it helps to remember the marketing mix as the "4 Ps") is making products available to customers in the quantities desired. Blockbuster realizes that its distribution network has to change for the company to stay competitive. People are less likely to drive to pick up DVDs when they have the option to receive them in the mail or watch them online. Because of this, the company has altered the way it distributes movies and video games.[17] To better compete with companies like Netflix and cable's on-demand services, Blockbuster has gone online. It now battles Netflix on its own territory by offering a combination mail order and online video and game rental business. Intermediaries, usually wholesalers and retailers, perform many of the activities required to move products efficiently from producers to consumers or industrial buyers. These activities involve transporting, warehousing, materials handling, and inventory control, as well as packaging and communication.

Critics who suggest that eliminating wholesalers and other middlemen would result in lower prices for consumers do not recognize that eliminating intermediaries would not do away with the need for their services. Other institutions would have to perform those services, and consumers would still have to pay for them. In addition, in the absence of wholesalers, all producers would have to deal directly with retailers or customers, keeping voluminous records and hiring people to deal with customers.

promotion Promotion is a persuasive form of communication that attempts to expedite a marketing exchange by influencing individuals, groups, and organizations to accept goods, services, and ideas. Promotion includes advertising, personal selling, publicity, and sales promotion, all of which we will look at more closely in Chapter 13.

The aim of promotion is to communicate directly or indirectly with individuals, groups, and organizations to facilitate exchanges. When marketers use advertising and other forms of promotion, they must effectively manage their promotional resources and understand product and target-market characteristics to ensure that these promotional activities contribute to the firm's objectives. Increases in gas prices can provide some companies with promotional opportunities. For example, Callaway Golf offered an

Promotions can take interesting twists. In 2009, Australia's Queensland Islands garnered millions of dollars in free publicity via a "Best Job in the World" contest. The winner, a Brit whose "job" it was to be the islands' "caretaker," received $150,000 and six months rent-free on the beautiful islands.

"The aim of promotion is to communicate directly or indirectly with individuals, groups, and organizations to facilitate exchanges."

"Increase Your Driving Distance" giveaway in which customers are eligible to win a $100 gas card with the purchase of certain golf clubs.[18]

Most major companies have set up Web sites on the Internet to promote themselves and their products. The home page for Betty Crocker, for example, offers recipes; meal planning; the company's history; descriptions of its 200 products; online shopping for complementary items such as dinnerware, linens, and gifts; and the ability to print a shopping list based on recipes chosen or ingredients on hand in the consumer's kitchen. The Web sites for The Gap and Old Navy provide consumers with the opportunity to purchase clothing and other items from the convenience of their homes or offices. Some sites, however, simply promote a company's products but do not offer them for sale online.

 LO5

Investigate how marketers conduct marketing research, and study buying behavior.

MARKETING RESEARCH AND INFORMATION SYSTEMS

Before marketers can develop a marketing mix, they must collect in-depth, up-to-date information about customer needs. **Marketing research** is a systematic, objective process of getting information about potential customers to guide marketing decisions. Such information may include data about the age, income, ethnicity, gender, and educational level of people in the target market; their preferences for product features; their attitudes toward competitors' products; and the frequency with which they use the product. For example, Toyota's marketing research on Generation Y drivers (born between 1977 and 1994) found that they practically live in their cars, and many even keep a change of clothes handy in their vehicles. As a result of this research, Toyota designed its Scion as a "home on wheels" with a 15-volt outlet for plugging in a computer, reclining front seats for napping, and a powerful audio system for listening to MP3 music files, all for a starting price of just over $16,000.

Pick our panel.

When it comes to picking the right panel for your research project, there are a lot of boogers out there. If you're looking for the one destination you can count on to deliver high quality panel at a price that won't leave a bad taste in your mouth, you've come to the right place. Our actively managed panel can help you lick any sized project faster than you can say, "mmmgood."

Pick a winner.

Opinion Outpost. *Your destination for online panel*

(801)373-7735

a service of

Western Watts

www.westernwatts.com

To get in touch with what consumers want, companies often hire firms such as Opinion Outpost, a survey research data collection company that asks survey-panel respondents to share their opinions on various products and services.

expenses. Outside the organization, data are readily available through private or public reports and census statistics, as well as from many other sources. Computer networking technology provides a framework for companies to connect to useful databases and customers with instantaneous information about product acceptance, sales performance, and buying behavior. This information is important to planning and marketing strategy development.

Two types of data are usually available to decision makers. **Primary data** are observed, recorded, or collected directly from respondents. If you've ever participated in a telephone survey about a product, recorded your TV viewing habits for A. C. Nielsen or Arbitron, or even responded to a political opinion poll, you provided the researcher with primary data. Primary data must be gathered by researchers who develop a method to observe phenomena or research respondents. Many companies use "mystery shoppers" to visit their retail establishments and report on whether the stores are adhering to the companies' standards of service. Some use digital cameras and computer equipment to document their observations of store appearance, employee effectiveness, and customer treatment. These mystery shoppers provide valuable information that helps companies improve their organizations and refine their marketing strategies. The state of Nebraska used focus groups as part of its effort to develop a formal marketing campaign. Among other things, focus groups suggested the state promote its history and natural beauty.[19] With surveys, respondents are sometimes untruthful in order to avoid seeming foolish or ignorant.

Some methods for marketing research use passive observation of consumer behavior and open-ended questioning techniques. Called ethnographic or observational research, the approach can help marketers determine what consumers really think about their products and how different ethnic or demographic groups react to them.

Secondary data are compiled inside or outside the organization for some purpose other than changing the current situation. Marketers typically use information compiled by the U.S. Census Bureau and other government agencies, databases created by marketing research firms, and sales and other internal reports to gain information about customers.

The marketing of products and the collecting of data about buying behavior—information on what people actually buy and how they buy it—represent the marketing research of the future. New information technologies are changing the way businesses learn about their customers and market their products. Interactive multimedia research, or *virtual testing,* combines sight, sound, and animation to facilitate the testing

Marketing research is vital because the marketing concept cannot be implemented without information about customers.

A marketing information system is a framework for accessing information about customers from sources both inside and outside the organization. Inside the organization, there is a continuous flow of information about prices, sales, and

● **BUYING BEHAVIOR** the decision processes and actions of people who purchase and use products

● **PERCEPTION** the process by which a person selects, organizes, and interprets information received from his or her senses

● **LEARNING** changes in a person's behavior based on information and experience

● **ATTITUDE** knowledge and positive or negative feelings about something

● **PERSONALITY** the organization of an individual's distinguishing character traits, attitudes, or habits

of concepts as well as packaging and design features for consumer products. Computerization offers a greater degree of flexibility, shortens the staff time involved in data gathering, and cuts marketing research costs. The evolving development of telecommunications and computer technologies is allowing marketing researchers quick and easy access to a growing number of online services and a vast database of potential respondents. The online research industry is valued at $4 billion.[20] Many companies have created private online communities and research panels that bring consumer feedback into the companies 24 hours a day.

Look-Look.com is an online real-time service that provides accurate and reliable information research and news about trendsetting youths ages 14 to 30. With this age group spending an estimated $140 billion a year, many companies are willing to shell out an annual subscription fee of about $20,000 for access to these valuable data. Look-Look pays more than 35,000 handpicked, prescreened young people from all over the world to e-mail the company information about their styles, trends, opinions, and ideas.[21]

Other companies are finding that quicker, less expensive online market research is helping them develop products faster and with greater assurance that the products will be successful.

BUYING BEHAVIOR

Carrying out the marketing concept is impossible unless marketers know what, where, when, and how consumers buy; marketing research into the factors that influence buying behavior helps marketers develop effective marketing strategies. **Buying behavior** refers to the decision processes and actions of people who purchase and use products. It includes the behavior of both consumers purchasing products for personal or household use and organizations buying products for business use. Marketers analyze buying behavior because a firm's marketing strategy should be guided by an understanding of buyers. People view pets as part of their families, and they want their pets to have the best of everything. Iams, which markets the Iams and Eukanuba pet food brands, recognized this trend and shifted its focus. Today, it markets high-quality pet food, fancy pet treats, sauces, and other items that allow pet lovers to spoil their pets.[22]

Both psychological and social variables are important to an understanding of buying behavior.

Psychological Variables of Buying Behavior

Psychological factors include the following:

- **Perception** is the process by which a person selects, organizes, and interprets information received from his or her senses, as when hearing an advertisement on the radio or touching a product to understand it better.

- Motivation, as we said in Chapter 10, is an inner drive that directs a person's behavior toward goals. A customer's behavior is influenced by a set of motives rather than by a single motive. A buyer of a home computer, for example, may be motivated by ease of use, ability to communicate with the office, and price.

- **Learning** brings about changes in a person's behavior based on information and experience. If a person's actions result in a reward, he or she is likely to behave the same way in similar situations. If a person's actions bring about a negative result, however—such as feeling ill after eating at a certain restaurant—he or she probably will not repeat that action.

- **Attitude** is knowledge and positive or negative feelings about something. For example, a person who feels strongly about protecting the environment may refuse to buy products that harm the earth and its inhabitants.

- **Personality** refers to the organization of an individual's distinguishing character traits, attitudes, or habits. Although market research on the relationship between personality and buying behavior has been inconclusive, some marketers believe that the type of car or clothing a person buys reflects his or her personality.

Social Variables of Buying Behavior

Social factors include **social roles,** which are a set of expectations for individuals based on some position they occupy. A person may have many roles: mother, wife, student, executive. Each of these roles can influence buying behavior. Consider a woman choosing an automobile. Her father advises her to buy a safe, gasoline-efficient car such as a Volvo. Her teenage daughter wants her to buy a cool car such as a Toyota Prius; her young son wants her to buy a Ford Escape to take on camping trips. Some of her colleagues at work say she should buy a hybrid to help the environment. Thus, when she decides which car to buy, the woman's buying behavior may be affected by the opinions and experiences of her family and friends and by her roles as mother, daughter, and employee.

Other social factors include reference groups, social classes, and culture.

- **Reference groups** include families, professional groups, civic organizations, and other groups with which buyers identify and whose values or attitudes they adopt. A person may use a reference group as a point of comparison or a source of information. A person new to a community may ask other group members to recommend a family doctor, for example.

● **SOCIAL ROLES** a set of expectations for individuals based on some position they occupy

● **REFERENCE GROUPS** groups with which buyers identify and whose values or attitudes they adopt

● **SOCIAL CLASSES** a ranking of people into higher or lower positions of respect

● **CULTURE** the integrated, accepted pattern of human behavior, including thought, speech, beliefs, actions, and artifacts

- **Social classes** are determined by ranking people into higher or lower positions of respect. Criteria vary from one society to another. People within a particular social class may develop common patterns of behavior. People in the upper-middle class, for example, might buy a Lexus or a Cadillac as a symbol of their social class.

- **Culture** is the integrated, accepted pattern of human behavior, including thought, speech, beliefs, actions, and artifacts. Culture determines what people wear and eat and where they live and travel. Many Hispanic Texans and New Mexicans, for example, buy *masa trigo,* a flour mixture used to prepare tortillas, which are basic to Mexican cuisine.

Understanding Buying Behavior

Although marketers try to understand buying behavior, it is extremely difficult to explain exactly why a buyer purchases a particular product. The tools and techniques for analyzing consumers are not exact. Marketers may not be able to determine accurately what is highly satisfying to buyers, but they know that trying to understand consumer wants and needs is the best way to satisfy them. In an attempt to better understand consumer behavior, Procter & Gamble sent video crews into about 80 households all around the world. The company, maker of Tide, Crest, Pampers, and many other consumer products,

hoped to gain insights into the lifestyles and habits of young couples, families with children, and empty nesters. Participants were taped over a four-day period and were paid about $200 to $250 a day. The behaviors caught on tape may lead the company to develop new products or change existing ones to meet consumers' needs better and give the company a competitive advantage over its rivals.[23] Procter & Gamble furthered its real-life research and enhanced its online credentials with the BlogHer conference, which was held in Chicago to promote the Swiffer WetJet mop. The events participants blogged, Tweeted and posted pictures on Facebook—all of which was free publicity for the company.[24]

  L06

Summarize the environmental forces that influence marketing decisions.

THE MARKETING ENVIRONMENT

A number of external forces directly or indirectly influence the development of marketing strategies; the following political, legal, regulatory, social, competitive, economic, and technological forces constitute the marketing environment.

- *Political, legal, and regulatory forces*—laws and regulators' interpretation of laws; law enforcement and regulatory activities; regulatory bodies, legislators and legislation, and political actions of interest groups. Specific laws, for example, require that advertisements be truthful and that all health claims be documented.

- *Social forces*—the public's opinions and attitudes toward issues such as living standards, ethics, the environment, lifestyles, and quality of life. For example, social concerns have

Marketers like Benetton want their ads to appeal to a consumer's self-concept. The message: "I want to be like them, so I should buy Benetton's products."

led marketers to design and market safer toys for children.

- *Competitive and economic forces*—competitive relationships, unemployment, purchasing power, and general economic conditions (prosperity, recession, depression, recovery, product shortages, and inflation).

- *Technological forces*—computers and other technological advances that improve distribution, promotion, and new-product development.

Marketing environment forces can change quickly and radically, which is one reason marketing requires creativity and a customer focus. Recently the concern about climate change, global warming, and the impact of carbon emissions on the environment has led to social concerns leading businesses to rethink marketing strategies. Possibly the most important concern is to make businesses, consumers and governments consider carbon emissions and the effect their purchases have. Escalating fossil fuel use in economies such as China and India has placed strong upward pressure on oil prices. China's fast development has made it the planet's largest contributor to greenhouse gases. As Figure 12.4 indicates, the public believes that government, individuals, and businesses are all responsible for leading the way in green practices. The result has been government initiatives such as tax credits for hybrid cars; increased use of reusable bags over plastic ones; and more products are available that are easy to recycle and that consume less energy. The average American generates about 5 tons of greenhouse gases annually. Many people are disturbed by this statistic and have resolved to take actions that reduce their energy usage and their impact on the environment through the use of carpooling, driving hybrid cars, using Energy Star products, and even washing their clothes in cold water instead of hot. In addition to fueling the demand for low-energy products, these developments are accelerating the development of renewable energy such as solar and wind.[25]

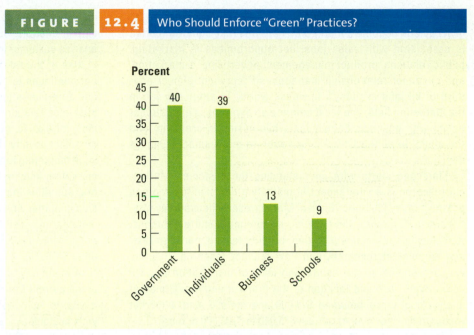

FIGURE 12.4 Who Should Enforce "Green" Practices?

When asked who should be in charge of enforcing environmentally sound practices in the United States, respondents said:

Source: "Leadind the Way in Green Practices," *USA Today Snapshots*®, June 3, 2008, p. A1.

Because such environmental forces are interconnected, changes in one may cause changes in others. Consider that because of evidence linking children's consumption of soft drinks and fast foods to health issues such as obesity, diabetes,

The makers of prestige products hope to sell their products not only to members of the upper class but to people who want to be like them.

SO YOU WANT A JOB IN MARKETING

You probably did not think as a child how great it would be to grow up and become a marketer. That's because marketing often is associated with sales jobs, but opportunities in marketing, public relations, product management, advertising, e-marketing, and customer relationship management represent almost one-third of all jobs in today's business world. To enter any job in the marketing field, you must balance an awareness of customer needs with business knowledge while mixing in creativity and the ability to obtain useful information to make smart business decisions.

Marketing starts with understanding the customer. Marketing research is a vital aspect in marketing decision making and presents many job opportunities. Market researchers survey customers to determine their habits, preferences, and aspirations. Activities include concept testing, product testing, package testing, test-market research, and new-product research. Salaries vary, depending on the nature and level of the position as well as the type, size, and location of the firm. An entry-level market analyst may make between $24,000 and $50,000, and a market research director may earn from $75,000 to $200,000 or more.

One of the most dynamic areas in marketing is direct marketing, in which a seller solicits a response from a consumer by using direct communications methods such as telephone, e-mail, mail, and catalogs. Jobs in direct marketing include buyers, catalog managers, research/mail-list managers, and order fulfillment managers. Most positions in direct marketing involve planning and market analysis. Some require the use of databases to sort and analyze customer information and sales history.

Use of the Internet for retail sales is growing and the Internet continues to be very useful for business-to-business sales, and so e-marketing offers many career opportunities, including customer relationship management (CRM). CRM helps companies market to customers through relationships, maintaining customer loyalty. Information technology plays a huge role in such marketing jobs, as you need to combine technical skills and marketing knowledge to communicate effectively with customers. Job titles include e-marketing manager, customer relationship manager, and e-services manager. A CRM customer service manager may receive a salary of $40,000 to $45,000, and experienced individuals in charge of online product offerings may earn up to $100,000.

A job in any of these marketing fields requires a strong sense of the current trends in business and marketing. Customer service is vital to many aspects of marketing, and so the ability to work with customers and communicate about their needs and wants is important. Marketing is everywhere, from the corner grocery or local nonprofit organization to the largest multinational corporations, making it a shrewd choice for an ambitious and creative person. We will discuss additional job opportunities in marketing in Chapter 13.

---

and osteoporosis, marketers of such products have experienced negative publicity and calls for legislation regulating the sale of soft drinks in public schools.

Although the forces in the marketing environment are sometimes called uncontrollables, they are not totally so. A marketing manager can influence some environmental variables. For example, businesses can lobby legislators to dissuade them from passing unfavorable legislation. Figure 12.5 shows the variables in the marketing environment that affect the marketing mix and the buyer. ■

FIGURE 12.5 The Marketing Mix and the Marketing Environment

Political, Legal, and Regulatory Forces

Social Forces

Product

Promotion

Customer

Price

Distribution

Technological Forces

Competitive and Economic Forces

Marketing Environment

Team Exercise

Form groups and assign the responsibility for finding examples of companies that excel in one dimension of the marketing mix (price, product, promotion, and distribution). Provide several company and product examples and explain why these would be exemplary cases. Present your research to the class.

CHECK OUT www.mhhe.com/FerrellM2e

for study materials including Interactive Exercises, Quizzes, iPod downloads, and video.

Dimensions of Marketing Strategy

13

introduction Creating an effective marketing strategy is important. Getting just the right mix of product, price, promotion, and distribution is critical if a business is to satisfy its target customers and achieve its own objectives (implement the marketing concept).

In Chapter 12, we introduced the concept of marketing and the various activities important in developing a marketing strategy. In this chapter, we'll take a closer look at the four dimensions of the marketing mix—product, price, distribution, and promotion—used to develop the marketing strategy. The focus of these marketing mix elements is a marketing strategy that builds customer relationships and satisfaction.

THE MARKETING MIX

The key to developing a marketing strategy is to maintain the right marketing mix that satisfies the target market and creates long-term relationships with customers. To develop meaningful customer relationships, marketers have to develop and manage the dimensions of the marketing mix to give their firm an advantage over competitors. Successful companies offer at least one dimension of value that surpasses all competitors in the marketplace in meeting customer expectations. However, this does not mean that a company can ignore the other dimensions of the marketing mix; it must maintain acceptable, and if possible distinguishable, differences in the other dimensions as well.

Wal-Mart, for example, emphasizes price ("Save money, live better"). Procter & Gamble is well known for its promotion of top consumer brands such as Tide, Cheer, Crest, Ivory, and Head & Shoulders. Domino's Pizza is recognized for its superiority in distribution after developing the largest home delivery pizza company in the world and its innovative new product introductions.

DID YOU KNOW?

Domino's Pizza delivery drivers cover 9 million miles a week delivering 400 million pizzas a year.[1]

●● ● **LO1**

Describe the role of product in the marketing mix, including how products are developed, classified, and identified.

PRODUCT STRATEGY

As mentioned previously, the term *product* refers to goods, services, and ideas. Because the product is often the most visible of the marketing mix dimensions, managing product decisions is crucial. In this section, we'll consider product development, classification, mix, life cycle, and identification.

Developing New Products

Each year thousands of products are introduced, but few of them succeed. The drug company Pfizer's Animal Health Group released Slentrol, a weight-loss drug for dogs. The drug controls a dog's appetite and blocks fat. The drug is meant as a weight loss tool for dogs with a medical condition or an owner who cannot resist feeding the dog too much or cannot give the dog more

> ## "Each year thousands of products are introduced, but few of them succeed."

While he was attending Yale in 1966, Fred Smith, the founder of Federal Express, wrote a paper about his idea for the business. However, his professor said the concept would never fly. After watching how the U.S. military's logistics worked while serving in Vietnam, Smith later got FedEx off the ground.

exercise.[2] Before introducing a new product, a business must follow a multistep process: idea development, the screening of new ideas, business analysis, product development, test marketing, and commercialization. A firm can take considerable time to get a product ready for the market: it took more than 20 years for the first photocopier, for example. First announced as a concept car in January 2007, the General Motors Volt will be radically different from any car on the road today when it is launched in 2010. It is an extended-range electric vehicle with a 161-horsepower engine and enough power to go from 0 to 60 miles per hour in 8.5 seconds.[3]

idea development New ideas can come from marketing research, engineers, and outside sources such as advertising agencies and management consultants. Microsoft has a separate division—Microsoft Research—where scientists devise the technology of the future. The division has more than 700 full-time employees who work in a university-like research atmosphere. Research teams then present their ideas to Microsoft engineers who are developing specific products. As we said in Chapter 12, ideas sometimes come from customers, too. Other sources are brainstorming and intracompany incentives or rewards for good ideas. New ideas can even create a company. Las Vegas–based Shuffle Master, for example, grew out of entrepreneur Mark Breeding's card-shuffling machine. The Shuffle Master is on 12,000 of the 40,000 tables in casinos around the world.[4]

new idea screening

The next step in developing a new product is idea screening. In this phase, a marketing manager should look at the organization's resources and objectives and assess the firm's ability to produce and market the product. Important aspects to be considered at this stage are consumer desires, the competition, technological changes, social trends, and political, economic, and environmental considerations. Basically, there are two reasons new products succeed: They are able to meet a need or solve a problem better than products already available or they add variety to the product selection currently on the market. Bringing together a team of knowledgeable people, including design, engineering, marketing, and customers, is a great way to screen ideas. Using the Internet to encourage collaboration is the next sea of innovation for marketers to screen ideas. After many ideas were screened, Heinz Ketchup introduced Heinz kid-targeted Silly Squirts with three cool drawing nozzles to keep kids amused and entertained at dinner. In addition, Easy Squeeze upside-down bottles added to convenience.[5] Most new-product ideas are rejected during screening because they seem inappropriate or impractical for the organization.

business analysis

Business analysis is a basic assessment of a product's compatibility in the marketplace and its potential profitability. Both the size of the market and competing products are often studied at this point. The most important question relates to market demand: How will the product affect the firm's sales, costs, and profits?

product development

If a product survives the first three steps, it is developed into a prototype that should reveal the intangible attributes it possesses as perceived by the consumer. Product development is often expensive, and few product ideas make it to this stage. New-product research and development costs vary. Adding a new color to an existing item may cost $100,000 to $200,000, but launching a completely new product can cost millions of dollars. The Coca-Cola Co. reduced the time and cost of product development research by 50 percent when it created an online panel of 100 teenagers and asked them how to remake

its Powerade sports drink.[6] During product development, various elements of the marketing mix must be developed for testing. Copyrights, tentative advertising copy, packaging, labeling, and descriptions of a target market are integrated to develop an overall marketing strategy.

test marketing

Test marketing is a trial minilaunch of a product in limited areas that represent the potential market. It allows a complete test of the marketing strategy in a natural environment, giving the organization an opportunity to discover weaknesses and eliminate them before the product is fully launched. Consider Seasons 52, the latest concept restaurant developed by Darden Restaurants Inc., the world's largest casual dining company. Seasons 52 boasts a seasonally inspired menu with the freshest goods available served in a casual atmosphere. Seasons 52 targets those who are striving to live fit, active lives and are concerned about the quality and nutrition of their food. All menu items at Seasons 52 have fewer than 475 calories, significantly lower than the food in competing restaurants; are nutritionally balanced; and are not fried. Darden test-marketed the concept in various cities around Florida and Georgia to experiment with menu, advertising, pricing and brand awareness, and now boasts restaurants in eleven locations, including in New Jersey and Illinois.[7] ACNielsen assists companies in test marketing their products. Figure 13.1 shows the permanent sites as well as custom locations for test marketing.

FIGURE 13.1 ACNielsen Market Decisions

Market Decisions
Test Market Locations

Portland
Boise
Peoria
Colorado Springs
Evansville
Lexington
Charleston
Tucson

◆ Permanent Test Markets ("Data Markets")

★ Additional "Custom" Test Markets

Source: "Test Marketing," ACNielsen (n.d.), www.acnielsen.com/services/testing/test1.htm (accessed August 28, 2009). Reprinted with permission of ACNielsen Market Decisions.

commercialization **Commercialization** is the full introduction of a complete marketing strategy and the launch of the product for commercial success. During commercialization, the firm gears up for full-scale production, distribution, and promotion. After Baskin-Robbins's sales of a new soft serve ice cream did well in test markets, the company planned its largest new-product roll-out in decades. Soft-serve ice cream is a risky move by the company, which has long branded itself on the hand-scooped variety, but soft serve represents one of ice cream's few growth areas. In summer 2008, soft-serve vanilla ice cream was in about half of Baskin Robbins's domestic stores, expanding to all 2,400 U.S. stores by 2009.[8]

Classifying Products

Products are usually classified as either consumer products or business products. **Consumer products** are for household or family use; they are not intended for any purpose other than daily living. They can be further classified as convenience products, shopping products, and specialty products on the basis of consumers' buying behavior and intentions.

- *Convenience products,* such as eggs, milk, bread, and newspapers, are bought frequently, without a lengthy search, and often for immediate consumption. Consumers spend virtually no time planning where to purchase these products and usually accept whatever brand is available.

- *Shopping products,* such as furniture, audio equipment, clothing, and sporting goods, are purchased after the consumer has compared competitive products and "shopped around." Price, product features, quality, style, service, and image all influence the decision to buy.

- *Specialty products,* such as ethnic foods, designer clothing and shoes, art, and antiques, require even greater research and shopping effort. Consumers know what they want and go out of their way to find it; they are not willing to accept a substitute.

Business products are used directly or indirectly in the operation or manufacturing processes of businesses. They are usually purchased for the operation of an organization or the production of other products; thus, their purchase is tied to specific goals and objectives. They too can be further classified:

- *Raw materials* are natural products taken from the earth, oceans, and recycled solid waste. Iron ore, bauxite, lumber, cotton, and fruits and vegetables are examples.

- *Major equipment* covers large, expensive items used in production. Examples include earth-moving equipment, stamping machines, and robotic equipment used on auto assembly lines.

- *Accessory equipment* includes items used for production, office, or management purposes which usually do not become part of the final product. Computers, fax machines, calculators, and hand tools are examples.

- *Component parts* are finished items that are ready to be assembled into the company's final products. Tires, window glass, batteries, and spark plugs are component parts of automobiles.

- *Processed materials* are things used directly in production or management operations but not readily identifiable as component parts. Varnish, for example, is a processed material for a furniture manufacturer.

- *Supplies* include materials that make production, management, and other operations possible, such as paper, pencils, paint, and cleaning supplies.

- *Industrial services* include financial, legal, marketing research, security, janitorial, and exterminating services.

Furniture and other higher-priced goods and services are shopping goods. Consumers conduct extensive searches for these goods and gather a lot of information about them before buying them.

FIGURE	13.2	Colgate-Palmolive's Product Mix and Product Lines

Product Mix →

Product Lines

Oral Care	Personal Care	Household Care	Pet Nutrition
Toothpaste	Men's antiperspirant/deodorant	Dishwashing	Science diet
Toothbrushes	Women's antiperspirant/deodorant	Fabric conditioner	Prescription diet
Kids' products	Bar soap	Household cleaners	
Whitening products	Body wash	Institutional products	
Over the counter	Liquid hand wash		
From the dentist	Toiletries for men		

Source: Colgate Products, www.colgate.com/app/Colgate/US/Corp/Products.cvsp (accessed June 17, 2007).

Purchasers decide whether to provide these services internally or to acquire them from an outside supplier.

Product Line and Product Mix

Product relationships within an organization are of key importance. A **product line** is a group of closely related products that are treated as a unit because of similar marketing strategy. At Colgate-Palmolive, for example, the oral-care product line includes Colgate toothpaste, toothbrushes, and dental floss. A **product mix** is all the products offered by an organization. Figure 13.2 displays a sampling of the product mix and product lines of the Colgate-Palmolive Company.

Product Life Cycle

Like people, products are born, grow, mature, and eventually die. Some products have very long lives. Ivory Soap was introduced in 1879 and is still popular. In contrast, a new computer chip is usually outdated within a year because of technological breakthroughs and rapid changes in the computer industry. There are four stages in the life cycle of a product: introduction, growth, maturity, and decline (Figure 13.3). The stage a product is in helps determine marketing strategy. While pickup trucks have historically sold very well in the United States, sales have reached the maturity stage, declining after a peak in 2004. The percentage of new vehicles sold reveals more car sales than truck sales. As oil prices increase, consumers are looking for better gas mileage, and the demand for fuel-efficient cars is on the rise. Figure 13.4 shows sales numbers of hybrid vehicles. Hybrid vehicles have been in the introductory stage, filling only around 3 percent of market share, but with continued demand are now passing into a strong growth stage.[9]

In the *introductory stage,* consumer awareness and acceptance of the product are limited, sales are zero, and profits are negative. Profits are negative because the firm has spent money on research, development, and marketing to launch the product. During the introductory stage, marketers focus on making consumers aware of the product and its benefits. When Procter & Gamble introduced the Tide Stainbrush to reach the 70 percent of consumers who pretreat stains when doing laundry, it employed press releases as well as television and magazine advertising to make consumers aware of the new product.[10] Sales accelerate as the product enters the growth stage of the life cycle.

Will high gas prices and concern for the environment mark the end of the product life cycle for monster-size SUVs such as Hummers?

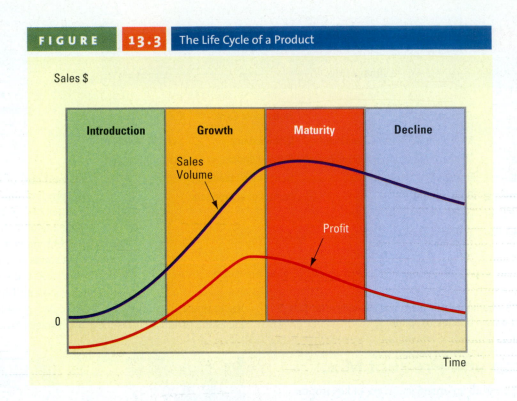

FIGURE 13.3 The Life Cycle of a Product

Sales $

| Introduction | Growth | Maturity | Decline |

Sales Volume

Profit

0

Time

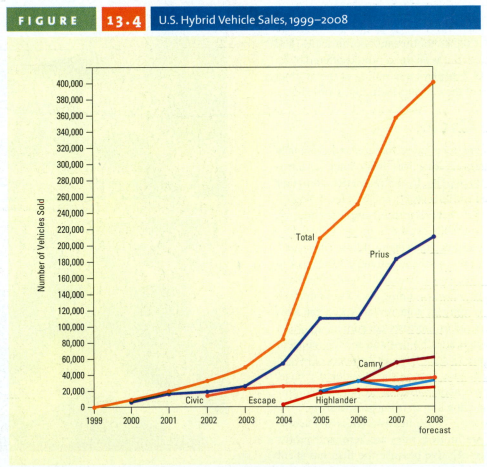

FIGURE 13.4 U.S. Hybrid Vehicle Sales, 1999–2008

Number of Vehicles Sold

Total

Prius

Camry

Civic   Escape   Highlander

1999 2000 2001 2002 2003 2004 2005 2006 2007 2008 forecast

Source: "April 2008 Dashboard: Hybrids Sales Defy Recession," *HybridCars.com,* May 13, 2008, www.hybridcars.com/market-dashboard/april-2008-hybrids-defy-recession.html (accessed June 25, 2008).

In the *growth stage*, sales increase rapidly and profits peak, then start to decline. One reason profits start to decline during the growth stage is that new companies enter the market, driving prices down and increasing marketing expenses. Consider Apple's iPod, the most popular digital music player with more than 70 percent of the music player market. Since its launch, more than 6 billion songs have been downloaded from its iTunes music store, and it is currently selling and renting more than 50,000 movies per day. Its iTunes music store surpassed Best Buy and Wal-Mart to become the biggest music retailer in the United States. iTunes has more than 20 million unique visitors a month.[11] During the growth stage, the firm tries to strengthen its position in the market by emphasizing the product's benefits and identifying market segments that want these benefits.

Sales continue to increase at the beginning of the *maturity stage*, but then the sales curve peaks and starts to decline while profits continue to decline. This stage is characterized by severe competition and heavy expenditures. In the highly competitive snack food industry, Quaker is converting mature products to single-serve lower-calorie treats. 100-calorie packs were a smash success for Quaker and competitor Kraft, so now rivals across the industry are introducing 90-, 80-, even 60-calorie versions of mature products in hopes of maintaining sales.[12]

During the *decline stage*, sales continue to fall rapidly. Profits also decline and may even become losses as prices are cut and necessary marketing expenditures are made. As profits drop, firms may eliminate certain models or items. To reduce expenses and squeeze out any remaining profits, marketing expenditures may be cut back, even though such cutbacks accelerate the sales decline. Finally, plans must be made for phasing out the product and introducing new ones to take its place. Unfortunately for Mattel, the 50-year-old Barbie Doll has seen her status and sales slide as she has been replaced on retail shelves with more edgy products such as Bratz. Barbie became vulnerable from competition not only from Bratz but from American Girl and the growth of toy sales in stores such as Wal-Mart and Target when they choose to allocate shelf space to products they considered more profitable.[13]

Identifying Products

Branding, packaging, and labeling can be used to identify or distinguish one product from others. As a result, they are key

During the *decline stage*, sales continue to fall rapidly. Profits also decline and may even become losses as prices are cut and necessary marketing expenditures are made.

marketing activities that help position a product appropriately for its target market.

branding

Branding is the process of naming and identifying products. A *brand* is a name, term, symbol, design, or combination that identifies a product and distinguishes it from other products. Consider that Google, iPod, and TiVo are brand names that are used to identify entire product categories, much as Xerox has become synonymous with photocopying and Kleenex with tissues. Protecting a brand name is important in maintaining a brand identity. The world's 10 most valuable brands are shown in Table 13.1. The brand name is the part of the brand that can be spoken and consists of letters, words, and numbers—such as WD-40 lubricant. A *brand mark* is the part of the brand that is a distinctive design, such as the silver star on the hood of a Mercedes or McDonald's golden arches logo. A **trademark** is a brand that is registered with the U.S. Patent and Trademark Office and is thus legally protected from use by any other firm.

Two major categories of brands are manufacturer brands and private distributor brands. **Manufacturer brands** are brands initiated and owned by the manufacturer to identify products from the point of production to the point of purchase. Kellogg's, Sony, and Texaco are examples. **Private distributor brands,**

TABLE 13.1 The 10 Most Valuable Brands in the World

Rank	Brand	Brand Value ($ millions)	Brand Value Change
1.	Google	100,039	16%
2.	Microsoft	76,249	8%
3.	Coca-Cola	67,625	16%
4.	IBM	66,622	20%
5.	McDonald's	66,575	34%
6.	Apple	63,113	14%
7.	China Mobile	61,283	7%
8.	General Electric	59,793	–16%
9.	Vodafone	53,727	45%
10.	Marlboro	49,460	33%

Source: "2009 100 Most Powerful Brands," Millward Brown Optimor, http://www.millwardbrown.com/Sites/Optimor/Media/Pdfs/en/BrandZ/BrandZ-2009-Report.pdf (accessed September 1, 2009).

● **GENERIC PRODUCTS**
products with no brand
name that often come in
simple packages and carry
only their generic name

● **PACKAGING** the external
container that holds and
describes the product

● **LABELING** the presentation of important information on a package

which may be less expensive than manufacturer brands, are owned and controlled by a wholesaler or retailer, such as Kenmore appliances (Sears) and Sam's grocery products (Wal-Mart and Sam's Wholesale Club). The names of private brands do not usually identify their manufacturer. While private-label brands were once considered cheaper and poor quality, such as Wal-Mart's Ol'Roy dog food, many private-label brands are increasing quality and image and competing with national brands. Target hired architect Michael Graves to design its private-label products, including kitchen appliances such as blenders and coffee pots. Martha Stewart designed a line of home fashions for K-Mart. Other firms, such as JC Penney and Wal-Mart, are also following the trend.[14] Manufacturer brands are fighting hard against private distributor brands.

Another type of brand that has developed is **generic products**—products with no brand name at all. They often come in plain, simple packages that carry only the generic name

ally branded. This branding policy ensures that the name of one product does not affect the names of others, and different brands can be targeted at different segments of the same market, increasing the company's market share (its percentage of the sales for the total market for a product). Another approach to branding is to develop a family of brands with each of the firm's products carrying the same name or at least part of the name. Gillette, Sara Lee, and IBM use this approach.

packaging The **packaging,** or external container that holds and describes the product, influences consumers' attitudes and their buying decisions. A survey of over 1,200 consumers found that 40 percent are willing to try a new product based on its packaging.[15] It is estimated that consumers' eyes linger only 2.5 seconds on each product on an average shopping trip; therefore, product packaging should be designed to attract and hold consumers' attention.

A package can perform several functions, including protection, economy, convenience, and promotion. Beverage manufacturers have been redesigning their bottles to make them more convenient for consumers and to promote them to certain markets. Scientists videotaped people drinking from different types of bottles and made plaster casts of their hands. They found that the average gulp is 6.44 ounces and that half the population would rather suck liquid through a pop-up top than drink it. Packaging also helps create an overall brand image. In an effort to improve packaging, reduce waste, and increase customer satisfaction, Amazon.com lets customers rate packaging on their orders. It is part of the company's Frustration Free Packaging Initiative, and is popular with consumers.[16]

labeling Labeling, the presentation of important information on the package, is closely associated with packaging. The content of labeling, often required by law, may include ingredients or content, nutrition facts (calories, fat, etc.), care instructions, suggestions for use (such as recipes), the manufacturer's address and toll-free number, Web site, and other useful information. McDonald's introduced packaging that lets you know the nutritional value of Big Macs as well as other products. It was the first fast-food chain to adopt the initiative.[17] This information can have a strong impact on sales. The labels of many products, particularly food and drugs, must carry warnings, instructions, certifications, or manufacturers' identifications.

Generic products like these appeal to consumers who are less concerned about quality and consistency but want lower prices.

of the product—peanut butter, tomato juice, aspirin, dog food, and so on. They appeal to consumers who may be willing to sacrifice quality or product consistency to get a lower price.

Companies use two basic approaches to branding multiple products. In one, a company gives each product within its complete product mix its own brand name. Warner-Lambert, for example, sells many well-known consumer products—Dentyne, Chiclets, Listerine, Halls, Rolaids, and Trident—each individu-

TABLE 13.2 Customer Satisfaction with Airlines

Airline	2008 Score	% Change from Previous Year
Southwest	79	4.0
All others	75	0.0
American	62	3.3
Continental	62	-10.1
Delta	60	1.7
Northwest	57	-6.6
United	56	0.0
US Airway Group	54	-11.5

Source: The American Customer Satisfaction Index, www.theacsi.org/index
.php?option=com_content&task=view&id=147&Itemid=155&i=Airlines (accessed March 24, 2009).

tries. The latest results showed that overall customer satisfaction rose to 75.2 (out of a possible 100), with increases in some industries balancing drops in others. Customer satisfaction with the airline industry dropped to its lowest point since 2001, while wireless telephone service stayed at an all-time high for the second year in a row. Table 13.2 shows the top 10 airlines in the Airline Quality Rankings. Southwest was ranked highest with 79 percent customer satisfaction, while U.S. Airways had the largest decline in score, falling 11.5 percent from the previous year.[18] Services are becoming a larger part of international competition. As shown in Figure 13.5, many consumers shop for green products (associated with quality) even during a recession.

product quality Quality reflects the degree to which a good, service, or idea meets the demands and requirements of customers. Quality products are often referred to as reliable, durable, easily maintained, easily used, a good value, or a trusted brand name. The level of quality is the amount of quality a product possesses, and the consistency of quality depends on the product maintaining the same level of quality over time.

Quality of service is difficult to gauge because it depends on customers' perceptions of how well the service meets or exceeds their expectations. In other words, service quality is judged by consumers, not the service providers. A bank may define service quality as employing friendly and knowledgeable employees, but the bank's customers may be more concerned with waiting time, ATM access, security, and statement accuracy. Similarly, an airline traveler considers on-time arrival, on-board food service, and satisfaction with the ticketing and boarding process. The University of Michigan Business School's National Quality Research Center annually surveys customers of more than 200 companies and provides quarterly results for selected indus-

Coca-Cola's trademark varies from country to country. But the overall look is retained through use of similar letterforms and style, even with different alphabets.

1. Arabic
2. French
3. Japanese
4. Thai
5. Spanish
6. Chinese
7. Hebrew
8. Polish

Coca-Cola is one of the most valuable brands in the world.

Kombucha Just May Cure What Ails You

In 1995, when G. T. Dave was a teenager, his mother was diagnosed with breast cancer. As a natural supplement to treatment, she drank Kombucha tea, which she and her son credit with her recovery. Although Dave was young, he was determined to share Kombucha with others. He began by brewing the tea at home. Kombucha is an ancient Chinese beverage, called by the Chinese the Tea of Immortality and the elixir of life, which has been used for thousands of years. Kombucha is cultured for 30 days, during which time enzymes, probiotics, amino acids, antioxidants, and polyphenols grow. The end result resembles a mushroom—a light brown, tough gelatinous disk. It is a living thing that regenerates, and samples can be used to create future batches. Although Dave's Kombucha company is much larger now, he still creates the drink in small batches, using his first cultures. Dave began distributing his Kombucha locally door to door, but he now sells his products to stores nationwide. People throughout the United States and worldwide swear by this unique beverage.[19] ❖

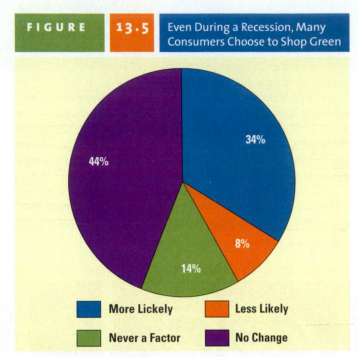

FIGURE 13.5 Even During a Recession, Many Consumers Choose to Shop Green

- More Lickely (34%)
- Less Likely (8%)
- Never a Factor (14%)
- No Change (44%)

Source: 2009 Cone Consumer Environmental Survey, January 29–30.

The quality of services provided by businesses on the Internet can be gauged by consumers on such sites as ConsumerReports.org and BBBOnline. The subscription service offered by ConsumerReports.org provides consumers with a view of e-commerce sites' business, security, and privacy policies. BBBOnline is dedicated to promoting responsibility online. The Web Credibility Project focuses on how health, travel, advocacy, news, and shopping sites disclose business relationships with the companies and products they cover or sell, especially when such relationships pose a potential conflict of interest.[20] Quality can be associated with where the product is made. For example, "Made in U.S.A." labeling can be perceived as a different value and quality. As Table 13.3 indicates, there are differences in the perception of quality and value between the U.S. consumers and Europeans when they compare products made in the United States, Japan, Korea and China.[21]

LO2

Define price and discuss its importance in the marketing mix, including various pricing strategies a firm might employ.

PRICING STRATEGY

Previously, we defined price as the value placed on an object exchanged between a buyer and a seller. Buyers' interest in price stems from their expectations about the usefulness of a product or the satisfaction they may derive from it. Because buyers have limited resources, they must allocate those resources to obtain the products they most desire. They must decide whether the benefits gained in an exchange are worth the buying power sacrificed. Almost anything of value can be assessed by a price. Many factors may influence the evaluation of value, including time constraints, price levels, perceived quality, and motivations to use available information about prices.[22] Indeed, consumers vary in their response to price: Some focus solely on the lowest price, while others consider quality or the prestige associated with a product and its price. As Figure 13.6 indicates, price is a major factor in deciding where to shop. However, some types of consumers are increasingly "trading up" to more status-conscious products, such as automobiles, home appliances, restaurants, and even pet food, yet remain price-conscious for other products such as cleaning and grocery goods. This trend has benefited marketers such as Starbucks, Sub-Zero, BMW, and Petco—which can charge premium prices for high-quality, prestige products—as well as Sam's Clubs and Costco—which offer basic household products at everyday low prices.[23]

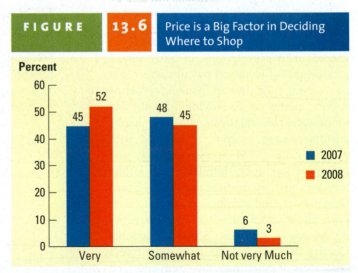

FIGURE 13.6 Price is a Big Factor in Deciding Where to Shop

Percent

	2007	2008
Very	45	52
Somewhat	48	45
Not very Much	6	3

Source: "USA Today Snapshot," *USA Today*, February 24, 2009, p. A1.

TABLE 13.3 Perceived Quality and Value of Products Based on Country of Origin*

	Made in U.S.A.		Made in Japan		Made in Korea		Made in China	
	Value	Quality	Value	Quality	Value	Quality	Value	Quality
U.S. adults	4.0	4.2	3.2	3.2	2.6	2.4	2.8	2.4
Western Europeans	3.3	3.4	3.5	3.5	2.8	2.4	2.9	2.4

*On a scale of 1 (low) to 5 (high).

Source: "American Demographics 2006 Consumer Perception Survey," *Advertising Age*, January 2, 2006, p. 9. Data by Synovate.

Price is a key element in the marketing mix because it relates directly to the generation of revenue and profits. In large part, the ability to set a price depends on the supply of and demand for a product. For most products, the quantity demanded goes up as the price goes down, and as the price goes up, the quantity demanded goes down. Changes in buyers' needs, variations in the effectiveness of other marketing mix variables, the presence of substitutes, and dynamic environmental factors can influence demand. New demand has greatly increased prices for industrial-grade diamonds as jewelers have turned to the impure gems, typically used for drill bits and saws, as a fashion statement. Even diamond giant De Beers has turned to the fashion, with is Talisman collection of flawed-diamond jewelry priced up to $675,000 and making up a quarter of all De Beers jewelry sales in the United States.[24]

Price is probably the most flexible variable in the marketing mix. Although it may take years to develop a product, establish channels of distribution, and design and implement promotion, a product's price may be set and changed in a few minutes. Under certain circumstances, of course, the price may not be so flexible, especially if government regulations prevent dealers from controlling prices.

Pricing Objectives

Pricing objectives specify the role of price in an organization's marketing mix and strategy. They usually are influenced not only by marketing mix decisions but also by finance, accounting, and production factors. Maximizing profits and sales, boosting market share, maintaining the status quo, and survival are four common pricing objectives.

Specific Pricing Strategies

Pricing strategies provide guidelines for achieving the company's pricing objectives and overall marketing strategy. They specify how price will be used as a variable in the marketing mix. Significant pricing strategies relate to the pricing of new products, psychological pricing, and price discounting.

pricing new products

Setting the price for a new product is critical: The right price leads to profitability; the wrong price may kill the product. In general, there are two basic strategies to setting the base price for a new product. **Price skimming** is charging the highest possible price that buyers who want the product will pay. Porsche Cayenne S V8, for example, has a starting price of $57,900, considerably higher than that of other sport utility vehicles.[25] This strategy allows the company to generate much-needed revenue to help offset the costs of research and development. Conversely, a **penetration price** is a low price designed to help a product enter the market and gain market share rapidly. For example, when Industrias Añaños introduced Kola Real to capitalize on limited supplies of Coca-Cola and Pepsi Cola in Peru, it set an ultralow penetration price to appeal to the poor who predominate in the region. Kola Real quickly gained market share in the Peruvian market, and spread to other South and Central American markets, where it is called Big Cola. Kola Real has made inroads in Asia as well, with distribution in Thailand and aims to take on the Chinese market. In all, Kola Real's penetration pricing strategy has allowed it to quickly take on much larger competitors in 12 international markets.[26] Penetration pricing is less flexible than price skimming; it is more difficult to raise a penetration price than to lower a skimming price. Penetration pricing is used most often when marketers suspect that competitors will enter the market shortly after the product has been introduced.

● **PRICE SKIMMING** charging the highest possible price that buyers who want the product will pay

● **PENETRATION PRICE** a low price designed to help a product enter the market and gain market share rapidly

Levi's Blue Jeans Go Green

Levi Strauss & Co. has long been known for its 501s, affordable prices, and premium denim clothing. Yet in an attempt to break into a hot market, Levi's traditional blue has gone green—eco-friendly green, that is. According to the research group Mintel, about 36 percent of Americans regularly purchase "green" products. As a result, many companies are switching to earth-friendly packaging and new production methods that conserve energy. In 2006, Levi's introduced environmentally friendly jeans made from 100 percent organic cotton and natural dyes.

At $250, the initial selling price of Levi's eco-friendly jeans was too high for many consumers. Since then they have become significantly more affordable. This raises the question: Why is going green so expensive? In Levi's case, it was the organic cotton. For cotton to be certi-fied organic, it cannot be genetically modified and must be pesticide- and fungicide-free. Most cotton in the United States is genetically modified. Many companies are turning to farmers overseas, but certification for those farmers can also be a challenge.

Despite the expense, many are willing to pay more to support farmers committed to harvesting with organic methods, and companies are spending big bucks to promote their stance on going green. As a result, organic cotton farming is increasing. According to the Organic Trade Association, global organic cotton farming grew 152 percent during the 2007–2008 year alone. This increase in supply has decreased organic cotton prices, allowing companies like Levi's to offer their organic jeans at more affordable prices. This combination of lower prices and high demand makes Levi's commitment to eco-friendly clothing appear to be a good long-term investment.[27] ❖

Q: **Discussion Questions**

1. Why can companies charge a premium price for green products?

2. What else might Levi's do to increase its offering of moderately priced green products?

3. How much more would you be willing to pay for environmentally friendly clothing such as Levi's new green jeans?

● **PSYCHOLOGICAL PRICING** encouraging purchases based on emotional rather than rational responses to the price

● **DISCOUNTS** temporary price reductions, often employed to boost sales

● **MARKETING CHANNEL** a group of organizations that moves products from their producer to customers; also called a channel of distribution

● **RETAILERS** intermediaries who buy products from manufacturers (or other intermediaries) and sell them to consumers for home and household use rather than for resale or for use in producing other products

● **WHOLESALERS** intermediaries who buy from producers or from other wholesalers and sell to retailers

psychological pricing

Psychological pricing encourages purchases based on emotional rather than rational responses to the price. For example, the assumption behind *even/odd pricing* is that people will buy more of a product for $9.99 than for $10 because it seems to be a bargain at the odd price. The assumption behind *symbolic/prestige pricing* is that high prices connote high quality. Thus the prices of certain fragrances are set artificially high to give the impression of superior quality. Some over-the-counter drugs are priced high because consumers associate a drug's price with potency.

price discounting

Temporary price reductions, or **discounts,** are often employed to boost sales. Although there are many types, quantity, seasonal, and promotional discounts are among the most widely used. Quantity discounts reflect the economies of purchasing in large volume. Seasonal discounts to buyers who purchase goods or services out of season help even out production capacity. Promotional discounts attempt to improve sales by advertising price reductions on selected products to increase customer interest. Often promotional pricing is geared to increased profits. Taco Bell, with its reputation for value, has been labeled the "best-positioned U.S. brand" to do well in a recession economy as consumers look for cheaper fast food options. Taco Bell capitalized on this by adding a "Why pay more?" menu of 11 items priced below $1.[28] McDonald's, however, is having trouble balancing its own "dollar menu" with profits. Franchisees have cited rising commodity costs and an increase in the minimum wage for sharply cutting their profit margins on dollar menu items. As consumers increasingly turn to these lower-priced options, McDonald's owner/operators are finding it difficult to keep up.[29]

●● LO3

Identify factors affecting distribution decisions, such as marketing channels and intensity of market coverage.

DISTRIBUTION STRATEGY

The best products in the world will not be successful unless companies make them available where and when customers want to buy them. In this section, we will explore dimensions of distribution strategy, including the channels through which products are distributed, the intensity of market coverage, and the physical handling of products during distribution.

Marketing Channels

A **marketing channel,** or channel of distribution, is a group of organizations that moves products from their producer to customers. Marketing channels make products available to buyers when and where they desire to purchase them. Organizations that bridge the gap between a product's manufacturer and the ultimate consumer are called *middlemen,* or intermediaries. They create time, place, and ownership utility. Two intermediary organizations are retailers and wholesalers.

Retailers buy products from manufacturers (or other intermediaries) and sell them to consumers for home and household use rather than for resale or for use in producing other products. Toys 'Я' Us, for example, buys products from Mattel and other manufacturers and resells them to consumers. Retailing usually

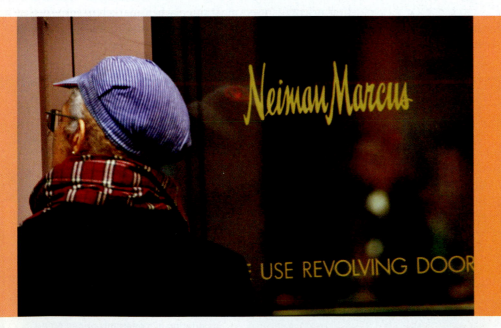

During the latest recession, upscale retailers such as Neiman Marcus brought out lower-priced product lines to attract shoppers. But that strategy is risky because it can "cheapen" a company's brands in the eyes of consumers.

occurs in a store, but the Internet, vending machines, mail-order catalogs, and entertainment, such as going to a Chicago Bulls basketball game, also provide opportunities for retailing. With more than 200 million Americans accessing the Internet, online sales are estimated to reach more than $300 billion by the year 2011.[30] By bringing together an assortment of products from competing producers, retailers create utility. Retailers arrange for products to be moved from producers to a convenient retail establishment (place utility). They maintain hours of operation for their retail stores to make merchandise available when consumers want it (time utility). They also assume the risk of ownership of inventories (ownership utility). Table 13.4 describes various types of general merchandise retailers.

Today, there are too many stores competing for too few customers, and as a result, competition between similar retailers has never been more intense. In addition, retailers face challenges such as shoplifting, as indicated in Table 13.5. Further, competition between different types of stores is changing the nature of retailing. Supermarkets compete with specialty food stores, wholesale clubs, and discount stores. Department stores compete with nearly every other type of store, including specialty stores, off-price chains, category killers, discount stores, and online retailers. Many traditional retailers, such as Wal-Mart and Macy's, have created online shopping sites to retain customers and compete with online-only retailers. One of the best-known online-only, or cyber, merchants is Amazon.com. Amazon offers millions of products from which to choose, all from the privacy and convenience of the purchaser's home. In some cases, Web merchants offer wide selections, ultra-convenience, superior service, knowledge, and the best products. More detail on the Internet's effect on marketing was presented in Chapter 4.

Wholesalers are intermediaries who buy from producers or from other wholesalers and sell to retailers. They usually do not sell in significant quantities to ultimate consumers. Wholesalers perform the functions listed in Table 13.6.

Wholesalers are extremely important because of the marketing activities they perform, particularly for consumer products. Although it is true that wholesalers can be eliminated, their functions must be passed on to some other entity, such as the producer, another intermediary, or even the customer. Wholesalers help consumers and retailers by buying in large quantities, then selling to retailers in smaller quantities. By stocking an assortment of products, wholesalers match products to demand.

supply chain management In an effort to improve distribution channel relationships among manufacturers and other channel intermediaries, supply chain

> ● ● **Although it is true that wholesalers can be eliminated, their functions must be passed on to some other entity, such as the producer, another intermediary, or even the customer.**

TABLE 13.5 Stealing from Stores

Shoplifters in United States	23 million
Amount retailers lose per year	More than $10 billion
Percent of shoplifters who are adults	75%

Source: "Shoplifting Statistics," www.shopliftingprevention.org/WhatNASPOffers/NRC/PublicEducStats.htm (accessed March 24, 2009).

TABLE 13.4 General Merchandise Retailers

Type of Retailer	Description	Examples
Department store	Large organization offering wide product mix and organized into separate departments	Macy's, JCPenney, Sears
Discount store	Self-service, general merchandise store offering brand name and private brand products at low prices	Wal-Mart, Target
Supermarket	Self-service store offering complete line of food products and some nonfood products	Kroger, Albertson's, Winn-Dixie
Superstore	Giant outlet offering all food and nonfood products found in supermarkets, as well as most routinely purchased products	Wal-Mart Supercenters
Hypermarket	Combination supermarket and discount store, larger than a superstore	Carrefour
Warehouse club	Large-scale, members-only establishments combining cash-and-carry wholesaling with discount retailing	Sam's Club, Costco
Warehouse showroom	Facility in a large, low-cost building with large on-premises inventories and minimum service	Ikea
Catalog showroom	Type of warehouse showroom where consumers shop from a catalog and products are stored out of buyers' reach and provided in manufacturer's carton	Service Merchandise

Source: William M. Pride and O. C. Ferrell, *Marketing: Concepts and Strategies*, 2008, p. 428. Copyright 2008 by Houghton Mifflin Company. Reprinted with permission.

We'll keep you
on course.

Any trucking company can haul goods or materials. Put simply, we're dedicated to keeping your supply chain on par with your performance goals. By partnering with Ruan, you will enjoy customized solutions and service that bolsters your efficiency and your bottom line. At the end of the day, you'll have less to worry about and more time to concentrate on other important matters.

- Dedicated Contract Carriage
- Bulk Transportation
- Ruan Certified Brokerage Services
- Integrated Services

For more information, contact us at (866) RUAN NOW or visit our Web site, ruan.com.

RUAN
DEDICATION THAT MOVES YOUR BUSINESS

Ruan is a trucking company that helps companies keep their supply chain moving efficiently.

viewed as the number-one crisis that could decrease revenue.[32]

The focus shifts from one of selling to the next level in the channel to one of selling products *through* the channel to a satisfied ultimate customer. Information, once provided on a guarded, "as needed" basis, is now open, honest, and ongoing. Perhaps most important, the points of contact in the relationship expand from one-on-one at the salesperson–buyer level to multiple interfaces at all levels and in all functional areas of the various organizations.

channels for consumer products Typical marketing channels for consumer products are shown in Figure 13.7. In Channel A, the product moves from the producer directly to the consumer. Farmers who sell their fruit and vegetables to consumers at roadside stands use a direct-from-producer-to-consumer marketing channel.

In Channel B, the product goes from producer to retailer to consumer. This type of channel is used for products such as college textbooks, automobiles, and appliances. In Channel C, the product is handled by a wholesaler and a retailer before it reaches the consumer. Producer-to-wholesaler-to-retailer-to-consumer marketing channels distribute a wide range of products, including refrigerators, televisions, soft drinks, cigarettes, clocks, watches, and office products. In Channel D, the product goes to an agent, a wholesaler, and a retailer before going to the consumer. This long channel of distribution is especially useful for convenience products. Candy and some produce are often sold by agents who bring buyers and sellers together.

Services are usually distributed through direct marketing channels because they are generally produced *and* consumed simultaneously. For example, you cannot take a haircut home for later use. Many services require the customer's presence and participation: The sick patient must visit the physician to receive treatment; the child must be at the day care center to receive care; the tourist must be present to sightsee and consume tourism services.

management creates alliances between channel members. In Chapter 9, we defined supply chain management as connecting and integrating all parties or members of the distribution system to satisfy customers. It involves long-term partnerships among marketing channel members working together to reduce costs, waste, and unnecessary movement in the entire marketing channel in order to satisfy customers.[31] It goes beyond traditional channel members (producers, wholesalers, retailers, customers) to include *all* organizations involved in moving products from the producer to the ultimate customer. In a survey of business managers, a disruption in the supply chain was

TABLE 13.6 Major Wholesaling Functions

Supply chain management	Creating long-term partnerships among channel members
Promotion	Providing a sales force, advertising, sales promotion, and publicity
Warehousing, shipping, and product handling	Receiving, storing, and stockkeeping
	Packaging
	Shipping outgoing orders
	Materials handling
	Arranging and making local and long distance shipments
Inventory control and data processing	Processing orders
	Controlling physical inventory
	Recording transactions
	Tracking sales data for financial analysis
Risk taking	Assuming responsibility for theft, product obsolescence, and excess inventories
Financing and budgeting	Extending credit
	Making capital investments
	Forecasting cash flow
Marketing research and information systems	Providing information about market
	Conducting research studies
	Managing computer networks to facilitate exchanges and relationships

Source: William M. Pride and O. C. Ferrell, *Marketing: Concepts and Strategies,* 2008, p. 389. Copyright 2008 by Houghton Mifflin Company. Reprinted with permission.

channels for business products

In contrast to consumer goods, more than half of all business products, especially expensive equipment and technically complex products, are sold through direct marketing channels. Business customers like to communicate directly with producers of such products to gain the technical assistance and personal assurances that only the producer can offer. For this reason, business buyers prefer to purchase expensive and highly complex mainframe computers directly from IBM, Cray, and other mainframe producers. Other business products may be distributed through channels employing wholesaling intermediaries such as industrial distributors and/or manufacturer's agents.

Intensity of Market Coverage

A major distribution decision is how widely to distribute a product—that is, how many and what type of outlets should carry it. The intensity of market coverage depends on buyer behavior, as well as the nature of the target market and the competition. Wholesalers and retailers provide various intensities of market coverage and must be selected carefully to ensure success. Market coverage may be intensive, selective, or exclusive.

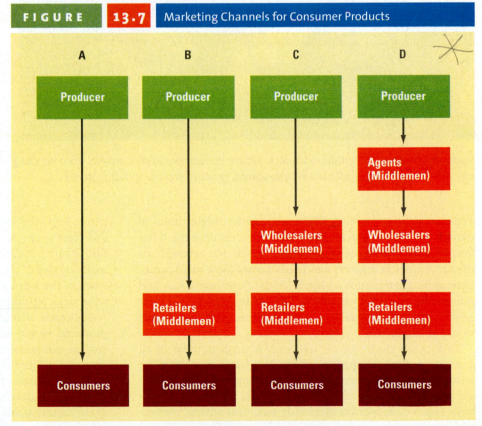

FIGURE 13.7 Marketing Channels for Consumer Products

Intensive distribution makes a product available in as many outlets as possible. Because availability is important to purchasers of convenience products such as bread, milk, gasoline, soft drinks, and chewing gum, a nearby location with a minimum of time spent searching and waiting in line is most important to the consumer. To saturate markets intensively, wholesalers and many varied retailers try to make the product

Redbox's intensive distribution strategy allows consumers to rent movies from vending machines conveniently located in restaurants, grocery stores, and drugstores.

available at every location where a consumer might desire to purchase it. Zoom Systems provides robotic vending machines for products beyond candy and drinks. Zoom has several hundred machines in airports and hotels across the United States, some selling items such as Apple iPods, Neutrogena hair and skin products and Sony products. The vending machines accept credit cards and allow sales to occur in places where storefronts would be impossible.[33]

Selective distribution uses only a small number of all available outlets to expose products. It is used most often for products that consumers buy only after shopping and comparing price, quality, and style. Many products sold on a selective basis require salesperson assistance, technical advice, warranties, or repair service to maintain consumer satisfaction. Typical products include automobiles, major appliances, clothes, and furniture.

Exclusive distribution exists when a manufacturer gives an intermediary the sole right to sell a product in a defined geographic territory. Such exclusivity provides an incentive for a dealer to handle a product that has a limited market. Exclusive distribution is the opposite of intensive distribution in that products are purchased and consumed over a long period of time, and service or information is required to develop a satisfactory sales relationship. Products distributed on an exclusive basis include high-quality musical instruments, yachts, airplanes, and high-fashion leather goods.

Physical Distribution

Physical distribution includes all the activities necessary to move products from producers to customers—inventory control, transportation, warehousing, and materials handling. Physical distribution creates time and place utility by making products available when they are wanted, with adequate service and at minimum cost. Both goods and services require physical distribution. Many physical distribution activities are part of supply chain management, which we discussed in Chapter 9; we'll take a brief look at a few more now.

transportation Transportation, the shipment of products to buyers, creates time and place utility for products, and thus is a key element in the flow of goods and services from producer to consumer. The five major modes of transportation used to move products between cities in the United States are railways, motor vehicles, inland waterways, pipelines, and airways.

Railroads offer the least expensive transportation for many products. Heavy commodities, foodstuffs, raw materials, and coal are examples of products carried by railroads. Trucks have greater flexibility than railroads because they can reach more locations. Trucks handle freight quickly and economically, offer door-to-door service, and are more flexible in their packaging requirements than are ships or airplanes. Air transport offers speed and a high degree of dependability but is the most

● **WAREHOUSING** the design and operation of facilities to receive, store, and ship products

● **MATERIALS HANDLING** the physical handling and movement of products in warehousing and transportation

● **INTEGRATED MARKETING COMMUNICATIONS** coordinating the promotion mix elements and synchronizing promotion as a unified effort

● **ADVERTISING** a paid form of nonpersonal communication transmitted through a mass medium, such as television commercials, magazine advertisements, and online ads

● **ADVERTISING CAMPAIGN** designing a series of advertisements and placing them in various media to reach a particular target market

expensive means of transportation; ships are the least expensive and slowest form. Pipelines are used to transport petroleum, natural gas, semiliquid coal, wood chips, and certain chemicals. Many products can be moved most efficiently by using more than one mode of transportation.

Factors affecting the selection of a mode of transportation include cost, capability to handle the product, reliability, and availability, and, as suggested, selecting transportation modes requires trade-offs. Unique characteristics of the product and consumer desires often determine the mode selected.

warehousing
Warehousing is the design and operation of facilities to receive, store, and ship products. A warehouse facility receives, identifies, sorts, and dispatches goods to storage; stores them; recalls, selects, or picks goods; assembles the shipment; and, finally, dispatches the shipment.

Companies often own and operate their own private warehouses that store, handle, and move their own products. They can also rent storage and related physical distribution services from public warehouses. Regardless of whether a private or a public warehouse is used, warehousing is important because it makes products available for shipment to match demand at different geographic locations.

materials handling
Materials handling is the physical handling and movement of products in warehousing and transportation. Handling processes may vary significantly due to product characteristics. Efficient materials-handling procedures increase a warehouse's useful capacity and improve customer service. Well-coordinated loading and movement systems increase efficiency and reduce costs.

Importance of Distribution in a Marketing Strategy

Distribution decisions are among the least flexible marketing mix decisions. Products can be changed over time; prices can be changed quickly; and promotion is usually changed regularly. But distribution decisions often commit resources and establish contractual relationships that are difficult, if not impossible, to change. As a company attempts to expand into new markets, it may require a complete change in distribution. Moreover, if a firm does not manage its marketing channel in the most efficient manner and provide the best service, a new competitor will evolve to create a more effective distribution system.

 L04

Specify the activities involved in promotion, as well as promotional strategies and promotional positioning.

PROMOTION STRATEGY

The role of promotion is to communicate with individuals, groups, and organizations to facilitate an exchange directly or indirectly. It encourages marketing exchanges by attempting to persuade individuals, groups, and organizations to accept goods, services, and ideas. Promotion is used not only to sell products but also to influence opinions and attitudes toward an organization, person, or cause. The state of Texas, for example, has successfully used promotion to educate people about the costs of highway litter and thereby reduce littering. Most people probably equate promotion with advertising, but it also includes personal selling, publicity, and sales promotion. The role that these elements play in a marketing strategy is extremely important.

The Promotion Mix

Advertising, personal selling, publicity, and sales promotion are collectively known as the promotion mix because a strong promotion program results from the careful selection and blending of these elements. The process of coordinating the promotion mix elements and synchronizing promotion as a unified effort is called **integrated marketing communications.** In planning promotional activities, an integrated marketing communications approach results in the desired message for customers. Different elements of the promotion mix are coordinated to play their appropriate roles in delivery of the message on a consistent basis.

advertising
Perhaps the best-known form of promotion, **advertising** is a paid form of nonpersonal communication transmitted through a mass medium, such as television commercials, magazine advertisements, and online ads. Commercials featuring celebrities, customers, or unique creations (the Energizer Bunny, for example) serve to grab viewers' attention and pique their interest in a product. Table 13.7 shows companies that spent more than $1 billion on ads in the United States in one year.

An **advertising campaign** involves designing a series of advertisements and placing them in various media to reach a particular target audience. The basic content and form of an advertising campaign are a function of several factors. A product's features, uses, and benefits affect the content of the campaign message and individual ads. Characteristics of the people in the target audience—gender, age, education, race, income, occupation, lifestyle, and other attributes—influence both content and form. When Procter & Gamble promotes Crest toothpaste to children, the company emphasizes daily brushing and cavity control, whereas it promotes tartar control

" ADVERTISING MEDIA ARE THE VEHICLES OR FORMS OF COMMUNICATION USED TO REACH A DESIRED AUDIENCE. "

TABLE 13.7 Top 10 Leading National Advertisers

Organization	Advertising Expenditure ($ Millions)
1. Procter & Gamble Co.	5230.1
2. AT&T	3207.3
3. General Motors Corp.	3101.1
4. Verizon Communications	3016.1
5. Time Warner	2962.1
6. Ford Motor Co.	2525.2
7. GlaxoSmithKline	2456.9
8. Johnson & Johnson	2408.8
9. Walt Disney Co.	2293.3
10. Unilever	2245.8

Source: Marketer Trees 2008, *Advertising Age,* June 2008, http://adage.com/marketer trees08update/ (accessed August 28, 2009).

and whiter teeth when marketing to adults. To communicate effectively, advertisers use words, symbols, and illustrations that are meaningful, familiar, and attractive to people in the target audience.

An advertising campaign's objectives and platform also affect the content and form of its messages. If a firm's advertising objectives involve large sales increases, the message may include hard-hitting, high-impact language and symbols. When campaign objectives aim at increasing brand awareness, the message may use much repetition of the brand name and words and illustrations associated with it. Thus, the advertising platform is the foundation on which campaign messages are built.

Advertising media are the vehicles or forms of communication used to reach a desired audience. Print media include newspapers, magazines, direct mail, and billboards, and electronic media include television, radio, and cyber ads. Newspapers, television, and direct mail are the most widely used advertising media. Figure 13.8 shows advertising spending by different media categories over time. Note how spending has increased across all categories, especially for the Internet and television.

Choice of media influences the content and form of the message. Effective out-door displays and short broadcast spot announcements require concise, simple messages. Magazine and newspaper advertisements can include considerable detail and long explanations. Because several kinds of media offer geographic selectivity, a precise message can be tailored to a particular geographic section of the target audience. For example, a company advertising in *Time* might decide to use one message in the New England region and another in the rest of the nation. A company may also choose to advertise in only one region. Such geographic selectivity lets a firm use the same message in different regions at different times.

The use of online advertising is increasing. However, advertisers are demanding more for their ad dollars and proof that they are working. Certain types of ads are more popular than pop-up ads and banner ads that consumers find annoying. One technique is to blur the lines between television and online advertising. TV commercials may point viewers to a Web site for more information, where short "advertainment" films continue the marketing message. When godaddy.com's 2008 Super Bowl commercial was rejected by Fox for being too racy, it left the racy version on its Web site. The TV commercial that aired showed people watching the original commercial featuring race car driver Danica Patrick online.[34] To reach a younger demographic, BMW created a 30-minute online mockumentary film featuring a fictional town in Bavaria

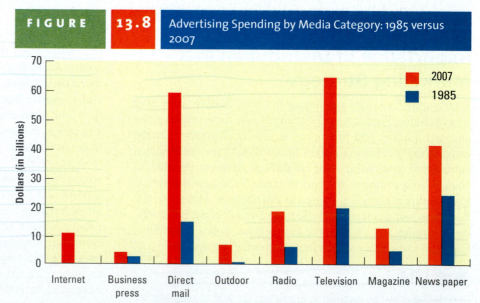

FIGURE 13.8 Advertising Spending by Media Category: 1985 versus 2007

Sources: "Ad Spending Totals by Media," *Advertising Age,* June 25, 2007, p. S-15; Robert J. Coen, "Coen: Little Ad Growth," *Advertising Age,* May 6, 1991, pp. 1, 16.

attempting to catapult a BMW car across the Atlantic using a giant ramp. The humorous take created strong buzz on the Web and led to articles in *The Wall Street Journal* and on CNN .com.[35]

Infomercials—typically 30-minute blocks of radio or television air time featuring a celebrity or upbeat host talking about and demonstrating a product—have evolved as an advertising method. Toll-free numbers and Web site addresses are usually provided so consumers can conveniently purchase the product or obtain additional information. Although many consumers and companies have negative feelings about infomercials, apparently they get results.

personal selling

Personal selling is direct, two-way communication with buyers and potential buyers. For many products—especially large, expensive ones with specialized uses, such as cars, appliances, and houses—interaction between a salesperson and the customer is probably the most important promotional tool.

Personal selling is the most flexible of the promotional methods because it gives marketers the greatest opportunity to communicate specific information that might trigger a purchase. Only personal selling can zero in on a prospect and attempt to persuade that person to make a purchase. Although personal selling has a lot of advantages, it is one of the most costly forms of promotion. A sales call on an industrial customer can cost as much as $200 or $300.

There are three distinct categories of salespersons: order takers (for example, retail sales clerks and route salespeople), creative salespersons (for example, automobile, furniture, and insurance salespeople), and support salespersons (for example, customer educators and goodwill builders who usually do not take orders). For most of these salespeople, personal selling is a six-step process:

1. *Prospecting:* Identifying potential buyers of the product.

2. *Approaching:* Using a referral or calling on a customer without prior notice to determine interest in the product.

3. *Presenting:* Getting the prospect's attention with a product demonstration.

4. *Handling objections:* Countering reasons for not buying the product.

5. *Closing:* Asking the prospect to buy the product.

6. *Following up:* Checking customer satisfaction with the purchased product.

publicity

Publicity is nonpersonal communication transmitted through the mass media but not paid for directly by the firm. A firm does not pay the media cost for publicity and is not identified as the originator of the message; instead, the message is presented in news story form. Obviously, a company can benefit from publicity by releasing to news sources newsworthy messages about the firm and its involvement with the public. Many companies have *public relations* departments to try to gain favorable publicity and minimize negative publicity for the firm.

Although advertising and publicity are both carried by the mass media, they differ in several major ways. Advertising messages tend to be informative, persuasive, or both; publicity is mainly informative. Advertising is often designed to have an immediate impact or to provide specific information to persuade a person to act; publicity describes what a firm is doing, what products it is launching, or other newsworthy information but seldom calls for action. When advertising is used, the

People Across America Catch the Twitter Bug

Want to tell the world what you are doing? The social networking site Twitter can help. By asking the question "What are you doing?," Twitter allows users to tell their friends, families, and other associates about moments in their daily lives. Twitter users post messages of up to 140 characters about their lives through SMS, instant messaging, or the Twitter Web site. Twitter is not your traditional company. Currently located in a South Park, San Francisco, warehouse, it was started when founders Biz Stone and Evan Williams created a podcasting company. They later removed the podcasting elements, leaving behind only the social-networking parts. Twitter was officially born. Twitter can be used to post something as simple as "I'm catching some zzz's in class," to President Obama's

"We just made history" on election night, to a San Francisco writer saying his house was being broken into. People are catching the "tweeting" bug, including Oprah, who tweeted for the first time on her show.

Even marketers are joining the Twitter bandwagon. Companies are finding Twitter to be an effective communications tool for attracting consumers. Bradsdeals.com, a site that identifies online shopping deals, posts company updates on Twitter. Within two months, the company attracted 2,500 followers. NASA tweets to inform people about its space shuttle flights. Bakeries are tweeting to tell customers when fresh cookies are available.

Of course, with the success of Twitter has come criticism as well. Some feel that many Twitter users post mundane details of their

lives just to kill time. Yet these complaints have not dulled Twitter's success. With two-thirds of online users visiting social-networking sites like Twitter, the Twitter craze may not fade any time soon.[36] ❖

Q: Discussion Questions

1. How would you describe Twitter as a product?

2. Do you think that Twitter is a good brand name that helps to identify the product?

3. Describe how Twitter is promoting its product.

organization must pay for media time and select the media that will best reach target audiences. The mass media willingly carry publicity because they believe it has general public interest. Advertising can be repeated a number of times; most publicity appears in the mass media once and is not repeated.

Advertising, personal selling, and sales promotion are especially useful for influencing an exchange directly. Publicity is extremely important when communication focuses on a company's activities and products and is directed at interest groups, current and potential investors, regulatory agencies, and society in general.

A variation of traditional advertising is buzz marketing, in which marketers attempt to create a trend or acceptance of a product. Companies seek out trendsetters in communities and get them to "talk up" a brand to their friends, family, co-workers, and others. Toyota, for example, parked its new Scions outside of raves and coffee shops, and offered hip-hop magazine writers the chance for test drives to get the "buzz" going about the new car.[37] Other marketers using the buzz technique include Hebrew National ("mom squads" grilled the company's hot dogs), Hasbro Games (fourth and fifth-graders tantalized their peers with Hasbro's POX electronic game), and Chrysler (its retro PT Cruiser was planted in rental fleets). The idea behind buzz marketing is that an accepted member of a particular social group will be more credible than any form of paid communication.[38] The concept works best as part of an integrated marketing communication program that also includes traditional advertising, personal selling, sales promotion, and publicity.

A related concept is viral marketing, which describes the concept of getting Internet users to pass on ads and promotions to others. Viral marketing is appealing to many companies because it allows them to compound their advertising impact cheaply. If a brand can get thousands of people to view an ad placed on YouTube, it is reaching many more people more cheaply than it would through other marketing channels.

sales promotion   Sales promotion involves direct inducements offering added value or some other incentive for buyers to enter into an exchange. The major tools of sales promotion are store displays, premiums, samples and demonstrations, coupons, contests and sweepstakes, refunds, and trade shows. Sales promotions are generally easier to measure and less expensive than advertising. More than $331 billion in potential consumer savings was distributed through coupons, with more than 2.6 billion coupons redeemed. Coupon inserts in newspapers made up about 89 percent of the distribution,

with 92.5 percent of all coupons distributed via methods sent directly to the home (direct mail, newspaper, magazine, etc).[39] While coupons can be a valuable tool in sales promotion, they cannot be relied on to stand alone, but should be part of an overall promotion mix. Sales promotion stimulates customer purchasing and increases dealer effectiveness in selling products. It is used to enhance and supplement other forms of promotion. Test drives allow salespersons to demonstrate vehicles, which can help purchase decisions. Sampling a product may also encourage consumers to buy. PepsiCo, for example, used sampling to promote its Sierra Mist soft drink to reach more than 5 million potential consumers at well-traveled sites such as Times Square and Penn Station.[40] In a given year, almost three-fourths of consumer product companies may use sampling.

Promotion Strategies: To Push or To Pull

In developing a promotion mix, organizations must decide whether to fashion a mix that pushes or pulls the product (Figure 13.9). A **push strategy** attempts to motivate intermediaries to push the product down to their customers. When a push strategy is used, the company attempts to motivate wholesalers and retailers to make the product available to their customers. Sales personnel may be used to persuade intermediaries to offer the product, distribute promotional materials, and offer special promotional incentives for those who agree to carry the product. Industrial products, such as computer parts, generally use more of a push strategy, although Intel branded its microchip and attempted to use a pull strategy by enticing consumers to seek out computers that used Intel chips. A **pull strategy** uses promotion to create consumer demand for a product so that consumers exert pressure on marketing channel members to make it available. For example, when the Coca-Cola Company launched its new hybrid energy soda VAULT, the company gave away samples throughout the United States via sampling teams in VAULT-branded International CXTs, the world's largest production pickup trucks. They distributed ice-cold VAULT at concerts and targeted retail outlets, sporting events, and other locations.[41] Such sampling prior to a product rollout encourages consumers to request the product from their favorite retailer.

A company can use either strategy, or it can use a variation or combination of the two. The exclusive use of advertising indicates a pull strategy. Personal selling to marketing channel members indicates a push strategy. The allocation of promotional resources to various marketing mix elements probably determines which strategy a marketer uses.

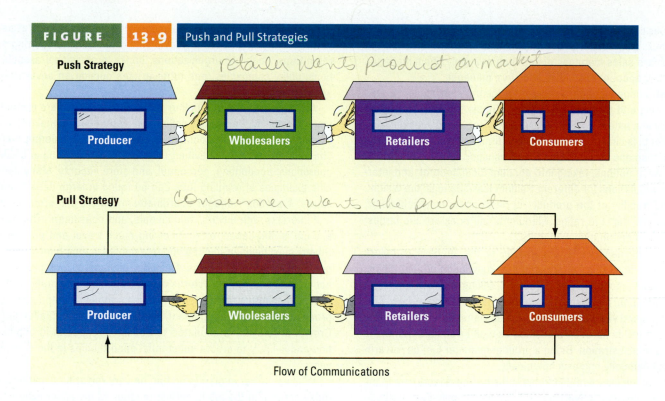

FIGURE 13.9 Push and Pull Strategies

Push Strategy

retailer wants product on market

Producer — Wholesalers — Retailers — Consumers

Pull Strategy

consumer wants the product

Producer — Wholesalers — Retailers — Consumers

Flow of Communications

Objectives of Promotion

The marketing mix a company uses depends on its objectives. It is important to recognize that promotion is only one element of the marketing strategy and must be tied carefully to the goals of the firm, its overall marketing objectives, and the other elements of the marketing strategy. Firms use promotion for many reasons, but typical objectives are to stimulate demand, stabilize sales, and inform, remind, and reinforce customers.

Increasing demand for a product is probably the most typical promotional objective. Stimulating demand, often through advertising and sales promotion, is particularly important when a firm is using a pull strategy.

Another goal of promotion is to stabilize sales by maintaining the status quo—that is, the current sales level of the product. During periods of slack or decreasing sales, contests, prizes, vacations, and other sales promotions sometimes are offered to customers to maintain sales goals. Advertising is often used to stabilize sales by making customers aware of slack use periods. For example, auto manufacturers often provide rebates, free options, or lower-than-market interest rates to stabilize sales and thereby keep production lines moving during temporary slowdowns. A stable sales pattern allows the firm to run efficiently by maintaining a consistent level of production and storage and utilizing all its functions so that it is ready when sales increase.

An important role of any promotional program is to inform potential buyers about the organization and its products. A major portion of advertising in the United States, particularly in daily newspapers, is informational. Providing information about the availability, price, technology, and features of a product is very important in encouraging a buyer to move toward a purchase decision. Nearly all forms of promotion involve an attempt to help consumers learn more about a product and a company.

Promotion is also used to remind consumers that an established organization is still around and sells certain products that have uses and benefits. Often advertising reminds customers that they may need to use a product more frequently or in certain situations. Pennzoil, for example, has run television commercials reminding car owners that they need to change their oil every 3,000 miles to ensure proper performance of their cars.

Reinforcement promotion attempts to assure current users of the product that they have made the right choice and tells them how to get the most satisfaction from the product. Also, a company could release publicity statements through the news media about a new use for a product. Additionally, firms can have salespeople communicate with current and potential customers about the proper use and maintenance of a product—all in the hope of developing a repeat customer.

Promotional Positioning

Promotional positioning uses promotion to create and maintain an image of a product in buyers' minds. It is a natural result of market segmentation. In both promotional positioning and market segmentation, the firm targets a given product or brand at a portion of the total market. A promotional strategy helps differentiate the product and make it appeal to

SO YOU WANT TO BE A MARKETING MANAGER

Many jobs in marketing are closely tied to the functions of the marketing mix: distribution, product, promotion, and price. Often the job titles are sales manager, distribution or supply chain manager, advertising account executive, and store manager.

A distribution manager arranges for the transportation of goods within firms and through marketing channels. Transportation can be costly and time is always an important factor, and so minimizing their effects is vital to the success of a firm. Distribution managers must choose one or a combination of transportation modes from a vast array of options, taking into account local, federal, and international regulations for different freight classifications; the weight, size, and fragility of the products to be shipped; time schedules; and loss and damage ratios. Manufacturing firms are the largest employers of distribution managers.

A product manager is responsible for the success or failure of a product line. This requires general knowledge of advertising, transportation modes, inventory control, selling and sales management, promotion, marketing research, packaging, and pricing. Frequently, several years of selling and sales management experience are prerequisites for such a position as well as college training in business administration. Being a product manager can be rewarding both financially and psychologically.

Some of the most creative roles in the business world are in the area of advertising. Advertising pervades our daily lives as businesses and other organizations try to grab our attention and tell us about what they have to offer. Copywriters, artists, and account executives in advertising must have creativity, imagination, artistic talent, and expertise in expression and persuasion. Advertising is an area of business in which a wide variety of educational backgrounds may be useful, from degrees in advertising to journalism or liberal arts degrees. Common entry-level positions in an advertising agency are found in the traffic department, account service (account coordinator), and the media department (media assistant). Advertising jobs are also available in many manufacturing or retail firms, nonprofit organizations, banks, professional associations, utility companies, and other arenas outside an advertising agency.

Although a career in retailing may begin in sales, there is much more to retailing than simply selling. Many retail personnel occupy management positions, focusing on selecting and ordering merchandise, promotional activities, inventory control, customer credit operations, accounting, personnel, and store security. Many specific examples of retailing jobs can be found in large department stores. A section manager coordinates inventory and promotions and interacts with buyers, salespeople, and consumers. The buyer's job is fast-paced, often involving much travel and pressure. Buyers must be open-minded and foresighted in their hunt for new, potentially successful items. Regional managers coordinate the activities of several retail stores within a specific geographic area, usually monitoring and supporting sales, promotions, and general procedures. Retail management can be exciting and challenging. Growth in retailing is expected to accompany growth in population and is likely to create substantial opportunities in the coming years.

While a career in marketing can be very rewarding, marketers today agree that the job is getting tougher. Many advertising and marketing executives say the job has gotten much more demanding in the last 10 years, viewing their number-one challenge as balancing work and personal obligations. Other challenges include staying current on industry trends or technologies, keeping motivated/inspired on the job, and measuring success. If you are up to the challenge, you may find that a career in marketing is just right for you to utilize your business knowledge while exercising your creative side as well.

a particular market segment. For example, to appeal to safety-conscious consumers, Volvo heavily promotes the safety and crashworthiness of Volvo automobiles in its advertising. Volkswagen has done the same thing with its edgy ads showing car crashes. Promotion can be used to change or reinforce an image. Effective promotion influences customers and persuades them to buy. ∎

Team Exercise

Form groups and give each team an opportunity to search for examples of convenience products, shopping products, specialty products, and business products. How are these products marketed? Provide examples of any ads you find to show examples of the promotional strategies for these products. Report your findings to the class.

CHECK OUT www.mhhe.com/FerrellM2e

for study materials including Interactive Exercises, Quizzes, iPod downloads, and video.

ACCOUNTING & FINANCIAL STATEMENTS

CHAPTER FOURTEEN

Introduction

Accounting, the financial "language" that organizations use to record, measure, and interpret all their financial transactions and records, is very important in business. All businesses—from a small family farm to a giant corporation—use the language of accounting to make sure they use their money wisely and plan for the future. Nonbusiness organizations such as charities and governments also use accounting to demonstrate to donors and taxpayers how well they are using their funds and meeting their stated objectives.

This chapter explores the role of accounting in business and its importance in making business decisions. First, we discuss the uses of accounting information and the accounting process. Then, we briefly look at some simple financial statements and accounting tools that are useful in analyzing organizations worldwide.

LO1

Define accounting, and describe the different uses of accounting information.

THE NATURE OF ACCOUNTING

Simply stated, **accounting** is the recording, measurement, and interpretation of financial information. Large numbers of people and institutions, both within and outside businesses, use accounting tools to evaluate organizational operations. The Financial Accounting Standards Board has been establishing standards of financial accounting and reporting in the private sector since 1973. Its mission is to establish and improve standards of financial accounting and reporting for the guidance and education of the public, including issuers, auditors, and users of financial information. However, the accounting scandals at the turn of the century resulted when many accounting firms and businesses failed to abide by generally accepted accounting principles. More than 1,000 firms ultimately reported flaws in their financial statements between 1997 and 2002; in 2002 alone, a record 330 companies chose to restate their earnings to avoid further questions.[1] Consequently, the federal government has taken a greater role in making rules, requirements, and policies for accounting firms and businesses through the Securities and Exchange Commission's Public Company Accounting Oversight Board. For example, Ernst & Young, a leading accounting firm, was barred from undertaking new audit clients for six months as a penalty for abusing the agency's auditor-independence rules.[2]

To better understand the importance of accounting, we must first understand who prepares accounting information and how it is used.

Accountants

Many of the functions of accounting are carried out by public or private accountants.

public accountants Individuals and businesses can hire a **certified public accountant (CPA),** an individual who has been certified by the state in which he or she practices

DID YOU KNOW?

Corporate fraud costs the average company nearly $3 million a year.[4]

to provide accounting services ranging from the preparation of financial records and the filing of tax returns to complex audits of corporate financial records. Certification gives a public accountant the right to express, officially, an unbiased opinion regarding the accuracy of the client's financial statements. Most public accountants are either self-employed or members of large public accounting firms such as Ernst & Young, KPMG, Deloitte & Touche, and Pricewaterhouse Coopers, together referred to as "the Big Four." In addition, many CPAs work for one of the second-tier accounting firms that are about one-third the size of the Big Four firms, as illustrated in Table 14.1. The accounting scandals at the turn of the century, combined with more stringent accounting requirements legislated by the Sarbanes-Oxley Act, have increased job prospects for accountants and students with accounting degrees as companies and accounting firms hire more auditors to satisfy the law and public demand for greater transparency.

With the demise of Arthur Andersen there have been concerns about one of the remaining Big Four accounting firms failing. The U.S. Chamber of Commerce published a report calling for regulators and policy makers to keep such an event from happening again to maintain competition and availability of accountants.[3]

A growing area for public accountants is *forensic accounting*, which involves analyzing financial documents in search of fraudulent entries or financial misconduct. Functioning as much like detectives as like accountants, forensic accountants have been used since the 1930s. In the wake of the accounting scandals of the early 2000s, many auditing firms are rapidly adding or expanding forensic or fraud-detection services. Additionally, many forensic accountants root out evidence of "cooked books" for federal agencies such as the

TABLE 14.1 The Top Accounting Firms in the United States

Company	Revenues (millions)*
"Big Four"	
Deloitte	10,982
PricewaterhouseCoopers	7,464
Ernst & Young	7,561
KPMG	5,357
Second-Tier Firms	
Grant Thornton	1,075
BDO Sideman	659
Moss Adams	315

*Rankings are 2009; revenue is 2008.

Source: "Top Accounting Firms–2009, Vault Top 40 Most Prestigious," www.vault.com/nr/finance_rankings/accounting_rankings.jsp?accounting2009=2 (accessed March 24, 2009); "IPA's 2008 Top 100 Firms," The Platt Consulting Group, www.plattgroupllc.com/top100_2008.pdf (accessed March 24, 2009).

Federal Bureau of Investigation or the Internal Revenue Service. The Association of Certified Fraud Examiners, which certifies accounting professionals as *Certified Fraud Examiners (CFEs),* has grown to more than 50,000 members.[5]

private accountants Large corporations, government agencies, and other organizations may employ their own **private accountants** to prepare and analyze their financial statements. With titles such as controller, tax accountant, and internal auditor, private accountants are deeply involved in many of the most important financial decisions of the organizations for which they work. Private accountants can be CPAs and may become **certified management accountants (CMAs)** by passing a rigorous examination by the Institute of Management Accountants.

Accounting or Bookkeeping?

The terms *accounting* and *bookkeeping* are often mistakenly used interchangeably. Much narrower and far more mechanical than accounting, bookkeeping is typically limited to the routine, day-to-day recording of business transactions. Bookkeepers are responsible for obtaining and recording the information that accountants require to analyze a firm's financial position. They generally require less training than accountants. Accountants, in contrast, usually complete course work beyond their basic four- or five-year college accounting degrees. This additional training allows accountants not only to record financial information, but to understand, interpret, and even develop the sophisticated accounting systems necessary to classify and analyze complex financial information.

The Uses of Accounting Information

Accountants summarize the information from a firm's business transactions in various financial statements (which we'll look at in a later section of this chapter) for a variety of stakeholders, including managers, investors, creditors, and government agencies. Many business failures may be directly linked to ignorance of the information "hidden" inside these financial statements. Likewise, most business successes can be traced to informed managers who understand the consequences of their deci-

sions. While maintaining and even increasing short-run profits is desirable, failure to plan sufficiently for the future can easily lead an otherwise successful company to insolvency and bankruptcy court.

Basically, managers and owners use financial statements (1) to aid in internal planning and control and (2) for external purposes such as reporting to the Internal Revenue Service, stockholders, creditors, customers, employees, and other interested parties. Figure 14.1 shows some of the users of the accounting information generated by a typical corporation.

internal uses **Managerial accounting** refers to the internal use of accounting statements by managers in planning and directing the organization's activities. Perhaps management's greatest single concern is **cash flow,** the movement of money through an organization on a daily, weekly, monthly, or yearly basis. Obviously, for any business to succeed, it needs to generate enough cash to pay its bills as they fall due. However, it is not at all unusual for highly successful and rapidly growing companies to struggle to make payments to employees, suppliers, and lenders because of an inadequate cash flow. One common reason for a so-called cash crunch, or shortfall, is poor managerial planning.

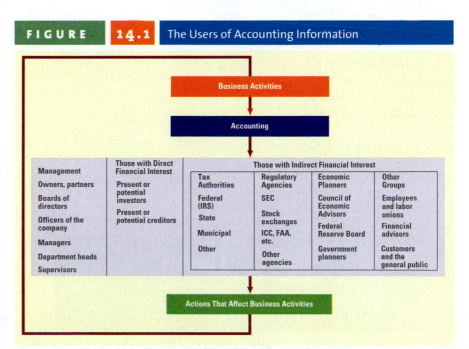

FIGURE 14.1 The Users of Accounting Information

Source: Belverd E. Needles, Henry R. Anderson, and James C. Caldwell, *Principles of Accounting,* 4th edition. Copyright © 1990 by Houghton Mifflin Company. Reprinted with permission.

Managerial accountants help companies make better internal financial decisions.

External suppliers, such as Huron Consulting Group, can provide diverse accounting services for clients.

Managerial accountants also help prepare an organization's **budget,** an internal financial plan that forecasts expenses and income over a set period of time. It is not unusual for an organization to prepare separate daily, weekly, monthly, and yearly budgets. Think of a budget as a financial map, showing how the company expects to move from Point A to Point B over a specific period. While most companies prepare *master budgets* for the entire firm, many also prepare budgets for smaller segments of the organization such as divisions, departments, product lines, or projects. "Top-down" master budgets begin at the top and filter down to the individual department level, while "bottom-up" budgets start at the department or project level and are combined at the chief executive's office. Generally, the larger and more rapidly growing an organization is, the greater will be the likelihood that it will build its master budget from the ground up.

Regardless of focus, the major value of a budget lies in its breakdown of cash inflows and outflows. Expected operating expenses (cash outflows such as wages, materials costs, and taxes) and operating revenues (cash inflows in the form of payments from customers) over a set period are carefully forecast and subsequently compared with actual results. Deviations between the two serve as a "trip wire" or "feedback loop" to launch more detailed financial analyses in an effort to pinpoint trouble spots and opportunities.

external uses Managers also use accounting statements to report the business's financial performance to outsiders. Such statements are used for filing income taxes, obtaining credit from lenders, and reporting results to the firm's stockholders. They become the basis for the information provided in the official corporate **annual report,** a summary of the firm's financial information, products, and growth plans for owners and potential investors. Although these reports frequently are presented between slick, glossy covers prepared by major advertising firms, the single most important component of an annual report is the signature of a certified public accountant attesting that the required financial statements are an accurate reflection of the underlying financial condition of the firm. Financial statements meeting these conditions are termed *audited*. The primary external users of audited accounting information are government agencies, stockholders and potential investors, and lenders, suppliers, and employees.

Federal, state, and local governments (both domestic and overseas) require organizations to file audited financial statements concerning taxes owed and paid, payroll deductions for employees, and, for corporations, new issues of securities (stocks and bonds). Even nonprofit corporations and other nonbusiness organizations may

A CORPORATION'S STOCKHOLDERS USE FINANCIAL STATEMENTS TO EVALUATE THE RETURN ON THEIR INVESTMENT AND THE OVERALL QUALITY OF THE FIRM'S MANAGEMENT TEAM

be required to file regular financial statements. Like individuals, well-managed companies generally try to minimize their taxable income by using accepted accounting practices. Usually, accounting practices that reduce taxes also reduce reported profits. By reducing taxes, the firm increases the cash available to the firm that can be used for many purposes, such as plant expansion, debt retirement, and repurchase of common stock.

A corporation's stockholders use financial statements to evaluate the return on their investment and the overall quality of the firm's management team. As a result, poor financial statements often result in changes in top management. Potential investors study the financial statements in a firm's annual report to determine whether the company meets their investment requirements and whether the returns from a given firm are likely to compare favorably with those of other similar companies.

Banks and other lenders look at financial statements to determine a company's ability to meet current and future debt obligations if a loan or credit is granted. To determine this ability, a lender examines a firm's cash flow to assess its ability to repay a loan quickly with cash generated from sales. A lender is also interested in the company's profitability and indebtedness

to other lenders. Short-term creditors focus on a firm's ability to pay off loans quickly; long-term lenders focus on profitability and indebtedness.

Labor unions and employees use financial statements to establish reasonable expectations for salary and other benefit requests. Just as firms experiencing record profits are likely to face added pressure to increase employee wages, employees are unlikely to grant employers wage and benefit concessions without considerable evidence of financial distress.

 L02

Demonstrate the accounting process.

THE ACCOUNTING PROCESS

Many view accounting as a primary business language. It is of little use, however, unless you know how to "speak" it. Fortunately, the fundamentals—the accounting equation and the double-entry bookkeeping system—are not difficult to learn.

> ## "Many view accounting as a primary business language."

Mark-to-Market Accounting

Mark-to-market accounting contributed to the problems banks faced in the 2008–2009 financial crisis. It requires companies to mark their assets to the market price that existed on that day, which makes sense for futures traders because they buy assets at a fixed future price. However, mark-to-market accounting has been abused recently, most notably by Enron. Enron misused mark to market by tabulating anticipated future profits as real, thereby driving up the company's appearance of profitability. This was clearly a misuse of the accounting technique.

Mark to market also does not work well when trading stops because a market price cannot be determined then. When a market dries up, as the mortgage-backed securities market did in late 2008, no active trading occurs and prices do not exist. Banks had mortgages and other

assets and debts that were technically marketable, but investors perceived that there was a high level of risk involved and did not want to invest. If the banks marked their assets to zero or 20 cents on the dollar, they would have been because of grossly undervaluing those instruments. Unfortunately, banks were forced to write down assets the mark-to-market rule and wrote off billions of dollars of losses.

To help ease the problems on Wall Street, Congress pressured the Securities and Exchange Commission and the Federal Accounting Standards Board to relax the mark-to-market rules, which they did to allow the use of discounted cash flow models to value these assets. These models give banks more accounting flexibility so that they do not have to mark down valuations drastically in times of crisis.[6] ❖

 Discussion Questions

1. How would you describe the mark-to-market accounting method? (Use your own words.)

2. Why did mark-to-market accounting methods affect the value of companies so greatly during the financial crisis?

3. Is it a good idea to relax mark-to-market rules to give companies more flexibility with accounting procedures during times of crisis?

These two concepts serve as the starting point for all currently accepted accounting principles.

The Accounting Equation

Accountants are concerned with reporting an organization's assets, liabilities, and owners' equity. To help illustrate these concepts, consider a hypothetical floral shop called Anna's Flowers, owned by Anna Rodriguez. A firm's economic resources, or items of value that it owns, represent its assets—cash, inventory, land, equipment, buildings, and other tangible and intangible things. The assets of Anna's Flowers include counters, refrigerated display cases, flowers, decorations, vases, cards, and other gifts, as well as something known as "goodwill," which in this case is Anna's reputation for preparing and delivering beautiful floral arrangements on a timely basis. Liabilities, in contrast, are debts the firm owes to others. Among the liabilities of Anna's Flowers are a loan from the Small Business Administration and money owed to flower suppliers and other creditors for items purchased. The owners' equity category contains all the money that has ever been contributed to the company that never has to be paid back. The funds can come from investors who have given money or assets to the company, or it can come from past profitable operations. In the case of Anna's Flowers, if Anna were to sell off, or liquidate, her business, any money left over after selling all the shop's assets and paying off its liabilities would constitute her owner's equity. The relationship between assets, liabilities, and owners' equity is a fundamental concept in accounting and is known as the accounting equation:

$$\text{Assets} = \text{Liabilities} + \text{Owner's equity}$$

Double-Entry Bookkeeping

Double-entry bookkeeping is a system of recording and classifying business transactions in separate accounts to maintain the balance of the accounting equation. Returning to Anna's Flowers, suppose Anna buys $325 worth of roses on credit from the Antique Rose Emporium to fill a wedding order. When she records this transaction, she will list the $325 as a liability or a debt to a supplier. At the same time, however, she will also record $325 worth of roses as an asset in an account known as "inventory." Because the assets and liabilities are on different sides of the accounting equation, Anna's accounts increase in total size (by $325) but remain in balance:

$$\text{Assets} = \text{Liabilities} + \text{Owners' equity}$$
$$\$325 = \$325$$

Thus, to keep the accounting equation in balance, each business transaction must be recorded in two separate accounts.

In the final analysis, all business transactions are classified as assets, liabilities, or owners' equity. However, most organizations further break down these three accounts to provide more specific information about a transaction. For example, assets may be broken down into specific categories such as cash, inventory, and equipment, while liabilities may include bank loans, supplier credit, and other debts.

Figure 14.2 shows how Anna used the double-entry bookkeeping system to account for all of the transactions that took place in her first month of business. These transactions include her initial investment of $2,500, the loan from the Small Business Administration, purchases of equipment and inventory, and the purchase of roses on credit. In her first month of business, Anna generated revenues of $2,000 by selling $1,500 worth of inventory. Thus, she deducts, or (in accounting notation that is appropriate for assets) *credits,* $1,500 from inventory and adds, or *debits,* $2,000 to the cash account. The difference between Anna's $2,000 cash inflow and her $1,500 outflow is represented by a credit to owners' equity, because it is money that belongs to her as the owner of the flower shop.

The Accounting Cycle

In any accounting system, financial data typically pass through a four-step procedure sometimes called the **accounting cycle.** The steps include examining source documents, recording transactions in an accounting journal, posting recorded transactions, and preparing financial statements. Figure 14.3 shows how Anna works through them. Traditionally, all these steps were performed using paper, pencils, and erasers (lots of erasers!), but today the process is often fully computerized.

step one: examine source documents

Like all good managers, Anna Rodriguez begins the accounting cycle by gathering and examining source documents—checks, credit-card receipts, sales slips, and other related evidence concerning specific transactions.

step two: record transactions

Next, Anna records each financial transaction in a **journal,** which is basically just a time-ordered list of account transactions. While most businesses keep a general journal in which all transactions are recorded, some classify transactions into specialized journals for specific types of transaction accounts.

step three: post transactions

Anna next transfers the information from her journal into a **ledger,** a book or computer program with separate files for each account. This process is known as *posting*. At the end of the accounting period (usually yearly, but occasionally quarterly or monthly), Anna prepares a *trial balance*, a summary of the balances of all the accounts in the general ledger. If, upon totalling, the trial balance isn't correct (that is, the accounting equation is not in balance), Anna or her accountant must look for mistakes (typically an error in one or more of the ledger entries) and correct them. If the trial balance is correct, the accountant can then begin to prepare the financial statements.

step four: prepare financial statements

The information from the trial balance is also used to prepare the company's financial statements. In the case of public corporations and certain other organizations, a CPA must *attest*, or certify, that the organization followed generally accepted accounting principles in preparing the financial statements. When these statements have been completed, the organization's books are "closed," and the accounting cycle begins anew for the next accounting period.

FINANCIAL STATEMENTS

The end results of the accounting process are a series of financial statements. The income statement, the balance sheet, and the statement of cash flows are the best-known examples of financial statements. These statements are provided to stockholders and potential investors in a firm's annual report as well as to other relevant outsiders, such as creditors, government agencies, and the Internal Revenue Service.

It is important to recognize that not all financial statements follow precisely the same format. The fact that different organizations generate income in different ways suggests that when it comes to financial statements, one size definitely does not fit all. Manufacturing firms, service providers, and nonprofit organizations each use a different set of accounting principles or rules upon which the public accounting profession has agreed. As we have already mentioned, these are sometimes referred to as *generally accepted accounting principles (GAAP)*. Each country has a different set of rules that the businesses within that country are required to use for their accounting process and financial statements. Moreover, as is the case in many other disciplines, certain concepts have more than one name. For example, *sales* and *revenues* are often interchanged, as are *profits, income*, and *earnings*. Table 14.2 lists a few common equivalent terms that should help you decipher their meaning in accounting statements.

 L03

Examine the various components of an income statement to evaluate a firm's "bottom line."

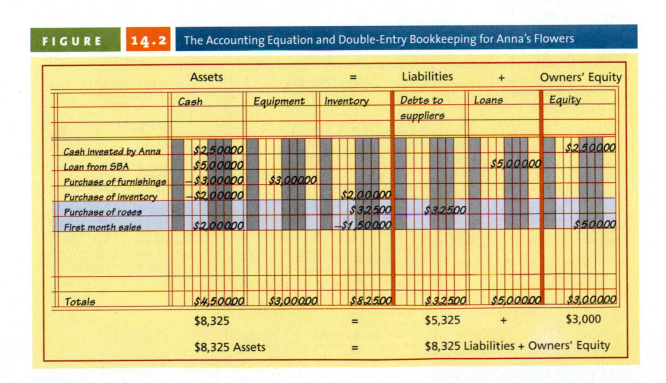

FIGURE 14.2 The Accounting Equation and Double-Entry Bookkeeping for Anna's Flowers

	Assets			=	Liabilities	+	Owners' Equity
	Cash	Equipment	Inventory		Debts to suppliers	Loans	Equity
Cash invested by Anna	$2,500.00						$2,500.00
Loan from SBA	$5,000.00					$5,000.00	
Purchase of furnishings	−$3,000.00	$3,000.00					
Purchase of inventory	−$2,000.00		$2,000.00				
Purchase of roses			$325.00		$325.00		
First month sales	$2,000.00		−$1,500.00				$500.00
Totals	$4,500.00	$3,000.00	$825.00		$325.00	$5,000.00	$3,000.00

$8,325 = $5,325 + $3,000

$8,325 Assets = $8,325 Liabilities + Owners' Equity

FIGURE 14.3 The Accounting Process for Anna's Flowers

Step 1:
Source documents show that a transaction took place.

Receipt Anna's Flowers	
July 7 Wedding floral arrangements	$500.00
Consultation services	250.00

Step 2:
The transaction is recorded in the journal.

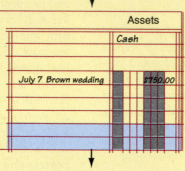

Assets

Cash

July 7 Brown wedding $750.00

Step 3:
The transaction is posted to the general ledger under the appropriate account (asset, liability, or some further breakdown of these main accounts).

Date		Explanation	PR	Debit	Credit	Balance Debit	Balance Credit
2009							
July	1		1	2,000		2,000	
	3		1		1,250		1,250
	4		1				
	7	Brown wedding	1		750		750
	14		1				

Step 4: At the end of the accounting period, the ledger is used to prepare the firm's financial statements.

Anna's Flowers
Income Statement
December 31, 2009

Revenues:		
Net sales		$123,850
Consulting		73,850
Total revenues		$197,700
Expenses:		
Cost of goods sold	$72,600	
Selling expenses	37,700	
General and admin.	18,400	
Other expenses	5,600	
Total expenses		134,300
Net income		$ 63,400

Anna's Flowers
Balance Sheet
December 31, 2009

Assets
Current assets:

Cash	$17,850	
Accounts receivable	10,200	
Merch. Inventory	8,750	
Tot. assets		$36,800
Property and Equipment		
Equipment	11,050	
Office building	73,850	
Tot. prop. & equip.		84,900
Total assets		$121,700

Liabilities and Owner's Equity
Current liabilities

Accounts payable	$12,600	
Tot. cur. liabilities		12,600
Long-term liabilities		
Mortgage payable		23,600
Total liabilities		36,200
Owner's equity:		
Anna Rodriguez, capital		$ 85,500
Tot. liabilities and owners' equity		$ 121,700

Anna's Flowers
Annual Budget
for 2009

	Sales	Consulting	Total
January	10,500	4,500	15,000
February	10,000	5,500	15,500
March	10,800	5,700	16,500
April	10,100	6,050	16,150
May	12,000	6,000	18,000
June	12,100	6,250	18,350
July	13,000	6,600	19,600
August	9,950	6,000	15,950
September	9,700	6,200	15,900
October	9,900	7,000	16,900
November	8,500	7,150	15,650
December	7,300	6,900	14,200
Annual	$123,850	$73,850	$197,700

The Income Statement

● INCOME STATEMENT a fianancial report that shows an organization's profitability over a period of time—month, quarter, or year

The question, "What's the bottom line?" derives from the income statement, where the bottom line shows the overall profit or loss of the company after taxes. Thus, the **income statement** is a financial report that shows an organization's profitability over a period of time, be that a month, quarter, or year. By its very design, the income statement offers one of the clearest possible pictures of the company's overall revenues and the costs incurred in generating those revenues. Other names for the income statement include profit and loss (P&L) statement and operating statement. A sample income statement with line-by-line explanations is presented in Table 14.3, while Table 14.4 presents the income statement of Starbucks. The income statement indicates the firm's profitability or income (the bottom line), which is derived by subtracting the firm's expenses from its revenues.

TABLE 14.2 Equivalent Terms in Accounting

Term	Equivalent Term
Revenues	Sales
	Goods or services sold
Gross profit	Gross income
	Gross earnings
	Gross margin
Operating income	Operating profit
	Earnings before interest and taxes (EBIT)
	Income before interest and taxes (IBIT)
Income before taxes (IBT)	Earnings before taxes (EBT)
	Profit before taxes (PBT)
Net income (NI)	Earnings after taxes (EAT)
	Profit after taxes (PAT)
Income available to common stockholders	Earnings available to common stockholders

TABLE 14.3 Sample Income Statement

The following exhibit presents a sample income statement with all the terms defined and explained.

Company Name for the Year Ended December 31	
Revenues (sales)	Total dollar amount of products sold (includes income from other business services such as rental-lease income and interest income).
Less: Cost of goods sold	The cost of producing the goods and services, including the cost of labor and raw materials as well as other expenses associated with production.
Gross profit	The income available after paying all expenses of production.
Less: Selling and administrative expense	The cost of promoting, advertising, and selling products as well as the overhead costs of managing the company. This includes the cost of management and corporate staff. One noncash expense included in this category is depreciation, which approximates the decline in the value of plant and equipment assets due to use over time. In most accounting statements, depreciation is not separated from selling and administrative expenses. However, financial analysts usually create statements that include this expense.
Income before interest and taxes (operating income or EBIT)	This line represents all income left over after operating expenses have been deducted. This is sometimes referred to as operating income because it represents all income after the expenses of operations have been accounted for. Occasionally, this is referred to as EBIT, or earnings before interest and taxes.
Less: Interest expense	Interest expense arises as a cost of borrowing money. This is a financial expense rather than an operating expense and is listed separately. As the amount of debt and the cost of debt increase, so will the interest expense. This covers the cost of both short-term and long-term borrowing.
Income before taxes (earnings before taxes—EBT)	The firm will pay a tax on this amount. This is what is left of revenues after subtracting all operating costs, depreciation costs, and interest costs.
Less: Taxes	The tax rate is specified in the federal tax code.
Net income	This is the amount of income left after taxes. The firm may decide to retain all or a portion of the income for reinvestment in new assets. Whatever it decides not to keep it will usually pay out in dividends to its stockholders.
Less: Preferred dividends	If the company has preferred stockholders, they are first in line for dividends. That is one reason their stock is called "preferred."
Income to common stockholders	This is the income left for the common stockholders. If the company has a good year, there may be a lot of income available for dividends. If the company has a bad year, income could be negative. The common stockholders are the ultimate owners and risk takers. They have the potential for very high or very poor returns because they get whatever is left after all other expenses.
Earnings per share	Earnings per share is found by taking the income available to the common stockholders and dividing by the number of shares of common stock outstanding. This is income generated by the company for each share of common stock.

revenue Revenue is the total amount of money received (or promised) from the sale of goods or services, as well as from other business activities such as the rental of property and investments. Nonbusiness entities typically obtain revenues through donations from individuals and/or grants from governments and private foundations. Starbucks' income statement (see Table 14.4) shows one main source of income: sales of Starbucks' products.

For most manufacturing and retail concerns, the next major item included in the income statement is the **cost of goods sold,** the amount of money the firm spent (or promised to spend) to buy and/or produce the products it sold during the accounting period. This figure may be calculated as follows:

$$\text{Cost of Goods Sold} = \text{Beginning inventory} + \text{Interim purchases} - \text{Ending inventory}$$

Let's say that Anna's Flowers began an accounting period with an inventory of goods for which it paid $5,000. During the period, Anna bought another $4,000 worth of goods, giving the shop a total inventory available for sale of $9,000. If, at the end of the accounting period, Anna's inventory was worth $5,500,

TABLE 14.4 Consolidated Statements of Earnings for Starbucks (in thousands, except earnings per share)

Fiscal Year Ended	Sept 30, 2007	Oct 1, 2006	Oct 2, 2005
Net revenues:			
Company-operated retail	$7,998,265	$6,583,098	$5,391,927
Specialty:			
Licensing	1,026,338	860,676	673,015
Foodservice and other	386,894	343,168	304,358
Total specialty	1,413,232	1,203,844	977,373
Total net revenues	9,411,497	7,786,942	6,369,300
Cost of sales including occupancy costs	3,999,124	3,178,791	2,605,212
Store operating expenses	3,215,889	2,687,815	2,165,911
Other operating expenses	294,136	253,724	192,525
Depreciation and amortization expenses	467,160	387,211	340,169
General and administrative expenses	489,249	479,386	361,613
Total operating expenses	8,465,558	6,986,927	5,665,430
Income from equity investees	108,006	93,937	76,648
Operating income	1,053,945	893,952	780,518
Net interest and other income	2,419	12,291	15,829
Earnings before income taxes	1,056,364	906,243	796,347
Income taxes	383,726	324,770	301,977
Earnings before cumulative effect of change in accounting principle	672,638	581,473	494,370
Cumulative effect of accounting change for FIN 47, net of taxes	—	17,214	—
Net earnings	$ 672,638	$ 564,259	$ 494,370
Per common share:			
Net earnings—basic	$ 0.90	$ 0.74	$ 0.63
Net earnings—diluted	$ 0.87	$ 0.71	$ 0.61
Weighted average shares outstanding:			
Basic	749,763	766,114	789,570
Diluted	770,091	792,556	815,417

Source: media.corporate-ir.net/media_files/irol/99/99518/2007AR (accessed September 18, 2008).

the cost of goods sold during the period would have been $3,500 ($5,000 + $4,000 - $5,500 = 3,500). If Anna had total revenues of $10,000 over the same period of time, subtracting the cost of goods sold ($3,500) from the total revenues of $10,000 yields the store's **gross income or profit** (revenues minus the cost of goods sold required to generate the revenues): $6,500. For Starbucks, cost of goods sold was slightly more than $2.6 billion in 2005. Notice that Starbucks calls it cost of sales, rather than cost of goods sold. This is because Starbucks buys raw materials and supplies and produces drinks.

expenses
Expenses are the costs incurred in the day-to-day operations of an organization. Three common expense accounts shown on income statements are (1) selling, general, and administrative expenses; (2) research, development, and engineering expenses; and (3) interest expenses (remember that the costs directly attributable to selling goods or services are included in the cost of goods sold). Selling expenses include advertising and sales salaries. General and administrative expenses include salaries of executives and their staff and the costs of owning and maintaining the general office. Research and development costs include scientific, engineering, and marketing personnel and the equipment and information used to design and build prototypes and samples. Interest expenses include the direct costs of borrowing money.

The number and type of expense accounts vary from organization to organization. Included in the general and administrative category is a special type of expense known as **depreciation,** the process of spreading the costs of long-lived assets such as buildings and equipment over the total number of accounting periods in which they are expected to be used. Consider a manufacturer that purchases a $100,000 machine expected to last about 10 years. Rather than showing an expense of $100,000 in the first year and no expense for that equipment over the next nine years,

the manufacturer is allowed to report depreciation expenses of $10,000 per year in each of the next 10 years because that better matches the cost of the machine to the years the machine is used. Each time this depreciation is "written off" as an expense, the book value of the machine is also reduced by $10,000. The fact that the equipment has a zero value on the firm's balance sheet when it is fully depreciated (in this case, after 10 years) does not necessarily mean that it can no longer be used or is economically worthless. Indeed, in some industries, machines used every day have been reported as having no book value whatsoever for over 30 years.

net income
Net income (or net earnings) is the total profit (or loss) after all expenses including taxes have been deducted from revenue. Generally, accountants divide profits

Firms depreciate, or spread out the costs of, their assets over a certain number of accounting periods.

into individual sections such as operating income and earnings before interest and taxes. Starbucks, for example, lists earnings before income taxes, net earnings, and earnings per share of outstanding stock (see Table 14.4). Like most companies, Starbucks presents not only the current year's results but also the previous two years' income statements to permit comparison of performance from one period to another.

temporary nature of the income statement accounts

Companies record their operational activities in the revenue and expense accounts during an accounting period. Gross profit, earnings before interest and taxes, and net income are the results of calculations made from the revenues and expenses accounts; they are not actual accounts. At the end of each accounting period, the dollar amounts in all the revenue and expense accounts are moved into an account called "Retained Earnings," one of the owners' equity accounts. Revenues increase owners' equity, while expenses decrease it. The resulting change in the owners' equity account is exactly equal to the net income. This shifting of dollar values from the revenue and expense accounts allows the firm to begin the next accounting period with zero balances in those accounts. Zeroing out the balances enables a company to count how much it has sold and how many expenses have been incurred during a period of time. The basic accounting equation (assets = liabilities + owners' equity) will not balance until the revenue and expense account balances have been moved or "closed out" to the owners' equity account.

One final note about income statements: You may remember from Chapter 5 that corporations may choose to make cash payments called dividends to shareholders out of their net earnings. When a corporation elects to pay dividends, it decreases the cash account (in the assets category) as well as a capital account (in the owners' equity category). During any period of time, the owners' equity account may change because of the sale of stock (or contributions/withdrawals by owners), the net income or loss, or from the dividends paid.

  LO4

Interpret a company's balance sheet to determine its current financial position.

The Balance Sheet

The second basic financial statement is the **balance sheet,** which presents a "snapshot" of an organization's financial position at a given moment. As such, the balance sheet indicates what the organization owns or controls and the various sources of the funds used to pay for these assets, such as bank debt and owners' equity.

The balance sheet takes its name from its reliance on the accounting equation: Assets *must* equal liabilities plus owners' equity. Table 14.5 provides a sample balance sheet with line-by-line explanations. Unlike the income statement, the balance sheet does not represent the result of transactions completed over a specified accounting period. Instead, the balance sheet is, by definition, an accumulation of all the financial transactions conducted by an organization since its founding. Following long-established traditions, items on the balance sheet are listed on the basis of their original cost less accumulated depreciation, rather than their present values.

Balance sheets are often presented in two different formats. The traditional balance sheet format placed the organization's assets on the left side and its liabilities and owners' equity on the right. More recently, a vertical format, with assets on top followed by liabilities and owners' equity, has gained wide acceptance. Consolidated balance sheets for 2006 and 2007 are presented in Table 14.6. In the sections that follow, we'll briefly

Paperless Banking Helps Save the Planet

Online banking became popular in the early 2000s, but today we are discovering that it is environmentally friendly as well as easy to use and convenient. To become an eco-friendly banking customer, Javelin & Strategy Research recommends doing away with paper statements, converting to direct deposit, using online banking services, and ditching receipts and deposit envelopes. According to payitgreen.org, one household can save 6.6 pounds of paper and avoid the use of 4.5 gallons of gasoline, the release of 63 gallons of wastewater, and the production of 171 pounds of greenhouse gas emissions annually by making the switch. If 20 percent of households got involved, it would save 150,939,615 pounds of paper and avoid the use of 102,945,600 gallons of gasoline and the production of 3,920,802,916 pounds of greenhouse gas emissions.

Sounds great—so why are three out of four households still receiving paper statements? Javelin attributes this to customer confusion resulting from a lack of information and suggests that banks push green banking and help their customers make the switch. The PayIt-Green Alliance—made up of banking institutions such as Bank of America, SunTrust Bank, Capital One, and 13 other banks—aims to do just that by offering assistance and information via payitgreen.org. As an added bonus, online bankers are more likely to spot fraud and identity theft than are those using paper. At a time when protecting the earth is critical, it's great to know that making a small change can have such a large impact—bank online and go green![7] ❖

Q: Discussion Questions

1. What are the important benefits of electronic accounting and financial statements?

2. Why is it so difficult to persuade consumers to switch to electronic-only statements?

3. What are the advantages of online banks to society?

TABLE 14.5 Sample Balance Sheet

The following exhibit presents a balance sheet in word form with each item defined or explained.

Typical Company December 31	
Assets	This is the major category for all physical, monetary, or intangible goods that have some dollar value.
Current assets	Assets that are cash or are expected to be turned into cash within the next 12 months.
Cash	Cash or checking accounts.
Marketable securities	Short-term investments in securities that can be converted to cash quickly (liquid assets).
Accounts receivable	Cash due from customers in payment for goods received. These arise from sales made on credit.
Inventory	Finished goods ready for sale, goods in the process of being finished, or raw materials used in the production of goods.
Prepaid expense	A future expense item that has already been paid, such as insurance premiums or rent.
Total current assets	The sum of the preceding accounts.
Fixed assets	Assets that are long term in nature and have a minimum life expectancy that exceeds one year.
Investments	Assets held as investments rather than assets owned for the production process. Most often the assets include small ownership interests in other companies.
Gross property, plant, and equipment	Land, buildings, and other fixed assets listed at original cost.
Less: Accumulated depreciation	The accumulated expense deductions applied to all plant and equipment over their life. Land may not be depreciated. The total amount represents in general the decline in value as equipment gets older and wears out. The maximum amount that can be deducted is set by the U.S. Federal Tax Code and varies by type of asset.
Net property, plant, and equipment	Gross property, plant, and equipment minus the accumulated depreciation. This amount reflects the book value of the fixed assets, not their value if sold.
Other assets	Any other asset that is long term and does not fit into the preceding categories. It could be patents or trademarks.
Total assets	The sum of all the asset values.
Liabilities and stockholders' equity	This is the major category. Liabilities refer to all indebtedness and loans of both a long-term and short-term nature. Stockholders' equity refers to all money that has been contributed to the company over the life of the firm by the owners.
Current liabilities	Short-term debt expected to be paid off within the next 12 months.
Accounts payable	Money owed to suppliers for goods ordered. Firms usually have between 30 and 90 days to pay this account, depending on industry norms.
Wages payable	Money owed to employees for hours worked or salary. If workers receive checks every two weeks, the amount owed should be no more than two weeks' pay.
Taxes payable	Firms are required to pay corporate taxes quarterly. This refers to taxes owed based on earnings estimates for the quarter.
Notes payable	Short-term loans from banks or other lenders.
Other current liabilities	The other short-term debts that do not fit into the above categories.
Total current liabilities	The sum of the preceding accounts.
Long-term liabilities	All long-term debt that will not be paid off in the next 12 months.
Long-term debt	Loans of more than one year from banks, pension funds, insurance companies, or other lenders. These loans often take the form of bonds, which are securities that may be bought and sold in bond markets.
Deferred income taxes	A liability owed to the government but not due within one year.
Other liabilities	Any other long-term debt that does not fit the preceding two categories.
Stockholders' equity	The following categories are the owners' investment in the company.
Common stock	The tangible evidence of ownership is a security called common stock. The par value is stated value and does not indicate the company's worth.
Capital in excess of par (a.k.a. contributed capital)	When shares of stock were sold to the owners, they were recorded at the price at the time of the original sale. If the price paid was $10 per share, the extra $9 per share would show up in this account at 100,000 shares times $9 per share, or $900,000.
Retained earnings	The total amount of earnings the company has made during its life and not paid out to its stockholders as dividends. This account represents the owners' reinvestment of earnings into company assets rather than payments of cash dividends. This account does not represent cash.
Total stockholders' equity	This is the sum of the preceding equity accounts representing the owner's total investment in the company.
Total liabilities and stockholders' equity	The total short-term and long-term debt of the company plus the owner's total investment. This combined amount *must* equal total assets.

TABLE 14.6 Consolidated Balance Sheets (in thousands, except share data)

Fiscal Year Ended	Sept 30, 2007	Oct 1, 2006
Assets		
Current assets:		
Cash and cash equivalents	$ 281,261	$ 312,606
Short-term investments—available-for-sale securities	83,845	87,542
Short-term investments—trading securities	73,588	53,496
Accounts receivable, net	287,925	224,271
Inventories	691,658	636,222
Prepaid expenses and other current assets	148,757	126,874
Deferred income taxes, net	129,453	88,777
Total current assets	1,696,487	1,529,788
Long-term investments—available-for-sale securities	21,022	5,811
Equity and other investments	258,846	219,093
Property, plant and equipment, net	2,890,433	2,287,899
Other assets	219,422	186,917
Other intangible assets	42,043	37,955
Goodwill	215,625	161,478
Total Assets	$5,343,878	$4,428,941
Liabilities and Shareholders' Equity		
Current liabilities:		
Commercial paper and short-term borrowings	$710,248	$700,000
Accounts payable	390,836	340,937
Accrued compensation and related costs	332,331	288,963
Accrued occupancy costs	74,591	54,868
Accrued taxes	92,516	94,010
Other accrued expenses	257,369	224,154
Deferred revenue	296,900	231,926
Current portion of long-term debt	775	762
Total current liabilities	2,155,566	1,935,620
Long-term debt	550,121	1,958
Other long-term liabilities	354,074	262,857
Total liabilities	3,059,761	2,200,435
Shareholders' equity:		
Common stock ($0.001 par value)—authorized, 1,200,000,000 shares; issued and outstanding, 738,285,285 and 756,602,701 shares, respectively, (includes 3,420,448 common stock units in both periods)	738	756
Other additional paid-in-capital	39,393	39,393
Retained earnings	2,189,366	2,151,084
Accumulated other comprehensive income	54,620	37,273
Total shareholders' equity	2,284,117	2,228,506
Total Liabilities and Shareholders' Equity	$5,343,878	4,428,941

Source: media.corporate-ir.net/media_files/irol/99/99518/2007AR (accessed September 18, 2008).

● **CURRENT ASSETS** assets that are used or converted into cash within the course of a calendar year

● **ACCOUNTS RECEIVABLE** money owed a company by its clients or customers who have promised to pay for the products at a later date

● **CURRENT LIABILITIES** a firm's financial obligations to short-term creditors, which must be repaid within one year

● **ACCOUNTS PAYABLE** the amount a company owes to suppliers for goods and services purchased with credit

● **ACCRUED EXPENSES** is an account representing all unpaid financial obligations incurred by the organization

describe the basic items found on the balance sheet; we'll take a closer look at a number of these in Chapter 16.

assets All asset accounts are listed in descending order of *liquidity*—that is, how quickly each could be turned into cash. **Current assets,** also called short-term assets, are those that are used or converted into cash within the course of a calendar year. Thus, cash is followed by temporary investments, accounts receivable, and inventory, in that order. **Accounts receivable** refers to money owed the company by its clients or customers who have promised to pay for the products at a later date. Accounts receivable usually includes an allowance for bad debts that management does not expect to collect. The bad-debts adjustment is normally based on historical collections experience and is deducted from the accounts receivable balance to present a more realistic view of the payments likely to be received in the future, called net receivables. Inventory may be held in the form of raw materials, work-in-progress, or finished goods ready for delivery.

Long-term, or fixed assets represent a commitment of organizational funds of at least one year. Items classified as fixed include long-term investments, plant and equipment, and intangible assets, such as corporate "goodwill," or reputation, as well as patents and trademarks.

liabilities As seen in the accounting equation, total assets must be financed either through borrowing (liabilities) or through owner investments (owners' equity). **Current liabilities** include a firm's financial obligations to short-term creditors, which must be repaid within one year, while long-term liabilities have longer repayment terms. **Accounts payable** represents amounts owed to suppliers for goods and services purchased with credit. For example, if you buy gas with a BP credit card, the purchase represents an account payable for you (and an account receivable for BP). Other liabilities include wages earned by employees but not yet paid and taxes owed to the government. Occasionally, these accounts are consolidated into an **accrued expenses** account, representing all unpaid financial obligations incurred by the organization.

owners' equity Owners' equity includes the owners' contributions to the organization along with income earned by the

The owners' equity portion of a balance sheet includes the money a company's owners have invested in the firm.

organization and retained to finance continued growth and development. If the organization were to sell off all of its assets and pay off all of its liabilities, any remaining funds would belong to the owners. Not surprisingly, the accounts listed as owners' equity on a balance sheet may differ dramatically from company to company. As mentioned in Chapter 5, corporations sell stock to investors, who become the owners of the firm. Many corporations issue two, three, or even more different classes of common and preferred stock, each with different dividend payments and/or voting rights. Because each type of stock issued represents a different claim on the organization, each must be represented by a separate owners' equity account, called contributed capital.

The Statement of Cash Flow

The third primary financial statement is called the **statement of cash flow,** which explains how the company's cash changed from the beginning of the accounting period to the end. Cash, of course, is an asset shown on the balance sheet, which provides a snapshot of the firm's financial position at one point in time. However, many investors and other users of financial statements want more information about the cash flowing into and out of the firm than is provided on the balance sheet to better understand the company's financial health. The statement of cash flow takes the cash balance from one year's balance sheet and compares it to the next while providing detail about how the firm used the cash. Table 14.7 presents Starbucks' statement of cash flows.

[**"Owners' equity includes the owners' contributions to the organization along with income earned by the organization and retained to finance continued growth and development."**]

TABLE 14.7   Starbucks Consolidated Statements of Cash Flows (in thousands)

Fiscal Year Ended	Sept 30, 2007	Oct 1, 2006	Oct 2, 2005
Operating Activities:			
Net earnings	$ 672,638	$ 564,259	$ 494,370
Adjustments to reconcile net earnings to net cash provided by operating activities:			
Cumulative effect of accounting change for FIN 47, net of taxes	—	17,214	—
Depreciation and amortization	491,238	412,625	367,207
Provision for impairments and asset disposals	26,032	19,622	19,464
Deferred income taxes, net	(37,326)	(84,324)	(31,253)
Equity in income of investees	(65,743)	(60,570)	(49,537)
Distributions of income from equity investees	65,927	49,238	30,919
Stock-based compensation	103,865	105,664	—
Tax benefit from exercise of stock options	7,705	1,318	109,978
Excess tax benefit from exercise of stock options	(93,055)	(117,368)	—
Net amortization of premium on securities	653	2,013	10,097
Cash provided/(used) by changes in operating assets and liabilities:			
Inventories	(48,576)	(85,527)	(121,618)
Accounts payable	36,068	104,966	9,717
Accrued compensation and related costs	38,628	54,424	22,711
Accrued taxes	86,371	132,725	14,435
Deferred revenue	63,233	56,547	53,276
Other operating assets and liabilities	(16,437)	(41,193)	(6,851)
Net cash provided by operating activities	1,331,221	1,131,633	922,915

(continued)

TABLE 14.7 *(concluded)*

Investing Activities:			
Purchase of available-for-sale securities	(237,422)	(639,192)	(643,488)
Maturity of available-for-sale securities	178,167	269,134	469,554
Sale of available-for-sale securities	47,497	431,181	626,113
Acquisitions, net of cash acquired	(53,293)	(91,734)	(21,583)
Net purchases of equity, other investments and other assets	(56,552)	(39,199)	(7,915)
Net additions to property, plant and equipment	(1,080,348)	(771,230)	(643,296)
Net cash used by investing activities	(1,201,951)	(841,040)	(220,615)
Financing Activities:			
Repayments of commercial paper	(16,600,841)	—	—
Proceeds from issuance of commercial paper	17,311,089	—	—
Repayments of short-term borrowings	(1,470,000)	(993,093)	—
Proceeds from short-term borrowings	770,000	1,416,093	277,000
Proceeds from issuance of common stock	176,937	159,249	163,555
Excess tax benefit from exercise of stock options	93,055	117,368	—
Principal payments on long-term debt	(784)	(898)	(735)
Proceeds from issuance of long-term debt	548,960	—	—
Repurchase of common stock	(996,798)	(854,045)	(1,113,647)
Other	(3,505)	—	—
Net cash used by financing activities	(171,887)	(155,326)	(673,827)
Effect of exchange rate changes on cash and cash equivalents	11,272	3,530	283
Net increase/(decrease) in cash and cash equivalents	(31,345)	138,797	28,756
Cash and Cash Equivalents:			
Beginning of period	312,606	173,809	145,053
End of the period	$ 281,261	$ 312,606	$ 173,809
Supplemental Disclosure of Cash Flow Information:			
Cash paid during the period for:			
Interest, net of capitalized interest	$ 35,294	$ 10,576	$ 1,060
Income taxes	$ 342,223	$ 274,134	$ 227,812

Source: media.corporate-ir.net/media_files/irol/99/99518/2007AR (accessed September 18, 2008).

The change in cash is explained through details in three categories: cash from (used for) operating activities, cash from (used for) investing activities, and cash from (used for) financing activities. *Cash from operating activities* is calculated by combining the changes in the revenue accounts, expense accounts, current asset accounts, and current liability accounts. This category of cash flows includes all the accounts on the balance sheet that relate to computing revenues and expenses for

Beltane Farm's Goat Cheeses Win Awards and Fulfill a Dream

Paul Trubey always wanted to raise goats. After moving to Connecticut, Trubey took a job teaching Latin at a local school, with the goal of eventually moving to Massachusetts and starting a farm with his partner. Then he met co-worker Dorothy Joba, who ran Highwater Farm. Trubey began working for Joba on nights and weekends and started making goat milk cheese. Eventually, Trubey decided to become a professional cheesemaker, forming Highwater Dairy LCC. Trubey had to learn the ins and outs of finance and accounting quickly because he soon started selling at the region's farmer's markets and to retail stores and restaurants. Trubey's chevre won a blue ribbon in the American Cheese Society's national competition. As sales grow, it becomes even more important to understand accounting methods and financial statements, something Trubey learned through running his business.[8] ❖

the accounting period. If this amount is a positive number, as it is for Starbucks, the business is making extra cash that it can use to invest in increased long-term capacity or to pay off debts such as loans or bonds. A negative number may indicate a business that is still in a growing stage or one that is in a declining position with regard to operations.

Cash from investing activities is calculated from changes in the long-term or fixed asset accounts. If this amount is negative, as is the case with Starbucks, the company is purchasing long-term assets for future growth. A positive figure indicates a business that is selling off existing long-term assets and reducing its capacity for the future.

Finally, *cash from financing activities* is calculated from changes in the long-term liability accounts and the contributed capital accounts in owners' equity. If this amount is negative, the company probably is paying off long-term debt or returning contributed capital to investors. As in the case of Starbucks, if this amount is positive, the company is either borrowing more money or raising money from investors by selling more shares of stock.

 L05

Analyze financial statements, using ratio analysis, to evaluate a company's performance.

RATIO ANALYSIS: ANALYZING FINANCIAL STATEMENTS

The income statement shows a company's profit or loss, while the balance sheet itemizes the value of its assets, liabilities, and owners' equity. Together, the two statements provide the

Ratio analysis, calculations that measure an organization's financial health, brings the complex information from the income statement and balance sheet into sharper focus so that managers, lenders, owners, and other interested parties can measure and compare the organization's productivity, profitability, and financing mix with other similar entities.

As you know, a ratio is simply one number divided by another, with the result showing the relationship between the two numbers. Financial ratios are used to weigh and evaluate a firm's performance. Interestingly, an absolute value such as earnings of $70,000 or accounts receivable of $200,000 almost never provides as much useful information as a well-constructed ratio. Whether those numbers are good or bad depends on their relation to other numbers. If a company earned $70,000 on $700,000 in sales (a 10 percent return), such an earnings level might be quite satisfactory. The president of a company earning this same $70,000 on sales of $7 million (a 1 percent return), however, probably should start looking for another job!

Looking at ratios in isolation is probably about as useful and exciting as staring at a blank wall. It is the relationship of the calculated ratios to both prior organizational performance and the performance of the organization's "peers," as well as its stated goals, that really matters. Remember, while the profitability, asset utilization, liquidity, debt ratios, and per share data we'll look at here can be very useful, you will never see the forest by looking only at the trees.

Profitability Ratios

Profitability ratios measure how much operating income or net income an organization is able to generate relative to its assets, owners' equity, and sales. The numerator (top number) used in these examples is always the net income after taxes.

> **"Profitability ratios measure how much operating income or net income an organization is able to generate relative to its assets, owners' equity, and sales."**

means to answer two critical questions: (1) How much did the firm make or lose? and (2) How much is the firm currently worth based on historical values found on the balance sheet?

Common profitability ratios include profit margin, return on assets, and return on equity. The following examples are based on the 2007 income statement and balance sheet for Starbucks,

You can look on Web sites like Yahoo! Finance under a company's "key statistics" link to find financial ratios, such as the firm's return on assets, return on equity, and current ratios. Other ratios require a closer look at the company's financial statements.

as shown in Tables 14.4 and 14.6. Except where specified, all data are expressed in millions of dollars.

The **profit margin,** computed by dividing net income by sales, shows the overall percentage profits earned by the company. It is based solely on data obtained from the income statement. The higher the profit margin, the better the cost controls within the company and the higher the return on every dollar of revenue. Starbucks' profit margin is calculated as follows:

$$\text{Profit margin} = \frac{\$672,638}{\$9,411,487} = 7.15\%$$

Thus, for every $1 in sales, Starbucks generated profits of almost 8 cents.

Return on assets, net income divided by assets, shows how much income the firm produces for every dollar invested in assets. A company with a low return on assets is probably not using its assets very productively—a key managerial failing. By its construction, the return on assets calculation requires data from both the income statement and the balance sheet.

$$\text{Return on assets} = \frac{\$672,638}{\$5,343,878} = 12.59\%$$

In the case of Starbucks, every $1 of assets generated a return of 12.59 percent, or profits of just over 12.5 cents.

Stockholders are always concerned with how much money they will make on their investment, and they frequently use the return on equity ratio as one of their key performance yardsticks. **Return on equity** (also called return on investment [ROI]), calculated by dividing net income by owners' equity, shows how much income is generated by each $1 the owners have invested in the firm. Obviously, a low return on equity means low stockholder returns and may indicate a need for immediate managerial attention. Because some assets may have been financed with debt not contributed by the owners, the value of owners' equity is usually considerably lower than the total value of the firm's assets. Starbucks' return on equity is calculated as follows:

$$\text{Return on equity} = \frac{\$672,638}{\$2,284,117} = 29.45\%$$

For every dollar invested by Starbucks stockholders, the company earned a 29.45 percent return, or 29.45 cents per dollar invested.

Asset Utilization Ratios

Asset utilization ratios measure how well a firm uses its assets to generate each $1 of sales. Obviously, companies using their assets more productively will have higher returns on assets

● **ASSET UTILIZATION RATIOS** ratios that measure how well a firm uses its assets to generate each $1 of sales

● **RECEIVABLES TURNOVER** sales divided by accounts receivable

● **INVENTORY TURNOVER** sales divided by total inventory

● **TOTAL ASSET TURNOVER** sales divided by total assets

● **LIQUIDITY RATIOS** ratios that measure the speed with which a company can turn its assets into cash to meet short-term debt

● **CURRENT RATIO** current assets divided by current liabilities

● **QUICK RATIO (ACID TEST)** a stringent measure of liquidity that eliminates inventory

than will their less efficient competitors. Similarly, managers can use asset utilization ratios to pinpoint areas of inefficiency in their operations. These ratios (receivables turnover, inventory turnover, and total asset turnover) relate balance sheet assets to sales, which are found on the income statement.

The **receivables turnover,** sales divided by accounts receivable, indicates how many times a firm collects its accounts receivable in one year. It also demonstrates how quickly a firm is able to collect payments on its credit sales. Obviously, no payments mean no profits. Starbucks collected its receivables 32.7 times per year. The reason the number is so high is that most of Starbucks' sales are for cash, not credit.

$$\text{Receivables turnover} = \frac{\$9,411,497}{\$287,925} = 32.69$$

Inventory turnover, sales divided by total inventory, indicates how many times a firm sells and replaces its inventory over the course of a year. A high inventory turnover ratio may indicate great efficiency but may also suggest the possibility of lost sales due to insufficient stock levels. Starbucks' inventory turnover indicates that it replaced its inventory over 13.6 times per year, or once per month.

$$\text{Inventory turnover} = \frac{\$9,411,497}{\$691,658} = 13.61$$

Total asset turnover, sales divided by total assets, measures how well an organization uses all its assets in creating sales. It indicates whether a company is using its assets productively. Starbucks generated $1.76 in sales for every $1 in total corporate assets.

$$\text{Total asset turnover} = \frac{\$9,411,497}{\$5,343,878} = 1.76$$

Liquidity Ratios

Liquidity ratios compare current (short-term) assets to current liabilities to indicate the speed with which a company can turn its assets into cash to meet debts as they fall due. High liquidity ratios may satisfy a creditor's need for safety, but ratios that are too high may indicate that the organization is not using its current assets efficiently. Liquidity ratios are generally best examined in conjunction with asset utilization ratios because high turnover ratios imply that cash is flowing through an organization very quickly—a situation that dramatically reduces the need for the type of reserves measured by liquidity ratios.

The **current ratio** is calculated by dividing current assets by current liabilities. Starbucks' current ratio indicates that for every $1 of current liabilities, the firm had $0.79 of current assets on hand. This number may appear troublesome, and it is a ratio on which the company should keep a close watch. This ratio seems to be low because Starbucks uses short-term commercial paper for much of its financing. If it used long-term debt, the current ratio would be greater than $1.

$$\text{Current ratio} = \frac{\$1,696,487}{\$2,155,566} = 0.79$$

The **quick ratio** (also known as the acid test) is a far more stringent measure of liquidity because it eliminates inventory, the least liquid current asset. It measures how well an organization can meet its current obligations without resorting to the sale of its inventory. In 2007, Starbucks had just 47 cents invested in current assets (after subtracting inventory) for every $1 of current liabilities.

$$\text{Quick ratio} = \frac{\$1,004,829}{\$2,155,566} = 0.47$$

Debt Utilization Ratios

Debt utilization ratios provide information about how much debt an organization is using relative to other sources of capital, such as owners' equity. Because the use of debt carries an interest charge that must be paid regularly regardless of profitability, debt financing is much riskier than equity. Unforeseen negative events such as recessions affect heavily indebted firms to a far greater extent than those financed exclusively with owners' equity. Because of this and other factors, the managers of most firms tend to keep debt-to-asset levels below 50 percent. However, firms in very stable and/or regulated industries, such as electric utilities, often are able to carry debt ratios well in excess of 50 percent with no ill effects.

The **debt to total assets ratio** indicates how much of the firm is financed by debt and how much by owners' equity.

To find the value of Starbucks' total debt, you must add current liabilities to long-term debt and other liabilities.

$$\text{Debt to total assets} = \frac{\$3,059,7617}{\$5,343,878} = 57.26\%$$

Thus, for every $1 of Starbucks' total assets, 57.26 percent is financed with debt. The remaining 42.74 percent is provided by owners' equity.

The **times interest earned ratio,** operating income divided by interest expense, is a measure of the safety margin a company has with respect to the interest payments it must make to its creditors. A low times interest earned ratio indicates that even a small decrease in earnings may lead the company into financial straits.

$$\text{Times interest earned} = \frac{\$1,053,945}{\$35,294} = 29.86$$

Per Share Data

Investors may use **per share data** to compare the performance of one company with another on an equal, or per share, basis. Generally, the more shares of stock a company issues, the less income is available for each share.

Earnings per share is calculated by dividing net income or profit by the number of shares of stock outstanding. This ratio is important because yearly changes in earnings per share, in combination with other economywide factors, determine a company's overall stock price. When earnings go up, so does a company's stock price—and so does the wealth of its stockholders.

$$\text{Diluted earnings per share} = \frac{\$672,638}{\$770,091} = 0.87 \ (2007)$$

$$= \frac{\$564,259}{\$792,556} = 0.71 \ (2006)$$

We can see from the income statement and these calculations that Starbucks' basic earnings per share increased from $0.71 in 2006 to $0.87 in 2007. You can see from the income statement that diluted earnings per share include more shares than the basic calculation; this is because diluted shares include

potential shares that could be issued due to the exercise of stock options or the conversion of certain types of debt into common stock. Investors generally pay more attention to diluted earnings per share than to basic earnings per share.

Dividends per share are paid by the corporation to the stockholders for each share owned. The payment is made from earnings after taxes by the corporation but is taxable income to the stockholder. Thus, dividends result in double taxation: The corporation pays tax once on its earnings, and the stockholder pays tax a second time on his or her dividend income. Starbucks has never paid a dividend, and so the calculation of dividends per share does not apply in this case.

Industry Analysis

We have used McDonald's as a comparison to Starbucks because there are no real national and international coffee houses that compete with Starbucks on the same scale. While McDonald's is much larger than Starbucks in terms of sales, they both have a national and international presence and to some extent compete for the consumer's dollars. Table 14.8 shows that while McDonald's earns more profit per dollar of sales, Starbucks earns more dollars per dollar of invested assets. Table 14.8 shows that McDonald's is more profitable than Starbucks on all three measures of profitability. Starbucks was faced with rising raw coffee prices in 2008 and a slower growth rate because of the

TABLE 14.8 Industry Analysis

	Starbucks	McDonald's
Profit margin	7.15%	10.51%
Return on assets	12.59%	8.15%
Return on equity	29.45%	15.67%
Receivable turnover	32.69×	21.64×
Inventory turnover	13.61×	182.30×
Total asset turnover	1.76×	0.78×
Current ratio	0.79×	0.80×
Quick ratio	0.47×	0.77×
Debt to total assets	57.26%	48.01%
Times interest earned	29.86×	9.46×
Earnings per share	$ 0.87	$ 1.98
Dividends per share	$ 0.00	$ 1.50

By tracking and analyzing the financial data of 18 million-plus U.S. businesses, BizMiner.com is able to deliver industry analysis information to its online subscribers.

Do you like numbers and finances? Are you detail-oriented, a perfectionist, and highly accountable for your decisions? If so, accounting may be a good field for you. If you are interested in accounting, there are always job opportunities available regardless of the state of the economy. Accounting is one of the most secure job options in business. Of course, becoming an accountant is not easy. You will need at least a bachelor's degree in accounting to get a job, and many positions require additional training. Many states demand coursework beyond the 120 to 150 credit hours collegiate programs require for an accounting degree. If you are really serious about getting into the accounting field, you will probably want to consider getting a master's in accounting and taking the CPA exam. The field of accounting can be complicated, and the extra training provided through a master's in accounting program will prove invaluable when you go out looking for a good job. Accounting is a volatile discipline that is affected by changes in legislative initiatives.

With corporate accounting policies changing constantly and becoming more complex, accountants are needed to help keep a business running smoothly and within the bounds of the law. In fact, the number of jobs in the accounting and auditing field is expected to increase 18 percent between 2006 and 2016, with over 1.5 million jobs in the United States alone by 2016. Jobs in accounting tend to pay quite well, with the national average salary standing at just over $57,000 annually. If you go on to get a master's degree in accounting, expect to see an even higher starting wage. In 2006, accountants with a bachelor's degree received an average opening offer of $47,618, while employees with a master's degree were offered $49,277. Of course, your earnings could be higher or lower than these averages, depending on where you work, your level of experience, the firm, and your particular position.

Accountants are needed in the public and private sectors, in large and small firms, and in for-profit and not-for-profit organizations. Accountants in firms are generally in charge of preparing and filing tax forms and financial reports. Public sector accountants are responsible for checking the veracity of corporate and personal records in order to prepare tax filings. Basically, any organization that has to deal with money and/or taxes in one way or another will be in need of an accountant, for in-house service or occasional contract work. Requirements for audits under the Sarbanes-Oxley Act and rules from the Public Company Accounting Oversight Board are creating more jobs and increased responsibility to maintaining internal controls and accounting ethics. The fact that accounting rules and tax filings tend to be complex virtually assures that the demand for accountants will never decrease.[9]

recession. As the high-priced alternative, Starbucks has begun to lose business to cheaper competitors such as McDonald's and Dunkin Donuts, which both offer cheaper coffee. Both companies have very little accounts receivable relative to the size of their sales. McDonald's pushes off much of its inventory holding costs on its suppliers and so has much less inventory per sales dollar compared with Starbucks. Because McDonald's has very little inventory, its quick ratio and current ratios are almost the same and are much higher than those of Starbucks. This is of little consequence to the financial analyst because both companies have high times interest earned ratios, with Starbucks significantly higher than McDonald's. Starbucks earns less per share than McDonald's, but McDonald's pays a dividend and Starbucks does not. In summary, both companies are in good financial health, and it is hard to say which company is better managed. One thing for sure, if Starbucks could earn the same profit margin as McDonald's, it would improve its other profitability ratios dramatically. ■

Team Exercise

You can look at Web sites such as Yahoo! Finance (http://finance .yahoo.com/) under a company's "key statistics" link to find many of its financial ratios, such as return on assets and return on equity. Have each member of your team look up a different company and explain why you think there are differences in the ratio analysis for these two ratios among the selected companies.

CHECK OUT www.mhhe.com/FerrellM2e

for study materials including Interactive Exercises, Quizzes, iPod downloads, and video.

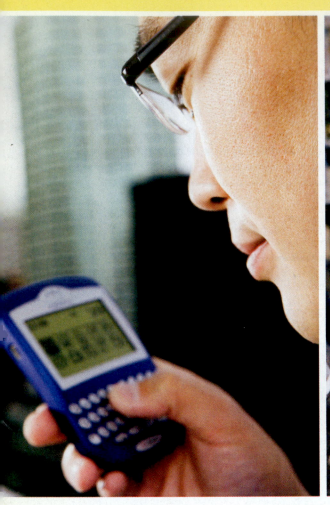

Money & The Financial System

15

Introduction

From Wall Street to Main Street—both overseas and at home—money is the one tool used to measure personal and business income and wealth. Not surprisingly, **finance** is the study of money: how it's made, how it's lost, and how it's managed. This chapter introduces you to the role of money and the financial system in the economy. Of course, if you have a checking account, automobile insurance, a college loan, or a credit card, you already have personal experience with some key players in the financial world.

We begin our discussion with a definition of money and then explore some of the many forms money may take. Next, we examine the roles of the Federal Reserve Board and other major institutions in the financial system. Finally, we explore the future of the finance industry and some of the changes likely to occur over the course of the next several years.

● ● LO1

Define money, its functions, and its characteristics.

MONEY IN THE FINANCIAL SYSTEM

Strictly defined, **money** is anything generally accepted in exchange for goods and services. Materials as diverse as salt, cattle, fish, rocks, shells, and cloth as well as precious metals such as gold, silver, and copper have long been used by various cultures as money. Most of these materials were limited-supply commodities that had their own value to society (for example, as a preservative or as jewelry). The supply of these commodities therefore determined the supply of "money" in that society. The next step was the development of "IOUs," or slips of paper that could be exchanged for a specified supply of the underlying commodity. "Gold" notes, for instance, could be exchanged for gold, and the money supply was tied to the amount of gold available. While paper money was first used in North America in 1685 (and even earlier in Europe), the concept of *fiat money*—a paper money not readily convertible to a precious metal such as gold—did not gain full acceptance until the Great Depression in the 1930s. The United States abandoned its gold-backed currency standard largely in response to the Great Depression and converted to a fiduciary, or fiat, monetary system. In the United States, paper money is really a government "note" or promise, worth the value specified on the note.

Functions of Money

No matter what a particular society uses for money, its primary purpose is to enable a person or organization to transform a desire into an action. These desires may be for entertainment actions, such as party expenses; operating actions, such as paying for rent, utilities, or employees; investing actions, such as buying property or equipment; or financing actions, such as for starting or growing a business. Money serves three important functions: as a medium of exchange, a measure of value, and a store of value.

> **" No matter what a particular society uses for money, its primary purpose is to enable a person or organization to transform a desire into an action. "**

For centuries, people on the Micronesian island of Yap have used giant round stones, like the ones shown here, for currency. The stones aren't moved, but their ownership can change.

medium of exchange Before fiat money, the trade of goods and services was accomplished through *bartering*—trading one good or service for another of similar value. As any school-age child knows, bartering can become quite inefficient—particularly in the case of complex, three-party transactions involving peanut butter sandwiches, baseball cards, and hair barrettes. There had to be a simpler way, and that was to decide on a single item—money—that can be freely converted to any other good upon agreement between parties.

measure of value As a measure of value, money serves as a common standard or yardstick of the value of goods and services. For example, $2 will buy a dozen large eggs and $25,000 will buy a nice car in the United States. In Japan, where the currency is known as the yen, these same transactions would cost about 200 yen and 2 million yen, respectively.

Money, then, is a common denominator that allows people to compare the different goods and services that can be consumed on a particular income level. While a star athlete and a "burger-flipper" are paid vastly different wages, each uses money as a measure of the value of his or her yearly earnings and purchases.

store of value As a store of value, money serves as a way to accumulate wealth (buying power) until it is needed. For example, a person making $500 per week who wants to buy a $500 computer could save $50 per week for each of the next 10 weeks. Unfortunately, the value of stored money is directly dependent on the health of the economy. If, due to rapid inflation, all prices double in one year, the purchasing power value of the money "stuffed in the mattress" will fall by half. By contrast, "mattress savings" buy more when prices fall as they did for more than 52 months in Hong Kong between 1999 and 2005.

Characteristics of Money

To be used as a medium of exchange, money must be acceptable, divisible, portable, stable in value, durable, and difficult to counterfeit.

acceptability To be effective, money must be readily acceptable for the purchase of goods and services and for the settlement of debts. Acceptability is probably the most important characteristic of money: If people do not trust the value of money, businesses will not accept it as a payment for goods and services, and consumers will have to find some other means of paying for their purchases.

divisibility In light of the widespread use of quarters, dimes, nickels, and pennies in the United States, it is no surprise that the principle of divisibility is an important one. With barter, the lack of divisibility often makes otherwise preferable trades impossible, as would be an attempt to trade a steer for a loaf of bread. For money to serve effectively as a measure of value, all items must be valued in terms of comparable units—dimes for a piece of bubble gum, quarters for laundry machines, and dollars (or dollars and coins) for everything else.

portability Clearly, for money to function as a medium of exchange, it must be easily moved from one location to the next. Large colored rocks could be used as money, but you couldn't carry them around in your

DID YOU KNOW?

Experts estimate that more than $130 million in counterfeit U.S. bills is circulating around the world.[2]

wallet. Paper currency and metal coins, in contrast, are capable of transferring vast purchasing power into small, easily carried (and hidden!) bundles. Few Americans realize it, but more U.S. currency is in circulation outside the United States than within. Currently, about $725 billion of U.S. currency is in circulation, and the majority is held outside the United States.[1]

stability Money must be stable and maintain its declared face value. A $10 bill should purchase the same amount of goods or services from one day to the next. The principle of stability allows people who wish to postpone purchases and save their money to do so without fear that it will decline in value. As mentioned earlier, money declines in value during periods of inflation, when economic conditions cause prices to rise. Thus, the same amount of money buys fewer and fewer goods and services. In some countries, particularly in Latin America, people spend their money as fast as they can to keep it from losing any more of its value. Instability destroys confidence in a nation's money and its ability to store value and serve as an effective medium of exchange. Ultimately, people faced with spiraling price increases avoid the increasingly worthless paper money at all costs, storing all their savings in the form of real assets such as gold and land.

durability Money must be durable. The crisp new dollar bills you trade at the music store for the hottest new CD will make their way all around town for about 20 months before

To prevent counterfeiting, the U.S. Treasury continues to redesign its currency and coins, using sophisticated printing and stamping methods that are hard to duplicate.

TABLE 15.1 The Life Expectancy of Paper Currency

Denomination of Bill	Life Expectancy (Years)
$ 1	1.8
$ 5	1.3
$ 10	1.5
$ 20	2
$ 50	4.6
$100	7.4

Source: "How Currency Gets into Circulation" www.newyorkfed.org/aboutthefed/fedpoint/fed01.html (accessed March 24, 2009); Barbara Mikkelson, Snopes, February 6, 2008, www.snopes.com/business/money/pennycost.asp (accessed March 24, 2009).

being replaced (see Table 15.1). Were the value of an old, faded bill to fall in line with the deterioration of its appearance, the principles of stability and universal acceptability would fail (but, no doubt, fewer bills would pass through the washer!). Although metal coins, due to their much longer useful life, would appear to be an ideal form of money, paper currency is far more portable than metal because of its light weight. Today, coins are used primarily to provide divisibility.

difficulty to counterfeit Finally, to remain stable and enjoy universal acceptance, it almost goes without saying that money must be very difficult to counterfeit—that is, to duplicate illegally. Every country takes steps to make counterfeiting difficult. Most use multicolored money, and many use specially watermarked papers that are virtually impossible to duplicate. Counterfeit bills represent less than 0.02 percent of the currency in circulation in the United States,[3] but it is becoming increasingly easier for counterfeiters to print money with just a modest inkjet printer. This illegal printing of money is fueled by hundreds of people who often circulate only small amounts of counterfeit bills. To thwart the problem of counterfeiting, the U.S. Treasury Department redesigned the U.S. currency, starting with the $20 in 2003, and the $50 in 2004, and the $10 in 2006. For the first time, U.S. money includes subtle colors in addition to the traditional green, as well as enhanced security features, such as a watermark, security thread, and color-shifting ink.[4] In 2006 the new Jefferson nickel was introduced, showing a profile of the nation's third president. Due to the increased price of metals, it costs 5.73 cents to make the 5 cent piece. President Lincoln was the first president to appear on a coin when the Lincoln penny was introduced in 1909. As Figure 15.1 indicates, it costs more than a penny to manufacture a penny, resulting in a call to discontinue it.

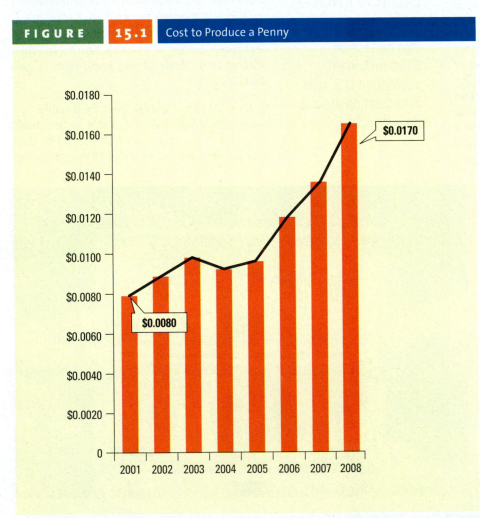

FIGURE 15.1 Cost to Produce a Penny

$0.0170

$0.0080

2001 2002 2003 2004 2005 2006 2007 2008

Source: *USA Today,* July 7, 2006, p. 2B; Barbara Mikkelson, Snopes, February 6, 2008, http://www.snopes.com/business/money/pennycost.asp (accessed March 24, 2009).

● ● LO2

Describe various types of money.

Types of Money

While paper money and coins are the most visible types of money, the combined value of all the printed bills and all the minted coins is actually rather insignificant compared with the value of money kept in checking accounts, savings accounts, and other monetary forms.

You probably have a **checking account** (also called a demand deposit), money stored in an account at a bank or other financial institution that can be withdrawn without advance notice. One way to withdraw funds from your account is by writing a *check*, a written order to a bank to pay the indicated individual or business the amount specified on the check from money already on deposit. Figure 15.2 explains the significance of the numbers found on a typical U.S. check. As legal instruments, checks serve as a substitute for currency and coins and are preferred for many transactions due to their lower risk of loss. If you lose a $100 bill, anyone who finds or steals it can spend it. If you lose a blank check, however, the risk of catastrophic loss is quite low. Not only does your bank have a sample of your signature on file to compare with a suspected forged signature, but you can render the check immediately worthless by means of a stop-payment order at your bank.

There are several types of checking accounts, with different features available for different monthly fee levels or specific minimum account balances. Some checking accounts earn interest (a small percentage of the amount deposited in the account that the bank pays to the depositor). One such interest-bearing checking account is the *NOW (negotiable order of withdrawal) account* offered by most financial institutions. The interest rate paid on such accounts varies with the interest rates available in the economy but is typically quite low (ranging between .05 and 1 percent).

Savings accounts (also known as time deposits) are accounts with funds that usually cannot be withdrawn without advance notice and/or have limits on the number of withdrawals per period. While seldom enforced, the "fine print" governing most savings accounts prohibits withdrawals without two or three days' notice. Savings accounts are not generally used for transactions or as a medium of exchange, but their funds can be moved to a checking account or turned into cash.

Money market accounts are similar to interest-bearing checking accounts, but with more restrictions. Generally, in exchange for slightly higher interest rates, the owner of a money market account can write only a limited number of checks each month, and there may be a restriction on the minimum amount of each check.

Certificates of deposit (CDs) are savings accounts that guarantee a depositor a set interest rate over a specified interval of time as long as the funds are not withdrawn before the end of the interval—six months, one year, or seven years, for example. Money may be withdrawn from these accounts prematurely only after paying a substantial penalty. In general, the longer

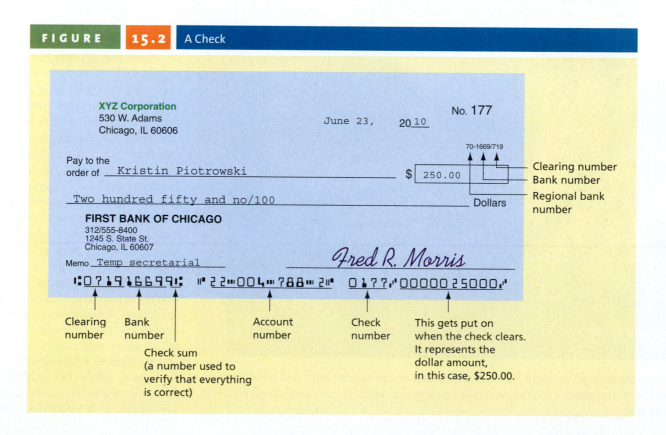

FIGURE 15.2 A Check

the term of the CD, the higher the interest rate it earns. As with all interest rates, the rate offered and fixed at the time the account is opened fluctuates according to economic conditions.

Credit cards allow you to promise to pay at a later date by using preapproved lines of credit granted by a bank or finance company. They are a popular substitute for cash payments because of their convenience, easy access to credit, and acceptance by merchants around the world. Indeed, it is difficult today to find stores (and even some governmental services, such as state license plate branches) that do not accept credit cards. The institution issuing the credit card guarantees payment of a credit charge to merchants, less a small transaction fee, typically between 2 and 5 percent of the purchase, and assumes responsibility for collecting the money from the cardholder.

With few exceptions, credit cards allow cardholders great flexibility in paying off their purchases. Some people always pay off their monthly charges as they come due, but many others take advantage of the option of paying a stated minimum monthly amount with interest charges, based on yearly interest rates, added to the balance until it has been paid in full. For years, credit card companies lured clients with offers to lock in low fixed rates, sending the message for people who carry a balance on their card—and most people do—that there is no need to worry that the interest rate will rise without any warning. Today, more than half of all credit cards carry variable interest rates, a level that hadn't been reached since the 1990s. According to Bankrate.com, about 55 percent of all cards have variable rates, up from 38 percent in 2003.[5] Average annual fees for the privilege of carrying specific credit cards are an important source of money for issuing banks and can sometimes reach $60 to $100 per year, although bank cards are increasingly available with no annual charge; reward cards generally charge a higher fee, which can be up to $200. Credit card issuers also charge a fee for converting from one nation's currency to another when the cardholder uses the card in another country.

● ● **It is estimated that banks, credit card issuers, and retailers lose more than a billion dollars annually to credit card fraud.**

Two major credit cards—MasterCard and Visa—represent the vast majority of credit cards held in the United States. More than half of the market is controlled by the industry's "Big Five"—Citigroup, MBNA, First USA, American Express, and Discover.[6] Banks are not the only issuers of credit cards. American Express has long been the dominant card company in the travel and entertainment market, with millions of cards outstanding. Unlike most bank cards, the original green American Express Card requires cardholders to pay their entire balances in full each month. However, American Express has expanded its card portfolio to include traditional credit cards.

Major department stores—Sears, JCPenney, Macy's, Saks Fifth Avenue, and others—offer their own credit cards to encourage consumers to spend money in their stores. Unlike the major credit cards discussed, these "private label" cards are generally accepted only at stores associated with the issuing company.

It is estimated that banks, credit card issuers, and retailers lose more than a billion dollars annually to credit card fraud, which includes lost or stolen cards, counterfeit cards, Internet purchases made with someone else's account number, and identity theft—the most devastating of all credit card frauds. Identity theft (also known as application or true name fraud) involves the assumption of someone else's identity by a criminal who then charges in the victim's name. Another concern is the amount of debt that Americans owe to credit card issuers. In an average month, Americans owe a collective $735 billion in credit card debt, while the British owe, $105 billion and the Australians owe $19 billion. That works out to about

In 2008, the U.S. government imposed restrictions on the interest rates and other fees credit card companies can impose on their customers, which include both consumers and businesses.

$2,300 for each U.S. man, woman, and child, $1,616 for each Briton, and $950 for each Australian.[7]

A **debit card** looks like a credit card but works like a check. The use of a debit card results in a direct, immediate, electronic payment from the cardholder's checking account to a merchant or other party. While they are convenient to carry and profitable for banks, they lack credit features, offer no purchase "grace period," and provide no hard "paper trail." Debit cards are gaining more acceptance with merchants, and consumers like debit cards because of the ease of getting cash from an increasing number of ATM machines. Financial institutions also want consumers to use debit cards because they reduce the number of teller transactions and check processing costs. Indeed, debit cards have become the most popular form of payment for grocery and gasoline purchases and at "big-box" retailers like Best Buy.[8] Some cash management accounts at retail brokers like Merrill Lynch offer deferred debit cards. These act like a credit card but debit to the cash management account once a month. During that time, the cash earns a money market return.

Traveler's checks, money orders, and cashier's checks are other common forms of "near money." Although each is slightly different from the others, they all share a common characteristic: A financial institution, bank, credit company, or neighborhood currency exchange issues them in exchange for cash and guarantees that the purchased note will be honored and exchanged for cash when it is presented to the institution making the guarantee.

● ● LO3

Specify how the Federal Reserve Board manages the money supply and regulates the American banking system.

THE AMERICAN FINANCIAL SYSTEM

The U.S. financial system fuels our economy by storing money, fostering investment opportunities, and making loans for new businesses and business expansion as well as for homes, cars, and college educations. This amazingly complex system includes banking institutions, nonbanking financial institutions such as finance companies, and systems that provide for the electronic transfer of funds throughout the world. Over the past 20 years, the rate at which money turns over, or changes hands, has increased exponentially. Different cultures place unique values on saving, spending, borrowing, and investing. The combination of this increased turnover rate and increasing interactions with people and organizations from other countries has created a complex money system. First, we need to meet the guardian of this complex system.

The Federal Reserve System

The guardian of the American financial system is the **Federal Reserve Board,** or "the Fed," as it is commonly called, an independent agency of the federal government established in 1913 to regulate the nation's banking and financial industry. The Federal Reserve System is organized into 12 regions, each with a Federal Reserve Bank that serves its defined area (Figure 15.3). All the Federal Reserve banks except those in Boston

Just as it takes a while for water from a faucet to heat up, it takes a while for the Fed's monetary policies to have an effect on economic activity.

and Philadelphia have regional branches. The Cleveland Federal Reserve Bank, for example, is responsible for branch offices in Pittsburgh and Cincinnati.

The Federal Reserve Board is the chief economic policy arm of the United States. Working with Congress and the president, the Fed tries to create a positive economic environment capable of sustaining low inflation, high levels of employment, a balance in international payments, and long-term economic growth. To this end, the Federal Reserve Board has four major responsibilities: (1) to control the supply of money, or monetary policy; (2) to regulate banks and other financial institutions; (3) to manage regional and national checking account procedures, or check clearing; and (4) to supervise the federal deposit insurance programs of banks belonging to the Federal Reserve System.

monetary policy   The Fed controls the amount of money available in the economy through **monetary policy.**

Without this intervention, the supply of and demand for money might not balance. This could result in either rapid price increases (inflation) because of too little money or economic recession and a slowdown of price increases (disinflation) because of too little growth in the money supply. In very rare cases (the depression of the 1930s) the United States has suffered from deflation, where the actual purchasing power of the dollar has increased as prices declined. To effectively control the supply of money in the economy, the Fed must have a good idea of how much money is in circulation at any given time. This has become increasingly challenging because the global nature of our economy means that more and more U.S. dollars are circulating overseas. Using several different measures of the money supply, the Fed establishes specific growth targets which, presumably, ensure a close balance between money supply and money demand. The Fed fine-tunes money growth by using four basic tools: open market operations, reserve requirements, the discount rate, and credit controls (see Table 15.2). There is generally a log of 6 to 18 months before the effect of these charges shows up in economic activity.

FIGURE 15.3   Federal Reserve System

Boundaries of Federal Reserve Districts
Boundaries of Federal Reserve Branch Territories
✪ Board of Governors of the Federal Reserve System
○ Federal Reserve Bank Cities
● Federal Reserve Branch Cities
■ Federal Reserve Bank Facility

TABLE 15.2 Fed Tools for Regulating the Money Supply

Activity	Effect on the Money Supply and the Economy
Buy government securities	The money supply increases; economic activity increases.
Sell government securities	The money supply decreases; economic activity slows down.
Raise discount rate	Interest rates increase; the money supply decreases; economic activity slows down.
Lower discount rate	Interest rates decrease; the money supply increases; economic activity increases.
Increase reserve requirements	Banks make fewer loans; the money supply declines; economic activity slows down.
Decrease reserve requirements	Banks make more loans; the money supply increases; economic activity increases.
Relax credit controls	More people are encouraged to make major purchases, increasing economic activity.
Restrict credit controls	People are discouraged from making major purchases, decreasing economic activity.

Open market operations refer to decisions to buy or sell U.S. Treasury bills (short-term debt issued by the U.S. government; also called T-bills) and other investments in the open market. The actual purchase or sale of the investments is performed by the New York Federal Reserve Bank. This monetary tool, the most commonly employed of all Fed operations, is performed almost daily in an effort to control the money supply.

When the Fed buys securities, it writes a check on its own account to the seller of the investments. When the seller of the investments (usually a large bank) deposits the check, the Fed transfers the balance from the Federal Reserve account into the seller's account, thus increasing the supply of money in the economy and, ideally, fueling economic growth. The opposite occurs when the Fed sells investments. The buyer writes a check to the Federal Reserve, and when the funds are transferred out of the

the Fed establishes and enforces banking rules that affect monetary policy and the overall level of the competition between different banks.

purchaser's account, the amount of money in circulation falls, slowing economic growth to a desired level.

The second major monetary policy tool is the **reserve requirement,** the percentage of deposits that banking institutions must hold in reserve ("in the vault," as it were). Funds so held are not available for lending to businesses and consumers. For example, a bank holding $10 million in deposits, with a 10 percent reserve requirement, must have reserves of $1 million. If the Fed were to reduce the reserve requirement to, say, 5 percent, the bank would need to keep only $500,000 in reserves. The bank could then lend to customers the $500,000 difference between the old reserve level and the new lower reserve level, thus increasing the supply of money. Because the reserve requirement has such a powerful effect on the money supply, the Fed does not change it very often, relying instead on open market operations most of the time.

General Electric the Financial Giant

Most people think of General Electric as a maker of lightbulbs and appliances. GE also makes jet engines, power turbines, and medical-imaging machines and owns NBC. General Electric Capital, a division of GE, is one of the largest financial companies in the United States. It is the second largest leaser of airplanes in the world and one of the biggest commercial and consumer lenders. It currently accounts for 37 percent of GE's revenue and 33 percent of its profits. The commercial lending and leasing division alone accounts for about $230 billion in assets, while consumer finance, which includes private-label credit cards, accounts for $183 billion in assets.

General Electric Capital is not regulated by the Federal Reserve. It has the ability to use money from GE industrial divisions to shore

up its lending and financial arm. During the financial meltdown, investors became more and more worried that GE would go the way of Bank America and Citibank. For example Bank America's common stock price went from a high of $55 in 2007 to a low of $3 in March 2009 and CitiGroup's stock went from a high of $57 to a low of $.97 during the same period. General Electric's common stock went from a high of $42 in 2007 to $5.73 in March 2009. Investors were worried that GE didn't have enough capital and might default on its loans. Even though GE raised over $50 billion in capital through public markets, investors were still nervous. GE had over $45 billion in cash on its balance sheet, but that wasn't enough to calm the market. By May 2009 the stock had rallied to $13. Check out its progress as you read this story.[9] ❖

Q: **Discussion Questions**

1. Why were investors so concerned about the future of GE Capital?

2. Why do you think investors provided GE Capital with $50 billion through public markets during the 2008–2009 financial crisis?

3. Look up the price of GE stock today and use it to evaluate current investor confidence.

The third monetary policy tool, the **discount rate,** is the rate of interest the Fed charges to loan money to any banking institution to meet reserve requirements. The Fed is the lender of last resort for these banks. When a bank borrows from the Fed, it is said to have borrowed at the "discount window," and the interest rates charged there are often higher than those charged on loans of comparable risk elsewhere in the economy. This added interest expense, when it exists, serves to discourage banks from borrowing from the Fed.

When the Fed wants to expand the money supply, it lowers the discount rate to encourage borrowing. Conversely, when the Fed wants to decrease the money supply, it raises the discount rate. The increases in interest rates that occurred in the United States from 2003 through 2006 were the result of more than 16 quarter-point (0.25 percent) increases in the Fed discount rate. The purpose was to keep inflation under control and to raise rates to a more normal level as the economy recovered from the recession of 2001. Not surprisingly, economists watch changes in this sensitive interest rate as an indicator of the Fed's monetary policy.

The final tool in the Fed's arsenal of weapons is **credit controls**—the authority to establish and enforce credit rules for financial institutions and some private investors. For example, the Fed can determine how large a down payment individuals and businesses must make on credit purchases of expensive items such as automobiles, and how much time they have to finish paying for the purchases. By raising and lowering minimum down payment amounts and payment periods, the Fed can stimulate or discourage credit purchases of "big ticket" items. The Fed also has the authority to set the minimum down payment investors must use for the credit purchases of stock. Buying stock with credit—"buying on margin"—is a popular investment strategy among individual speculators. By altering the margin requirement (currently set at 50 percent of the price of the purchased stocks), the Fed can effectively control the total amount of credit borrowing in the stock market.

the financial crisis During the financial crisis of 2008–2009, the Fed used every tool at its disposal. It lowered the discount rate to almost zero, it expanded the money supply, and it did some things it had never done before. It agreed to buy and sell financial assets in markets that had become frozen and nonfunctioning. By making markets, it created liquidity for many of the financial institutions that could not sell assets such as mortgage-backed securities and commercial paper. The Fed also guaranteed loans so that investors loaning money to financial institutions had the full faith and credit of the U.S. government behind the loans. These were powers the Fed had the ability to use but never needed to use until the crisis. The lessons learned from the Great Depression of the 1930s motivated the Federal Reserve as well as the U.S. Treasury to act fast and in concert with the $700 billion stimulus passed by Congress. The lessons from the past indicated that a speedy response would be much more successful than the usual slow government response in past recessions. Time will tell whether all the actions taken had the desired result.

regulatory functions The second major responsibility of the Fed is to regulate banking institutions that are members of the Federal Reserve System. Accordingly, the Fed establishes and enforces banking rules that affect monetary policy and the overall level of the competition between different banks. It determines which nonbanking activities, such as brokerage services, leasing, and insurance, are appropriate for banks and which should be prohibited. The Fed also has the authority to approve or disapprove mergers between banks and the formation of bank holding companies. Increasingly, mergers between banks are crossing international waters. For example, Frances's BNP Paribas acquired United California Bank and Honolulu based BancWest Corp., while the Royal Bank of Scotland, through its Citizens Financial Group subsidiary, purchased Pittsburgh's Mellon Financial and Philadelphia's Commonwealth Bancorp.[10] In an effort to ensure that all rules are enforced and correct accounting procedures are being followed at member banks, surprise bank examinations are conducted by bank examiners each year.

check clearing The Federal Reserve provides national check processing on a huge scale. Divisions of the Fed known as check clearinghouses handle almost all the checks written against a bank in one city and presented for deposit to a bank in a second city. Any banking institution can present the checks it has received from others around the country to its regional Federal Reserve Bank. The Fed passes on the checks to the appropriate regional Federal Reserve Bank, which then sends the checks to the issuing bank for payment. With the advance of electronic payment systems and the passage of the Check Clearing for the 21st Century Act (Check 21 Act), checks can now be processed in a day. The Check 21 Act allows banks to clear checks electronically by presenting an electronic image of the check. This eliminates mail delays and time-consuming paper processing.

depository insurance The Fed is also responsible for supervising the federal insurance funds that protect the deposits of member institutions. These insurance funds will be discussed in greater detail in the following section.

Banking Institutions

Banking institutions accept money deposits from and make loans to individual consumers and businesses. Some of the most important banking institutions include commercial banks, savings and loan associations, credit unions, and mutual savings banks. Historically, these have all been separate institutions. However, new hybrid forms of banking institutions that perform two or more of these functions have emerged over the last two decades. The following banking institutions all have one thing in common: They are businesses whose objective is to earn money by managing, safeguarding, and lending money to others. Their sales revenues come from the fees and interest they charge for providing these financial services.

● ● LO4

Compare and contrast commercial banks, savings and loan associations, credit unions, and mutual savings banks.

commercial banks The largest and oldest of all financial institutions are **commercial banks,** which perform a variety of financial services. They rely mainly on checking and savings accounts as their major source of funds and use only a portion of these deposits to make loans to businesses and individuals. Because it is unlikely that all the depositors of any one bank will want to withdraw all their funds at the same time, a bank can safely loan out a large percentage of its deposits.

Today, banks are quite diversified and offer a number of services. Commercial banks make loans for virtually any conceivable legal purpose, from vacations to cars, from homes to college educations. Banks in many states offer *home equity loans,* by which home owners can borrow against the appraised value of their already purchased homes. Banks also issue Visa and MasterCard credit cards and offer CDs and trusts (legal entities

Chase completed a merger with Bank One in 2004, making it the second largest bank in the United States behind Citigroup. JPMorgan was created through a merger with Chase Manhattan Bank and JPMorgan, and Bank One acquired many Midwestern banks, with its biggest acquisition being First Chicago Corp.

savings and loan associations Savings and loan associations (S&Ls), often called "thrifts," are financial institutions that primarily offer savings accounts and make long-term loans for residential mortgages. A mortgage is a loan made so that a business or individual can purchase real estate, typically a home; the real estate itself is pledged as a guarantee (called *collateral*) that the buyer will repay the loan. If the loan is not repaid, the savings and loan has the right to repossess the property. Before the 1970s, S&Ls focused almost exclusively on real estate lending and accepted only savings accounts. Today, following years of regulatory changes, S&Ls compete directly with commercial banks by offering many types of services.

Savings and loans have gone through a metamorphosis since the early 1990s, after having almost collapsed in the 1980s. Congress passed legislation that allowed more competition

[**". . . banks are quite diversified and offer a number of services."**]

set up to hold and manage assets for a beneficiary). Many banks rent safe deposit boxes in bank vaults to customers who want to store jewelry, legal documents, artwork, and other valuables. In 1999 Congress passed the Financial Services Modernization Act, also known as the Gramm-Leach-Bliley Bill. This act repealed the Glass Steagall Act, which was enacted in 1929 after the stock market crash and prohibited commercial banks from being in the insurance and investment banking business. This puts U.S. commercial banks on the same competitive footing as European banks and provides a more level playing field for global banking competition. The stimulus for the Gramm-Leach-Bliley Bill was probably the merger of Citibank and Travelers Insurance. With its Salomon Smith Barney investment bank and brokerage units, Travelers Insurance, when combined with Citibank, became the largest financial services company in the United States. As commercial banks and investment banks have merged, the landscape has changed. Consolidation remains the norm in the U.S. banking industry. For example JPMorgan

between banks and savings and loans. The problem was the owners and managers of the savings and loans did not know how to behave like a bank, and they did not have the products necessary to compete. Then, Congress passed laws in 1986 that took away many of the tax benefits of owning real estate, which caused investment in real estate to slow considerably and stimulated defaults that were spurred by a poor economy. Developers defaulted on loans, and the S&L managers who had lent the money for these high-risk ventures found themselves holding billions of dollars of virtually unsellable real estate properties.

Despite the efforts of the Federal Savings and Loan Insurance Corporation—which we discuss in more detail shortly—there were not enough funds to bail out the industry. Eventually, the insurance fund ran out of money, and Congress created the Resolution Trust Corporation (RTC) in 1989 to help the industry work its way out of trouble. At a cost of hundreds of billions of dollars, the RTC cleaned up the industry and, with its task completed, was dissolved by 1998.

credit unions

A **credit union** is a financial institution owned and controlled by its depositors, who usually have a common employer, profession, trade group, or religion. The Aggieland Credit Union in College Station, Texas, for example, provides banking services for faculty, employees, and current and former students of Texas A&M University. A savings account at a credit union is commonly referred to as a share account, while a checking account is termed a share draft account. Because the credit union is tied to a common organization, the members (depositors) are allowed to vote for directors and share in the credit union's profits in the form of higher interest rates on accounts and/or lower loan rates.

While credit unions were originally created to provide depositors with a short-term source of funds for low-interest consumer loans for items such as cars, home appliances, vacations, and college, today they offer a wide range of financial services. Generally, the larger a credit union is, the more sophisticated its financial service offerings will be.

mutual savings banks

Mutual savings banks are similar to savings and loan associations, but, like credit unions, they are owned by their depositors. Among the oldest financial institutions in the United States, they were originally established to provide a safe place for the savings of particular groups of people, such as fishermen. Found mostly in New England, they are becoming more popular in the rest of the country as some S&Ls have converted to mutual savings banks to escape the stigma created by the widespread S&L failures in the 1980s.

insurance for banking institutions

The **Federal Deposit Insurance Corporation (FDIC),** which insures individual bank accounts, was established in 1933 to help stop bank failures throughout the country during the Great Depression. In the past the FDIC insured all bank accounts up to $100,000, but because of overriding fears about bank solvency, it raised the insured amount to $250,000 during the financial crisis. This increase was temporary and originally was meant to last two years, but there is always the possibility that it could be made permanent. The insured accounts cover nearly 8,000 member institutions that pay insurance premiums to the FDIC. While most major banks are insured by the FDIC,

After running billboards criticizing large banks for taking government bailout funds, Worthington National, a small Texas bank, received millions of dollars in new deposits.

If You Ask Denny Buchanan, He Will Tell You Independent Bank Is the Way to Go

In 2005 Denny Buchanan acquired $7.5 million in equity capital and launched Independent Bank of Austin. It was profitable within three months and had a $1.4 million profit after one year. The bank performed so well, that after 18 months it had $100 million in assets.

The bank avoided the traps of the 2008–2009 subprime crisis and remained profitable. According to analysts, a move toward smaller banks occurs a few years after a round of industry consolidation as a backlash against banks growing so large. In 2007, Independent Bank was ranked the number one bank

in return on average equity (ROE) out of all banks founded in 2005. Buchanan attributes Independent Bank's success to the company's services, prompt lending decisions and competitive rates, and the maintenance of quality customer relationships.[11] ❖

small institutions in some states may be insured by state insurance funds or private insurance companies. Should a member bank fail, its depositors can recover all of their funds, up to $250,000. Amounts over $250,000, while not legally covered by the insurance, are in fact usually covered because the Fed understands very well the enormous damage that would result to the financial system should these large depositors withdraw their money. The *Federal Savings and Loan Insurance Corporation (FSLIC)* insured thrift deposits before its insolvency and failure during the S&L crisis of the 1980s. Now, the insurance functions once overseen by the FSLIC are handled directly by the FDIC through its Savings Association Insurance Fund. The **National Credit Union Association (NCUA)** regulates and charters credit unions and insures their deposits through its National Credit Union Insurance Fund.

When they were originally established, Congress hoped that these insurance funds would make people feel secure about their savings so that they would not panic and withdraw their money when news of a bank failure was announced. The "bank run" scene in the perennial Christmas movie *It's a Wonderful Life,* when dozens of Bailey Building and Loan depositors attempted to withdraw their money (only to have the reassuring figure of Jimmy Stewart calm their fears), was not based on

mere fiction. During the Great Depression, hundreds of banks failed and their depositors lost everything. The fact that large numbers of major financial institutions failed in the 1980s and 1990s—without a single major banking panic—underscores the effectiveness of the current insurance system. While the future may yet bring unfortunate surprises, most depositors go to sleep every night without worrying about the safety of their savings.

 LO5

Distinguish among nonbanking institutions such as insurance companies, pension funds, mutual funds, and finance companies.

Nonbanking Institutions

Nonbank financial institutions offer some financial services, such as short-term loans or investment products, but do not accept deposits. These include insurance companies, pension funds, mutual funds, brokerage firms, nonfinancial firms, and finance companies. Table 15.3 lists other diversified financial services firms.

Bank runs like this one at Indymac still occur. To reinstill confidence in banks after the economic meltdown, in 2008 the FDIC temporarily increased deposit insurance from $100,000 to $250,000 per depositor.

diversified firms Recently, a growing number of tradition-ally nonfinancial firms have moved onto the financial field. These firms include manufacturing organizations, such as General Motors and General Electric, that traditionally confined their financial activities to financing their customers' purchases. GE, in particular, has been so successful in the financial arena that its credit sub-sidiary now accounts for more than 30 percent of the company's revenues and earnings. Not every nonfinancial firm has been success-ful with its financial ventures, however. Sears, the retail giant, once commanded an imposing financial network composed of real estate (Coldwell Banker), credit card (Discover Card), and brokerage (Dean Witter Reynolds) companies, but losses of hundreds of millions of dollars forced Sears to dismantle

TABLE 15.3 Leading Diversified Financial Services Firms

Company	Revenues (millions)
General Electric	183,207
Fannie Mae	22,652
International Assets Holding	18,359
Freddie Mac	12,392
Marsh & McLennan	11,587
Aon	8,406
SLM	7,689
Ameriprise Financial	7,149

Source: "Fortune 500: Diversified Financials," *Fortune,* May 4, 2009, p. 49.

by individual objectives and tolerance for risk. The interest earned by all these investments may be deferred tax-free until retirement.

> # "... a growing number of traditionally nonfinancial firms have moved onto the financial field."

its network. The very prestigious brokerage firm Morgan Stan-ley acquired Dean Witter Discover, thus creating one of the largest investment firms in the country—in a league with Smith Barney and Merrill Lynch. Perhaps the moral of the story for firms like Sears is "stick to what you know."

insurance companies Insurance companies are businesses that protect their clients against financial losses from certain specified risks (death, injury, disability, accident, fire, theft, and natural disasters, for example) in exchange for a fee, called a premium. Because insurance premiums flow into the companies regularly but major insurance losses can-not be timed with great accuracy (although expected risks can be assessed with considerable precision), insurance companies generally have large amounts of excess funds. They typically invest these or make long-term loans, particularly to businesses in the form of commercial real estate loans.

pension funds Pension funds are managed invest-ment pools set aside by individuals, corporations, unions, and some nonprofit organizations to provide retirement income for members. One type of pension fund is the *individual retirement account (IRA),* which is established by individuals to provide for their personal retirement needs. IRAs can be invested in a variety of financial assets, from risky commodities such as oil and cocoa to low-risk financial "staples" such as U.S. Treasury securities. The choice is up to each person and is dictated solely

In 1997, Congress revised the IRA laws and created a Roth IRA. Although similar to a traditional IRA in that investors may contribute $3,000 per year, the money in a Roth IRA is considered an after-tax contribution. When the money is withdrawn at retirement, no tax is paid on the distribution. The Roth IRA is beneficial to young people who can allow a long time for their money to compound and who may be able to have their parents or grandparents fund the Roth IRA with gift money.

Most major corporations provide some kind of pension plan for their employees. Many of these are established with bank trust departments or life insurance companies. Money is deposited in a separate account in the name of each individual employee, and when the employee retires, the total amount in the account can be either withdrawn in one lump sum or taken as monthly cash payments over a defined period (usually for the remaining life of the retiree). Both corporate-sponsored pen-sion funds and individually managed pension funds usually are invested in financial assets such as stocks and bonds. During the financial crisis, the stock market dropped over 50 percent from peak to trough, and many pension funds felt the pain. Funds that were conservatively invested suffered less than did funds invested mostly in common stocks. Many corporate-and state-sponsored pension funds suffered large losses and became underfunded, which meant they did not have enough assets to pay off their pension obligations. This is why everybody is hop-ing for a stock market recovery.

● **MUTUAL FUND** an investment company that pools individual investor dollars and invests them in large numbers of well-diversified securities

● **BROKERAGE FIRMS** firms that buy and sell stocks, bonds, and other securities for their customers and provide other financial services

● **FINANCE COMPANIES** businesses that offer short-term loans at substantially higher rates of interest than banks

Social Security, the largest pension fund, is publicly financed. The federal government collects Social Security funds from payroll taxes paid by both employers and employees. The Social Security Administration then takes these monies and makes payments to those eligible to receive Social Security benefits—the retired, the disabled, and the young children of deceased parents.

mutual funds

A **mutual fund** pools individual investor dollars and invests them in large numbers of well-diversified securities. Individual investors buy shares in a mutual fund in the hope of earning a high rate of return and in much the same way people buy shares of stock. Because of the large numbers of people investing in any one mutual fund, the funds can afford to invest in hundreds (if not thousands) of securities at any one time, minimizing the risks created by any single security that does not do well. Mutual funds provide professional financial management for people who lack the time and/or expertise to invest in particular securities, such as government bonds. While there are no hard-and-fast rules, investments in one or more mutual funds are one way for people to plan for financial independence at the time of retirement.

Like most financial institutions, mutual funds are regulated and in recent years have come under closer scrutiny because of a scandal precipitated by questionable activities at some fund companies. Starting at the turn of the 21st century, the Securities and Exchange Commission (SEC) worked to rapidly implement rules and regulations for the $7.5 trillion mutual fund industry to curtail abuses that gave large traders an advantage over small investors. The problem stems from practices such as late trading and market timing—the rapid buying and selling of fund shares—which can lower the overall performance of a fund and result in higher costs for small investors.[12]

A special type of mutual fund called a *money market fund* invests specifically in short-term debt securities issued by governments and large corporations. Although they offer services such as check-writing privileges and reinvestment of interest income, money market funds differ from the money market accounts offered by banks primarily in that the former represent a pool of funds, while the latter are basically specialized, individual checking accounts. Money market funds usually offer slightly higher rates of interest than bank money market accounts.

brokerage firms

Brokerage firms buy and sell stocks, bonds, and other securities for their customers and provide other financial services. Larger brokerage firms like Merrill Lynch, Charles Schwab, and A. G. Edwards offer financial services unavailable at their smaller competitors. Merrill Lynch, for example, offers the Merrill Lynch Cash Management Account (CMA), which pays interest on deposits and allows clients to write checks, borrow money, and withdraw cash much like a

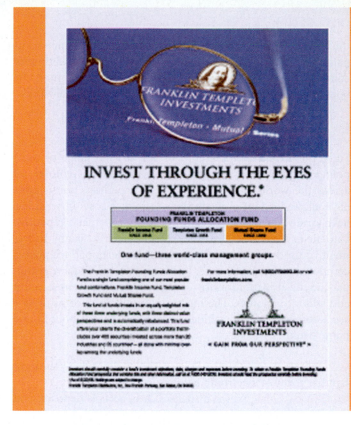

Rather than buy individual stocks and bonds themselves, small investors often purchase mutual funds, which are run by professional financial managers.

commercial bank. The largest of the brokerage firms (including Merrill Lynch) have developed so many specialized services that they may be considered financial networks—organizations capable of offering virtually all the services traditionally associated with commercial banks.

finance companies

Finance companies are businesses that offer short-term loans at substantially higher rates of interest than banks. Commercial finance companies make loans to businesses, requiring their borrowers to pledge assets such as equipment, inventories, or unpaid accounts as collateral for the loans. Consumer finance companies make loans to individuals. Like commercial finance companies, these firms require some sort of personal collateral as security against the borrower's possible inability to repay their loans. Because of the high interest rates they charge and other factors, finance companies typically are the lender of last resort for individuals and businesses whose credit limits have been exhausted and/or those with poor credit ratings. Major consumer finance companies include Household Finance and Wells Fargo. All finance companies—commercial or consumer—obtain their funds by borrowing from other corporations and/or commercial banks.

Electronic Banking

Since the advent of the computer age, a wide range of technological innovations has made it possible to move money all across the world electronically. Such "paperless" transactions have allowed financial institutions to reduce costs in what has been (and what appears to continue to be) a virtual competitive battlefield. **Electronic funds transfer (EFT)** is any movement of funds by means of an electronic terminal, telephone, computer, or magnetic tape. Such transactions order a particular financial institution to subtract money from one account and add it to another. The most commonly used forms of EFT are automated teller machines, automated clearinghouses, and home banking systems.

automated teller machines Probably the most familiar form of electronic banking is the **automated teller machine (ATM),** which dispenses cash, accepts deposits, and allows balance inquiries and cash transfers from one account to another. ATMs provide 24-hour banking services—both at home (through a local bank) and far away (via worldwide ATM networks such as Cirrus and Plus). Rapid growth, driven by both strong consumer acceptance and lower transaction costs for banks (about half the cost of teller transactions), has led to the installation of hundreds of thousands of ATMs worldwide. Table 15.4 presents some interesting statistics about ATMs.

automated clearinghouses Automated **clearinghouses (ACHs)** permit payments such as deposits or withdrawals to be made to and from a bank account by magnetic computer tape. Most large U.S. employers, and many others worldwide, use ACHs to deposit their employees' paychecks directly to the employees' bank accounts. While direct deposit is used by only 50 percent of U.S. workers, nearly 100 percent of Japanese workers and more than 90 percent of European workers utilize it. The largest user of automated clearinghouses in the United States is the federal government, with 99 percent of federal government employees and 65 percent of the private workforce receiving their pay via direct deposit. More than 82 percent of all Social Security payments are made through an ACH system. More than 2.3 billion business-to-business ACH payments were made.

The advantages of direct deposits to consumers include convenience, safety, and potential interest earnings. It is estimated that more than 4 million paychecks are lost or stolen annually, and FBI studies show that 2,000 fraudulent checks

Bank of America Stakeholders Support Sustainability

Bank of America faced a difficult financial situation throughout 2008–2009. In the middle of a global banking crisis related to subprime loans and customers defaulting on loans, BofA, was forced to accept a $20 billion government rescue. Shareholders were concerned about the quality of leadership and decision making at BofA, and they approved a proposal to split the positions of chairman of the board and CEO. This came in response to the financial crisis and BofA's decision to acquire the failing Merrill Lynch and Country-wide Financial. A scandal emerged regarding $3.6 billion in bonuses paid to Merrill executives, which contributed to the massive losses associated with that bank. The government provided a $20 billion bailout to help BofA cope with the losses associated with its weak financial position.

For two decades, BofA has focused on achieving energy efficiency, reducing emissions, and limiting waste, even in the wake of its financial meltdown–related troubles. BofA maintains a strong commitment to sustainability in addition to addressing concerns over its financial performance, a stance shareholders support. The company offers customers eco-friendly products and services such as Brighter Planet Visa and online banking to reduce paper use. BofA is active in communities, promoting energy efficiency and environmental responsibility. The company committed $20 billion over 10 years to aid businesses addressing global climate change, create loans for companies developing renewable energy, and create new jobs. BofA won California's 2008 Governor's Environmental and Economic Leadership Award (GEELA) for its focus on melding environmental stewardship with long-term company management. This award was issued to BofA because of its involvement in solar school initiatives, the creation of Clean Renewable Energy Bonds, and the preservation of redwood forests.

Although BofA admits that its focus on protecting the environment is for profit and economic growth, it also acknowledges that it is the responsible stance to take. BofA intends to maintain its sustainability efforts even in recessionary times.[13] ❖

Q: Discussion Questions

1. How does BofA balance sustainability and performance during a difficult financial time?

2. What does BofA gain from continuing to invest in sustainability?

3. Do you think that being recognized and winning environmental awards will help BofA become more profitable?

TABLE 15.4 ATM Fact Sheet

- An ATM costs between $9,000 and $50,000, depending on the functions it has been designed to perform.
- An ATM costs between $12,000 and $15,000 in annual maintenance costs, such as cash replenishment, servicing, telephone costs, and rent.
- The top four ATM owners are Bank of America, Cardtronics, JPMorgan Chase, and Wells Fargo.
- In 2007, there were 415,321 ATMs in the United States.
- Transactions at these machines totaled $14.9 billion.
- 21% of Americans prefer to bank via ATMs.
- The first ATM was in use in 1969 at the Chemical Bank in Long Island, NY.

Source: ATM Fact Sheet, 2008 ABA issue Summary, American Bankers Association, www.texasbankers.com/pdfs/2ATM_Facts.pdf (accessed March 24, 2009).

are cashed every day in the United States. Checks can never be lost or stolen with direct deposit. The benefits to businesses include decreased check-processing expenses and increased employee productivity. Research shows that businesses that use direct deposit can save more than $1.25 on each payroll check processed. Productivity could increase by $3 to $5 billion annually if all employees were to use direct deposit rather than taking time away from work to deposit their payroll checks.

online banking With the growth of the Internet, banking activities may now be carried out on a computer at home or at work, or through wireless devices such as cell phones and PDAs anywhere there is a wireless "hot point." Consumers and small businesses can now make a bewildering array of financial transactions at home or on the go 24 hours a day. Functioning much like a vast network of personal ATMs, computer networks such as America Online allow their subscribers to make sophisticated banking transactions, buy and sell stocks and bonds, and purchase products and airline tickets without ever leaving home or speaking to another human being. Many banks allow customers to log directly into their accounts to check balances, transfer money between accounts, view their account statements, and pay bills via a home computer or other Internet-enabled devices. Computer and advanced telecommunications technology have revolutionized world commerce. The online banking market is a rapidly growing sector of the banking industry, with more than 51 million Americans already signed on.[14]

 LO6

Investigate the challenges ahead for the banking industry.

Challenge and Change in the Commercial Banking Industry

In the early 1990s, several large commercial banks were forced to admit publicly that they had made some poor loan decisions. Bank failures followed, including that of the Bank of New England, the third-largest bank failure in history. The vibrant economic growth in the 1990s substantially improved what had been a rather bleak picture for many financial institutions. Better management, combined with better regulation and a robust economy, saved commercial banks from the fate of the S&Ls. Indeed, low inflation rates meant low interest rates on deposits, and high employment led to very low loan default rates. Combined, these factors helped make the 1990s one of the most profitable decades in the history of the banking industry.

The banking industry continued to change in the 2000s, and with the passage of the Gramm-Leach-Bliley Bill, banks are expected to continue their "urge to merge." Now that banks are allowed to offer insurance, brokerage, and investment banking services, there will be a hunt to find likely merger partners that will expand their customer reach and the services they are able to offer. On the other side of the coin, even as banks such as Bank of America continue to become national banks with offices in more than half the states, small community banks continue to start up to serve the customer who still wants personal service. The ability of these small banks to buy state-of-the-art technology from nonbank service providers allows them to offer Internet banking and many sophisticated services at competitive costs. They also provide a local face and service to the consumer who is more and more likely to be unwelcome at some large banks that cater to corporations and wealthy individuals.

CitiBank is one of the largest international banks in the world and has locations in Asia, Latin America, Europe, and of course North America. People living in Manila can use CitiBank's online banking services from abroad, and CitiBank customers can pay their bills on the Internet while traveling around the world in addition to having access to their money with a CitiBank ATM card. Banking will continue to become more international with large banks such as the Dutch ABN-AMRO bank continuing to acquire banking assets in the United States. For instance in Chicago, ABN-AMRO owns LaSalle Bank, and The Bank of Montreal owns The Harris Bank.

Indeed, the recent trend toward ever bigger banks and other financial institutions is not happening by chance alone.

SO YOU'RE INTERESTED IN FINANCIAL SYSTEMS OR BANKING

You think you might be interested in going into finance or banking, but it is so hard to tell when you are a full-time student. Classes that seem interesting when you take them might not translate in an interesting work experience after you graduate. A great way to see if you would excel at a career in finance is to get some experience in the industry. Internships, whether they are paid or unpaid, not only help you figure out what you might want to do after you graduate, they are a great way to build up your résumé, put your learning to use, and start generating connections within the field. For example, for the past four years, Pennsylvania's Delaware County District Attorney's Office has been accepting business students from Villanova University for a six-month internship. The students work in the economic-crime division, analyzing documents of people under investigation for financial crimes ranging from fraud to money laundering. The students get actual experience in forensic accounting and have a chance to see whether this is the right career path for them. On top of that, the program has saved the county an average of $20,000 annually on consulting and accounting fees, not to mention that detectives now have time to take on larger caseloads. Michael Busby, a student who completed the program, spent his six months investigating a case in which the owner of a sewage treatment company had embezzled a total of $1 million over the course of nine years. Busby noted that the experience helped him gain an understanding of how different companies handle their financial statements, as well as how accounting can be applied in forensics and law enforcement.

Internship opportunities are plentiful all over the country, although you may need to do some research to find them. To start, talk to your program advisor and your professors about opportunities. Also, you can check the Web sites of companies where you think you might like to work to see if they have any opportunities available. City, state, and federal government offices often provide student internships as well. No matter where you end up interning, the real-life skills you pick up, as well as the résumé boost you get, will help you find a job after you graduate. When you graduate, commercial banks and other financial institutions offer major employment opportunities. In 2008–2009, a major downturn in the financial industry resulted in mergers, acquisitions, and financial restructuring for many companies. While the immediate result was a decrease in job opportunities, as the industry recovers, there will be many challenging job opportunities available.[15]

Financial services may be an example of a "natural oligopoly," meaning that the industry may be best served by a few very large firms rather than a host of smaller ones. As the largest U.S. banks merge into even larger international entities, they will erase the relative competitive advantages now enjoyed by the largest foreign banks. It is by no means implausible that the financial services industry of the year 2020 will be dominated by 10 or so internationally oriented "megabanks."

Rapid advances and innovations in technology are challenging the banking industry and requiring it to change. As we said earlier, more and more banks, both large and small, are offering electronic access to their financial services. ATM technology is rapidly changing, with machines now dispensing more than just cash. Online financial services, ATM technology, and bill presentation are just a few of the areas where rapidly changing technology is causing the banking industry to change as well. ■

Team Exercise

Mutual funds pool individual investor dollars and invest them in a number of different securities. Go to http://finance.yahoo.com/ and click on top-performing funds by criteria such as sector, style, and strategy.

Assume that your group has $100,000 to invest in mutual funds. Select five funds in which to invest, representing a balanced (varied industries, risk, etc.) portfolio, and defend your selections.

CHECK OUT www.mhhe.com/FerrellM2e

for study materials including Interactive Exercises, Quizzes, iPod downloads, and video.

learning OBJECTIVES

LO1 Describe some common methods of managing current assets.

LO2 Identify some sources of short-term financing (current liabilities).

LO3 Summarize the importance of long-term assets and capital budgeting.

LO4 Specify how companies finance their operations and manage fixed assets with long-term liabilities, particularly bonds.

LO5 Discuss how corporations can use equity financing by issuing stock through an investment banker.

LO6 Describe the various securities markets in the United States.

financial management

A N D

SECURITIES
MARKETS

INTRODUCTION While it's certainly true that money makes the world go round, financial management is the discipline that makes the world turn more smoothly. Indeed, without effective management of assets, liabilities, and owners' equity, all business organizations are doomed to fail—regardless of the quality and innovativeness of their products. Financial management is the field that addresses the issues of obtaining and managing the funds and resources necessary to run a business successfully. It is not limited to business organizations: All organizations, from the corner store to the local nonprofit art museum, from giant corporations to county governments, must manage their resources effectively and efficiently if they are to achieve their objectives.

In this chapter, we look at both short- and long-term financial management. First, we discuss the management of short-term assets, which companies use to generate sales and conduct ordinary day-to-day business operations. Next, we turn our attention to the management of short-term liabilities, the sources of short-term funds used to finance a business. Then, we discuss the management of long-term assets such as plant and equipment and the long-term liabilities such as stocks and bonds used to finance these important corporate assets. Finally, we look at the securities markets, where stocks and bonds are traded.

LO1

Describe some common methods of managing current assets.

MANAGING CURRENT ASSETS AND LIABILITIES

Managing short-term assets and liabilities involves managing the current assets and liabilities on the balance sheet (discussed in Chapter 14). Current assets are short-term resources such as cash, investments, accounts receivable, and inventory. Current liabilities are short-term debts such as accounts payable, accrued salaries, accrued taxes, and short-term bank loans. We use the terms *current* and *short term* interchangeably because short-term assets and liabilities usually are replaced by new assets and liabilities within three or four months, and always within a year. Managing short-term assets and liabilities sometimes is called **working capital management** because short-term assets and liabilities continually flow through an organization and are thus said to be "working."

Managing Current Assets

The chief goal of financial managers who focus on current assets and liabilities is to maximize the return to the business on cash, temporary investments of idle cash, accounts receivable, and inventory.

managing cash A crucial element facing any financial manager is effectively managing the firm's cash flow. Remember that cash flow is the movement of money through an organization on a daily, weekly, monthly, or yearly basis. Ensuring that sufficient (but not excessive) funds are on hand to meet the company's obligations is one of the single most important facets of financial management.

Idle cash does not make money, and corporate checking accounts typically do not earn interest. As a result, astute money managers try to keep just enough cash on hand, called **transaction balances,** to pay bills—such as employee wages, supplies, and utilities—as they fall due. To manage the firm's cash and ensure that enough cash flows through the organization quickly and efficiently, companies try to speed up cash collections from customers.

To accelerate the collection of payments from customers, some companies have customers send their payments to a **lockbox,** which is simply an address for receiving payments, instead of directly to the company's main address. The manager of the lockbox, usually a commercial bank, collects payments directly from the lockbox several times a day and deposits them into the company's bank account. The bank can then start clearing the checks and get the money into the company's checking account much more quickly than it could if the payments had been submitted directly to the company. However, there is no free lunch: The costs associated with lockbox systems make them worthwhile only for companies that receive thousands of checks from customers each business day.

Large firms with many stores or offices around the country, such as Household International (parent company of the well-known finance company Household Finance), frequently use electronic funds transfer to speed up collections. Household Finance's local offices deposit checks received each business day into their local banks, and at the end of the day, Household's corporate office initiates the transfer of all collected funds to its central bank for overnight investment. This technique is especially attractive for major international companies, which face slow and sometimes uncertain physical delivery of payments and/or less-than-efficient check-clearing procedures.

More and more companies are now using electronic funds transfer systems to pay and collect bills online. It is interesting that companies want to collect cash quickly but pay out

Firms and individuals can buy and redeem T-bills and other government securities from the U.S. Department of the Treasury at www.treasurydirect.com.

cash slowly. When companies use electronic funds transfers between buyers and suppliers, the speed of collections and disbursements increases to one day. Only with the use of checks can companies delay the payment of cash quickly and have a three- or four-day waiting period until the check is presented to their bank and the cash leaves their account.

investing idle cash

As companies sell products, they generate cash on a daily basis, and sometimes cash comes in faster than it is needed to pay bills. Organizations often invest this "extra" cash, for periods as short as one day (overnight) or for as long as one year, until it is needed. Such temporary investments of cash are known as **marketable securities.** Examples include U.S. Treasury bills, certificates of deposit, commercial paper, and Eurodollar loans. Table 16.1 summarizes a number of different marketable securities used by businesses and some sample interest rates on those investments as of June 23, 2006. The safety rankings are relative. While all the listed securities are very low risk, the U.S. government securities are the safest.

You can see that interest rates declined during the two periods presented. Because of the recession and the financial crisis, the Federal Reserve lowered interest rates to almost zero in an attempt to stimulate the economy and boost borrowing. The rates of 2006 are what one would expect in a normal economy, while the rates in 2009 are artificially depressed. Investors will not get much return on their idle cash in this low-interest-rate environment.

Many large companies invest idle cash in U.S. **Treasury bills (T-bills),** which are short-term debt obligations the U.S. government sells to raise money. Issued weekly by the U.S. Treasury, T-bills carry maturities of one week to one year. U.S. T-bills are generally considered to be the safest of all investments and are called risk free because the U.S. government will not default on its debt.

Commercial certificates of deposit (CDs) are issued by commercial banks and brokerage companies. They are available in minimum amounts of $100,000 but are typically in units of $1 million for large corporations investing excess cash. Unlike consumer CDs (discussed in Chapter 15), which must be held until maturity, commercial CDs may be traded before maturity. Should a cash shortage occur, the organization can simply sell the CD on the open market and obtain needed funds.

One of the most popular short-term investments for the largest business organizations is **commercial paper**—a written promise from one company to another to pay a specific amount of money. Because commercial paper is backed only by the name and reputation of the issuing company, sales of commercial paper are restricted to only the largest and most financially stable companies. As commercial paper is frequently bought and sold for durations of as short as one business day, many "players" in the market find themselves buying commercial paper with excess cash on one day and selling it to gain extra money the following day.

Some companies invest idle cash in international markets such as the **eurodollar market,** a market for trading U.S. dollars in foreign countries. Because the Eurodollar market originally was developed by London banks, any dollar-denominated deposit in a non-U.S. bank is called a eurodollar deposit, regardless of whether the issuing bank is actually located in Europe, South America, or anyplace else. For example, if you travel overseas and deposit $1,000 in a German bank, you will have "created" a eurodollar deposit in the amount of $1,000. Since the U.S. dollar is accepted by most countries for international trade, these dollar deposits can be used by international companies to settle their accounts. The market created for trading such investments offers

TABLE 16.1 Short-Term Investment Possibilities for Idle Cash

Type of Security	Maturity	Seller of Security	Interest Rate 6/23/2006	Interest Rate 6/6/09	Safety Level
U.S. Treasury bills	90 days	U.S. government	4.80%	.18%	Excellent
U.S. Treasury bills	180 days	U.S. government	5.05	.30	Excellent
Commercial paper	30 days	Major corporations	5.14	.28	Very good
Certificates of deposit	90 days	U.S. commercial banks	5.40	.46	Very good
Certificates of deposit	180 days	U.S. commercial banks	5.43	.80	Very good
Eurodollars	90 days	European commercial banks	5.48	1.25	Very good

Source: www.federalreserve.gov/releases/h15/current (accessed June 3, 2009).

firms with extra dollars a chance to earn a slightly higher rate of return with just a little more risk than they would face by investing in U.S. Treasury bills.

maximizing accounts receivable

After cash and marketable securities, the balance sheet lists accounts receivable and inventory. Remember that accounts receivable is money owed to a business by credit customers. For example, if you charge your Shell gasoline purchases, until you actually pay for them with cash or a check, they represent an account receivable to Shell. Many businesses make the vast majority of their sales on credit, and so managing accounts receivable is an important task.

Walmart electronically shares its inventory information with its suppliers: When the stock of products runs low, the suppliers are alerted electronically to ship more of it to Walmart.

Each credit sale represents an account receivable for the company, the terms of which typically require customers to pay the full amount due within 30, 60, or even 90 days from the date of the sale. To encourage quick payment, some businesses offer some of their customers discounts of 1 to 2 percent if they pay off their balance within a specified period of time (usually between 10 and 30 days). Late payment charges between 1 and 1.5 percent serve to discourage slow payers from sitting on their bills forever. The larger the early payment discount offered is, the faster customers will tend to pay their accounts. Unfortunately, while discounts increase cash flow, they also reduce profitability. Finding the right balance between the added advantages of early cash receipt and the disadvantages of reduced profits is no simple matter. Similarly, determining the optimal balance between the higher sales likely to result from extending credit to customers with less than sterling credit ratings and the higher bad-debt losses likely to result from a more lenient credit policy is also challenging. Information on company credit ratings is provided by local credit bureaus, national credit-rating agencies such as Dun and Bradstreet, and industry trade groups.

optimizing inventory

While the inventory that a firm holds is controlled by both production needs and marketing considerations, the financial manager has to coordinate inventory purchases to manage cash flows. The object is to minimize the firm's investment in inventory without experiencing production cutbacks as a result of critical materials shortfalls or lost sales due to insufficient finished goods inventories. Every dollar invested in inventory is a dollar unavailable for investment in some other area of the organization. Optimal inventory levels are determined, in large part, by the method of production. If a firm attempts to produce its goods just in time to meet sales demand, the level of inventory will be relatively low. If, in contrast, the firm produces materials in a constant, level pattern, inventory increases when sales decrease and decreases when sales increase. One way companies are attempting to optimize inventory is through the use of radio frequency identification (RFID) technology.

The automobile industry is an excellent example of an industry driven almost solely by inventory levels. Because it is inefficient to continually lay off workers in slow times and call them back in better times, Ford, General Motors, and Chrysler try to set and stick to quarterly production quotas. Automakers typically try to keep a 60-day supply of unsold cars. During particularly slow periods, however, it is not unusual for inventories to exceed 100 days of sales. When sales of a particular brand fall far behind the average and inventories build up, production of that model may be canceled, as General Motors did with its Oldsmobile marque. Before eliminating a brand outright, however, automakers typically try to "jump-start" sales by offering rebates, special financing incentives, or special lease terms—all of which GM tried without success.

Although less publicized, inventory shortages can be as much of a drag on potential profits as too much inventory. Not having an item on hand may send the customer to a competitor—forever. Complex computer inventory models are frequently employed to determine the optimum level of inventory a firm should hold to support a given level of sales. Such models can indicate how and when parts inventories should be ordered so that they are available exactly when required—and not a day before. Developing and maintaining such an intricate production and inventory system is difficult, but it can often prove to be the difference between average profits and spectacular ones.

 L02

Identify some sources of short-term financing (current liabilities).

Managing Current Liabilities

While having extra cash on hand is a delightful surprise, the opposite situation—a temporary cash shortfall—can be a crisis. The good news is that there are several potential sources of short-term funds. Suppliers often serve as an important source through credit sales practices. Also, banks, finance companies, and other organizations offer short-term funds through loans and other business operations.

accounts payable Remember from Chapter 14 that accounts payable is money an organization owes to suppliers for goods and services. Just as accounts receivable must be managed actively to ensure proper cash collections, so too must accounts payable be managed to make the best use of this important liability.

The most widely used source of short-term financing, and therefore the most important account payable, is **trade credit**—credit extended by suppliers for the purchase of their goods and services. While varying in formality, depending on both the organizations involved and the value of the items purchased, most trade credit agreements offer discounts to organizations that pay their bills early. A supplier, for example, may offer trade terms of "1/10 net 30," meaning that the purchasing organization may take a 1 percent discount from the invoice amount if it makes payment by the 10th day after receiving the bill. Otherwise, the entire amount is due within 30 days. For example, pretend that you are the financial manager in charge of payables. You owe Ajax Company $10,000, and it offers trade terms of 2/10 net 30. By paying the amount due within 10 days, you can save 2 percent of $10,000, or $200. Assume you place orders with Ajax once per month and have 12 bills of $10,000 each per year. By taking the discount every time, you will save 12 times $200, or $2,400, per year. Now assume you are the financial manager of Gigantic Corp., and it has monthly payables of $100 million per month. Two percent of $100 million is $2 million per month. Failure to take advantage of such trade discounts can, in many cases, add up to large opportunity losses over the span of a year.

bank loans Virtually all organizations—large and small—obtain short-term funds for operations from banks. In most instances, the credit services granted to these firms take the form of a line of credit or fixed dollar loan. A **line of credit** is an arrangement by which a bank agrees to lend a specified amount of money to the organization upon request—provided

Deceit and Derivatives Cause Company Destruction

Bear Stearns survived the Great Depression but met its ruin in 2008. Two things caused the doom of this 85-year-old company: subprime mortgages and derivatives. Like many financial institutions, Bear Stearns, a global investment bank and securities brokerage firm, invested heavily in subprime mortgages. However, Bear Stearns misrepresented information to achieve its success. The company had reported client information inaccurately on some loan applications to make them appear less risky.

After securing the loans, Bear Stearns sold the debt to other institutions. Bear Stearns agreed to insure the debt that it sold to other companies in the form of a financial instrument called a derivative. The derivatives were supposed to be backed by cash flows from the loans. This allowed Bear Stearns to move the risk onto investors. In November 2007, Bear Stearns had $13.4 trillion in derivatives. There was just one problem: When the economic downturn hit, the cash flows from the loans dried up and the bank could not make good on its promise to "bail out" investors. The situation was made worse by the misconduct of executives Ralph Cioffi and Matthew Tannin. As the company's hedge funds were failing, those executives deceived investors by portraying the funds as great investments. A month later, the funds collapsed, losing $1.6 billion in investor assets. Although the U.S. government attempted to save Bear Stearns, the damage was irrevocable. It was bought by JP Morgan at $10 a share, a far cry from its previous 52-week high of $133.20 per share. Cioffi and Tannin were arrested, but this did little to recover the billions in investor assets they helped lose.[1] ❖

 Discussion Questions

1. What were the ethical issues at Bear Stearns?

2. Should Bear Stearns be held responsible for its executives who engaged in misconduct? Or should those executives be considered rogues who were operating outside the company?

3. Why do you think the stock value of Bear Stearns dropped so rapidly?

● **SECURED LOANS** loans backed by collateral that the bank can claim if the borrowers do not repay them

● **UNSECURED LOANS** loans backed only by the borrowers' good reputation and previous credit rating

● **PRIME RATE** the interest rate that commercial banks charge their best customers (usually large corporations) for short-term loans

that the bank has the required funds to make the loan. In general, a business line of credit is very similar to a consumer credit card, with the exception that the preset credit limit can amount to millions of dollars.

In addition to credit lines, banks make **secured loans**—loans backed by collateral that the bank can claim if the borrowers do not repay the loans—and **unsecured loans**—loans backed only by the borrowers' good reputation and previous credit rating. Both individuals and businesses build their credit ratings from their history of borrowing and repaying borrowed funds on time and in full. The three national credit-rating services are Equifax, TransUnion, and Experian. A lack of credit history or a poor credit history can make it difficult to get loans from financial institutions. The *principal* is the amount of money borrowed; *interest* is a percentage of the principal that the bank charges for use of its money. As we mentioned in Chapter 15, banks also pay depositors interest on savings accounts and some checking accounts. Thus, banks charge borrowers interest for loans and pay interest to depositors for the use of their money. In addition, these loans may include origination fees.

The **prime rate** is the interest rate commercial banks charge their best customers (usually large corporations) for short-term loans. While for many years loans at the prime rate represented funds at the lowest possible cost, the rapid development of the market for commercial paper has dramatically reduced the importance of commercial banks as a source of short-term loans. Today, most "prime" borrowers are actually small and medium-size businesses.

The interest rates on commercial loans may be either fixed or variable. A variable or floating-rate loan offers an advantage when interest rates are falling but represents a distinct disadvantage when interest rates are rising. Between 1999 and 2004, interest rates plummeted, and borrowers refinanced their loans with low-cost fixed-rate loans. Nowhere was this more visible than in the U.S. mortgage markets, where homeowners lined up to refinance their high-percentage home mortgages with lower-cost loans, in some cases as low as 5 percent on a 30-year loan. Mortgage interest rates returned to 6.5 percent during 2006 and 6.0 percent during 2008 and then fell below 5 percent in 2009. One of the causes of the financial crisis was the collapse in housing prices combined with rising mortgage rates from 2004 through 2008. Many subprime borrowers (those with low credit scores were considered high-risk borrowers) used floating-rate loans to buy their houses. As interest rates went up, so did

Businesses often find it easier to loan money if they are willing to back the loan with collateral—such as buildings and equipment that lenders can take possession of should the loans go into default.

their monthly mortgage payments. Many of those borrowers could not afford the increase in payments and stopped paying their mortgages completely. In these circumstances, the bank or mortgage company ended up foreclosing on the loan and taking possession of the house. As more and more borrowers defaulted on their loans, those financial institutions lost more and more money. Eventually, the banks put the houses back on the market at reduced prices, and that caused housing prices to decline even more. In areas where the housing prices were very inflated, such as Arizona, Florida, Nevada, and California, prices fell as much as 40 to 50 percent in some neighborhoods. The housing bubble is only one of the causes of the financial crisis. By 2009, mortgage rates on 30-year conventional mortgages (which require a 20 percent down payment) were less than 5 percent; more borrowers refinanced their home loans, and the prices of houses started to find a bottom.

nonbank liabilities Banks are not the only source of short-term funds for businesses. Indeed, virtually all financial institutions, from insurance companies to pension funds, from money market funds to finance companies, make short-term loans to many organizations. The largest U.S. companies also actively engage in borrowing money from the eurodollar and commercial paper markets. As was noted earlier, both of these funds' sources are typically slightly less expensive than bank loans.

In some instances, businesses actually sell their accounts receivable to a finance company known as a **factor,** which gives the selling organizations cash and assumes responsibility for collecting the accounts. For example, a factor might pay $60,000 for receivables with a total face value of $100,000 (60 percent of the total). The factor profits if it can collect more than what it paid for the accounts. Because the selling organization's customers send their payments to a lockbox, they may have no idea that a factor has bought their receivables.

Additional nonbank liabilities that must be efficiently managed to ensure maximum profitability are taxes owed to the government and wages owed to employees. Clearly, businesses are responsible for many different types of taxes, including federal, state, and local income taxes, property taxes, mineral rights taxes, unemployment taxes, Social Security taxes, workers' compensation taxes, excise taxes, and more! While the public tends to think that the only relevant taxes are on income and sales, many industries must pay other taxes that far exceed those levied against their income. Taxes and employees' wages represent debt obligations of the firm, which the financial manager must plan to meet as they fall due.

● ● **LO3**

Summarize the importance of long-term assets and capital budgeting.

MANAGING FIXED ASSETS

Up to this point, we have focused on the short-term aspects of financial management. While most business failures are the result of poor short-term planning, successful ventures must also consider the long-term financial consequences of their actions. Managing the long-term assets and liabilities and the owners' equity portion of the balance sheet is important for the long-term health of a business.

Long-term (fixed) assets are expected to last for many years— production facilities (plants), offices, equipment, heavy machinery, furniture, automobiles, and so on. In today's fast-paced world, companies need the most technologically advanced, modern facilities and equipment they can afford. Automobile, oil refining, and transportation companies are dependent on fixed assets.

Modern and high-tech equipment carries high price tags, and the financial arrangements required to support these investments are by no means trivial. Leasing is just one approach to financing. Obtaining major long-term financing can be challenging for even the most profitable organizations. For less successful firms, such challenges can prove nearly impossible. One approach is leasing assets such as equipment, machines, and buildings. In the case of leasing or not taking ownership but paying a fee for usage, potential long-term assets can be taken off the balance sheets as a debt. Still, the company has the asset and an obligation to pay money that is a contractual obligation. Leases are associated with $1.25 trillion in off-the-balance-sheet obligations, and the Securities and Exchange Commission is considering changing accounting rules to make future cash obligations more visible.[2] We'll take a closer look at long-term financing in a moment, but first let's address some issues associated with fixed assets, including capital budgeting, risk assessment, and the costs of financing fixed assets.

Capital Budgeting and Project Selection

One of the most important jobs performed by a financial manager is to decide what fixed assets, projects, and investments will earn profits for the firm beyond the costs necessary to fund them. The process of analyzing the needs of the business and selecting the assets that will maximize its value is called **capital budgeting,** and the capital budget is the amount of money budgeted for investment in such long-term assets. But capital budgeting does not end with the selection and purchase of a particular piece of land, equipment, or major investment. All assets and projects

● **FACTOR** a finance company to which businesses sell their accounts receivable—usually for a percentage of the total face value

● **LONG-TERM (FIXED) ASSETS** production facilities (plants), offices, and equipment—all of which are expected to last for many years

● **CAPITAL BUDGETING** the process of analyzing the needs of the business and selecting the assets that will maximize its value

FIGURE 16.1 How Often Is Budgeting and Planning Unreliable?

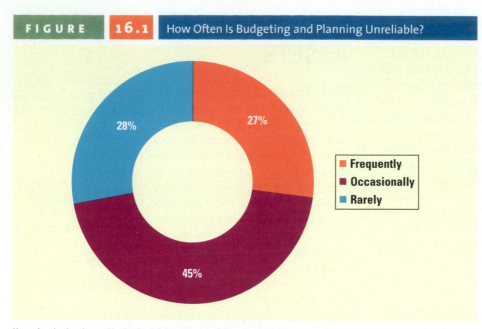

- **Frequently** 27%
- **Occasionally** 45%
- **Rarely** 28%

How often is planning and budgeting information unrealistic or irrelevant?

Source: Don Durfee, "By the Numbers: Alternative Budgeting," *CFO,* June 2006, p. 28.

FIGURE 16.2 Qualitative Assessment of Capital Budgeting Risk

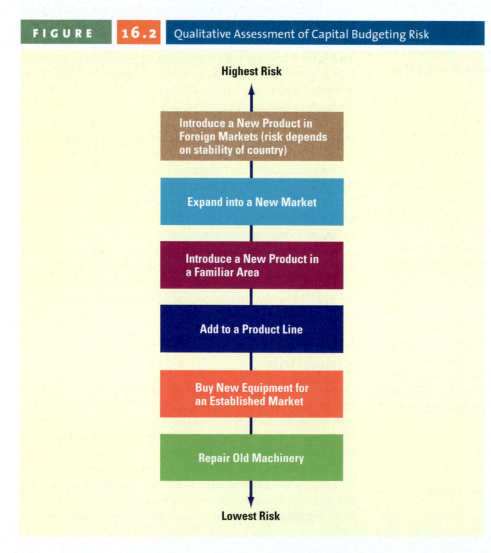

Highest Risk

Introduce a New Product in Foreign Markets (risk depends on stability of country)

Expand into a New Market

Introduce a New Product in a Familiar Area

Add to a Product Line

Buy New Equipment for an Established Market

Repair Old Machinery

Lowest Risk

must be reevaluated continually to ensure their compatibility with the organization's needs. As Figure 16.1 indicates, financial executives believe most budgeting activities are occasionally or frequently unrealistic or irrelevant. If a particular asset does not live up to expectations, management must determine why and take necessary corrective action. Budgeting is not an exact process, and managers must be flexible when new information is available.

Assessing Risk

Every investment carries some risk. Figure 16.2 ranks potential investment projects according to estimated risk. In considering investments overseas, risk assessments must include the political climate and economic stability of a region. The decision to introduce a product or build a manufacturing facility in England would be much less risky than a decision to build one in the Middle East, for example.

Not apparent from Figure 16.2 are the risks associated with time. The longer a project or asset is expected to last, the greater its potential risk because it is hard to predict whether a piece of equipment will wear out or become obsolete in 5 or 10 years. Predicting cash flows one year down the road is difficult, but projecting them over the span of a 10-year project is a gamble.

The level of a project's risk is also affected by the stability and competitive nature of the marketplace and the world economy as a whole. IBM's latest high-technology computer product is far more likely to become obsolete overnight than is a similar $10 million investment in a manufacturing plant. Dramatic changes in the marketplace are not uncommon. Indeed, uncertainty created by the rapid devaluation of Asian currencies in the late 1990s wrecked a host of assumptions in literally hundreds of projects worldwide. Financial managers must constantly consider such issues when making long-term decisions about the purchase of fixed assets.

Pricing Long-Term Money

The ultimate profitability of any project depends not only on accurate assumptions about how much cash it will generate but also on its financing costs. Because a business must pay interest on money it borrows, the returns from any project must cover not only the costs of operating the project but also the interest expenses for the debt used to finance its construction. Unless an organization can effectively cover all of its costs—both financial and operating—it eventually will fail.

Clearly, only a limited supply of funds is available for investment in any particular enterprise. The most efficient and profitable companies can attract the lowest-cost funds because they typically offer reasonable financial returns at very low relative risks. Newer and less prosperous firms must pay higher costs to attract capital because these companies tend to be quite risky. One of the strongest motivations for companies to manage their financial resources wisely is that they will, over time, be able to reduce the costs of their funds and in so doing increase their overall profitability.

In our free-enterprise economy, new firms tend to enter industries that offer the greatest potential rewards for success. However, as more and more companies enter an industry, competition intensifies, eventually driving profits down to average levels. The digital music player market of the early 2000s provides an excellent example of the changes in profitability that typically accompany increasing competition. When Apple introduced its iPod player, it earned very high returns, boosted by paid music downloads from its iTunes online service. Early on, Apple dominated the market with a 40 percent share of digital music player sales and 70 percent of legal paid music downloads. These high returns, coupled with the growing interest in music downloads, spurred competing firms such as Dell, Samsung, Creative, and Rio Nitrus to introduce players with new features or lower prices. Creative, for example, markets a 40-gigabyte player for $200 less than the 40-gigabyte iPod. It is difficult to maintain market dominance in the consumer electronics industry for extended periods of time. Some have even suggested that Apple spin off its iPod business through an initial public offering.[3] The same is true in the personal computer market. With increasing competition, prices have fallen dramatically since the 1990s. Even Dell and Gateway, with their low-cost products, have moved into other markets, such as servers and televisions, to maintain growth in a maturing market. Weaker companies have failed, leaving the most efficient producers/marketers scrambling for market share. The expanded market for personal computers dramatically reduced the financial returns generated by each dollar invested in productive

assets. The "glory days" of the personal computer industry—the time in which fortunes could be won and lost in the space of an average-sized garage—have long since passed into history. Personal computers have essentially become commodity items,

> ## "Budgeting is not an exact process, and managers must be flexible when new information is available."

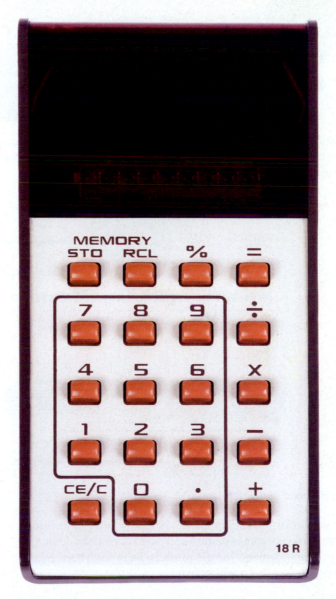

In the 1960s and 1970s, consumers paid hundreds of dollars for basic-function calculators such as this one. But over time, as more competitors enter the market, the prices of products generally drop.

FINANCING WITH LONG-TERM LIABILITIES

Established firms like Apple have an edge when it comes to borrowing at a low cost to develop their products. Startup firms generally must pay more for their capital because lenders view them as being higher risk.

An IBM bond certificate.

As we said earlier, long-term assets do not come cheap, and few companies have the cash on hand to open a new store across town, build a new manufacturing facility, research and develop a new lifesaving drug, or launch a new product worldwide. To develop such fixed assets, companies need to raise low-cost, long-term funds to finance them. Two common choices for raising these funds are attracting new owners (*equity financing*), which we'll look at in a moment, and taking on long-term liabilities (*debt financing*), which we'll look at now.

Long-term liabilities are debts that will be repaid over a number of years, such as long-term bank loans and bond issues. These take many different forms, but in the end, the key word is *debt*. Companies may raise money by borrowing it from commercial banks or other financial institutions in the form of lines of credit, short-term loans, or long-term loans. Many corporations acquire debt by borrowing money from pension funds, mutual funds, or life-insurance funds.

Companies that rely too heavily on debt can get into serious trouble should the economy falter; during these times, they may not earn enough operating income to make the required interest payments (remember the times interest earned ratio in Chapter 14). In severe cases when the problem persists too long, creditors will not restructure loans but instead sue for the interest and principal owed and force the company into bankruptcy.

Bonds: Corporate IOUs

Aside from loans, much long-term debt takes the form of **bonds,** which are debt instruments that larger companies sell to raise long-term funds. In essence, the buyers of bonds (bondholders) loan the issuer of the bonds cash in exchange for regular interest payments until the loan is repaid on or before the specified maturity date. The bond itself is a certificate, much like an IOU, that represents the company's debt to the bondholder. Bonds are issued by a wide variety of entities, including corporations; national, state, and local governments; public utilities; and nonprofit corporations. Most bondholders

and profit margins for companies in this industry have shrunk as the market becomes mature and new PC versions do little to unleash new demand for the product. Sales have been falling, and profits have been falling faster.

 L04

Specify how companies finance their operations and manage fixed assets with long-term liabilities, particularly bonds.

need not hold their bonds until maturity; the existence of active secondary markets of brokers and dealers allows for the quick and efficient transfer of bonds from owner to owner.

The bond contract, or *indenture*, specifies all the terms of the agreement between the bondholders and the issuing organization. The indenture, which can run more than 100 pages, specifies the basic terms of the bond, such as its face value, the maturity date, and the annual interest rate. Table 16.2 briefly explains how to determine these and more things about a bond from a bond quote, as it might appear in *The Wall Street Journal*. The face value of the bond, its initial sales price, is typically $1,000. After this, however, the price of the bond on the open market will fluctuate along with changes in the economy (particularly changes in interest rates) and in the creditworthiness of the issuer. Bondholders receive the face value of the bond along with the final interest payment on the maturity date. The annual interest rate (often called the *coupon rate*) is the guaranteed percentage of face value that the company will pay to the bond owner every year. For example, a $1,000 bond with a coupon rate of 7 percent would pay $70 per year in interest. In most cases, bond indentures specify that interest payments be made every six months. In the preceding example, the $70 annual payment would be divided into two semiannual payments of $35.

In addition to the terms of interest payments and maturity date, the bond indenture typically covers other important areas, such as repayment methods, interest payment dates, procedures to be followed in case the organization fails to make the interest payments, conditions for the early repayment of the bonds, and any conditions requiring the pledging of assets as collateral.

Types of Bonds

Not surprisingly, there are a great many different types of bonds. Most are **unsecured bonds,** meaning that they are not backed by specific collateral; such bonds are termed *debentures*. **Secured bonds,** in contrast, are backed by specific collateral that must be forfeited if the issuing firm defaults. Whether secured or unsecured, bonds may be repaid in one lump sum or with many payments spread out over a period of time. **Serial bonds,** which are different from secured bonds, are actually a sequence of small bond issues of progressively longer maturity. The firm pays off all of the serial bonds as they mature. **Floating-rate bonds** do not have fixed interest payments; instead, the interest rate changes with current interest rates otherwise available in the economy.

TABLE 16.2 A Basic Bond Quote

Bonds	Cur Yld	Vol	Close	Net Chg
ATT 8 ⅛ 22	7.9	121	102 ½	. . . .
IBM 7 ½ 13	6.7	2	112	+1 ½
(1) (2) (3)	(4)	(5)	(6)	(7)

(1) **Bond**—the name or abbreviation of the name of the company issuing the bond; in this case, IBM.

(2) **Annual Interest Rate**—the annual percentage rate specified on the bond certificate: IBM's is 7.5 percent, and so a $1,000 bond will earn $75 per year in interest.

(3) **Maturity date**—the bond's maturity date; the year in which the issuer will repay bondholders the face value of each bond; 2013.

(4) **Current yield**—percentage return from interest, based on the closing price (column 6); if you buy a bond with a $1,000 par value at today's closing price of 112.00 ($1,120) and receive $75 per year, your cash return will be 6.7 percent.

(5) **Volume**—the number of bonds trading during the day; 2.

(6) **Close**—the closing price; 112.00 112 percent of $1,000 par value or $1,120 per bond.

(7) **Change**—change in the price from the close of the previous trading day; IBM's went up 1½ percent of its $1,000 par value, or $15.00 per bond.

RealKidz Clothing Is Ready for Take-off

Merrill Guerra always used to have trouble finding clothing for her plus-size daughter, Gabi, and she was not alone. With one-third of all U.S. children overweight or obese, plus-size children's clothing is a $6.2 billion industry, with growth of 41 percent expected by 2012. Guerra started RealKidz Clothing in 2007 to fill the need for age-appropriate plus-size clothes.

Many companies have been reluctant to produce clothing for overweight children partly because of the extra space larger clothes take up in the store and partly because companies do not want to be seen as condoning an epidemic of childhood obesity. Guerra hopes to bypass these potentially sensitive issues by combining her clothing business with a social network for parents to help their families make healthy lifestyle changes. She stresses that people need to concentrate on being healthy and feeling good but that part of that is dressing well.[4] ❖

In recent years, a special type of high-interest-rate bond has attracted considerable attention (usually negative) in the financial press. High-interest bonds, or **junk bonds** as they are popularly known, offer relatively high rates of interest because they have higher inherent risks. Historically, junk bonds have been associated with companies in poor financial health and/or startup firms with limited track records. In the mid-1980s, however, junk bonds became a very attractive method of financing corporate mergers; they remain popular today with many investors as a result of their very high relative interest rates. But higher risks are associated with those higher returns (upward of 12 percent per year in some cases), and the average investor would be well advised to heed those famous words: Look before you leap!

price is called *capital in excess of par*. Except in the case of some very low-priced stocks, the capital in excess of par account is significantly larger than the par value account. Table 16.3 briefly explains how to gather important information from a stock quote as it might appear in *The Wall Street Journal* or on the NASDAQ Web site.

Preferred stock was defined in Chapter 5 as corporate ownership that gives the stockholder preference in the distribution of the company's profits but not the voting and control rights accorded to common stockholders. Thus, the primary advantage of owning preferred stock is that it is a safer investment than common stock.

All businesses exist to earn profits for their owners. Without the possibility of profit, there can be no incentive to risk investors' capital and succeed. When a corporation has profits left over after paying all its expenses and taxes, it has the choice of retaining all or a portion of its earnings and/or paying them out to its shareholders in the form of dividends. **Retained earnings** are

> ## A second means of long-term financing is through equity.

L05

Discuss how corporations can use equity financing by issuing stock through an investment banker.

FINANCING WITH OWNERS' EQUITY

A second means of long-term financing is through equity. Remember from Chapter 14 that owners' equity refers to the owners' investment in an organization. Sole proprietors and partners own all or a part of their businesses outright, and their equity includes the money and assets they have brought into their ventures. Corporate owners, by contrast, own stock or shares of their companies, which they hope will provide them with a return on their investment. Stockholders' equity includes common stock, preferred stock, and retained earnings.

Common stock (introduced in Chapter 5) is the single most important source of capital for most new companies. On the balance sheet, the common stock account is separated into two basic parts—common stock at par and capital in excess of par. The *par value* of a stock is simply the dollar amount printed on the stock certificate and has no relation to actual *market value*—the price at which the common stock is currently trading. The difference between a stock's par value and its offering

reinvested in the assets of the firm and belong to the owners in the form of equity. Retained earnings are an important source of funds and are, in fact, the only long-term funds that a company can generate internally.

When the board of directors distributes some of a corporation's profits to the owners, it issues them as cash dividend payments. But not all firms pay dividends.

Many fast-growing firms retain all of their earnings because they can earn high rates of return on the earnings they reinvest. Companies with fewer growth opportunities typically pay out large proportions of their earnings in the form of dividends, thereby allowing their stockholders to reinvest their dividend payments in higher-growth companies. Table 16.4 presents a sample of companies and the dividend each paid on a single share of stock. As shown in the table, when the dividend is divided by the price the result is the **dividend yield.** The dividend yield is the cash return as a percentage of the price but does not reflect the total return an investor earns on the individual stock. If the dividend yield is 3.79 percent on Campbell Soup and the stock price increases by 10 percent from $26.38 to $29.02, the total return will be 13.79 percent. This would represent a capital gain of 10 percent plus the cash dividend payment of 3.79 percent. It is not clear that stocks with high dividend yields are better investments than stocks that pay low or no dividends. Most large companies pay their stockholders dividends on a quarterly basis. Small, fast-growing companies often retain their earnings for reinvestment in the firm rather than paying out a portion to stockholders.

TABLE 16.3 A Basic Stock Quote

1 Stock Price 52 Week		2	3	4	5	6	7	8
Hi	Low	Stock	Sym	Div	Yld. %	Vol	Close	Net Chg
70.60	51.50	Nike	NKE	0.92	1.35	2,934,372	68.39	+1.01
33.49	16.05	Skechers USA	SKX	0.00	0	1,000,241	24.65	+0.79
27.76	12.83	Timberland	TBL	0.00	0	429,555	19.05	+0.79
31.21	19.85	Wolverine Worldwide	WWW	0.44	1.52	311,697	28.87	+0.27

1. The **52-week high and low**—the highest and lowest prices, respectively, paid for the stock in the last year; for Nike stock, the highest was $70.60 and the lowest price was $51.50.

2. **Stock**—the name of the issuing company. When followed by the letters "pf," the stock is preferred stock.

3. **Symbol**—the ticker tape symbol for the stock; NKE.

4. **Dividend**—the annual cash dividend paid to stockholders; Nike paid a dividend of $0.92 per share of stock outstanding.

5. **Dividend yield**—the dividend return on one share of common stock; 1.35%.

6. **Volume**—the number of shares traded on this day: 2,934,372.

7. **Close**—Nike's last sale of the day was for $68.39.

8. **Net Change**—the difference between the previous day's close and the close on the day being reported; Nike was up $1.01.

Source: finance.yahoo.com/q?s, May 29, 2008.

TABLE 16.4 Estimated Common Stock Price-Earnings Ratios and Dividends for Selected Companies

Ticker Symbol	Company Name	Price Per Share	Dividend Per Share	Dividend Yield	Earnings Per Share	Price Earnings Ratio (P-E)
ANF	Abercrombie & Fitch	$74.07	$0.70	0.95%	$5.20	14.24
AXP	American Express	46.75	0.72	1.54	3.33	14.04
AAPL	Apple	186.69	0.00	0.00	4.85	38.49
CPB	Campbell Soup	33.21	0.88	2.65	2.11	15.74
DIS	Disney	33.81	0.35	1.04	2.22	15.23
F	Ford	6.71	0.00	0.00	−1.14	NA
HOG	Harley Davidson	40.52	1.32	3.26	3.80	10.66
HD	Home Depot	27.71	0.90	3.25	2.37	11.69
MCD	McDonald's	59.48	1.50	2.52	2.15	27.67
PG	Procter & Gamble	65.47	1.60	2.44	3.38	19.37
LUV	Southwest Airlines	13.18	0.02	0.15	0.78	16.90
SBUX	Starbucks	18.33	0.00	0.00	0.84	21.82

Earnings per share are for the latest 12-month period and do not necessarily match year-end numbers.

NA—not applicable because of negative earnings

Source: finance.yahoo.com/q?s, May 29, 2008.

INVESTMENT BANKING

A company that needs more money to expand or take advantage of opportunities may be able to obtain financing by issuing stock. The first-time sale of stocks and bonds directly to the public is called a *new issue*. Companies that already have stocks or bonds outstanding may offer a new issue of stock to raise additional funds for specific projects. When a company offers its stock to the public for the very first time, it is said to be "going public," and the sale is called an *initial public offering*.

New issues of stocks and bonds are sold directly to the public and to institutions in what is known as the **primary market**—the

● **PRIMARY MARKET** the market where firms raise financial capital

● **SECONDARY MARKETS** stock exchanges and over-the-counter markets where investors can trade their securities with others

● **INVESTMENT BANKING** the sale of stocks and bonds for corporations

● **SECURITIES MARKETS** the mechanism for buying and selling securities

A McGraw-Hill stock certificate.

market where firms raise financial capital. The primary market differs from **secondary markets,** which are stock exchanges and over-the-counter markets where investors can trade their securities with other investors rather than the company that issued the stock or bonds. Primary market transactions actually raise cash for the issuing corporations, while secondary market transactions do not.

Investment banking, the sale of stocks and bonds for corporations, helps such companies raise funds by matching people and institutions that have money to invest with corporations in need of resources to exploit new opportunities. Corporations usually employ an investment banking firm to help sell their securities in the primary market. An investment banker helps firms establish appropriate offering prices for their securities. In addition, the investment banker takes care of the myriad details and securities regulations involved in any sale of securities to the public.

Just as large corporations such as IBM, General Motors, and Microsoft have a client relationship with a law firm and an accounting firm, they also have a client relationship with an investment banking firm. An investment banking firm can provide advice about financing plans, dividend policy, or stock repurchases, as well as advice on mergers and acquisitions. Many now offer additional banking services, making them "one-stop shopping" banking centers. When Chrysler merged with Daimler-Benz, both companies used investment bankers to help them value the transaction. Each firm wanted an outside opinion about what it was worth to the other. Sometimes mergers fall apart because the companies cannot agree on the price each company is worth or the

structure of management after the merger. The advising investment banker, working with management, often irons out these details. Of course, investment bankers do not provide these services for free. They usually charge a fee between 1 and 1.5 percent of the transaction. A $20 billion merger can generate between $200 and $300 million in investment banking fees. The merger mania of the late 1990s allowed top investment bankers to earn huge sums. Unfortunately, this type of fee income is dependent on healthy stock markets, which seem to stimulate the merger fever among corporate executives.

While the function of investment bankers won't change, the structure of the industry changed dramatically with the financial meltdown. Bear Sterns was acquired by JPMorganChase, and Lehman Brothers was allowed to go bankrupt by the government. Merrill Lynch was bought by Bank America to avoid bankruptcy, and Morgan Stanley and Goldman Sachs became bank holding companies so that they would qualify for loan guarantees by the Federal Reserve and the Federal Citizen Information Center (FCIC). No large independent investment banking firms are left on Wall Street. They have become banks or been acquired by banks. They will still perform the same functions, but with a smaller amount of debt (financial leverage) and most likely smaller returns.[6]

● ● **L06**

Describe the various securities markets in the United States.

THE SECURITIES MARKETS

Securities markets provide a mechanism for buying and selling securities. They make it possible for owners to sell their stocks and bonds to other investors. Thus, in the broadest sense, stocks and bonds markets may be thought of as providers of liquidity—the ability to turn security holdings into cash quickly and with minimal expense and effort. Without liquid securities markets, many potential investors would sit on the sidelines rather than invest their hard-earned savings in securities. Indeed, the ability to sell securities at well-established market prices is one of the very pillars of the capitalistic society that has developed over the years in the United States.

Unlike the primary market, in which corporations sell stocks directly to the public, secondary markets permit the trading of previously issued

DID YOU KNOW?

If you bought one share of Johnson and Johnson stock at its initial public offering price of $37.50 and reinvested the dividends, you would now have over $900,000. This comes out to a 17.1 percent return on an annual basis. You would have 2,500 shares because of stock splits.[5]

securities. There are many different secondary markets for both stocks and bonds. If you want to purchase 100 shares of Du Pont common stock, for example, you must purchase this stock from another investor or institution. It is the active buying and selling by many thousands of investors that establishes the prices of all financial securities. Secondary market trades may take place on organized exchanges or in what is known as the over-the-counter market. Many brokerage houses exist to help investors with financial decisions, and many offer their services through the Internet. One such broker is Paine Webber. Its site offers a wealth of information and provides educational material to individual investors.

Stock Markets

Stock markets exist around the world in New York, Tokyo, London, Frankfort, Paris, and other locations. The two biggest stock markets in the United States are the New York Stock Exchange (NYSE) and the NASDAQ market. There are smaller markets such as the American Stock Exchange, the Chicago Stock Exchange, and exchanges in Philadelphia, Boston, Cincinnati, and Los Angeles.

Exchanges used to be divided into organized exchanges and over-the-counter markets, but during the last several years, dramatic changes have occurred in the markets. Both the NYSE and NASDAQ became publicly traded companies. They were previously not-for-profit organizations but are now for-profit companies. Additionally, both exchanges bought or merged with electronic exchanges, the NYSE with Archipelago and the NASDAQ with Instinet. Electronic trading is faster and less expensive than floor trading (where brokers meet to transact business) and now accounts for most of the stock trading done worldwide.

In an attempt to expand its markets, NASDAQ acquired more than 25 percent of the London Stock Exchange in 2006, and the New York Stock Exchange countered by agreeing to merge with Euronext, a large European electronic exchange that trades options and futures contracts as well as common stock. Both the NYSE and NASDAQ have expanded their reach, their product line, and their ability to trade around the world. What we are witnessing is the globalization of the world's financial markets.

Traditionally, the NASDAQ market has been an electronics market, and many of the large technology companies such as Microsoft, Oracle, and Apple Computer trade on the NASDAQ market. The NASDAQ operates through dealers who buy and sell common stock (inventory) for their own accounts. The NYSE has traditionally been a floor-traded market where brokers meet at trading posts on the floor of the New York Stock Exchange to buy and sell common stock. The brokers act as agents for their clients and do not own their own inventory. This traditional division between the two markets is becoming less significant as the exchanges become electronic.

The Over-the-Counter Market

Unlike the organized exchanges, the **over-the-counter (OTC) market** is a network of dealers all over the country linked by computers, telephones, and Teletype machines. It has no central location. While many very small new companies are traded on the OTC market, many very large and well-known concerns trade there as well. Indeed, thousands of shares of the stocks of companies such as Apple Computer, Intel, and Microsoft are traded on the OTC market every day. Further, because most corporate bonds and all U.S. securities are traded over the counter, the OTC market regularly accounts for the largest total dollar value of all the secondary markets.

Measuring Market Performance

Investors, especially professional money managers, want to know how well their investments are performing relative to the market as a whole. Financial managers also need to know how their companies' securities are performing compared with their competitors'. Thus, performance measures—averages and indexes—are very important to many different people. They not only indicate the

The Ups and Downs and Ups of Investing in First Solar

First Solar, Inc., has been working to perfect an affordable alternative to fossil fuels since 1999. By tapping into the sun's rays, First Solar has earned over $6 billion in contracts to provide solar project developers, system integrators, and public utilities with its cadmium telluride solar cells and panels. Much of First Solar's early business focused on Germany, which is the world's leader in solar power, but business is growing rapidly in the United States thanks to this country's investment tax credit.

While it may be obvious that a company involved in alternative fuel is committed to the environment, First Solar goes beyond many of its peers. Solar energy is renewable and clean. Using it conserves natural resources and reduces greenhouse gas emissions. However, many companies use perfluorinated gases such as nitrogen triflouride, which emits high levels of greenhouse gas, to manufacture solar cells. First Solar does not use those gases, focusing instead on less harmful options. The company also manages the entire life cycle of its products from raw materials sourcing through the collection and recycling of old products.

First Solar's management is determined to eliminate all unnecessary costs, and this generally has yielded successes beyond Wall Street's or even the company's own predictions. First Solar's financial results have been excellent. During the 2008–2009 recession the company stock fluctuated between $85 and $301 but generally increased in value. With cheaper solar energy and innovations on the horizon, as well as a president in office who supports clean energy, the future seems bright for companies like First Solar.[7] ❖

Q: Discussion Questions

1. Why did First Solar stock fluctuate over such a wide range in 2008 and 2009?

2. Because First Solar sells a product that is important to sustainability, does that mean its stock might be considered to have added value?

3. Look up the stock price of First Solar (FSLR) and evaluate its current stock performance.

performance of a particular securities market but also provide a measure of the overall health of the economy.

Indexes and averages are used to measure stock prices. An *index* compares current stock prices with those in a specified base period, such as 1944, 1967, or 1977. An *average* is the average of certain stock prices. The averages used are usually not simple calculations, however. Some stock market averages (such as the Standard and Poor's Composite Index) are weighted averages in which the weights employed are the total market values of each stock in the index (in this case 500). The Dow Jones Industrial Average is a price-weighted average. Regardless of how they are constructed, all market averages of stocks move closely together over time.

Many investors follow the activity of the Dow Jones Industrial Average very closely to see whether the stock market has gone up or down. Table 16.5 lists the 30 companies that currently make up the Dow. Although these companies are only a small fraction of the total number of companies listed on the New York Stock Exchange, because of their size they account for about 25 percent of the total value of the NYSE.

The numbers listed in an index or average that tracks the performance of a stock market are expressed not as dollars but as a number on a fixed scale. If you know, for example, that the Dow Jones Industrial Average climbed from 860 in August 1982 to a high of 14,198 in late 2007, you can calculate that the value of the DJIA increased about 16.5 times during that 25-year period, making it one of the highest rate of return periods in the history of the stock market. Of course, if you look at Figure 16-3, you can tell that it had a few bumps on the way to its peak. You can see the collapse of the market with the Internet bubble of 2000–2003, when the DJIA hit 8,000 and then recovered to its new high.

Unfortunately, this good fortune didn't last because after the Internet bubble came the housing bubble and the financial crisis. This brought the market to its knees, and the DJIA plummeted to a low of 6,470 in March 2009. This was a 54 percent decline in the market which brought back fears of the Great Crash of 1929 and the Depression that followed. If you look at the long-term trend line, you can see that the market was off its trend line on the high side and was probably overvalued. However, at 6,470 it was below the trend line and probably undervalued. It recovered to 8,400 by May 2009.

In general, over the long term, stock markets follow the growth of the economy and the general growth of corporate profits. In the short term markets are subject to the emotions of investors, which can range between fear and greed. A period of large increases in stock prices is called a *bull market,* with the bull symbolizing an aggressive, charging market and rising stock prices. A declining market is called a *bear market,* with the bear symbolizing sluggish, retreating activity or even hibernation. When stock prices decline very rapidly, as they did in the 2007–2009 period, the market is said to *crash.* In general, the market usually returns to its long-term trend. As young investors, you should focus on the long-term trend, not the short-term volatility. The problem is that investors have egos and most are optimistic enough to think they can call the ups and downs in the market. Research shows however, that very few investors can do this and that famous investors such as Warren Buffet have made their billions with long-term investments.

For investors to make sound financial decisions, it is important that they stay in touch with business news, markets, and indexes. Of course, business and investment publications such as *The Wall Street Journal, BusinessWeek, Fortune, Forbes,* and *Money* offer this type of information. Many Internet sites,

> # [Many investors follow the activity of the Dow Jones Industrial Average very closely to see whether the stock market has gone up or down.]

TABLE 16.5   The 30 Stocks in the Dow Jones Industrial Average

3M	Du Pont	McDonald's
Alcoa	ExxonMobil	Merck
Altria	General Electric	Microsoft
American Express	Hewlett-Packard	Pfizer
American International Group	Home Depot	Procter & Gamble
AT&T	Honeywell	Travelers
Boeing	IBM	United Technologies
Caterpillar	Intel	Verizon
Cisco	Johnson & Johnson	Wal-Mart
Coca-Cola	JPMorgan Chase	Walt Disney

FIGURE 16.3 The Dow Jones Industrial Average, 1999–2009

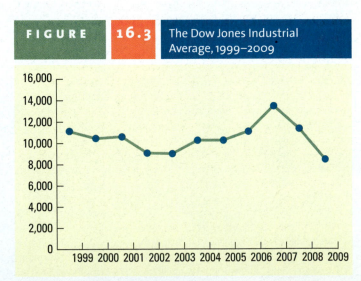

*Numbers taken on July 1 or the nearest trading day of each year.

Source: "Market Overview," Yahoo Finance, http://finance.yahoo.com/marketupdate/overview.

SO YOU WANT TO WORK IN FINANCIAL MANAGEMENT OR SECURITIES

Taking classes in financial and securities management can provide career options ranging from managing a small firm's accounts receivable, to handling charitable giving for a multinational, to investment banking, to stock brokerage. We have entered into a less certain period for finance and securities jobs, however. In the world of investment banking, the past few years have been especially challenging. Tens of thousands of employees from Wall Street firms have lost their jobs. This phenomenon is not confined to New York City, leaving the industry with a lot fewer jobs around the country. This type of phenomenon is not unique to the finance sector. In the early 2000s the tech sector experienced a similar downturn, from which it has subsequently largely recovered. Undoubtedly, markets will bounce back and job creation in finance and securities will increase again—but until that happens, the atmosphere across finance and securities will be more competitive than it has been in the past. However, this does not mean that there are no jobs. All firms need financial analysts to determine whether a project should be implemented, when to issue stocks and bonds, and when to initiate loans. These and other forward-looking questions such as how to invest excess cash must be addressed by financial managers. Economic uncertainty in the financial and securities market has made for more difficulty in finding the most desirable jobs.

Why this sudden downturn in financial industry prospects? A lot of these job cuts came in response to the subprime lending fallout and subsequent bank failures such as that of Bear Stearns, which alone lost around 7,000 employees. All these people will be looking for new jobs in new organizations, increasing the competitive level in a lot of different employment areas. For young job seekers with relatively little experience, this may result in a great deal of frustration. However, by the time you graduate, the job market for finance majors could be in recovery and rebuilding with new employees. Uncertainty results in hiring freezes and layoffs but leaves firms lean and ready to grow when the cycle turns around, resulting in hiring from the bottom up.

Many different industries require people with finance skills, so do not despair if you have a difficult time finding a job in exactly the right firm. Most students switch companies a number of times over the course of their careers. Many organizations require individuals trained in forecasting, statistics, economics, and finance. Even unlikely places such as museums, aquariums, and zoos need people who are good with numbers. It may require some creativity, but if you are committed to a career in finance, look to less obvious sources, not just large financial firms.[8]

including CNN/Money, Yahoo finance, and MSN Money, among others, offer up-to-date information. Many sites offer searchable databases of information by topic, company, or keyword. However investors choose to receive and review business news, doing so is a necessity in today's market.

If you would like to start investing, it is always advantageous to start out when you are young. The longer you let your money compound, the more you have as you get older. For example, one dollar invested at 10 percent for 30 years would grow to $17.45. If you let that dollar grow for a total of 40 years, it would be worth $42.25, and at 50 years it would be worth $117.40. If a 20-year-old starts investing and continues to put one dollar per year into an investment earning 10 percent, after 50 years that $50 will be worth $1,164. ■

Team Exercise

Compare and contrast financing with long-term liabilities such as bonds with financing with owners' equity, typically retained earnings, common stock, and preferred stock. Form groups and suggest a good mix of long-term liabilities and owners' equity for a new firm that makes wind turbines for generating alternative energy and would like to grow quickly.

CHECK OUT www.mhhe.com/FerrellM2e

for study materials including Interactive Exercises, Quizzes, iPod downloads, and video.

Chapter 1

1. Hewlett-Packard, "HP Recycles Nearly 250 Million Pounds of Products in 2007—50 Percent Increase over 2006," February 5, 2008, **www.hp.com/hpinfo/newsroom/press/2008/080205a .html** (accessed June 1, 2009).

2. **www.cummins.com,** "Community Involvement Teams," Cummins Diesel, South Africa CIT, **www.cummins.com/cmi/content.jsp?site Id=1&langId=1033&menuId=82&overviewId=5&anchorId=393 &index=2&menuIndex=0** (accessed May 31, 2006).

3. "Diversity Pipeline Alliance," **www.diversitypipeline.org/public/ publicpage.asp?WCE=C=32IK=S221485** (accessed April 21, 2009).

4. "U-Haul Lends a Helping Hand to Arkansas Tornado and Flood Victims, with 30 Days of Free Storage," News Release U-Haul International, Inc., **www.primenewswire.com/newsroom/news .html?d=139560** (accessed April 21, 2009).

5. Chris Isidore, "NASCAR Goes Hollywood," May 25, 2006, **http:// money.cnn.com/2006/05/26/commentary/column_sportsbiz/ sportsbiz/index.htm** (accessed June 1, 2006).

6. Riva Richmond, "Update-Google CEO: Rising Competition Is Expanding Market," May 31, 2006, **http://money.cnn.com/services/ tickerheadlines/for5/200605311542DOWJONESDJONLINE001020_ FORTUNE5.htm** (accessed June 1, 2006).

7. Elaine Appleton, "Roll Out the Fine Carpet," *INC,* April, 2008, **www.inc.com/magazine/20080401/business-for-sale-roll-out-the- fine-carpet.html** (accessed April 21, 2009).

8. Elizabeth M. Whelan, "Kellogg's: A Sad Cereal Sellout," June 17, 2009, *New York Post,* **www.nypost.com/seven/06172007/postopinion/ opedcolumnists/kelloggs__a_sad_cereal_sellout_opedcolumnists_ elizabeth_m__whelan.htm** (accessed June 1, 2009).

9. Preston Lerner, "The Future Is Now," *Automobilemag.com,* March 2008, pp. 46–52; Kim Reynolds, "First Drive: 2008 Tesla Road-ster," *Motor Trend,* 2008, **www.motortrend.com/roadtests/alternative/ 112_0803_2008_tesla_roadster** (accessed February 22, 2008); Mike Adams, "Review: Tesla Motors Pioneers All-Electric Perfor-mance Sports Car," *Flixya.com,* March 23, 2007, **www.flixya.com/ post/tavatchaibt/10020/Tesla_Motors_pioneers_all-electric performance** (accessed February 18, 2008); "Electric Power," Tesla Motors, **www.teslamotors.com/performance/electric_power.php** (accessed February 22, 2008); **www.teslamotors.com/media/press_/room** (accessed April 1, 2009); Elon Musk, "Tesla Motors Update," February 12, 2009, **www.teslamotors.com/blog2/?p=70** (accessed April 1, 2009).

10. "Health and Wellness "(n.d.), **www.fritolay.com/fl/flstore/cgi-bin/ health_wellness.htm?** (accessed June 1, 2006).

11. **www.whymilk.com/celebrityarchive.htm** (accessed June 1, 2006).

12. Toddi Guttner, "In the Venture Drought, an Oasis," *Business-Week,* July 16, 2001, pp. 86E2, 86E4.

13. "About Bill Daniels" **www.danielsfund.org/BillDaniels/index.asp** (accessed June 1, 2009).

14. Greg Farrell and Noelle Knox, "Record: 1 Million Homes in Foreclosure," *USA Today,* March 7, 2008, p. B1.

15. "Leading With Patents" in United States Patent and Trademark Office. *United States Patent and Trademark Office Performance and Accountability Report Fiscal Year 2006* (n.d.), **www.uspto .gov/web/offices/com/annual/2006/200 message director.html** (accessed May 29, 2007).

16. "Zimbabwe Inflation Hits 165,000%," *BBC.com,* April 16, 2008, **http://news.bbc.co.uk/1/hi/business/7351086.stm** (accessed April 21, 2009).

17. Treasury Direct, "Debt to the Penny and Who Holds It," March 27, 2008, **www.treasurydirect.gov/NP/BPDLogin?application=np** (accessed April 21, 2009).

18. Home Depot 2008 Annual Report, "Letter to Shareholders," **www.homedepotar.com/html/downloads/HD_Annual_Report_2008 .pdf** (accessed April 24, 2009), pp. 2–3; Lowe's 2008 Annual Report, "Letter to Shareholders," **http://lowes.com/lowes2/assets/ ar_html/HTML1/002.htm** (accessed April 24, 2009), pp. 2–4; "The Home Depot to Present at Bank of America-Merrill Lynch 2009 Consumer Conference" Home Depot, March 5, 2009, **http://phx .corporate-ir.net/phoenix.zhtml?c=63646&p=RssLanding&cat= news&id=1266482** (accessed April 24, 2007); Mary Ellen Lloyd, "Lowe's Popularity Can't Beat Home Depot's Locations—Survey," *Dow Jones Newswires,* September 5, 2007; Jennifer Waters, "Home Depot, Lowe's Facing Up to Challenges," *MarketWatch,* July 9, 2007, **www.marketwatch.com/news/story/goldman-sees-buying- opportunity-rivals/story.aspx?guid=\{84525FAB-C31A-4368-86B9- 1254A5BA7652}** (accessed September 27, 2007); "Healthier Home, Happier You," Lowe's, April 8, 2009, **www.lowes.com/ lowes/lkn?action=frameSet&url=lowes.mediaroom.com/index .php?s=company_overview** (accessed April 24, 2009); "Battle for the Wallets of American Homeowners: The Home Depot vs. Lowe's," **www.retailforward.com, www.retailforward.com/Marketing/ BattlefortheWallets_ReportOverview.pdf** (accessed September 27, 2007); "Fortune 500 2008," *CNN Money,* **http://money.cnn.com/ magazines/fortune/fortune500/2008/full_list/** (accessed April 24, 2009).

19. "Women in the Labor Force, 1900–2002," *InfoPlease* (n.d.), **www .infoplease.com/ipa/A0104673.html** (accessed March 9, 2004).

20. Taco Chic Salsa, "The Origins of Taco Chic Salsa," **http:// tacochicsalsa.com/html/history.htm** (accessed April 19, 2009).

21. "About the Hershey Co.," **www.thehersheycompany.com/about/** (accessed April 21, 2009).

22. "About Us," **www.walmartstores.com/aboutus** (accessed April 21, 2009).

23. Tom McNichol, "Building a Wiki World," *Business 2.0,* March 2007, pp. 102–108; Jonathan Dee, "All the News That's Fit to Print Out," *The New York Times,* July 1, 2007, **www.nytimes.com/ 2007/07/01/magazine/01WIKIPEDIA-t.html?ex=1189828800&en= b2e607ab370a06f8&ei=5070** (accessed September 13, 2007); Daniel Terdiman, "Growing Pains for Wikipedia," *News.com,* December 7, 2005, **www.news.com/2102-1025_3-5981119.html? tag=st.util.print** (accessed September 13, 2007).

24. Karen Richardson, Liam Pleven, and Amir Efrati, "Jury Con-victs Five of Fraud in Gen Re, AIG Case," February 26, 2008, **http://online.wsj.com/article/SB120396729370091225.html? mod=relevancy** (accessed June 1, 2009).

25. Dennis Schaal, "100 Best Corporate Citizens 2008," *The CRO,* **www.thecro.com/node/615** (accessed April 21, 2009).

26. Ronald Alsop, "Corporate Scandals Hit Home," *The Wall Street Journal,* February 18, 2004, **http://online.wsj.com.**

27. Lindsey Gerdes, "Where Undergrads Dream of Working," *Busi-nessWeek Online,* May 23, 2008, **www.businessweek.com/ managing/content/may2008/ca20080523_988667.htm?chan= search** (accessed June 19, 2008).

Chapter 2

1. Greg Farrell, "Lay, Skilling Found Guilty," *USA Today,* May 26, 2006, pp. A1, B1; *The New York Times* coverage of the Enron trial, **www.nytimes.com/business/businessspecial3/index.html?adxnnl= 1&adxnnlx=1147986237-z56Vd16RUkp6eHnHTTXBHw** (accessed May 18, 2006).

2. Ronald Alsop, "Corporate Scandals Hit Home," *The Wall Street Journal,* February 18, 2004, **http://online.wsj.com.**

3. Carrie Johnson, "Jury Acquits HealthSouth Founder of All Charges," June 29, 2005, p. A01, **www.washingtonpost.com/ wp-dyn/content/article/2005/06/28/AR2005062800560.html** (accessed June 2, 2006).

4. O. C. Ferrell, John Fraedrich, Linda Ferrell, *Business Ethics: Ethical Decision Making and Cases,* 6th ed. (Boston: Houghton Mifflin, 2005), p. 7.

5. David Callahan, as quoted in Archie Carroll, "Carroll: Do We Live in a Cheating Culture?" *Athens Banner-Herald,* February 21, 2004, **www.onlineathens.com/stores/022204/bus_20040222028.shtml.**

6. Jenny Anderson, "3 Executives under Fire on Exit Pay," *The New York Times,* March 8, 2008, pp. B1, B4.

7. John Lyman, "Who Is Scooter Libby? The Guy Behind the Guy," *Center for American Progress.* October 28, 2005.

8. Laurie P. Cohen and Amir Efrati, "Spitzer Engulfed in Sex Scandal," *The Wall Street Journal,* March 11, 2008, p.A1.

9. "Colorado Places Barnett on Administrative Leave," *SI.com,* February 19, 2004, **http://sportsillustrated.cnn.com/.**

10. Mark Long, "Jimmy Johnson's Crew Chief Thrown Out of Daytona 500," urlStarTribune.com, February 13, 2006, **www.star tribune.com/694/story/244568.html.**

11. Ferrell, Fraedrich, Ferrell, *Business Ethics.*

12. "National Business Ethics Survey 2007: An Inside View of Private Sector Ethics," Ethics Resource Center, **http://www.ethics.org** (accessed April 21, 2009).

13. "Stop Workplace Bullying!," **www.bullyfreeworkplace.org/id27 .html** (accessed April 21, 2009).

14. Peter Lattman, "Boeing's Top Lawyer Spotlights Company's Ethical Lapses," *The Wall Street Journal,* Law Blog., Januray 30, 2006, **blogs.wsj.com/law/2006/01/31/boeings-top-lawyer-rips- into-his-company** (accessed March 31, 2006).

15. Janet Guyon, "Jack Grubman Is Back. Just Ask Him," *Fortune,* May 16, 2005. pp. 119–26.

16. "Three Ex-IBM Korea Officials Are Sentenced," *The Wall Street Journal,* February 18, 2004, **http://online.wsj.com.**

17. "Transparency International 2008 Corruption Perception Index," Transparency International, **www.transparency.org/policy_research/ surveys_indices/cpi/2008** (accessed March 9, 2009).

18. "Pens and Post-Its Among Most Pilfered Office Supplies, Says New Vault Survey," November 16, 2005, **www.vault.com/nr/ newsmain.jsp?nr_page=3&ch_id=420&article_id=25720773** (accessed June 2, 2006).

19. David Whelan, "Only the Paranoid Resurge," *Forbes,* April 10, 2006.

20. Yuri Kageyama, "Mitsubishi Motors Says Massive Defect Cover-ups Were Intentional," *Boston Globe,* August 22, 2000, **www .boston.com;** "Mitsubishi Cover-up May Bring Charges," *Detroit News,* August 23, 2000, **www.det-news.com/2000/autos/0008/23/ b03-109584.htm.**

21. Michael Josephson. "The Biennial Report Card: The Ethics of American Youth." Josephson Institute of Ethics, press release, **www.josephsoninstitute.org/survey2004/** (accessed August 11, 2005).

22. James Bandler and Nicholas Varchaver with Doris Burke, "How Bernie Did It," *Fortune,* May 11, 2009, pp. 50–71; Tom Hays, "Trustee: Nearly 9,000 Claims in Madoff Case," *The Associated Press,* May 15, 2009, **www.google.com/hostednews/ap/article/ ALeqM5iVRaRYcWFCQgMxBfNtbcfT98Zr4QD986AAL01** (accessed May 15, 2009); Robert Frank and Tom Lauricella, "Madoff Created Air of Mystery," *The Wall Street Journal,* December 20, 2008, **http://online.wsj.com/article/SB122973208705022949.html** (accessed December 23, 2008).

23. "Teens Respect Good Business Ethics." *USA Today,* Snapshots, December 12, 2005, p. 13-1.

24. Marianne Jennings, "An Ethical Breach by Any Other Name," *Financial Engineering News.* January/February 2006.

25. "The 'Skinny Pills' Do Not Make You Skinny, Says the FTC," Federal Trade Commission, press release, February 4, 2004, **www.ftc.gov/opa/2004/02/skinnypill.htm.**

26. "Campaign Warns about Drugs from Canada," *CNN,* February 5, 2004, **www.cnn.com;** Gardiner Harris and Monica Davey, "FDA Begins Push to End Drug Imports," *The New York Times,* January 23, 2004, p. C1.

27. "Briefing: Tobacco Packaging and Labelling," Information Resource Center, **http://infolink.cancerresearchuk.org/publicpolicy/ briefings/prevention/tobacco** (accessed July 31, 2006).

28. 2005 National Business Ethics Survey (Washington, D.C.: Ethics Resource Center, 2005), p. 43.

29. Susan Pullman, "Ordered to Commit Fraud, A Staffer Balked, Then Caved," *The Wall Street Journal,* June 23, 2003, **http:// online.wsj.com.**

30. Blake Morrison, "Ex-USA Today Reporter Faked Major Stories," *USA Today,* March 19, 2004, **www.usatoday.com/.**

31. Thomas M. Jones, "Ethical Decision Making by Individuals in Organizations: An Issue-Contingent Model," *Academy of Management Review* 2 (April 1991), pp. 371–73.

32. Sir Adrian Cadbury, "Ethical Managers Make Their Own Rules," *Harvard Business Review* 65 (September–October 1987), p. 72.

33. Ferrell, Fraedrich, and Ferrell, pp. 174–75.

34. Ethics Resource Center.

35. Ethics Resource Center, "The 2007 National Business Ethics Survey," **www.ethics.org/research/NBESOffers.asp** (accessed April 21, 2009).

36. Richard Lacavo and Amanda Ripley, "Persons of the Year 2002— Cynthia Cooper, Coleen Rowley, and Sherron Watkins," *Time,* December 22, 2002, **www.time.com/personofth-year/2002.**

37. Ferrell, Fraedrich, and Ferrell, p. 13.

38. John Galvin, "The New Business Ethics," **SmartBusinessMag.com,** June 2000, p. 99.

39. Archie B. Carroll, "The Pyramid of Corporate Social Responsibility: Toward the Moral Management of Organizational Stakeholders," *Business Horizons* 34 (July/August 1991), p. 42.

40. Bryan Walsh, "Why Green Is the New Red, White and Blue," *Time,* April 28, 2008, p. 46.

41. Walsh, p. 46.

42. Walsh, p. 54.

43. Alan Beattie, "Countries Rush to Restrict Trade in Basic Foods," *Financial Times,* April 2, 2008, p.1.

44. Laura Petrecca, "Marketing Efforts May End up in a Green Blur," *USA Today,* April 22, 2008, p. 10B.

45. Alexandra Zendrian, "Workers' Employers Not Green Enough," *Inc.,* April 17, 2008, **www.inc.com/news/articles/2008/04/green .html** (accessed April 21, 2009).

46. Ferrell, Fraedrich, and Ferrell, pp. 13–19.

47. Rachel Emma Silverman, "On-the-Job Cursing: Obscene Talk Is Latest Target of Workplace Ban," *The Wall Street Journal,* May 8, 2001, p. B12.

48. "Business Discover the Value in Fighting AIDS," *Milwaukee Journal Sentinel,* March 14, 2004, via World Business Council for Sustainable Development, **www.wbcsd.org/Plugins/DocSearch/details .asp. . .;** Lucia Mutikani, "German Automakers Tackle S. Africa AIDS Scourge," Reuters News Service, as reported in *Forbes,* January 22, 2004, **www.forbes.com/business/newswire/2004/01/22/ rtr1221795.html.**

49. Wendy Zellner, "No Way to Treat a Lady?" *BusinessWeek,* March 3, 2003, pp. 63–66.

50. Laura Judy, "Green from the Ground Up," *Atlanta Home Improvement,* January 2006, **www.homeimprovementmag.com/ Articles/2006/06Jan_ground_up.html** (accessed June 15, 2007); "EarthCraft House Program," "Green Fast Facts: Did You Know . . .," **www.atlantahomebuilders.com/education/earthcraft.cfm** (accessed October 5, 2007); Melanie Lindner, "Living Green" EarthCraft House," *Atlanta Intown Newspaper,* January 2007, **www.atlantaintownpaper.com/features/EarthCraftHouseJAN07.php** (accessed October 5, 2007); EarthCraft House, **www.earthcraf thouse.com/index.htm** (accessed April 3, 2009).

51. Chad Terhune, "Jury Says Home Depot Must Pay Customer Hurt by Falling Merchandise $1.5 Million," *The Wall Street Journal,* July 16, 2001, p. A14.

52. Charales Haddad and Brian Grow, "Wait a Second—I Didn't Order That!" *BusinessWeek,* July 16, 2001, p. 45.

53. The Pickens Plan, **www.pickensplan.com;** "T. Boone Pickens: 2008 *Success* Achiever of the Year," *Success Magazine,* **www.successmagazine.com/2008-success-achiever-of-the-year/ PARAMS/article/682** (accessed May 28, 2009); Kimberley A. Strassel, "From Here to There," *The Wall Street Journal,* March 9, 2009, **http://online.wsj.com/article/SB1236549103 94364885.html** (accessed May 28, 2009).

54. Judy, "Green from the Ground Up," *Atlanta Home Improvement,* January 2006, **www.homeimprovementmag.com/articles/2006/ 06Jan_ground_up.html** (accessed April 21, 2009); EarthCraft House, **www.earthcrafthouse.com** (accessed October 5, 2007); "Earthcraft House Program," "Green Fast Facts: Did You Know . . .," **www.atlantahomebuilders.**

55. Lauren Etter, "Earth Day: 36 Years on, Plenty of Concerns Remain," *The Wall Street Journal,* April 22–23, 2006, p.A7.

56. Etter, "Earth Day: 36 Years on, Plenty of Concerns Remain."

57. Etter, "Earth Day: 36 Years on, Plenty of Concerns Remain."

58. "Diamant Corporation Furthers National Consumer Awareness Efforts as British Prime Minister Gordon Brown Announces Tougher Measures to Drastically Reduce the Society's Dependence on Single-Use Plastic Bags," *Marketwire,* March 25, 2008, **http://findarticles.com/p/articles/mi_pwwi/is_200803/ai_n24951380/** (accessed April 21, 2009).

59. Matthew Knight, "Plastic Bags Fly into Environmental Storm," *CNN.com,* March 17, 2008, **http://edition.cnn.com/2007/TECH/ 11/14/fsummit.climate.plasticbags/index.html** (accessed April 21, 2009).

60. "Whole Foods to Sack Disposable Plastic Grocery Bags," January 22, 2008, **www.wholefoodsmarket.com/cgi-bim/print1Opt .cgi?url=/pressroom/pr_01-22-08.html** (accessed March 17, 2008).

61. Alan K. Reichert, Marion S. Webb, and Edward G. Thomas, "Corporate Support for Ethical and Environmental Policies: A Financial Management Perspective," *Journal of Business Ethics* 25 (2000), pp. 53–64.

62. "Trend Watch," *Business Ethics,* March/April 2001, p. 8.

63. David & Lynch "Corporate America Warms to Fight Against Global Warming," *USA Today,* June 1, 2006, p. B1.

64. Amy Standen, "Bulging at the Waste," *Terrain,* Winter 2003, **www .ci.sf.ca.us/sfenvironment/articles_pr/2003/article/110003_2.htm.**

65. "GreenChoice: The #1 Green Power Program in America," Austin Energy (n.d.), **www.austinenergy.com/Energy%20Efficiency/Pro grams/Green%20Choice/index.htm** (accessed February 24, 2004).

66. "Certification," Home Depot (n.d.), **www.homedepot.com/HDUS/ EN_US/corporate/corp_respon/certification.shtml** (accessed April 6, 2004).

67. "Yes, We Have No Bananas: Rainforest Alliance Certifies Chiquita Bananas," *AgJournal* (n.d.), **www.agjournal.com/story.cfm?story _id_1047** (accessed April 6, 2004).

68. "Charity Holds Its Own in Tough Times (Giving USA 2003: The Annual Report on Philanthropy for the Year 2002)," American Association of Fundraising Council, press release, June 2003, **http://aafrc.org/press_releases/trustreleases/charityholds.html.**

69. Mark Calvey, "Profile: Safeway's Grants Reflect Its People," *San Francisco Business Times,* July 14, 2003, **http://sanfrancisco .bizjournals.com/sanfrancisco/stories/2003/07/14/focus9.html.**

70. "About Avon," Avon (n.d.), **www.avoncompany.com/about/** (accessed February 25, 2004); "The Avon Breast Cancer Crusade," Avon (n.d.), **www.avoncompany.com/women/avoncrusade/** (accessed February 25, 2004).

71. "Take Charge of Education," Target (n.d.), **http://target.com/ common/page.jhtml;jsessionid=GWORM5AQSLBLDLARAAVWW 4FMCEACU1IX?content=target_cg_take_charge_of_education** (accessed February 25, 2004).

72. "Who Really Pays for CSR Initiatives," *Environmental Leader,* February 15, 2008, **www.environmentalleader.com/2008/02/15/ who-really-pays-for-csr-initiatives/** (accessed April 21, 2009); "Global Fund," **www.joinred.com/Learn/HowRedWorks/GlobalFund .aspx** (accessed April 21, 2009).

73. Reena Jana, "The Business of Going Green," *Business Week* Online, June 22, 2007, **www.businessweek.com/innovate/content/ jun2007/id20070622_491833.htm?chan=search** (accessed June 19, 2008).

74. Avery Johnson, "Pfizer Will Pull Some Lipitor Ads in Wake of Probe," *The Wall Street Journal,* February 26, 2008, **http:// online.wsj.com/article/SB120396972593291395.html** (accessed June 1, 2009); Vanessa Aristide, "Pfizer Voluntarily Withdraws Lipitor Advertising Featuring Dr. Robert Jarvik," Pfizer press release, February 25, 2008, **http://mediaroom.pfizer.com/portal/ site/pfizer/?ndmViewId=news_view&newsId=20080225006247& newsLang=en** (accessed June 1, 2009).

Chapter 3

1. "Getting to Know Us," McDonald's, **www.aboutmcdonalds.com** (accessed June 1, 2009).

2. "About Us," Starbucks, **www.starbucks.com/aboutus/company-factsheet.pdf** (accessed June 1, 2009).

3. Dexter Roberts and David Rocks, "China: Let a Thousand Brands Bloom," *BusinessWeek*, October 17, 2005, pp. 58, 60.

4. Nandini Lakshman, "Subcontinental Drift: More Westerners Are Beefing Up Their Resumes with a Stint in India," *BusinessWeek*, January 16, 2006, pp. 42–43.

5. "2007 Annual Trade Highlights, Dollar Change from Prior Year," U.S. Census Bureau, Foreign Trade Statistics, **www.census.gov/foreign-trade/statistics/highlights/annual.html** (accessed April 21, 2009).

6. Dexter Roberts and David Rocks, "China: Let a Thousand Brands Bloom," *BusinessWeek*, October 17, 2005, pp. 58, 60.

7. "2007 Annual Trade Highlights, Dollar Change from Prior Year," U.S. Census Bureau, Foreign Trade Statistics.

8. Robert E. Scott and David Ratner, "Trade Picture," Economic Policy Institute, February 10, 2006, **www.epinet.org/content.cfm/webfeatures_econindicators_tradepict20060210** (accessed April 21, 2009); "2007 Annual Trade Highlights, Dollar Change from Prior Year," U.S. Census Bureau, Foreign Trade Statistics.

9. Roberts and Rocks, "China: Let a Thousand Brands Bloom."

10. J. Bonasia, "For Web, Global Reach Is Beauty—and Challenge," *Investor's Business Daily*, June 13, 2001, p. A6.

11. Yuri Kageyama, "Japan Imports American Culture via Calories," *Marketing News*, May 1, 2007, p. 11; Dan Hilton, "Japan's Junk-Food Obsession," *CBC News*, July 5, 2006, **www.cbc.ca/news/viewpoint/vp_hilton/20060705.html** (accessed September 20, 2007); Joanne Lutynec, "American Junk Food Big Hit in Japan," *Slashfood*, April 4, 2007, **www.slashfood.com/2007/04/04/american-junk-food-is-a-big-hit-in-japan** (accessed September 20, 2007); "Tokyo Queues for You," *J@pan Inc.*, July 3, 2008, www.japaninc.com/mgz_july_/2008_krispy_kreme_marketing_in_japan (accessed April 24, 2009).

12. Stan Beer, "Global Software Piracy Cost US$40 billion in 2006: BSA," *IT Wire*, May 15, 2007, **www.itwire.com.au/content/view/12171/53/** (accessed June 7, 2007).

13. Alan Beattie, "Countries Rush to Restrict Trade in Basic Foods," *The Financial Times*, April 2, 2008, p. 1.

14. Helene Cooper, "WTO Rules Against U.S.'s Quota on Yarn from Pakistan in Latest Textiles Setback," *The Wall Street Journal*, April 27, 2001, p. A4.

15. "WTO Panel Rules U.S. Duties on Canadian Lumber Are Illegal," *The Wall Street Journal*, March 22, 2004, **http://online.wsj.com**.

16. Julie Bennett, "Product Pitfalls Proliferate in Global Cultural Maze," *The Wall Street Journal*, May 14, 2001, p. B11.

17. Greg Botelho, "2003 Global Influentials: Selling to the World," *CNN*, December 9, 2003, **www.cnn.com**.

18. Slogans Gone Bad, **www.joe-ks.com/archives_apr2004/slogans_gone_bad.htm** (accessed June 6, 2006).

19. Sydney B. Leavens, "Father-Daughter Ad Breaks Latino Mold," *The Wall Street Journal*, p. B7.

20. Nutriset Company Web site, **www.nutriset.fr/index.php?option=com_frontpage&Itemid=1** (accessed April 7, 2009); Conscious Management Scandinavia, "Nutriset: Hope for Undernourished," **www.lots.mindo.com/EN/news.aspx?id=330** (accessed October 23, 2007); Nutriset Company Website, "Plumpy-nut," **www.nutriset.fr/index.php?option=com_content&task=view&id=30&Itemid=28** (accessed October 23, 2007); World Hunger Education Service, "World Hunger Facts 2007," **www.worldhunger.org/articles/Learn/world%20hunger%20facts%202002.htm** (accessed October 23, 2007); Anderson Cooper, "A Life Saver Called "Plumpynut" *CBS News, 60 Minutes* October 21, 2007, **www.cbsnews.com/stories/2007/10/19/60minutes/main3386661_page3.shtml** (accessed October 23, 2007); Medicins Sans Frontieres, Doctors Without Borders, "Malnutrition, MSF Warns More Food Will Not Save Malnourished Children," October 10, 2007, **www.doctorswithoutborders.org/news/malnutrition/** (accessed October 23, 2007).

21. Bonasia, "For Web Global Reach Is Beauty—and Challenge."

22. Jim Hopkins, "Other Nations Zip by USA in High-Speed Net Race," *USA Today*, January 19, 2004, pp. 1B, 2B.

23. "What Is the WTO," World Trade Organization (n.d.), **www.wto.org** (accessed February 25, 2004).

24. "WTO: U.S. Steel Duties Are Illegal," *USA Today*, November 10, 2003, **http://usatoday.com**.

25. "Bush Ends Steel Tariffs," *CNNMoney*, December 4, 2003, **http://cnnmoney.com**.

26. "NAFTA," Office of the United States Trade Representative, **http://www.ustr.gov/trade-agreements/free-trade-agreements/north-american-free-trade-agreement-nafta** (accessed September 25, 2009).

27. "NAFTA," Office of the United States Trade Representative.

28. "Canada: The World Factbook," CIA, **https://www.cia.gov/library/publications/the-world-factbook/geos/ca.html** (accessed September 25, 2009).

29. CIA, *The World Fact Book*. "Trade with Canada: 2006"; U.S. Bureau of the Census, **www.census.gov/foreign-trade/balance/c1220.html** (accessed April 21, 2009).

30. "Top 10 Countries with which the U.S. Trades," U.S. Census Department, **http://www.census.gov/foreign-trade/top/dst/2009/06/balance.html** (accessed September 25, 2009).

31. "Mexico: The World Factbook," CIA, **https://www.cia.gov/library/publications/the-world-factbook/geos/mx.html** (accessed September 25, 2009).

32. Felipe Calderón Hinojosa, "Mexico's Road," *The Economist*, November 15, 2007, p. 48.

33. Harold Sirkin, "Mexico: A Better Choice than China?" Businessweek, March 13, 2009, **http://www.businessweek.com/managing/content/mar2009/ca20090313_410106.htm?campaign_id=rss_daily** (accessed September 25, 2009).

34. "Mexico: The World Factbook."

35. "Antecedents of the FTAA Process," Free Trade Area of the Americas (n.d.), **www.ftaa-alca.org/View_e.asp** (accessed February 25, 2004); "FTAA Fact Sheet," Market Access and Compliance, U.S. Department of Commerce (n.d.), **www.mac.doc.gov/ftaa2005/ftaa_fact_sheet.html** (accessed November 3, 2003).

36. "Archer Daniels to File NAFTA Claim Against Mexico," *Inbound Logistics*, October 2003, p. 30.

37. "Top 10 Countries with which the U.S. Trades," U.S. Census Department.

38. "Europe in 12 Lessons," http://europa.eu/abc/12lessons/lesson_2/index_en.htm (accessed April 21, 2009).

39. Stanley Reed, with Ariane Sains, David Fairlamb, and Carol Matlack, "The Euro: How Damaging a Hit?" *BusinessWeek,* September 29, 2003, p. 63; "The Single Currency," *CNN* (n.d.), www.cnn.com/SPECIALS/2000/eurounion/story/currency/ (accessed July 3, 2001).

40. "Microsoft Hit by Record EU Fine," *CNN,* March 24, 2004, www.cnn.com.

41. "About APEC," www.apec.org/content/apec/about_apec.html (accessed April, 2009).

42. Smith and Lindblad, "Mexico: Was NAFTA Worth It?"

43. Clay Chandler, "China Is Too Darn Hot!" *Fortune,* November 10, 2003, pp. 39–40; Clay Chandler, "How to Play the China Boom," *Fortune,* December 22, 2003, pp. 141, 142.

44. David J. Lynch, "The IMF Is Tired . . . Fund Struggles to Reinvent Itself," *USA Today,* April 19, 2006. p. B1.

45. Brad Fishman, "International Trade Shows: The Smartest Ticket for Overseas Research," International Franchise Association (n.d.), www.franchise.org/news/fw/april03c.asp (accessed July 27, 2001).

46. Ben Worthen, "The Crazy World of Outsourcing," *WSJ.com,* February 25, 2008, http://blogs.wsj.com/biztech/2008/02/25/the-crazy-world-of-outsourcing/?mod=relevancy (accessed April 21, 2009).

47. "Bank of America to Outsource 1,000 Jobs to India," [Albany] *Business Review,* February 18, 2004, www.bizjournals.com/albany/stories/2004/02/16/daily18.html.

48. Nick Easen, "Firms Get Savvy About Outsourcing," *CNNMoney,* February 18, 2004, www.cnn.com.

49. Walter B. Wriston, "Ever Heard of Insourcing?" commentary, *The Wall Street Journal,* March 24, 2004, p. A20.

50. "Bharti of India Will Outsource IT Needs to IBM," *The Wall Street Journal,* March 29, 2004, http://online.wsj.com.

51. Jason Bush, "GM: On the Road to Russia," *BusinessWeek,* January 19, 2004, p. 14.

52. "What We're About," NUMMI (n.d.), www.nummi.com/co_info.html (accessed February 26, 2004).

53. Sharon Silk Carty, "Ford Plans to Park Jaguar, Land Rover with Tata Motors," *USA Today,* March 26, 2008, p B1.

54. O. C. Ferrell, John Fraedrich, and Linda Ferrell, *Business Ethics,* 6th ed. (Boston: Houghton Mifflin, 2005), pp. 227–30.

55. Kim Jung Min, "Asian Company's Perfume Passes French Smell Test," *The Wall Street Journal,* March 19, 2004, http://online.wsj.com.

56. Vanessa O'Connell, "Exxon 'Centralizes' New Global Campaign," *The Wall Street Journal,* July 11, 2001, p. B6.

57. Michael Zhao, "60-Mile Wi-Fi," *Forbes,* April 9, 2007; "Bio for Eric Brewer," UC Berkeley, www.cs.berkeley.edu/~brewer/bio.html (accessed August 15, 2007).

58. Export.gov, www.export.gov/comm_svc/about_home.html (accessed February 9, 2006), CIBER *Web,* http://CIBERWEB.msu.edu (accessed February 9, 2006).

Chapter 4

1. "Wikipedia: About," 2009, http://en.wikipedia.org/wiki/Wikipedia:About (accessed April 21, 2009).

2. www.cosmetics.com (accessed July 17, 2009).

3. Roger W. Ferguson, Jr., "Remarks by Vice Chairman Roger W. Ferguson, Jr.," American Economic Association meeting, January 4, 2004, San Diego, California, available at www.federalreserve.gov/boarddocs/speeches/2004/200401042/default.htm.

4. Edward P. Lazear and Katherine Baicker, "America at Work," *The Wall Street Journal Online,* May 8, 2006, http://online.wsj.com/article/SB114705083956846285-searchhtml?KEYWORDS=productivity+adds+to+GDP&COLLECTION=wsjie/6month, (accessed July 17, 2009).

5. Jodh Tyrangiel, "Radical Remix," *Time,* October 15, 2007, p. 60.

6. "Data," *Webopedia,* October 28, 2003, www.webopedia.com/TERM/D/data.html.

7. "On Strike, Virtually," *The Economist,* March 15, 2008, p. 80; Tim Stevens, "Students Stage Virtual Protest on Facebook," *Switched,* August 31, 2007, www.switched.com/2007/08/31/students-stage-virtual-protest-on-facebook (accessed April 3, 2008); "Designer Takes Anti-Fur protest to Virtual World," *MSNBC.com,* June 29, 2007, www.msnbc.msn.com/id/19506442/print/1/displaymode/1098 (accessed April 3, 2008); "Stop Global Warming," www.stopglobalwarming.org (accessed April 13, 2009); Moveon.org, www.moveon.org (accessed April 14, 2009).

8. "Anheuser Busch Goes Full Tilt," August 8, 2005, www.anheuser-busch.com/Press/Archive05.html (accessed July 17, 2009).

9. "OnStar Experience," www.onstar.com/US-english/jsp/explore/index (accessed July 17, 2009).

10. "About IRI," Information Resources Inc. (n.d.), us.infares.com/About/tabid/59/Default.aspx (accessed July 17, 2009); "On-line Purchases of Consumer Packaged Goods on the Rise," study by Information Resources Inc., *DSN Retailing Today,* June 4, 2001.

11. Information Resources Inc, Company Overview, http://us.infores.com/page/about/company_overview (accessed June 8, 2006).

12. "How Duke Helps Students Connect," April 5, 2004, *BusinessWeek Online,* www.businessweek.com/bschools/content/apr2006/bs2006045_8177.htm?campaign_id=search (accessed July 17, 2009).

13. Edward C. Baig, "Livescribe Pulse Digital Pen Brings Your Notes to Life," *USA Today,* May 8, 2008, p. B1.

14. Adam Wright, "Mobile Phones Could Soon Rival the PC as the World's Dominant Internet Platform," April 18, 2006, www.ipsos-na.com/news/pressrelease.cfm?id=3040# (accessed April 22, 2009).

15. "Surge in Chinese Internet Users," *The BBC News,* January 14, 2009, http://news.bbc.co.uk/2/hi/asia-pacific/7827765.stm (accessed April 22, 2009).

16. www.epicurious.com (accessed April 22, 2009).

17. www.bluetooth.com/bluetooth (accessed April 22, 2009).

18. Leslie Cauley, "Deal Shakes Up Wireless World," *USA Today,* May 7, 2008, p. B1; Leslie Cauley, "Big Investors Join Clearwire's WiMax Plan for Wireless Nation," *USA Today,* May 8, 2008, p. B3.

19. FCC Consumer Facts, "VOIP/Internet Voice," www.fcc.gov/cgb (accessed April 22, 2009).

20. "Wal-Mart Is Dead Serious About RFID," CIO.com, January, 18, 2008, www.cio.com/article/173702/Wal_Mart_Is_Dead_Serious_About_RFID (accessed April 22, 2009).

21. "Shaping the Future Mobile Information Society," International Telecommunication Union (n.d.), www.itu.int/osg/spu/ni/futuremovile (accessed April 22, 2009).

22. Josh Quitter, "How Jeff Bezos Rules the Retail Space," *Fortune,* May 5, 2008, pp. 127–32.

23. John Gaffney, "How Do You Feel about a $44 Tooth-Bleaching Kit?" *Business 2.0,* October 2001, p. 126; Stephanie Stahl and John Soat, "Feeding the Pipeline: Procter & Gamble Uses IT to Nurture New Product Ideas," *Information Week,* February 24, 2003, **www.informationweek.com/story/showArticle.jhtml;–jsession id=4SA2EIBSJYSZCQSNDBGCKHY?articleID=8700568&pgno=1.**

24. Jefferson Graham, "Veoh Aims to Be One-Stop Shop for Net TV Viewers," *USA Today,* February 27, 2008, p. B8.

25. Moira Herbst, "The Comy Pinkflip Epidemic," *BusinessWeek* October 21, 2008, **www.businessweek.com/bwdaily/dnflash/content/oct 2008/db 20081020-022633.html** (accessed June 1, 2009).

26. Michael J. Mandel and Robert D. Hof, "Rethinking the Internet," *BusinessWeek,* March 26, 2001, p. 118.

27. Dennis K. Berman, "Business.com Could Hit Jackpot on Auction Block," *The Wall Street Journal,* June 22, 2007, p. B3; "About Us," *Business.com,* **www.business.com/info/press/index.asp** (accessed April 7, 2008); Giselle Abramovich, "R.H. Donnelley to Buy Business.com," *DMNews,* July 31, 2007, **www.dmnews.com/cms/dm-news/ad-agencies/41964.html** (accessed April 7, 2008); "Domain Name," **Wikipedia.org, http://en.wikipedia.org/wiki/Domain_name** (accessed April 7, 2008); Lisa LaMotta, "The Most Expensive Web Addresses," *Forbes.com,* June 29, 2007, **www.forbes.com/entrepreneurs/2007/06/28/google-news-corp-ent-tech-cx_ll_0629webaddresses.html** (accessed April 7, 2008).

28. Peter Passi, "Goodbye, Waiting Rooms," April 8, 2006, **http://www.duluthsuperior.com/mld/duluthsuperior/news/14295747.htm** (accessed June 14, 2006).

29. Mandel and Hof, "Rethinking the Internet," *BusinessWeek,* March 26, 2001, p. 118.

30. "How It Works," *The Wall Street Journal,* May 21, 2001, p. R8.

31. Mandel and Hof, "Rethinking the Internet."

32. *BusinessWeek,* special supplement, February 28, 2000, p. 74.

33. Anjali Cordeiro, "Online Market Lets Companies Buy and Sell Ideas," *The Wall Street Journal Online,* **http://online.wsj.com/article/SB120882814463933399.html** (accessed June 1, 2009).

34. Quitter, "How Jeff Bezos Rules the Retail Space."

35. Travel Industry Association of America, "Leading Travel Industry Consumer Survey Reports Significantly More Travelers Plan and Book Trips Online," November 16, 2005, **www.tia.org/pressmedia/pressrec.asp?Item=689** (accessed June 14, 2006).

36. Jayne O'Donnell, "Online Buyers Crack the Code on Deals," *USA Today,* April 4, 2008, p. B3.

37. Tessa Romita. "Sky's the Limit for Airlines Online," *Business 2.com,* January 23, 2001, p. 4.

38. Adapted from Judy Strauss and Raymond Frost, *Emarketing,* 2nd ed. (Upper Saddle River, NJ: Prentice-Hall, 2001).

39. Adapted from William M. Pride and O.C. Ferrell, *Marketing,* 13th ed. (Boston: Houghton Mifflin, 2005).

40. **www.olay.com/clubolay/intro.htm** (accessed June 15, 2006).

41. O. C. Ferrell, Michael D. Hartline, and George H. Lucas, Jr., *Marketing Strategy* (Fort Worth, TX: Dryden, 2002), p. 97.

42. **www.salesforce.com/products/sales-force-automation.jsp** (accessed July 17, 2009).

43. Edward Prewitt, "How to Build Customer Loyalty in an Internet World," *CIO,* January 1, 2002, **www.cio.com/archive/010102/loyalty_content.html.**

44. Eve M. Caudill and Patrick E. Murphy, "Consumer Online Privacy: Legal and Ethical Issues," *Journal of Public Policy & Marketing,* 19 (Spring 2000), pp. 7–12.

45. **www.truste.org/about/fact_sheet.php** (accessed July 17, 2009).

46. Better Business Bureau Online (n.d.), **www.bbbonline.org/** (accessed July 17, 2009).

47. Thomas Claburn, "Spam Made up 94% of all E-Mail in December," *InformationWeek,* January 29, 2007, **http://www.informationweek.com/showArticle.jhtml;jsessionid=4H4VB4FGNIKEWQSNDLRSKHSCJUNN2JVN?articleID=197001430** (accessed June 17, 2009).

48. "Gmail Uses Google's Innovative Technology to Keep Spam out of Your Inbox," Google, 2009, **www.google.com/mail/help/fight spam/spamexplained.html** (accessed May 5, 2009).

49. Tim Hanrahan and Jason Fry, "Spammers, Human Mind Do Battle Over Spelling," *The Wall Street Journal,* February 9, 2004, **http://online.wsj.com.**

50. "EU Orders Anti-Spam Legislation," *CNN,* April 1, 2004, **www.cnn.com.**

51. "FTC Releases List of Top Consumer Fraud Complaints in 2007," January 13, 2008, **www.ftc.gov/opa/2008/02/fraud.shtm** (accessed April 22, 2009).

52. Andrea Chipman, "Stealing You," *The Wall Street Journal,* April 26, 2004, **http://online.wsj.com.**

53. Christine Dugas, "Identity Theft on the Rise," USA Today, May 11, 2001, p. 3B.

54. 2007 Identity Fraud Survey Report, **www.javelinstrategy.com/uploads/701.R_2007IdentityFraudSurveyReport_Brochure.pdf** (accessed April 22, 2009).

55. Jack McCarthy, "National Fraud Center: Internet Is Driving Identity Theft," *CNN,* March 20, 2000, **www.cnn.com.**

56. Juan Carlos Perez, "Biggest Security Threat? Insiders," *PC World,* October 2, 2002, **www.pcworld.com/news/article/0,aid,105528,00.asp.**

57. Fifth Annual BSA and IDC Global Software Piracy Study, **http://global.bsa.org/idcglobalstudy2007/** (accessed April 22, 2009).

58. "States Approve Effective Date for Sales Tax Simplification Agreement," **www.govtech.net/news/news.php?id=94929#** (accessed June 15, 2006).

59. Alan Rappeport, "Second Life's John Zdanowski," *CFO,* October 2007, pp. 46–48; "Gartner Gives Second Life a Dose of Virtual Reality," *TechCentral.ie,* **www.techcentral.ie/article.aspx?id=11873** (accessed March 18, 2008); Mike Shields, "CNN Goes Virtual," *Mediaweek,* Oct. 29, 2007, **www.mediaweek.com/mw/current/article_display.jsp?vnu_content_2.=1003664347** (accessed March 18, 2008); "Economic Status," Second Life, **http://secondlife.com/whatis/economy_stats.php** (accessed March 18, 2008); "What Is Second Life?," **http://secondlife.com/whatis/** (accessed March 18, 2008).

Chapter 5

1. Max Chafkin, "Gordon Segal of Crate and Barrel," *Inc.,* May 2008, **www.inc.com/magazine/2008501/gordon-segal-of-crate-and-barrel.html** (accessed April 22, 2009).

2. The Entrepreneurs's Help Page, **www.tannedfeet.com/sole_proprietorship.htm** (accessed April 22, 2009); Kent Hoover, "Startups Down for Women Entrepreneurs, Up for Men," *San Francisco Business Times,* May 2, 2008, **http://sanfrancisco.bizjournals.com/sanfrancisco/stories/2008/05/05/smallb2.html** (accessed April 22, 2009).

3. Maggie Overfelt, "Start-Me-Up: The California Garage," *Fortune Small Business,* July/Aug. 2003, **www.fortune.com/fortune/smallbusiness/articles/0,15114,475872,00.html.**

4. Jason Norman, "Best Buy to Stock E-Bikes in Select Stores," *Bicycle Retailer,* April 29, 2009, **www.bicycleretailer.com/news/newsDetail/2648.html** (accessed May 19, 2009); Christine Wurst, "Electric Bikes Gain Speed and Popularity," May 15, 2009, **www.ebikes.ca/faq.shtml** (accessed May 19, 2009); "FAQ," ebikes.ca, **www.ebikes.ca/faq.shtml** (accessed May 19, 2009); "Electric Bikes," Schwinn Quality, **www.schwinnbike.com/usa/eng/Products/Electric/All/** (accessed May 19, 2009); "A2B," Ultra Motor A2B, **http://sanfrancisco.goa2b.us/products/a2b** (accessed May 19, 2009); "Our Vision," Ultra Motor A2B, **www.ultramotor.com/uk/about_us/** (accessed May 19, 2009); Julio Ojeda-Zapata, "Riders of Electric Bicycles Plug in and Pedal," *TwinCities.com,* May 17, 2009, **www.twincities.com/ci_12383680** (accessed May 22, 2009).

5. "1: Digital Artists Agency," Business 2.0, April 2004, p. 90.

6. Linda Tischles, "Join the Circus," *Fast Company,* July 2005, pp. 53–58.

7. "BP's Russian Oil Row Intensifies," *BBC News,* June 9, 2008, **http://news.bbc.co.uk/2/hi/business/7443380.stm** (accessed June 1, 2009).

8. Megan Kamerick, "Santa Fe Trio Builds Furniture Business on Rich Tradition," *New Mexico Business Weekly,* June 8–14, 2007, p. 13; *Taos Furniture,* **www.taosfurniture.com** (accessed September 1, 2007).

9. U.S. Bureau of the Census, *Statistical Abstract of the United States 2003* (Washington, D.C.: U.S. Government printing office, 2004).

10. Deborah Orr, "The Secret World of Mars," *Forbes,* April 28, 2008, **www.forbes.com/2008/04/28/billionaires-mars-wrigley-biz-billies-cz_do_0428marsfamily_print.html** (accessed April 22, 2009).

11. Shlomo Reifman, "America's Largest Private Companies," *Forbes,* November 8, 2007, **www.forbes.com/business/2007/11/08/largest-private-companies-biz-privates07-cx_sr_1108privateintro.html** (accessed April 22, 2009).

12. David Kiley, "Ford Family Celebrates 100 Years of Cars," *USA Today,* June 10, 2003, pp. 1B, 2B.

13. "Intrepid Potash," *MSN Money,* IPO Central, **http://moenycentral.hoovers.com/global/msn/index.xhtml?pageid=10021&PDate=M:2008:4** (accessed April 22, 2009).

14. Bree Fowler, "Daimler Reaches Deal on Final Split from Chrysler," *Chron.com,* April 27, 2009, **www.chron.com/disp/story.mpl/business/6395359.html** (accessed April 30, 2009).

15. O. C. Ferrell, John Fraedrich, and Linda Ferrell, *Business Ethics: Ethical Decision Making and Cases,* 6th ed. (Boston: Houghton Mifflin, 2005), p. 84.

16. Julie Daum, "Board Talent Getting Scarcer," *BusinessWeek Online,* January 29, 2008, **www.businessweek.com/print/managing/content/jan2008/ca20080129_376288.htm** (accessed June 1, 2009).

17. Joseph Nathan Kane, *Famous First Facts,* 4th ed. (New York: The H. W. Wilson Company, 1981), p. 202.

18. Camille Jensen, "ESOP Companies Mark the Fortune 100 Liss," February 6, 2009, **www.axiomnews.c2/News archives/2009/February/February06.html** (accessed June 1, 2009).

19. David Kiley, "Audi, VW Must Share a U.S. Factory," *BusinessWeek Online,* May 7, 2008, **www.businessweek.com/lifestyle/content/may2** (accessed June 1, 2009).

20. Robert D. Hisrich and Michael P. Peters, *Entrepreneurship,* 5th ed. (Boston: McGraw-Hill, 2002), pp. 315–16.

21. Ariel Nelson, "Mars Acquisition of Wrigley: 3rd Biggest Deal of 2008," *CBNC.com,* April 28, 2008, **http://www.cnbc.com/id/24351497** (accessed June 9, 2008); "Hershey Shares Jumps Amid New Venture Talk," *Reuters,* May 27, 2008, **http://uk.reuters.com/article/UK_HOTSTOCKS/idUKN2731687420080527** (accessed June 9, 2008).

22. Ariel Nelson, "Mars Acquisition of Wrigley: 3rd Biggest Deal of 2008," *CBNC.com,* April 28, 2008, **www.cnbc.com/id/24351497** (accessed April 22, 2009); "Hershey Shares Jump Amid New Venture Talk," *Reuters,* May 27, 2008, **http://uk.reuters.com/article/UK_HOTSTOCKS?idUKN2731687420080527** (accessed April 22, 2009).

23. Alex Crippen, "Busch Tapping Buffet?," *CNBC.com,* June 16, 2008, **www.cnbc.com/id/25190248** (accessed June 1, 2009).

24. "What Is Community Supported Agriculture and How Does It Work?," *Local Harvest,* **www.localharvest.org/csa.jsp** (accessed April 10, 2009); "Community-Supported Agriculture," *Wikipedia,* **http://en.wikipedia.org/wiki/Community-supported_agriculture** (accessed February 18, 2008); "Community Supported Agriculture at Indian Line Farm," **www.indianlinefarm.com/csa.html** (accessed February 25, 2008).

Chapter 6

1. "About SBA," Small Business Administration, **http://sba.gov/aboutsba/index.html** (accessed August 10, 2009).

2. "Environmentalism: What We Do," Patagonia, **www.patagonia.com/web/us/patagonia.go?assetid=2329** (accessed June 1, 2009).

3. "Data on Small Businesses," SBA, **http://www.sba.gov/advo/research/data.html** (accessed August 10, 2009).

4. Center for Women's Business Research, "Key Facts about Women Owned Business," **www.nfwbo.org/facts/index.php** (accessed April 27, 2009).

5. "Minority Business Fast Facts Profiles," Minority Business Development Agency, November 8, 2007, **www.mbda.gov/minoritybizfacts/?bucket_id=789** (accessed April 27, 2009).

6. Jose M. Ledon, "A One-Stop Developer," *Fortune,* May 5, 2008, p. S14.

7. "Frequently Asked Questions," SBA, **http://web.sba.gov/faqs/faqindex.cfm?areaID=24** (accessed August 10, 2009).

8. "Data on Small Businesses," SBA, **http://www.sba.gov/advo/research/data.html,** (accessed August 10, 2009).

9. "Sky Car," Moller, **http://www.moller.com/skycar.htm** (accessed August 10, 2009).

10. Lindsay Blakely, "One Man Brands," *Money.CNN.com,* July 6, 2007, **http://money.cnn.com/galleries/2007/biz2/0706/gallery.building_brands.biz2/** (accessed June 1, 2009).

11. "How to Finance a New Business," *Consumer Reports,* April 2008, **www.consumerreports.org/cro/money/credit-loan/how-to-finance-a-new-business/overview/how-to-finance-a-new-business-ov.htm** (accessed June 1, 2009).

12. Peter Svensson, "U.S. Economy Grows at a Slower Pace," *Washingtonpost.com,* June 5, 2006, **www.washingtonpost.com/wp-dyn/content/article/2006/06/05/AR2006060500376.html** (accessed August 10, 2009).

13. News release, "PRO-TEC Coating Company Wins Prestigious Malcolm Baldrige National Quality award," *ProTecCoating.com,* November 21, 2007, **www.proteccoating.com/pdf/PRO-TEC-Baldrige Award.pdf** (accessed April 27, 2009).

14. Jessie Hempel, "How Facebook Is Taking Over Our Lives," *Money.CNN.com,* February 16, 2009, **http://money.cnn.com/2009/02/16/technology/hempel_facebook.fortune/index.htm.** (accessed June 1, 2009).

15. "Small Business Statistics."

16. Nitasha Tiku, "Making the Most of a Brush With Fame," *Inc.,* August 2007, p.19; Recycline company Web site, **www.recycline.com/** (accessed December 4, 2007); "Recycline: Sitting on Mainstream's Doorstep," Sustainable Is Good, **www.sustainableisgood.com/blog/2007/03/recycline_produ.html** (accessed December 4, 2007); "FACTBOX: Five Facts about Entrepreneur Eric Hudson," December 23, 2008, **www.reuters.com/article/deborahCohen/idUSTRE4BM4YR20081223** (accessed April 10, 2009).

17. Dana Knight, "Big-Headed Guy Gets a Big Idea for Sunglasses," *USA Today,* March 21, 2006, **http://www.usatoday.com/money/smallbusiness/2006-03-21-fatheadz-usat_x.htm** (accessed August 10, 2009).

18. "You're Not the Boss of Me Now," *Weekend Today,* October 21, 2005, **msnbc.msn.com/id/9762771/** (accessed August 10, 2009).

19. "Startup Failure Rates," Small Business Trends, April 28, 2008, **http://smallbiztrends.com/2008/04/startup-failure-rates.html** (accessed August 10, 2009).

20. Emily Lambert, "Pesticide Prince," *Forbes,* April 9, 2007, pp. 68–70; "About Us," AgriStar, Albaugh, Inc., **www.albaughinc.com/aboutus.htm** (accessed September 14, 2007).

21. "Spring 2005 Interland Business Barometer," *USA Today,* Snapshots, October 26, 2005.

22. Jennifer Martin, "From Cow Pies to Cow Pots: A Creative Way to Manage Farm Waste," Cooperative State Research, Education, and Extension Service, July 17, 2007, **www.csrees.usda.gov/newsroom/research/2007/cowpots.html,** (accessed June 1, 2009).

23. Robert Tomsho, "Ask the Volk Family: 30 Million Turkeys Can't Be Wrong," *The Wall Street Journal,* November 22, 2005, p. A1; **www.volkenterprises.com/about_us/index.html,** "About Us," (accessed August 10, 2009).

24. Nick Hodge, "Solar Energy Venture Capital," *Wealth Daily,* January 23, 2008, **www.wealthdaily.com/articles/solar-venture-capital/1120** (accessed April 27, 2009).

25. Susan McGee, "A Chorus of Angels," *Inc.,* January 2004, **www.inc.com/magazine/20040101/finance.html.** (accessed August 10, 2009).

26. Thomas W. Zimmerer and Norman M. Scarborough, *Essentials of Entrepreneurship and Small Business Management,* 4th ed. (Upper Saddle River, NJ: Pearson Prentice Hall, 2005), pp. 118–24.

27. Ibid.

28. "About SCORE," SCORE, **http://www.score.org/explore_score.html** (accessed August 10, 2009).

29. Adapted from "Tomorrow's Entrepreneur," *Inc. State of Small Business,* 23, no. 7 (2001), pp. 80–104.

30. "The Boomer Stats," Baby Boomer HQ, **www.bbhq.com/bomrstat.htm** (accessed August 10, 2009).

31. Molly Smith, "Managing Generation Y as They Change the Workforce," *Reuters,* January 8, 2008, **www.reuters.com/article/pressRelease/idUS129795+08-Jan-2008+BW20080108** (accessed April 27, 2009).

32. Jeffrey Passal and D'Vera Cohn, "Immigration to Play Lead Role in Future U.S. Growth," **http://pewresearch.org/pubs/729/united-states-population-projections** (accessed April 27, 2009).

33. Kelly Crow, "The Oldest Crop," *The Wall Street Journal,* June 8, 2007, pp. W1, W10; Mark Potter, "The Dinosaurs of South Dakota," *MSNBC.com,* September 20, 2007, **www.msnbc.msn.com/id/20894357** (accessed February 22, 2008); Joanne Fox, "Fossil Hunters Really Dig Their Hobby," *Sioux City Journal,* September 25, 2007, **www.siouxcityjournal.com/articles/2007/09/25/news/top/e6cd21c5655fde5886257361000d4cd8.txt** (accessed February 22, 2008).

34. Paul Brown, "How to Cope with Hard Times," *The New York Times,* June 10, 2008, **www.nytimes.com/2008/06/10/business/smallbusiness/10toolkit.html?_r=1&ref=smallbusiness&oref=slogin** (accessed June 25, 2008).

35. Gifford Pinchott III, *Intrapreneuring* (New York: Harper & Row, 1985), p. 34.

Chapter 7

1. Peter Sanders, "Boeing Yet to Clear Dreamliner's Takeoff," *Wall Street Journal,* July 23, 2009, **http://online.wsj.com/article/SB124826216575571813.html** (accessed August 10, 2009).

2. Denese McDonald, "Partners in Success," *Fortune,* May 5, 2008, p. S12.

3. Alex Taylor III, "Can This Car Save Ford?," *Fortune,* May 5, 2008, pp. 170–173.

4. "Celestial Difference," Celestial Seasonings, **www.celestialseasonings.ca/en/index.php/celestial/** (accessed August 10, 2009).

5. Procter & Gamble R&D Mission, **www.pg.com/science/rdmission.jhtml** (accessed August 10, 2009).

6. "Points of Light Institute Honors Deloitte," Points of Light, June 24, 2009, **http://www.pointsoflight.org/current-news/points-light-institute-honors-deloitt** (accessed August 10, 2009).

7. Kathryn Kranhold, "His Bright Idea: Dominate Energy-Saving Light Bulbs," *The Wall Street Journal,* December 27, 2007, pp. B1–B2; Julie Scelfo, "Any Other Bright Ideas?," *The New York Times,* January 10, 2008, **www.nytimes.com/2008/01/10/garden/10lighting.html?ex=1357621200&en=e017408dffab6416&ei=5088&partner=rssnyt&emc=rss** (accessed August 10, 2009); TCP School Program, "About TCP," "FAQ," **http://schoolprograms.tcpi.com, www.tcpi.com/corp/press_releases.aspx** (accessed August 10, 2009).

8. Kelly Kurt, "Tulsa Bids Zebco Fishing Reels Farewell," *Chicago Tribune,* March 11, 2001, section 5, p. 7.

9. G. Tomas, M. Hult, David W. Cravens, and Jagdish Sheth, "Competitive Advantage in the Global Marketplace: A Focus on Marketing Strategy," *Journal of Business Research* 51 (January 2001), p. 1.

10. Telis Demos, "Copter Crisis," *Fortune,* May 12, 2008, p. 20.

11. Vivienne Walt, "Oil Is Plentiful, Demand Weak. Why are Gas Prices Going Up?," *Time*, May 29, 2009, **www.time.com/time/world/article/0,8599,1901446,00.html** (accessed August 10, 2009).

12. **www.aboutreuters.com/productsinfo/**(accessed June 12, 2006).

13. Michelle Maynard, "A Primer on the GM Bankruptcy," *The New York Times*, June 1, 2009, **www.nytimes.com/2009/06/02/business/02primer.html?ref=business** (accessed August 10, 2009).

14. John Shepler, "Managing After Downsizing," JohnShepler.com (n.d.), **www.johnshepler.com/articles/managedown.html** (accessed August 10, 2009).

15. "The Big Picture," *BusinessWeek*, July 16, 2001, p. 12.

16. "ASPO-USA Response to Exxon Mobil Peak Oil Advertisement," March 3, 2006, Association for the Study of Peak Oil & Gas-USA, **www.aspo-usa.com/news.cfm?nd=1468** (accessed August 10, 2009).

17. "2008 Catalyst Census of Women Corporate Officers and Top Earners of the Fortune 500," Catalyst, **http://www.catalyst.org/file/241/08_census_cote_final.pdf** (accessed August 10, 2009).

18. David Kiley, "Ghosn Hits Accelerator," *BusinessWeek*, May 12, 2008, p. 46.

19. Steve Ulfeldfer, "Chief Privacy Officers: Hot or Not?," Computerworld Security, March 15, 2004, **http://www.computerworld.com/s/article/91168/CPOs_Hot_or_Not_** (accessed August 10, 2009).

20. Pearl Meyer, "Executive Pay: What Really Makes Sense," *BusinessWeek Online*, April 24, 2008, **www.businessweek.com/managing/content/apr2008/ca20080424_081309.htm** (accessed August 10, 2009).

21. Annie Finnigan, "Different Strokes," *Working Woman*, April 2001, p. 44.

22. "Developing Colleagues with Passion," *Inbound Logistics*, April 2004, p. 14.

23. "Improved Health of Employees and Financial Bottom Line Demonstrated Through Innovative Pilot Program at Daimler Chrysler Canada's Windsor Assembly Plant," **http://www.pfizer.ca/english/newsroom/press%20releases/default.asp?s=1&releaseID=194** (accessed August 10, 2009).

24. "Corporate Information," **www.google.com/corporate/facts.html** (accessed June 12, 2006); "The Google Culture," **www.google.com/corporate/culture.html** (accessed August 10, 2009).

25. "Tougher to Be a Leader," *USA Today* Snapshot, March 6, 2006, p. B1.

26. Carol J. Llomis, "Can Anyone Run Citigroup?" *Fortune*, May 5, 2008, pp. 81–84.

27. Bank of America Assumes $16.6B in Countrywide Debt," *Dayton Business Journal*, November 10, 2008, **www.bizjournals.com/dayton/stories/2008/11/10/daily7.html** (accessed November 14, 2008); Carl Gutierrez, "Countrywide's New Bad News," *Forbes*, March 10, 2008, **www.forbes.com/markets/2008/03/10/countrywide-fbi-mortgage-markets-equity-cx_cg_0310markets26.html** (accessed August 10, 2009); "Judge Rules Mozilo and Countrywide Execs Must Face Multi-Million Dollar Federal Lawsuit," *The New York Times*, May 22, 2008, **www.nytimes.com/2008/03/07/business/07cnd-pay.html?_r=1&oref=slogin;** Maria Bartiromo, "Countrywide Feels the Heat." *BusinessWeek*, August 29, 2007, **www.businessweek.com/bwdaily/dnflash/content/aug2007/db20070829_117563.htm?chan=search** (accessed August 10, 2009).

28. Chad Terhune and Joann S. Lublin, "Coca-Cola Considers 4 Outsiders as Search for New CEO Intensifies," *The Wall Street Journal*, April 9, 2004, **http://online.wsj.com/article/SB108146176363878403.html?mod=googlewsj** (accessed August 10, 2009).

29. "Coca-Cola Names E. Neville Isdell Chairman and Chief Executive Officer Elect," Coca-Cola, press release, May 4, 2004, **http://www.cocacolasabco.com/index.php?option=com_content&view=article&id=47:coca-cola-names-e-neville-isdell-chairman-and-chief-executive-officer-elect&catid=18:newsroom&Itemid=64** (accessed August 10, 2009).

30. Pallavi Gogoi, "Big Soda's Sticky End," *BusinessWeek Online*, May 4, 2006, **www.businessweek.com/investor/content/may2006/pi20060504_428474.htm?campaign_id=search** (accessed August 10, 2009).

31. Kara Scannell, "Wharton Offers Students a Tough Course in Combat," *Wall Street Journal*, June 5, 2001, **http://online.wsj.com/article/SB991691641700579064.html?mod=googlewsj** (accessed August 10, 2009).

32. Kerrie Unsworth, "Unpacking Creativity," *Academy of Management Review*, 26 (April 2001), pp. 289–97.

33. *Harvard Business Review* 60 (November–December 1982), p. 160.

34. Amelia Patterson, "Fallen Forests Salvaged," *Colorado Biz Magazine*, September 2007, pp. 34–36; "About Dennie Ibbotson and Laughing Sun Custom Handcarved Signs and Doors," *Laughing Sun*, **www.handcarveddoors.com/info.html** (accessed May 9, 2008); D.A. Leatherman, I. Aguayo, and T. M. Mehall, "Mountain Pine Beetle," *Colorado State University Extension—Horticulture*, **www.ext.colostate.edu/pubs/insect/05528.html** (accessed August 10, 2009).

35. "Client List," Nierenberg Group, Inc., **http://www.nierenberggroup.com/bm/clients/index.shtml** (accessed August 10, 2009).

36. **www.selfmarketing.com/about.html** (accessed August 10, 2009).

37. "2007 National Employment and Wage Estimates," Bureau of Labor Statistics, **www.bls.gov/oes/current/oes_nat.htm#b11-0000** (accessed August 10, 2009); "Career Guide to Industries 2008–2009 Edition: Management and Business and Financial Operations Occupations," *Bureau of Labor Statistics*, **www.bls.gov/oco/oco1001.htm** (accessed August 10, 2009).

Chapter 8

1. Michael O'Neill, "From Wharton to War," *Fortune*, June 12, 2006, pp. 105–108.

2. Benjamin Fulford, "The Tortoise Jumps the Hare," *Forbes*, February 2, 2004, pp. 53–56.

3. Kevin Kingsbury, "Merck Agrees to Pay $58 to Settle Vioxx Advertising Claims," *The Wall Street Journal*, May 20, 2008, **http://online.wsj.com/article/SB121130041562407333.html** (accessed August 11, 2009).

4. Ashley Petry, "Ethical, and Profitable," *Indianapolis Star Online*, May 19, 2008, **www.indystar.com/apps/pbcs.dll/article?AID=/20080519/BUSINESS05/805190323** (accessed August 11, 2009).

5. Adam Smith, *Wealth of Nations* (New York: Modern Library, 1937; originally published in 1776).

6. Jyoti Thottam, "When Execs Go Temp," *Time*, April 26, 2004, pp. 40–41.

7. Chris Perttila, "Keep It Simple," *Entrepreneur*, February 2006, pp. 60–64.

8. Dennis Hays, "Kodak's Faraci Named President, Chief Operating Officer," *Photo News Today*, September 24, 2007, **www.photonewstoday.com/?p=7890** (accessed August 11, 2009).

9. Peter Gumbel, "Big Mac's Local Flavor," May 2, 2008, **http://money.cnn.com/2008/04/29/news/companies/big_macs_local.fortune/index.htm** (accessed August 11, 2009).

10. Gary Hamel, "What Google, Whole Foods Do Best," *CNN.com*, September. 26, 2007, **http://money.cnn.com/2007/09/26/news/companies/management_hamel.fortune/index.htm,** (accessed August 11, 2009).

11. Sandra Bretting, "Growing a Market for a Unique Product," *The Houston Chronicle*, March 9, 2008, p. D6; "Green Garlic," *gourmetsleuth.com*, **www.gourmetsleuth.com/greengarlic.htm** (accessed August 11, 2009); Gourmet Country Farm Web site, **www.gourmetcountryfarm.com** (accessed August 11, 2009).

12. Jon R. Katzenbach and Douglas K. Smith, "The Discipline of Teams," *Harvard Business Review* 71 (March–April 1993), pp. 111–20.

13. Ibid.

14. Leah Buchanan, "When Absence Makes the Team Grow Stronger," *Inc.*, June 2008, p. 40.

15. Darryl Haralson and Adrienne Lewis, "USA Today Snapshots," *USA Today*, April 26, 2001, p. B1.

16. "Our Task Force Report," The Coca-Cola Company, 2006, **http://www.thecoca-colacompany.com/ourcompany/task_force_report_2006.pdf** (accessed August 11, 2009).

17. Julia Chang, "A View from the Top," *Sales & Marketing Management*, February 2004, p. 19.

18. Jerry Useem, "What's That Spell? TEAMWORK," *Fortune*, June 12, 2006, p. 66.

19. Jia Lynnyang, "The Power of Number 4.6," *Fortune*, June 12, 2006, p. 122.

20. Nicole Miller, "UW-Madison's Product Development Team Beats the Odds," *College of Architecture and Life Sciences News*, January 3, 2006, **http://news.cals.wisc.edu/newsDisplay.asp?id=1445** (accessed August 11, 2009).

21. Richard S. Wellins, William C. Byham, and Jeanne M. Wilson, *Empowered Teams: Creating Self-Directed Work Groups That Improve Quality, Productivity, and Participation* (San Francisco: Jossey-Bass Publishers, 1991), p. 5.

22. Josh Kyatt, "The Soul of a New Team," *Fortune*, June 12, 2006. pp. 134–150.

23. Peg Kelly, "Vampire Meetings and How to Slay Them," *WebPro News*, January 7, 2003, **http://www.webpronews.com/topnews/2003/01/07/vampire-meetings-and-how-to-slay-them** (accessed August 11, 2009).

24. Fulford, "The Tortoise Jumps the Hare."

25. "Intranet Design Annual 2009: Year's Ten Best Intranets," Nielson Norman Group, **http://www.nngroup.com/reports/intranet/design/** (accessed August 11, 2009).

26. Stacy Perman, "Concrete Decision," *BusinessWeek*, February/March 2007; Rick Hampson, "Tree Roots Can't Ravage This Sidewalk," *USAToday*, **www.usatoday.com/news/nation/2006-09-19-sidewalks_x.htm** (accessed August 20, 2008); **www.rubbersidewalks.com** (accessed August 11, 2009); Rebecca Adler Warren, "Bright Green Ideas," April 2009, *More*, **www.rubbersidewalks.com/pdf/MoreGreenEntrepreneurs_April09.pdf** (accessed August 11, 2009).

27. Candice Novak, "7 Ways Your Email Can Get you Fired," *U.S. News and World Report*, August 4, 2008, **http://www.usnews.com/articles/business/careers/2008/08/04/7-ways-your-e-mail-can-get-you-fired.html** (accessed August 11, 2009).

28. "New Products Add Fun and Humor to Employee Training," Business Wire, February 29, 2005, via BNet, **http://findarticles.com/p/articles/mi_pwwi/is_20050229/ai_mark02027866/** (accessed August 11, 2009).

29. Michelle Kessler, "Dell Reverses, Steps into Wal-Mart," *USA Today*, May 25, 2007, p. B1–B2; Peter Svensson, "Dell to Sell Desktops at Nation's Top Retailer," *The Miami Herald*, (May 25, 2007), p. 6C; Erica Ogg, "What Wal-Mart Means to Dell," *News.com*, May 25, 2007, **http://news.com.com/What+Wal-Mart+means+to+Dell/2100-1042_3-6186402.html** (accessed August 11, 2009); Jessica Davis, "Analyst: Dell's Wal-Mart Choice 'Creative," *eWeek Channel Insider*, May 25, 2007, **www.channelinsider.com/article/Analyst+Dells+WalMart+Choice+Creative/208346_1.aspx** (accessed August 11, 2009); "Wal-Mart Salutes Schools Through 'Earth Day, Every Day' School Challenge," *Wal-Mart*, April 3, 2009, **http://walmartstores.com/FactsNews/NewsRoom/9064.aspx** (accessed August 11, 2009).

30. Erika Germer, "Huddle Up," *Fast Company*, December 2000, p. 86.

31. Tamar Lewin, "Chevron Settles Sexual Harassment Charges," *The New York Times*, February 22, 1995, **http://www.nytimes.com/1995/02/22/us/chevron-settles-sexual-harassment-charges.html** (accessed August 11, 2009).

Chapter 9

1. Valerie A. Zeithaml and Mary Jo Bitner, *Services Marketing*, 3rd ed. (Boston: McGraw-Hill/Irwin, 2003), p. 7.

2. Bruce Horovitz, "A Whole New Ballgane in Grocery Shopping," *USA Today*, March 9, 2005, p. B1; **http://www.usatoday.com/money/industries/food/2005-03-08-wholefoods-cover-usat_x.htm** (accessed August 11, 2009).

3. Dan Reed, "Jet Blue Tries to Bounce Back from Storm of Trouble," *USA Today*, June 7, 2007, pp. 1B–2B; Steve Huettel, "Jet Blue Issues Fliers Bill of Rights," *St. Petersburg Times*, February 20, 2007, **www.sptimes.com/2007/02/20/news_pf/Business/Jet_Blue_issues_flier.shtml** (accessed Mar. 17, 2008); Lior Arussy, "Effective Customer Complaints Handling," "Focus: Customer," *CRMXchange*, April 2007, **www.crmxchange.com/focus_customer/april07.asp** (accessed August 11, 2009).

4. Tahl Raz, "A Recipe for Perfection," *Inc.*, July 2003, pp. 36–38.

5. Leonard L. Berry, *Discovering the Soul of Service* (New York: The Free Press, 1999), pp. 86–96.

6. Zeithaml and Bitner, *Services Marketing*, pp. 3, 22.

7. Bernard Wysocki Jr., "To Fix Health Care, Hospitals Take Tips from the Factory Floor," *The Wall Street Journal*, April 9, 2004, **http://online.wsj.com/article/SB108146068260878363.html?mod=googlewsj** (accessed August 11, 2009).

8. Ibid.

9. Jean Halliday, "Nissan Delves into Truck Owner Psyche," *Advertising Age*, December 1, 2003, p. 11.

10. Faith Keenan, "Opening the Spigot," *BusinessWeek e.biz,* June 4, 2001, **www.businessweek.com/magazine/content/01_23/b3735616.htm.**

11. "Agricultural Export Benefits from Standardized Production," China.org, December 24, 2003, **www.china.org.cn/english/2003/Dec/83203.htm.**

12. Sue Kirchhoff, "Manufactured Homes—and Their Owners—Gain New Respect," *USA Today,* August 8, 2005 p. 13.

13. Stanley Holmes, "Boats as Big as the Ritz," *BusinessWeek,* April 26, 2004, **http://www.businessweek.com/magazine/content/04_17/b3880115_mz070.htm** (accessed August 11, 2009).

14. Kiri Blakeley,"Entrepreneurs: Shoes with Soul," "Fancy Footwork," *Forbes,* April 9, 2007; "MINK Shoes Story," "Rebecca Brough Bio," **www.minkshoes.com/story** (accessed August 11, 2009).

15. Press Release, "Honda Enhances Flexible Manufacturing Network in North America," Honda of American Mfg., Inc., October 13, 2008, **http://www.ohio.honda.com/pressroom/View_Release.cfm?articleid=172** (accessed August 11, 2009).

16. Hershey, "Hershey's Chocolate Kisses," (n.d.), **www.hersheys.com/products/kisses.shtml** (accessed August 11, 2009).

17. "Gbout Schwob," **www.aboutschwob.com** (accessed June 1, 2009).

18. "Tesla Motors Building Car Plant in New Mexico," *Silicon Valley/San Jose Business Journal,* February 20, 2007, **http://albuquerque.bizjournals.com/sanjose/stories/2007/02/19/daily19.html** (accessed August 11, 2009). Thomas Munro, "Tesla Motors Backs out of NM Deal," *New Mexico Business Weekly,* June 30, 2008, **http://www.bizjournals.com/albuquerque/stories/2008/06/30/daily11.html** (accessed August 11, 2009).

19. "Shopping for Subsidies: How Wal-Mart Uses Taxpayer Subsidies to Finance its Never-Ending Growth," Good Jobs First, May 2004, **http://www.goodjobsfirst.org/pdf/wmtstudy.pdf** (accessed August 11, 2009).

20. Press Release, "Robot Orders Down Sharply in First Half of 2009," Robotics Online, August 6, 2009, **http://www.robotics.org/content-detail.cfm/Industrial-Robotics-News/Robot-Orders-Down-Sharply-in-First-Half-of-2009/content_id/1637** (accessed August 11, 2009).

21. Laura Wilcox, "Surgeons Learning Robotics," e-Health Source of the Herald Dispatch, August 10, 2009, **http://www.herald-dispatch.com/life/healthsource/x1562572807/No-Headline** (accessed August 11, 2009).

22. O. C. Ferrell and Michael D. Hartline, *Marketing Strategy* (Mason, OH: South-Western, 2008), p. 256.

23. John Edwards, "Orange Seeks Agent," *Inband Logistics,* January 2006, pp. 239–242.

24. Ferrell and Hartline, *Marketing Strategy,* p. 256.

25. Bob Daniell, John Tracy, and Simon Kaye, "Made in China: Perspectives on the Global Manufacturing Giant," *Inbound Logistics,* March 2008, pp. 46–49.

26. Bruce Nussbaum, "Where Are the Jobs?" *BusinessWeek,* March 22, 2004, pp. 36–37.

27. Lisa H. Harington, "Balancing on the Rim," *Inband Logistics,* January 2006, pp. 168–170.

28. "Opinion Research Corporation, Survey of 1,012 Respondents," *USA Today Snapshots,* Public Influence on Outsourcing. October 4, 2005, p. B1.

29. *Air Travel Consumer Report,* Office of Aviation Enforcement and Proceedings, August 2009, **http://airconsumer.dot.gov/reports/2009/August/200908ATCR.PDF** (accessed August 11, 2009).

30. Alex Taylor III, "Wheeler Dealer," *Fortune,* October 15, 2007, pp. 50; Kellen Schetter, "Smart Car Offers Drivers New High MPG Option," *Greencar.com,* 2008, **www.greencar.com/features/smart-car** (accessed August 11, 2009); Michelle Krebs, "Smart Moves: Microcar Goes for Big Splash," *Auto Observer,* July 3, 2007, **www.autoobserver.com/2007/07/smart-moves-mic.html** (accessed March 17, 2008); FAQ, Smart Car America, **www.smartcarofamerica.com/faqs** (accessed August 11, 2009); *GasBuddy.com* (accessed August 11, 2009); Leila Abboud, "Small European Cars Shine," *The Wall Street Journal,* December 2, 2008, **http://online.wsj.com/article/SB122817265705770477.html** (accessed August 11, 2009).

31. Christopher Lawton, "The War on Product Returns," *The Wall Street Journal,* May 8, 2008, p. D1.

32. Ibid

33. Philip B. Crosby, *Quality Is Free: The Art of Making Quality Certain* (New York: McGraw-Hill, 1979), pp. 9–10.

34. Nigel F. Piercy, *Market-Led Strategic Change* (Newton, MA: Butterworth-Heinemann, 1992), pp. 374–385.

35. Hershey, "Hershey's Chocolate Kisses."

36. "Employment Opportunities," Careers in Supply Chain Management, **www.careersinsupplychain.org/career-outlook/empopp.asp** (accessed August 11, 2008).

Chapter 10

1. John Bishop, "The High Cost of Turnover," Ezine @rticles, March 13, 2007, **http://ezinearticles.com/?The-High-Cost-of-Turnover&id=486954** (accessed August 12, 2009).

2. Grey Carperter and Oliver Wyman, "The Totol Financial Import of Employee absences," October 2008, Marsh, Merces, Kroll, **www.Kronos.com/AbsenceAnonymous/media/Mercer-Survey-Highlights.pdf** (accessed August 13, 2009).

3. "Why individual incentives?," Marriot Hotels **http://www.marriott.com/incentives/incentive-travel-programs.mi,** (accessed August 12, 2009); "Teamwork Incentive Program," Washington Secretary of State, **http://www.secstate.wa.gov/productivityboard/tip.aspx** (accessed August 12, 2009).

4. "Why Individual Incentives?" **http://marriott.com/incentives/Travel.mi** (accessed June 20, 2006); "Teamwork Incentive Program," **www.secstate.wa.gov/productivityboard/tip.aspx** (accessed August 13, 2009).

5. "2009 Executive PayWatch," AFL-CIO, **http://www.aflcio.org/corporatewatch/paywatch/** (accessed August 12, 2009).

6. James Park, "You're Hired!," *Entrepreneur.com,* October 2007, **www.entrepreneur.com/article/printthis/184466.html** (accessed August 13, 2009); "Our Companies," Emerging Demographics, Inc., **www.emergingdemographics.com/our_companies.htm** (accessed August 13, 2009); "Management," *HireWorkers.com,* **www.hireworkers.com/management.php** (accessed August 13, 2009); "Pricing and Information for Hiring Help," *HireWorkers.com,* **www.hireworkers.com/hire_now.php** (accessed August 13, 2009); "About Us," *HireWorkers.com,* **www.hireworkers.com/AboutUs.php** (accessed August 13, 2009); "Online Service Allows Low-Wage Jobseekers to Access Recruitment Service by Phone in Multiple Languages," *PRNNewswire,* May 30, 2007, **www.java.sys-con.com/read/382561_p.htm** (accessed August 13, 2009).

7. "Comfort Means Productivity for Office Workers," October 20, 2004, **www.ergoweb.com/news/detail.cfm?id=1004** (accessed August 13, 2009).

8. Abraham Maslow, *Motivation and Personality* (New York: Harper & Row, 1954).

9. "Global Workforce Studies Highlights Alarming Trends," Hudson Institute, September 19, 2000, **http://www.hudson.org/index.cfm?fuseaction=publication_details&id=697** (accessed August 12, 2009).

10. John Tschohl, "Empowerment: The Key to Customer Service," **http://www.bizonline-content.com/BizResourceOnline/Wachovia/displayarticle.asp?id=54&clientid=8&categoryid=4** (accessed August 12, 2009).

11. Douglas McGregor, *The Human Side of Enterprise* (New York: McGraw-Hill, 1960), pp. 33–34.

12. Ibid, pp. 47–48.

13. "Meet Ray Anderson," The Purpose Prize, Civic Ventures, **www.purposeprize.org/finalists/finalists2007/anderson.cfm** (accessed August 13, 2009); Interface, Inc., Annual Report 2006, pp. 3–4, 7–8, 13–14, **http://library.corporate-ir.net/library/11/112/112931/items/242191/Interface_AR06.pdf** (accessed August 13, 2009); Who We Are/Founder, Interface, Inc., **www.interfaceinc.com/who/founder.html** (accessed August 13, 2009); Jennifer Beck, "Business Hero: Ray Anderson," **www.myhero.com/myheroaprint.asp?hero=r_anderson** (accessed August 13, 2009); Interface press releases, **www.interfaceglobal.com/Media-Center/Press-Releases.aspx** (accessed August 3, 2009).

14. Jon L. Pierce, Tatiana Kostova, and Kurt T. Kirks, "Toward a Theory of Psychological Ownership in Organizations, *Academy of Management Review* 26, no. 2 (2001), p. 298.

15. Jeanne Sahadi, "Where the (Best) 6-Figure Jobs Are," *CNNMoney.com,* **http://money.cnn.com/2006/07/13/pf/six_fig_farthest/index.htm** (accessed August 13, 2009).

16. The National Association for Shoplifting Prevention, **www.shopliftingprevention.org/The Issue.htm** (accessed August 13, 2009).

17. Archie Carroll, "Carroll: Do We Live in a Cheating Culture?" *Athens Banner-Herald,* February 21, 2004, **www.onlineathens.com/stories/022204/bus_20040222028.shtml.**

18. Geoff Colvin, "How Top Companies Breed Stars," September 20, 2007, **http://money.cnn.com/magazines/fortune/fortune_archive/2007/10/01/100351829/index.htm** (accessed August 13, 2009).

19. Amy Wrzesniewski and Jen E. Dutton, "Crafting a Job: Revisioning Employees as Active Crafters of Their Work," *Academy of Management Review* 26, no. 2 (2001), p. 179.

20. My Guides USA.com, "Which Jobs Offer Flexible Work Schedules?" **http://jobs.myguidesusa.com/answers-to-my-questions/which-jobs-offer-flexible-work-schedules?/** (accessed August 13, 2009).

21. Adam Geller, "Employers Cut 'Work/Life' Programs," *Sun,* October 23, 2003, **www.thesunlink.com/redesign/2003–10–23/business/290909.shtml.**

22. Larry Muhammad, "Help for the Helpers," *[Louisville] Courier-Journal,* April 20, 2004, **www.courier-journal.com/features/2004/04/20/helpers.html.**

23. "Annual Survey Shows Americans Are Working from Many Different Locations Outside Their Employer's Office," October 4, 2005, **www.workingfromanywhere.org/news/pr100405.htm** (accessed August 13, 2009).

24. "Telecommuting Benefits Documented," **www.telecommutect.com/content/benifits.htm** (accessed August 13, 2009)

25. "HR Executives Split on Telecommuting," *USA Today,* March 1, 2006, p. B1.

26. Stephanie Armour, "Telecommuting Gets Stuck in the Slow Lane," *USA Today,* June 25, 2001, pp. 1A, 2A.

27. Ron Mott, "For Best Buy Workers, a 'Racial' Orientation," *NBC Nightly News with Brian Williams,* **www.msnbc.msn.com/id/3032619/#23960059** (accessed August 13, 2009); Zac Bissonnette, "Best Buy Workers Make a Serious Commitment to Diversity," *BloggingStocks,* April. 6, 2008, **www.bloggingstocks.com/2008/04/06/best-buy-workers-makes-a-serious-commitment-to-diversity** (accessed August 13, 2009); Best Buy Corporate Responsibility, **http://69.12.100/csr/people.asp;** "Diversity," Best Buy Career Center, **http://69.12.100/CareerCenter/Diversity.asp** (accessed August 13, 2009); "Culture," Best Buy Career Center, **http://69.12.100/CareerCenter/Culture.asp** (accessed August 13, 2009); "About the Museum," National Civil Rights Museum, **www.civilrightsmuseum.org/about/about.asp** (accessed August 13, 2009); Sarah Boehle, "Best Buy Gets Innovative with Women's Leadership," *MANAGEsmarter,* December 16, 2008, **www.managesmarter.com/msg/content_display/training/e3iaa83ea53feec6959a9b57fba9188f7ac?imw=Y** (accessed August 13, 2009).

Chapter 11

1. Procter & Gamble, "U.S. Recruiting process," **www.pg.com/jobs/recruitblue/recprocess.shtml** (accessed August 13, 2009).

2. Ibid.

3. Jerry Bowles, "Putting Supplier Diversity to Work," *BusinessWeek,* April 16, 2007, pp. 68–69; "AT&T," **www.att.com** (accessed August 13, 2009); "AT&T Selected as the No. 1 Organization for Multicultural Business Opportunities," **www.attsuppliers.com/diversity.asp** (accessed August 13, 2009); "NMSDC Announces Top Regional Minority Suppliers," National Minority Supplier Development Council, **www.nmsdc.org/news/2007_NMSDC_%20Regional_%20Suppliers_of_%20the_Year.pdf** (accessed August 13, 2009); "Corporate Profile," *AT&T,* **www.att.com/gen/investor-relations?pid=5711** (accessed August 13, 2009); "Citizenship and Sustainability," *AT&T,* **www.att.com/gen/corporate-citizenship?pid=7753** (accessed August 13, 2009).

4. "What Does Employee Alcohol & Drug Use Cost Your Business," DWI Resource Center, **www.dwiresourcecenter.org/bizcenter/workplace/cost.shtml** (accessed August 13, 2009).

5. Associated Press, "Food Network Chef Fired After Resume Fraud," *USA Today,* March 3, 2008, **www.usatoday.com/news/nation/2008-03-03-chef-fired_N.htm** (accessed August 13, 2009).

6. "Charge Statistics FY 1992 through FY 2008," Equal Employment Opportunity Commission (n.d.), **www.eeoc.gov/stats/charges.html** (accessed August 13, 2009).

7. Joseph Daniel McCool, "Diversity Pledge Ring Hollow," *BusinessWeek,* February 5, 2008, **www.businessweek.com/managing/content/feb2008/ca2008025_080192.htm?chan=search** (accessed August 13, 2009).

8. Stephen Bastien, "12 Benefits of Hiring Older Workers," *Entrepreneur.com,* September 20, 2006, **www.entrepreneur.com/humanresources/hiring/article167500.html** (accessed August 13, 2009).

9. Ellen Wulfhorst, "U.S. Gender Pay Gap Emerges Early, Study Finds," *Reuters,* April 23, 2007, **www.reuters.com/article/topNews/idUSN2029109620070423** (accessed August 13, 2009).

10. Michael Sanserino and Cari Tuna, "Companies Strive Harder to Please Customers," *Wall Street Journal,* July 27, 2009, **http://online.wsj.com/article/SB124864862273182247.html** (accessed August 13, 2009).

11. "US Career Advice Functions," Procter & Gamble, **http://www.pg.com/jobs/jobs_us/cac/functions.shtml** (accessed August 13, 2009).

12. Creative Group survey of 125 advertising executives and 125 senior marketing executives; "What Is the Greatest Benefit for Students or Graduates in an Internship Program, Aside from Pay?" *USA Today Snapshots,* May 5, 2009, p. B1.

13. Patrick Thibodeau, "Best Buy Settles Age Discrimination Lawsuit with Former IT Workers," *Computerworld,* June 26, 2007, **www.computerworld.com/action/article.do?command=viewArticleBasic&articleId=9025759** (accessed August 13, 2009).

14. Maury A. Peiperl, "Getting 360-Degree Feedback Right," *Harvard Business Review,* January 2001, pp. 142–48.

15. Chris Musselwhite, "Self Awareness and the Effective Leader," *Inc.com,* **www.inc.com/resources/leadership/articles/20071001/musselwhite.html** (accessed August 13, 2009).

16. Laura Lorber, "A Corporate Culture Makeover," *The Wall Street Journal,* **http://online.wsj.com/article/SB120827656392416609.html** (accessed August 13, 2009).

17. Anne Fisher, "Workplace: Turning Clock Watchers into Stars," *Fortune,* March 8, 2004, **www.fortune.com.**

18. Associated Press, "General Motors Downsizing Plants, Cars," *Herald Net,* **www.heraldnet.com/article/20080604/BIZ/91714729** (accessed August 13, 2009); **GMReinvention.com** (accessed August 13, 2009).

19. "2008 Corporate Social Responsibility Report," CVS/CareMark, **http://info.cvscaremark.com/sites/cvscaremark.com/files/2008_CVS_Caremark_CSR_Report.pdf** (accessed August 13, 2009).

20. U.S. Department of Labor, "Minimum Wage," **http://www.dol.gov/dol/topic/wages/minimumwage.htm** (accessed April 28, 2009).

21. "About," The Working Poor Families Project," **http://www.workingpoorfamilies.org/about.html** (accessed August 13, 2009).

22. "100 Best Companies to Work for 2008," *Fortune,* **http://money.cnn.com/magazines/fortune/bestcompanies/2008/snapshots/7.html** (accessed August 13, 2009); Starbucks 2006 Annual Report, pp. 11–15, **http://media.corporate-ir.net/media_files/irol/99/99518/reports/StarbucksAnnualReport.pdf** (accessed August 13, 2009); Starbucks 2007 Annual Report, p. 7; "OCA Declares Victory in Its 'Frankenbucks' Campaign," Organic Consumers Association, **http://organicconsumers.org/Starbucks/index.cfm** (accessed August 13, 2009); Sonia Narang, "Carbon with That Latte?," *Forbes,* July 3, 2007, **www.forbes.com/2007/07/02/starbucks-emissions-environment-biz-cz_sn_0703green_carbon.html** (accessed August 13, 2009); **www.starbucks.com**; Company fact sheet, **www.starbucks.com/aboutus/Company_Factsheet.pdf** (accessed May 6, 2009).

23. David Kiley, "Crafty Basket Makers Cut Downtimes, Waste," *USA Today,* May 10, 2001, p. C1.

24. "Kele & Co: First Innovative Jewelry Company in Direct Sales," May 5, 2008, **www.24-7pressrelease.com/press-release/kele-co-the-first-innovative-jewelry-company-in-direct-sales-48835.php** (accessed August 13, 2009).

25. "Advantages," DreamMaker Remodeling, **http://www.dreamaker-remodel.com/franchiseopportunities/advantages.cfm** (August 13, 2009).

26. Winston Wood, "Work Week," *The Wall Street Journal,* May 1, 2001, p. A1.

27. "Employer Costs for Employee Compensation," U.S. Bureau of Labor Statistics, March 12, 2008, **www.bls.gov/news.release/ecec.nr0.htm** (accessed August 13, 2009).

28. Marilyn Odesser-Torpey, "The Benefits Advantage," *QSR* (n.d.), **www.qsrmagazine.com/issue/62/benefits.phtml** (accessed August 13, 2009).

29. "#38. Microsoft, 100 Best Companies to Work For, 2009," *Fortune,* **http://money.cnn.com/magazines/fortune/bestcompanies/2009/snapshots/38.html** (accessed August 13, 2009); Todd Bishop, "Microsoft trims benefits to cut costs," *Seattle Pi,* May 20, 2004, **http://www.seattlepi.com/business/174131_msftbenefit20.html** (accessed August 13, 2009).

30. Jesse Russell, "Despite Union Percentage Declines, Union Workers Make More Money," *Workers Independent News,* January 31, 2007, **www.laborradio.org/node/5182** (accessed August 13, 2009).

31. "Southern California Strike," UFCW, **http://www.ufcw.org/your_industry/retail/strike_updates/index.cfm** (accessed August 13, 2009).

32. "Work Stoppages Involving 1,000 or More Workers, 1947–2008," U.S. Department of Labor, February 11, 2009, **www.bls.gov/news.release/wkstp.t01.htm** (accessed August 13, 2009).

33. Jason Dean, "The Forbidden City of Terry Gou," *The Wall Street Journal,* August 11–12, 2007, pp. A1, A5; Luisa Kroll, "The World's Billionaires: #160 Terry Gou," *Forbes.com,* March 5, 2008, **www.forbes.com/lists/2008/10/billionaires08_Terry-Gou_X28Q.html** (accessed August 13, 2009); "The Information Technology Top 100: #2 Hon Hai Precision Inc.," *BusinessWeek,* **www.businessweek.com/it100/2005/company/HONHI.htm** (accessed August 13, 2009).

34. Jena McGregor, "Women: Nearing a Majority at Work?," *Businessweek,* August 11, 2009, **http://www.businessweek.com/careers/managementiq/archives/2009/08/women_nearing_a.html** (accessed August 13, 2009).

35. Annie Finnigan, "Different Strokes," *Working Woman,* April 2001, p. 44.

36. Feliciano Garcia, "US West Has the Tool," *Fortune,* July 10, 2000, p. 198.

37. Taylor H. Cox, Jr., "The Multicultural Organization," *Academy of Management Executives* 5 (May 1991), pp. 34–47; Marilyn Loden and Judy B. Rosener, *Workforce America! Managing Employee Diversity as a Vital Resource* (Homewood, IL: Business One Irwin, 1991).

Chapter 12

1. Sean Gregory, "Cool Runnings," *Time,* October 15, 2007, pp. Global 9–10.

2. Lisa McLaughlin, "Paper, Plastic or Prada?," *Time,* August 13, 2007, pp. 49–51; Megha Bahree, "Bag Lady," *Forbes,* November 26, 2007, **http://members.forbes.com/forbes/2007/1126/109.html** (accessed August 17, 2009); Carolyn Sayre, "Just Say No to Plastic Bags: The Global Warming Survival Guide," *Time,* **www.time.com/time/specials/2007/environment/article/0,28804,1602354_1603074_1603179,00.html** (accessed August 17, 2009); Kathreen Ricketson, "Plastic Fantastic? Recycled Jewelry," *Treehugger,*

February 21, 2007, **www.treehugger.com/files/2007/02/plastic_fantastic.php** (accessed August 17, 2009); Maurye Audet, "Homestead Diva: New Ways to Recycle Plastic Bags," *Hub-Pages,* **http://hubpages.com/hub/Recycle-Plastic-Bags** (accessed August 17, 2009).

3. **www.mcdonalds.com/usa/eat/nutrition_info/simplesteps.html** (accessed August 17, 2009).

4. Marguerite Higgins, "McDonalds Labels Nutrition," *The Washington Times,* October 26, 2005, **washingtontimes.com/business/20051025-102731-2213r.htm** (accessed August 17, 2009).

5. Michael Treacy and Fred Wiersema, *The Discipline of Market Leaders* (Reading, MA: Addison Weslsey, 1995), p. 176.

6. "Customer Is King—Says Who," *Advertising Age,* April 15, 2006, p. 4.

7. Matthew Miller, "Playing Cupid to the Rich and Famous," *Forbes,* May 30, 2007, **www.forbes.com/entrepreneurs/management/2007/05/30/matchmaking-small-business-ent-manage-cx_mm_0530match.html?feed=rss_entrepreneurs_entremgmt** (accessed August 17, 2009); *Samantha's Table,* **www.samanthastable.com** (accessed February 5, 2008).

8. Wallace Witkowski, "Mars, Incorporated Completes Acquisition of Wm. Wrigley Jr. Company," *IT News,* October 6, 2008, **http://www.itnews.it/news/2008/1006225001848/mars-incorporated-completes-acquisition-of-wm-wrigley-jr-company.html** (accessed August 17, 2009).

9. "Dell targets students with new netbook," *Business Mirror,* June 29, 2009, **http://businessmirror.com.ph/component/content/article/52-technology/12418-dell-targets-students-with-new-netbook.html** (accessed August 17, 2009).

10. "Fastest Growing Demographic on Facebook: Women Over 55," *Inside Facebook,* February 2, 2009, **http://www.insidefacebook.com/2009/02/02/fastest-growing-demographic-on-facebook-women-over-55/** (accessed August 17, 2009).

11. Mya Frazier, "Staples Gains Footing in Hispanic Market," *Advertising Age,* April 3, 2006, p. 58.

12. Courtney E. Counts, "Interactivism Allows Consumers to Co-Create, Grows Loyalty," *Marketing News,* October 1, 2006, p. 6.

13. Moon Ihlwan, "Samsung's Plan to Widen its Range," *Business-week,* August 24 and 31, 2009, p. 30.

14. Charles Passy, "Your Scoop Is in the Mail," *The Wall Street Journal,* May 25, 2001, pp. W1, W6.

15. Dean Reynolds, "The Price of the Perfect Name? $350," *ABC News,* July 10, 2007, **http://abcnews.go.com/print?id=3363739** (accessed August 17, 2009); *Baby Naming Central,* **www.babynamingcentral.com** (accessed August 17, 2009); *Name Structures,* **http://namepower101.com** (accessed August 17, 2009); Alexandra Alter, "The Baby-Name Business," *The Wall Street Journal,* June 22, 2007, pp. W1, W12.

16. "The Coca Cola Company Fact Sheet," **www.TheCoca-Cola Company.com/our company/pdf/Company_Fact_Sheet.pdf** (accessed August 17, 2009).

17. John Simons, "Don't Count blockbuster Out," *Money.CNN.com,* March 6, 2008, **http://money.cnn.com/2008/03/06/technology/simons_blockbuster.fortune/index.htm?section=money_technology** (accessed August 17, 2009).

18. Laura Petrecca, "Marketers Say 'Tanks' for Buying with Gifts of Gas," *USA Today,* June 4, 2008, p. 3B.

19. "Focus Groups in Nebraska Help Market Tourism," *Marketing News,* January 6, 2003, p. 5.

20. "Online Research Spending Predicted to Grow to $4 Billion," GMI press, June 14, 2005, **http://www.gmi-mr.com/about-us/news/archive.php?p=2005-06-14** (accessed August 17, 2009).

21. Look-Look, **http://www.look-look.com/look/pdfs/presskit.pdf** (accessed August 17, 2009).

22. Diane Brady, "Pets Are People Too, You Know," *BusinessWeek,* November 28, 2005, p. 114.

23. Emily Nelson, "P&G Checks Out Real Life," *The Wall Street Journal,* May 17, 2001, p. B1.

24. "Procter & Gamble's real-life promo builds online cred," *Smart-Brief on Social Media,* July 27, 2009, **http://www.smartbrief.com/news/socialmedia/storyDetails.jsp?issueid=1056F1BE-F925-44C5-AEEE-738FF9E7F319&copyid=3C5727F9-6C0A-483F-8CC1-4D890879F76D&brief=socialmedia&sb_code=rss&&campaign=rss** (accessed August 17, 2009).

25. Bryan Walsh, "Why Green Is the New Red, White and Blue," *Time,* April 28, 2008, pp. 45–48; Denis Ryan, "Taking the Green change," *The Vancouver Sun,* May 31, 2008, pp.136–137.

Chapter 13

1. **www.dominos.com/Public-EN/site+Content/secondary/inside+dominos/pizza+particulars/** (accessed June 14, 2006).

2. William Hupp, "The Dog Days of Dieting," *Advertising Age,* April 14, 2008, p. 14.

3. Michelle Krebs, "2007 Detroit Auto Show: Chevrolet Volt," *Edmunds,* January 7, 2007, **www.edmunds.com/insideline/do/Features/articleId=119088?mktcat=chevrolet-volt-pricing-ad-copy&kw=chevrolet+volt+pricing+ad+copy&mktid=gc47736448** (accessed August 28, 2009).

4. Amy Barrett, with Christopher Palmeri and Stephanie Anderson Forest, "Hot Growth Companies," *BusinessWeek,* June 7, 2004, pp. 86–90.

5. Judann Pollack, "The Endurance Test, Heinz Ketchup," *Advertising Age,* November 14, 2005, p. 39.

6. Faith Keenan, "Friendly Spies on the Net," *BusinessWeek e.biz,* July 9, 2001, p. EB27.

7. Seasons 52, **www.seasons52.com** (accessed August 28, 2009).

8. Bruce Horovitz, "Scooping Out New Territory: Soft Serve," *USA Today,* May 8, 2008, p. 3B.

9. "Light Truck Sales Plummet in 2008," *Green Car Congress,* June 3, 2008, **www.greencarcongress.com/2008/06/light-truck-sal.html** (accessed August 28, 2009); "April 2008 Dashboard: Hybrids Sales Defy Recession," *HybridCars.com,* May 13, 2008, **www.hybridcars.com/market-dashboard/april-2008-hybrids-defy-recession.html** (accessed August 28, 2009).

10. New Release, "Revolving Power of Tide StainBrush is Latest Tool in "Revolution" Against Stains," Proctor & Gamble Investor, **http://www.pginvestor.com/phoenix.zhtml?c=104574&p=irol-newsArticle&ID=628887&highlight=** (accessed August 28, 2009).

11. Philip Elmer-DeWitt, "How to Grow the iPod as the MP3 Player Market Shrinks," *Fortune.com,* January 29, 2008, **http://apple20.blogs.fortune.cnn.com/2008/01/29/beyond-the-incredible-shrinking-ipod-market/** (accessed August 28, 2009); "iTunes Store

Tops Over Five Billion Songs Sold," *Apple.com*, www.apple.com/pr/library/2008/06/19itunes.html (accessed August 28, 2009); Charles Gaba, "iPod Sales Quarterly and Total," *Mac Vs PC System Shootout*, www.systemshootouts.org/ipod_sales.html (accessed August 28, 2009).

12. Bruce Horovitz, "Snacks: Does This Bag Make Me Look Fat?," *USA Today*, February 20, 2008, p B1.

13. T. L. Stanley, "Barbie Hits the Skids," *Advertising Age*, October 31, 2005, pp. 1, 33.

14. Michael Fielding, "Private-Label Brands Use New Tools to Compete," *Marketing News*, May 15, 2006, p. 11.

15. Alessandra Galloni, "Advertising," *The Wall Street Journal*, June 1, 2001, p. B6.

16. Ina Steiner, "Amazon.com Lets Customers Rate Packaging," Auction Bytes, August 28, 2009, http://www.auctionbytes.com/cab/abn/y09/m08/i28/s04 (accessed August 28, 2009).

17. Pallavi Gogoi, "McDonald's New Wrap," *BusinessWeek*, February 17, 2006, www.businessweek.com/print/bwdaily/dnflash/feb2006/nf20060217_8329_db016.htm?chan=db (accessed August 28, 2009).

18. "ACSI: Customer Satisfaction Halts Slide, Glimmer of Hope for the Economy?," *American Customer Satisfaction Index*, May 20, 2008, www.theacsi.org/images/stories/images/news/0508Q1.pdf (accessed August 28, 2009); Joe Kleinsasser, "AirTran Takes Top AQR Spot; Industry Score Falls To New Low," *This Is Wichita State*, April 16, 2008, www.wichita.edu/thisis/wsunews/news/?nid=182 (accessed August 28, 2009).

19. Katy McLaughlin, "Kombucha Grows On You, Some Say, Like a Fungus," *The Wall Street Journal*, June 23–24, 2007, pp. A-1, A-7; Conan Milner, "Kombucha, Part 1," *The Epoch Times*, March 16, 2007, http://en.epochtimes.com/news/7-3-16/52931.html (accessed August 28, 2009); Conan Milner, "Kombucha, Part 2," *The Epoch Times*, March 22, 2007, http://en.epochtimes.com/news/7-3-22/53236.html (accessed August 28, 2009); "What Can Kombucha Do for Me?," www.gtskombucha.com (accessed August 28, 2009); "The Story Behind the Bottle," www.gtskombucha.com (accessed August 28, 2009).

20. Stephanie Miles, "Consumer Groups Want to Rate the Web," *The Wall Street Journal*, June 21, 2001, p. B13.

21. "American Demographics 2006 Consumer Perception Survey," *Advertising Age*, January 2, 2006, p. 9. Data by Synovate.

22. Rajneesh Suri and Kent B. Monroe, "The Effects of Time Constraints on Consumers' Judgments of Prices and Products," *Journal of Consumer Research* 30 (June 2003), pp. 92+.

23. Linda Tischler, "The Price Is Right," *Fast Company*, November 2003, pp. 83+.

24. Andy Stone, "Drill Bits Are Forever," *Forbes*, December 10, 2007, p. 200.

25. "All Cayenne Models," Porsche, www.porsche.com/usa/models/cayenne/ (accessed August 28, 2009).

26. Ricardo Castillo Mireles, "In Mexico, Big Cola is the Real Thing," Logistics Today, March 2, 2004, http://logisticstoday.com/operations_strategy/outlog_story_6366/index.html (accessed August 28, 2009); Fernando Chevarría León, "Los genios de las botellas (The Genies in the Bottles)," América Economía, August 28, 2009, http://www.americaeconomia.com/327024-Los-genios-de-las-botellas.note.aspx (accessed August 28, 2009).

27. Reena Jana, "Green Threads for the Eco Chic," *BusinessWeek*, September 27, 2006, www.businessweek.com/print/innovate/content/sep2006/id20060927_111136.htm (accessed August 28, 2009); Laura McClure, "Green Jeans," *Reader's Digest*, June 2007, p. 21; "Levi's Brand Launches 100% Organic Cotton Jeans," www.levistrauss.com, July 5, 2006, www.levistrauss.com/News/PressReleaseDetail.aspx?pid=784 (accessed August 28, 2009); "Levi's Eco," *Levi's*, http://us.levi.com/family/index.jsp?categoryId=3146907&cp=3146849.3146902 (accessed August 28, 2009); Mintel International, "Mintel Finds Fewer Americans Interested in Going "Green" During Recession," *Yahoo!Finance*, February 20, 2009, http://finance.yahoo.com/news/Mintel-Finds-Fewer-Americans-bw-14426203.html (accessed August 28, 2009); "Organic Cotton Facts," *Organic Trade Association*, February 2009, www.ota.com/organic/mt/organic_cotton.html (accessed August 28, 2009).

28. Emily Bryson York, "Taco Bell Tops Yum Portfolio After Tough Year," *Advertising Age*, May 12, 2008, p. 16.

29. Emily Bryson York, "McD's Dollar-Menu Fixation Sparks Revolt," *Advertising Age*, June 2, 2008, p. 1.

30. "2009 Statistical Abstract: Online Retail Sales," U.S. Census Bureau, http://www.census.gov/compendia/statab/cats/wholesale_retail_trade/online_retail_sales.html (accessed August 28, 2009).

31. O. C. Ferrell and Michael D. Hartline, *Marketing Strategy* (Mason, OH: South-Western, 2005), p. 215.

32. "Top Threats to Revenue," *USA Today*, February 1, 2006, p. A1.

33. Brad Howarth, "Hear This, iPods from a Vending Machine," *The Sydney Morning Herald*, November 14, 2006, www.smh.com.au/news/biztech/hear-this-ipods-from-a-vending-machine/2006/11/13/1163266481869.html (accessed August 28, 2009).

34. Jonathon Ramsey, "Danica Patrick's GoDaddy.com Ad Banned from Super Bowl Because of Beavers," *autoblog.com*, January 24, 2008, www.autoblog.com/2008/01/24/danica-patricks-godaddy-com-ad-banned-from-super-bowl-because-o/ (accessed August 28, 2009).

35. Stephanie Kang, "BMW Ran Risk With Silent Role in Mockumentary," *The Wall Street Journal*, June 20, 2008, p. B5.

36. Brad Wilson. Bradsdeals home page. http://bradsdeals.com/ (accessed August 28, 2009); Michael S. Malone. "The Twitter Revolution." *The Wall Street Journal*. April 18, 2009, p. A11; Ann Meyer. "Facebook, Twitter, Other Social Media Help Drive Business for Small Firms." *Chicagotribune.com*, April 27, 2009, www.chicagotribune.com/business/chi-mon-minding-social-media-042apr27,0,7593202.story (accessed August 28, 2009); Bill Pride and O.C. Ferrell, *Marketing*. Boston, MA: Houghton-Mifflin, 2010.

37. Michael J. Weiss, "To Be About to Be," *American Demographics* 25 (September 2003), pp. 29–36.

38. Gerry Khermouch and Jeff Green, "Buzz Marketing," *BusinessWeek*, July 30, 2001, pp. 50–56.

39. PRNewswire, "New Research Reveals Surge in Online Activity and Overall Coupon Usage as Year Progresses," March 11, 2009, www.reuters.com/article/pressRelease/idUS191459+11-Mar-2009+PRN20090311 (accessed August 28, 2009).

40. Kate MacArthur, "Sierra Mist: Cie Nicholson," *Advertising Age,* November 17, 2003, p. S-2.

41. "Coca-Cola North America Announces the Launch of VAULT," February 17, 2006, **www2.coca-cola.com/presscenter/newprod ucts_vault.html** (accessed August 28, 2009).

Chapter 14

1. "Post-Enron Restatements Hit Record," *MSNBC,* January 21, 2003, **www.msnbc.com/news/862325.asp.**

2. "Break up the Big Four?" *CFO,* June 1, 2004, **www.cfo.com/article/ 1,5309,14007%7C%7CM%7C926,00.html**, (accessed August 28, 2009).

3. Laura Demars, "Protectionist Measures," *CFO,* March 2006, p. 18.

4. Beth Braverman, "Corporate Fraud Cost is Up 22% at Average Biz," Financial Week, September 14, 2008, **http://www .financialweek.com/apps/pbcs.dll/article?AID=/20080914/ REG/809149995/1049/COMPLIANCE** (accessed August 28, 2009).

5. "About the ACFE," Association of Certified Fraud Examiners, **http://www.acfe.com/about/about.asp** (accessed August 28, 2009).

6. Andrew Ross Sorkin, "Suspending Mark-to-Market: Bad Policy, Bad Time," *The New York Times DealBook Blog,* March 31, 2009, **http://dealbook.blogs.nytimes.com/2009/03/31/suspending -mark-to-market-bad-policy-bad-time/?scp=1&sq=mark %20to%20market%20accounting&st=cse** (accessed August 28, 2009); Floyd Norris, "Banks Get New Leeway in Valuing Their Assets," *The New York Times,* April 2, 2009, **www.nytimes .com/2009/04/03/business/03fasb.html?scp=2&sq=mark %20to%20market%20accounting&st=cse.** (accessed August 28, 2009).

7. Jessica C. Kraft, "Paperless Banking Is Good for your Green," *RiverWired.com*, June 10, 2008, **www.riverwired.com/blog/ paperless-banking-good-your-green** (accessed August 28, 2009); "Motivating Consumer Adoption of Green-Paperless-Banking," *paymentsnews.com*, June 2008, **www.paymentsnews .com/2008/06/motivating-cons.html** (accessed August 28, 2009); *payitgreen.org* (accessed August 28, 2009).

8. Nicholas Day, "Wheeling Down the CT Cheese Trail," *The Hartford Advocate,* October18, 2007, pp. 19–21; "About Us," *Beltane Farm,* **www.beltanefarm.com** (accessed August 28, 2009); *Saxelby Cheesemongers,* **www/saxelbycheese.com** (accessed August 28, 2009).

9. "Occupational Outlook Handbook 2008–2009: Accountants and Auditors," *Bureau of Labor Statistics,* **www.bls.gov/oco/ ocos001.htm** (accessed August 28, 2009).

Chapter 15

1. "How Currency Gets into Circulation," Federal Reserve Bank of New York (n.d.), **www.newyorkfed.org/aboutthefed/fedpoint/fed01 .html** (accessed August 31, 2009).

2. Barbara Hagenbaugh, "It's Too Easy Being Green," *USA Today,* May 13, 2003, **http://www.usatoday.com/money/industries/banking/ 2003-05-12-newmoney_x.htm** (accessed August 31, 2009).

3. Ibid.

4. "About the Redesigned Currency," United States Currency and Bills, **http://www.moneyfactory.gov/newmoney/main.cfm/currency/ aboutNotes?CFID=1013794&CFTOKEN=63947712** (accessed August 31, 2009).

5. Jane J. Kim, "The Credit-Card Catapult," *The Wall Street Journal,* March 25–26, 2006, p. B1.

6. Emily Thornton, Heather Timmons, and Joseph Weber, "Who Will Hold the Cards," *BusinessWeek,* March 19, 2001, p. 90.

7. "Card Debt," Card Trak, May 2004, **http://cardweb.com/cardtrak/ pastissues/may2004.html** (accessed August 31, 2009).

8. David Breitkopf, "MasterCard, Pulse Report Wider Use of Debit Cards," *American Banker,* May 17, 2004, p. 5.

9. General Electric, **www.ge.com**; General Commercial Finance, **http://gecommercialfinance.gecapsol.com/cms/servlet/cmsview/ ComFin_Corp/prod/en/main/index.html**; GE Capital, **http://gecapsol .com/cms/servlet/cmsview/GE_Capital_Solutions/prod/en/index .html** (accessed August 31, 2009).

10. Ian Rowley, "Banking on U.S. Acquisitions," *CFO,* February 2003, pp. 79–80.

11. Jeremy Quittner, "I Am My Own Banker," *Business Week,* February/March 2007, p. 16; "Lakeway's Independent Bank Earns Top National Ranking," *Lake Travis Business,* April 26, 2007, **www .ibankaustin.com/3004-01-IBA/UserFiles/File/LTV%201%20Ranking .pdf** (accessed August 31, 2009); Press release, "Independent Bank of Austin (TX), SSB, 2nd Qtr. Net Profit up 16.6%; Assets, Loans, Deposits Rise Sharply at Lakeway, Georgetown Operations; Bank Adds Employees, Announces HQ Construction Progress," *Press Release Newswire,* **www.prweb.com/releases/2007/7/prweb542320 .htm** (accessed August 31, 2009).

12. Christine Dugas, "Officials Order New Mutual Fund Reforms," *USA Today,* February 12, 2004, **http://www.usatoday.com/money/ perfi/funds/2004-02-12-secfunds_x.htm** (accessed August 31, 2009).

13. Bank of America 2008 Annual Report, p. 16; "Bank of America Wins Top Environmental Leadership Award from California Governor," *TradingMarkets.com,* November 26, 2008, **www .tradingmarkets.com/.site/news/Stock%20News/2051715/** (accessed August 31, 2009); Jonathan Stempel, "Bank of America Creates Environmental Banking Team," Reuters, February 12, 2008, **www.reuters.com/article/companyNewsAndPR/ idUSN1225091020080212** (accessed August 31, 2009).

14. "Number of U.S. Online Banking Customers Continues to Grow," IT News Online, April 21, 2009, **http://www.itnewsonline .com/showprnstory.php?storyid=42376** (accessed August 31, 2009).

15. "CSI Pennsylvania," *CFO Magazine,* March 2008, p. 92.

Chapter 16

1. Andrew Ross Sorkin, "JP Morgan Pays $2 a Share for Bear Stearns," *The New York Times,* March 17, 2008, **www.nytimes .com/2008/03/17/business/17bear.html** (accessed September 1, 2009); Bear Stearns, **www.bearstearns.com;** Investor Relations, **www.bearstearns.com/sitewide/investor_relations/index.htm.**

2. Tim Reason, "Hidden in Plain Sight," *CFO,* August 2005, p. 59.

3. Alex Salkever, "It's Time for an iPod IPO," *BusinessWeek,* May 5, 2004, **www.businessweek.com.**

4. Aili McConnon, "Bigger Kids Want to Dress Cool, Too," *BusinessWeek,* June 30, 2008, p. 62; *RealKidz,* **www.realkidzclothing.com;** Kathrine Yung, "Funding Isn't Child's Play," *Detroit Free Press,* June 15, 2008, **www.freep.com/apps/pbcs.dll/article?AID=/20080615/BUSINESS06/806150553** (accessed September 1, 2009); Special Health Issue: "Our Super-Sized Kids," *Time,* June 23, 2008.

5. Geoff Colvin and Jessica Shambora, "J&J: Secrets of Success," *Fortune ,* May 4, 2009, p. 118.

6. "Rebuilding the Banks, A Special Report on International Banking," *The Economist,* May 16, 2009, pp. 3–20.

7. First Solar, **http://www.firstsolar.com** (accessed September 1, 2009); Gene Marcial, "First Solar's Bright Future," *BusinessWeek,* August 9, 2009, **http://www.businessweek.com/investor/content/aug2009/pi2009087_955238_page_2.htm** (accessed September 1, 2009); "First Solar, Inc." Google Finance, **http://www.google.com/finance?q=NASDAQ%3AFSLR** (accessed September 1, 2009).

8. Vincent Ryan, "From Wall Street to Main Street," *CFO,* June 2008, pp. 85–86.

CREDITS

Chapter 12

p. 226–227, © BananaStock/JupiterImages.

p. 228, © FilmMagic/Getty Images.

p. 231, © AP Photo/Brian Kersey.

p. 234, Courtesy of J&D's.

p. 237, © image 100/Alamy.

p. 238, Courtesy of Western Wats.

p. 240, © Benetton Group SPA; Photo by Oliviero Toscani.

p. 241, © Copyright 1997 IMS Communications Ltd/Capstone Design. All Rights Reserved.

Chapter 13

p. 244–245, © BananaStock/JupiterImages.

p. 246, © Stephane De Sakutin/AFP/Getty Images.

p. 248, © PhotoLink/Getty Images.

p. 249, © The McGraw-Hill Companies, Inc./Lars A. Niki, photographer.

p. 252, © Cathy Melloan/PhotoEdit.

p. 253, Courtesy The Coca-Cola Company.

p. 256, © Getty Images.

p. 258, Courtesy of Ruan.

p. 260, © Getty Images.

Chapter 14

p. 268–269, © Fancy Photography/Veer.

p. 272 top, © Digital Vision/Getty Images.

p. 272 bottom, Courtesy of Huron Consulting Group.

p. 279, © Stockbyte/Punchstock Images.

p. 283, © Royalty-Free/Corbis.

p. 287, Reproduced with permission of Yahoo! Inc. © 2009 Yahoo! Inc. YAHOO! and the YAHOO! Logo are registered trademarks of Yahoo! Inc.

Chapter 15

p. 292 left, © Beathan/Corbis.

p. 292–293, © BananaStock/PictureQuest.

p. 293 right, © BananaStock/JupiterImages.

p. 294, Courtesy Yap Tourism Bureau.

p. 295, © AP Photo/Lee Jin-man.

p. 298, © Getty Images/Photodisc.

p. 299, © Imagemore Co., Ltd./Corbis.

p. 304, Courtesy of Worthington National Bank. Photo by Glen Ellman.

p. 305, © AFP/Getty Images.

p. 307, Courtesy of Franklin Templeton Investments.

Chapter 16

p. 312, © Getty Images/Digital Vision.

p. 314, Courtesy of the U.S. Department of the Treasury, Bureau of the Public Debt.

p. 316, © The McGraw-Hill Companies, Inc./John Flournoy, photographer.

p. 318, © IMS Communications Ltd./Capstone Design/Flatearth Images.

p. 321, © Paul Springett/Alamy.

p. 322 top, © Getty Images.

p. 322 bottom, Courtesy International Business Machines Corporation.

p. 326, © The McGraw-Hill Companies, Inc.

M

MacArthur, Kate, 345
Macy's, 298
MADD (Mothers Against Drunk Driving), 4
Madoff, Bernie, 25, 29
Magnuson-Mass Warranty (FTC) Act (1975), 50
Malcolm Baldrige National Quality Award, 116, 183–184
Malone, Michael S., 344
Management
  areas of, 138–139
  career options in, 146
  controlling function of, 135
  directing function of, 134
  explanation of, 130
  functions of, 6
  importance of, 130
  levels of, 135–138
  organizing function of, 133
  planning function of, 130–133
  reality of, 145–147
  span of, 157
  staffing function of, 133–134
Management information systems (MIS), 77–78
Managerial accounting, 271–272
Managers
  administrative, 139
  analytical skills of, 142
  background of, 142–143
  compensation for, 146
  conceptual skills of, 141–142
  decision-making role of, 143–145
  explanation of, 130
  financial, 137
  first-line, 137, 138
  human relations skills of, 142
  human resources, 138–139
  inexperienced, 119–120
  influence of, 30–31
  informational technology, 139
  leadership skills for, 139–141
  marketing, 139
  middle, 137–138
  production and operations, 138
  resources for, 120–121
  roles of, 31, 140
  technical expertise of, 141
  top, 135–137
Mandel, Michael J., 335
Manning, Eli, 7
Manning, Peyton, 7
Manufacturer, 172
Manufacturing
  computer-assisted, 177
  computer-integrated, 178
  as element of management, 6
  explanation of, 170
  flexible, 178
  small-business, 116
Manufacturing economy, 17
MapQuest, 85
Maquiladoras, 65
Marcial, Gene, 346
Marketable securities, 315
Marketing
  buzz, 264
  career options in, 242, 266

environmental, 34
environment for, 241–243
exchange relationship in, 228–229
explanation of, 228
functions of, 6–7, 227, 229–230
nature of, 228–230
test, 247
Marketing channels
  for business products, 259
  for consumer products, 258
  explanation of, 256–257
  supply chain management and, 257–258
Marketing concept
  evolution of, 231–232
  explanation of, 230–231
Marketing economy, 17
Marketing information system, 236, 238–239
Marketing managers, 138
Marketing mix
  distribution and, 236, 256–261
  environment and, 242, 243
  explanation of, 235, 236
  price and, 236, 255
  product and, 235–236
  promotion and, 237
Marketing orientation, 232
Marketing research
  explanation of, 230, 236, 237
  function of, 237–238, 242
  primary data and, 238
  secondary data and, 238–239
Marketing strategy
  explanation of, 232
  importance of distribution in, 236
  market mix development and, 235–237
  target market selection and, 233–235
Markets
  explanation of, 233
  target, 233–235
Market segmentation
  approaches to, 233–234
  bases for, 235
  explanation of, 233
Market segments, 233
Mark-to-mark accounting, 273
Mars, 232
Mars, Forrest, Sr., 101–102
Martin, Jennifer, 337
Martin Marietta, 109
Marx, Karl, 8
Maslow, Abraham, 193–195, 341
Maslow's hierarchy of needs, 193–195
MasterCard, 298
Material-requirements planning (MRP), 180, 181
Materials handling, 261
Matlack, Carole, 334
Matrix structure, 159–160
Matsushita, 71, 150, 163
Mattel, 94, 251
Maynard, Michelle, 338
Mayo, Elton, 192
Maytag, 200
MBNA, 298
McCarthy, Jack, 335
McCartney, Stella, 77
McClendon, Aubrey K., 136

McClure, Laura, 344
McConnon, Aili, 346
McCool, Joseph Daniel, 341
McDonald, Denese, 337
McDonald's, 18, 56, 60, 62, 84, 115, 118, 122, 150, 156, 157, 173, 179, 182, 183, 230, 252, 289–290
McGee, Susan, 337
McGraw-Hill Companies, 208, 326
McGregor, Douglas, 195, 196, 341
McGregor, Jena, 342
McLaughlin, Katy, 344
McLaughlin, Lisa, 342
McNichol, Tom, 330
Mediation, 43
Medtronic, 193
Mehail, T. M., 338
Mellon, Andrew, 18
Mellon Financial, 302
Merck & Co., 150
Merger mania, 109
Mergers
  explanation of, 108
  negative aspects of, 111
  trends in, 109–110
Merrell, Paula, 120
Merrill Lynch, 25, 83, 132, 307, 326
Mesa Petroleum Company, 38
Mexico, 65
Meyer, Ann, 344
Meyer, Pearl, 338
MGM Entertainment, 102
Microsoft Corporation, 18, 40, 116–117, 136, 246, 327
Middle managers, 137–138
Miles, Stephanie, 344
Millennials, 124
Miller, Matthew, 343
Miller, Nicole, 339
Milner, Conan, 344
Min, Kim Jung, 334
Minimum wage, 215
Mini-trial, 44
Minorities. *See also* Cultural diversity; Diversity
  buying power of, 234
  as small-business owners, 115
  in workforce, 210, 221–222
Mireles, Ricardo Castillo, 344
Mission, 131
Mitsubishi Motors, 29, 71
Mixed economies, 10
Model Business Corporation Act, 101
Modified capitalism, 9, 10, 18
Modular design, 175
Moen, 174
Moller, 115
Monetary policy, 300–302
Money
  characteristics of, 295–296
  explanation of, 294
  functions of, 294–295
  pricing long-term, 320–321
  types of, 296–299
Money market accounts, 297
Money market funds, 307
Monopolistic competition, 12
Monopoly, 12
Monroe, Kent B., 344
Montana Rugs and Furniture, 6
MooShoes, Inc., 40

Morale, 190
Morgan, J. P., 18
Morgan Stanley, 306, 326
Morrison, Blake, 331
Mortgage interest rates, 318–319
Moss Adams, 270
Motivation
  explanation of, 190
  Hawthorne studies of, 192–193
  historical perspectives on, 191–192
Motivational factors (Herzberg), 195
Motivation strategies
  behavior modification as, 199
  importance of, 201
  job design as, 199–201
Motivation theories
  classical theory, 191–192
  equity theory, 198
  expectancy theory, 198
  Herzberg's two-factor theory, 195
  Maslow's hierarchy of needs, 193–195
  McGregor's Theory X and Theory Y, 195–197
  Theory Z, 197–198
Motorola, 40
Motor vehicles
  design of, 174
  electric, 6
  inventory management for, 316–317
  pollution from, 38–39
  quality and, 183, 184
  smart car, 183
Mott, Ron, 341
Mozilo, Angelo, 25, 141
MTC, 51
MTV, 36
Muhammad, Larry, 341
Multidivisional structure, 159
Multimedia messaging services (MMS), 81
Multinational corporations (MNCs), 70–71
Multinational strategy, 71
Multisegment approach, 234–235
Munro, Thomas, 340
Murphy, Patrick E., 335
Murphy Business & Financial Corp., 122
Musk, Elon, 6, 330
Musselwhite, Chris, 342
Mutikani, Lucia, 332
Mutual funds, 307
Mutual savings banks, 304
MyCustoms.com, 60
Myers-Briggs Type Indicator, 208–209
MySpace.com, 117
MySQL, 162

N

Naik, Dilip, 157
Nakamura, Kunio, 150, 163
Names, 235
Napster, 12
Narang, Sonia, 342
NASCAR, 6, 26
NASDAQ, 327
National Aeronautics and Space Administration (NASA), 103

active review card

The Dynamics of Business and Economics

chapter one

IN A NUTSHELL

Goals, activities, and participants make up the fundamentals of business. Understanding the basics of economics and applying them to the United States' economy will further your understanding of how business works and provide a framework for learning about business.

The following questions will test your take-away knowledge from this chapter. How many can you answer?

LO.1. Define basic concepts such as business, product, and profit.

LO.2. Identify the main participants and activities of business and explain why studying business is important.

LO.3. Define economics and compare the four types of economic systems.

LO.4. Describe the role of supply, demand, and competition in a free-enterprise system.

LO.5. Specify why and how the health of the economy is measured.

LO.6. Trace the evolution of the American economy and discuss the role of the entrepreneur in the economy.

Did your answers include the following important points?

LO.1. Define basic concepts such as business, product, and profit.

- A business is an organization or individual that seeks a profit by providing products that satisfy people's needs.
- A product is a good, service, or idea that has both tangible and intangible characteristics that provide satisfaction and benefits.
- Profit, the basic goal of business, is the difference between what it costs to make and sell a product and what a customer pays for it.

LO.2. Identify the main participants and activities of business and explain why studying business is important.

- The three main participants in business are owners, employees, and customers, but others—government regulators, suppliers, social groups, etc.—are also important.
- Management involves planning, organizing, and controlling the tasks required to carry out the work of the company.
- Marketing refers to those activities—research, product development, promotion, pricing, and distribution—designed to provide goods and services that satisfy customers.
- Finance refers to activities concerned with funding a business and using its funds effectively, and studying business can help you prepare for a career and become a better consumer.

LO.3. Define economics and compare the four types of economic systems.

- Economics is the study of how resources are distributed for the production of goods and services within a social system, and an economic system describes how a particular society distributes its resources.
- Communism is an economic system in which the people, without regard to class, own all the nation's resources, while in a socialist system, the government owns and operates basic industries but individuals own most businesses.

- Under capitalism, individuals own and operate the majority of businesses that provide goods and services.
- Mixed economies have elements from more than one economic system; most countries have mixed economies.

LO.4. Describe the role of supply, demand, and competition in a free-enterprise system.

- Supply is the number of goods or services that businesses are willing to sell at different prices at a specific time.
- Demand is the number of goods and services that consumers are willing to buy at different prices at a specific time.
- Competition is the rivalry among businesses to persuade consumers to buy goods or services.

LO.5. Specify why and how the health of the economy is measured.

- A country measures the state of its economy to determine whether it is expanding or contracting and whether the country needs to take steps to minimize fluctuations.
- One commonly used measure is gross domestic product (GDP), the sum of all goods and services produced in a country during a year.
- A budget deficit occurs when a nation spends more than it takes in from taxes.

LO.6. Trace the evolution of the American economy and discuss the role of the entrepreneur in the economy.

- The American economy has evolved through the early economy, the Industrial Revolution, the manufacturing economy, the marketing economy, and the service- and Internet-based economy of today.
- Entrepreneurs play an important role because they risk their time, wealth, and efforts to develop new goods, services, and ideas that fuel the growth of the American economy.

Practical Application

LO.1.

- When purchasing a product, the consumer is actually buying its anticipated benefits and _____.
- If a business is to be successful in the long run, it must treat its customers, employees, and community with social _____.
- The goal of business is to earn _____.

LO.2.

- _____ involves activities designed to provide goods and services that fulfill needs and desires of consumers.
- When a business fails or does not make a profit, _____ have the most to lose.
- Advertising, personal selling, coupons, and sweepstakes are forms of _____.

LO.3.

- Private property, profits, independent business decisions, and choice are rights associated with _____.
- Factors of production are _____.
- Resources may be _____.

LO.4.

- Agricultural commodities are usually sold under _____.

- Monopolies that function in a capitalistic economy are likely to have a process determined by _____.
- If an economist is analyzing the quantity of goods or services that businesses are willing to sell at different prices at specific times, the focus is on _____.

LO.5.

- A severe recession may turn into a(n) _____.
- _____ is the sum of all goods and services produced in a country during a year.
- A(n) _____ happens when a nation spends more than it takes in from taxes.

LO.6.

- The early economy of the United States was marked by colonists who operated a society based primarily on _____.
- In the history of the American economy, the period or stage following the Industrial Revolution was known for its emphasis on _____.
- Trends have gradually changed the United States to a(n) _____ economy focused on making life easier for busy consumers.

ANSWERS LO1•satisfaction •responsibility •a profit LO2•Marketing •owners •promotion LO3•free enterprise •resources used to produce goods and services •human LO4•pure competition •government regulation •supply LO5•depression •Gross domestic product •budget deficit LO6•agriculture •manufacturing •service

active review card

chapter two

Business Ethics and Social Responsibility

IN A NUTSHELL

You must understand the role of ethics and social responsibility in making good business decisions. Learning to recognize business ethics issues, how businesses can improve their ethical behavior, and the impact of how companies respond to these issues is the basis of social responsibility.

The following questions will test your take-away knowledge from this chapter. How many can you answer?

LO.1. Define business ethics and social responsibility and examine their importance.

LO.2. Detect some of the ethical issues that may arise in business.

LO.3. Specify how businesses can promote ethical behavior.

LO.4. Explain the four dimensions of social responsibility.

LO.5. Debate an organization's social responsibilities to owners, employees, consumers, the environment, and the community.

Did your answers include the following important points?

LO.1. Define business ethics and social responsibility and examine their importance.

- The principles and standards that determine acceptable conduct in business organizations are defined as business ethics.
- A business's obligation to maximize its positive impact and minimize its negative impact on society illustrates the concept of social responsibility.
- Business ethics relates to an individual's or a work group's decisions that society evaluates as right or wrong, whereas social responsibility is a broader concept that concerns the impact of the entire business's activities on society.
- Socially responsible businesses win the trust and respect of their employees, customers, and society and increase profits.
- Ethics is important in business because it builds trust and confidence in business relationships.

LO.2. Detect some of the ethical issues that may arise in business.

- An ethical issue is an identifiable problem, situation, or opportunity requiring a person or organization to choose from among several actions that must be evaluated as right or wrong.
- Ethical issues can be categorized in the context of their relation with conflicts of interest, fairness and honesty, communications, and business associations.

LO.3. Specify how businesses can promote ethical behavior.

- Businesses can promote ethical behavior by employees by limiting their opportunity to engage in misconduct.

- Formal codes of ethics, ethical policies, and ethics training programs reduce the incidence of unethical behavior by informing employees what is expected of them and providing punishments for those who fail to comply.

LO.4. Explain the four dimensions of social responsibility.

- The four dimensions of social responsibility are economic (being profitable), legal (obeying the law), ethical (doing what is right, just, and fair), and voluntary (being a good corporate citizen).

LO.5. Debate an organization's social responsibilities to owners, employees, consumers, the environment, and the community.

- Businesses must maintain proper accounting procedures, provide all relevant information about the performance of the firm to investors, and protect the owners' rights and investments.
- In relations with employees, businesses are expected to provide a safe workplace, pay employees adequately for their work, and treat them fairly.
- Consumerism refers to the activities undertaken by independent individuals, groups, and organizations to protect their rights as consumers.
- Increasingly, society expects businesses to take greater responsibility for the environment, especially with regard to animal rights, as well as water, air, land, and noise pollution.
- Many businesses engage in activities to make the communities in which they operate better places for everyone to live and work.

Practical Application

LO.1.

- If a very successful professional football team has been ignoring the players' use of illegal muscle-building steroids, the owners should begin focusing on improving the organization's _____.
- Ethical violations destroy _____.
- The Sarbanes-Oxley Act was passed to _____.

LO.2.

- If the owner of a toy store seeking a price reduction gives the manager of a toy manufacturing company a new personal computer, the toy-store owner is using the _____ approach to influence the manufacturer's decision making.
- If a corporate manager makes a decision that results in personal financial benefit while the company's owners lose financially, this is an ethical issue related to _____.
- _____ is an example of ethical consideration within business relationships.

LO.3.

- _____ occurs when an employee exposes an employer's wrongdoing to outsiders.

- A set of formalized rules and standards that describe what a company expects of its employees is called a(n) _____.
- According to the text, ethical decisions in an organization are influenced by (1) individual moral standards, (2) the influence of managers and co-workers, and (3) _____.

LO.4.

- Being profitable relates to _____ social responsibility.
- Consumers vote against firms they view as socially irresponsible by not _____.
- Philanthropic contributions made by a business to a charitable organization represent _____ social responsibility.

LO.5.

- Businesses must first be responsible to _____.
- Many of the laws regulating safety in the workplace are enforced by _____.
- _____ assures the fair treatment of consumers who voice complaints about a purchased product.

ANSWERS LO1•ethics •trust •help restore confidence in Corporate America LO2•bribery •conflicts of interest •keeping company secrets LO3•Whistleblowing •code of ethics •the opportunity to engage in misconduct LO4•economic •buying their products •voluntary LO5•their owners •OSHA •The right to be heard

active review card

Business in a Borderless World

chapter three

IN A NUTSHELL

To learn about business in a global marketplace, you need to understand the nature of international business, including barriers to and promoters of trade across international boundaries. You must also consider the levels of organizational involvement in international business and the strategies used for trading across national borders.

The following questions will test your take-away knowledge from this chapter. How many can you answer?

LO.1. Explore some of the factors within the international trade environment that influence business.

LO.2. Investigate some of the economic, legal-political, social, cultural, and technological barriers to international business.

LO.3. Specify some of the agreements, alliances, and organizations that may encourage trade across international boundaries.

LO.4. Summarize the different levels of organizational involvement in international trade.

LO.5. Contrast two basic strategies used in international business.

Did your answers include the following important points?

LO.1. Explore some of the factors within the international trade environment that influence business.

- International business is the buying, selling, and trading of goods and services across national boundaries.
- Importing is the purchase of products and raw materials from another nation; exporting is the sale of domestic goods and materials to another nation.
- A nation's balance of trade is the difference in value between its exports and its imports: a negative balance of trade is a trade deficit.
- An absolute or comparative advantage in trade may determine what products a company from a particular nation will export.

LO.2. Investigate some of the economic, legal-political, social, cultural, and technological barriers to international business.

- Companies engaged in international trade must consider the effects of economic, legal, political, social, and cultural differences between nations.
- Wide-ranging legal and political barriers include differing laws (and enforcement), tariffs, exchange controls, quotas, embargoes, political instability, and war.
- Ambiguous cultural and social barriers involve differences in spoken and body language, time, holidays, and other observances and customs.

LO.3. Specify some of the agreements, alliances, and organizations that may encourage trade across international boundaries.

- Among the most important promoters of international business are the General Agreement on Tariffs and Trade, the World Trade Organization, the North American Free Trade Agreement, the European Union, the Asia-Pacific Economic Cooperation, the World Bank, and the International Monetary Fund.

LO.4. Summarize the different levels of organizational involvement in international trade.

- Countertrade agreements occur at the import/export level and involve bartering products for other products, and a trading company links buyers and sellers in different countries to foster trade.
- Licensing and franchising occurs when one company allows a foreign company to use its name, products, patents, brands, trademarks, raw materials, and production process in exchange for a flat fee or royalty.
- Contract manufacturing occurs when a company hires a foreign company to produce a specified volume of the firm's product and allows the final product to carry the domestic firm's name. In a joint venture companies work as a partnership and share the costs and operation of the business.
- Direct investment involves purchasing overseas production and marketing facilities, whereas outsourcing involves transferring manufacturing to countries where labor and supplies are cheap. A multinational corporation is one that operates on a worldwide scale, without ties to any one nation or region.

LO.5. Contrast two basic strategies used in international business.

- A multinational strategy customizes products, promotion, and distribution according to cultural, technological, regional, and national differences, while a global strategy (globalization) standardizes products for the whole world, as if it were a single entity.

Practical Application

LO.1.
- When a Chicago-based company buys coffee from Colombia, it is _____.
- The difference between the flow of money into and out of a country is called its _____.
- The United States has a comparative advantage in producing _____.

LO.2.
- The United States' prohibition of imported Cuban cigars is an example of a(n) _____.
- A group of nations or companies that band together to act as a monopoly is known as a _____.
- When a country devalues its currency, this encourages the sale of its _____.

LO.3.
- The _____ makes short-term loans to member countries with trade deficits and provides foreign currencies to member nations.
- The _____ is the largest source of advice and assistance with loans for developing countries.

- _____ is a member nation of APEC.

LO.4.
- An intermediary, or middleman, who markets goods in another country is acting as a(n) _____.
- PepsiCo allows a Canadian firm to use its name, formula, and brands in return for a royalty. This arrangement is known as _____.
- A major advantage of exporting through an agent is that the company does not have to deal with _____.

LO.5.
- Standardizing products for the whole world as if it were a single entity is a characteristic of _____ strategy.
- When Lever Brothers changes the formula of its bar soap to match different countries' water conditions and washing habits, this is an example of a _____.
- Customizing products, promotion, and distribution according to cultural, technological, and national differences indicates a _____.

IN A NUTSHELL

In examining e-business as a strategy to improve business performance and create competitive advantage, a successful business will need to understand the role and impact of technology in an information-driven economy, manage that information, and be aware of the legal and social issues associated with information technology and e-business.

The following questions will test your take-away knowledge from this chapter. How many can you answer?

LO.1. Summarize the role and impact of technology in the global economy.

LO.2. Specifiy how information is managed and explain a management information system.

LO.3. Describe the Internet and explore its main uses.

LO.4. Define e-business and discuss the e-business models.

LO.5. Identify the legal and social issues of information technology and e-business.

Did your answers include the following important points?

LO.1. Summarize the role and impact of technology in the global economy.

- Technology relates to the application of knowledge, including the processes and procedures to solve problems, perform tasks, and create new methods to obtain desired outcomes.
- A driving force in the advancement of economic systems, technology has dramatically affected economic productivity.

LO.2. Specifiy how information is managed and explain a management information system.

- A management information system (MIS) is used for organizing and transforming data into information that can be used for decision making.
- The purpose of the MIS is to obtain data from both internal and external sources to create information that is easily accessible and structured for user-friendly communication to managers.
- The MIS breaks down time and location barriers, making information available when and where it is needed to solve problems.

LO.3. Describe the Internet and explore its main uses.

- The Internet is a global information system that links many computer networks together.
- It is used mainly for communication, information, entertainment, and e-business.

LO.4. Define e-business and discuss the e-business models.

- E-business carries out the goals of business through the utilization of the Internet.
- The three major e-business models are business-to-business (use of the Internet for transactions and communications between organizations), business-to-consumer (delivering products and services directly to individual consumers through utilization of the Internet), and consumer-to-consumer (markets in which consumers market goods and services to each other through utilization of the Internet).

LO.5. Identify the legal and social issues of information technology and e-business.

- Growth of information technology, the Internet, and e-business have generated many legal and social issues, including concerns about privacy, identity theft, and protection of intellectual property and copyrights.

Practical Application

LO.1.

- _____ relates to processes and applications that create new methods to solve problems, perform tasks, and manage communication.
- The amount of output per hour of work is known as _____.
- Today, economic productivity is based more on _____ than on any other advance.

LO.2.

- Businesses often engage in _____ efforts to improve data flow and the usefulness of information.
- _____ includes meaningful and useful interpretation of data and knowledge that can be used in making decisions.
- _____ is a major business resource that should be viewed as an asset to be developed and distributed to managers.

LO.3.

- The global information system that links many computer networks together is known as the _____.
- _____ is the most popular use of the Internet in the United States.
- The process of _____ allows users to carry on one or more real-time conversations simultaneously.

LO.4.

- Businesses that transact business on the Internet are often called _____.
- _____ uses the Internet to carry out marketing activities, including buying and selling activities conducted online.
- The use of the Internet for transactions and communications between organizations is known as _____ e-business.

LO.5.

- _____ occurs when criminals obtain personal information that allows them to impersonate someone else in order to use their credit to obtain financial accounts and make purchases.
- The _____ law was passed in 1998 to protect copyrighted materials on the Internet and limit the liability of online service providers.
- _____ is intended to simplify state sales tax laws and tax collection procedures.

IN A NUTSHELL

Sole proprietorship, partnership, and corporation are three primary forms of business that are used in traditional business, online-only business, or a combination of both. Other forms of business include S corporations, limited liability companies, and cooperatives. In organizing a business, it is helpful to understand the advantages and disadvantages of these forms of business, as well as business trends.

The following questions will test your take-away knowledge from this chapter. How many can you answer?

LO.1. Define and examine the advantages and disadvantages of the sole proprietorship form of organization.

LO.2. Identify two types of partnership and evaluate the advantages and disadvantages of the partnership form of organization.

LO.3. Describe the corporate form of organization and cite the advantages and disadvantages of corporations.

LO.4. Define and debate the advantages and disadvantages of mergers, acquisitions, and leveraged buyouts.

Did your answers include the following important points?

LO.1. Define and examine the advantages and disadvantages of the sole proprietorship form of organization.

- The most common form of business is the sole proprietorship. The advantages of this form of business include easy and inexpensive to form, allow a high level of secrecy, all profits belong to the owner, the owner has complete control over the business, government regulation is minimal, taxes are paid only once, and the business can be closed easily.
- Disadvantages include owner may have to use personal assets to borrow money, sources of external funds are difficult to find, the owner must have many diverse skills, the survival of the business is tied to the life of the owner and his or her ability to work, qualified employees are hard to find, and wealthy sole proprietors pay a higher tax rate than they would under the corporate form of business.

LO.2. Identify two types of partnership and evaluate the advantages and disadvantages of the partnership form of organization.

- Partnerships may be general or limited and offer the following advantages: easy to organize, may have higher credit ratings because partners may have more combined wealth, partners can specialize, partnerships can make decisions faster than larger businesses, and government regulations are few.
- Disadvantages include general partners have unlimited liability for the debts of the partnership, partners are responsible for each other's decisions, the death or termination of one partner requires a new partnership agreement, it is difficult to sell a partnership interest at a fair price, the distribution of profits may not correctly reflect the amount of work done by each partner, and partnerships cannot find external sources of funds as easily as large corporations.

LO.3. Describe the corporate form of organization and cite the advantages and disadvantages of corporations.

- A corporation, which is owned by stockholders, is a legal entity created by the state, whose assets and liabilities are separate from those of its owners. They are chartered by a state through articles of incorporation and have a board of directors made up of corporate officers or people from outside the company.
- Advantages include owners have limited liability, ownership (stock) can be easily transferred, corporations are long-lasting, raising money is easier, and expansion into new businesses is simpler.
- Disadvantages include the company is taxed on its income and owners pay a second tax on any profits received as dividends, forming a corporation can be expensive, keeping trade secrets is difficult because so much information must be made available to the public and to government agencies, and owners and managers are not always the same and can have different goals.

LO.4. Define and debate the advantages and disadvantages of mergers, acquisitions, and leveraged buyouts.

- A merger occurs when two companies (usually corporations) combine to form a new company. An acquisition occurs when one company buys most of another company's stock, whereas in a leveraged buyout, a group of investors borrows money to acquire a company, using the assets of the purchased company to guarantee the loan.
- Advantages include they can help merging firms gain a larger market share in their industries, acquire valuable assets, and lower costs. They can also benefit stockholders by improving companies' market value and stock prices.
- Disadvantages include they can hurt companies if they force managers to focus on avoiding takeovers at the expense of productivity and profits, they may lead to a company to take on too much debt, and they can harm employee morale and productivity.

Practical Application

LO.1.
- One of the most popular and easiest to establish forms of business in the United States is the _____.
- Jane has discovered that she is bored working for others. She wants to open a business in which she will have maximum control and the least interference from government regulation. She should use the _____ form of business.
- _____ requires owners to perform many functions and possess diverse skills to make decisions.

LO.2.
- _____ is the least used form of business organization in the United States.
- The decision-making process in a partnership tends to be faster when the partnership is _____.
- _____ is an advantage of a partnership.

LO.3.
- Another often-used name for stockholder is _____.
- A private corporation is one that _____.
- The organizational form that many consider to be a blend of the best characteristics of corporations, partnerships, and sole proprietorships is the _____.

LO.4.
- When two companies combine to form a new company, it is called a(n) _____.
- When companies operating at different, but related, levels of an industry merge, it is known as a(n) _____.
- XYZ, Inc. is attempting to avoid a hostile takeover by a corporate raider by allowing stockholders to buy more shares of stock at prices lower than current market value. _____ method is being used to avoid the takeover.

active review card
Small Business, Entrepreneurship, and Franchising

chapter six

IN A NUTSHELL

A successful entrepreneur or small business owner understands the advantages and disadvantages of owning a small business, challenges facing small businesses today, and why small businesses succeed or fail.

The following questions will test your take-away knowledge from this chapter. How many can you answer?

LO.1. Define entrepreneurship and small business.

LO.2. Investigate the importance of small business in the U.S. economy and why certain fields attract small business.

LO.3. Specify the advantages of small-business ownership.

LO.4. Summarize the disadvantages of small-business ownership and analyze why many small businesses fail.

LO.5. Describe how you go about starting a small business and what resources are needed.

LO.6. Evaluate the demographic, technological, and economic trends that are affecting the future of small business.

LO.7. Explain why many large businesses are trying to "think small."

Did your answers include the following important points?

LO.1. Define entrepreneurship and small business.

- An entrepreneur is a person who creates a business or product and manages his or her resources and takes risks to gain a profit; entrepreneurship is the process of creating and managing a business to achieve desired objectives.
- A small business is one that is not dominant in its competitive area and does not employ more than 500 people.

LO.2. Investigate the importance of small business in the U.S. economy and why certain fields attract small business.

- Small businesses are vital to the American economy because they provide products, jobs, innovation, and opportunities.
- Retailing, wholesaling, services, manufacturing, and high technology attract small businesses because these industries are relatively easy to enter, require relatively low initial financing, and may experience less heavy competition.

LO.3. Specify the advantages of small-business ownership.

- Small-business ownership offers some personal advantages, including independence, freedom of choice, and the option of working at home.
- Business advantages include flexibility, the ability to focus on a few key customers, and the chance to develop a reputation for quality and service.

LO.4. Summarize the disadvantages of small-business ownership and analyze why many small businesses fail.

- Small businesses have many disadvantages for their owners, such as expense, physical and psychological stress, and a high failure rate.
- Small businesses fail for many reasons: undercapitalization, management inexperience or incompetence, neglect, disproportionate burdens imposed by government regulation, and vulnerability to competition from larger companies.

LO.5. Describe how you go about starting a small business and what resources are needed.

- Have an idea for developing a small business and devise a business plan to guide the development of the business. Then you must decide what form of business ownership to use and provide funds, using your own funds, funds retained from family and friends, financial institutions, other businesses in the form of trade credit, investors, state and local organizations, or the Small Business Administration.
- You must also decide whether to start a new business from scratch, buy an existing one, or buy a franchise operation.

LO.6. Evaluate the demographic, technological, and economic trends that are affecting the future of small business.

- Changing demographic trends that represent areas of opportunity for small businesses include more elderly people as baby boomers age; a large gain in the 11 to 28 age range known as echo boomers, millennials, or Generation Y; and an increasing number of immigrants to the United States.
- Technological advances and an increase in service exports have created new opportunities for small companies to expand their operations abroad, while trade agreements and alliances have created an environment in which small business has fewer regulatory and legal barriers.
- Economic turbulence presents both opportunities for and threats to the survival of small businesses.

LO.7. Explain why many large businesses are trying to "think small."

- Large companies are copying small businesses in an effort to make their firms more flexible, resourceful, and innovative, and improve the bottom line.
- This involves downsizing and intrapreneurship, where an employee takes responsibility for developing innovations of any kind within the larger organization.

Practical Application

LO.1.
- Small businesses are the heart of the U.S. economic and social system because _____.
- The Small Business Administration was established _____.
- This textbook uses the term small business to refer to an owner-managed business that employs not more than _____ people.

LO.2.
- Three-quarters of all new jobs created in the United States in recent years were generated by _____.
- In the context of starting a new business, a retailer differs from a manufacturer in that the retailer is less likely to make a heavy investment in _____.
- The fastest growing sector of the U.S. economy is represented by _____.

LO.3.
- When market conditions change rapidly, a small business usually has fewer layers of management to work through in making decisions. This advantage of small business is _____.
- One of the major reasons people want to own and operate their own business is to _____.
- A small business's ability to focus on narrow niches can help it develop _____.

LO.4.
- _____ is a disadvantage of small-business ownership.

- Although some businesses are less risky than others, overall the financial risks of running a small business are _____.
- Initially, the factor that probably affects a company's reputation more than anything else is poorly managed _____.

LO.5.
- Since Rachel Hollings decided to purchase the rights to own and operate a McDonald's fast-food restaurant rather than start her own operation, she is probably a(n) _____.
- A mortgage is an example of _____.
- Franchising first began in the United States within the _____ industry.

LO.6.
- The _____ segment of the population is probably the wealthiest in the United States.
- Many experts think that the _____ demographic is the market of the future.
- _____ industries are likely to continue to grow as baby boomers age.

LO.7.
- Reducing management layers, corporate staff, and work tasks to make a firm more flexible, resourceful, and innovative is known as _____.
- Individuals who take responsibility for the development of innovations of any kind within larger organizations are called _____.
- Downsizing helps firms become _____.

IN A NUTSHELL

A successful manager needs to possess certain skills and follow steps to effective decision making. In doing so, managers accomplish various functions and participate in differing levels and areas of management.

The following questions will test your take-away knowledge from this chapter. How many can you answer?

LO.1. Define management and explain its role in the achievement of organizational objectives.

LO.2. Describe the major functions of management.

LO.3. Distinguish among three levels of management and the concerns of managers at each level.

LO.4. Specify the skills managers need in order to be successful.

LO.5. Summarize the systematic approach to decision making used by many business managers.

Did your answers include the following important points?

LO.1. Define management and explain its role in the achievement of organizational objectives.

- Management is a process designed to achieve an organization's objectives by using its resources effectively and efficiently in a changing environment.
- Managers make decisions about the use of the organization's resources and are concerned with planning, organizing, staffing, directing, and controlling the organization's activities so as to reach its objectives.

LO.2. Describe the major functions of management.

- Planning is the process of determining the organization's objectives and deciding how to accomplish them. Organizing is the structuring of resources and activities to accomplish those objectives efficiently and effectively.
- Staffing obtains people with the necessary skills to carry out the work of the company.
- Directing is motivating and leading employees to achieve organizational objectives and controlling the process of evaluating and correcting activities to keep the organization on course.

LO.3. Distinguish among three levels of management and the concerns of managers at each level.

- Top management is responsible for the whole organization and focuses primarily on strategic planning. Middle management

develops plans for specific operating areas and carries out the general guidelines set by top management.

- First-line, or supervisory, management supervises the workers and day-to-day operations.
- Managers can also be categorized as to their area of responsibility: finance, production and operations, human resources, marketing, or administration.

LO.4. Specify the skills managers need in order to be successful.

- Managers need leadership skills, technical expertise, conceptual skills, analytical skills, and human relations skills.

LO.5. Summarize the systematic approach to decision making used by many business managers.

- A systematic approach to decision making follows these steps: recognizing and defining the situation, developing options, analyzing options, selecting the best option, implementing the decision, and monitoring the consequences.

Practical Application

LO.1.
- If a manager is concerned about doing work with the least cost and waste, her primary managerial concern is _____.
- _____ make decisions about the use of an organization's resources and are concerned with planning organizing, leading, and controlling the organization's activities.
- If a manager is organizing equipment within a factory setting, he is mainly involved with _____ resources.

LO.2.
- The type of planning conducted on a long-range basis by top managers is usually called _____.
- Dividing work into small units and assigning it to individuals are tasks related to _____.
- Giving people incentives to achieve objectives relates to the management function of _____.

LO.3.
- _____ are responsible for tactical planning that will implement the general guidelines established by top management.
- Decisions regarding adding new products, acquiring companies, and moving into foreign markets would most typically be made by _____.

- The levels of management form a _____.

LO.4.
- Joe met with all of his department heads to listen to their opinions about buying a new machine. Although they all thought it was a good idea, Joe did not buy the machine. Joe's leadership style is _____.
- To train employees, answer questions, and provide guidance in doing a task, managers need _____.
- When Karen uses authority and economic rewards as incentives to motivate workers, her leadership style is _____.

LO.5.
- Managers at XYZ Inc. have recognized declining sales on their ABC model product and must make a decision about what to do. Their next step is to _____.
- When analyzing options in the decision-making process, managers must consider the appropriateness and _____ of each option.
- Effective implementation of a major decision requires _____.

active review card

Organization, Teamwork, and Communication

IN A NUTSHELL

An organization's culture affects its operations. It is important in organizing a business to understand the development of structure, including how tasks and responsibilities are organized through specialization and departmentalization, as well as the different forms organizational structure may take.

The following questions will test your take-away knowledge from this chapter. How many can you answer?

LO.1. Define organizational structure and relate how organizational structures develop.

LO.2. Describe how specialization and departmentalization help an organization achieve its goals.

LO.3. Distinguish between groups and teams and identify the types of groups that exist in organizations.

LO.4. Determine how organizations assign responsibility for tasks and delegate authority.

LO.5. Compare and contrast some common forms of organizational structure.

LO.6. Describe how communication occurs in organizations.

Did your answers include the following important points?

LO.1. Define organizational structure and relate how organizational structures develop.

- Structure is the arrangement or relationship of positions within an organization; it develops when managers assign work activities to work groups and specific individuals and coordinate the diverse activities required to attain organizational objectives.
- Organizational structure evolves to accommodate growth, which requires people with specialized skills.

LO.2. Describe how specialization and departmentalization help an organization achieve its goals.

- Structuring an organization requires that management assign work tasks to specific individuals and groups. Under specialization, managers break labor into small, specialized tasks and assign employees to do a single task, fostering efficiency.
- Departmentalization is the grouping of jobs into working units.
- Businesses may departmentalize by function, product, geographic region, or customer, or they may combine two or more of these.

LO.3. Distinguish between groups and teams and identify the types of groups that exist in organizations.

- A group is two or more persons who communicate, have a common identity, and have a common goal, whereas a team is a small group whose members have complementary skills, a common purpose, goals, and approach, and who hold themselves mutually accountable.
- The major distinction is that individual performance is most important in groups, while collective work group performance counts most in teams.

- Special kinds of groups include task forces, committees, project teams, product-development teams, quality-assurance teams, and self-directed work teams.

LO.4. Determine how organizations assign responsibility for tasks and delegate authority.

- Delegation of authority means assigning tasks to employees and giving them the power to make commitments, use resources, and take whatever actions are necessary to accomplish the tasks.
- The extent to which authority is delegated throughout an organization determines its degree of centralization.

LO.5. Compare and contrast some common forms of organizational structure.

- Line structures have direct lines of authority that extend from the top manager to employees at the lowest level of the organization.
- A multidivisional structure gathers departments into larger groups called divisions. A matrix or project-management structure sets up teams from different departments, thereby creating two or more intersecting lines of authority.

LO.6. Describe how communication occurs in organizations.

- Communication occurs both formally and informally in organizations. Formal communication may be downward, upward, horizontal, and even diagonal.
- Informal communication takes place through friendships and the grapevine.

Practical Application

LO.1.

- The arrangement or relationship of positions within an organization is called _____.
- Dress codes, work habits, extracurricular activities, and stories are informal expressions of an organization's _____.
- The more people an organization has and the greater its specialization, the greater is its need for _____.

LO.2.

- _____ departmentalization arranges jobs around the needs of various types of customers.
- General Motors is organized into these groups: GMC Trucks, Chevrolet, Pontiac, Buick, and Cadillac. Its type of departmentalization is _____.
- Adam Smith illustrated improvements in efficiency through the application of _____.

LO.3.

- A temporary group of employees responsible for bringing about a particular change is a _____.
- Most of the essential work of business occurs in _____.
- A special type of project team formed to devise, design, and implement a new product is a _____.

LO.4.

- A organization with many layers of managers is considered to be _____.
- An organization operating in a complex and unpredictable environment is likely to be _____.
- When the decisions of a company are very risky and low-level mangers lack decision-making skills, the company will tend to _____.

LO.5.

- The _____ organizational form allows managers to specialize in the area for which they are responsible.
- The _____ organizational form is likely to be complex and expensive.
- Today's dynamic business environment has fostered a _____ form of organizational structure.

LO.6.

- When managers recognize that a grapevine exists, they should _____.
- Upward communication conveys _____.
- Downward communication conveys _____.

active review card

Managing Service and Manufacturing Operations

chapter nine

IN A NUTSHELL

Production and operations management involves planning and designing the processes that will transform resources into finished products, managing the movement of resources through the transformation process, and ensuring that the products are of the quality expected by customers.

The following questions will test your take-away knowledge from this chapter. How many can you answer?

LO.1. Define operations management and differentiate between operations and manufacturing.

LO.2. Explain how operations management differs in manufacturing and service firms.

LO.3. Describe the elements involved in planning and designing an operations system.

LO.4. Specify some techniques managers may use to manage the logistics of transforming inputs into finished products.

LO.5. Assess the importance of quality in operations management.

Did your answers include the following important points?

LO.1. Define operations management and differentiate between operations and manufacturing.

- Operations management (OM) is the development and administration of the activities involved in transforming resources into goods and services.
- The terms *manufacturing* and *production* are used interchangeably to describe the activities and processes used in making tangible products, whereas operations is a broader term used to describe the process of making both tangible and intangible products.

LO.2. Explain how operations management differs in manufacturing and service firms.

- Manufacturers and service firms both transform inputs and outputs, but service providers differ from manufacturers in several ways: They have greater customer contact because the service occurs at the point of consumption; their inputs and outputs are more variable than those of manufacturers; because of the human element, service providers are generally more labor intensive and their productivity measurement is more complex.

LO.3. Describe the elements involved in planning and designing an operations system.

- Operations planning relates to decisions about what products to make, for whom, and what processes and facilities are needed to produce them.
- Common facility layouts include fixed-position layouts, process layouts, and product layouts.
- Where to locate operations facilities is a crucial decision that depends on proximity to market, availability of raw materials,

availability of transportation, availability of power, climatic influences, availability of labor, and community characteristics.

- Technology is also vital to operations, particularly computer-assisted design, computer-assisted manufacturing, flexible manufacturing, robotics, and computer-integrated manufacturing.

LO.4. Specify some techniques managers may use to manage the logistics of transforming inputs into finished products.

- Logistics, or supply chain management, includes all the activities involved in obtaining and managing raw materials and component parts, managing finished products, packaging them, and getting them to customers.
- Common approaches to inventory control include the economic order quantity (EOQ) model, the just-in-time (JIT) inventory concept, and material-requirements planning (MRP).
- Logistics also includes routing and scheduling processes and activities to complete products.

LO.5. Assess the importance of quality in operations management.

- Quality is a critical element of operations management because low-quality products can hurt people and harm business.
- Quality control refers to the processes an organization uses to maintain its established quality standards.
- To control quality, a company must establish what standard of quality is desired and determine whether its products meet that standard through inspection.

Practical Application

LO.1.

- Viewed from the perspective of operations, the money used to purchase a carpenter's tools and the electricity used to run his power saw are _____.
- If an employee is involved with transforming resources into goods and services, then he is in _____.
- From an operations perspective, food sold at a restaurant and services provided by a plumbing company are _____.

LO.2.

- Money, employees, time, and equipment represent an airline's _____ to the transformation process.
- Actual performance of the service provider's product typically occurs _____.
- Compared to service providers, manufacturers generally _____.

LO.3.

- To facilitate operations planning, most firms use _____ to determine the kinds of goods and services to provide and the features they must possess.
- If ABC Computer Company is determining demand for its future products and how much consumers are willing to pay, the company probably will rely on _____.

- When a customer goes to a print shop to order business cards, the manufacturing process used would most likely be _____.

LO.4.

- Within organizations, purchasing is also referred to as _____.
- Materials that have been purchased to be used in making other products are included in _____.
- A planning system that schedules the precise quality of materials needed for production is called _____.

LO.5.

- Determining how many items are to be inspected is called _____.
- The degree to which a good or service meets the demands and requirements of customers is called _____.
- _____ is a philosophy that a uniform commitment to quality in all areas of an organization will promote a culture that meets customers' perceptions of quality.

active review card

Motivating the Workforce

chapter ten

IN A NUTSHELL

Managers who understand the needs and motivations of workers and strategies for motivating them can help workers reach higher levels of productivity, subsequently contributing to the achievement of organizational goals.

The following questions will test your take-away knowledge from this chapter. How many can you answer?

LO.1. Define human relations and determine why its study is important.

LO.2. Summarize early studies that laid the groundwork for understanding employee motivation.

LO.3. Compare and contrast the human-relations theories of Abraham Maslow and Frederick Herzberg.

LO.4. Investigate various theories of motivation, including Theories X, Y, and Z; equity theory; and expectancy theory.

LO.5. Describe some of the strategies that managers use to motivate employees.

Did your answers include the following important points?

LO.1. Define human relations and determine why its study is important.

- Human relations is the study of the behavior of individuals and groups in organizational settings. Its focus is what motivates employees to perform on the job.
- Human relations is important because businesses need to understand how to motivate their employees to be more effective, boost workplace morale, and maximize employees' productivity and creativity.

LO.2. Summarize early studies that laid the groundwork for understanding employee motivation.

- Time and motion studies by Frederick Taylor and others helped them analyze how employees perform specific work tasks in an effort to improve their productivity.
- Taylor and the early practitioners of the classical theory of motivation felt that money and job security were the primary motivations of employees; however, the Hawthorne Studies revealed that human factors also influence workers' behavior.

LO.3. Compare and contrast the human-relations theories of Abraham Maslow and Frederick Herzberg.

- Abraham Maslow defined five basic needs of all people and arranged them in the order in which they must be satisfied: physiological, security, social, esteem, and self-actualization.
- Frederick Herzberg divided the characteristics of jobs into hygiene factors and motivational factors.

- Herzberg's hygiene factors can be compared to Maslow's physiological and security needs; motivational factors may include Maslow's social, esteem, and self-actualization needs.

LO.4. Investigate various theories of motivation, including Theories X, Y, and Z; equity theory; and expectancy theory.

- Douglas McGregor contrasted two views of management: Theory X suggests workers dislike work, while Theory Y suggests that workers not only like work, but seek out responsibility to satisfy their higher-order needs.
- Theory Z stresses employee participation in all aspects of company decision making, while the equity theory indicates that how much people are willing to contribute to an organization depends on their assessment of the fairness, or equity, of the rewards they will receive in exchange.
- The expectancy theory states that motivation depends not only on how much a person wants something, but also on the person's perception if how likely her or she is to get it.

LO.5. Describe some of the strategies that managers use to motivate employees.

- Strategies for motivating workers include behavior modification and job design. Among the job design strategies businesses use are job rotations, job enlargement, job enrichment, and flexible scheduling strategies.

Practical Application

LO.1.
- An inner drive that directs behavior toward objectives is called _____.
- Good morale is likely to result in _____.
- To achieve organizational objectives, employees must have the ability, tools, and _____ to perform their jobs.

LO.2.
- Prior to the Hawthorne Studies, management theorists believed that the primary motivators of employees were job security and _____.
- The birth of the study of human relations can be traced to _____.
- The person primarily associated with the Hawthorne Studies was _____.

LO.3.
- According to Maslow, living life to the fullest is most closely associated with fulfilling one's _____ need.
- If a department store contest promises that the employee with the highest sales will be treated to dinner by the store manager, the store is helping its employees fulfill their _____ need.

- According to Maslow, an employee who goes to night school to get a college degree to minimize the chance of being laid off during a recession is motivated to fulfill her _____ need.

LO.4.
- Jim has learned that his company is offering a Hawaiian vacation to its best salesman. He almost won last year and really wants the trip. He is working very hard because he thinks he has a good chance to win. This exemplifies the _____ theory.
- Jack believes that he can get some extra work completed before the deadline by withholding his workers' vacation schedules until the job is completed. Jack could be described as _____.
- The approach that suggests that imagination, ingenuity, and creativity can help solve organizational problems is _____.

LO.5.
- A work system that allows employees to choose their starting and ending times as long as they are at work during a specified core period is called _____.
- _____ adds tasks to a job instead of treating each task as a separate job.
- When Kelly reprimands Sarah each time Sarah is late for work, Kelly is applying _____.

IN A NUTSHELL

Human resource managers need to plan for, recruit, and select qualified employees. Yet another aspect of the human resource manager's job is to train, appraise, compensate, and retain valued employees, which can present an added challenge among unionized and diverse employees.

The following questions will test your take-away knowledge from this chapter. How many can you answer?

LO.1. Define human resource management and explain its significance.

LO.2. Summarize the processes of recruiting and selecting human resources for a company.

LO.3. Discuss how workers are trained and their performance is appraised.

LO.4. Identify the types of turnover companies may experience, and explain why turnover is an important issue.

LO.5 Specify the various ways a worker may be compensated.

LO.6. Discuss some of the issues associated with unionized employees, including collective bargaining and dispute resolution.

LO.7. Describe the importance of diversity in the workforce.

Did your answers include the following important points?

LO.1. Define human resource management and explain its significance.

- Human resources, or personnel, management refers to all the activities involved in determining an organization's human resources needs and acquiring, training, and compensating people to fill those needs.
- It is concerned with maximizing the satisfaction of employees and improving their efficiency to meet organizational objectives.

LO.2. Summarize the processes of recruiting and selecting human resources for a company.

- The human resources managers must determine the firm's human resources needs, develop a strategy to meet those needs, and recruit qualified applicants from whom management will select the employees.
- Selection is the process of collecting information about applicants, using that information to decide which to hire, and putting potential hires through the process of application, interview, testing, and reference checking.

LO.3. Discuss how workers are trained and their performance is appraised.

- Training teaches employees how to do their job tasks, while development is training that augments the skills and knowledge of managers and professionals as well as current employees.
- Appraising performance involves identifying an employee's strengths and weaknesses on the job. Performance appraisals may be subjective or objective.

LO.4. Identify the types of turnover companies may experience, and explain why turnover is an important issue.

- A promotion is an advancement to a higher-level job with increased authority, responsibility, and pay. A transfer is a move to another job within the company, typically at the same level and wage.

- Separations occur when employees resign, retire, are terminated, or are laid off. Turnovers due to separation are expensive because of the time, money, and effort required to select, train, and manage new employees.

LO.5. Specify the various ways a worker may be compensated.

- Wages are financial compensation based on the number of hours worked or the number of units produced, while commissions are a fixed amount or percentage of a sale paid as compensation.
- Salaries are compensation calculated on a weekly, monthly, or annual basis, regardless of the number of hours worked or the number of items produced.
- Bonuses and profit sharing are types of financial incentives, while benefits are nonfinancial forms of compensation, such as vacation, insurance, and sick leave.

LO.6. Discuss some of the issues associated with unionized employees, including collective bargaining and dispute resolution.

- Collective bargaining is the negotiation process through which management and unions reach an agreement on a labor contract.
- If labor and management cannot agree on a contract, labor union members may picket, strike, or boycott the firm, while management may lock out striking employees, hire strikebreakers, or form employers' associations.
- In a deadlock, labor disputes may be resolved by a third party.

LO.7. Describe the importance of diversity in the workforce.

- When companies value and effectively manage their diverse workforces, they experience more productive use of human resources, reduced conflict, better work relationships among workers, increased commitment to and sharing of organizational goals, increased innovation and creativity, and enhanced ability to serve diverse customers.

Practical Application

LO.1.

- In some companies, the department that handles the human resources management function is still called _____.
- The document that contains an overview of a job's title, tasks, relationships with other jobs, physical and mental skills required, duties, and responsibilities is referred to as job _____.
- The qualifications required for a job are spelled out in a job _____.

LO.2.

- _____ tests are restricted to specific government jobs and those involving security or access to drugs.
- Professionals who specialize in luring qualified people away from other companies are known as _____.
- Recruiting for entry-level managerial and professional positions is often carried out _____.

LO.3.

- Subjective evaluation tools include _____.
- If Greta received her training by watching videotapes and discussing case studies, she most likely received _____ training.
- Joseph, a Ph.D., has worked in the Union Carbide research lab as a chemist for several years. He is currently participating in a series of management seminars at company expense. This is an example of _____.

LO.4.

- When Sandy Smith moved to a new job that involved more responsibility and an increase in compensation, she received a _____.

- Susan was terminated from her job by her employer, because she was repeatedly late to work. She _____.
- Human resources departments strive to _____.

LO.5.

- To motivate employees such as car salespersons to sell as much as they can, they are paid _____.
- June works at McDonald's twenty hours per week as a grill operator. She will probably be paid with the _____ compensation method.
- An employee stock ownership plan is _____.

LO.6.

- Workers seeking to improve pay and working conditions may join together to form a labor _____.
- _____ makes carrying out normal business operations difficult, if not impossible.
- If the negotiations between union and management representatives come to a standstill and a third party is brought in to make suggestions or propose solutions to help resolve the impasse, the third party would probably be a(n) _____.

LO.7.

- Age, gender, and race are _____ characteristics of diversity.
- Secondary characteristics of diversity _____.
- Having a diverse workforce has many benefits. One benefit is _____.

IN A NUTSHELL

Marketers develop marketing strategies to satisfy the needs and wants of their customers; they also need to consider buying behavior and use research to determine what consumers want to buy and why. Marketers also need to consider the impact of the environment on marketing activities.

The following questions will test your take-away knowledge from this chapter. How many can you answer?

LO.1. Define marketing and describe the exchange process.

LO.2. Specify the functions of marketing.

LO.3. Explain the marketing concept and its implications for developing marketing strategies.

LO.4. Examine the development of a marketing strategy, including market segmentation and marketing mix.

LO.5. Investigate how marketers conduct marketing research and study buying behavior.

LO.6. Summarize the environmental forces that influence marketing decisions.

Did your answers include the following important points?

LO.1. Define marketing and describe the exchange process.

- Marketing is a group of activities designed to expedite transactions by creating, distributing, pricing, and promoting goods, services, and ideas.
- Marketing facilitates exchange, the act of giving up one thing in return for something else. The central focus is to satisfy needs.

LO.2. Specify the functions of marketing.

- Marketing includes many varied and interrelated activities: buying, selling, transporting, storing, grading, financing, marketing research, and risk taking.

LO.3. Explain the marketing concept and its implications for developing marketing strategies.

- The marketing concept is the idea that an organization should try to satisfy customers' needs through coordinated activities that also allow it to achieve its goals.
- If a company does not implement the marketing concept by providing products that consumers need and want while achieving its own objectives, it will not survive.

LO.4. Examine the development of a marketing strategy, including market segmentation and marketing mix.

- A marketing strategy is a plan of action for creating a marketing mix for a specific target market. Some firms use a total-market approach, designating everyone as the target market.

- Most firms divide the total market into segments of people who have relatively similar product needs.
- A company using a concentration approach develops one marketing strategy for a single market segment, whereas a multisegment approach aims marketing efforts at two or more segments, developing a different marketing strategy for each segment.

LO.5. Investigate how marketers conduct marketing research and study buying behavior.

- Carrying out the marketing concept is impossible unless marketers know what, where, when, and how consumers buy; marketing research into the factors that influence buying behavior helps marketers develop effective marketing strategies.
- Marketing research is a systematic, objective process of getting information about potential customers to guide marketing decisions.
- Buying behavior is the decision processes and actions of people who purchase and use products.

LO.6. Summarize the environmental forces that influence marketing decisions.

- There are several forces that influence marketing activities: political, legal, regulatory, social, competitive, economic, and technological.

Practical Application

LO.1.
- James Johnson has developed a new product, found a store willing to sell it, and agreed to help promote the product's sale. He is engaging in _____.
- The exchange process is _____.
- When a customer hands the cashier $1 and receives a loaf of bread, _____ has occurred.

LO.2.
- When a storeowner spends a lot of money for new products that have yet to be proved sales items, the owner is engaging in the marketing function of _____.
- Marketers need to spend more effort understanding _____ to determine what products to market.
- Richard has acquired a supply of canned fruits and vegetables. He does not yet have a buyer for them, but he's using promotion and other activities to find a buyer. He is performing the marketing function of _____.

LO.3.
- The goal of the marketing concept is _____.
- _____ remains a major element of any strategy to develop and manage long-term customer relationships.
- During the Industrial Revolution, new technologies fueled strong _____.

LO.4.
- A plan of action for developing, pricing, distributing, and promoting products that meets the needs of a specific customer is a _____.
- People visiting a ski resort would be viewed by a ski equipment storeowner as the business's _____.
- The aim of _____ is to communicate directly or indirectly with individuals, groups, and organizations to facilitate exchanges.

LO.5.
- Marketing research is _____.
- _____ is a psychological variable of buyer behavior.
- _____ are the least expensive data to collect.

LO.6.
- Computers and advances that improve new-product development are associated with _____.
- Purchasing power, recession, and inflation are associated with _____.
- The public's opinions and attitudes toward living standards, ethics, and the environment are considered _____.

IN A NUTSHELL

There are four dimensions of marketing—product, price, distribution, and promotion. These elements are used to develop a marketing strategy that builds customer relationships and satisfaction.

The following questions will test your take-away knowledge from this chapter. How many can you answer?

LO.1. Describe the role of product in the marketing mix, including how products are developed, classified, and identified.

LO.2. Define price and discuss its importance in the marketing mix, including various pricing strategies a firm might employ.

LO.3. Identify factors affecting distribution decisions, such as marketing channels and intensity of market coverage.

LO.4. Specify the activities involved in promotion, as well as promotional strategies and promotional planning.

Did your answers include the following important points?

LO.1. Describe the role of product in the marketing mix, including how products are developed, classified, and identified.

- Products are among a firm's most visible contacts with consumers and must meet consumers' needs to be successful. New-product development is a multistep process including idea development, the screening of new ideas, business analysis, product development, test marketing, and commercialization.
- Products are classified as either consumer or business products. Consumer products can be further classified as convenience, shopping, or specialty products.
- The business product classifications are raw materials, major equipment, component parts, processed materials, supplies, and industrial services.
- Products can also be classified by the stage of the product life cycle. Identifying products includes branding, packaging, and labeling.

LO.2. Define price and discuss its importance in the marketing mix, including various pricing strategies a firm might employ.

- Price is the value placed on an object exchanged between a buyer and a seller. Pricing objectives include survival, maximization of profits and sales volume, and maintenance of the status quo.
- A firm may use price skimming or penetration pricing when introducing a new product. Psychological pricing and price discounting are other strategies.

LO.3. Identify factors affecting distribution decisions, such as marketing channels and intensity of market coverage.

- Making products available to customers is facilitated by middlemen or intermediaries, who bridge the gap between the producer of the product and its ultimate user.
- A marketing channel is a group of marketing organizations that directs the flow of products from producers to consumers.
- Market coverage relates to the number and variety of outlets that make products available to customers; it may be intensive, selective, or exclusive.

LO.4. Specify the activities involved in promotion, as well as promotional strategies and promotional planning.

- Promotion encourages marketing exchanges by persuading individuals, groups, and organizations to accept goods, services, and ideas. The promotion mix includes advertising, personal selling, publicity, and sales promotion.
- A push strategy attempts to motivate intermediaries to push the product down to the customers, whereas a pull strategy ties to create consumer demand for a product so that the consumers exert pressure on marketing channel members to make the product available.
- Typical promotion objectives are to stimulate demand, stabilize sales, and inform, remind, and reinforce customers. Promotional positioning is the use of promotion to create and maintain an image of the product in the mind of the buyer.

Practical Application

LO.1.

- The _____ stage in new-product development allows for a test of the marketing strategy.
- Most new product ideas are rejected during the _____ stage because they seem inappropriate for the organization.
- Industrial products such as wheels, batteries, and spark plugs for automobiles are classified as _____.

LO.2.

- The pricing policy that allows a company to cover the product's development cost most quickly is _____.
- _____ is the most flexible variable in the marketing mix.
- If a cosmetics company is selling eye shadow priced at $11.99 rather than $12.00, it is using _____.

LO.3.

- Wholesalers and retailers are referred to as intermediaries or _____.
- Services are usually distributed through _____.
- High-quality items such as musical instruments, sailboats, and airplanes would probably use _____ distribution coverage.

LO.4.

- When Ford pays a television network to air its commercial, it is using _____.
- When Chiquita uses newspaper ads to introduce its new fruit drink to consumers before introducing it to supermarkets, it uses _____.
- The form of communication that attempts to facilitate a marketing exchange by influencing people, groups, or organizations is _____.

IN A NUTSHELL

The use of accounting information and the accounting process is important in making business decisions. Understanding simple financial statements and accounting tools is useful in analyzing organizations worldwide.

The following questions will test your take-away knowledge from this chapter. How many can you answer?

LO.1. Define accounting and describe the different uses of accounting information.

LO.2. Demonstrate the accounting process.

LO.3. Decipher the various components of an income statement in order to evaluate a firm's "bottom line."

LO.4. Interpret a company's balance sheet to determine its current financial position.

LO.5. Analyze financial statements, using ratio analysis, to evaluate a company's performance.

Did your answers include the following important points?

LO.1. Define accounting and describe the different uses of accounting information.

- Accounting is the language businesses and other organizations use to record, measure, and interpret financial transactions.
- Financial statements are used internally to judge and control an organization's performance and to plan and direct its future activities and measure goal attainment.
- External organizations such as lenders, governments, customers, suppliers, and the Internal Revenue Service are major consumers of the information generated by the accounting process.

LO.2. Demonstrate the accounting process.

- Assets are an organization's economic resources; liabilities are debts the organization owes to others; owners' equity is the difference between the value of an organization's assets and liabilities.
- This principle can be expressed as the accounting equation: Assets = Liabilities + Owners' equity.
- The double-entry bookkeeping system is a system of recording and classifying business transactions in accounts that maintain the balance of the accounting equation.
- The accounting cycle involves recording transactions in a journal, posting transactions, and preparing financial statements on a continuous basis throughout the life of the organization.

LO.3. Decipher the various components of an income statement in order to evaluate a firm's "bottom line."

- The income statement indicates a company's profitability over a specific period of time. It shows the "bottom line," the total profit (or loss) after all expenses have been deducted from revenue.
- The cash flow statement details how much cash is moving through the firm and adds insight to the firm's "bottom line."

LO.4. Interpret a company's balance sheet to determine its current financial position.

- The balance sheet, which summarizes the firm's assets, liabilities, and owners' equity since its inception, portrays its financial position as of a particular point in time.
- Major classifications included in the balance sheet are current assets, fixed assets, current liabilities, long-term liabilities, and owners' equity.

LO.5. Analyze financial statements, using ratio analysis, to evaluate a company's performance.

- Ratio analysis is a series of calculations that brings the complex information from the income statement and the balance sheet into sharper focus so that managers lenders, owners, and other interested parties can measure and compare the organization's productivity, profitability, and financing mix with those of other similar entities.
- Ratios may be classified in terms of profitability, asset utilization, liquidity, debt utilization, and per share data.

Practical Application

LO.1.

- CPA stands for _____.
- John James is an accountant who is employed by a large department store chain in the tax department. He is probably a(n) _____.
- According to the text, one of financial managers' single greatest concerns is probably _____.

LO.2.

- The system of recording and classifying business transactions in separate accounts in order to maintain the balance of the accounting equation is called _____.
- The debts Anna's Flowers owes to the Small Business Administration and her company's suppliers represent _____.
- After gathering and analyzing source documents and recording each financial transaction in a journal, a financial manager, bookkeeper, or accountant next _____.

LO.3.

- The profits of a company are equal to the revenue minus _____.
- When an accountant allocates the cost of a piece of equipment over a period of time, this is called _____.
- An income statement shows _____.

LO.4.

- The financial statement that represents an accumulation of all of a company's transactions since it began is the _____.
- The owners' contributions to a company and all earnings retained to finance continued growth and product development are _____.
- A company's assets that can be easily converted into cash are called _____.

LO.5.

- Information found on the company's income statement and balance sheet is extracted from these documents and examined more closely through the use of _____.
- Barbara was asked to extend trade credit to a restaurant she hadn't serviced before. She asked to see its balance sheet to determine if it could pay its bills. She divided its current assets by its current liabilities to get its _____.
- Return on assets and return on equity are examples of a(n) _____ type of ratio.

ANSWERS LO1•Certified Public Accountant •private accountant •cash flow LO2•double-entry bookkeeping •liabilities •posts transactions to a ledger LO3•expenses •depreciation •revenues, expenses, and net income over a period of time LO4•balance sheet •owners' equity •current assets LO5•ratio analysis •current ratio •profitability

active review card

Money and the Financial System

chapter fifteen

IN A NUTSHELL

The Federal Reserve and other major financial institutions play significant roles in the financial system. In understanding finance, you need to consider the definition of money and the forms money may take. You also need to consider the future of the finance industry and the changes likely to occur over the course of the next several years

The following questions will test your take-away knowledge from this chapter. How many can you answer?

LO.1. Define money, its functions, and its characteristics.

LO.2. Describe various types of money.

LO.3. Specify how the Federal Reserve Board manages the money supply and regulates the American banking system.

LO.4. Compare and contrast commercial banks, savings and loan associations, credit unions, and mutual savings banks.

LO.5. Distinguish among nonbanking institutions such as insurance companies, pension funds, mutual funds, and finance companies.

LO.6. Investigate the challenges ahead for the banking industry.

Did your answers include the following important points?

LO.1. Define money, its functions, and its characteristics.

- Money is anything generally accepted as a means of payment for goods and services. Money serves as a medium of exchange, a measure of value, and a store of wealth.
- To serve effectively in these functions, money must be acceptable, divisible, portable, durable, stable in value, and difficult to counterfeit.

LO.2. Describe various types of money.

- Money may take the form of currency, checking accounts, or other accounts. Checking accounts are funds left in an account in a financial institution that can be withdrawn without advance notice.
- Other types of accounts include savings accounts, money market accounts, certificates of deposit, credit cards, and debit cards, as well as traveler's checks, money orders, and cashier's checks.

LO.3. Specify how the Federal Reserve Board manages the money supply and regulates the American banking system.

- The Federal Reserve Board regulates the U.S. financial system. The Fed manages the money supply by buying and selling government securities, raising or lowering the discount rate, raising or lowering bank reserve requirements, and adjusting down payment and repayment terms for credit purchases.
- It also regulates banking practices, processes checks, and oversees federal depository insurance for institutions.

LO.4. Compare and contrast commercial banks, savings and loan associations, credit unions, and mutual savings banks.

- Commercial banks are financial institutions that take and hold deposits in accounts for and make loans to individuals and businesses.
- Savings and loan associations are financial institutions that primarily specialize in offering savings accounts and mortgage loans. Mutual savings banks are similar to S&Ls, except that they are owned by their depositors.
- Credit unions are financial institutions owned and controlled by their depositors.

LO.5. Distinguish among nonbanking institutions such as insurance companies, pension funds, mutual funds, and finance companies.

- Insurance companies are businesses that protect their clients against financial losses due to certain circumstances, in exchange for a fee.
- Pension funds are investments set aside by organizations or individuals to meet retirement needs.
- Mutual funds pool investors' money and invest in large numbers of different types of securities, while brokerage firms buy and sell stocks and bonds for investors and finance companies make short-term loans at higher interest rates than banks.

LO.6. Investigate the challenges ahead for the banking industry.

- Future changes in financial regulations are likely to result in fewer but larger banks and other financial institutions.

Practical Application

LO.1.

- When a dollar bill is handled hundreds of times and is still being used, it has _____ characteristics.
- When used to accumulate wealth, money functions as a _____.
- When inflation is very high, people no longer believe that money is _____.

LO.2.

- Another name for a savings account is a(n) _____.
- In general, the longer the term of a certificate of deposit, the _____.
- The acronym NOW, when used in financial circles, stands for _____.

LO.3.

- To carry out its functions of controlling the supply of money, the Federal Reserve Board _____.
- The Federal Reserve is responsible for _____.
- When the Federal Reserve buys securities, it _____.

LO.4.

- If employees of a local school district conduct their financial business through the same financial institution that they own and only they are allowed to join, the institution is probably a(n) _____.
- The oldest and largest of all financial institutions are _____.
- The major difference between banks and credit unions is that _____.

LO.5.

- A mutual fund allows many small investors to _____.
- Insurance companies invest premiums from insured individuals and businesses or make short-term loans, particularly to businesses in the form of _____.
- _____ permits home computer users to conduct banking activities through their personal computers.

LO.6.

- The _____ made it possible for banks to offer insurance, brokerage, and investment banking services.
- Financial services may be an example of a(n) _____.

IN A NUTSHELL

Companies use short-term assets to generate sales and conduct ordinary day-to-day business operations and short-term liabilities to finance business. They also use long-term assets such as plant and equipment and long-term liabilities such as stocks and bonds to finance corporate assets. Financial management is dependent on the management of these assets and liabilities, as well as the trade of stocks and bonds.

The following questions will test your take-away knowledge from this chapter. How many can you answer?

LO.1. Describe some common methods of managing current assets.

LO.2. Identify some sources of short-term financing (current liabilities).

LO.3. Summarize the importance of long-term assets and capital budgeting.

LO.4. Specify how companies finance their operations and manage fixed assets with long-term liabilities, particularly bonds.

LO.5. Discuss how corporations can use equity financing by issuing stock through an investment banker.

LO.6. Describe the various securities markets in the United States.

Did your answers include the following important points?

LO.1. Describe some common methods of managing current assets.

- Current assets are short-term resources such as cash, investments, accounts receivable, and inventory, which can be converted to cash within a year.
- Financial managers focus on minimizing the amount of cash kept on hand and increasing the speed of collections through lockboxes and electronic funds transfer and by investing in marketable securities.
- Marketable securities include U.S. Treasury bills, certificates of deposit, commercial paper, and money market funds.
- Managing accounts receivable requires judging customer creditworthiness and creating credit terms that encourage prompt payment.
- Inventory management focuses on determining optimum inventory levels that minimize the cost of storing the ordering inventory without sacrificing too many lost sales due to stockout.

LO.2. Identify some sources of short-term financing (current liabilities).

- Current liabilities are short-term debt obligations that must be repaid within one year, such as accounts payable, taxes payable, and notes payable.
- Trade credit is extended by suppliers for the purchase of their goods and services, whereas a line of credit is an arrangement by which a bank agrees to lend a specified amount of money to a business whenever the business needs it.
- Secured loans are backed by collateral; unsecured loans are backed only by the borrower's good reputation.

LO.3. Summarize the importance of long-term assets and capital budgeting.

- Long-term or fixed assets are expected to last for many years, such as production facilities, offices, and equipment. Businesses need modern up-to-date equipment to succeed in today's competitive environment.

- Capital budgeting is the process of analyzing company needs and selecting the assets that will maximize its value; a capital budget is the amount of money budgeted for the purchase of fixed assets. Every investment in fixed assets carries some risk.

LO.4. Specify how companies finance their operations and manage fixed assets with long-term liabilities, particularly bonds.

- Two common choices for financing are equity financing and debt financing. Long-term liabilities are debts that will be repaid over a number of years, such as long-term bank loans and bond issues.
- A bond is a long-term debt security that an organization sells to raise money. The bond indenture specifies the provisions of the bond contract—maturity date, coupon rate, repayment methods, and others.

LO.5. Discuss how corporations can use equity financing by issuing stock through an investment banker.

- Owners' equity represents what owners have contributed to the company and includes common stock, preferred stock, and retained earnings.
- To finance operations, companies can issue new common and preferred stock through an investment banker that sells stocks and bonds to corporations.

LO.6. Describe the various securities markets in the United States.

- Securities markets provide the mechanism for buying and selling stocks and bonds. Primary markets allow companies to raise capital by selling new stock directly to investors through investment bankers.
- Secondary markets allow the buyers of previously issued shares of stock to sell them to other owners. Major secondary markets are the New York Stock Exchange, the American Stock Exchange, and the over-the-counter market.
- Investors measure stock market performance by watching stock market averages and indexes.

Practical Application

LO.1.

- Cash, marketable securities, accounts receivable, and inventory are also known as _____.
- In the area of short-term assets and liabilities, a word that is synonymous with "short term" is _____.
- Good financial managers minimize the amount of cash available to pay bills in _____.

LO.2.

- A finance company to which businesses sell their accounts receivable, usually for a percentage of the total face value, is known as a(n) _____.
- The most widely used source of short-term financing is _____.
- If the interest rate on a loan changes according to the daily average of the prime rate over the life of the loan, the interest rate is said to be _____.

LO.3.

- Plants, offices, and equipment are considered _____.
- Long-term assets can also be called _____ assets.
- When a company invests a lot of money in a particular project, it is concerned about the amount of risk involved. In general, the longer the expected life of a project or asset, the _____ the potential risk.

LO.4.

- _____ are a sequence of small bond issues of progressively longer maturity.
- Items such as a bond's value, date, and rate are specified in the _____.
- A method of long-term financing that requires repaying funds with interest is _____.

LO.5.

- The 52-week high and low are the highest and lowest prices, respectively, paid for a stock in the last _____.
- If a company retains all of its earnings, it will not pay _____.
- Corporations usually employ an investment banking firm to help sell their securities in _____.

LO.6.

- A(n) _____ is a sluggish, retreating market with declining stock prices.
- A(n) _____ compares current stock prices with those in a specified base period.
- Once a corporation's stock is publicly owned, owners can trade it in a(n) _____.